The Enemies of Paul: Demons, Satan, Betrayers, and Apostles

The Enemies of Paul: Demons, Satan, Betrayers, and Apostles

Risk Analysis and Recovery of Paul's Opponents in Thessaloniki, Galatia, and Corinth in the Context of the First Century

Roger S. Busse

FOREWORD BY
Stephen J. Patterson

RESOURCE *Publications* • Eugene, Oregon

THE ENEMIES OF PAUL: DEMONS, SATAN, BETRAYERS, AND APOSTLES
Risk Analysis and Recovery of Paul's Opponents in Thessaloniki, Galatia, and Corinth in the Context of the First Century

Copyright © 2018 Roger S. Busse. All rights reserved. Except for brief quotations in critical publications or reviews, no part of this book may be reproduced in any manner without prior written permission from the publisher. Write: Permissions, Wipf and Stock Publishers, 199 W. 8th Ave., Suite 3, Eugene, OR 97401.

Resource Publications
An Imprint of Wipf and Stock Publishers
199 W. 8th Ave., Suite 3
Eugene, OR 97401

www.wipfandstock.com

PAPERBACK ISBN: 978-1-5326-5916-4
HARDCOVER ISBN: 978-1-5326-5917-1
EBOOK ISBN: 978-1-5326-5918-8

Manufactured in the U.S.A.

This book is dedicated with love to my children, Josh, Kim, Hunter, and Sophia, and to my grandchildren, Andrew, Leah, Ava, and Nina.

I would like to thank Stephen J. Patterson for his continued encouragement and support, vigorous discussions, criticisms, and suggestions over the course of the last decade.

Helmut Koester, my teacher and friend for over thirty years, encouraged studies in risk analysis and the interpretation of Christian origins and the New Testament in its context.

Finally, I wish to express my heartfelt thanks for the continued support of my wife, Tami, whose critical thinking, critique, and contributions enriched this study and helped to drive my application of risk analysis to its most significant levels to date.

Christos Anesti

Contents

Foreword by Stephen J. Patterson | xi

Introduction | 1

1 Establishing the First-Century Risk Context of Paul's Enemies: From Saul of Tarsus to Paul the *Apostolos* | 6

2 The Enemies of Paul in Thessaloniki: Risk Analysis of Paul's First Letter to the Thessalonians | 19
    Recovering the *Sitz im Leben* 19
    Historical Evidence for Paul's Dangerous Path to Thessaloniki 23
    The Place of Composition 26
    Paul's Arrival 29
    Perilous Risk, Countermeasures and Practices 30
    Vocation as Eschatological Event 33
    Paul's Use of Sayings (*Logia*) of Jesus and the Risen Lord to Confront Enemies 36
    Crisis, Enemies and Paul's Mitigation of Perilous Risk 39
    The Composition of the *Ecclesia* 41
    The *Ecclesia* as Protection from Satan and Dark Forces 45
    The Perilous Risk of Abandoning Local and Civic Cults 48
    Letter as Charismatic and Eschatological Weapon against Satanic Enemies 53
    Demonic Enemies: From Death to Life 55
    Betrayers, Apostles, and James the Brother of Jesus 60
    The Risk of Joining the Cult of the Crucified Lord in the First-Century Roman World 65
    The Eschatology of Paul and the Relationship of 1 and 2 Thessalonians 68

Excursus: Paul and the *Logia* of Jesus: Precursor of the Conflict in Corinth | 71

CONTENTS

3 The Enemies of Paul in Corinth | 82

    Risk Analysis of Paul's Letter to the Corinthians 82
    Recovering the *Sitz im Leben* 82
    Assessing the Scope of the Perilous Risk Conflict and Crisis 85
    Apostoloi of the *Logia* and Authority for Rejecting Paul's *Euangelion* 88
    The Opponents' Countermeasures to Paul 89
    Paul's Countermeasures 91
    Logia Used to Oppose Paul: Paul's Claim to Authority over the *Logia* 91
    The Form of Paul's Risk Response to Opponents 93
    Paul's Direct Attack on the Perilous Risk Presented by Opponents 95
    Naming His Enemies and Rejecting Gnosis—the New *Soma* of God 97
    Gnosis, the Jerusalem *Apostoloi* and Battle over the *Logia* 102
    Perilous Risk Questions from Corinth 106
    Logia and Paul's Empowerment of Women in His *Ecclesiae* 110
    The Emerging Risk Profile of Paul's Opponents 113
    The Consumption of Demonic Food 118
    Paul as a Charlatan, Deceived, and a False *Apostolos* 125
    The *Apostolos* as Servant of *Agape* 130
    Allegory and the Wisdom of God: The New Seder and the *Logia* of Christ 133
    Veiling Women in the *Ecclesiae*: A Later Emendation to 1 Corinthians 141
    Paul's Warning to Opponents on Misuse of the *Logia* 144
    The Enemies of Paul Revealed in Chloe's Questions 147
    The *Ecclesia* and the Spirit of God 158
    The Legitimate *Charismata* 161
        Apostolos and Paul's Appointment by God as *Apostolos* of the Risen Christ
        Propheteia 163
        Didaskolos 165
        Glossolalia 172
    The More Excellent Way: Efficacious *Agape* as Mitigation to Satan and the Curse of Death 174
    The Mark of the Enemies: Branding and Tattoos 184
    The Power of *Agape* over All Enemies 190
    The Dim Mirror 195
    The Pursuit of *Agape* and Valid *Charismata* 200
    Perilous Risk for the Adherents 204
    Paul's Authority over the Opponents' *Glossolalia* 206
    The Practice of Prophecy in Paul's *Ecclesiae* and the *Logia* of Jesus Christ 208
    Conflict over the *Charismata* 211

Paul, Resurrection, and the Risen Lord   217
Mitigating the Perilous Risk of Salvific *Gnosis*: The Resurrection of Jesus   217
The Twelve, Oral Tradition, and Formation of the Gospel Narratives   223
Proof of the Resurrection: Paul's Additional Witnesses   225
James, the Brother of Jesus, as Paul's Opponent   229
The False *Apostoloi Christou* in Corinth   236
The Relationship between Kayfa, Paul, and James   239
Paul and John   241
The "Beloved Disciple" and Paul's "John" as the "Pillar"   245
The Resurrection Creed or the *Logia*   247
The Imminent Expectation of the *Parousia*: The Opponents' Deadly Danger   255
Baptism for the Dead   259
The Perilous Risks Faced by Paul and the Shame of His Enemies   262
The Nature of the Resurrected Body   267
Paul's Plea to His Adherents   274
The Collection for the *Agioi* in Jerusalem   274
Paul's Travel Plans and Return to Corinth   277
The Miracle in Ephesus: One of Three Events   280
Paul's Supporters in the Last Days   284
    Timothy   285
    Apollos   303
    Eschatological Relationships and *Agape*   304
    Stephanas, Titius Justus   306
    Fortunatus and Achaichus   310
    The Holy Kiss   311
    Those in Asia   312
    Prisca and Aquila   312
    Sosthenes and Paul's Signature   313
Paul's Curse on Enemies   313
Paul's Blessing on Adherents of the Way   314

Bibliography | 317

Foreword

ROGER BUSSE IS A banker who understands risk. He understands that people do not engage in risky action unless, of course, doing something else would pose even greater risks. When Mr. Busse first approached me with this basic banking insight as a strategy and theory for looking at early Christian texts, I was not sure what fruits it might yield. But with time I've begun to see where this approach might lead.

When classically trained scholars approach the texts of the New Testament they typically do so with a view to their deep theological meaning. The tradition of theological exegesis casts a long shadow over this exegetical tradition that is hard to escape. Moreover, it is usually assumed that the theological insights to be uncovered will be comprehensible, relevant and meaningful to modern interpreters. In the last century, Rudolf Bultmann saw that this was not necessarily so. The religious world of antiquity and the assumptions of ancient people are so different from those held by people in the modern world that little can be gleaned from these ancient texts without translation. Bultmann, famously, proposed demythologizing as a way of translating the claims of the New Testament into terms that would be comprehensible to modern believers. His method, largely misunderstood, created a great controversy, but it did not last. Karl Barth's method of theological exegesis proved far more popular and enduring. Barth's program of teasing out the meaning of the New Testament in terms of orthodox Christian doctrine was more palatable to Christian interpreters, and in many ways, it is still the dominant method of reading the New Testament today.

Roger Busse comes from an orthodox Christian background, but while taking a masters degree in early Christianity at Harvard Divinity School under the direction of Helmut Koester, the last doctoral student of Rudolf Bultmann, his eyes were opened to the same problem Bultmann's demythologizing meant to address seventy-five years ago—the difference separating the ancient world from the modern. Busse came to the realization that the concerns of twentieth-century theologians would not have been sufficient to motivate the followers of Jesus to engage in the risky behavior involved in joining with the fledgling Jesus movement. Why would young people reject their families, leave house and home behind, mix with disreputable figures, and ultimately declare their fealty to someone executed as a despicable criminal and enemy of the Roman empire? For a disputed fine point about the nature of grace? No. After all, modern interpreters and common believers don't generally respond to these texts by leaving their homes and families behind in favor of mendicant poverty or other radical measures. To the contrary, a conventional reading of the New Testament generally leads to a conventional life—even the life of a banker. No, the sort of risky behavior we see among the followers of Jesus must have been motivated by something else, something more.

What, then, could have motivated the radical measures taken by the followers of Jesus? As Busse began to explore the religious world of antiquity under the guidance of Koester and others, he came to a different answer. The ancient world was a world inhabited by (what people believed were) dangerous, demonic forces. The followers of Jesus believed that Jesus could handle them. He could exorcize demons, face down the prince of demons, and stand in the face of demonic agents, like Rome's legate, Pilate. And when the forces of evil put Jesus to death, he had the power to return from the dead and continue to wage war against these dark forces. To become part of the Jesus movement, the followers of Jesus had to believe that the present evil order was about to come to an end and the final battle was at hand. To modern readers, this is the stuff of *Ghostbusters*, but to ancients, it was real. The risks were just that great, so people like Peter and Andrew risked involvement with the executed, discredited *magus*, Jesus of Nazareth, to save their very lives.

In this volume, Busse turns his attention to Paul, asking more or less the same question: what motivated Paul, the respectable Roman provincial, to become involved in the thoroughly risky business of the Jesus movement. Paul, too, must have seen risks that far outweighed the risks that he took on by leaving home and family behind to wander among the ancient cities of the Roman empire promoting the veneration of a crucified criminal. If you read the letters of Paul carefully, not for their neoorthodox theological content, but looking for clues to Paul's own worldview, the answer soon becomes clear. Paul was a typical ancient person, who believed that the world was inhabited by supernatural forces devoted to good and evil. He believed that a decisive battle was about to take place and that he and his followers would be involved. Paul, in fact, was already involved. He saw himself as engaging demonic forces and his letters constantly refer to his weapons of choice. As Busse writes in the introduction to this volume,

> Paul's letters are so much more than simple stylistic, intellectual, rhetorical and emotional correspondences—they are filled and infused with dangerous mystical and charismatic powers feared in the ancient world that were intended to disable, mutilate or destroy opponents he believed to be satanic or demonic. Indeed, this was the world of prevalent, active dark forces and multilayered human and supernatural conflicts; of angels and demons at war; of *charismata* and *anathemata* (deadly curses and binding spells); and the

FOREWORD

imminent *parousia* (i.e., the coming of the Christ . . .), leading to the defeat of Satan and the curse of death.[1]

Busse's thesis is fairly straightforward: Paul took the radical step of joining the Jesus movement because he saw the gathering clouds and decided it was better to be on the right side of the conflict than the wrong side. In his own mystical experiences, God had revealed to him who the real warrior-hero was: Jesus of Nazareth, whom Paul calls Christ Jesus. Paul decided to take up the battle and his language reveals that he was thoroughly at home with the notion that great things were unfolding in the transcendent world around him.

This study is focused on the classical exegetical problem of identifying Paul's opponents, the figures who appear in virtually all of Paul's letters as sources of opposition to his mission. It is in addressing the opponents that Paul's language and methods become most readily identifiable as coming from the ancient world of magic, the battle between good and evil, between angels and demons. This represents a new approach to the problem of Paul's opponents. Most discussions focus on theological disputes or personal conflicts Paul might have had with his opponents. And these ideas are not necessarily disputed by Busse's work. It is, rather, that Paul's words reveal that there was so much more to this conflict than theology or personality. It was this something more that elicited his most ardent, heated prose: he believed that his opponents were one the wrong side of the war.

Busse is an outsider to New Testament scholarship. If you are expecting a rehearsal of familiar schools of thought and conventional approaches to old problems, you'll be disappointed with this work. If, however, you are willing to hear what an intelligent, attentive sojourner might have to say about texts we know as familiar, and yet still strange, I recommend this work and its author to you.

Stephen J. Patterson

George H. Atkinson Professor of Religious and Ethical Studies,
Willamette University

---

1. Busse, *Enemies of Paul*, 2.

Introduction

As established in *To Be Near the Fire* and *Jesus, Resurrected*,[1] risk analysis is highly effective in evaluating both the perilous risks and risk mitigations used by Jesus of Nazareth, Paul, and others evidenced in ancient documents, including the New Testament gospels and sources, noncanonical gospels and pseudepigraphical writings, Paul's undisputed letters, contemporary literature and the Jesus tradition. Historical core conflicts can be recovered, as well as ancillary findings as to the form and function of sayings, events, and literature. The level of risk conflict, evidenced in the scope and scale of countermeasures to neutralize enemies, demonstrates the severity and level of the threat. For example, to cast a death curse on an enemy[2] is conclusive evidence that equal deadly risk is present and threatened, and that the author of that perilous risk is a significant and powerful person who is dangerous and must be literally destroyed by turning them over to Satan. Paul's undisputed letters document this level of conflict, and make claim to efficacious powers and presence, and so, represent a decisive and transformative charismatic event that confronts opponents and enemies with heightened countermeasures that were familiar in the first-century world. This study extends the application of risk analysis to the undisputed letters of Paul addressed to various *ecclesiae* he formed and founded in nascent Christianity that were under attack. As with the previous studies, new risk findings abound that, when set in the context of the first half of the first century, deepen our understanding of that very alien world and the perilous risks that assaulted Paul in the contemporary setting.

Paul's conflicts with his enemies, human and otherwise, led him to employ efficacious powers, authority, *charismata* (spiritual gifts), coherent with his contemporary setting and situation, or *sitz im leben*.[3] These included soul and spirit transportation,

---

1. Busse, *To Be Near the Fire* and *Jesus, Resurrected*. Risk analysis has its roots in human conflict and mitigations to neutralize risk (see below), similar to conclusions rendered in the scientific analysis of "affect heuristic," confirmed in the research of Slovic et al., "Risk as Analysis," 311–22; see also Slovic and Weber, "Perception of Risk," 1–21.

2. Gal 1:8; 1 Cor 5:5; 16:22, and referenced in Phil 3:19; Rom 12:20.

3. *Charismata* (an efficacious gift of the Spirit) is Paul's characteristic term used to express efficacious powers he has at his disposal as an *apostolos*, many of which other adherents also experience

possession, visions and traces, speaking in angelic and demonic languages, free use and even rejection of Jesus' *logia*, exorcisms, special techniques to repel demonic attack (i.e., attempts by Satan and dark angels to kill him), the "holy kiss," as well as the darkest of what was considered black magic in the first century—casting a death curse on his enemies, calling on Satan and his demons to infect, harm or even kill them. Paul's letters are so much more than simply stylistic, intellectual, rhetorical and emotional correspondences[4]—they are filled and infused with dangerous mystical and charismatic powers feared in the ancient world that were intended to disable, mutilate or destroy opponents he believed to be satanic or demonic. Indeed, this was a world of prevalent, active dark forces and multilayered human and supernatural conflicts;[5] of angels and demons at war; of *charismata* and *anathemata* (deadly curses and binding spells);[6] and the immanent *parousia* (i.e., the coming of the Christ, like a king, also reflecting the imagery of the Sinai theophany,[7] or of Exodus 19, Isaiah 26–27 or Zechariah), leading to the defeat of Satan and the curse of death. The analogous *hemera kuriou*, "Day of the Lord," was coming like "a thief in the night,"[8] where the risen Christ would rescue his followers from Satan and the curse of death that had contaminated humans since Adam—even those who "slept" in a temporary state with Christ. Paul's enemies considered him and "evildoer,"[9] a dark magician, deceived and possessed by Satan, and so, a charlatan, profiteer and blasphemer.[10] On orders from powerful

---

and could employ (e.g., *propheteia, glossolalia, didaskolos*, described in detail later in the study). Paul's *charismata*, however, extend far beyond those of other adherents as will be noted, and included deadly curses. See Schutz, *Paul and the Anatomy of Apostolic Authority*, 250–64.

4. Koester, "First Thessalonians," 15–23.

5. See, e.g., Hull, *Hellenistic Magic*, 48–55. Hull presents a plethora of pagan writers who provide multiple examples of demonic activity, exorcisms, attacks by retributive ghosts, evil curses and spells in the Hellenistic world that were considered prevalent. Also see Ogden, *Magic*, 146, 149–52; Ogden translates and categorizes dozens of examples that are drawn from primary sources, many contemporaneous with Paul's activity.

6. See Gager, *Curse Tablets*, 3–30.

7. See Plevnik, *Paul and the Parousia*, 5–11.

8. Plevnik, *Paul and the Parousia*, 117–18. Plevik and other scholars demonstrated this to be from an earlier tradition, and that Paul is employing a saying or words (*logoi*) of Jesus. A similar saying is found in the *Gos. Thom.*, Saying 21, and in Q source, reflected in Luke 12:39. Matt 24:43; 1 Thess 5:2.

9. The accusations against Paul as possessed, satanic, a charlatan and practicing dark magic categorize him as an "evildoer," thereby making him susceptible to the same deadly risks faced by Jesus. See for example the accusations against Jesus, Luke 11:20, and especially John 18:28, 30. Jesus is portrayed not just as a criminal, but instead, as an "evildoer," a term in the ancient world equivalent to an illegal, dangerous dark magician. Pilate certainly knew Jesus' reputation as an exorcist and necromancer. It is he alone who ordered his crucifixion, a form of death known to neutralize retribution by the dead against their executioners (see below). Also see Smith, *Jesus the Magician*, 41, 109, 175. Smith states: "'Doer of Evil' = Magician: Codex *Theodosianus* IX.16.4; Codex *Justinianus* IX.18.7, citing Constantius; compare 1 Peter 4.15 and Tertullian, *Scorpiace* 12.3. Selwin, *1 Peter*, understood 4.15 correctly and cited Tacitus' use of *malefica*, Annals II.69."

10. Paul's enemies claimed he opposed the true salvific *euangelion* (gospel), discovered solely in the *logia* of the Living One, where salvific *gnosis* (knowledge) and *sophia* (wisdom) awakened and reunited the seeker with their divine origin, negating Paul's *euangelion* of the cross and coming *parousia*.

opponents who were well organized, viscous enemies tracked Paul in order to threaten and dissolve his *ecclesiae* (i.e., his churches). From Paul, the loss of an *ecclesia* was to face perilous risk. He was subject to divine condemnation, "woes" as he called them, which meant condemnation and exclusion from the coming *basileia tou Theou* (kingdom of God) by the Lord Jesus Christ, the very being he had once considered a minion of Beelzebul, but whom he now accepted as master. All was at risk, and Paul used every means and power available to him to neutralize his enemies.

The predestined *apostolos* of Christ,[11] Paul was terrified of catastrophic failure coming from infiltrators, spies and enemies. As such, to confront them Paul created something completely new—urgent correspondences that are efficacious, mystically powerful, deadly, even allowing him to be present via soul or spirit transportation to afflict his enemies. Each letter was dangerous immediately when read aloud, effecting *anathema* or death curses on his enemies, even if the enemy were James the brother of Jesus or angel of heaven.[12] Indeed, Jewish opponents from Palestine and Jerusalem, who claimed to be *apostoloi* and *pneumatikoi*[13] of salvific and efficacious *gnosis* (knowledge), gleaned from the *sophia* (wisdom)[14] of a special collection of *logia* (sayings) given by the Living One,[15] accused Paul of being an evildoer, and so, an *apostolos* of Satan. Consequently, it is difficult, if not impossible, to classify Paul's letters in any specific ancient literary genre.[16] Paul's undisputed correspondences are something completely new. They are eschatological, mystical and charismatic encounters with no direct contemporary parallels. As such, they are an invaluable, primary and fundamental source of information about the deadly conflict between Paul, *apostolos* of Christ, and the invaders and infiltrating enemies, whom Paul considered satanic. Countering his authority and claims, they considered Paul's *euangelion* of the cross and *pistis* (faith) to be evil deception, deadly and dangerous that must be neutralized, meaning both his satanic message and his existence. The methods they employed to

---

Patterson, *Gospel of Thomas and Christian Origins*, 245–46, 257, and "Paul and the Jesus Tradition," 23–41. Koester believes that 1 Cor 2:9 was from an early version of Q. See Robinson and Koester, *Trajectories*, 158–204, and *Ancient Christian Gospels*, 58–59. The saying of Jesus would indicate that competing views of its meaning are in play very early. See Davies, *Gospel of Thomas*, xxxiv, xxxv, Sayings 14 and 53. Also see Kloppenborg et al., *Q-Thomas Reader*, 102, Saying 65, the parable of the wicked tenants, a familiar situation in Galilee. Both Q and Thomas may have originated from a common salvific wisdom tradition of Jesus sayings. See Stephen Patterson, "Wisdom in Q," 194.

11. Gal 1:15.

12. Koester, "First Thessalonians," 15–23.

13. Koester, "Wisdom and Folly," 85; Koester goes even further in this identification: "That they were Gnostics, namely Jewish Gnostics, seems even more certain to me." This study will evaluate these identifications fully, as well as the self-designations employed by Paul's opponents in 1 and 2 Corinthians. Georgi, for example, holds that the opponents were gnostics in 1 Corinthians, but were not gnostics in 2 Corinthians (see below).

14. See Patterson, *Lost Way*, 22; evidence of this trajectory, similar to the trajectory found in Q and Thomas, is clearly present in 1 Corinthians.

15. Georgi, *Paul's Opponents*, 18–60.

16. Ibid., 16; see also Funk, "Apostolic *Parousia*," 249–69.

neutralize Paul are just as striking as the methods he employed. All of this is recoverable in its contemporary setting using risk analysis.

As noted in our previous studies, effective risk analysis, when applied to uncovering perilous risks and conflict, is generally framed in two methodological categories. The first is quantitative risk analysis, based on numbers, ratios, trends, and statistics. This method, which is associated with traditional mathematical due diligence, is obviously not fruitfully applied to the New Testament except for example in terms of word counts to help determine authorship. The second methodology is qualitative risk analysis. This method has real value in analyzing the New Testament context for evaluating the implications of this historical conflict. Qualitative risk analysis generally follows a standard evaluative pattern that is iterative. To begin with, there is a perception of what those in the industry call "perilous risk," or danger of immanent serious material harm, which is thought to be a real threat to the stability or survival of an entity under analysis. This threat is usually an assault on the entity's religious, social, economic, or political environment(s). Qualitative risk analysis assesses both the scope of those threats and the entity's vulnerability, then evaluates the effectiveness of potential measures employed to cancel them out. If they are successful, these countermeasures are usually patterned, replicated, or embellished by the entity, thereby attracting other adherents and standard practices. However, when countermeasures fail, devastation, catastrophe, or even physical harm or death can ensue.[17]

Where there are two conflicting entities, additional criteria apply that are particularly applicable. When two entities in a common historical context perceive one another as a perilous risk, the countermeasures each employs to cancel the other out almost always isolate a verifiable historical conflict. As noted, the level of risk conflict in these instances, evidenced in the scope and scale of countermeasures to neutralize enemies, demonstrates the severity and level of the threat. In other words, the intensity of the mitigations employed to neutralize risk is equal to the scope and danger of the opponent perceived, and so, can give rise to the identification of that opponent. In almost every case, the core risk issues are uncovered, and often they provide a basis for assessment of the factual nature of the escalating conflict and the countermeasures employed (e.g., actions, sayings, or events). Many times, obscure, distracting, or irrelevant issues (such as later embellishment and exaggeration of the original conflict) can be identified and set aside. The goal of each of these two conflicting entities is victory, rarely a negotiated settlement (which usually occurs only when perilous risk assures mutual annihilation). Even if a negotiated settlement is reached, it is usually temporary, since each opponent urgently seeks and ultimately employs any advantage to eliminate or neutralize their opponent. In case of failure, the entity or its followers may shift to a different strategy, usually more clandestine, in order to survive. Most interestingly, when this method is applied, the results can provide unqualified conclusions about the materiality and likelihood that risk events will or have occurred in

---

17. Busse, *Fire*, 5–7.

highly specific ways. The qualitative method is applicable to any historical conflicts of crisis and peril, even those set in a different cultural context, as long as that risk context can be adequately recovered.[18] This has important implications for the application of qualitative risk analysis to the New Testament. Qualitative risk analysis suggests conclusions as to the activities of Jesus and his contemporaries, including Paul, in countering perilous risk, all in a new context of historical risk and human conflict to cancel out competing perils. It can also provide clarity to the original conflict between Paul and his opponents, as well as to the nature and intent of his activity, including the sayings that defined that activity and resulted in his capture and execution. The pattern and methods of his activity are also made available by such means.

We will now apply this method to Paul and his opponents and the crises in the Thessalonian and Corinthian *ecclesiae* after establishing context, and reference the conflicts in Galatia and Philippi.

---

18. See Busse, *Fire*, 4–7, and *Jesus Resurrected*, 4n14. Risk analysis and human responses to perilous risks that have influenced the application of qualitative and quantitative risk analysis include classic and contemporary research. See Kahneman et al., *Judgment under Uncertainty*; Drabek, *Human Systems and Response to Disaster*; Fischoff et al., *Acceptable Risk*; Bernstein, *Against the Gods*; Burton, *Perception of Risk*; Pidgeon Framework," section 1; and Sunstein, "Laws of Fear."

Chapter 1

Establishing the First-Century Risk Context of Paul's Enemies
From Saul of Tarsus to Paul the *Apostolos*

THERE IS AN OMINOUS, ugly and even brutal history, one that Paul admits stood behind his later life as an *apostolos*; that is, when he was a young, violent and ambitious Pharisee,[1] a paid and commissioned "hit man" of the Jerusalem elite.[2] To them and to the early Jesus followers, he was known as Saul of Tarsus.[3] It was this Saul and his violent former life that must first be evaluated from a risk perspective, both to understand the perilous risks he perceived as present, as well as the methods he used to mitigate them—even if that mitigation was murder.[4] Indeed, the same Roman-sympathizers

---

1. See two opposing views of Pharisaism in the first century: Neusner, *From Politics*, 89–90, and Rivkin, *Hidden Revolution*, 72–75, 176, 242. Neusner advocates for a less political and aggressive Pharisaism, while Rivkin argues for a politically active and more powerful movement. Paul's own description of being zealous and a Pharisee would tend to support Rivkin's argument, as would his activity as a spy, infiltrator and murderer of Jesus' followers post-crucifixion for the Jerusalem elite.

2. The high priestly families, Scribes, the Herodian aristocracy and rich elite aligned with Rome were *de facto* Roman patrons, Busse, *Jesus Resurrected*, 32–34, 51–53, 56–59, 60–65, and *Fire*, 8–30, 70–75. There are multiple attestations to this view of the elite in Josephus, pagan historians and New Testament sources that will be cited in forthcoming discussions. See Hanson and Oakman, "Social Impact," 146–54. Saul carried "letters" of authority from his Roman-supported elite in Jerusalem. Letters were considered more than just words on paper. They carried power and presence (see also Koester, "First Thessalonians"), with the ability to disable most evil attacks through blessings, mitigating dark curses, or *logoi* (charismatic words of power in the name of a powerful master or Lord, see Origen, *Contra Celsus*, 6:40). Paul's letter to the Galatians and 1 Corinthians are filled with such powerful protective blessings and death curses (see Betz, *Galatians*, 352–53), with the ability to disable even evil from attack through a blessing, a curse, or words of power.

3. For a description of Tarsus in Cilicia, its economic and political power as a safe harbor and trade center, a favored Roman city by Augustus, wealth and influence (like that of Athens and Alexandria, per Dio Chrysostom), center of education, religion and Cynic and Stoic philosophy, please see Roetzel, *Paul*, 12–16. Paul does not mention Tarsus in any of his undisputed letters. Acts 22:3 provides this information, and caution must be exercised, as Acts provides other information about Paul that conflicts with his own letters, including the assertion that he was a Roman citizen (discussion to follow below). However, there is no reason to doubt Acts here, as Paul's familiarity with rhetoric and Stoic philosophy tend to confirm Tarsus as his home city. The city's syncretic nature is reflected in its coinage showing Greek gods and goddesses on the obverse and an inscription in Aramaic on the reverse.

4. Acts 22:4.

that orchestrated the capture, torture and execution of the "evildoer" Jesus, also authorized Saul to commit atrocities against Jesus' followers post-crucifixion, or in his own words, "annihilate them" (*eporthoun*),[5] as a zealous persecutor (*diokon*) of the church (*ecclesia*).[6] The mention of Saul's name in the early post-crucifixion period brought terror to Jesus' remaining exorcists and followers in Palestine and beyond.[7] His cruelty was, self-admittedly, legendary.

Jesus' enemies were abundant, powerful and deadly. The Jerusalem elite and their spies were particularly voracious in their fear of and desire to entrap and ritually destroy Jesus because they considered him an "evildoer," i.e., a dark magician.[8] Jesus' practice of necromancy, ability to control and converse with demons (and even Satan),[9] illegal exorcisms, use of curses, all led them to conclude he was a minion of or possessed by Beelzebul, Satan's dark angel, the prince of demons.[10] To his enemies, Jesus was not only in control of demonic forces, the untimely dead (*ahori*), and dead by violence (*biaeothanati*),[11] that could attack, infect and even kill, but was thought by Herod to have conjured the beheaded[12] John the Baptist's spirit for deadly retribution and evil against him.[13] No scholar contests that Jesus' enemies accused him of having authority over demons.[14] Indeed, Jesus was clearly perceived as a perilous risk to the elite in Jerusalem, whom he labeled satanic, "vipers and serpents,"[15] as he moved from village to village, exorcising demons. He left Galilee, entered Decapolis, encircled and then headed toward Jerusalem to confront them in the temple. In the context of the first-century world, as Beelzebul's minion and controlling the dark forces of Satan, Jesus was a deadly threat that must be neutralized.

As demonstrated in *Jesus, Resurrected*,[16] once spies witnessed Jesus employing necromancy in Bethany (considered the darkest of magical practices in the ancient world

---

5. Gal 1:13.
6. Phil 3:4–6.
7. Acts 9:26.
8. Busse, *Jesus Resurrected*, 1–13, 47–59; Smith, *Magician*, 33, 75–76.
9. Mark 1:12–13; Luke 4:1–13; Matt 4:1–11. Only Jesus could have shared these encounters, so they are self-admitted, and because of their problematic nature in their contemporary setting (Jesus conversed with Satan, feeding the Beelzebul controversy), have a claim to authenticity. Indeed, the nature of the encounter speaks to a vision or trance, which is consistent with the contemporary experiences of exorcists and charismatics like Jesus. For an excellent presentation on the scholarly debate and arguments for the authenticity of the tradition due to its problematic risk nature to the church, see Kimball, *Jesus' Exposition of the Old Testament*, 80–95.
10. See Busse, *Fire*, 54–59 (Mark 3:22).
11. Ogden, *Magic*, 149–55; Busse, *Jesus Resurrected*, 53.
12. Mutilation of John's body and beheading was thought to neutralize retribution by his ghost. It did not guaranty it, however, thus Herod's terror.
13. Mark 6:20; Busse, *Fire*, 54.
14. Ibid., 54–60, 88–89.
15. Matt 23:33, the equivalent of saying they were possessed by and under the control of Satan.
16. Busse, *Jesus Resurrected*, 4–5, 60–65.

The Enemies of Paul: Demons, Satan, Betrayers, and Apostles

and worthy of death under Roman law),[17] he was quickly captured with the help of their spy, informant and assassin, Judas Iscariot.[18] Jesus was then ritually killed under a divine curse to annihilate him, body and soul.[19] To ensure his retaliatory spirit had been neutralized and could not be conjured by his follower, Jesus was entombed in stone.[20] Saul certainly shared this dark view of Jesus, evidenced by his admission of brutal attacks on and participation in the murder of Jesus' followers, post-crucifixion

The use of informants, infiltrators and armed and dangerous spies by the Roman elite was rampant in Roman occupied Palestine.[21] Informants were not only expected to be in place and be well paid, but a network of spies and assassins was required of the Jerusalem elite by their Roman patrons and occupiers to keep the peace, or risk being displaced.[22] Certainly, the use of spies and paid informants was familiar to Saul—he not only was one, but he used others to locate followers of Jesus and then brutally attack or murder them on the spot.[23] He was deadly. The word *phonos*, meaning murder or killing, is directly applied to Saul, "breathing threats *and murder*."[24] Indeed, as striking as this may be, Saul's techniques and risk motivation were similar to those of Judas Iscariot.[25] Saul entered synagogue assemblies (as was his strategy as Paul) and feigned proclaiming Jesus to identify followers.[26] While it is shocking and disturbing to think of Saul and Judas as similar Roman sympathizers and murderous informants, unfortunately, the historical evidence seems incontrovertible. Saul and Judas were paid informants and assassins, out to destroy Jesus and his exorcists by any and all means possible so as to mitigate the danger of their dark powers to the elite, and both were successful in helping to murder both Jesus and some of his exorcists. This sobering reality means that both Saul and Judas perceived Jesus and his followers as a dangerous perilous risk, leading both to side with Rome and its powerful allies in Jerusalem. This is what makes Saul's transformation following his post-crucifixion encounter with Jesus so striking.

17. See Ogden, *Magic*, 277–99, for a comprehensive analysis of ancient Roman law and the illegal practices, and du Plessis, *Borkowski's Textbook*, 5–6, 29–30.

18. Busse, *Fire*, 27–30.

19. Supported by multiple sources, including the Dead Sea Scrolls, 4 Q 169 3–4, II (Pesher Nahum) and 11 QT LXIV, 7–12 (Temple Scroll); Thatcher, "I Have Conquered," 147–48; Busse, *Jesus Resurrected*, 47–52.

20. Ibid., 52–57.

21. Ibid., 153–54; Busse, *Fire*, 15–16, 20–29.

22. See Jeffries, *Graeco-Roman World*, 156–57.

23. Stephanus, Acts 7:54—8:2.

24. Acts 9:1.

25. Horsley and Hanson, *Bandits*, 30–33. This included brutal men like Judas Iscariot, an infiltrating paid informant and assassin of the elite (see Busse, *Fire*, 27–30). It is clear that Jerusalem was filled with political turmoil and intrigue for much of its Roman historical period, all of which was fostered by fearful concern over maintaining political control and power, as exemplified by Herod the Great slaughtering members of his own family.

26. A practice used by the Romans and Pilate, see Busse, *Fire*, 22–23.

Establishing the First-Century Risk Context of Paul's Enemies

Scholars universally accept that this Saul became the earliest and only direct witness (via his undisputed letters)[27] to have seen and have been possessed by the risen Jesus (i.e., "revealed" in him, *en emoi*),[28] as well as the Holy Spirit.[29] In fact, Paul describes multiple encounters of various types, and also acknowledges that his was not the first; several others had preceded him based on a chronological, extensive list of witnesses he provides in 1 Cor 15:1–8.[30] His authentic letters (usually engendered by a risk response to dangerous opponents infiltrating and trying to disband his *ecclesiae* [churches]) describe his own multiple ecstatic experiences. Remarkably, these encounters include spirit[31] and soul[32] transportation, possession,[33] attack by dark angels[34] and Satan,[35] ecstatic language,[36] and trances.[37] Paul was a charismatic Jew *par excellence* in his contemporary setting.[38] Even his letters carried mystical and charismatic powers; specifically curses[39] and blessings when read aloud that became immediately effective. They also include reference to his encounter with this executed Palestinian peasant Jew and crucified "evildoer" and exorcist, which he depicts as having seen, specifically not only in a vision, séance or trance familiar to his world,[40] nor in an ethereal encounter with a *Bi(ai)othanatori*,[41] but with his own eyes (*opthe*), as a visible, in some way a substantial manifestation where he was present.[42] Such an admission would be not only be shocking in the Roman world, but dangerous, leading to accusations that he too was a dark magician. And yet it was this event that created

27. Generally accepted by virtually all scholars: Galatians, 1 and 2 Corinthians, 1 Thessalonians, Philippians, Philemon, and most of Romans.

28. Gal 1:16.

29. See Patterson, *Beyond the Passion*, 119.

30. Koester, *Introduction*, 84.

31. 1 Cor 5:4.

32. 2 Cor 2:12; Paul describes his being lifted up to the place of redeemed humans in "heaven."

33. 1 Cor 14:1–25.

34. 2 Cor 12:7–10.

35. 1 Thess 2:18.

36. 1 Cor 14:18.

37. 2 Cor 12:2.

38. Vermes, *Jesus the Jew*, 74.

39. Busse, *Jesus Resurrected*, 213–15; Busse, *Fire*, 170; 1 Cor 5:7–12; Gal 1:8–9; 1 Cor 16:22.

40. For the historical context and variety of ecstatic expressions, see Smith, *Jesus the Magician*, 75–80; also Lewis for a broader definition of "trance" in *Ecstatic Religion*, 29–31, and then descriptions that correspond to Hellenistic and Roman settings such as 39–57.

41. A ghost, "those dead by violence." See Ogden, *Magic*, 146, 149–52.

42. The word "appeared" (*ophthe*) literally means that "he was seen" with the eyes, i.e., not as an indistinct vision *but was literally seen with the eyes of the individual, often in some form of materiality, and in historical time*. For discussion see Conzelmann, *Corinthians*, 256–57, and especially 257n74. Paul does not describe a human flesh-and-blood body or his recognizing Jesus by his wounds. His encounter was overwhelming because it was with a crucified, cursed, Jewish criminal that he despised. The later traditions of a bodily encounter with Jesus post-crucifixion, i.e., physically touching his wounds, was unknown to Paul.

perilous risk, so dramatic for Saul that he changed his name, abandoned his religious heritage (calling it "refuse"),[43] and adopted a starving, hunted, poor and wandering life, supporting himself as a subsistence worker, a tentmaker (or leatherworker), reflecting his lower caste.[44] He became a self-proclaimed *apostolos* of that Roman criminal, whom he claimed was now not only active, but his "master" and the Son of God.[45] This ecstatic event, in a world filled with capricious gods, ghosts, angels, demons and spirits, and a religious law that Saul once embraced but now claimed condemned one to death,[46] defined for the new man, Paul, the radical countermeasure to satanic power and the curse of death. Faith (*pistis*) in the crucified Jesus as risen by God was the only "way" to achieve safety and life, for the world would soon enter a divine cataclysmic judgment—the *parousia*—the "Day of the Lord" led by that crucified Jew, now Christ (*Christos*) and Lord (*kurios*). To refuse was to condemn oneself to satanic affliction,[47] a curse and annihilation—"woe to me," Paul says, if he refused to serve his master and Lord and publicly proclaim at great peril the efficacious *euangelion* (gospel).[48]

It was this perilous risk that led this young Jewish zealot[49] (one who not only publicly participated in but also led others to murder Jesus' fellow exorcists or violently arrest and attack sympathizers) to publicly announce he was both "in" (i.e., was one with), as well as possessed by the Spirit of Jesus—a shocking and perilous admission in the Roman world. More remarkably, he came to invoke the name of Jesus as protection from satanic attack, or employed it to make effective deadly curses with immediate consequences on its victims.[50] Paul's radical transformation now acknowledged that Beelzebul did not possess and control Jesus (as he, Saul, had most certainly had claimed in concert with the Jerusalem elite),[51] but that the Spirit

---

43. Phil 3:8.
44. Hock, "Paul's Tentmaking," 555–64.
45. Gal 2:20; 2 Cor 11:23–27.
46. 1 Cor 15:56.
47. Acts 9:9; 2 Cor 12:7.
48. 1 Cor 9:16: The mystical nature of the word itself, *euangelion*, as efficacious and salvific is fully described in the next section. Encountering and having faith, *pistis*, in the *euangelion*, was immediately impactful to Paul, saturating the adherent with power to neutralize the curse of death, dependent upon whether the adherent was found to be "in Christ" at the *parousia*. This efficacious effect of the *euangelion* is analogous to the introduction to the *Gospel of Thomas*, which says, "Whoever discovers the interpretation of these sayings will not taste death" (Saying 1). Unlike Thomas, which did not need a *parousia*, Paul's *euangelion* is cast in an eschatological tenor and, therefore, is effective only for adherents until and at the *parousia*.
49. Gal 1:14.
50. 1 Cor 5:4.
51. Mark 3:22; see Smith on the accusation of Jesus' opponents. Jesus was under control of Beelzebul, prince of demons: "Take that away, and all that remains is a collection of unrelated complaints, most of them not very serious; introduce it, and then these complaints can be seen as component elements of a comprehensive structure." Jesus was working for Satan according to the view of his opponents. Smith, *Jesus the Magician*, 31–32.

of God did.⁵² Only a transformative encounter with Jesus post-crucifixion, which included the threat of permanent blindness and a deadly curse,⁵³ can explain acceptance of heightened perilous risk. Consequently, assessing Paul's encounters from a risk perspective is not only imperative, but it is made possible through a contextual risk analysis of Paul's own letters.

There are at least four types of post-crucifixion encounters claimed by Paul. He states that he had seen Jesus with his own eyes, i.e., a manifestation of Jesus in a new *soma*, which he describes.⁵⁴ Paul also encounters Jesus in dreams,⁵⁵ where he receives instructions and words (*logoi*) of the Lord,⁵⁶ commands and *logia* (sayings).⁵⁷ He describes visions and revelations given by the Lord or the Spirit,⁵⁸ which include ecstatic transportation to heaven, again where he hears divine words (*logoi*) that he is forbidden from repeating.⁵⁹ Finally, Paul states that he can enter into Spirit possession, evoking ecstatic prophetic and angelic language and esoteric interpretations given to him by the Spirit or the Lord.⁶⁰ Paul reports all of these encounters in response to heightened perilous risk, i.e., as risk mitigations to neutralize opposing perilous risk.⁶¹ But fundamental to all of these was his encounter with the *soma* of Jesus, and the subsequent danger and deadly risk it brought to Paul daily,⁶² beginning with a narrow escape from Damascus and his flight to Arabia.⁶³

By Paul's own admission after this event, he, like Jesus before him, came to radically reject the Jerusalem elite.⁶⁴ He considered them evil and under the control of Satan and his demons. Remarkably, Paul's rejection of Jerusalem elite ultimately extended to certain leaders (even a "pillar") of the Jerusalem *ecclesia*, declaring that Satan had taken control.⁶⁵ His "apology" letter to the Galatian *ecclesiae* (i.e., the house churches

---

52. The contrast between two kinds of spirits, Beelzebul and the Holy Spirit that possesses Jesus, is clear in Mark, particularly implicit in Mark 3:20. See Robinson, *History in Mark*, 36. As Robinson points out, "The rarity of this identification in Mark [i.e., the Holy Spirit as empowering Jesus' actions] show the importance the present issue has for him."

53. Acts 9:9; perhaps again 2 Cor 12:7.

54. 1 Cor 9:1; 15:8; Gal 1:12, 16; Phil 3:8.

55. Acts 16:9; 18:9. These were the most common of interactions described by Ogden in *Magic* form contemporary sources, noted previously in our study.

56. 1 Cor 7 (in response to questions, where Paul cites his and the Lord's instructions).

57. 1 Cor 11:23.

58. Gal 1:12; 1 Cor 2:2–12; also perhaps 11:23, and certainly 15:51; 2 Cor 12:1–10; 1 Thess 4:15–17; Rom 1:17; 16:25.

59. 2 Cor 12:2–4.

60. Gal 4:6, Rom 8:15; for *glossolalia*, see 1 Cor 14:8.

61. 2 Cor 11:16–33.

62. 1 Cor 15:31.

63. 2 Cor 11:32.

64. Busse, *Jesus Resurrected*, 10; Carter, *Roman Empire*, 54–55.

65. Gal 6:13–15; Schweitzer asserts that Paul's accusation of possession and curse is leveled against Kayfa, James and John, who were the "super-apostles." See Schweitzer, *Mysticism of Paul*, 156–57.

in that province) reviling the infiltration of Yacob, the brother of Jesus (whose spies attempted to disband his assemblies) is literally a "magical letter" in that it contains an unconditional curse on the infiltrators, indeed a death curse (or a blessing of safety on the members of Paul's *ecclesiae*) immediately when read.[66] Those who had come to reject Paul and his *euangelion* were infected with a deadly curse—something in the Roman world considered dark magic, punishable by death under Roman law. In a startling implication, Paul's curse extended to Yacob, the brother of Jesus. And this wasn't a unique use of such power. Paul placed a deadly curse on a man in 1 Cor 5:3: "I have already judged . . . and give him over to Satan for the destruction of the flesh." By Paul's giving the man to Satan, he was practicing what was considered the "blackest of magic" in the ancient world.[67]

As an itinerant *apostolos* of Jesus Christ at war with powerful dark forces, Paul expected to be attacked by both demons and Satan and states he was constantly.[68] Yet he embraced this terrifying risk, and the risk of total annihilation because of his encounters with the risen Lord, and the salvific *euangelion*, or "Gospel" of God. Once received and accepted, one was mystically united with the risen Lord,[69] whether through the charismatic rite of baptism in water (*into which* evil was expelled and absorbed)[70] or by baptism and possession of the Spirit (which expelled or exorcised evil and any demons into places of wandering), but certainly through efficacious *pistis* in the *euangelion*. The practice of *agape* evidenced possession of the adherent by the Spirit of God,[71] thus ensuring protection from satanic forces and death. A new person, the *tekna tou Theou* (child of God),[72] began to emerge, like a new plant from a seed. This was the work of God, not Satan, the divine, not magic or sorcery. All "powers" of Paul's world would bow to this authority,[73] literally the most feared and terrifying enemies—every demon, the prince of demons, Beelzebul, evil spirits and the dead,

---

66. Betz, *Galatians*, 352–53.

67. See Morton, *Jesus the Magician*, 110.

68. Paul, 2 Cor 12:6–9; for Jesus, Luke 4:9, and other ecstatic experiences in the desert wilderness of Judea where expelled demons and even Satan were said to roam looking for victims.

69. Gal 2:19–21.

70. Busse, *Jesus, Resurrected*, 145–48. That Beelzebul haunted the waters is confirmed by Hull: "Beelzebul has a demonic child who haunts the Red Sea (*T. Sol.* 5.11) and has been trapped there against his will (*T. Sol.* 25.7)." See Hull, *Hellenistic Magic*, 104; also see Bar-Ilan, *Exorcism by Rabbis*: "Some springs have a complete family of spirits living in each; it is understood that hot springs, as in Tiberias (Galilee), are heated by spirits (acting on the basis of the commands of King Solomon). It can be generalized that there is hardly a source of water in the land of Israel without a spirit (one or more)." Bar-Ilan cites as additional support the *Pesachim* 112, p. 1, two baraitot: "The Rabbis learned: One should not drink water from rivers or lakes at night. And if he drinks, he risks his life because of the hazard. What hazard? The hazard of demons." Also cited by Bar-Ilan, "Haunted Springs," 153–70. See also Ferguson, *Baptism*, 56–93.

71. Gal 5:22–23.

72. Gal 3:26.

73. Phil 2:9–11.

malevolent and retributive ghosts, and even Satan who was "falling like lightening."[74] Those previously subject to harm, illness and deadly risk of attack from these capricious powers now fell under the protection of God and Jesus Christ until the *parousia* through *pistis* in the *euangelion* and the practice of divine *agape*.

Paul is certain that he will experience the "Day of the Lord Jesus" (*hemera kuriou*) during his lifetime, and this imminent, cataclysmic[75] event characterizes the tension between the current order of the world that is soon to collapse and the presence of the Lord and the general resurrection "at his coming [for] those who belong to Christ,"[76] meaning both those "who have fallen asleep" (death is not possible for those "in Christ"[77] through *pistis* in the *euangelion*), as well as those still alive. This event is then followed by a period of subjection of all powers to God and the delivery of the kingdom "by his son." It is Paul's expectation that the living believers *in Christ* addressed in each letter will soon experience a metamorphosis at the *parousia*,[78] literally "the coming," or "the presence," at the *hemera kuriou*; indeed, many of those who hear Paul's letter read aloud will experience the change (*allagesometha*) of their physical body, *the soma*, in a new spiritual *soma* and witness it with their own eyes:

> Lo! I tell you a mystery. We shall not all sleep, but we shall all be changed, in a moment, in the twinkling of an eye at the last trumpet. . . . For this perishable nature must put on the imperishable, and this mortal nature must put on immortal.[79] What is ". . . sown as a body [*soma*] natural and [is] raised a body [*soma*] spiritual."[80]

---

74. Luke 10:18.

75. 1 Cor 15:23–28: "But each in his own order; Christ, the first-fruits, then at his coming those who belong to Christ. Then comes the end, when he delivers the kingdom to God the Father after destroying every ruler and every authority and power. For he must reign until he has put all his enemies under his feet. The last enemy to be destroyed is death. (For God has put all things in subjection under his feet.) But when it says (all things are put in subjection under him), it is plain that he is expected who put all things all under him. When all things are subjected to him, then the Son himself will also be subjected to him who put all things under him, that God may be everything to everyone."

76. 1 Cor 15:13.

77. 1 Thess 4:14–17.

78. Donfried, *1 Thessalonians*, 85–86; Plevik, *Paul and the Parousia*, 3–13, correctly notes that *parousia* in Paul's accepted writings was not a technical term (as does Koester), as Paul uses it also to describe the coming of his colleagues. It is the context of the use that is important in understanding and proper interpretation. The cultural context of *parousia* is also helpful in that it is used to describe the arrival of a king, or Caesar, as savior—a joyous event. However, Paul only employs this word in an eschatological and apocalyptic setting. Plevik provides an excellent analysis of *parousia* that associates Paul's imagery with the Sinai theophany (Exod 19:10–18). The Lord comes down, trumpets blast, there is thunder and other imagery. This would have been an image that better fit the contextual background of Paul's Jewish background, and is found in other Jewish apocalyptic imagery.

79. 1 Cor 15:51–52a, 53.

80. 1 Cor 15:44b.

Paul's description of the resurrected (or transformed), body as "spiritual" has led to controversy.[81] To some scholars, transformation appears here to be purely spiritual, but when set in the context of the first century, evidence is quite the contrary. Paul is a Jew and Pharisee, and in verses too numerous to cite, Paul speaks of the body as the *soma*, which is a term for the body that a Pharisee understands *as the physical body*. He consistently alludes to the body in this way[82] and is also consistent in his statements as to the physical, holy (i.e., temple of the Holy Spirit), and sinful nature of the body from the perspective of a Pharisee. Further, the Pharisees were also insistent as to the physical resurrection of the *soma* at the end of the age.[83] His analogy of the seed dying to produce a more glorious body, and the body as a type of seed that must die to become "imperishable," as well as his description of the many types of plant, animal and material "*soma*" God has chosen and made, all refer to physical realities.[84]

Soma, is then a new but somehow material observable reality. For Paul, the resurrected body is a "spiritual *soma*" (*soma pneumatikon*), just as the food and drink that the Jews ate in the wilderness with Moses were "spiritual food and drink," i.e., material food and drink, but given by God's miracle, thus making it spiritual.[85] So it is with what is raised as "imperishable," meaning it is a spiritual *soma* whose characteristics are given by the miracle of God; but it is a material *soma*, not just ethereal spirit, and unlike anything known up to that time with the exception of the risen Jesus, which he witnessed. Some form of materiality after death was ascribed to various retributive ghosts and spirits, but usually as a vapor or dark smoke, sometimes a bodily materiality,[86] but not as Paul describes a divine, glorious, resurrected *soma*.[87] And as Paul says, "Christ was the first fruits,"[88] so the resurrected *soma* Paul is describing is similar to that of Jesus, *which Paul claims to have seen with his own eyes in its full glory*.[89] To be clear, what Paul has seen, he is describing—the *soma* of Jesus. If Paul were to have intended to teach only transformation into an ethereal spirit at the *parousia* day he would have been clear that this was "out of the body" (*soma*), just as he did when he recounted his experience being "caught away" to the "third heaven" (not "caught up" as in some translations; caught away is consistent with the ancient Jewish

---

81. Busse, *Jesus Resurrected*, 220–23.

82. 1 Corinthians refers to the *soma* thirty-five times, more than any other New Testament work.

83. This continued into the rabbinical period and is still one of thirteen fundamental tenets of current rabbinic Judaism.

84. 1 Cor 15:37–42.

85. 1 Cor 10:1–5.

86. Ogden, *Magic*, 149–55; see also Busse, *Jesus Resurrected*, 14–21.

87. Busse, *Jesus Resurrected*, 54, i.e., the example provided by Phlegon, about Philinnion, and also the physical attack of retributive spirits at tombs on victims.

88. 1 Cor 15:23.

89. 1 Cor 9:1; for other ancient examples, see Busse, *Jesus Resurrected*, 54–55, and Ogden, *Magic*, 159–60, as compared with phantasms and spirits. See examples in Ogden, *Magic*, 64–65, 146–47, 149–52, 161–62, 164–65, on tombs and encounters with ghosts and spirits there.

belief of the highest heaven being somewhere other than up or above): "I know a man in Christ who fourteen years ago was caught away to the third heaven—whether in the body or out of the body, I do not know, God, knows."[90] Paul knows and could explain the difference firsthand.

For Paul, being "in Christ" is a mystical experience and relationship that began at his first encounter and continued until his death: "The being-in-Christ is not conceived as a static partaking in the spiritual being of Christ, but as a real coexistence of his dying and rising again."[91] It is not something metaphorical, but his new reality, and it is distinctive from Hellenistic mysticism, "founded on the idea of deification" (which we will later find with his opponents in Corinth), as opposed to the Pauline fellowship with Christ, the divine and resurrected son, who will raise those at the *parousia* who are in him, that is possessed by his spirit.[92] Paul's mystical experience is grounded in the eschatology of the impending resurrection; that being in Christ is to mitigate the perilous risk of annihilation and the curse of death; and that every manifestation of this conflict with Satan and demons, or his triumph in the establishment and growth of his *ecclesiae* is because of his being in Christ as the last days unfold. This mystical relationship is captured in Galatians and certifies Paul's possession: "I am crucified with Christ, so I live no longer as I myself; rather it is Christ who lives in me" (Gal 2:19–20).[93]

From Beelzebul's Servant[94] to "Master" and "Lord"—*Euangelion* as Metamorphosis

We can extend this new risk understanding to specific words that in today's world are professed as "Scripture," versus how they were experienced as striking, numinous and efficacious in the alien world of the first century. Here is perhaps the most important example. According to Paul, transformation into a familial relationship with the divine, the *tekna tou Theou* (i.e., under the adoption and protection of God the father as *Abba'*), was made immediately possible in "Gospel," *euangelion*, a word not as we may understand it today, that is, as a noun, but as a powerful supernatural verb, saturated with life giving power that overwhelmed body and soul, and supplanted one's risk of death and the capricious threat of doom by Satan and his demons.[95] *Pistis* in the *euangelion* literally altered, transformed and mitigated one's peril, indeed, the certain outcome facing the *apistoi* (unbelievers), i.e., death,

---

90. 2 Cor 12:2–3.
91. Schweitzer, *Mysticism*, 13.
92. Ibid., 16.
93. Ibid., 120–28.
94. See Busse, *Fire*, 54–59.
95. E.g., Craffert, *Life*, 226, 302–3, and, indeed, his entire study for a complete analysis of the "alien" world of first-century Palestine.

meaning total annihilation. *Pistis* in the *euangelion* imbued one with divine protection, risk mitigation, and the sure hope of life (*elpis*), thereby making impotent all evil powers until the *parousia*.[96] The *euangelion* was the power God, the evidence of which began with the raising of Jesus, the "first fruits," as Christ.[97] The encounter with *euangelion* was an irreversible event that demanded a choice between God and Satan, and according to Paul, was undeniably deadly if rejected, as one fell under Satan's curse.[98] It created a cataclysmic shift in what perilous risk now represented to each that encountered it.[99] If the *euangelion* of Jesus Christ was rejected, or even altered,[100] one was *anathema*, permanently blemished, and nothing could be done to prevent it. This terrifying risk of rejecting the *euangelion* brought on such a deadly curse, one's complete and ultimate being was immediately to be considered void, useless, at an end, and would be consumed by evil.[101] The *euangelion* of Paul allowed rescue from Satan and the imminent judgment to come any day.

Only an analysis of the perilous risks that led this young, violent Jewish zealot[102] to radically change is capable of recovering the original historical context.[103] More, Paul's risk responses can be accurately analyzed: What could have led Paul to invoke the name of Jesus for protection against demons and spirits, or to combine the name of Jesus with "Lord [*kurios*] and *Christos* [Messiah]," or employ these more titular eponyms to assert the overwhelming supernatural power of his letters, usually written to repel opponents he announced were of Satan? By implication, why would Paul publicly reject the assertion that Beelzebul the prince of demons had possessed Jesus as he, Saul, had most claimed in concert with the Jerusalem elite),[104] and instead announce that it was the Spirit of God that possessed Jesus?[105] How does one explain this radical transformation, the acceptance of perilous risk and deadly dangers faced, that is, of Saul to Paul?

---

96. Rom 8:38.

97. 1 Cor 15:20.

98. 1 Cor 15:31.

99. Rom 7:24.

100. Gal 1:8, 2 Cor 11:4.

101. 1 Cor 15:8.

102. Gal 1:14; a man who not only publicly participated in, but led others to murder Jesus' exorcists, and violently attack and imprison sympathizers!

103. Gal 1:16.

104. Mark 3:22; see also Smith on the accusation of Jesus' opponents. Jesus was under control of Beelzebul, prince of demons: "Take that away, and all that remains is a collection of unrelated complaints, most of them not very serious; introduce it, and then these complaints can be seen as component elements of a comprehensive structure." Jesus was working for Satan according to the view of his opponents. Smith, *Jesus the Magician*, 31–32.

105. The contrast between two kinds of spirits, Beelzebul and the Holy Spirit that possesses Jesus, is clear in Mark, particularly implicit in Mark 3:20. See Robinson, *History in Mark*, 36. As Robinson points out, "The rarity of this identification in Mark [i.e., the Holy Spirit as empowering Jesus' actions] show the importance the present issue has for him."

Establishing the First-Century Risk Context of Paul's Enemies

Risk analysis leads to an unequivocally conclusion: Saul confronted a manifestation of a post-crucifixion Jesus, and was absolutely certain it was his hated enemy. There was no doubt. Saul, the hired informant and assassin of the Jerusalem elite—the man who had once labeled Jesus an "evildoer" and minion of Beelzebul; a criminal, one of the untimely dead; a *bi(ai)othanatoi* that had either vacated the tomb seeking retribution against the elite (including attacks by his surviving exorcists), or a ghost or spirit that could be conjured by followers who took his body and used spells and necromancy to access his dark powers—had encountered Jesus. It was a terrifying and shattering event that forever altered his understanding of perilous risk. The mitigation to this encounter was to annihilate Saul and all that he was, and become Paul and serve this risen master, allowing his to possess his being, or face the woe of annihilation. These are Paul's own words to describe his new perilous dilemma. Saul's orders to find and brutally eliminate any of Jesus' exorcists, a threat that risk analysis confirmed the Jerusalem elite believed urgent,[106] had led to this event.

Remarkably and ironically, it is the Roman cross that becomes Paul's central theme of salvation from the power of Satan and the curse of death; indeed, the very instrument that Saul believed had divinely cursed and eliminated the threat of Jesus the evildoer had instead become the instrument of salvation for both Greek and Jew. It was God's wisdom (*sophia*) and power (*dunamis*) that were demonstrated in the cross and resurrection, as opposed to human *gnosis* and *sophia*, which were impotent against Satan because they had originated from Satan. Death was overcome, and so Satan's reign was drawing to a close, yielding to the coming kingdom of God (*basileia tou Theou*). Paul declared that Jesus was God's son, both Lord and Christ, raised from the dead, and soon to come at the *parousia*, destroying all of God's enemies, the last of which being the infection of death. *Pistis* in the *euangelion* and the practice of *agape* imbued one with divine protection and security from these cataclysmic events about to unfold. Paul was at war with Satan, his demons and dark angels, or with the enemies that Satan had possessed or deceived to do his bidding. Satan intended to destroy Paul, and with him, the salvific *euangelion*. As we will discover, Paul's encounters with the risen Lord were multifaceted, and while many are complimentary to the reports in contemporary literature, most were considered to occur in the prevue of magicians, sorcerers, exorcists and those with dark powers. Consequently, Paul was at risk of attack from enemies, both human an otherwise—a reality he experienced.[107] He accepted this perilous risk because the alternative was unimaginable and deadly.

Paul, like Jesus, deliberately engaged in an epic battle against Satan, demonic forces and dark control.[108] And Paul, like Jesus, embraced a dangerous itinerant life, bearing the risks. Both were determined to overcome Satan and death, village-by-village,

---

106. Busse, *Jesus Resurrected*, 60–65.

107. 2 Cor 11:16–23; 1 Thess 2:18.

108. Busse, *Fire*, 70–88, 166–70; Bolt, "Life, Death and the Afterlife," 55–59; Smith, *Magician*, 126–27; Ogden, *Magic*, 152–53, 158.

synagogue by synagogue, and city by city. The similarities are striking, and their conflict with Satan and his demons in this itinerant war formed the basis of the perilous risk conflicts each confronted.[109] Most important, like Jesus, Paul was followed by spies, ridiculed, cursed, accused of illegal activities and being a charlatan, and was brutalized to near death, indeed, thought to be dead, for the sake of the efficacious *euangelion*. This conflict is evident in Paul's correspondences to the assemblies he founded, confronting all enemies, including those in Thessaloniki, Galatia, Corinth, and beyond. We now turn to assess Paul's enemies in the context of the first-century world and to develop a portrait of these deadly opponents, human and otherwise, he considered satanic using risk analysis.

---

109. Later writers, particularly Luke, extended this theme to its most extreme—Jesus brought the *euangelion* from Bethlehem to Jerusalem; the *apostoloi* and Paul took it from Jerusalem to Rome.

Chapter 2

The Enemies of Paul in Thessaloniki
Risk Analysis of Paul's First Letter to the Thessalonians

QUALITATIVE RISK ANALYSIS SUGGESTS conclusions as to the activities of Jesus and his contemporaries, in this case Paul, in countering perilous risk, all in a new context of historical risk and conflict to cancel out competing perils, human or otherwise. It can provide clarity to the original conflict between Paul and his opponents, as well as to the nature and intent of his activity, including the sayings, threats, curses and activities that defined that activity. The pattern and methods employed in their contemporary setting are also made available by such means. We will apply this method to Paul and his opponents and the crises in the Thessalonian *ecclesia* after establishing context.

Recovering the *Sitz im Leben*[1]

First Thessalonians is the earliest writing in the New Testament.[2] It is a remarkable historical document and an undisputed letter of Paul. Paul founded the nascent church (*ecclesia*) in the seaport of Thessaloniki,[3] a major city in the Roman province of Macedonia on the *Via Egnaita*.[4] It met in a private home on the first day of each week.[5] This was a prosperous port city, and (as was typical of Hellenistic Roman cities) a diverse metropolis with sections populated with various ethnicities, including a small Jewish

---

1. For the most recent and lauded scholarly study on Thessaloniki in an outstanding interdisciplinary volume, see Nasrallah et al., *From Roman to Early Christian Thessaloniki*.

2. Between 49–51 CE, or only fifteen to seventeen years after Paul's encounter with the risen Jesus.

3. The seaport was expanded significantly by the Romans, making Thessaloniki a major trade port in northern Greece, which is still operative; it was named after the wife of Cassander, Thessalonice ("Thassalian victory"), in 315 BCE.

4. There is evidence that a Jewish colony was established in Thessaloniki in the 1st century CE, supporting the early growth of Christianity with Paul's arrival.

5. This was a workday, similar to our Monday, but for the believer, the day of the resurrection and so the day of celebration; meetings were held either early in the morning before dawn, during the afternoon *siesta*, or after at the evening meal in the cool of the day. Since Paul indicates that their was drinking and drunkenness in Corinth (1 Cor 11:21), at the gathering, this was likely in the evening after a long and arduous workday.

sector that held a synagogue.⁶ The Romans allowed Jews to disperse throughout the empire, as Judaism was a legal religion. These Hellenistic synagogues were composed of merchants and tradesmen near the port, as well as common laborers and workers.⁷

Thessaloniki was not considered an intellectual center like Athens. Officials were known as the politarchs, or city counselors, both from local inscriptions and Acts 17:6. The city itself was pagan, protected by Kabiros and Tyche (further evidenced by the city's coins with their images). The significance of the cult of Kabiros to the city is undisputed by scholars,⁸ although specific rituals and practices are not fully known, and speculation, including millenarianism, has led to significant debate.⁹ There were several cults active in the time of Paul, particularly Egyptian cults worshiping various gods, such as Sarapis (the deeds of Sarapis are recorded in an inscription found there and a Sarapeion was discovered)¹⁰ and Isis, where a dedication from a woman, Phouphikia, for healing her hearing was discovered. Lastly, an inscription of dedication was noted, "Aulus Papius Chilon, who provided the meeting place."¹¹ In all, there are over sixty inscriptions to Egyptian deities that have been identified in excavations at Thessaloniki thus far. As Koester notes, "the . . . diversity of pagan religions is amazing."¹² A small aristocracy controlled the city. This led to a diversification of associations that dominated life in Thessaloniki.

> Due to the minority of aristocrats in the city, and having few opportunities to play an active role in local politics as individuals, the Thessalonians, especially those from the middle and lower strata of society, sought new collective identities as members of groups. . . . These identities were built upon common elements linking members, such as religious convictions, possibilities of professional cooperation, solidarity or even aesthetic preferences and were solidified through mechanisms such as celebrations, rituals and feasts, often memorial feasts.¹³

Undoubtedly, Paul gained adherents from such associations, particularly trade associations like his own (which he likely joined upon arrival). The vibrant diversity of such associations, as well as the numerous cults, mystery religions and temples, also speaks to the very alien world of Thessaloniki to our own, and the context within

---

6. Archaeological evidence however can only be dated to the fifth century via a Samaritan inscription, see Koester, *Paul*, 56–57.

7. Josephus mentions the presence of Jews in Macedonia when he cites a letter from Herod to Caligula in 10 CE.

8. Koester, "Archaeology and Paul," 40–41; Koester, "Egyptian Religion," 133–50.

9. Robert Jewett's conclusions of millenarianism in Thessaloniki (i.e., *Thessalonian Correspondence*) has been successfully challenged by Koester, *Paul*, 40–41, and others.

10. Ibid., 50–52; also see Koester, "Egyptian Religion," 133–50.

11. Koester, *Paul*, 53–54.

12. Ibid., 55.

13. Nigelis, "Voluntary Associations," 35–36.

which Paul drew adherents who sought escape, safety and salvation from capricious evil dark forces, curses, demons and retributive dead, Satan and death. The nascent Christian community in Thessaloniki was comprised of Hellenistic Jews, as well as Gentile converts to Judaism, called "God fearers," and Gentiles of these same strata, many of whom were subsistence workers.

Acts records that "*not a few of the leading women*" were also followers.[14] This is a critically important statement, as it provides a more complete understanding the earliest composition of Paul's *ecclesia*. It also confirms that women in the Roman world held prominent and influential positions and were financially powerful, even if their legal status remained inferior to that of men.[15] These positions of status gave them religious influence arising from this substantial wealth, which could include family or inherited fortunes (as widows), becoming benefactors.[16] Paul's authentic writings unquestionably confirm that he accepted and supported women leaders as equals (including *apostoloi*),[17] just as Jesus, who traveled with a contingent of followers that included women exorcists[18]—something completely unique.[19] This democratization of the gospel (*euangelion*) to all was consistent with Paul's statement in Galatians, "neither Jew nor Greek, *male or female*," and was likely a baptismal formula;[20] that is, there is a charismatic, mystical transformation, a new creation, that defies old presumptions of difference or separation, even social or sexual status—one becomes a new child of God, where God is ecstatically addressed as *Abba'*. Freedom from Satan's control, demonic possession and the curse of death was available to all through Paul's gospel.[21] The long disputed statement of Paul in Corinthians (see Chapter 3), that women should "keep silent in the church," has been convincingly shown by scholars

---

14. Acts 17:4; it is interesting to note that in Pisidian Antioch there were prominent and leading God-fearing women, but these women are said to have risen against Paul and Barnabas: "But the Jewish leaders incited the God-fearing women of high standing and the leading men of the city. They stirred up persecution against Paul and Barnabas, and expelled them from their region" (Acts 13:50). Women, while under many social restrictions, had a prominent and influential role in the Roman world as a result of inherited wealth, or marriage to powerful men.

15. Women could own property after the defeat of the Oppian laws (that included restrictions on women's rights), divorce, sponsor buildings and public projects and conduct businesses.

16. Although it is also certain in the male-dominated Roman society, her husband, her guardian or father significantly controlled the wealth of a woman; the widow may have had the most autonomy, although this is uncertain. There are no writings from women of the first century that address.

17. Gal 3:28.

18. See Busse, *Jesus, Resurrected*, 106–20.

19. Jesus and the Samaritan woman; Jesus first appearance to Mary in the garden, and the women that accompanied Jesus during his itinerant preaching tour.

20. Patterson, *Lost Way*, 227–28.

21. Gal 3:28: "There is neither Jew nor Greek, slave nor free, male nor female, for you are all one in Christ Jesus." While likely a baptismal formula (Patterson, *Lost Way*, 227–28), this is a remarkable democratization of social status among all believers, unheard of in contemporary Jewish society and rare in Greek religion, particularly given the legal status of slaves and women. The new community of Paul made no distinctions.

to be later emendation or addition based on a review of context alone.[22] All of Paul's undisputed and most influential letters reference women as equals in his ministry and missionary work and at all levels.[23] More, he acknowledges at least one woman, Junias, as a renowned *apostolos* before him, which means she had charismatic power, could exorcise demons, and had encountered a risen Jesus—all the attributes that Paul describes are required as an *apostolos* in 2 Corinthians.

Whatever their origin, the *sitz im leben* shared equally by Paul and his Thessalonian *ecclesia* is one of eschatological crisis, which is about to unfold; where cataclysmic changes are imminent, brought about by the impending *parousia*. The crisis upon them democratizes perilous risk for every adherent, even Paul. In 1 Thessalonians, he never claims to be their superior, even if an *apostolos* of the risen Lord, but like them as a witness to and participant in the conflict between God and his Son and Satan and his angels and demons in the last days of the age.[24] Indeed, acceptance of Paul's efficacious *euangelion* of the cross, reception of the *charismata*, and practice of *agape*, has led them all directly into perilous conflict with Satan and his demonic forces.[25]

Consequently, comprised of men and women, the *ecclesia* of Thessaloniki was small, perhaps two dozen believers. Socially, it was comprised primarily of those from lower strata, the local trades and subsistence workers (like Paul), a few wealthy women, some of who were patrons. It must not escape us that Paul and his adherents met secretly in a home, worshiped a crucified Jew who had been condemned and brutally and ritually executed by a Rome and the Jerusalem elite as an "evildoer" (i.e., a dark magician), and whose itinerant founder was literally chased from town to town, accused of blasphemy and being a charlatan. Their gatherings were dangerous, filled with perilous risk. Indeed, the risks to those in this community from local authorities, Jews and Gentiles, owners and employers, and related trade associations, all of whom could be fearful of this cultic association, inform against them or retaliate, were not just real, but inevitable. Were it not for the protection made possible by Paul's *euangelion* in the last days before the cataclysmic *parousia* and the arrival of Jesus Christ and kingdom of God (the mitigation to these perilous risks), adherents would be doomed and succumb to these risks and abandon the *ecclesia*. Paul knows this, and is terrified, for failure would mean his doom and his own judgment, "Woe to me!"[26] Paul's reassurance to these men and women who

---

22. 1 Cor 14:33b–36.

23. The list is undeniably supportive of this statement; the deaconess Phoebe (Rom 16:1 is a letter of recommendation for her), Prisca (the wife of Aquila, given equal status in the ministry of Paul, both in Corinth and Ephesus), Junias an apostle (the statement, "they are men" referring also to Junias is a mistranslation of the Greek); clearly Junias is a woman's name and she is an apostle that was "in Christ before me" (Rom 16:7); Paul's statement is more bold than the Cynics, who according to Antishenes said, "Virtue is the same for a man and a women," Diogenes Laertius, 6.12.

24. Koester, "Paul and the Thessalonians," 28.

25. Ibid.

26. 1 Cor 9:16–17.

The Enemies of Paul in Thessaloniki

face new crises and enemies is imperative. Correspondence then becomes eschatological presence and mystical power, not mere words and encouragement. It is a charismatic event.

Historical Evidence for Paul's Dangerous Path to Thessaloniki

According to Acts, Paul entered Europe for the first time as a result of an ecstatic dream or vision (*horama*), possibly a trance[27] (*ekstasis*) such as that attributed to Kayfa[28] in Joppa.[29] He had been prevented from entering various areas by the "spirit of Jesus"; i.e., encounters in visions or trances that prohibited travel.[30] An unidentified man of Macedonia (*aner tis en makedon*) is calling to him to come over and help (*boetheson hemin!*). Paul is in Troas and immediately responds, arriving by ship in Philippi.[31] Eventually, he arrives in Thessaloniki by land, but only after having been severely beaten and forced out of Philippi, the main city of the province to the north. Paul and Silas[32] had been tortured, i.e., repeatedly beaten with rods for advocating "customs [that] it is not lawful for us Romans to accept or practice,"[33] that is, he practiced illegal, dark magic, and religion. Paul had exorcised and silenced a spirit-possessed female servant or slave (*paidiske*) who was able to provide insight into the future in response to questions, which included dangers and perilous risks, thus providing invaluable insight worthy of substantial compensation. Her ecstatic speech was certainly like that of an "oracle," often considered a remarkable and welcome gift of the gods, but also at this time considered to be demonic possession and access to the underworld. Paul's exorcism debilitated her. Consequently, the exorcism was considered dark magic of an unknown religion, terrifying several of the local citizens, breaking Roman law, and infuriating her owners who made their living from compensation for her divinations.

Interestingly, the *paidiske* is described as having a *pythonos pneuma*, a "python spirit," thus representing a woman who had been possessed by the *python* god or a special demon, and so, had the power of insight associated with the cult of the Pythian

---

27. See also Busse, *Jesus Resurrected*, 213n11, n13, and additional references.

28. Simeon, son of Yonah, was renamed "the rock" by Jesus after being trained as his leading exorcist. In Greek, "the rock" is Petros, but in Aramaic, Kayfa, the "s" being added to adjust the Aramaic ending "a" implying a feminine ending, thereby making it masculine. Consequently, Kephas, commonly used by scholars, should be Kayfa, the original Aramaic, with the long "a." The other translation of Cephas improperly drops the hard "k" of Aramaic.

29. Acts 10:9–16.

30. Acts 16:7.

31. Acts 16:9.

32. Silas was sent back to Antioch with Paul and Barnabas to represent the apostles after the council of Jerusalem, Acts 15:36–40. Silas remained a loyal companion to Paul in his ministry and is mentioned in 1 Thess 1:2 and 2 Cor 1:19 as Silvanus, the full name.

33. Acts 16:21.

Apollo.[34] However, as noted, there were demons given access to future events by Satan, or the gods, while others were possessed and received oracles of the dead, or practiced rites near tombs.[35] While it is possible that she was somehow related to or was thought to be one like the sibyls or priestesses of Delphi known as the Pythia, none had ever been known to be slaves or servants to humans. In Ancient Greece, Delphi was the primary sanctuary of Apollo, the famous sacred precinct in the south central portion of Greece on the southwestern slope of Mt. Parnassus. The myth was that Apollo had slain the great python that guarded the navel of the earth for some heinous act it had committed.[36] Apollo had cast the dead python[37] into a rock cleft from which came a spring. From that time forward, fumes emitted were intoxicating to the Pythia. As they sat on a tripod in their sacred place (the remains of the site can be visited in Dephi to this day), the Pythia breathed in these fumes. The Pythia entered into a trance and were able to provide remarkably accurate guidance about the future.[38] It was believed that Apollo spoke through them. Indeed, what became known as the Delphic oracles were famous.[39] The Pythia had advised great kings, including Croesus, Oedipus, and Alexander the Great, and predicted the outcome of momentous battles and events. But, after the destruction of the temple of Delphi in 83 BCE, the oracle was in disrepair, its oracles thought errant, and so, its influence fell dramatically. Consequently, this *paidiske* of Philippi was most likely understood to have a demon of divination; she was thought possessed and given access to dead heroes, gods or spirits, or knew of entrances to the underworld where insight could be obtained.[40] Since this was a port city, many may have come from some distance and great expense to visit with her. As either a servant or slave, she would have been extremely valuable to her owners.

In the context of the first-century Roman world, when those known to be dangerous entered the city and a prophet or *paidiske* shouted out, such an overt action was dire, particularly for those whose demon was divination. The *paidiske's* demon was speaking as a herald, warning and threatening anyone who would be swayed.[41] Announcement that there were magicians present by a respected *paidiske* led to a

34. So named after the python defeated by Apollo at the site, which guarded the "navel" of the earth; originally, the site was known in ancient times as Krisa and later Delphi.

35. Ogden, "Oracles of the Dead," 167–87.

36. There are conflicting ancient accounts of what the python was or had done, from simply defying Apollo to rape.

37. I.e., *python* can be translated as "rot."

38. Despite the account by some Roman authors, it appears that the Pythia did not speak in riddles or metaphors. According to Plutarch, who also confirms that Apollo did not possess the oracle but instead gave them a spirit, which was their gift, whether learned or in the by nature, the Pythia spoke plainly and were clearly understood.

39. There is a long list of oracles from 630 BCE to 380 CE.

40. Ogden, "Oracles of the Dead," 180–85, and examples.

41. An example is the herald who, according to the Talmud, preceded Jesus and warned of his blasphemy and condemnation to be stoned, asking anyone who could speak for Jesus to come forward (*Sanhedrin* 43a; also see accusations, *Talmud Sanhedrin* 107b, *Sotah* 47a).

prescribed and severe Roman punishment—they were to be beaten with rods, imprisoned, and either killed or deported—exactly what actually happened in Philippi.[42] While Paul is said to have grown annoyed at the persistence of the *paidiske*, following them for several days and publicly calling out, "These are servants of the Most High God, and they are telling you *a* way to be saved [not *the* way]," Paul's exorcism of the demon was a shockingly violent expulsion (*paragello soi . . . exelthein*). He did so "in the name of Jesus Christ" (*en to onomato Jesou Christou*).[43] The exorcism took effect over the course of an hour. Only this risk context is plausible for what actually took place in Philippi—if she were attesting to their validity, as Acts suggests, the locals would have embraced Paul and Silas reputation.

In response to Paul's exorcism, the owners dragged Paul to the public marketplace, the *agora*, in the center of town, or more likely the *statsmarket*, the administrative center of Philippi. There, local officials heard accusations of magic and incited a retributive group of citizens to seize them. Paul was seriously attacked, then stripped (to ensure no amulets, spells or other items could be employed against them) and beaten with rods by the local police (perhaps the *rabdouchous*, officials called lictors who carried the *fasces*, a bundle of rods that surrounded a hatchet, before the counsels of Rome), under orders form the local magistrates. Surviving, they were jailed and put in painful stocks.[44] That the magistrate was notified is important. Only the presence of dark magicians or evildoers would result in such a rapid and dramatic response with this level of authority and prescribed Roman punishment. A beating with rods (*rabdizen*) was brutal and damaging. Rods were probably made from the smooth limbs of a tree bound together to form a strong wooden rod or pole. The beating was on the shoulders, back and legs causing intense pain and bruising. Acts 16:22–23, reports that the beating was repeated, and severe. It was likely intended to kill them.

According to Acts, by God's intervention (i.e., an earthquake) was Paul freed from a maximum-security cell. He, however, chose to remain in the prison, thereby saving the jailor who had decided to end his life due his fear of a mass prison escape for which the locals would have found him culpable. Ultimately, Paul was offered his freedom by the local magistrates, as Acts also reports that they believed his claim to be a citizen of Rome. But, as noted earlier, Paul could not have been a citizen. As such, the story that Paul demanded that the leaders of the city apologize, and they did, fearing the repercussions having violated the rights of a citizen, is a later embellishment.[45] Their quick expulsion from the city would be coherent with an earthquake that damaged the jail and cell, as it affirmed them as dangerous exorcists and magicians. The event in Philippi was most likely one of the three times Paul confirms

---

42. Wendt, "All the Temple Gates," 53–54 (citing Paulus, Sent. 5:23–15).

43. Acts 16:16–18.

44. Acts 16:23–24.

45. Paul could appeal to the Roman authorities under his rights for recompense against the local magistrates; they could be severely punished.

in his letters to the Corinthians that had been beaten with rods.[46] Paul left Philippi branded as a dark magician, possessed and dangerous. This was the reputation he carried with him as he entered Thessaloniki.

The Place of Composition

It is evident that Paul wrote 1 Thessalonians from Corinth between 49–51 CE, although some have argued for a date closer to 41 CE. The question of date is associated with Emperor Claudius's expulsion of the Jews from Rome. Acts reports[47] that Paul met up with two fellow tentmakers/leatherworkers in Corinth who were expelled under this edict, Prisca[48] and her husband, Aquila. Paul had moved on to Corinth to set up and organize his next *ecclesia* after a short visit to Athens, where he failed to gain any adherents. Like Thessaloniki, Corinth was a capital of a Roman province, in this case Achaia. Corinth too was a rich powerful seaport, benefiting from two harbors on the east and west sides of the isthmus near the city. Corinth had been destroyed by the Romans in 144 BCE, but was colonized by Julius Caesar with freemen from Italy, Greece and even Judeans in 44 BCE.[49] The city continued to attract significant migration. It was only a little over a century since it had been reestablished that Paul arrived. Some estimate that by 50 CE the population had risen to six hundred thousand, although this may be triple its actual size. The Isthmian games had been reinstated, which brought athletes from Greece and perhaps the entire Mediterranean region. Both the athletes and visitors who came required temporary housing. Archaeological studies have confirmed that there was a lack of permanent housing.[50] Tent shelters provided the primary accommodations for both, which was Paul's trade.

Upon his arrival in Corinth, Paul followed his standard practice of locating craftsmen in his trade, then joining a local guild or coworkers to sustain himself, and thus, his ministry.[51] According to Acts 18:1–8, Paul found Aquila and Prisca, husband and wife, tentmakers or leatherworkers. Paul sought out others in his trade, looking for shared shop space and work, and to gain entry to the local guild or association to attract adherents. Aquila and Prisca had recently arrived as a result of the edict of the Claudius, having been expelled from Rome along with all the Jews. Having come from Rome, it is apparent why they chose to migrate to one of the most important cities in the ancient world. As a Roman colony, the predominant language was likely Latin,

---

46. 2 Cor 11:25.

47. Acts 18:1–4.

48. As he calls her in his letter to the Romans; Priscilla in Acts.

49. Corinth was renamed *Colonia Laus Julia Corinthiensis*, "Corinth the praise of Julius."

50. Excavations in Isthmia, begun in the 1830s continuing again sporadically, and then in 1967–1976, and 1980–1989 no permanent structures that could accommodate the number of athletes and visitors were found dating from the mid-first century.

51. See above on the strong confirmation of this mission strategy, which was later confirmed as noted by Celsus.

not Greek, and more important, their trade was in high demand there. There was also a Jewish community. As was his modus operandi, Paul began speaking at the local synagogue on the Sabbath.

Corinth had a reputation as a rough and bawdy city with lax sexual standards. It was known as a slander when it was said, "You are nothing but a Corinthian" (i.e., *korinthiazesthai*).[52] Despite this reputation, Corinth was a perhaps the wealthiest and most diverse Hellenistic/Roman city due to its location as a powerful and prominent seaport. Located on a narrow isthmus, only three and one-half miles wide, between the Gulf of Corinth on its east to the Saronic Gulf on its west. Corinth also connected the Greek mainland to the Peloponnesus. Merchants preferred traversing their goods across the short land passage (i.e., across the narrow width of the isthmus), thereby avoiding the more treacherous circumnavigation around the Peloponnesus and cape Malea.[53] To do so, they employed smaller portage boats that were literally winched and lifted out of the seaport onto wooden carts, then rolled over a specially designed road to the opposite port, either Lechaeum or Cenchreae. As a result, Corinth was situated in a strategic location on this isthmus, which provided control of the shipping and merchant transport for much of the trade from Italy and Rome to the Mediterranean world, and beyond. A fortress stood eighteen hundred feet above the city, known as Acrocorinth, to reinforce is rights to control trade. On the high point of Acrocorinth was an ancient small temple of Aphrodite (52–33 feet, prostyle temple), said by Strabo (Geog. 8.6.21) to be notorious for temple prostitution, who "once owned a thousand temple-slaves, prostitutes, both men and women had dedicated to the goddess."[54] Other scholars have challenged this view, but Paul himself noted the immorality of the city (1 Cor 6:9–20; 7:1).

Since it was a Roman provincial capital and produced its own coinage,[55] Corinth maintained an administrative center, or state *agora*. The administrative center of the city was impressive, containing a *bouleuterion* (council house, official assembly house), *odeiona* (musical or poetry performances), *basilica* (courts, official offices, public assembly), and official sanctioned temples of Apollo, Octavia, and a public

---

52. There is an ancient Greek proverb also which states, "It is not every man who can afford a trip to Corinth," referring to sexual immorality, prostitution, gambling and drunkenness, as in later plays when a Corinthian appears it is only as a drunk man.

53. This route was infamous for shipwrecks and disasters—it is still regarded as treacherous by captains—the winds were treacherous as a ship passed the gulfs of Argolis, Lanconia and Messinia, then north past Mt. Ithome and the city of Olympia, finally entering the gulf of Calydon and finally the Gulf of Corinth, literally over four hundred miles of rugged coast. The mystery cult of Melikertes at Isthmia included rites to protect sailors from drowning, and the Isthmian games were said to be instituted in honor of Melikertes. See Koester, "Melikertes in Isthmia," in *Paul*, 180–91.

54. There were estimates of over one thousand temple prostitutes at the time of Paul's ministry in Corinth.

55. Prior to the Roman destruction of Corinth, the silver stater (8.3 grams, 20 mm across) that depicted the Corinthian-helmeted Athena with the winged Pegasus on the reverse was most common. Athena was replaced by Tiberius in the bronze coins of 14–37 CE.

theatre. The buildings were arranged around colonnaded stoa with marble walkways, multiple statues, honorary inscriptions and memorials. In the center of the state *agora* was the *bema*. The *bema*, also called the *rostrum*,[56] was a large, high,[57] blue and white marble-covered platform.[58] It was used for pronouncements, public address, and for the judgment of individuals prosecuted under Roman law.[59] The open area in front of the *bema* could easily accommodate over two hundred people. As Corinth was the capital of an imperial province a Roman governor or *proconsul* resided there. Paul was beaten and forcibly brought before the proconsul at the *bema*.[60] Paul's forced appearance occurred during the appointment of Gallio in 51–52 CE.[61] The dating is made possible by an inscription found in the sacred precincts of Delphi.[62] Emperor Claudius directed Gallio to facilitate the resettlement of high-standing Corinthians to Delphi to help repopulate it. This event helps provide the approximate date that Paul must have written 1 Thessalonians during his residence. However, if Claudius's edict to expel the Jews was in 41 CE as some scholars claim,[63] it is possible that Paul wrote the letter from Corinth during a much earlier visit. If so, the editor/author of Acts conflated two or more visits. Most scholars reject this view, that is, the blending visits within the itinerary of Acts. Thus, it appears that Paul must have composed 1 Thessalonians about this time while in Corinth. If so, 1 Thessalonians was composed by Paul roughly seventeen years after the first encounter with the risen Jesus, or about 51 CE.

---

56. The Bema measured about 3 meters, or 6.5 ft., high and 20 ft. wide.
57. Estimating the size was 40 ft. long, 20 ft. wide and at least 15 ft. high, it divided the stoa in half.
58. Most likely it was built in 30–44 CE.
59. Partial remains of the "seat" or platform are still standing today in the ruins of ancient Corinth.
60. Paul was attacked again by local Jews reacting to the split he brought to their synagogue, but in this case was brought before the highest authority in Achaia, Gallio.
61. Gallio (born 5 CE in Cordoba, Spain, as Marcus Novatus, see Tacitus, *Annals*, 15:73) was brother of the famous philosopher of the time Seneca, who interestingly dedicated a treatise to him. Seneca later became Nero's tutor. Gallio was raised by his father, Seneca, a famous rhetorician and likely was under his influence. He was sent to Rome and adopted by Lucius Junias Gallio, thus the change in name. He became proconsul under Claudius. His brother Seneca in his letter to Lucilius (*Seneca Letter 104*) was described as having a "sweet" disposition and was "loved" by many. He reportedly left Corinth due to a fever, which he attributed to the place, thus the need for his departure for health reasons. Jerome later reported that he committed suicide, likely forced to kill himself for complicity in the plot to kill Nero, i.e., the so-called Pisonian conspiracy (65 CE, the plot of Gaius Calpurius Piso, a Roman Statesman who wished to have himself proclaimed emperor after killing Nero).
62. Delphi is a sacred precinct of the god Apollo, where the temple treasuries of many cults and gods were housed, along with the mysterious and very famous oracle of Delphi, and as noted, the women Pythian seers, who provided guidance to kings and emperors, including Croesus and Alexander the Great.
63. Later scholars, such as Karl Donfreid, continue the debate; Donfreid, *Paul*, 99–118.

Paul's Arrival

Paul arrived in the seaport of Thessaloniki, a free city (as opposed to Philippi, a Roman city), with a population estimated at over two hundred thousand, walking along the *Via Egnatia* some seventy-nine miles from Philippi. Paul stopped (recovering from his beating) in the cities of Pydna, Apollonia and Amphipolis. Thessaloniki was located at a critical juncture where the *Via Egnatia* met the trade routes north to the Danube. Situated in a scenic natural harbor located at the end of the Thermatic Gulf and at the feet of the Kortiates mountains, Thessaloniki was one of the most important trade and commercial centers in Greece and was the Roman capital of province of Macedonia.[64]

According to Acts 17:1–9, Paul's time in Thessaloniki was short lived. He was forced to leave the city, once again due to local and violent Jewish opposition. Since Acts reports that they were able to gather "wicked" men from the *agora* to join with them in seizing Paul, the report may be suspect and opposition may have actually come from locals who knew Paul's reputation as an accused "evildoer," i.e., Gentiles. Here, Acts extends a recurrent theme of Jewish opposition to Paul, which while certainly probable, may be exaggerated and betray a theological bias against Jews. The accusations brought to officials (correctly named as *politarchas*), centered on Paul's proclaiming another king, and so sedition. However, the tradition confirms that Paul was known to proclaim a crucified Jew as risen Lord, i.e., an accused dark magician executed by Pontius Pilate, and that he was under the control of the spirit of Jesus. Indeed, Paul did demonstrate charismatic powers, "those of an apostle" in the cities he reached,[65] including exorcisms and other acts considered magical, and was known to place deadly curses on enemies in the name of Jesus, calling on satanic and demonic attack—the darkest of magic. Acts betrays more concern for these types of accusations using phrases such as, *oti oi ten oikoumenen houtoi kai enthade pereisin*, i.e., "these are the ones creating chaos," and *apenanti ton dogmaton kaisaro prattousin*, "these do contrary to the decrees of Caesar," such as the decrees against the practice of magic. Consequently, to proclaim Jesus as Christ and Lord was more than just sedition—it was to publicly announce union with dark forces opponents, which would be most concerning to Jew and Gentile alike, particularly the *politarchas*. More, Paul claimed cataclysmic forces were about to arrive, i.e., a *parousia* led by this very Jesus Christ who was coming to destroy all his enemies, and with it Caesar and Roman rule.

Acts 17:2 reports that Paul established an *ecclesia* in the home of a Jason after having spoken in the local synagogue on only three occasions (i.e., each Sabbath for three weeks, "as was his custom").[66] Paul's speaking in the local synagogue is historically plausible, as it was not uncommon for traveling Jews and teachers to be invited

---

64. Established as the capital of the Roman province of Macedon in 146 BCE.
65. 2 Cor 12:12; 1 Thess 1:5.
66. Acts 17:2.

to speak at the appointed time at the Sabbath services, particularly a Pharisee with Paul's training.[67] If in fact Paul was so effective in such a short time as to establish an *ecclesia* in the home of Jason (possibly relative of Paul?)[68] after only three presentations, it would be rather remarkable. Paul does state at the outset of his letter that the powerful influence of the Holy Spirit helped to establish the *ecclesia* there. However, Paul's comments in the letter imply a much longer period of time in Thessaloniki. More, there is nothing in 1 Thessalonians that leads one to assume that the *ecclesia* was composed solely of Jews at the time of writing, i.e., only Jews who had heard Paul speak in the local synagogue. It is very probable that the majority of the Jews who had at first accepted Paul's message had since turned away, leaving only Gentile and "God-fearing" believers. Paul states that the Thessalonians had left "idols" (i.e., demons that possessed idols, images, and sacred objects), and does not imply, as in Galatians, really anything concrete about Jewish adherents, nor does he provide Hebrew references or scriptural support for the *euangelion*, which would suggest the presence of Jews. Consequently, this would imply a much longer period of residence in Thessaloniki. It is interesting that the narrator of many sections of Acts, known as the "we" passages, are not evident in this section, thus, an eyewitness may not have been present. If so, Acts 16–27 may only included selected secondary reminiscences.

Perilous Risk, Countermeasures and Practices

Paul confirms that he worked in his trade while in Thessaloniki, further suggesting an established and more extended stay there. While he claims the right as an *apostolos* to make a demand for support,[69] he made no such claim on them and, instead, supported himself, so as to not be a *barei*, a heavy burden: "For you remember our labor and toil, brethren; we worked night and day, that we might not burden any of you, while we preached the gospel of God."[70] Paul's use of "night and day" confirms that he plied his portable trade of leatherworking or tent making. This trade demanded long days with many sleepless nights in tight quarters, often grueling conditions, just to earn a subsistence living. As a leatherworker, Paul was able to carry his box or bag of tools with him, and so was mobile. There is evidence that tentmakers' fingers and hands became swollen and arthritic, perhaps explaining why Paul signs his letter to the Galatians, "See with what large letters I am writing you."

---

67. That is, by way of his reported training under Gamaliel, a renown first-century CE rabbi in Jerusalem—although Paul himself does not name his teacher, he does say that he excelled in training beyond any of his colleagues; only the writer of Acts mentions Gamaliel, see above.

68. A Greek name, and possibly a relative of Paul, see Rom 16:21, "Timothy, my fellow worker greets you; so do Lucius and Jason and Sosipater, my kinsmen."

69. See 2:6, clearly a reference to a saying of Jesus—"the laborer is worthy of his hire"—and obviously practiced by some of the other apostles including Peter who was accompanied by his wife per Paul in 1 Cor.

70. 1 Thess 2:9.

Leatherworking and tent making were craftsman trades passed on father to son. Indeed, as a Pharisee, Paul's father would have ensured he apprenticed at an early age in his own trade, or one that would have insured he could remain financially independent and ritually pure.[71] The implications are clear. While Paul may have received a Jewish education, as he is well versed in the Septuagint, leatherworking or tent making confirm he was not from the elite class, nor likely a Roman citizen.[72]

Tradesmen such as Paul often followed the Roman army as they moved in the field, traveling to where they were garrisoned, i.e., to repair and make tanned goat or calf-skin tents, usually for the *contubernium* (eight-man tent group, standard in the legions) or other portable quarters (officer quarters), or they remained near military assemblages or in cities where tents were needed. In major population centers, leather workers and tentmakers also made awnings, leather harnesses and straps, as well as lodging tents near ports for sailors and travelers who landed, as the inns were notoriously dangerous. Temporary accommodations were also provided for sports festivals, such as the Pythian games, or those held in Corinth. Virtually every major population center had a need for similar expertise, whether repair or new work. As such, Paul's portable trade was a perfect compliment to itinerant travels, as he could arrive in a city and seek out members of his trade. Ron Hock has thoroughly described Paul's workplace ministry and itinerancy.[73] It is entirely possible that Paul was conducting a major portion of his teaching, and even exorcisms, while working in his trade to support himself.[74] Hock confirms this by looking at other historical parallels to the workshop setting of Paul's ministry. Upper-caste and wealthy Romans and Greeks held very low opinions of artisans and trade workers like Paul. But it was known that famous Cynic philosophers rose from a workshop setting,[75] and that Paul, an ecstatic exorcist (or magician to some) and charismatic Jew who urgently proclaimed a salvific way to mitigate impending peril and doom, may represent such a possibility to those visiting his workshop.

Since Paul refused support (unlike other wandering charismatics,[76] orators, teachers or philosophers who expected and received it), his *modus operandi* must have followed a similar pattern each time he entered a metropolis where he planed to take up his trade and board. After his arrival, Paul found other artisans in his trade using as reference others from the cities from which he had traveled.[77] Later evidence supporting this conclusion is found in *The True Word* of the second-century

---

71. Tent making and leatherworking were ritually acceptable trades, while tanning was not.
72. Roetzel, *Paul*, 20–25.
73. Hock, *Social Setting*, 9–121.
74. Paul's use of his sweat from handkerchiefs to expel demons causing illness, Acts 19:11–12, implies that Paul was known as an exorcist and sought out.
75. Hock, *Social Setting*, 37.
76. 1 Cor 9:5.
77. E.g., Aquila and Prisca when he went to Ephesus.

pagan writer, Celsus, who vehemently criticizes Christianity. He states Christianity was comprised of "wool-workers, cobblers, laundry workers, and the uneducated," i.e., those who had come into the community through trade associations. This confirms that there were associations of subsistence working artisans who practiced a workshop strategy just like that of Paul's.[78]

Once employed, likely in an established workshop with two to four other workers, Paul may have been allowed to sleep in the back of the workshop, or in the loft above the shop and share meals. He would then attend guild or trade meetings and Sabbath services. Synagogue assemblies must have included local Jews and Gentile "God-fearers" who were subsistence workers like Paul. Since Paul specifically refers to himself in 1 Thessalonians as an example to follow, and later instructs his recipients to "admonish the idlers," it is virtually certain that he did ply his trade and worked for his wages while there, and expected all of the Thessalonian adherents to do the same. Consequently, as in other cities he entered, Paul employed his itinerant strategy using his trade as an entry point and to support himself. Thus, his workshop setting was an integral part of his itinerant strategy.

No matter what may be said about the exact length of his stay, Paul was effective, as the result was the formation of a new *ecclesia*, composed of a handful to two dozen followers, men and women. His strategy of employing a dual tactic, i.e., a workplace ministry and Sabbath preaching, had been successful.[79] The recipients of his letter in Thessaloniki could not dispute it, evidenced by Paul's comfort in including such statements as indisputable.[80] Indeed, the Thessalonian adherents obviously acknowledged this success, for they were not only willing, but did suffer religious, social and perhaps even physical persecution for the Way. According to Paul: "For you suffered the same things from your own countrymen as they [i.e., the churches in Judea from the Jews]."[81] Here it is plainly stated (i.e., as an observable fact by Paul who was a witness to the difficulties facing the *ecclesia* in Jerusalem)[82] that the

---

78. Origin, *Against Celsus*, 3.44.

79. This was Paul's *modus operandi*, he would enter a metropolis and locate the synagogue, making himself and his training known, thereby being welcomed and offered to speak; then he would seek workshop employment in his trade, tent making, by contacting the local guild or other workers. It is possible that Paul's skills were advanced and afforded him immediate employment. Yet, Paul admits he works "night and day," thereby confirming that he shared the very difficult work and long hours, combined with minimal pay.

80. The point here is that these statements prove that Paul was an effective itinerant missionary, establishing new communities in major metropolitan areas that were even willing to withstand confrontation and persecution, even at the earliest stages—1 Thessalonians is a critical witness to Paul's successful strategy and the risk others were willing to take when becoming adherents.

81. 1 Thess 2:14.

82. Paul may have had the persecution of Herod Agrippa I in mind, about 44 CE, where he had James the brother of John beheaded, and attempted to destroy the early church in Jerusalem; this would have been only five years before Paul's letter to the Thessalonians.

Thessalonian persecution was equal to that experienced by those in Jerusalem—there was great risk, suffering and even physical peril.

Ironically, Paul's insistence on "working with one's own hands" is confirmation of an intense eschatological expectation as to the near term *parousia*: "Make it your ambition to lead a quiet life: You should mind your own business and work with your hands, just as we told you, so that your daily life *may win the respect* of outsiders and so that you will not be dependent on anybody."[83] Indeed, Paul's manual labor set *the* standard to follow, as Paul uses it to defend himself from personal attacks on his character by his opponents, including opponents in Corinth.[84] In no better way can the eschatological tension between the present and future be understood for Paul. Working at one's labor today confirmed the cataclysmic changes soon to come, for any change is unnecessary, even meaningless, in that one is called in the last days and in their current state. More important, sustaining one's current situation (unless a change can benefit service to the Lord) may influence change among those who witness reserve and peaceful life in the looming shadow of the *parousia*.[85]

Vocation as Eschatological Event

Paul employed the same word, *parousia*,[86] to describe the coming of Jesus as that contemporarily used to depict the pending arrival of a great ruler, a king or Caesar, to a Hellenistic city[87] (as noted, the coming of the Christ, like a king, also reflecting the imagery of the Sinai theophany,[88] or of Exodus 19, Isaiah 26–27 or Zachariah; in this case, the *parousia* led to the king's defeat of Satan and the curse of death). The analogous *hemera kuriou*, "Day of the Lord," was coming like "a thief in the night."[89] The anticipation of a king's arrival was real and intense, already felt and anticipated. Preparations were immediately put in place to honor the coming king—this was so active an expectation that everything was centered on that day, both joy and trepidation,

---

83. 1 Thess 4:11–12.

84. 2 Cor 11:7–11: "Was it a sin for me to lower myself in order to elevate you by preaching the gospel of God to you *free of charge*? I robbed other churches by receiving support from them so as to serve you. And when I was with you and needed something, I was not a burden to anyone, for the brothers who came from *Macedonia* supplied what I needed [the believers from the church in Thessaloniki most likely]. I have kept myself from being a burden to you in any way, and will continue to do so. As surely as the truth of Christ is in me, nobody in the regions of Achaia will stop this boasting of mine. Why? Because I do not love you? God knows I do!"

85. 1 Cor 7:17–24.

86. 1 Thess 4:15: "For this we say to you by the *word of the Lord*, that we who are alive and remain until the *coming* of the Lord will by no means precede those who are asleep."

87. Koester, "Paul's Eschatology," 59–60.

88. See Plevnik, *Paul and the Parousia*, 5–11.

89. Ibid., 117–18. Plevik and other scholars have shown this to be from an earlier tradition, and that Paul is employing a saying or words (*logoi*) of Jesus. A similar saying is found in the *Gospel of Thomas*, Saying 21, and in Q source, reflected in Luke 12:39; Matt 24:43; 1 Thess 5:2.

soon to come. For Paul, embracing the salvific gospel included working with one's own hands, showing love and mercy to one's neighbor, and living a peaceful life; all were *part of this preparation for the coming of the Lord*, but is was also to protect the adherent from Satan, demonic possession and evil intent of enemies, fully evident in the attacks on Paul by enemies, human and otherwise. To employ this imagery was clearly to draw from the vivid experience *of the Gentile converts*. But with the arrival of Caesar or a king, there was great risk and the potent of judgment and retribution for enemies. Jesus, as Paul notes, is coming, but the arrival portends prosecution, subjugation and annihilation of all enemies (including Satan), and then the kingdom!

Paul embraces this expectation. He radically reorients it by emphasizing *the coming of the crucified and resurrected Jesus of Nazareth* as Christ; it is he who has been appointed to deliver the kingdom to God after he destroys all of God's enemies, including death.[90] The image of a crucified Lord would be shocking, as the retributive dead sought revenge and justice, a very terrifying and real expectation in the ancient world.[91] But, according to Paul, it is this event that also offers hope and life to all who turn and embrace *pistis* in the resurrected Lord *and practice agape*, i.e., embracing faith that Jesus is Christ, working peacefully at one's vocation, and thereby, humbling oneself before God as a child through the practice of divine and efficacious love—it is this and only this that provides safety from evil and judgment at the *parousia*. For Paul, *it is Christ's imminent* presence that calls for preparation, for with the return comes cataclysmic judgment of enemies and the new age in the kingdom of God for adherents. Those who embrace *pistis* in Jesus as Christ are safe "from the wrath to come,"[92] and receive the gift of life, to "be with the Lord forever."[93] Consequently, Paul's contextual placement of "working with one's hands" in the intense expectation of the joy of the "coming" of the Lord, lifts one's work to eschatological preparation for the Lord's arrival; one's work becomes more than a vocation, it is a *charismatic act that identifies true adherents in the last days*. As such, all vocations of the children of Abba', *regardless of social standing*, become eschatological preparation for the coming of Jesus and arrival of the kingdom of God. Vocation is thereby transformed; it becomes evidence of transformation and preparation for the arrival of the Lord and the *parousia*. Adherents are participants in the imminent eschatological event.

While not by any means a chosen vocation, Paul includes slavery in this democratized list of those who could serve the gospel, and more important, were *equal brothers and sisters in the new age*.[94] However, if, as noted in Paul's letter to Philemon on behalf

---

90. See 1 Thess 5 and the earliest description of the order of the *parousia* in the New Testament.

91. Busse, *Jesus*, 12–17.

92. 1 Thess 1:10.

93. 1 Thess 4:15–17.

94. Recall that in Galatians, Paul tears down all barriers of social status ("neither Jew nor Greek, male nor female, slave or free") in the democratized *ecclesia* of God—this is true of all vocations as well, unless they detract or demean the Way (we will see this problem emerge radically in 1 Corinthians among Paul's enemies there).

of the slave Onesimus, one's vocation or social status could be bettered to advance the success in spreading the *euangelion*, then one should seek to *do so immediately*. It is in this context that Paul speaks to other issues of preparation, such as remaining single and his allowance of divorce from unbelievers—both facilitate one's effectiveness as a child of God and proclamation of the *euangelion*. Paul's identification of vocation as an eschatological event is something completely new. It demonstrates beyond doubt that Paul expected the *parousia* in his lifetime, and the peril of any failure to embrace itinerancy meant his doom. This is fully evidenced in the shocking metamorphosis of his vocation: The radical conversion from clandestine work as Saul, the paid spy, informant and murderer for the Roman sympathizing Jerusalem elite (perhaps even once using his trade as a means to infiltrate guilds, trade associations and artisan settings), to Paul the very public, itinerant eschatological exorcist who advocated an evildoer, a crucified Jewish magician, as his risen Lord. The acceptance of vocational change was most certainly to accept risk and perilous danger. This is what makes Paul's correspondence so compelling to analysts of risk.

Indeed, Paul states that he lives day to day, as if the end of the age is already present and tomorrow may be its last.[95] From the perspective of his Jewish heritage, Paul understood his appointment as the most urgent and terrifying in history—he has been chosen from *before birth* by God to serve him in this capacity in the last days. It is no wonder that he sees himself as completely unworthy, i.e., as "one untimely born."[96] He had not only encountered Jesus post-crucifixion, he continued to be in contact with his new Lord, the Christ.[97] Paul must be possessed by Christ to receive protection from Satan and his angels and demons, as well as provide his new adherents with urgent guidance and assurance, or he will lose an *ecclesia* and his "seal" as an *apostolos* and face doom.[98] Paul did not understand his position as glorious or higher than any other in the work of the Way, but as a tremendous burden.[99] Called a fool, stoned and left for dead, beaten, reviled, hungry and excommunicated from his own people and heritage, the risks that Paul embraced for the *euangelion* evidenced what other risks existed if he failed to accept this role and by the *work of his hands*. Paul is compelled to push himself everyday to his limits, to execute his strategy of missionary work from city to city using all of the tools given to him and to bear every physical and mental anguish necessary "for the sake of the gospel" and, as he so movingly states in Galatians, for "the Son who loved me."[100] But Paul is compelled to deliver all the hope laid upon him by his Lord and the Father: "Woe to me if I do not preach the gospel."[101]

95. 1 Thess 5:2.
96. See 1 Cor 15:1–10.
97. 1 Cor 11:23.
98. 1 Thess 4:15.
99. 2 Cor 10:12–18.
100. Gal 2:20.
101. This statement captures not a regret, but the reality and significance of his appointment and

Paul's Use of Sayings (*Logia*) of Jesus and the Risen Lord to Confront Enemies

The pre-advent death of adherents has fostered a crisis in the Thessalonian *ecclesia*. Indeed, the question urgently sent by messenger to Paul reflects more than a theological conundrum—there is serious dissonance creating perilous risk that threatens the survival of the *ecclesia*. Paul could lose his adherents to satanic forces. His response provides a definitive and powerful mitigation to the crisis if accepted, but more, it is important evidence as to how *apostoloi* such as Paul blended and melded sayings of the Lord, both pre- and post-crucifixion *logia*, to mitigate crises in the *stiz im leben* of various *ecclesiae* and to confront enemies, human or demonic. Paul's use of these *logia* in 1 Thessalonians confirms that eschatological tenets were still in oral formation at the time of its writing, the most dramatic example of which is Paul's presentation of *parousia*, which is strikingly different than the much later synoptic apocalypses, such as Mark 13,[102] which address risk crises facing those communities.

It is clear that Paul employed "words of the Lord" in debates and as *propaganda* to strengthen and confirm the cataclysmic and imminent eschatological crisis now unfolding.[103] He also used them to authenticate the divine origin of his charismatic powers and the efficacious *euangelion*; provide *paraenesis* and confirmation of rituals and practices; and to attack and curse (in the name of the Lord) enemies who corrupted and misused *logia* as under satanic influence. The Thessalonian subsistence laborers, patrons, artisans and those attending synagogue assemblies who heard Paul's preaching would have been confronted with selected *logia* almost immediately, particularly as he upended their social and religious worlds by revealing the true nature of the conflict. Some of the *logia* were already well established in oral form. For example, "For you yourselves know well that the *day of the Lord* will come like a *thief in the night*."[104] Here Paul references a saying attributed to Jesus of Nazareth spoken during his itinerant war on Satan in Palestine—a dire warning of the urgent nearness of the end of the age and kingdom of God that demands a response.[105] This is the earliest citation of *logoi* of Jesus of Nazareth in the New Testament, predating the earliest canonical gospel, Mark, by fifteen or more years.[106]

Since Paul encountered only the post-crucifixion Jesus, it is significant when he quotes *logia* from *the pre-crucifixion period of Jesus' war on Satan*, and it is very instructive how they are employed. Paul, as is evidenced in Galatians and other undisputed

---

its weighty responsibility as the age rapidly comes to its end.

102. Here Jesus is now associated with the Son of Man, bar nasha, a messianic and retributive figure of Jewish apocalypticism reflected in 4 Ezra and similar documents.

103. 1 Thess 4–5.

104. 1 Thess 5:2.

105. Luke 12:39–40.

106. 1 Thessalonians dates to about 49–51 CE, while Mark dates to 69–71 CE.

writings, had no need to rely on the past teachings or traditions about Jesus[107] since Jesus was risen Lord and was active in not only guiding, but providing charismatic powers and signs to punctuate the authority of his itinerant mission to spread the efficacious *euangelion*. Indeed, the signs, or proofs, of his divine appointment and legitimacy (and demonstration of the salvific power of the *euangelion*) via Spirit possession, exorcisms, curses and blessings, all validated his standing and authority also as an *apostolos* of the active, risen Lord. So, it is fitting here that when Paul provides instruction in relation to the advent of the end of the age, *he seamlessly blends logia spoken during Jesus' violent war on Satan and demonic imperialism*[108] *with new sayings from the risen Lord*, i.e., "by word of the Lord"; that is, pre-crucifixion *logia* are blended with sayings Paul has received by vision, trace, soul or spirit transportation to the "third heaven," or in dreams—all of which were considered equally valid with sayings he has heard circulating in oral tradition.[109] Most important, Paul freely introduces and interprets *logia* attributed to Jesus,[110] or that he received, to meet the *sitz im leben* present, particularly when confronting enemies, human or otherwise. Indeed, 1 Thessalonians is both testament to and validation of the trajectory of oral sayings traditions, and more, how sayings of the risen Lord entered into the oral tradition via *apostoloi*.[111] Thus, it is evident then that sayings Paul knew were from the pre-crucifixion period were used, adapted and applied with other *logia* as required. This means that some older sayings were retained only if they were useful, which provides clear evidence of form-critical assertions of an active and selective oral period of transmission of Jesus' *logia* that can be studied and sometimes accurately recovered with the *sitz im leben* of the early church. For example, Paul has introduced Jesus of Nazareth's saying, the "thief in the night," in formulating his answer to the Thessalonian crisis, i.e., the pre-advent death of adherents. Taking it from the context of Jesus' eschatological ministry,[112] Paul recontextualizes it by placing it within a new eschatological framework. Therefore, the new saying of the risen Lord (1 Thess 4:15) is now recontextualized to meet the concerns and needs (actually, the crisis) of the Thessalonians, i.e., it is adjusted as a dynamic oral saying that may be used by an *apostolic* authority, such as Paul, to address a new life setting. To explore this further, how is the Thessalonian life situation different than that of Jesus' war on Satan, and more, how has Paul adapted the saying to mitigate the risk of the new *sitz im leben*?

107. Reflected in the canonical gospels, other than items primarily related to the passion narrative, including the Last Supper, betrayal, crucifixion and resurrection, all of which are referenced.

108. Busse, *Fire*, 70–82.

109. Morton, *Magician*, 110.

110. This will be evidenced shortly, as well as in the risk analysis of Paul's adaptation and use of *logia* when battling his Corinthian opponents, who clearly claim their authority from a document that primarily consists of carefully selected *logia* of the Lord.

111. That is, *apostoloi* such as Paul or others, such as Didymas, Judas, Thomas, or James!

112. Jesus is here speaking of the arrival of God that is imminent and the inbreaking of the kingdom of God already becoming present, evidenced by "Satan falling like lightening."

The Enemies of Paul: Demons, Satan, Betrayers, and Apostles

To be clear, Paul has recast Jesus' urgent eschatological warning concerning the nearness of the kingdom of God, the perilous risk to those who reject his demand to resist Satan and demonic imperialism and embrace *agape* and the efficacious *euangelion* (i.e., *agape* as the only valid protection and charismatic sign of repentance and acceptance of the *euangelion*, and thus the mitigation to impending judgment and annihilation of God's satanic enemies), by inserting it into a new more comprehensive eschatological framework. This framework now includes what happens to adherents that have died before the *parousia*; that is, it attempts to neutralize the Thessalonian crisis. Thus, in response to the Thessalonian *sitz im leben*, Paul introduces a new saying of the risen Lord to mitigate the dissonance and risk emerging from the pre-advent death of adherents, and then incorporates the "thief in the night" saying from Jesus' war on Satan to remind them of the nearness of the *parousia* and necessity for a holy life (to be sober, act in *agape*, and be strong in *pistis*), so as to "obtain the hope [*elpida*] of salvation through our Lord Jesus Christ."[113] Those who practice this are *huioi photos*, "sons of light," and not *huioi hemeras ouk semen nuktos oude skotous*, "sons of night and darkness," i.e., deadly enemies, those of Satan.[114]

We learn a great deal from this "blending" of sayings. For Paul, there is no difference in the importance of the either saying; that is, no preeminence is given to sayings of Jesus from his war period, and in fact, there is some evidence that believers recast all of Jesus' sayings in the light of Easter, i.e., that Easter revealed their true and full meaning. This is why knowing "Christ in the flesh"[115] is immaterial to Paul. He is not just in contact with the risen Lord, the risen Lord's spirit possesses him as does the Holy Spirit.[116] Since the beginning, when God "revealed" his son to Paul,[117] the risen Jesus had been active, compelling him "to preach [the *euangelion*] among the Gentiles" given the now more urgent eschatological crisis. First Thessalonians confirms that the sayings tradition was a living, vibrant, orally malleable tradition in the hands of the *apostolos* Paul[118] who is establishing communities under both the commission and influence of the living Lord[119]—for the *parousia* is about to arrive. Consequently, Paul's authority to develop oral tradition and amend it is unlimited in support his *euangelion* of the cross. It is his right as an apostle.[120] Only he is authorized to define the eschatological outlook by appealing to the *logoi* of the

---

113. 1 Thess 5:8.

114. 1 Thess 5:5.

115. 2 Cor 5:16.

116. Gal 2:20; 4:6; Rom 5:5; 8:9–11; 1 Cor 2:4.

117. Gal 1:16.

118. Or for that matter, Paul's opponents, such as in Corinth who arrive with a written sayings document collected to foster their theological stance and radical behavior.

119. Gal 1:15–16.

120. Paul's contention that the divorce of believers from nonbelieving spouses in 1 Corinthians (only if they leave the believer, 1 Cor 7:16) and his refusal to take compensation for his ministry (for which he is accused of being a false apostle in 1 Cor 9:4–27).

Lord. Thus, 1 Thessalonians confirms that it was an apostolic practice to employ and amend sayings of the Lord to meet the situation in life of the early community, and this tradition continued in oral transmission until the compilation of the canonical gospels, Mark, Matthew, Luke and John, and even sources such as Q. Without allowing for this alien world, where demons, Satan and evil dominated and death was a curse, where the risen Lord was about to arrive with judgment of satanic enemies, we cannot fully grasp the power of Paul's use of *logia* of the risen Lord (the one who overcame Satan and death) as words of assurance.

In presenting the new eschatological framework, Paul defines the stages of the *parousia* in rather remarkable detail (see below), and through his presentation, he gives dramatic new hope to the adherents by mitigating risk, emphatically stating that those who have died are only "sleeping" (those who have died "in the Lord"). Paul confirms that the risen Lord has plainly told him that the dead in Christ are not lost or forgotten, but simply await the imminent *parousia*. Indeed, Paul provides remarkable comfort to the Thessalonians in crisis—that the "dead in Christ" are the first to be raised and enter eternal life. It is they who will be the ones leading the celebratory procession out to greet the arriving Lord. They are the first to hear the announcement of that the Day of the Lord has arrived with a shout and trumpet.

Crisis, Enemies and Paul's Mitigation of Perilous Risk

Timothy, who was sent to Thessaloniki by Paul from Athens to see if opponents from Philippi had turned the Thessalonians against them,[121] has returned to his master with troubling news. The Thessalonians were encountering persecution[122]—both verbal and physical attacks from opponents under the influence of Satan, or by demons themselves.[123] The full nature of the persecution is not clear, but it engendered Paul's charismatic correspondence, which includes warnings, powerful *logia* of the risen Lord, blessings and reminders of *charismata*, signs and wonders evidencing the Holy Spirit,[124] that if abandoned, mean satanic victory and death—the wrath to come.[125] As noted, the attack included the introduction of the dissonance by opponents concerning the death of adherents before the *parousia*, the earliest conflict over the delay of the *parousia* recorded in the New Testament. But more, Paul was named a deceiver, i.e., the illegal dark magician and charlatan seeking monetary gain just expelled from Philippi,[126] for which he was almost killed. He reminds them he "labored night and day" as a subsistence leather worker employing his itinerant strategy of workshop

121. 1 Thess 2:4–6.
122. 1 Thess 1:3b.
123. 1 Thess 3:3–5.
124. 1 Thess 1:6.
125. 1 Thess 1:10.
126. Implied by 1 Thess 2:2; see the previous discussion on Paul's rejection at Philippi.

infiltration into the local trade or guild previously discussed.[127] It is clear most of the adherents have rejected such charges against Paul, and still hold him to be divinely empowered by the risen Lord to overcome demonic attack, the infection of death and wrath of God evidenced by the signs he performed there and the protection he and the risen Lord can provide. Nonetheless, they have requested he return as soon as possible.[128] *Agape* permeates Paul's opening comments, emphasizing the relationship they share—children, father and familial references, signifying the efficacious presence of divine practices, and thus, protection from demonic attack and peril.

Like his Thessalonian adherents, Paul expects to be alive for the *parousia*. In the interim, both he and the adherents are mystically saturated with divine protection, i.e., divine *agape*, providing safety from the annihilation of satanic forces and death. *Pistis* in the *euangelion* and the practice of *agape*, which is the penultimate command of the Lord,[129] inoculates the adherent and assures that body, soul and spirit are safe: "May the God of peace himself sanctify you wholly; and may your spirit and soul *and body* be kept sound and blameless at the coming of the Lord Jesus Christ."[130] Those who accept the *euangelion* of Paul of Tarsus are thus imbued with this mystical protection from the curse and infection of death, as the *parousia* was immanent. Yet, if so, why had some died?

It is critical to grasp the dissonant impact death had on Paul's adherents. Virtually all of Paul's Gentile adherents had abandoned the rituals and rites of other cults and mystery religions that were thought to afford protection from evil forces and assure an afterlife. More, by embracing Paul's *euangelion* and practicing what many of his enemies considered abhorrent cultic rituals (such as digesting the blood and flesh of a crucified risen Lord so as to unite one with the one many considered a possessed magician and necromancer), they were adopting a dangerous, marginal, if not illegal cult. It was considered heretical by many Jews and Gentiles, but particularly by Rome and the civic authorities sympathetic to the empire, including the Jerusalem elite that captured and had him brutalized and ritually executed, and appointed hit men, informants and assassins such as Saul to annihilate followers of Jesus in Palestine. Both the Thessalonian persecution and the debilitating questions about Paul's legitimacy and death of adherents confirmed they were not safe, but instead, were in perilous risk. Failure to explain the experience of death prior to the *parousia*, or place death in the context of the sweeping eschatological events unfolding, likely would mean the loss of the Thessalonian community to Satan—a catastrophic failure for Paul, placing at risk the safety of his body, soul and spirit, undercutting his legitimacy of his appointment as the emissary of Jesus Christ.

---

127. 1 Thess 2:9.
128. Clearly to Paul's relief.
129. Gal 5:14.
130. 1 Thess 5.

And so, Paul begins framing his risk mitigation response by appealing to an unassailable, powerful authority—the risen Lord: "We declare by the *word of the Lord*,"[131] meaning, he appeals to an encounter he has recently had with the risen Lord, not *logia* or traditions that originated during Jesus' war on Satan. This is immensely important—Paul is clearly asserting that the living, active Lord not only anticipated their crisis, but that the risen Jesus Christ has exclusively given his *apostolos* an authoritative vision encounter and revelation to convey, perhaps secretly to the Thessalonian adherents, the coming events.[132] What follows then is an apocalypse, and specifically the eschatological sequence of events that will soon unfold with the imminent return of Christ with the kingdom of God. That this was a revelatory vision or trace is confirmed by how Paul describes what he witnessed in it, that is, stark and striking visual imagery of the *parousia* like that of a king or Caesar to a city, but here coming from heaven to earth. Jewish imagery is evident, such as the trumpet and accompanying angels and arch. The vision Paul received, spoken by *logoi* of the Lord, is recounted:

> According to the *Lord's word*, we tell you that we who are still alive, who are left until the coming of the Lord, will certainly not precede those who have fallen asleep. For the Lord himself will come down from heaven, with a loud command, with the voice of the archangel and with the trumpet call of God, and the dead in Christ will rise first. After that, we who are still alive and are left will be caught up together with them in the clouds to meet the Lord in the air. And so we will be with the Lord forever.[133]

Even the dead in Christ are saturated with mystical protection until the *parousia*. There is nothing to fear. Paul has powerfully mitigated the perilous risk of pre-advent death, making death the most honored state of being for adherents of the *euangelion*; it is they who will first be raised to meet the Christ at the *parousia*.

The Composition of the *Ecclesia*

The composition of the *ecclesia* in Thessaloniki underscores its radical eschatological outlook and concomitant practices. Paul appoints temporary leaders: "those who labor among you and are over you [or literally 'taking the lead']."[134] This is terminology familiar to leadership in a trade association or guild in the ancient world (see below), not a defined ecclesiastical order, such as that described in the pseudepigraphical 1 and 2 Timothy. Indeed, this language is further evidence of Paul's urgent strategy of infiltrating trades and guilds to gain adherents in the spread of the *euangelion*. The lack of hierar-

---

131. 1 Thess 4:21.

132. It appears in no other undisputed letters of Paul.

133. 1 Thess 4:15–17.

134. 1 Thess 2:18; it is interesting that satanic opposition to Paul's progress could not be stopped, but "hindered," meaning that the eschatological overturning of God's enemies had begun.

chical structure in Thessaloniki confirms Paul's intense eschatological expectation—the *parousia* is imminent and overseers are all that are necessary there.[135] As such, those who "took the lead" and their specific leadership functions are not identified, other than ensuring the efficacious practice of *agape*. The eschatological conflict of the last days was fully engaged: Paul's deep concern about persecution and his need to send Timothy back from Athens to check on their condition and his inability to return because Satan was attacking him,[136] provides context for the conflicts being experienced. Paul's use of the phrase *enekopsen hemas ho satanas* is not a euphemism—Satan and his demons are confronting Paul, and by inference, the Thessalonian adherents. Their "labor" is most certainly urgent support for the immediate needs of the other adherents under attack, as well as collection of money for the commune in Jerusalem.[137]

Agape was the efficacious, cohesive and distinctive element of Paul's *ecclesia* in Thessaloniki, and its practice was expected and essential to permeate all relationships as a very real and potent guard and shield against aggressive demonic attacks—as long as *agape* was practiced, divine charisma was evident.[138] Those "taking the lead" were the *men and women* Paul perceived as having the *charismata* of *agape*, and by their example they would bond the adherents to the risen Lord, and having been possessed by the spirit of Christ survive ridicule, physical attack by humans and demons, social persecution and even pre-advent death. In fact, so successful were they in expressly demonstrating the characteristics of *agape* that the Thessalonian *ecclesia* had become well known throughout "all of Macedonia[139] and Achaia."[140] Paul instructs the adherents to follow these leaders in matters of import. They are authorized to "admonish," instruct and correct, the *ecclesia* as if "brothers and sisters," specifically in right behavior and the practice of *agape*. Paul's instruction implies that these leaders are accountable to his apostolic authority and charismatic powers, including the power to bless and curse.

Since Paul practiced his trade "night and day" just to survive, and so, was forced to explain his encounter with a crucified and risen Jew and the urgent *euangelion* he was charged to deliver while in the arduous workshop setting of Thessaloniki,[141] it is certain that many of his first adherents (if not the majority) came from subsistence

---

135. It is interesting that, unlike Paul's other letters, there are no named local believers in the salutation or conclusion to the letter like those found in other letters of Paul (e.g., see Rom 16 that has a long list of specific names and greetings).

136. 1 Thess 2:18.

137. Acts 6:1–7.

138. 1 Thess 5:8, Paul uses the imagery of putting on armor, including the "breastplate of faith and love," perhaps indicating that some of the adherents may have been artisans that supplied the Roman army, or repaired equipment, and would be familiar with these items. More likely, *pistis* and *agape* are the efficacious protection from satanic and demonic attack, and so, they are the eschatological armor of the war against Satan.

139. Macedonia is the Roman province of Greece, with Thessaloniki as its capital—this would imply that there were other ecclesia in the province beyond Philippi that had believers.

140. That is, Greece.

141. As noted, much longer than the three weeks implied by Acts.

laborers like himself, both men and women, Gentile and Jew; in other words, the leatherworkers or tentmakers,[142] as well as those of other trades who interacted with them.[143] Paul was of a fringe and unknown cult, making it impossible for him to initially demand support, despite his later claim he could have done so; and frankly, most who worked with Paul had little. But the protection he offered to escape capricious gods, retributive ghosts, curses, demonic attack, illness and even death, combined with the radical social changes that he explained were about to unfold for these struggling workers with the arrival of the *parousia* (i.e., what was thought before Paul's arrival to be an unimaginable escape from generational hunger, poverty and social oppression) were enormously appealing to those desperate, exhausted workers. The offer of freedom from the fear of death and generational poverty, the promise of divine adoption as a son or daughter of God in a new kingdom of justice and mercy, were overwhelming. More, Paul's promises were confirmed by *charismata* and signs he demonstrated "in power" by the Holy Spirit and risen Lord, including expulsion of demonic illness through the application of sweat clothes and handkerchiefs taken from his shop to those possessed by demons. For those new adherents, there were no cult tribute payments required any longer, no commitment of wages to associations,[144] only expectations of support to "brothers and sisters"—in essence a modest redistribution of subsistence wages to a new *ecclesia*. As such, Paul's remarkable *euangelion* was worthy of taking perilous religious, social and personal risks, which could threaten starvation and even arrest and death. Paul's own recounting of his sordid history of brutality and violence and his metamorphosis to *apostolos* of the risen Lord were likewise compelling—he was worse than any of them, and yet he received mercy and appointment. Indeed, he was *the* example for these artisans to follow and emulate, particularly in the practice of divine *agape*. Paul would willingly suffer hardships and subsistence existence, even demonic attack, beatings and attempts destroy him, because the Day of the Lord was immanent. With *pistis* and *agape*, the new adherent, like Paul, was saturated with divine protection, and just in time. This was all that was required to receive not only protection but also *elpis* (hope) and adoption as the last days of the current age hurdled to a catastrophic close.

These artisans were of the uneducated and poor, trapped in generational economic slavery, seen as lower caste and even socially fringe workers. They lived harsh lives with little sleep or food and clothing, and often worked along side slaves, as depicted

---

142. It is not clear that Prisca and Aquila for example were Christians when Paul met them in Corinth; he may have brought them to the Way, having sought out fellow Jews and tentmakers.

143. Origen, *Against Celsus*, 3.44; Celsus, a second-century pagan opponent of Christianity, confirms that even in the second century, the workshop ministry of artisans led others to the ecclesia, and more, that the membership was comprised of artisans, women, salves and uneducated lower class. This is late, but critical confirmation that Paul's first membership was from fellow craftsmen and women and artisans.

144. Barclay, *Pauline Churches*, 110.

in funerary inscriptions.[145] Young children were put to work as soon as they were able, and for long days and nights. Artisans had few rights and virtually none were Roman citizens. Their bodies often bore the signs of labor and hardship, and they often died young.[146] They had been trained and worked in their trade from childhood by their fathers or other relatives to provide for extended families living in cramped, small apartments, or *insulae*, or in the loft of the workshop itself in exchange for wages. There is strong evidence of trade guilds or associations in larger cities, such as Thessaloniki, where workers gathered, worshiped, as well as collected fees for member gatherings, feasts and even burials, There were financial tributes paid to a patron god, its sanctuary or temple and the priest. Paul spoke at meetings of the trade guilds (where work was assigned). These guilds were often affiliated with local cults and feasts of both foreign and local gods. As a result, other artisans or craftsmen may have also joined with the early adherents who had worshiped the same god or deity.[147] Still, clients of higher social status, individuals and political or military representatives, came to the workshop and had their favorite artisans.[148] Certainly, tents and temporary living quarters were needed for visitors, sailors (near their ships), or tourists and athletes who attended special games; particularly the Isthmian games, where there is ample evidence for substantial tent making there during Paul's time.[149]

Paul also drew members from the local Jewish assembly. As an invited speaker on the Sabbath at the local synagogue, Paul may have convinced Jews to the peril present and crisis at hand, as well Gentile "God-fearers," i.e., Gentiles who aligned themselves with the Jewish faith and God of Israel.[150] Indeed, his converts in Corinth reportedly included leaders, such as the "president" of the synagogue, or other Jewish administrators and leaders. While the range of social standing among the Jews was certainly mixed, but Paul acknowledges that the majority were low status.[151]

145. Such as the funerary inscription of Lucius Cornelius Atimetas, see Hawkins, "Cotracts, Coercion and Boundaries," 36–39.

146. Paul's own admission, "See with what large letters I write, I Paul, with my own hand," Gal 6:11, confirming the arthritis or damage in his hands from years of toil and labor as a leatherworker.

147. See also *EGT*, 41.

148 Acts 18:3, Priscilla is mention equally with her husband Prisca as tentmakers, or leatherworkers. Paul "went to see them, and because he was a tentmaker like them, he stayed and worked with them." This confirms Paul's missionary strategy was also operative in Corinth when he arrived, i.e., to see out Jews and tentmakers and then strike up his workshop ministry and find residence among this craftsmen.

149. Koester, "Archaeology and Paul," 38–39; also see Koester, *Cities of Paul*. I was a participant in this project in 1995 with Helmut and other selected graduate students, as well as Professors David Mitten, François Bovon and Karen King.

150. Acts 18:4–8; Paul attracted the leader of the synagogue, Crispus.

151. 1 Cor 1:26–29: "Brothers and sisters, think of what you were when you were called. Not many of you were wise by human standards; not many were influential; not many were of noble birth. But God chose the foolish things of the world to shame the wise; God chose the weak things of the world to shame the strong. God chose the lowly things of this world and the despised things—and the things that are not—to nullify the things that are, so that no one may boast before him."

Local women who were benefactors, particularly widows or those with wealth and social status, sponsored local cults, assemblies, and perhaps some supported a synagogue in Thessaloniki.[152] Women held distinctive roles, including civic and religious titles[153] based on inscription in multiple Roman cities from the period of Paul's itinerant travels. Their participation indicated a very diverse socioeconomic mix of adherents. The overseers whom Paul selected could have been women or men, their primary duty being the unity through *agape*. The adherents entered into ecstatic prayer together (Paul recommends that they pray constantly),[154] communal and individual acts of *agape, charismata*, including prophesying (i.e., the interpretation of Hebrew Scripture and words of the Lord to their *sitz im leben*),[155] recited the Lord's Prayer (i.e., a mystical union with God as Father, and call for protection from Satan and kingdom to arrive), and celebrated a cultic meal (a union with the risen Lord via the ingestion of the body and blood of Jesus, the risen Lord—not dissimilar to the efficacious nature of some cultic meals contemporary with Paul's activity; those guilty of not partaking properly were cursed). The binding force of the *ecclesia* was *pistis* in the efficacious *euangelion* and constant practice of *agape* and "brotherly love," permeated by an intense eschatological expectation of the imminent *parousia*. Paul appeals for respect and *agape*, as the overseers of the Thessaloniki *ecclesia* represented a cross class social and gender status, various religious and cult affiliation origins, citizens, slave and artisans.[156]

The *Ecclesia* as Protection from Satan and Dark Forces[157]

With regard to understanding the *sitz im leben* of Paul's letter to the Thessalonian *ecclesia*, the leaders were overseeing an *interim and loosely knit organization of democratized adherents never before gathered*, one that stood between the present day and the end of the age soon to arrive. Clearly, the new social fabric introduced by Paul in the community of *agape* was unlike any of its time—the new adopted "children" of God the Father, *a free people*; free from the "wrath to come" and "free from fear of death."[158] It was a community of equals, brothers and sisters, or as Paul later describes in Galatians, *the sons and daughters of God*.[159] They were now bound together as family by divine *agape*,

---

152. Kraemer, *Her Share*, 174; Brooten, *Women Leaders*, 15–64, 141–44; also see Kraemer, *Maenads, Martyrs, Matrons*, 27–32, 90–99.
153. Kloppenborg, "Collegia and Thiasoi," 16–30.
154. 1 Thess 5:17.
155. 1 Cor 14:34–35.
156. 1 Thess 5:12.
157. Koester, "Apostle and Church," 25–28.
158. 1 Thess 1:10.
159. See Gal 3:26.

united by rites and practice as members of the body of Christ, most perfectly expressed by the practice of *agape* among the adherents, no matter social status.[160]

This new social unification, primarily of lower castes, poor and socially fringe men and women that made up the mysterious cultic associations of the crucified Lord, were often reviled, ridiculed and violently opposed. Considered more than just offensive to ruling authorities (from Jerusalem to Rome), these *ecclesiae* were sought out by Jewish opponents who followed wandering itinerants such as Paul from metropolis to metropolis, vociferously rejecting his crucified Galilean Jew as Messiah, instead naming him an evildoer like his master, a charlatan who worshiped a necromancer and magician and practice dark magic himself.[161] Consequently, both Jewish and Gentile adherents who joined these cultic gatherings were susceptible to unpredictable levels of persecution, as well as demonic attacks, including the hurling of curses and evil spells cast by enemies; what Paul terms "much affliction."[162] Indeed, Paul's adherents were known to await the retributive return of a condemned Jew, a crucified Roman criminal, naming him Lord and Savior, which are the same titles applied to divine Caesar, Soter and Pontifex Maximus.[163] So offensive, it is understandable why adherents were considered seditious, dangerous, a perilous risk—a bizarre religious cult,[164] and illegal. Roman historians deemed adherents of the cult associates of dark magic, meaning that any informer could reap monetary reward, and that immediate physical abuse of adherents was tolerated.[165] Mobs formed and civic unrest accompanied the spread of the "superstition" because the local populace and administrators feared demonic attack and evil that they believed accompanied practices.[166] There was legitimate concern, as even Paul's own letters included curses and turning opponents

---

160. 1 Thess 3:6–8; 3:12; 4:9–12. See also Koester, "Apostle and Church," 27–28.

161. This rejection extended back into Jesus' ministry when it was asked by the religious elite in Jerusalem, "Can anything good come from Nazareth," later extended into the sarcastic slur against the followers of Jesus after Easter, "the Nazarenes," and lastly expressed in the rejection of Jesus noted here.

162. 1 Thess 1:6.

163. *Soter* translates as the Savior, the keeper and protector of Rome and the people. *Pontifix* was the term of Lord and Ruler, head of the state religion of Rome, later more fully expressed in the combined divinities Roma and Deified Caesar, physically represented in the singular Temple of Dea Roma and Divus Julius (dedicated as a great honor, such as in the metropolis of Ephesus, twice honored, i.e., twice Nikorate); this ultimately led to emperor worship, i.e., devotion and oblation to the emperor as divine. This is the practice that Christians later rejected to perform (as well as a rejection of Jesus as Lord), that led to their execution under Nero (56–66 CE), perhaps Domitian (93–96 CE), and later Trajan (113 CE), as evidenced in the letters of Pliny.

164. The eating of flesh and drinking of blood, i.e., the Lord's Supper, was completely misunderstood by contemporary Romans, such as Pliny the Younger.

165. See Tacitus, *Annals* 15:44, 2–8.

166. This unrest was caused by riots and turmoil between Jews over the incursion of the Way into synagogues, which disrupted major Jewish communities; for the Romans, such as Tacitus, the issue was not the entry of Christianity, but simply conflicts between the various sects of Judaism, particularly between those who were led by Crestus (most certainly a derivative form of Christ, misunderstood by Tacitus), and other Jews; see Tacitus, *Annals* 15:44, 2–8.

over to Satan for destruction of the flesh. Yet, despite this intense affliction, Gentile adherents nonetheless "turned from idols to serve a living and true God,"[167] and thus, likely had withdrawn from many important and familiar social events, celebrations and relationships that were linked to pagan worship, and, as a result were excluded from traditional activities and civic festivals as well. Why would Paul's adherents have publicly withdrawn if they knew the risks?

Paul carefully describes his adherents' withdrawal from popular and familiar social and religious relationships and associations as a decision to "reject *idols*" (i.e., *eidolon*). In Paul's world, such a withdrawal was radical and seditious, as most considered cult and temple idols as divinely possessed, and associations protected by a cult deity. Consequently, Paul's choice of this word is intentional and shocking. They had served lifeless stone *cult statues and deities that were possessed by or under the control of demons*, and whose exploits were founded on lies and demonic ethereal worlds of deceit. Adherents now embraced servitude[168] to the "true and living God,"[169] whose "son" was murdered on a cross by the very persecutors they encountered,[170] but who was raised from the dead—an event witnessed or experienced in visions, trances, ecstatic journeys to the third heaven, not only by Paul and other *apostoloi* (most of who were still living), but by dozens of others that would attest to it, and risked their lives for it. It is these persecutors who were deceived and controlled by satanic forces.[171] The enemies of Christ would meet justice and judgment at the *parousia*. The demonic enemies of God, including these persecutors, were about to be destroyed, leaving only the people "of the light."

Paul then confirms the divine source of his *euangelion*. He reminds the Thessalonians that his *euangelion* came with "power and in the Holy Spirit and with full conviction."[172] In other words, the adherents encountered charismatic events of protection and safety from evil—what only God would provide: Exorcisms and control over afflicting demons of the dead, satanic dark angles and evil entities and spirits; possession by *glossolalia*, speaking in angelic tongues, praising their salvific future, *agape*, and the risen Lord; ecstatic dreams, visions and trances; protection from cast curses and evil spells (including cursed fluids slipped to them thought to be poison and infectious). That demonic activity was thought rampant and deadly in the ancient Hellenistic world has been demonstrated, as demonic possession, exorcism, spells, the

---

167. 1 Thess 1:9.

168. The Greek word is *douleuein*, committed as a slave to a master.

169. Paul's description of the Way and God in many letters, including 1 Thessalonians.

170. This was later documented in 1 Cor 15:1–8, where the earliest listing of resurrection appearances is presented by Paul in a very early formulaic statement of faith, meaning that the statement predated Paul, and so, it was circulating orally (including the allusion to the appearance to over five hundred at one time) a quarter of a century before the first gospel, Mark (69–71 CE), was composed.

171. Hull, *Hellenistic Magic*, 48–54.

172. The absolute assurance by witnessing these events, whatever they may have been—Paul cites what must be well known to the Thessalonians and is indisputable.

attack of ghosts and evil spirits, have been well documented among pagan writers of the first and second centuries.[173] These were all events familiar to their *sitz im leben*. But Paul's adherents were afforded remarkable protection from all of these, given as signs and proof of divine activity, and only experienced when an adherent of Paul's *ecclesia*. Their *pistis* in the efficacious *euangelion*,[174] or as Paul terms it from the outset, "their work of faith"[175] as "adherents"[176] practicing *agape*, ensured not only safety from demons and Satan, but adoption (divine and protective relationship) of God, and a rescue from the judgment to come—not just for those Thessalonians who are alive, but for those adherents who have died, but are simply "asleep"—indeed, it is these who would be first to greet the Lord at the *parousia*. Paul addresses his letter to the whole community of the Thessalonians, ". . . in God the Father and the Lord Jesus Christ" (1:1), not to individuals.[177] They are united in *pistis* and *elpis*, bonded as family and *agape*. They are experiencing satanic distress and persecution as they await justice and hope, which is also proof of their divine status. Indeed, it is the Thessalonians *as a community*, Paul states, who are exercising the most profound characteristics of brotherly love desired by God.[178] Of all of Paul's undisputed letters, this is the only *ecclesia* cited as *the example* for others to follow.

The Perilous Risk of Abandoning Local and Civic Cults

Which contemporary cults and deities active in Thessaloniki would Gentile adherents have rejected, and would they have posed a threat to Paul and his adherents? Certainly, some must have abandoned the city's patron deity, Cabirus (or Kabeiros), once popular with the subsistence and working classes.[179] While details about the cult and its practices are disputed, it is certain that the cult of Cabirus worshiped a bearded young male god, son of Vulcan and Cabira, who was murdered by his two brothers. Initiate rites included cultic baptism uniting one with the god, forgiveness of sins following a confession, and protection and divine aid to the working class (artisans and craftsmen), as well as rescue for the hopeless. Cabirus appeared on the city coins with

---

173. Hull, *Hellenistic Magic*, 48–54.

174. Again, for Paul, the foundation of justification before God as Abba' is faith alone in the *euangelion* of forgiveness, mercy and love, as proclaimed by the son, who died as an expiation for sin, but was raised, and on whose faith and love for those who embrace the salvific *euangelion*, safety and life with the Father.

175. 1 Thess 1:2.

176. 1 Thess 2:10.

177. This will be more fully discussed below by analyzing Paul's use of the term *ecclesia*, or assembly, which he applies to the community of the Thessalonians.

178. 1 Thess 1:7; 4:9–12.

179. Pictured on coins with a rhyton (drinking flask), and hammer, symbol of the working class, the artisans and craftsmen.

Tyche,[180] also protector of the city. Cabirus is shown holding what appears to be a hammer, signifying his association with craftsmen. In other inscriptions of Cabirus, two crossed hammers accompanied the image of the god.

Once the central and preferred deity and protector of the Thessalonian working classes,[181] the cult of Cabirus was apparently appropriated by the upper classes, the wealthy and elite, and then eventually by the city's ruling class, thereby nullifying his exclusive connection with protection of workers and laborers. This was unwelcomed and resulted in the disenfranchisement of artisans and craftsmen, creating significant social animosity. Indeed, there is evidence that the civic leaders of Thessaloniki, the *politarchs*, changed their titles to the *Cabiri*, further offending workers and artisans. While the power of a god was generally enhanced through association with the rich and powerful in the Hellenistic and Roman worlds,[182] this was not the case in Thessaloniki. The loss of the cultic deity by the working class disrupted membership and support at cultic associations of Cabirus and led to an intense resentment of the elite. Thessaloniki was a large seaport and the capital of Macedonia. It had been awarded local autonomy with powerful leaders, and was a center of trade center with merchants and likely several artisan and craftsmen associations, including Cabirus.[183] The well-defined segmentation of the classes and social distancing between the elite and "those who worked with their hands" was pronounced. Seizing the cult of Cabirus was understood as demeaning.[184] This made the introduction of a new cult for slaves, artisans and the working class not only appealing, but also necessary to ensure full protection and safety from the evil and hardships that were being encountered.

Consequently, the absorption of the cult by the elite emptied it of its exclusive power for workers. Subsistence working artisans would have gravitated to a new working-class cult, Paul's *euangelion*, brought to the city by an artisan with charismatic powers, practicing initiate baptism, promising protection from demonic affliction, forgiveness, democratized adoption as a son or daughter of God, and salvation in a coming *parousia* of judgment and justice. Paul's *ecclesia* also provided relief from cultic fees. This was an efficacious *euangelion*, not simply aid or protection of the working class, but much more, rescue and deliverance from death, and life in God's new kingdom. An executed young man and artisan, a *carpenter*, was the Son of God. He had been betrayed by a man considered his brother and was murdered by the elite. But he was raised by his father, was elevated to Christ, the Lord, and savior for all, particularly

---

180. Tyche was the Greek goddess of prosperity and protector of cities in the Hellenistic world; Fortuna was her Roman counterpart; Tyche was the protector of Thessaloniki, like Cabirus—one protector of the civic society and the other for the working people of this important port city; see full discussion on the cult of Cabirus below.

181. The craftsmen and artisans.

182. This is because it was assumed that their prayers were readily heard by the god.

183. This is most probably how Paul was able to find work and support himself—finding his trade association, i.e., his guild association in Thessaloniki.

184. Although, as noted above, Paul expects this for *all* the Thessalonian believers.

the lowly and disenfranchised. Uniting with the risen Lord, Jesus Christ, in cultic practices, including the mystical ingestion of his body and blood, ensured that every adherent would escape the catastrophe that was imminent if they shared in the practice of divine *agape* for each other. They would be raised like him. While rescue was available to all classes, *it was particularly made available and attractive to the working classes, as Paul emphatically demonstrates through personal example of "working with his own hands"*—something he expects of all Thessalonians, as Paul emphasizes it to be an expression of divine *agape*, assuring safety for the adherent. Paul, *the artisan tentmaker*, had not only encountered Jesus only a few years before, but was commanded by him to become and itinerant artisan and to urgently spread the *euangelion* before the *parousia*. The *euangelion* was therefore the message and power of "the true and *living* God," confirmed, as Paul notes, through powerful evidence of Holy Spirit among the Thessalonians in the *charismata* they witnessed.

For these working-class artisans and craftsmen, turning from cult of Cabirus meant conversion *to a more powerful association*, and one that was expecting the presence of the Lord, "like a thief in the night," any day, as well as judgment against the wicked, which must have been thought to include the elite. Paul's success indicates there was indeed a significant disenfranchisement of working artisans and craftsmen from the rule of the elite and the unjust social order; the *euangelion* provided the risk mitigation to this crisis in the *sitz im leben* of these men and women. This new collection of adherents would have been a cohesive social group due to the trade and class associations they already shared; they were, thus, more likely able to withstand economic pressures and social distress from outside sources, perhaps even from the Cabiri, and other leaders of the city. This new artisan and craftsmen association would also explain Paul's use of the term *ecclesia* to describe their assembly, which in the Greco-Roman world is a term used to describe a political or social gathering. Instead of their association being the *ecclesia* of Calibri, or in a trade association associated with the protective deity, they were the "*ecclesia* of the Thessalonians in God the Father and the Lord Jesus Christ" (1:1). It is possible that this *ecclesia* actually strengthened in the face of persecution, perhaps even attracting widespread adherents of the working class, and more important, economically survived or thrived through mutual support and by the necessity of their skills in the city. These factors explain again why Paul addresses the Thessalonians as a collective group.

Another very popular cult that had spread throughout the Greco-Roman world was the cult of Isis. Isis, also known as the Phrygian Cybele to the Romans, was originally an Egyptian deity often portrayed as a crowned mother holding a child. She had sway over life and death, black magic, physical healing,[185] fertility and was the protector of children and women, as well as mother goddess. On a more fundamental basis,

---

185. There are multiple representations of her healings via votive offerings found dating to the first century, including in Thessaloniki. These are ears, feet, arms in sculpted form with statements confirming the healing by the goddess and expression of thanks.

the cult of Isis was centered on rebirth and safety, providing protection from capricious events, curses and black magic, and painful death. Egyptian religion in general was extremely popular in the Roman world, particularly in trade and cultural centers such as Thessaloniki. Contemporaneous with Paul's activity, the cult of Isis in Thessaloniki had absorbed multiple attributes of Greco-Roman female deities, particularly as her cult spread from metropolis to metropolis. Among these attributes was her standing as patron goddess of sailors, and since the temple cult was commonly found in seaports, Thessaloniki undoubtedly had its own sanctuary, established and financed by seamen and local merchants. Indeed, several inscriptions related to the Isis cult have been found in excavations there—more than any other cultic temple.

The myth was ancient and well known. Following the murder and dismemberment of her husband, Osiris, Isis searched the earth, collecting his body parts, and through various practices and cunning, she was able to bring about his rebirth—a resurrection and regeneration of her murdered husband. Cultic initiation inferred a promise of eternal life and rebirth for the initiate, all under the proven power of the goddess Isis (via her husband's rebirth) and her protection. Some priests of Isis[186] were thought to have the power to heal and perform magic, including the ability to influence and control even the weather. Most interesting is the role of women and the apparent equality implied by the female deity and cultic practices. Since social status was democratized in Paul's *ecclesia*, and this included the equal standing of men and women as the new *sons and daughters of God*,[187] it is possible that former adherents of the cult of Isis were attracted to the *euangelion*.[188]

Yet, it is more likely that these women were wealthy patrons of artisans and tradesmen and were attracted to the *ecclesia* because this association and related interest in the new *ecclesia* these artisans had formed, now associated with the risen Lord and God. If Paul, a tentmaker, taught in his workshop setting and worked with those of his own trade, and had also been invited to speak to other artisan and trade associations at a sponsored gathering in a tradesmen building or hall,[189] perhaps a trade organization such as an *ecclesia*, *Paul may have won over complete trade and artisan groups*, thereby forming a newly combined *ecclesia* "in God, the Father, and the Lord Jesus Christ," as opposed to in Cabirus or Isis. The *parousia*, that is, the heralded and celebratory arrival of the Lord, greeting him like a king in joy outside the city gates,[190] more akin to the

---

186. Both men and women priests and priestesses.

187. Evidenced in Paul's letter to the Galatians (3:28) and appointment of women to important roles in his mission work—see Paul's letter to the Romans and the role of Phoebe (16:1–2), as well as other women prominently mentioned, Junias the apostle (16:7).

188. Many of the attributes and practices within the cult would have found strong parallel in Paul's democratized *ecclesia*; that is, all but cultic elitism, e.g., the priesthood and special standing. Paul's proclamation emphasized a risen Lord, but also, the immediate presence of this Lord arriving in history—the cult did not have an eschatological expectation.

189. For example, was this something similar to the "Hall of Tyrannus" in Ephesus?

190. 1 Thess 4:17.

Sinai theophany (the Lord's coming down with trumpets, thunder and lightening),[191] was joyous, but more, imminent, making Paul's urgent appeal to members of any other cult dangerous not to embrace. Indeed, Paul himself was a compelling witness to the risen Jesus, for he murdered adherents before his post-crucifixion encounter. Paul stood as a witness to these events, demonstrated *charismata* and powers, exorcised demons of illness and madness. More, the risen Lord was active with Paul. Cultic members of Cabirus and Isis therefore encountered "the living God."

Other cults, such as the cult of Dionysus, the Hellenistic deity blended with the Egyptian god Osiris, the same murdered husband resurrected by Isis, are more difficult to directly associate with Paul's success in obtaining adherents to his new *ecclesia*.[192] The cult participated in ecstatic revelry and debauchery, sometimes leading to frenzy so outrageous that violent murder occurred. It is possible that Paul indirectly references this cult by way of criticism when he describes the need to live a quiet life, to be sober and remain a "son of the light,"[193] not of "darkness." While this comment is most reminiscent of the Essenes, as reflected in the Dead Sea Scrolls (i.e., the dualistic contrast of light and darkness, and particularly the *War of the Sons of Light and Sons of Darkness*),[194] this may be a reference to a cultic ritual within certain mystery religions, where an initiate is isolated in the dark inner chamber of a sanctuary, and having experience a vision or some other ecstatic experience, was brought forth as if reborn or to new life.

Indeed, the *ecclesia* of Jesus Christ was a new association that democratized social standing and asserted that one's class, wealth or standing in this world as irrelevant. The adherent, as the child of God and member of the new community and kingdom called together by God,[195] was the "new Israel,"[196] the "saints," *agios*, literally the "holy ones."[197] They greet each other with a "holy kiss" (*en phelimati agapes*),[198] not just the common greeting in the Mediterranean world.[199] This was the same kiss that Jesus of Nazareth used to provide protection and bless his exorcists—we know this because it is how Jesus was betrayed by one of his own, i.e., Judas. The kiss carried with it a blessing or curse in the ancient world. Judas' kiss was to disarm and curse Jesus for

191. Plevnik, *Paul and the Parousia*, 9–11.

192. This may have been an issue in Corinth, however. Paul has to admonish the Corinthians about drunkenness at the community's love feast, which clearly points to new believers who may have participated in the cult of Dionysus. Wine was used abundantly to induce a mystic and intoxicated state, indicative of being possessed by the spirit of the god. Through intoxication, the participant returns to their uninhibited natural state of ecstasy, where one is free of social constraints and connected to life and other initiates in a democratized cult of life. The cult was therefore popular with the fringes of society; slaves, women, foreigners, poor, and the lawless.

193. 1 Thess 5:5.

194. See Allegro, *Dead Sea Scrolls*.

195. 1 Thess 2:12.

196. See Gal 3:29.

197. 1 Thess 1:1.

198. See Rom 16:16; certainly a practice in all of Paul's churches.

199. Luke 7:45.

capture, disabling his ability to retaliate.[200] Indeed, this kiss was used to convey dark magic, a death curse. Paul knows of the "holy kiss," i.e., tradition and practice that continued among the *apostoloi* of Jesus, marking it as a familial sign of divine *agape* and protection among the adherents.

Letter as Charismatic and Eschatological Weapon against Satanic Enemies

As noted, 1 Thessalonians is the oldest document in the New Testament, predating the Gospel of Mark by fifteen to twenty years. Paul employs the most common literary form of his day, the personal letter carried by messenger. But clearly as this study has shown, certain elements it contains transform it into a new and powerful apostolic community *document of personal authority and eschatological presence* to confront enemies, human and otherwise. From this perspective, Paul transforms the letter into a new literary genre, a dynamic, efficacious eschatological and charismatic document that can be used to ward off demons, place a curse on enemies, bless and protect adherents, and even confront Satan. In it, *Paul is present, as is the power of the risen Lord*. Paul affirms this in the Corinthian letter: "For though absent in the body I am present in spirit, and as if present, I have already pronounced judgment in the name of the Lord Jesus Christ,"[201] i.e., the reading of his letter and his words make both him and his authority "in the name [presence] of the Lord" present. It is his own voice speaking to them; it is his "spirit" there, in that moment with the adherents. Thus, the letter is an eschatological event: "I adjure [command] you by the Lord that this letter be read to all of the brethren."[202] This is one example of soul transportation, where in speaking, the individual was present, likely believed to be in a trance and with the hearer in its reading.

The importance of this new and powerful literary form introduced by Paul cannot be overemphasized. Through Paul, the common letter was transformed into a charismatic and eschatological proclamation and presence genre, which included efficacious weapons against satanic enemies awarded to him by the risen Lord, as well as protection for adherents, something that the gospels themselves eventually took over. When the apostolic period ended in the middle to later half of the first century, the absence of the powerful personal eschatological presence of the *apostoloi*, which included Paul's letters to his *ecclesiae*, were replaced by the genre of the literary form of the proclamation gospel, which were fostered by the *sitz im leben* of the

---

200. John 12:6: this passage, designating Judas as a "thief," is very old. It shows that Judas Iscariot (the false exorcist, known as the strangler, see Busse, *Jesus Resurrected*, 227) was known to be a liar, covering up his actual intent with deceiving words. He was a paid infiltrator and assassin, much like Saul before his encounter with the risen Jesus. It is often forgotten that he was the "keeper of the bag," see John 13:9. Consequently, he left with much more that his contract bounty money. He had taken everything from the disciples and from Jesus, and gladly so.

201. 1 Cor 5:5.

202. 1 Thess 5:17.

communities they served through the collection of oral traditions that had circulated for decades. The presence of the Lord, who once directed and communicated with his *apostoloi*, was now captured in traditions about this itinerant activity, death, burial and resurrection, and the future promise of his return and reward to the faithful. These oral traditions became crystallized in literary gospels, and so were unassailable and salvific. The dynamic *euangelion* of Paul that had brought the eschatological crisis and his mitigation through *pistis*, *elpis* and *agape* directly to the believer with the fluidity and adaptation of oral traditions and *logia*, all in the intense eschatological context of an imminent *parousia* pressing the demand for decision, was now captured in the literary gospel genre, both the canonical and noncanonical trajectories. Paul's presence and charismatic authority stood behind his letter's efficacious powers as an *apostoloi* of Jesus Christ, while Jesus, the risen Lord and Christ and Holy Spirit's direct authority stood behind that of the gospels. *Euangelion* was shifted back once again to Jesus with the passing of time and the delay of the *parousia*. As such, the void created by Paul's absence, the loss of the *apostoloi* and transference of personal charismatic letters and eschatological assurances to *paraenesis* and instruction, was filled by collecting oral lore and traditions about Jesus that survived and circulated among the *ecclesiae* because they had mitigated conflicts, crisis and needs of their *sitz im leben*—the parables, *logia*, *novella* and others—and were still useful to the remaining nascent Christian communities of the later first and early second centuries. Most were organized around the core salvific event, i.e., the passion narrative, but others were as ancient and were formed around a salvific collection of *logia* of the risen Lord given to an apostolic authority. Paul is emphatic as to his personal voice and presence with them, particularly when he shifts to the first person: ". . . with great desire to see you face to face; because we wanted to come to you—*I Paul*, again and again—but Satan hindered us."[203] The Gospel of John captures this same personal eschatological presences: "This is the disciple who testifies to these things and who wrote them down. We know that his testimony is true," adding, "These are written that you may believe that Jesus is the Messiah, the Son of God, and that by believing you may have life in his name." The *Gospel of Thomas*: "These are the secret sayings which the living Jesus spoke and which Didymas Judas Thomas wrote down. And he said, 'Whoever finds the interpretation of these sayings will not experience death.'" Thus, Paul's letters are intimate communications of personal presence and authority framed by the urgent eschatological context of the living Lord's impending arrival, *made fully present by the apostle's words*. The gospel genre understood the power of presence represented in Paul's letters. Consequently, Paul's letters and the powerful presence they were known to create influenced the creation of the gospel genre—to encounter the voice of Jesus of Nazareth and have his presence until his return: "This is the beginning of good

---

203. 1 Thess 2:18. This is the eschatological conflict between God and Satan. For Koester, Satan wants to destroy God's work, namely, *agape* and the efficacious gospel that makes that possible. Koester, "Apostle and Church," 28.

news of Jesus the Messiah, the Son of God";[204] "In the beginning was the Word, and the Word was face to face with God, and the Word was God."[205]

In reading the Thessalonian correspondence, one can still sense the personal and powerful presence of Paul and wonder at the eschatological fervor heard again as his voice is given life through the letter's reading, just as in the first century. Indeed, Paul's thoughts, words and world traverse time in an instant and invade consciousness, however foreign and alien that world may be now, filled with demons, spirits and black magic that both Jesus and Paul were accused of conducting, and which they had both confronted in the battle to overthrow Satan and announce the coming kingdom of God.

Demonic Enemies: From Death to Life

What was Paul's strategy in addressing the crisis in Thessaloniki? While much subtler than his aggressive, emotional, even angry defense of his gospel in the letter to the Galatians (i.e., "let them—the Jewish Christians sent from James—be cursed!" Gal 1:9), it is clear that Paul is on the *defensive in 1 Thessalonians*. To properly discern the reason for the defense, it is important to set the context.

At the outset, Paul sets the stage for his defense by lauding the Thessalonians for their exhibited *pistis*, *agape* and demonstrated "steadfastness of *elpis* in our Lord Jesus Christ" (1:3). Paul implies that the conduct of the community since his departure has surely demonstrated that they are on safe from perilous risk at the *parousia*. They have withstood, thus far, the persecution and challenges faced, as well as a return to servicing demons that possess idols—at least most of them. Of course, the only way Paul would known is through the report of Timothy, who, at Paul's request, traveled from Athens (possibly implied by the letter [3:1]): "Therefore, when we could bear it no longer, we were willing to be left behind in Athens alone and we sent Timothy," or as Acts reflects, from Beroea (see Acts 17:14, "Then the brethren immediately sent Paul off on his way to the sea, but Silas and Timothy remained there"),[206] to check on the condition of the *ecclesia* of Thessaloniki.

Timothy would have traveled approximately 320 arduous miles if by road from Athens, only a small part of which would have been on the *via Egnatia*. If by foot, and the standard daily travel distance was approximately fifteen to twenty miles, his trip would have taken twenty-five to thirty days. If by sea, assuming about eighty miles depending on weather, a week to a week and a half, having stopped at various ports along the route. The *Via Egnatia*[207] was a very sophisticated Roman *odos*, or commer-

---

204. Mark 1:1.

205. John 1:1.

206. If he traveled from Beroea, Timothy would have had about a forty-five-mile journey, about half of which was on the superior via Egnatia.

207. This road named after the proconsul who ordered its construction, Gauis Egnatius, begun

cial and military road that stretched from the Black Sea in the east across hundreds of miles[208] to the ancient seaport of Dyrrachium to the west on the Adriatic, where, directly across from Italy, it continued on the *Via Appia*,[209] or Appian Way, to Rome. The *Via Egnatia* was an extremely well-engineered commercial highway. Begun in the second century BCE, this was one of the first major Roman roads built outside of Italy using proven techniques (e.g., of the *Via Appia*).[210] It had exacting specifications to ensure its reliability and stability despite various terrain and seasonal weather conditions, from bedrock in the mountains using only cobblestone pavers to the valley and plains with up to four layers of fill, drainage and even and clay waterproofing. Sections of *via Egnatia* are still visible today. If Timothy did come from Athens, which seems almost certain since Paul himself confirms this in the letter, he more likely came by sea than by road, however. Nonetheless, using land or sea, this was a long journey, which explains why Timothy caught up with Paul many weeks later in his new center of ministry, Corinth.

The sending of Timothy was clearly a significant commitment of precious resources in the battle of God over Satan and death, as well a difficult personal separation for Paul. But that was of no consequence—the eschatological standing of the *ecclesia* was a paramount importance, and Timothy, Paul's most devoted personal aide, must be spared (even risked) for a return mission, carrying a powerful eschatological letter to prevent its demise from attack by opponents and enemies. Not only was Timothy one of Paul's most trusted colleagues (i.e., like a son, unlike Silas and Barnabas),[211] he was Paul's most trusted designate, informant and charismatic enforcer of all those in his itinerant entourage of "fellow-workers" (*synergo*).[212] Timothy was a young adult, when Paul arrived in the rural Lystra,[213] a small city or village in comparison to Antioch or Iconium,[214] and likely, because of his Jewish mother, either heard of or personally witnessed Paul's teaching and success in urgently garnering adherents, particularly from the Gentile "God-fearers" and subsistence working artisans. Eunice may have been an

---

around 130 BCE, but more likely in more complete form by 146 CE.

208. In total, approximately 520 miles.

209. Named after Appius Claudias Caecus, the Roman Censor, or tax collector, who began the road in about 310 BCE.

210. The archaeology of the road is interesting and exact, as portions of the road exist to this day and dozens of location have been excavated and recorded.

211. Barnabas was Paul's mentor, when Paul was the "fellow-worker."

212. That Paul sent Timothy on this mission is a clear indication of his confidence in his ability and talent, as well as his inspiration, to expound Scripture related to the significance of Jesus of Nazareth as the fulfillment of prophecy.

213. Around 46 to late 47 CE.

214. Iconium, part of Roman Galatia, was a Phrygian city, named after the Greek myth relating the recreation of humans out of mud and a divine breath by Prometheus and Athena after a great flood destroyed all humanity, i.e., "*icons*," *eikones*, or images.

artisan,[215] as she became an adherent.[216] Paul had only just escaped from the threat of stoning in Iconium, likely for both blasphemy and accusations of practicing magic and deception, following a sorcerer who was a minion of Beelzebul. Jewish opponents violently rejected Paul, and gathering a mob (who would have joined in the attack if he were thought to be evil and dangerous), some of the "God-fearers" attempted to kill him.[217] Indeed, the exorcism of a demon in Lystra, at first hailed in the rural "Lycaonian language" as the work of the gods[218] Zeus (the Lyconian patron deity) and Hermes,[219] was instead said by his enemies to be black magic by possession of the evildoer, Jesus. The same violent Jews from Iconium, now accompanied by Jews from Antioch (perhaps from James, see below), arrived to silence him. In the context of perilous risk, the decision to send violent emissaries after Paul confirms the risk that was perceived he presented to his enemies, a fact too often forgotten. The distance from Antioch to Iconium was about ninety miles, but it was only eighteen miles from Iconium to Lystra. This means that the total distance covered from Antioch to Lystra would have taken less than ten days for the opponents to reach Paul and murder him. There he was grabbed, violently brutalized and then stoned as a blasphemer and so, dark magician and evildoer, until he was presumed dead from head wounds. His body was dragged out of the city and thrown into the municipal refuse pile to be eaten by the dogs and

---

215. See Acts 14:11–15, the encounter of Paul and Lydia, the merchant of highly prized and valuable purple cloth, outside the city walls at a "place of prayer." The river to which Acts refers can only have been a stream that flowed most likely from the spring, as there are no major rivers within the allowed Sabbath's day walk. Eunice could have similarly encountered Paul as a merchant or artisan in a meeting place, since Lystra was too small to have a synagogue (to form a synagogue, ten Jewish men who were the heads of households were required). This may indicate that Paul sought out "places of prayer" were there was no synagogue, and because they were visited by Jewish women, or may have been a location where Hellenistic-Roman women who were artisans gathered together to pray with them.

216. Eunice, *Eunike* (Greek for "good victory"), was married to a pagan (Acts 16:1), and since the male of the family was unavailable to teach the torah, she apparently took up this task. While this may be assumed as a normal practice, it is not well attested in contemporaneous literature. More, it would be unusual for a woman to have been taught the torah, other than for her obligations (per the *halachah*), the *mitzvahs*, the Sabbath, purity, etc. My speculation is that this was a family event that began with Lois, Eunice's mother, also a Jew, and was expanded by her to incorporate more than just her obligations.

217. Acts 14:2: "But the Jews who refused to believe stirred up the other Gentiles and poisoned their minds against the brothers."

218. The local priests of Zeus brought a bull and were ready to decorate it with garlands and sacrifice it for a public feast—this indicates the impressive response of Lystra to the healing, i.e., only Zeus could perform! It is interesting to note that Acts 14:12 states that the locals called Barnabas Zeus, clearly indicating that he was considered the leader, and Paul, Hermes the messenger of Zeus, the one who likely was the charismatic and pronounced the healing.

219. Zeus and Hermes to be exact. The identification of the Lycaonian language is remarkably accurate, as the inhabitants of Lystra spoke their own distinct language and dialect. This indicates that the tradition in Acts 16 has claim to having been written by an eyewitness, or was received from one who was present.

birds (an implied curse fit for a blasphemer).[220] Paul somehow survived and regained consciousness,[221] then immediately returned to the city, gathered his things, then left the next day for Derbe.[222] Later, upon his return to Lystra (about three years later), Paul added Timothy to his itinerate missionary team, circumcising him, as he continued through Asia Minor and on to Troas, then on to Macedonia.[223]

The Thessalonians would have been more than impressed with the return visit of Paul's "son" and personal envoy. It should not escape us that Timothy was also imbued with *charismata* (charismatic gifts) and *dunamis* (power), which included his authority to activate and employ deadly curses, either his own, or those of Paul (see below). The term "beloved son" then should not detract from Timothy's own abilities to instruct and admonish, condemn and curse, which Paul recognizes.[224] Paul's sending of Timothy demonstrated his fear that satanic enemies had been successful in disbanding the *ecclesia*.[225] If so, Paul was in perilous risk as well, i.e., the loss of an *ecclesia* meant he had failed the risen Lord and was susceptible to doom.[226]

Paul concludes his introductory comments with reference to their turning from "idols," i.e., as noted, the satanic demons that possessed images and icons said to be images of the gods, heroes, rulers or religious figures[227] (see also 2 Cor 10:20);[228] Paul is deliberate in his choice of words. He compares service to "idols" with service to the living and true God. Paul's adherents "wait for the Son from heaven whom he [God], raised from the dead, Jesus, who delivers us from the wrath to come."[229] Only adherents to Paul's *euangelion* forgo the wrath of God awaiting those entangled with demonic idols—divine judgment and the curse of annihilation and death. Servicing idols, even attending cultic rituals or events, place one in a position of perilous risk. This statement is of immense import, as it underscores one of the key elements of

---

220. Acts 14:8.

221. He likely awoke from being unconscious.

222. Originally, Derbe was thought to be only a day's distance from Lystra, or about fifteen to eighteen miles. More recent archaeological evidence has shown it to be some sixty miles away, or a four-day journey. This means that Paul made a painful, exhausting and difficult trip, having just been stoned and certainly near death—quite remarkable.

223. Acts 16:1.

224. According to 2 Timothy (2 Tim 3:15; see the discussion below on the authenticity of this letter), Timothy was well verses in the Scriptures, the Septuagint, and so would be able to interpret and apply them to the events in Jesus' life and resurrection.

225. 1 Thess 1:4.

226. 1 Thess 3:1.

227. Paul confirms demonic possession of idols, cultic worship and mystery religious rites: "You cannot drink the cup of the Lord and the cup of demons; you cannot partake of the table of the Lord and the table of demons" (1 Cor 10:21). Paul lists idolatry as equivalent to sorcery (Gal 5:19–21). Worshipers of idols and demons would not inherit the kingdom of God (1 Cor 6:9). This is a theme from ancient Judaism that Paul knows well from his training (Ps 106:36–37).

228. A common belief in the ancient world, also reflected in 1 John 5:21 and Rev 9:20.

229. 1 Thess 1:9.

The Enemies of Paul in Thessaloniki

Paul's letter at the outset. Paul *is always intentional in his choice of words*, particularly in the first few sentences of every letter, just as in Galatians and 1 Corinthians.[230] Here Paul presents Jesus, the historical crucified man, as the one whom God raised from the dead, now the "son from heaven," the one who stands above all demonic powers that will be destroyed, along with their followers.[231]

In eschatological language, Paul then reminds the *ecclesia* that the *last days are already upon them*, indeed at the door coming "like a thief in the night [as noted, quoting a *logia* of Jesus]," and that it is Jesus, the risen Lord, whose near presence will protect them from justice and the judgment events to come if they hold fast to *pistis, elpis,* and *agape*.[232] It is no accident that Paul now employs references to sayings of Jesus and biographical materials to strengthen his authoritative relationship and affinity with Jesus, the risen Lord. The list of sayings is impressive.[233] Paul mixes pre- and post-crucifixion sayings. As to biographical material, Paul does not hesitate to name Jesus' murderers, the Jerusalem elite, emphasizing the risk faced by all in the final days from even Jesus' enemies.[234] Paul, on the authority of his apostleship and relationship with the risen Lord then is free to insert his own instructions with *logia* of Jesus. Paul is an *apostolos*, whose words and instructions are unassailable. Paul is the unequivocal interpreter of Jesus' *logia* and traditions in the midst of the eschatological crisis. Paul speaks for Jesus, the risen Lord: "Aspire to live quietly, mind your own affairs and work with your own hands as we charged you."[235]

For Paul, the danger and risks evidenced in their persecution only confirms the legitimacy of the *euangelion* and that they are joined to the Lord himself, i.e., suffering for the *euangelion* is eschatological confirmation of inclusion in the cataclysmic events unfolding. Paul reminds the Thessalonians that they *received and embraced the euangelion in affliction*, which is the nature of the eschatological struggle already present;[236] just as Paul and Jesus had suffered, and so had become "examples to all the adherents in Macedonia and Achaia . . . so that your faith in God has gone forth everywhere."[237] Suffering and faith are linked to the *nature of the eschatological transformation in process*. They are transferring from certain judgment and satanic anni-

---

230. See above Gal 1:1–10.

231. Similar to the hymn in Phil 2:5–11; if other powers do not bend the knee and submit, they are enemies and by implication would be cast out or destroyed.

232. 1 Thess 5:2.

233. Sayings from the *risen* Jesus; abstain from unchastity, take a wife in holiness and honor, do not defraud a brother in business (4:3–6): Sayings from Jesus *pre-Easter ministry*; love your brother as yourself and love one another, the nearness of the end as like a thief in the night and the certainty of the end like the travail that comes on a woman with child (4:9–10; 5:2–4).

234. 2:14–15, although many scholars reject this section as a later addition as a polemic against the Jews.

235. 1 Thess 4:11.

236. See 2:6, more explicitly described as to the severity in 2:14–16.

237. 1 Thess 1:8.

hilation to life, from darkness to light, and their rescue and judgment are near! The conflict and suffering of the adherents unites them together as the new community, *the ecclesia* of God, those who embrace the conflict, for it will be swept away with the arrival of the risen Lord soon.

Betrayers, Apostles, and James the Brother of Jesus

Jewish opponents from Philippi have tracked Paul to Thessaloniki, passing through Amphipolis and Apollonia along the way, most assuredly to threaten adherents and disrupt and dissolve the *ecclesiae* he formed.[238] Paul considers these opponents, and any that oppose him, satanic. As a result of their arrival and incursion in Thessaloniki, not long after Paul's departure for Athens, it appears that virtually all of the Jewish adherents have abandoned Paul, clearly all the Jewish artisans and craftsmen with whom he worked. Acts reports that Jewish opponents in Philippi raised a mob, physically forcing his expulsion from the city with the cooperation of city officials. Jason, Paul's host (and perhaps a relative), had been beaten and dragged from his home.[239] It was he, not Paul who was then attacked at his home by this mob, which indicates he was considered to be harboring an illegal and dangerous dark magician.

This incursion by Paul's violent enemies into the Thessalonian *ecclesia* provides insight into their *modus operandi*. Just as Paul employed an incursion strategy as he entered a metropolis, so too did his deadly enemies. Indeed, 1 Thessalonians suggests that they not only aggressively disrupted the lives of Jewish converts, threatening their already tenuous subsistence existence (i.e., just has Paul did when he persecuted the adherents in Jerusalem and Syria),[240] they also similarly persecuted and pursued the Gentile followers in every way possible, naming them associates of a crucified, demonized Jew and dark magician, worthy of expulsion from local trade or guild, and perhaps brutalization and death under Roman law. The social unrest and disruption created by legal representatives of an imperially recognized religion, Judaism, who were armed with authoritative letters, provided them immunity and the supportive attention of local magistrates and officials. Undoubtedly, this reflected Paul's own deadly and effective strategy in Palestine as a spy and assassin of the elite in Jerusalem as Saul. Flight or death, or minimally expulsion or the threat of starvation of the adherent and

---

238. Paul's familiar statement, "To the Jew first and then to the Gentile" (Rom 1:16), may also reflect the conflict with his opponents and their *modus operandi*, i.e., to attack the Jewish believers in the gospel first, then turn to the Gentiles to obliterate the small and nascent communities and ensure their destruction—not unlike Paul's own activity in the Judean and Syrian *ecclesia* among the Jews and Gentile "God-fearers." Was this their slogan that Paul adopts, or was it his own from his former life as a violent persecutor of the Way that reflects their effort. Has Paul taken this slogan from his former life and now applied it to believers who embrace the gospels? The slogan must have had an origin.

239. Acts 17:1–9.

240. Thus, the question to Paul on what happens to those who die before the *parousia*, i.e., the opponents point out the incongruity of Paul's promise of salvation and life, but then the still normal death of believers before the event.

his or her family (including the extended family), was an unmitigated perilous risk. Indeed, Jason, a Gentile, was with Paul when he wrote his letter to the Romans from Corinth, meaning, he was forced to flee Philippi,[241] just as others in Thessaloniki must had been forced out of their city.

First Thessalonians confirms that Paul's enemies had been successful in threatening and terrorizing Jewish converts and "God fearers." There are virtually no references to Hebrew Scripture, and the language and terminology used are reflective of a non-Jewish audience. The crisis over the pre-advent death of adherents is further evidence. Paul's enemies cited these deaths as shattering proof that Paul was a deceiver, illegal magician and charlatan. More, he took money and left the city, abandoning them. In fact, during Paul's stay in Thessaloniki he received at least two monetary offerings of support, and he demanded that they abandoned the city and other cults, converting cult and festival fees to him. As his enemies certainly did say, Paul was "turning the world upside down." For this they were under severe persecution and in danger: "For when we were with you we told you beforehand that we were to suffer affliction; just as it has come to pass."[242] While Paul had warned of enemies, it is apparent that he did not provide the full detail of the charges brought against him until the Thessalonian correspondence:[243] "Error," meaning heresy, which could only come with perversion of Scripture and practices considered satanic (the proclamation of worship for an "evildoer," condemned as under Roman law and executed as a dark magician, with accompanying *charismata* assumed to be provided by Satan by them); "uncleanliness," not just following Jewish dietary laws and eating with Gentiles, but eating meat sacrificed to idols and participating in new, illegal cultic practices that were forbidden (eating the body and blood of an evildoer to absorb his power);[244] "pleasing men," deceit, as well as rejecting Jewish circumcision of Greek God-fearers and, thus, proper conversion under the laws and traditions of Judaism;[245] "guile," or treacherous deception, perhaps using exorcism and magic, or also Paul deceiving Jews by misusing Scripture to support Jesus as the Christ, and perhaps his manipulating divine Scripture to his own personal gain—namely, forming a community to provide himself with monetary support and wealth; "words of flattery . . . or cloak for greed," also was a charge by the his Jewish opponents in Galatia.[246] What is striking is that enemies who risked dangerous travel, were commissioned and paid by powerful

241. Rom 16:21; Romans was written between 55–59 CE, i.e., only three to four years after Paul's arrival in Thessaloniki.

242. 1 Thess 3:4.

243. 1 Thess 2:3–11.

244. Yet, Paul does not here cite the confrontation he had with Peter in Antioch as he did in the later Galatian correspondence—this would do nothing for his argument since it is not addressed to Jews.

245. Gal 1:10.

246. Gal 1:1, 10–11, supporting the use of the word "guile" as well; also see Gal 6:17, Paul is able to show physical marks of his suffering for his faith if anyone wishes.

The Enemies of Paul: Demons, Satan, Betrayers, and Apostles

authorities (carrying letters authorizing their actions); verbally attacked, threatened, used economic coercion to socially dismantle assemblies; physically beat and even murdered to stop Paul, the evildoer; would use such benign language Paul quotes. This would suggest that Paul attenuated the accusations.

Nonetheless, based on the language and similarities of the accusations with the letter to the Galatians, Paul's enemies are most certainly the Jews that tracked him to Galatia and then Philippi, indeed, those who had violently opposed him in Antioch and Lystra, namely, followers of James the brother of Jesus, the Jerusalem elite, or a combination that may suggest collusion.[247] The troubling and unresolved mystery as to who Paul's opponents were that tracked him from city to city, and why the Jerusalem *ecclesia* was now free from persecution and could hold a "council" only a few years after persecution and murder of followers, presents a startling suggestion: Was James, head of the Jerusalem *ecclesia*, in collusion with the Jerusalem elite so as to mitigate perilous risk and ensure their survival until the *parousia*? Did James and others agree to remain quiet, worship in the temple and support and exorcise demons for the poor? Was this the arrangement following the murder of James the brother of John in 44 CE and death of Herod? It would seem so. Paul was certainly vocal and a disrupter of Diaspora synagogues. He had deserted the Jerusalem elite, having been their informer and murderer of Jesus-followers, proclaiming the crucified Jew now as Lord and Christ. Paul was confrontational with the Jerusalem elite, local synagogue leaders, trade guild members, *apostoloi*, fellow itinerants and even James the brother of Jesus. Paul literally created havoc virtually everywhere, and performed exorcisms in the name of the condemned and crucified evildoer, thought possessed by Beelzebul. There had been multiple attempts to kill him for sedition, illegal magic, blasphemy, and greed. Clearly, Paul's aggressive *euangelion* led to his separation from and schism with James the brother of Jesus at the Jerusalem council (i.e., despite the gloss in Acts, they were at odds; Paul curses anyone, including James, that opposes his *euangelion* within months of that meeting—see Chapter 3, "James, the Brother of Jesus, as Paul's Opponent"). Paul learned that James' spies dismantled his *ecclesiae* in Galatia. His public confrontation with Kayfa in Antioch ended his relationship with Kayfa and the Twelve. Paul was then forced to leave Antioch, beginning his second itinerant mission about 49 CE. Thereafter, Paul was clearly followed by spies and paid informants, and then a team of aggressive and viscous infiltrators capable of murder. The intentional destruction of Paul's *ecclesiae*, which were considered to reflect the most abhorrent practices of satanic deception and magic (the same charges brought against Jesus), would explain multiple problematic issues that have plagued scholarship for generations, and why traditions about James correctly identify him with salvific wisdom sayings, his own and those of

---

247. How else can we explain Paul's attackers were not wreaking havoc on the Jerusalem *ecclesia* control of James? Indeed, James "the righteous" was said by Josephus to worship in the temple daily and remained unhindered until a change in procurators and high priest a decade later when he was murdered.

The Enemies of Paul in Thessaloniki

Jesus, and teachings about righteousness and living a quiet life. Ultimately, Paul was named a charlatan, an evildoer and deceiver, dangerous and was to be silenced. Only those authorized by James, with the acknowledgment of the Jerusalem elite, could have been so effective. James was therefore an enemy of Paul.

Since Paul is writing to remaining adherents, i.e., only Gentiles, and so cannot appeal to Scripture in addressing the charges brought against him, he turns instead to his observable behavior they witnessed. He rejects the charge that he is a profiteering charlatan (and so, a magician charging fees for services) by reminding the Thessalonians that he supported himself during his time there, and by implication, did not charge for any exorcisms arising from use of his sweat cloths or handkerchiefs.[248] He eased their burden, did not make claim to financial support (a reference to a saying of Jesus, "the worker is worthy of his hire"),[249] even though he could do so. Interestingly, Paul then compares his care for the adherents to a nurse (*trophos*, i.e., not "mother" as in some translations) who cares for her children, or to a father's loving care of a child, both clear examples of responsible and earnest concern for the innocent familiar to the structure of Gentile households.[250] These references, both to the beloved household nurse of a Gentile home and adoptive father under Roman law would have resonated with both female and male Gentile adherents, underscoring the true devotion and depth of Paul's care for them.

Paul's ultimate defense as to his good character is the Thessalonians themselves, as they "have become imitators of the *ecclesia* of God in Christ Jesus in Judea,"[251] that is, they mirror the practices of the very *ecclesia* founded by the other apostles who lived, ate and prayed with Jesus of Nazareth, and had witnessed and been with the risen Lord *like Paul*. Paul's reference is additional support that his enemies must come from Jerusalem, and any claim they make to Paul's errant, deceptive behavior is void because he mirrors the practices there, even the practices of James. How can they who "work with their hands" and practice *agape* as brothers and sisters of the eschatological and democratized *ecclesia* tolerate any opponents' vicious attacks on him? How can they accept their characterization of him as a charlatan, or as one who had abandoned them once he had played out his fable for monetary gain? Their personal experience with him was incongruous with these charges, and that is why Timothy's cautious but positive report of their fidelity to Paul set the conciliatory tone of this

---

248. 1 Thess 2:9.

249. Luke 10:7.

250. The role of the nurse for the young children in the Gentile household, usually a slave that is charged with their care and upbringing, is well documented in the ancient world. She was treated with great respect, as a close and intimate associate of the female head of the house, was a revered member of the family. Paul here references the work of a slave in serving the children as duty and charge, but with the same love and respect with which they would be familiar. Paul's reference to a female example may indicate that his Gentile audience *represented a large group of women*.

251. 1 Thess 2:14.

letter (as opposed to Galatians and 1 and 2 Corinthians). His Jewish enemies had only been successful with Jewish adherents.

Paul concludes this section with a much-disputed but shocking condemnation of *these specific Jewish opponents*, again confirming they come from Jerusalem and have connections with the Jerusalem elite: "For you suffered the same things from your own countrymen as they did for the Jews, who killed both the Lord Jesus and the prophets and drove us out and displease God and oppose all men by hindering us from speaking to the Gentiles that they may be saved—so always to fill up the measure of their sins."[252] While some scholars debate whether Paul wrote this section, it is coherent with the context of the letter, and is as vehement a charge as the curse (*anathema*), he brings on the Jewish *opponents sent from James* who have attempted to disband all of his *ecclesiae* in the province of Galatia.[253] These statements are certainly Paul's own.

Consequently, Paul's condemnation of the Jewish enemies and elements of his defense confirm that he is speaking to Gentile adherents. When Paul describes the Jews in such terse and unforgiving terms, he is clearly speaking *about the specific group of Jews who track and oppose him*, not the Jewish people, or the Hebrews by descent from Abraham, or even Jews of the Diaspora. The Jews who trouble the Thessalonians are the same who "*killed [apokteinanton], the Lord Jesus and the prophets and drove us out.*"[254] *Those that troubled Paul are equated in the most severe words with the enemies and murders of Jesus himself*, the very same elite that hired Saul to track down Jesus-sympathizers, the Jerusalem elite. Interestingly, Paul, a Jew, is the earliest witness in the New Testament to name those held responsible for the murder of Jesus—*it is not the Romans that Paul identifies as the killers of Jesus*, but the worst of the Jews, as horrendous as the contract killers, Jewish sympathizers with Rome—the same Jewish opponents who infiltrated in Thessaloniki.[255] Paul's comments here confirm that the Gentiles had heard the account of Jesus' capture and crucifixion, the role the Jewish leaders. They have now encountered these same vicious men and experienced the same perilous risks. The *letter then presupposes at least a rudimentary understanding of the events that led to Jesus' death* later captured in the passion narrative. This section is then also the earliest witness to the formation and oral transmission of this narrative. Paul, like Jesus, expects to suffer and perhaps be murdered, but it is the Son of God who will rescue him, just as he will rescue the Gentile adherents from death: "I have been crucified with Christ and I no

252. 1 Thess 2:15.
253. Gal 1:8.
254. 1 Thess 2:15.

255. This realization is extremely important because at one time, Paul was endorsed by the Jerusalem elite, including the High Priest. Paul had no doubt who was responsible for handing Jesus over—it was Jews that were like him when he was violently trying to destroy the ecclesia, and not the Romans who were to blame—we must not forget Paul was a Jew.

longer live, but Christ lives in me. The life I now live in the body, I live by faith in the Son of God, who loved me and gave himself for me."²⁵⁶

Paul is distraught and agonizes over the possible loss of the *ecclesia*.²⁵⁷ Paul has absolutely no basis of "boasting" if he fails for he has been compelled by the risen Lord to find those separated from God and imbue them with the *euangelion* before the *parousia* for face his own woe: "For if I preach the gospel I have nothing to boast for I am under compulsion. Woe to me if I do not preach the gospel."²⁵⁸ All Paul can do is express his own eschatological crisis by asking the question, what is my "*hope or joy or crown of boasting* before our Lord Jesus at his coming," where he adds about the Thessalonians, "Is it not you? For you are our glory and joy."²⁵⁹ They are Paul's assurance of safety at the *parousia*, his mitigation of perilous risk of judgment and rejection on the "Day of the Lord."

The Risk of Joining the Cult of the Crucified Lord in the First-Century Roman World

Based on the writings of ancient Roman historians and apologists, such as Flavius Josephus,²⁶⁰ execution on a Roman cross was fraught with political, social and religious implications that were devastating, not just for the condemned,²⁶¹ but also for the family, and for generations to come. Indeed, risking the cross, universally accepted as one of Jesus' authentic sayings, was much more that a metaphor for being willing to take a chance or press one's conviction. As shocking as Jesus' *logoi* to *pick up the cross* were to a Palestinian Jew,²⁶² it was equally as shocking and as meaningful to the Gentile—and this fact is often lost. The Gentile adherent too had to accept not only the possible fate of the cross and its horrendous form of death, but its horrible repercussions as one of the untimely dead, a wandering spirit, susceptible to control by evil and demonic forces.²⁶³ Crucifixion, forbidden for Roman citizens, still surely

---

256 Gal 2:20.

257. The letter to Philemon is exactly this in every way.

258. 1 Cor 8:16.

259. 1 Thess 2:19–20.

260. See *Antiquities* 18:10, Judas the Galilean and the results of his revolt.

261. As noted, complete separation from God for the Jew.

262. Faith must be so completely trusting, the fullest expression of which can only be compared to the complete love and trust of a small child for the parent, that the Jew is even willing to literally pick up a cross beam and risk total separation from God for the sake of the good news—only this renders one right before God, not merit or works of any kind; for a Jew to consider submitting to the risk of the cross was abhorrent. The tension between the Jews and the Romans contemporaneous with Jesus was so strong that the lack of trustworthiness meant speaking about "taking up" the cross was tantamount to a revolutionary cry! The Jews were mistreated and detested by Pilatus, and anyone suggesting that one should "take up your cross" would certainly be considered a rebel, arrested and summarily executed.

263. In fact, Gentile crucifixion was brutally experienced in Rome and elsewhere in the empire

The Enemies of Paul: Demons, Satan, Betrayers, and Apostles

meant for the majority of the Gentile adherents real perilous risk, as they were poor and of the lower castes, slaves and subsistence workers like Paul. Publicly accepting as master a rebellious crucified Galilean Jewish criminal was clearly seditious, evidenced by mass persecution and execution of Christians less than two decades later by Nero. Paul notes that to Gentiles it was "folly,"[264] i.e., not simply foolishness, but perilous danger. The juxtaposition of *pistis* and *elpis* with risk acceptance of crucifixion brings to clarity the danger accepted by Paul's adherents. Only a worse peril and alternative would lead one to accept such horrendous risk.

Contextual analysis of the risk accepted by Jewish or Gentile adherents only serves to underscore the peril accepted by Paul's adherents. Contemporary mystery cults reenacted mythical encounters of initiates in the realm of the gods, included salvific language similar to Paul's *euangelion* (e.g., *resurrection* and *salvation*), as well as rituals for initiates to assure union with the god or spirit and transference to life.[265] There was evidential proof provided, such as hearing the voice of the god and *glossolalia*, trance, vision or spiritual encounters, healings and other *charismata*, as well as participation in efficacious cultic meals that afforded protection to adherents. But these were *legal religions*, approved and condoned by Rome, and none carried the risk of crucifixion and a cursed death because all allowed for the emperor oblation, worship and adoration. None elevated a condemned, crucified "evildoer," a Jewish Galilean peasant and magician charged with sedition and black magic, to master, as well as acknowledged possession by that Lord. Jesus Christ demanded that all bend a knee to him—sedition. While Paul demonstrated *charismata* and signs that validated his relationship with this risen Lord and confirmed his urgent call for efficacious *pistis* in the *euangelion*, it was the salvific offer to the lower classes to become adopted by God before the end of the age and the cataclysmic judgment and justice that were soon to come that drew adherents willing to accept a perilous risk—the hopeless and fringe of society, the artisans, slaves, outcasts, the socially disenfranchised and poor. Harsh, brutal lives would soon end, and a new kingdom was imminent for them. Paul's affirmation that protection from evil and demonic forces already afflicting and killing them would cease, demonstrated in his *charismata* and by those who joined his *ecclesia*, demonstrated that Paul's adherents had turned to "the living God." Indeed, the *euangelion* and presence of the Lord assured them that the end of the age was near, the evidence of which was the death and resurrection of Jesus of Nazareth, *raised by*

---

only about fifteen years after this letter was written, during the reign of Nero, and again under Domitian and then Trajan.

264. 1 Cor 1:23.

265. The list of cults that had a dying and rising god included Asclepius, Orpheus, Osiris, and Dionysius to name a few—but all were initiated into a mythological event of another world, not the world of history with dozens, if not hundreds, of living witnesses to the event in this world. This was Paul's very point—God is the "living God" who intervened in history to bring about safety and salvation to all without elaborate rites and practices, simply by faith.

THE ENEMIES OF PAUL IN THESSALONIKI

the living God and Father;[266] an event witnessed in by dozens, *both Jews and Greeks*, most of whom were still alive.[267] The democratize *ecclesia* of Jew and Greek, slave and free, women and men, demonstrated transference now and a vision of what was to soon come. The union and protection was assured by the practice of *agape* and filial love. This new way provided significant mitigation to the daily risks and hopelessness of these men and women. To die like Jesus, even on a cross, was to gain life, i.e., there was nothing to lose and everything to gain as the current age was coming to a close. The end of the age was at hand, time was rushing to an end: God's peace and justice were soon to arrive with the *parousia* and presence of the resurrected Jesus, the Lord. The Thessalonians would soon greet the Son of God, a craftsman and pious man executed by evil men, who had been resurrected as Lord and Savior.

That *pistis* in the efficacious *euangelion* and practice of *agape* with *elpis* in the imminent and salvific *parousia* emptied the Roman cross of its power to destroy and curse its victims, was the most startling symbol imaginable in Paul's time. It was shocking—but that it had just happened, and that there were dozens of witnesses to prove its truth, which was overwhelming. Indeed, if God made the cross the symbol of power and life, not death, then what ultimate danger was there for those who, like Jesus, were of God? The *euangelion* was most the most dissonant reversal of expectations of its time. The illegality and risk to adherents of Paul's *ecclesiae* were fully mitigated by the imminent promise and proof of this reversal and reward—death was not death, it was sleep, awaiting the risen Lord. The cross and its curse no longer carried its dark powers. As Paul says to the Thessalonians, "For God has not destined us for wrath, but to obtain salvation through our Lord Jesus Christ, who died for us so that whether we wake or sleep we might live with him."[268] The cross is divine wisdom, the power of God, powerless to annihilate the faithful, and now the remarkable symbol of hope and life.

The eschatological struggle for the "children of light" was fully engaged. The enemies of God were retaliating successfully against the *euangelion*. Paul states, "Because we wanted to come to you—I, Paul, again and again [with great emphasis]—but Satan hindered us."[269] Demonic attack and suffering were part of the pangs of the end of the age: "For when we were with you, we told you beforehand that we were to suffer affliction; just as it had come to pass, and you know."[270] Thus, Paul counted it as a blessing to share in the suffering of Jesus[271]—it was as Jesus' predicted and it reflected the reality

---

266. The early movement was simply called "the way," or "the way of the Lord" (Acts 9:2; 18:26; 19:9, 23; 24:4, 14, 22).

267. See the earliest list of witnesses, including "five hundred" brethren, in Paul's recount, 1 Cor 15:1–9.

268. 1 Thess 5:9–10.

269. 1 Thess 2:18.

270. 1 Thess 3:4.

271. Gal 6:17.

of the crisis and eschatological conflict at hand. As Hans Conzelmann states, "It is the time of the church, the proclamation of the death of Christ, of faith, of hope."[272]

The Eschatology of Paul and the Relationship of 1 and 2 Thessalonians

Second Thessalonians has long been challenged as non-Pauline. An examination of the letter makes clear the issues for debate. First, the Paul of 2 Thessalonians has a much different eschatological view of the *parousia*. Second Thessalonians emphasizes vengeance and retribution: "When the Lord Jesus is revealed from heaven with his mighty angels in flaming fire, inflicting vengeance on those who do not know God and upon those who do not obey the gospel of our Lord Jesus."[273] Clearly, this image is drawn from a different apocalyptic genre that is foreign to Paul, one that represents the later stage of the development of Mark and Q and the *bar nasha*, or Son of Man traditions.[274] Second, and more telling, the Paul of 1 Thessalonians expects the presence of Jesus to come "like a thief in the night," meaning *soon and unexpectedly*, whereas the Paul of 2 Thessalonians provides a rather detailed description of the sequence of events that will precede the *parousia*. The incongruity between these two views simply cannot be reconciled. Second Thessalonians also assumes that Paul has fully described these events to the *ecclesia*, which is impossible given the context of 1 Thessalonians: "Let no one deceive you in any way; for that day will not come unless rebellion comes first, and the man of perdition, who opposes and exalts himself against every so-called god or object o worship, so that he take his seat in the temple of God, proclaiming himself to be God."[275] This description is a clear reference to the desolating sacrilege of Daniel,[276] which appears only in a late apocalypse inserted into Mark 13 associated with predictions as to the destruction of Jerusalem and the temple being witnessed in 70 CE. The writer of Daniel describes in obscure prophetic and apocalyptic language the decisive violation of the temple by a false foreign king who takes his place in it. He is the deceiver and destroyer of God's people, the most profound enemy of God in the last days before the faithful are delivered and the general resurrection occurs. Daniel has this king's rule ended, but not before he has completed his profane act.

Scholars have long associated Daniel with the conquest and domination of Palestine by the Seleucid ruler, Antiochus IV Epiphanes (i.e., his self-proclaimed title of "god manifest"). In 167 BCE Antiochus was returning through Israel from Egypt, having failed to conquer Alexandria. The events that led to his withdrawal, while obscure, are revealing as to Roman power and influence, even in the second century BCE. Antiochus was within reach of conquering Egypt, preparing an assault on Alexandria,

---

272. Conzelmann, *Corinthians*, 270.
273. 2 Thess 1:7b–8.
274. Dating to 65–70 CE (Mark), and in its later phase of development 65–75 CE (Q).
275. 2 Thess 2:3–4.
276. Dan 9:27 (11:31 and also 12:11).

The Enemies of Paul in Thessaloniki

when a single Roman ambassador, Gaius Popillius Laenas[277] met him on the road at the head of his army. This lone ambassador handed "god manifest" some tablets on which were written orders to withdraw. Gaius simply stood there and told him to leave Egypt immediately or consider himself at war with the Roman Senate. Livy reports that Antiochus read the tablets ordering this departure, but hesitated and stated that he would call a council to consider it. Gaius literally drew a line in the sand around Antiochus stating that he wanted an answer before he stepped over the line, otherwise war was declared. Antiochus withdrew.

On the return to Syria, furious and unrepentant, he used the occasion to attack and sack Jerusalem. He desecrated the temple of Jerusalem by dedicating it to the Olympian Zeus[278] and sacrificing all unclean animals on the Jewish altar. He forbade the practice of the Jewish religion, and, according the 2 Maccabees, he slaughtered innocent women and children, killed thousands and enslaved tens of thousands. His persecution continued until driven out by the Jews who revolted, led by Judas Maccabeus. Second Thessalonians embraces this language likely due to a historical event of similar proportion, such as the pending destruction of Jerusalem or encirclement of it by the Romans, and then combines it with the Son of Man imagery similar to IV Ezra: "And then the lawless one will be revealed, and the Lord Jesus will slay him with the breath of his mouth and destroy him by his appearing and his coming."[279] Clearly, the eschatological outlook of 2 Thessalonians is completely foreign to other undisputed writings of Paul,[280] and is dissimilar to Paul's understanding of the position of the adherent and imminent *parousia*. Paul's adherents look forward to the *parousia* in the hope salvation. In 2 Thessalonians, the adherent is chosen and "saved from the beginning" (2:13).[281] For the writer of 2 Thessalonians, the historical events being experienced are expressed in much different Jewish apocalyptic language.

Some scholars defend the letter as Pauline, correlating contemporaneous historical events with Paul's activity. For example, the 2 Thessalonians may refer to actions taken by the Emperor Caligula, who in 40 CE attempted to place a statue of himself in the temple of Jerusalem. But if so, Paul would either be looking back on this event, which would make a reference awkward, or it is an event unfolding, but such an early date for the Thessalonians correspondence is unlikely. Consequently, the language of 2 Thessalonians and blending with a Jewish apocalyptic genre of literature places the letter about the time of the destruction of Jerusalem under Titus.[282] By then, Paul had been

---

277. Livy 45:12.
278. 2 Macc 6:1–11.
279. 2 Thess 2:8.
280. See also 1 Cor 15 on the historical events of Jesus witnessed resurrection.
281. 2 Thess 2:13.
282. The siege began during the Passover on April 14, 70 CE, and was completed with the burning of the temple by September 8, but not before the legions had sacrificed to their Roman standards in the holy of holies (Josephus, *Jewish War*, 6:220–70).

executed. Indeed, according to 2 Thessalonians, a spurious letter arrived and purported to be from Paul that claimed that the "day of the Lord has come."[283] The writer of 2 Thessalonians then describes how the Day of the Lord has not yet come because it will be preceded by a definitive sequence of events that are discernible, obviously reflecting current cataclysmic events *such as Jerusalem being surrounded*.

Other differences between the letters are evident. For example, it is clear that 1 Thessalonians accurately reflects the personal relationship, issues, and intimate history of Paul's experiences as a persecuted *apostolos* of Jesus that would have been familiar to the Thessalonians, even the description of his expulsion form Philippi. Why include these events in the letter had they not occurred, i.e., they are problematic and so would be omitted if untrue. Also, analysis shows the 1 Thessalonians is coherent with the social, political and religious context that would have accompanied Paul's mission there and conversion of a large number of Gentiles, primarily craftsman and artisans. More, our analysis has demonstrated that there were few if any Jewish converts remaining following the infiltration of Paul's enemies, so Jewish apocalyptic terminology would have been completely foreign to the recipients if Paul.

Therefore, it is clear that 2 Thessalonians was written in the name of Paul, to usurp his authority, to clarify for an apocalyptic community witnessing monumental events, such as the destruction of Jerusalem. The writer wished to explain, like many apocalyptic texts, that hard times and suffering, especially unprecedented difficulties and injustice, would soon be rectified by a powerful vengeful angelic or heavenly being, such as the Son of Man, who, for the writer of 2 Thessalonians, is Jesus. Consequently, 2 Thessalonians is pseudepigraphical,[284] i.e., written by another author who uses Paul's name. The letter confirms the continuing influence the name of Paul had for well over one hundred years before the first collection of his letters was assembled, i.e., by the mid-second century.[285] It may contain authentic elements, but the differences make full reconciliation improbable.

---

283. 2 Thess 2:2.

284. Written between CE 67 to CE 110.

285. Clement 47:1, Ignatius of Antioch, Marcion (the accused heretic, excommunicated from the Roman Church in 144 CE, who first assembled Paul's letters in to a collection), 2 Pet 3:15–16, all before 145 CE.

Excursus: Paul and the *Logia* of Jesus
Precursor to the Conflict in Corinth

As noted, 1 Thessalonians demonstrates that Paul is able to employ "words of the Lord," *logia*, and reinterpret them to support his itinerant effort in both establishing and maintaining (including defending in crisis) the *ecclesiae* he establishes throughout the Roman world, appealing to his witness of and ongoing engagement with the risen Lord. Examples of Paul's use of Jesus' sayings, both pre- and post-crucifixion, demonstrate fully the malleability of the Jesus' tradition during this oral period of expansion. Indeed, various readings, including scholarly works on the history of the Jesus sayings tradition (i.e., the history, transmission, interpretation and collection of Jesus' sayings),[1] recent research on Jewish sects contemporaneous with Jesus and Paul,[2] and countless articles investigating noncanonical gospels[3] all point to a vibrant period in the formation of the oral and nascent early collection of written *logia* during and after Paul's itinerant ministry. Confirmation that this included noncanonical sayings of Jesus is indisputably found in 1 Corinthians. In 1 Cor 2:9, Paul introduces a passage with the words "as it is written." Typically, Paul used this introduction only for written scriptural references drawn from the Jewish writings in the Torah or Prophets. The verse that follows, "What no eye has seen, nor ear heard nor the heart of man conceived, what God has prepared for those who love him," has no clear parallel in Jewish literature.[4] The only direct parallel is found in a document known as the *Gospel of Thomas* (i.e., *Gos. Thom.* 17), a noncanonical writing that reached its final form between 100 and 150 CE, but may date its more primitive form to as early as the 60s.[5]

Thomas is a collection of 114 sayings attributed to Jesus that were given to Judas Didymos (Greek for the twin), Thomas, presumably the same person as the Apostle

1. Robinson and Koester, *Trajectories*.

2. Work on the Dead Sea Scrolls by Geza Vermes, John Allegro, and also noticing the work of John Strugnell of Harvard Divinity School.

3. Most notably, Helmut Koester, also of Harvard Divinity School.

4. Isa 64:4 is sometimes cited, but it is clearly *not* the passage Paul is quoting; the lack of parallels includes rabbinic materials according to Conzelmann, *I Corinthians*, 63–64.

5. See Robinson and Koester, *Trajectories*, 186.

Thomas mentioned in all three synoptic gospels, and the "doubting" Thomas of the Gospel of John.[6] This is also the same Thomas who, when Jesus said that he would return to Judea where his life was in great danger, said bravely to the disciples, "Let us also go, that we might die with him."[7] Later at the Last Supper, Jesus tells the disciples it is time for his glorification and departure[8] and that he must go to his Father.[9] Thomas responds, "Lord, we do not know where you are going; how can we know *the way*?" Thomas' question, followed by Phillip's additional request ("Lord, show us the Father so that we may be satisfied"), elicits Jesus' detailed description of the believer's relationship with the Father that comes about through belief in him as the son and his soon-to-come glorification as the Son of Man. By following Jesus' commandments to love and by keeping his words (*logia*), guided by the Counselor, also called the Spirit of Truth and Holy Spirit, who "will teach you all things, and bring to your remembrance all that I have said to you" (14:26), the believer receives the love of the Father, but even more, in a beautifully simple but powerful statement, Jesus says, ". . . and we will come to him [i.e., to the Father, a future event] and make our home with him [in the kingdom]" (14:23).[10] Unfortunately, it is difficult to find a direct connection between these events in John (the sayings are in a narrative framework), and the *Gospel of Thomas* (which has virtually no narrative framework, and no direct link to 1 Cor 2:9).

Thomas purports to contain the "secret sayings" given to Thomas by "the living Jesus." This designation of Jesus would imply that the sayings given to Thomas came from the risen Jesus, or certainly, the glorified Jesus, however, Saying 12 says that at least some were spoken during his itinerant activity: "The disciples said to Jesus, 'We know that your are going to leave us. Who will be our leader?' Jesus said to them, 'No matter where you are you are to go to James the Just, for whose sake heaven and earth came into being.'" Of course, James the Just is none other than the brother of Jesus of Nazareth. For the *Gospel of Thomas* and its community, James is not only the sole and exclusive apostolic authority of the legitimate Jesus movement, he is the final arbiter of which of Jesus' *logia* are to be retained. It is he who decides if they are efficacious and what their meaning may be to this community, as only Jesus' words contain salvation. No one may interpret them differently. This is an extraordinary claim to James' apostolic power and the existence of a salvific sayings trajectory that stands a distinct from the Synoptic Gospels and predates them. More, for the community of the *Gospel of Thomas*, there is no other apostle that can question James. He is the exclusive legitimate guardian of the *logia* of Jesus.

---

6. John 20:24, Thomas says he will only believe if he physically touches the wounds of Jesus—which he does and exclaims, "my Lord and my God."
7. John 11:16.
8. John 13:31.
9. "And you know where I am going," John 14:4.
10. John 14:25.

Excursus: Paul and the Logia of Jesus

The extant copy of *Thomas* is in Coptic, which is Egyptian transcribed into the Greek alphabet (with the addition of seven new characters), and was bound in the codex, or papyrus-bound book. The document itself was found near the town of Nag Hammadi, Egypt, in an earthen jar by a farmer in 1945.[11] This was just one of many documents found (twelve bound papyrus codices and eight loose pages), most of which are attributed by scholars to the *gnostic genre*. Gnosticism was an emerging wisdom and cosmological religion, where revelation of the true state of oneself as being trapped by an evil god in this material and doomed world, frees both the mind and soul to attain reunification with the true god (there are many iterations of this, including the true god as reigning in the seventh heaven). Thus, *wisdom sayings* that provide such a revelation were extremely popular and of immense import to the adherents of Gnosticism, and so also to the Thomas community. The *Gospel of Thomas* then represents a Christian element of Gnosticism, where Jesus, the *Living One*, is divine revealer of the saving truth as son of the one true God through his sayings. As such, Jesus' wisdom and revelatory statements tend to have a more ethereal tone, perhaps better described as esoteric wisdom sayings about discovering one's true nature, and by doing so, salvation and freedom are obtained.

There is no narrative or biographical framework in the *Gospel of Thomas*, no *eschatological emphasis* on the return of Jesus with the kingdom like "a thief in the night," no reference to the crucifixion or cross (in fact, Jesus in the historical sense is no longer of import), nothing whatsoever as to the resurrection, and certainly nothing about the Son of Man, or the coming Son of Man. Instead, *it is Jesus' words* that contain life and power and that lead the adherent to eternal revelation and salvation through knowledge of one's true state, or *gnosis*. Thus, the *Gospel of Thomas* is nothing like the other canonical gospels in form or content, which subjugated the sayings and activity of Jesus to the central message of faith that led to the cross and God's resurrection and inauguration of the end of the age. However, both the canonical gospels and *Thomas* make an equal claim to provide salvation to the believer, and this is critically important in understanding the development of early Christianity and the beginning of the Christology of the New Testament. A saving encounter with the good news of the canonical gospels (and the ministry of Paul), meant a high risk, trusting, *faithful* response to the event of God in the historical cross and resurrection of Jesus of Nazareth, and full commitment to him as Lord and Christ;[12] a commitment in a world where powerful opponents, including Roman authorities, considered Jesus to be possessed by Beelzebul and crucified as a dark magician, and "evildoer." In the case of *Thomas*, a saving encounter was achieving true wisdom or gnosis, or *faith* in the revelation and immediate salvation provided through Jesus words; by gaining wisdom and understanding of one's true nature through Jesus' secret sayings; "Whoever discovers the interpretation

---

11. Some scholars believe that *Thomas* and the other Nag Hammadi documents were found in a grave and not in an earthen jar, particularly those who have visited the site.

12. Koester, "Wisdom and Folly," 82.

of these sayings will not taste death" (Saying 2). The sayings in the *Gospel of Thomas* are, in fact, a form of good news, *but to only a select few*, i.e., those who have access to the "secret sayings" and, more important, have the ability to "discover their interpretation"; and so, the good news is not a democratized invitation to the lost, the hopeless, poor, or those without merit, power and health as in the Synoptic Gospels. That this good news is "secret" and must be "discovered" means *that it is elitist* and, more importantly, one obtains *salvation by merit* of obtaining gnosis.

These *trajectories* then would have been operating in parallel to each other, likely being disseminated by designated, authorized "apostles." Consequently, those who found saving power in the wisdom sayings of Jesus by discovering their hidden meaning as to one's true nature and origin, that his sayings were filled with life as he was the Living One (and likely there were those who encountered him as the Living One), these adherents and their emissaries (authorized apparently by James, or whose authority was later tied to the Apostle James, which is more likely, just as pseudepigraphical letters were later ascribed to Paul), would have been quite active as itinerant charismatics contemporaneous with Paul.

Since each trajectory made a direct claim to the authority of Jesus,[13] they were *ultimately on a collision course*. More specifically, the canonical gospels are intended to elicit faith and hope in the proclaimed in the good news of Jesus of Nazareth, that is, the good news of the Father's forgiveness and unbounded love and justification only by limitless trust and faith in his love, evidenced by the crucifixion and resurrection, later combined with faith in the imminent presence of the resurrected Lord, i.e., an intense eschatological viewpoint. Mark is expecting the near arrival of the vengeful Son of Man, i.e., Jesus, to destroy God's enemies. Luke-Acts establishes the return of Jesus as distant and far in the future while the church takes full form and reaches the entire world. Thomas refocuses that faith into a reliance on the saving power of the words alone and their revelation of one's true nature. One resurrection is future (and has started with Jesus), while the other is immediate salvation through *gnosis*, brought about by revelation and understanding the truth as revealed in the secret words and sayings of Jesus: "The Gnosticism of the Gospel of Thomas appears to be a direct continuation of the eschatological sayings of Jesus. But the disclosure of the mysterious presence of the kingdom is no longer an eschatological event; it has become a matter of interpretation of Jesus words: '. . . whoever finds the explanation of these words will not taste death.'"[14] In Thomas, salvation is immediate.

This eschatological orientation of sayings in *Thomas* often reflect a historical period in Jesus' ministry that were experienced by the very first adherents who were at risk by following him, where, as Saying 16 notes, "Perhaps people think that I have come

---

13. Koester and Robinson in their collection of articles, *Trajectories*, describe just what these paths represent, namely, expressions of faith that found their root in the sayings of Jesus, i.e., the "living one" and Son of God.

14. Saying 1, see Robinson and Koester, *Trajectories*, 175.

to cast peace on the world; they do not know that I have come to cast conflicts upon the world—fire, sword, and war." This saying has often been dismissed in inconsistent with Jesus' activity for Abba' and the unbounded love of God. On the contrary, Jesus recognized that the message would bring division and possibly violence, i.e., he was at war with Satan, demonic imperialism and demons that had polluted the land.[15] As such, despite significant differences between the canonical gospels and *Thomas*, one cannot preclude the possibility that many Thomas sayings (over half of which have parallels in the canonical gospels), include sayings of Jesus of Nazareth and have a claim to historical validity, that is, they, like many of the canonical sayings, originated from his ministry and work, but were reinterpreted or took a different trajectory.

Some of the Thomas sayings, when compared to the synoptic parallels, appear to be in a form that is earlier (e.g., Saying 16), i.e., a more difficult reading, or a more "primitive" in form. Indeed, as established in the foregoing chapters, Paul was in communication with Jesus, the risen Lord, and was receiving instructions, "words of the Lord," and so Thomas sayings may have come from this fluid and rich period of interaction with the risen Jesus, who for Thomas was "the Living One." As Koester notes, "The basis of the Gospel of Thomas is a sayings collection which is more primitive than the canonical gospels, even though its basic principal is not related to the creed of the passion and resurrection."[16] Certainly, a collection of sayings like those found in *Thomas* would indicate that, like the now lost Q sayings source, there were written documents focused on preserving only the sayings of Jesus, or *logia*, and that they began to be formed very early. Those who had tendencies to understand the *logia* as revelatory would ultimately preserve such wisdom sayings, forming collections of similar sayings and developing them theologically over time by adding attributions (i.e., the source of the sayings, Judas Didymas Thomas), and the promise of salvation. Again, "Whoever discovers the interpretation of these sayings will not taste death." Thomas is a pure representative of both genres—the sayings collection and gnostic-wisdom logia.

Thus, the oral period of transmission, from Jesus' ministry through the apostolic period and sayings of the risen Jesus until the early second century (reaching its peak with the composition of the Gospel of Mark in about 64–80 CE), must have included sayings that were pulled into many trajectories, including the gospel proclamation represented by the synoptic traditions (Matthew, Mark and Luke), and revelatory wisdom traditions (Thomas). It is probable that there were such sayings collections circulating as early as 40–50 CE that were still in formation within early communities.[17] Confirmation that these collections were in written form very early is clearly

---

15. See Busse, *Fire*, 40–53.
16. Robinson and Koester, *Trajectories*, 186.
17. In fact, some sayings may have been contained in letters of recommendation sent to specific communities, similar to that carried by Paul and Barnabas according to Acts 15:22–29, and certainly by Paul's opponents in Corinth, 2 Cor 3:1 and 2:17.

demonstrated in the well-developed and theologically layered written source used by Matthew and Luke, namely Q, which appears to have gone through various iterations (i.e., the earliest version likely did not include the Son of Man traditions added later as the destruction of Jerusalem was both imminent and witnessed; see above, used as a source along side the Gospel of Mark). Q became so completely absorbed in Matthew and Luke (as early as 70–85 CE), that it is now "lost" as a separate document. But its absence today as a separate document is paralleled by dozens of other early Christian writings, now found only in the quotations of later writers.

Consequently, literary and historical analysis of the trajectories of early Christian faith and belief, evidenced just by the Synoptics, John, Q and Thomas, confirm that there were competing claims to (1) authority (i.e., as to the apostolic source of the tradition thereby linking the sayings to a direct witness and hearer of Jesus—in other words, that it can be traced to Jesus) (2) the object of faith (e.g., faith in the historical event of the cross and resurrection, or in the power of Jesus' wisdom and words to save),[18] and (3) eschatology and the nature of salvation (as in Thomas, the saving power of the words of Jesus now versus the return and presence of the Lord). *Indeed, the collision of competing interpretations based on the use of Jesus' sayings must have occurred early-on, particularly as migrating adherents infiltrated established communities, or when itinerant apostoloi, such as Paul (or Kayfa, or Apollos, or "Superlative Apostles"), entered and taught a "new gospel."* While Paul had no need to appeal to written list of sayings of the Lord, as he was under the commission and active guidance of the risen Jesus and Holy Spirit, he is undeniably able to cite authoritative support for his *euangelion* by appealing to sayings that are known to have come both from Jesus' earthly ministry and later from the risen Lord directly to him.[19] Thus, Paul's authority was still fluid and operative among his *ecclesia* as the authoritative conduit of the gospel and sayings of Jesus without distinction to time (i.e., Jesus earthly ministry or as risen Lord) or appeal to a written document of wisdom logia that fostered salvation. For Paul, sayings were a natural part of his work that was being guided by the risen Lord, nothing more. Sayings had not been yet crystallized in Paul's *ecclesia*—they had an apostle. So then, for those that collected *logia*, the focus was on the authoritative interpretation of the oral and written wisdom sayings of the Living Lord. By implication then, there were those who had attained such an ability and made this claim, and would not only proselytize but defend this faith approach as the only true and valid way of salvation, and share these written "secret" sayings documents. The fact that Paul plainly cites the aforementioned saying of Jesus found only in the *Gospel of Thomas* (1 Cor 2:9; this saying may have been in an earlier sayings collection, but likely in the same genre of salvation wisdom), and, as noted, prefaces it with "as it is

---

18. Koester, "Wisdom and Folly," 82–83.

19. See above, 1 Thess 4, where Paul attributes his description of the parousia to "the word of the Lord," that is, the risen Lord Jesus, in response to the crisis of death within the community and the subsequent questions that have been posed to Paul by the Thessalonians.

Excursus: Paul and the Logia of Jesus

written," may provide dramatic insight into the first encounter of these competing expressions of faith in the cosmopolitan city of Corinth—in the very *ecclesia* founded by Paul. And so, it is important to ascertain evidence from 1 Corinthians that may validate the collision of tradition and authority—that 1 Cor 2:9 / Thomas 17 may provide the first confirmed evidence of confrontation between emerging faith expressions within early Christianity.

What is clear from reading 1 Corinthians is that the metropolis and the *ecclesia* were fertile ground for primitive forms of Christology and theological development that significantly challenged Paul, particularly from the distance of Ephesus, his new missionary center.[20] He was once again facing opposition (1 Corinthians chs. 1–4), and new challenges of immorality (ch. 5), as well as the failure to practice *agape* (ch. 6), troubling written questions (chs. 7–8), and another defense of the legitimacy of his apostleship (ch. 9). Paul attacked the error of adherents considering themselves free from morality, but allowed eating meat offered to idols if it did not disturb other followers (ch. 10). He allowed a distinctly unique practice, unheard of outside of the letter of 1 Corinthians—the practice of baptism for the dead. The trouble he faced brought by opponents was met with emotion as well as sarcastic condemnation of those who claimed they were already "kings," i.e., they had achieved salvation.[21] In addition, it is apparent that there had been well-known, famous apostles and teachers who either visited Corinth, or whose followers (apparently initiated into the Way by baptism), had become affiliated with adherents of the *ecclesia*; namely Kayfa (a leader of the apostles and first, according to Paul, of the male apostles to encounter the resurrected Jesus according to 1 Cor 15:5), and Apollos (the "eloquent" Alexandrian Jew noted in Acts 18:24–28, who had built up the *ecclesia* in Ephesus, and who was "well versed in the scriptures," Acts 18:24).

Apollos had come to Corinth after having received a strong recommendation from the *ecclesia* in Ephesus. It is revealing that the author of Acts describes Apollos as "eloquent" (in Greek, *logios*), meaning well educated and, most likely, trained in interpretation and teaching of Jewish Scripture.[22] Thus, the use of the term "eloquent" also implies that Apollos is an influential speaker, that is, fluent and *persuasive words* (*logia*). Apollos may have introduced John's baptism, which included different rites, including removal of clothing, stamping on those garments to signify putting off the

---

20. The distance from Corinth to Ephesus was approximately 210 nautical miles. Paul either left by ship to Piraeus or from Corinth. According to *Parallel Lives: Sulla* (26.1) the journey, with favorable winds and currents, was only three days. If Paul would have returned by land, it would have taken him several weeks, and he would then have stopped at Borea, Thessaloniki, Philippi by land, crossed to Asia Minor by sea and stopped at Troas, before completing his journey to Ephesus.

21. 1 Cor 4:8.

22. Alexandria, Egypt, his city of origin, was famous for its library, the greatest of the ancient world, centers of learning, and philosophers, including Philo of Alexandria, a Hellenistic Jew who allegorically interpreted the torah to make it applicable to current times.

past, and water immersion, accompanied by special words.[23] But the thrust of Paul's interest is in Apollos' preaching. Clearly, it is possible that as a well-known interpreter of Scripture and teacher, Apollos may have introduced an oral or written collection of *logia*, or Jesus sayings including wisdom sayings, and provided interpretation that was centered in salvation wisdom.[24] Again, the passage in Acts provides information that, while "he had been instructed in the *way of the Lord*, and he spoke accurately the things [*ta*], concerning the Lord [his sayings?]," he did not *know* of the baptism of Jesus, only that of John the Baptist. Could this mean that Apollos was accurate and eloquent (*logios*) in educating others in the sayings (*logia*) of Jesus, but had not been exposed to Paul's salvific *euangelion* of the faith, *pistis*, in the crucifixion, death and resurrection of Jesus, now Christ, the one coming with the *parousia*? For Paul, all *logia* of Jesus can only be properly rendered and applied if set within the context of his *euangelion* to serve the *ecclesia*. Jesus' *logia* by themselves, particularly grouped in an esoteric and exclusivist collection, were neither the complete revelation of the *euangelion*, nor could contain the miraculous activity of the risen Lord evident in his ministry or witnessed among the adherents—the signs and wonders among them.[25] In fact, for Paul, such collections were dangerously errant, if not satanic (see below), resulting in esoteric elitism and rejection of the *euangelion*.[26]

While it is possible that Apollos taught wisdom-salvation using the *logia* of Jesus, and also the practice of *agape*, also founded on Jesus' sayings, it must only remain as pure speculation, as the historical and literary evidence is not only circumstantial, other facts speak against it. And so, it is unlikely that Apollos is the transmitter of the saying in 1 Cor 2:9, or for that matter, that his teaching is the source of the many problems that had arisen in the community, but it is clear that his name is prominently mentioned by Paul numerous times.[27] Apollos was highly regarded by Paul, as in all of his references he takes a respectful tone. In fact, many times in 1 Corinthians, Paul ties Apollos productively to his ministry and how he has helped foster growth. This would lend support to the view that Apollos did not fully grasp the central element of the cross and justification by faith alone, but once he understood, he became an accepted itinerant missionary in the "camp" of Paul and Kayfa, witnesses to the risen Christ. Why else would Paul place Apollos in the same company as he and Kayfa at the outset of his letter? Certainly, Paul would not do this if Apollos were considered an opponent. Paul was never hesitant to publicly chastise or curse his opponents; or, as is later evident in 1 Corinthians, proclaim himself as literally present in spirit (as the words were

---

23. Patterson, *Lost Way*, 225–30.
24. Ibid., 222–25.
25. 1 Thess 1:5–6.
26. 1 Cor 4:6–7.

27. 1 Cor 1:12 as a baptizer like Paul; also, that Apollos built upon the foundation of Paul's work; 3:6, Paul uses an analogy of nature, Paul planted the seed and Apollos "watered," but God gave the growth.

Excursus: Paul and the Logia of Jesus

being read from his letter), and, as a result, pronounce judgment and condemnation on troublemakers as if he were.[28] But, there is no such condemnation of Apollos. Paul's letter demonstrates that the *ecclesia* of Corinth represented a complex amalgamation of early and emerging beliefs and personalities that created the greatest challenge so far experienced in Paul's missionary work for the risen Lord.

Removing Apollos as the possible source and proponent of a wisdom-salvation faith, the question remains as to whether the situation in Corinth, evidenced by the independent and noncanonical saying of Jesus in 2:9, is associated with the *introduction of written sayings source that had a different theological basis than faith of the cross*. Do Saying 17 and the content of Paul's letter to the Corinthians provide sufficient evidence that an early form of *gnosis*, supported by a primitive sayings document, has been introduced into his community? The key to answering this question is, once again, to be found in the occasion of the letter to the Corinthians, namely identifying Paul's "opponents" in Corinth.

Paul founded the Corinthian *ecclesia* only two to three years before he wrote a series of letters, including a first letter now lost mentioned in 1 Cor 5:9. The letters were written over another one- to two-year period, and show an intensely deteriorating situation between Paul and certain adherents, largely outsiders that have infiltrated the *ecclesia* after Paul departed for his next missionary objective, Ephesus. There were perhaps eight letters in all: Letter 1 (the lost letter mentioned in 1 Cor 5:9), Letter 2 (1 Corinthians itself, although several sections of the letter are clearly later insertions),[29] Letter 3 (2 Cor 2:14—6:13), Letter 4 (2 Cor 10–12), Letter 5 (2 Cor 1:1—2:13), Letter 6 (2 Cor 8), Letter 7 (2 Cor 9), Letter 8 (remaining fragments in 2 Cor 6:14–7:1). In reviewing 1 Corinthians and the composition of the community of adherents implied by its content (including the attempts of the opponents to eradicate Paul's gospel and eschatology by disrupting and dividing the community), it becomes clear that Paul had employed his familiar mission strategy in founding the *ecclesia*, namely: (1) Paul's workshop ministry is successful in attracting other artisans, craftsmen and skilled workers to the Way from local pagan cults, temples and mystery religions, and (2) he has also been successful in drawing God-fearers and other Jews to the Way as a result of his speaking in the local synagogue on the Sabbath; this includes wealthy women (just as in Thessaloniki), who were benefactors to the local synagogue. The new, democratized community embraces the faith of Jesus and accepts him as risen Lord. This acceptance is based on Paul's proclamation (i.e., the perilous risk of death and expected eschatological events mitigated by faith in Paul's gospel of the cross), as well as validating experience through charismatic events and activities (e.g., exorcisms, healings, heavenly language), which include Paul's own visions, dream, soul trans-

---

28. 1 Cor 5:4.

29. Particularly Paul's order that women be silent in the church—this is clearly not from Paul, as will be demonstrated below; Paul fully utilized women as equal, even superior members of the *ecclesiae* (Rom 16:7).

portation and perhaps trance encounters with the risen Lord. Paul's proclamation is centered on the historical event of the cross and the resurrection as God's decisive act and entry into human history,[30] the coming end of the age with the arrival of the risen Lord, and the imminent general resurrection and establishment of the kingdom of God for his children who practice *agape*. The resurrection of Jesus confirms the inauguration of the Way of God and inbreaking of God's kingdom. The practice of *agape* is the binding, divine practice of the adherents, the uniting force of the community in the intense eschatological setting of crisis and persecution, hope and yearning, as the last days unfold before the imminent presence of the risen Lord.

The *ecclesia* is the radically democratized, intense eschatological community of new equals[31] with only an informal and temporary leadership left in place by Paul, those who are chosen to sponsor a house church until the Lord comes.[32] This leadership is guided by the command to love and to admonish errant practices where love is void and this behavior disrupts the peaceful, "quiet life" they are to lead, "working with their own hands" (which by example draws others to the community).[33] The *agape* feast, the central, weekly celebration of the communal meal both anticipating the Lord's return and the overcoming of the curse of death (i.e., by uniting with death in the cultic meal, body and blood, they receive protection from satanic and demonic control and the curse of death, Jesus having been raised), is established as the central focus of the gatherings. As the community urgently expects the end of the age, it sometimes provides support to Paul to assist in his continuing itinerant missionary work as the crisis of the last days intensifies.

And then, as Paul is active in Ephesus, outside opponents arrive and dramatically disrupt Paul's assembly, directly attacking his authority, the accuracy of his teaching and content of his gospel, his eschatology, and his character. This is all based on "words of the Lord" and who has the authority to employ them, which source of those words is valid (a written source, such as a sayings list similar to Thomas or Paul's active encounters with the risen Lord as an *apostolos*), and what eschatological stance of the adherent achieves by accepting them. In the case of 1 Corinthians, there is a distinctly new competing interpretation of Jesus and his words that rejects Paul's gospel, its authority, the basis of faith and, thus, the "Way" salvation to God—in the history of early Christianity this is *the primitive battle for "orthodoxy"* with each "camp" *defining its opponents as dangerous*. So clearly, 1 Corinthians reflects a familiar occasion to Paul's letters, the same that led to the composition of Galatians and

---

30. As Abba', father to his new adopted children, the new Israel.

31. The composition of the community is radical in its historical setting, crossing barriers of gender, social class, social order, religion, philosophy, even politics (exchanging Divine Caesar as Savior and protector for Jesus of Nazareth, Savior, Lord and also Christ).

32. Obviously, Chloe and other leaders of house churches in Corinth who are to serve and admonish, occasionally bringing the whole *ecclesia* together, perhaps for the love feasts.

33. Including Paul's admonition to "make it your ambition [your passion and drive] to live peacefully," "working with your own hands," 1 Thess 4:11.

Thessalonians, namely, strong opposition to Paul's gospel. In this case, the opposition and the response it engendered brings to light the fragility of the community, its weaknesses as it finds its way in the new faith, and its struggle to firm up its identify as a new, radically democratized, *ecclesia* composed of rich and poor, Jew and Gentile, male and female, slave and free.[34]

---

34. 1 Cor 1:26; see also Gal 3:28.

Chapter 3

The Enemies of Paul in Corinth

Risk Analysis of Paul's Letter to the Corinthians

As noted, qualitative risk analysis suggests conclusions as to the activities of Jesus and his contemporaries in countering perilous risk when historical context can be recovered. It can effectively assess human conflict to cancel out competing perils. It can provide clarity to the original conflict between opponents, as well as to the nature and intent of actions, methods and techniques employed, such as authoritative correspondence, the use of Jesus' sayings and charismatic practices, curses, soul transportation, visions and trances, as well as post-crucifixion encounters with Jesus. The perilous risk conflict between Paul and his opponents in 1 Thessalonians could be recovered. In 1 Thessalonians, Paul and his opponents each considered the other to be agents of Satan, and subject to the curse of death. It is recovery of this perilous risk context that fully reveals the desperate and deadly nature of the conflict and the specific activities used to neutralize it. The patterns and methods of Paul's activity, eschatology and charismatic prowess are also made available in the very alien and foreign world of the first-century Roman and Hellenistic milieu. We will next apply risk analysis to Paul and his opponents and the crises in the Corinthian *ecclesia* after attempting to recover the *sitz im leben*, or historical context.

Recovering the *Sitz im Leben*

To begin, Chloe's "people" (literally "those of Chloe") bring word of aggressive factionalism in Corinth (i.e., "I am of Paul, I am of Kayfa, I am of Apollos"), introduced by intruders.[1] Chloe is Greek and a woman's name.[2] Paul's use of the term "those of Chloe" would mean that Chloe likely had sent her servants or freemen at some expense to notify Paul of the emerging crisis. She is most certainly a head of house—the

---

1. 1 Cor 1:12.

2. The name was commonly used to describe the goddess Demeter, and is translated as the "young one, the green sprout"; it is possible that Paul gave this name to indicate her new faith, as Paul did give new names to some of the new believers.

owner of property, a *domus* (home), and employed servants and slaves—and therefore is a wealthy widow, emancipated, a merchant, or has inherited her rights and wealth from father or family. She was what Roman law designated as *sui iuris*, her "own woman," which was common and legally protected, that is, the right of a woman to own property, which afforded official protections and social standing. If she were a financial "patron" then she had substantial wealth at her disposal, and, just as noted for some of the women in Thessaloniki, she may have supported religious or secular gatherings, such as cults or social associations, which were popular at the time. The term would often be used for women who were benefactors of temples. Indeed, Phoebe, the deaconess of Cenchreae is so designated (*protstatis*), by Paul in his recommendation letter for her to the Roman *ecclesia*.[3] Women could not vote or hold political office although there is substantial evidence via inscriptions they held significant official positions, including civic and religious leadership roles. There are numerous examples where women exerted powerful influence. Paul simply mentions Chloe by name, there is no need to describe her, meaning everyone in the Corinthian *ecclesiae* knew her. Paul's citation is another clear confirmation and testament *to the significant role of women in the early church*, which Paul encouraged and consistently enforced. The democratization of leadership and equality in the early church included women in all of Paul's *ecclesiae*.

It is possible that Chloe's home was the central place of cultic gathering and meals (the *Eucharist*). If it was not, Chloe's home was certainly one of the more important *ecclesiae* in the city, which met the first day of each week (the tradition of keeping the day of post-crucifixion encounters as the day of assembly). Since Corinth was a recolonized Roman metropolis, her home would have followed the design plan of a *domus*, or Roman villa. The structure of the Roman *domus* provides a tantalizing insight. In some designs was a large area in the front of the *domus* that included one or more artisan shops. These could be rented out, or were used by the owner to employ artisans to produce items for their merchant and trade activity. Paul may have worked in the shop in front of Chloe's *domus*. If so, Chloe may have been among Paul's first adherents, perhaps a merchant of leather and tents for the nearby athletic games, the Roman garrison, or for domestic use, It would have been possible that she employed Aquila and Prisca, as well as Paul, i.e., slaves and artisans. Toward the back interior of the *domus* itself was a *peristylium*, or larger rectangle garden or fountain area that would be surrounded by columns with rooms around it. The *peristylium* in many excavated home in Ephesus, Pompei and other Roman cities was easily able to hold between twenty to as many as fifty. The number of adherents in Corinth, evidenced by the myriad of issues at the time of Paul's writing, suggests a larger gathering than fifty. There may have been multiple *ecclesiae*,[4] but Paul does command that "the whole church" come together at the letter's reading, as it contained multiple charismatic ac-

3. Rom 16:1–2.
4. 1 Cor 16:9.

tions, from soul transportation to curses for the assembly.[5] Chloe may have provided her *domus* for this event, particularly since Paul was answering the urgent questions she had sent on behalf of fellow adherents.[6]

The intruders into the *ecclesiae* of Corinth at first appear to be unlike those Paul confronted, and then cursed, in Galatia or Thessaloniki. For example, they do not overtly demand Gentiles be circumcised and strictly adhere to dietary laws, as in Galatia.[7] It is clear that something much more complicated and ominous is present, as Paul seems to have underestimated the perilous risk they present. This is confirmed by the number of letters he issued after 1 Corinthians (as many as nine), as well as a "painful" confrontation during a subsequent encounter.

Paul considered his enemies in Corinth satanic and demon-possessed intruders, evidenced by those he cursed for evil practices and turned over to Satan for destruction—what was considered to be the darkest of magic in the ancient world.[8] For Paul, the perilous risk they represented was the most dangerous he had yet encountered from Satan. The conflict represented a deadly crisis, i.e., the survival of the *ecclesiae* and his salvific *euangelion*, and so also for himself, the *apostolos* of that *euangelion*. They claimed the sole right and privilege of immediate salvific powers through an exclusivist charismatic "awakening" provided by esoteric wisdom (*sophia*), and knowledge (*gnosis*), mystically accessed in special rites and *logia* of the Risen One. Some of these *logia* were employed to vociferously condemn Paul as dangerous, a false *apostolos*, and so, an evildoer and deceiver of Satan. Paul's enemies only recognized the efficacious power of *logia* as imbuing adherents with immediate salvific protection, if accompanied by certain expelling rituals performed by apostolic mystagogues whom Paul sarcastically labeled "super-apostles." Paul clearly accepts many of their *logia* to be on par with Hebrew Scripture (e.g., 2:9, a saying only found in the *Gospel of Thomas*, Saying 17), but he subjugates all *logia* to his apostolic authority and his *euangelion* of the cross and practice of *agape*, cursing anyone who that denies it is of God. All *logia* must be interpreted in light of the *euangelion* and impending *parousia*. The intensity of the eschatological conflict between Paul and his enemies is striking, and underscores the very alien world of Paul and his contemporaries to our own. Both claimed authority of the risen Lord, and both threatened the other with curses, death and annihilation in order to mitigate the perilous and deadly risks of being deceived and owned by Satan.

In sum, there was significant conflict over the interpretive authority of *logia*, as well as if they held salvific and efficacious power, and if so, which *apostoloi* held

---

5. 16:23, such as the house of Gaius.

6. Is this why she is well known by all, meaning, she had been with the *ecclesia* since the beginning? Most likely, it is.

7. See previous discussions on Paul's enemies in Galatia.

8. 1 Cor 5:5; not unlike Gal 5:12, perhaps a curse, where Paul wishes the Galatian insurrectionist would mutilate themselves, meaning, emasculate themselves!

ultimate power over them. Paul's enemies assert a radical eschatology that only Jesus' *logia* made accessible, where discovering one's true nature affords immediate salvation through a radical form of charismatic *gnosis*. This sacred, divine knowledge yielded an awakening that imbued the individual with the salvation revealed in Jesus' *logia* alone. The characteristics, nature and danger of this risk conflict can now be more fully explored.

Assessing the Scope of the Perilous Risk Conflict and Crisis

As in his retributive, charismatic dispatches to the Galatian and Thessalonian *ecclesiae*, Paul immediately addresses an emerging risk crisis, this time in Corinth, which once again results from outside intrusion. Other *apostoloi* have targeted and infiltrated Paul's *ecclesiae*, introducing esoteric rites, charismatic practices and a radical eschatology of salvific *gnosis*, all of which reject Paul, his *euangelion* of the cross and an imminent *parousia*. As proof of their divine appointment, status and authority, these *apostoloi* publicly exhibit dramatic *charismata*, primarily *glossolalia*, which Paul's adherents admire. A mystical baptismal ceremony conducted by one of the *apostoloi* is required for entry into the cult. The initiate receives a mystical rebirth from death to life, allowing them access to secret *logia* of the Living One. Once fully initiated, adherents can then be baptized for the dead, a form of mystical necromancy and salvific rite. That Paul does not practice the rite of initiate baptism (other than occasionally), and yet claims to be an *apostolos*, impugns his legitimacy. Following the initiate baptism, these *apostoloi* begin to share a private collection of *logia* from the Living One, Jesus. These *logia* provide a charismatic awakening as to one's true divine origin, as well as the perilous risk of remaining or returning to ignorance, i.e., to be under Satan's deception and in ignorance (i.e., death). The reception of charismatic enlightenment through *sophia* (divine wisdom), and salvific *gnosis* contained in the *logia*, possesses the adherent with a cloak of divinity, freeing them from this world's doom and Satan. They can feast without fear of demonic possession at any pagan cultic meal, even engaged in unlawful sexual relationships, now as libertines to ridicule the world and display their prowess. Their new status is evidenced by *charismata*, confirming that unification with the divine and the Living One has been achieved.

To gain entry into Paul's *ecclesiae*, the *apostoloi* carry written licenses with testimonies, i.e., charismatic letters of endorsement purportedly from other notable *apostoloi*. They endorse each by name as true *apostoloi* of the Living One, empowered to provide adherents with exclusive possession of powerful *logia* and *gnosis* so as to escape the satanic world of deception, doom and death. Paul is not on that list. His enemies dispute his *charismata*, his claim to be an *apostoloi*, and scoff at his *euangelion* of the cross and *parousia*. Paul is an evildoer, a magician, whose claim of a future *parousia* is intended only to secure a subsistence living, absconding funds in the name of Jesus Christ, the future messiah he claims is still to return. This is not the Living One, whose salvific *logia* provide *sophia* and efficacious *gnosis*. They note that Paul quickly departs to other cities using the same deceptions, leaving his adherents not only poor but in worse peril, subject to persecution and attack from human and demonic enemies, and still doomed to remain in satanic ignorance.

Paul's defense of his *euangelion* and *charismata* is defiant:

> Therefore, you do not lack any spiritual gift as you eagerly wait for our Lord Jesus Christ to be revealed. He will keep you strong to the end, so that you will be blameless on the day of our Lord Jesus Christ.[9]

By verse 7, it is apparent that Paul is being challenged by this new and radicalized eschatology that has no reliance on Paul's *euangelion* of the cross, resurrection and future *parousia*, i.e., the Day of the Lord, is still to come. Safety and salvation are accessible immediately to the adherent via esoteric and salvific *gnosis* and *sophia* drawn from the *logia* of Jesus.[10] This is the earliest evidence of vying eschatologies and *apostoloi* in nascent Christianity. For Paul, the crisis is fraught with perilous risk. To lose adherents is to jeopardize his apostleship,[11] and thus bring doom on himself. If Paul's *ecclesiae* are in peril, so is his life, spirit and soul.

Paul's response is emphatic: The "day of the Lord" is yet to come for his adherents. That day includes the judgment of actions in the interim between reception of the *euangelion* in *pistis* (with the practice of *agape* and forgiveness), and the presence of the Lord, who will bring the God's judgment and deliver the kingdom *only to Paul's faithful*: "He will keep you strong to the end, so that you will be blameless" (1:8).[12] And so for Paul, there is great risk between the time of faithful acceptance of his efficacious *euangelion* and the future intervention of God, so near: "God, who has called you into fellowship with his son Jesus Christ the Lord, is faithful."[13] As in Galatians, any other *euangelion* is satanic deception.[14] After reaffirming the still future presence of the Lord, judgment and hope of salvation from the curse of death, Paul declares that they have received all spiritual gifts *and gnosis* now available; that is, there is nothing secret, nothing hidden from them, they know all there is to know and that it is sufficient to achieve salvation: ". . . that you were enriched in every way by him in all speaking and knowledge . . . so that you were deficient in no gift."[15] Paul

---

9. 1 Cor 7b–8.

10. See Patterson, *Lost Way*, 22; as noted, evidence of this trajectory, similar to the trajectory found in Q and Thomas, is clearly present in 1 Corinthians.

11. 1 Cor 9:2. As the "seal" of his apostleship, he is validated and is good standing with the risen Lord, who has directed his itinerant activity. To fail is to fall under a possible curse and death.

12. 1 Cor 1:8.

13. Ibid.

14. 2 Cor 11:13; Paul equates his enemies deception with the serpent, Satan, who deceived and condemned the innocent Eve to death with his cunning.

15. 1 Cor 1:5.

is setting the stage to subjugate any *charismata* and *logia* practiced or employed by his enemies to his own *euangelion*.

Paul's followers are therefore in crisis. They are characterized by these intruding "super-apostles" as trapped in the deadly ignorance of this world, and, therefore, are at perilous risk—*all because of Paul*. The wisdom-salvation *gnosis* accessed through their *logia* collection of the Living One is unassailable. Clearly these efficacious *logia* reveal the truth of one's divine nature. This awakening and *gnosis* brings "life," which is immediate once achieved, just as represented in the *logia* collection of the *Gospel of Thomas*: "Whoever discovers the interpretation of these sayings will not taste death."[16] It is a promise of efficacious transformation to life with discovery of the *sophia* contained in the *logia*. Such sayings sources were charismatic encounters, not unlike the Gospel of Mark's introduction to the *euangelion* of the cross: "This is the beginning of the gospel of Jesus Christ." The *euangelion* here is a charismatic word of transformation for those that accept it. This is particularly true for Paul, where the word *euangelion* is more than a noun; it is a powerful verb—an event that is encountered—filled with saving power. Both Paul and his enemies assert from the outset the salvific power of either the *logia*, which is immediate, or the saving event of the passion and empty tomb, which becomes active with the *parousia* for those who have held to this *pistis* and its *elpis*.

Drawing from Paul's introductory and defensive comments alone, Paul's enemies claim sole authority to access protection and life. Salvation then is exclusivist, restricted to those who can properly understand and mystically absorb the *logoi* of the living Jesus. The solitary individual achieves salvation, that is, salvation is achieved by an individual's own interaction and transformation via *gnosis*; i.e., to discover *saving gnosis* in Jesus' sayings, and once realized, be free. Any claim of a future judgment or action by God is not just unnecessary and moot; it is deceptive and question begging.

Consequently, the exclusive authority these opponents claim is unlike any found in the *sitz im leben* of the Thessaloniki or Galatian *ecclesiae*. They dismiss and accuse self-proclaimed *apostoloi* such as Paul as charlatans, as deadly ignorant with their emphasis on pending events. Paul affirms this attack on him and the *euangelion*:

> Now if Christ is preached as raised from the dead, how can some of you say that there is no resurrection of the dead . . . But if there is no resurrection of the dead, then Christ has not been raised, if Christ is not raised the our preaching is in vain . . . We are even found to be misrepresenting God.[17]

Paul concludes with the sad state of affairs for all *apostoloi* if his opponents are correct: "If for this life only we have hoped in Christ, we are of all men most to be pitied."[18] His enemies agreed.

16. Ibid.
17. 1 Cor 15:12, 15.
18. 1 Cor 15:19.

On whose authority did they make such remarkable claims and call for rejection of Paul as a charlatan? Only an appeal to the authoritative *logia* of an active, risen Jesus, the "Living One,"[19] combined with charismatic acts demonstrating their direct access to the authority of Jesus and the endorsement of an undisputed leader, would suffice. Calling themselves *apostoloi*[20] implies they had been appointed to provide access to salvation and safety from the curse of death through mystical initiation into *gnosis* and the transformative power of Jesus' *logia*.[21] Who gave them this *gnosis* and power, and letters of recommendation?[22]

Apostoloi of the *Logia* and Authority for Rejecting Paul's *Euangelion*

In bypassing Paul, the opponents/infiltrators confirm that he was illegitimate and vehemently reject him as a weak, errant, dangerous charlatan, despite his claim of once having received the "right hand of fellowship."[23] As noted, those relationships had since evaporated (if they ever existed as Paul presumed). It was public knowledge that Paul and James were at enmity. In Galatians, Paul confirms that James the brother of Jesus sent spies, i.e., authoritative intruders and infiltrators, into his Galatian *ecclesiae*. They ridiculed and condemned him and attempted to dismantle his *ecclesiae*—they likely succeeded. Paul places a deadly curse on these enemies opponents that by implication included James.[24] Indeed, he hoped that the curse would drive them mad, so that they mutilate themselves by emasculation, a sign of demonic possession.[25]

Clearly, Paul was followed and then hunted by his enemies—in Galatia, Macedonia and now in Corinth. Such *apostoloi* must have appealed to an authority all would have understood as being undisputed, one who could affirm the legitimacy of *logia* of the Living One—a name, perhaps also on a letter of recommendation, one with intimate knowledge of Jesus and his salvific *logia*. Who better a source than James, the brother of Jesus, Paul's deadly opponent in Galatia, and Thessaloniki?[26] In fact, the *Gospel of Thomas specifically cites James as its apostolic authority* of the efficacious

---

19. *Gos. Thom.*, Saying 1.

20. 2 Cor 11:13.

21. Georgi, *Paul's Opponents*, 38–39: Paul's later terminus with his post-crucifixion encounter with Jesus as being the end of apostolic appointments is intended to invalidate other claims (1 Cor 15:8). But more, Georgi notes that this terminus means that faith, *pistis*, is not "enveloped in a timeless, mystical experience of identity [like his opponents' claim], but that faith also has a past and thereby the dimension of time." This links the event of an encounter with the risen Jesus with time, and so, a future, i.e., the *parousia*, which for Paul is an essential element of true salvific faith.

22. 2 Cor 3:1–3.

23. Gal 2:9.

24. Gal 1:8; 2:4.

25. Gal 5:12.

26. *Gos. Thom.* 12: The disciples said to Jesus, "We know that you are going to leave us. Who will be our leader?" Jesus said to them, "No matter where you are you are to go to James the Just, for whose sake heaven and earth came into being."

logia. It is he who "rules over them," and so, is the interpretive authority of its powerful, salvific *logia*, which are specifically labeled as "secret sayings of the living Jesus,"[27] given to a second, and subordinate apostle, Didymus Judas Thomas. By implication, Thomas has access to the living Jesus, more so than other apostles, particularly Paul who knows nothing of them!

A claim to possess powerful *logia* of Jesus is actually a direct link to the powerful *logia* of Jesus as an exorcist, that is, where his *logia*, including special commands, esoteric language, prayers and techniques, took control and drove out demons, which included the infection of death, i.e., Satan's ultimate power. The *logia* of Paul's enemies do the same, and the continuity is rather remarkable, pointing to a very early trajectory of itinerants who carried such words of authority and knowledge, but now from the "Living One," i.e., the risen Jesus. Still exorcising in Jesus' name post-crucifixion is one thing, but these *apostoloi* employ Jesus' name and his words to transform the adherent from ignorance (death) to life—there is no need for a future return and judgment, death has been expelled! Like Jesus' exorcisms that provided liberation from the demons and death, now, as risen Lord the Living One, they provide liberation from the curse of death. *The charismatic exorcist Jesus has become the charismatic Lord of salvation.* Paul evidences knowledge of certain sayings of Jesus, but clearly, he was unfamiliar with their salvific use.[28] According to these itinerants, without embracing the techniques they employ and *gnosis* of the *logia* of Jesus they control, any Jesus-follower is in perilous danger. Adherence to Paul's gospel is to remain under a curse and Satan's control.

The Opponents' Countermeasures to Paul

Paul's enemies have not only taken residence in Corinth alongside Paul's adherents, they have formed their own distinct *ecclesia* and are conducting a mystical or charismatic baptismal rite.[29] They begin their effort to discredit and dismantle Paul's errant teachings and ministry almost immediately. The itinerant "super-apostles," carry with them the aforementioned letter of recommendation,[30] undoubtedly giving them immediate access to shelter and food, affording them an extended stay. The length of their stay reflects a period when itinerants could still claim housing and long-term support. The Didache (50–70 CE) confirms that this became a problem with wandering itinerant *apostoloi* who arrived in a village, town or metropolis. Apparently, many made a claim to onerous, extended support. The Didache insists that hospitality

27. *Gos. Thom.*, Introductory Saying.
28. *Gos. Thom.*, Saying 12.
29. See the discussion of creedal formula used by Paul, and possibly his opponents, recovered by Patterson; Patterson, *Lost Way*, 225–30.
30. 2 Cor 3:2–3.

be offered only briefly, not longer than three days (12:2).[31] Since the controversy between Paul and the super-apostles extended into the multiple letters now contained in 2 Corinthians, they must have remained in Corinth for months. Paul is quick to point out that he did not make claim to support, while they claim it is their right, certainly referring to the *logoi* of Jesus.[32]

The *apostoloi* next rebuke Paul's *euangelion* by appealing to their superior authority and standing.[33] Not only do they have a persuasive letter of recommendation from James, they make claim to their elite ancestry, i.e., as "pure" Israelites, who are separate and merit this secret knowledge—they have a superior "spirit."[34] Paul states, perhaps in his fourth letter, that it is not the risen Lord Jesus or the Spirit of God the opponents proclaim, it is the message of Satan, consequently, it is a perilous risk for any who turn to their path. As such, Paul echoes their charge against him. Indeed, Paul dismisses this "superior knowledge" as demonic deceit, for the Corinthians adherents have already received "all things" from the apostle who truly *understands and knows* God, and God's son, the risen Lord, who is still to come:[35]

> For if some one comes and preaches another Jesus other than the one we preached, or if you receive a different spirit from the one you received, or if you accept a different gospel from the one you accepted, *you submit to him easily* [i.e., the influence of Satan and his deception]. I think that I am not the least inferior to the superlative apostles. Even if I am unskilled in speaking, I am not in knowledge; in every way we have made this plain to you in all things.[36]

For Paul, the opponents are of Satan (11:14–16). His warning here is not dissimilar to that in Galatians, which includes a deadly curse:

> But even if we or an angel of heaven should preach a gospel contrary to the one we preached to you, let him be under God's curse![37]

Consequently, these opponents threaten the charismatic protection, unity and integrity of the Corinthian *ecclesia* by introducing a completely contrary power of escape from death and judgment based on a claim of personal, elitist enlightenment through the revelation and charismatic power of Jesus' *logia*, a mystical transformation that is

---

31. Patterson on the Didache (*Gospel of Thomas and Jesus*, 173): "Of course today, when the similarities between the Didache and Barnabas, or the Shepherd of Hermas, are no longer taken as proof that the Didache is literarily dependent upon these documents, the trend is to date the Didache much earlier, at least by the end of the first century or the beginning of the second, and in the case of Jean-P. Audet, as early as 50–70 C.E."

32. Luke 10:7.
33. 2 Cor 12:11–13.
34. 2 Cor 11:21–23a.
35. 2 Cor 10–12, in full assault on the staying power, if not growing strength, of his opponents.
36. 2 Cor 11:4–6.
37. Gal 1:8.

immediately salvific. This is the basis of their attack on Paul, and forms the foundation of their countermeasures to neutralize him.

Paul's Countermeasures

This threat far exceeds a risk of just disunity. The arrival and disruption of the Corinthian opponents represents a devastating development. Paul has no choice due to distance (now residing in Ephesus)[38] than use every means possible to quickly intercede and neutralize his opponents, including the use of what would be considered dark magic—curses—and a séance or "presence" by soul transportation, where a believer is possessed by the spirit of Paul.[39] Paul goes so far as to name the invaders as *God's opponents*, placing them in the camp of Satan, and thus possessed and controlled demonic powers. Paul characterizes the invasion of the Corinthian *ecclesiae* as *an eschatological event of disruption*, the conflict of good and evil, the children of light and darkness, confirming the end of the age is not only confirmed, but rapidly approaching:

> And what I do I will continue to do, in order to undermine the claim of those who would like to claim that in their boasted mission they work on the same terms as we do. For such men are *false apostles, deceitful workmen, disguising themselves as apostles of Christ. And no wonder, for even Satan disguises himself as an angel of light.*[40]

The conflict is reminiscent of Paul's statement in 1 Thessalonians on the eschatological battle that is being waged in the last days: "For we wanted to come to you—certainly I, Paul, did, again and again—but Satan stopped us."[41] This is not a mythic confrontation, or a battle in another realm or cosmos, but one that Paul witnesses, feels, anguishes over daily, and suffers—Paul is under attack by Satan. This is a battle between Satan, his demons and the Son of God and Paul.

Logia Used to Oppose Paul: Paul's Claim to Authority over the *Logia*

As noted, Paul's opponents claim exclusive salvific authority. Proselytes must participate in a secret baptismal ritual of initiation and transformation[42] performed by a specially appointed *pnuematikos*, or mystigogue, what Paul calls also a "super-apostle,"

---

38. As noted, 210 nautical miles if by direct course (see above on Sulla), or three dangerous days of sailing. More likely the trip would have taken him north to Troas and across to Macedonia to Thessaloniki, then south to Philippi by land, then by ship to Athens and then to Corinth (again, unless the land route was taken)—approximately a two to three month trip.
39. 1 Cor 5:4.
40. 2 Cor 11:12–14.
41. 1 Thess 2:18.
42. 1 Cor 1:12–15.

apparently a Hebrew male[43] who becomes their "guardian."[44] These rites allow the initiate access to powerful esoteric *logia* of divine knowledge, divine *gnosis*, which is efficacious and revelatory (i.e., it unveils their true state and risk status), and when discerned and accepted is salvific, as it frees one from deadly deception, indeed satanic deception, and *agnosis* that dooms one to a curse of death. For Paul, adherence solely to the torah is deadly ignorance, for all who hold the law to be salvific are subject its curse of death,[45] while for the opponents, Paul's gospel is steeped in ignorance and falsehoods, and so those who follow him are under the very curse of death he claims is mitigated by his *euangelion*. Paul is an evil, empty, deceptive charlatan. Awaiting Paul's *parousia* is the lie of this charlatan who wants money, or, minimally, who is himself deceived and doomed!

This salvific *gnosis* can only be obtained post-baptism through mystical exposure, likely through exoteric rites, to an exclusive collection of Jesus' *logia*, although Paul clearly has heard or even read some of the sayings.[46] It is possible to recreate a partial list of the *logia* (see below), which were probably in an early written form,[47] but not yet in a well-developed theological sequence or order that can be recovered.[48] This collection would predate the canonical gospels by almost two decades. In the opponents' collection, the *logia* stand alone, acting as direct conduits to salvation, while the *logia* of the canonical gospels are contextualized by the passion narrative and promised return of Jesus as Christ, or *bar nasha*, the retributive apocalyptic Son of Man.

It is interesting to note that in this early oral stage of circulation, Jesus' sayings were malleable and being placed into collections, along with events and traditions. Paul does just this in 1 Corinthians 11, blending the *Eucharist* traditions with *logia* of Jesus, an early form of the passion narrative. Various early Christian groups and communities circulated both so as to address needs, mitigate crises, establish authority or explain events in relation to their varying eschatological expectations or, such as in the case of the opponents in 1 Corinthians, esoteric practices. As noted in 1 Thessalonians 4, Paul blends sayings of the Lord (both pre- and post-crucifixion) with his eschatological schema. Sayings, whether from the activity of Jesus pre or post-crucifixion, carried equal weight. Indeed, 1 Corinthians confirms the ability to

43. See Georgi, *Paul's Opponents*, 18–60. Paul's identification of his opponents in Corinth as Hebrews actually signifies a term understood as indicating the mysteries of the Hebrew practices and rites, even the use of the Hebrew language, which in other ancient authorities are compared to mystery and cult rites of Hellenistic religions.

44. 1 Cor 4:15.

45. For Paul, ignorance through the practice of the law can only bring death. This is not totally dissimilar to the opponents' claim that adherence to Paul's gospel of Jesus' death, burial and resurrection, with the general resurrection to come, is false, and therefore deadly! Both claim exclusivity.

46. 1 Cor 4:6.

47. 1 Cor 4:6. John Strugnell viewed this as a scribal emendation, i.e., Strugnell, *A Plea*, but the entire conflict is centered in a collection in Jesus' *logia*.

48. This order could reveal a theological motif, as well as practices and esoteric interpretations that would further unravel the mystery of Paul's opponents in Corinth.

The Enemies of Paul in Corinth

trace the use of *logia* in ascertaining their history and *sitz im leben*, a process that has been successfully and convincingly demonstrated by Bultmann and others in the synoptic and certain portions of the Johannine traditions.[49] In this case, the practices, authority and salvific power of Paul's opponents are rooted in their exclusive *gnosis* and brought to light by their unique interpretation of specific *logia*, which have been acknowledged by an undisputed authority—certainly one of the many trajectories of primitive Christian beliefs that held equal claim to having originated with Jesus, the risen Lord and son of God. Paul never denies the *logia* are legitimate sayings of Jesus, but he vehemently disputes how the opponents have employed them. He was not a member of Jesus' band of exorcists during his war on Satan, so he cannot dispute the validity of any sayings that originated during this period—he knows this. Yet, he freely adapts the *logia* to *euangelion* because of his active and *ongoing experience of the risen Lord*, i.e., Paul claims has more than a list of esoteric sayings, he is possessed by and in contact with the risen Lord.

The Form of Paul's Risk Response to Opponents

Sections of the letter clearly show they were dictated to a scribe, as there are brief memory lapses, corrections, as well as strong emotional statements that betray an oral composition.[50] The correspondence is of course organized around Paul's vehement response to those he considered satanic aggressive agitators and opponents, including answers to questions clearly intended to impugn Paul's legitimacy, thereby dismantling his *ecclesia*. Despite the crisis and risk challenge confronting him, 1 Corinthians is well constructed. There is evidence of some significant redaction by later editors (see below), but overall it is a singular composition (unlike 2 Corinthians, which is comprised of at least seven letters).

The letter is aggressive, charismatic and threatening, and fully displays Paul's apologetic skills. It includes the rather shocking blend of warnings and threats coupled with dramatic charismatic actions hurled at opponents, including death curses, soul transportation and possession, and judgmental condemnations. Paul is clear in asserting that his words carry the authority, indeed the very voice, of the risen Lord, and so they are indisputably authoritative and efficacious.

Characteristic of his "crisis letters," Paul immediately reveals the nature of the catastrophe faced in the first few sentences. In this case, not only are the fatally errant eschatology of the opponents[51] but also the devastating impact that these teachings

---

49. Most notably, Bultmann, *History*, and Koester, *Ancient Christian Gospels*.

50. Notice how Paul says he baptized no one except Crispus (1:14), and then recalls he did (1:16), a mistake a writer would have corrected, just as Paul did either in his dictation, or by hand.

51. "Already you are filled! Already you have become rich! Without us you have become kings!" 4:8a.

have already had on Paul's adherents made evident.[52] In an aggressive assault on the opponents, Paul asserts that those who reject their radical claims (i.e., as already saved) underscore their alliance with the apostle that initiated them into the protective *pistis* of Jesus and powerful salvific *euangelion* of the cross and resurrection—only they are safe. Paul's *euangelion* is incontrovertible, unassailable and protects from Satan's power and doom. Indeed, in a startling, if not radical statement, not even baptism, particularly that practiced by his enemies, is important to Paul, only the *euangelion* of the cross that obliterated the curse of death. Only *pistis* and resulting *agape*, whose validity is evidenced by the *charismata* given by the Holy Spirit, imbue adherents with protection from demons, Satan and the curse of death until the *parousia*. For Paul, charismatic baptismal rites, initiation into secret *gnosis* of the *logia* (which hinges on their superior, mystical power and authority as "kings"), and denial of the *parousia*, are the powerful deception of Satan, disguised as an "angel of light"—even if they appeal to the *logia* of the Lord.[53] Paul has received all knowledge and mysteries, including secret mysteries given that he cannot utter during his transportation by vision, trance or soul travel to the third heaven, i.e., the place where God and the risen Jesus dwell.

Paul demands unity and exclusivity, i.e., that adherents remain under the powerful protection of the *euangelion*, warning that it is *not* the apostle or mysterious charismatic rites of baptism that vitiate doom ("What then is Apollos? What then is Paul? Servants through whom you believed, as the Lord assigned to each"),[54] but efficacious *pistis* in the broken curse of death evidenced by the resurrection of the Lord and now Christ from the cross. *Pistis* and *agape* are the death breaking power of God over Satan, the mystical protection for adherents until the *parousia*:

> When I came to you, brethren, I did not come proclaiming to you the testimony [mysteries] of God in superior *logia* [selected sayings of Jesus?] or *gnosis*. For I decided to know nothing among [i.e., share *gnosis* with you] you except Jesus Christ and him crucified.[55]

Paul asserts that he has already revealed all of the "secrets and hidden wisdom of God,"[56] that is, the event of the cross and act of God in the resurrection and coming *parousia*: "that your faith might *not rest in the gnosis of men* but in the power of God."[57] By implication, the use of any *logia* is invalid until understood as conveying

---

52. It is possible that the opponents practice baptism as an initiation into their salvation-gnosis. It is noteworthy that Simon Magus and, later, Dositheus, are said to have been followers of John the Baptist (just as was Apollos). More will be said to this later.

53. 1 Cor 1:10—4:7.

54. 1 Cor 3:5.

55. 1 Cor 2:1.

56. 1 Cor 2:7.

57. 1 Cor 2:5b.

the power of the cross and faith in its salvific power! They cannot stand alone or apart from the cross.[58]

Paul charges his opponents with total deception, even murder—if these super-apostles truly understood God's wisdom (*sophia*), they would have not "crucified the Lord of Glory."[59] Paul shockingly accuses these infiltrators, Jews clearly from Jerusalem, as having originally resisted Jesus, and so participating in and being complicit with his murder. Legitimate *apostolos* embrace Paul's gospel: "For Christ did not send me to baptize, but preach the gospel, not with eloquent wisdom, lest the cross of Christ be emptied of its power."[60] Jesus' *logia* are therefore authoritative, but for Paul they are subservient to the *euangelion* and charismatic power of the cross—any other use or application of them is dangerous.

As Paul makes clear, he, Kayfa and Apollos are the true "stewards of the mysteries of God," who are "trustworthy";[61] if they are not, they are at risk, as they will be judged by the Lord soon when all will be revealed. By including Kayfa as one who is trustworthy, Paul confirms that the infiltrators must have come from James (as in Galatia and Thessaloniki). Paul admonishes those who have held to his *euangelion* and their apostle: "Therefore, do not pronounce judgment before the time, before the Lord comes, who will bring to light the things now hidden in darkness and will disclose the purposes of the heart."[62] The infiltrators are thus deceivers in darkness, possessed and of Satan.

Paul's Direct Attack on the Perilous Risk Presented by Opponents

Paul addresses the infiltrators forcefully. It is possible to still detect the emotion and sarcasm in his voice even across twenty centuries.[63] Paul sternly warns that he will personally come and face them with a punishing "rod" if necessary, a metaphor for the very serious and real threat he presents is to their safety in the last days before the *parousia*, i.e., "rod," the very weapon used to beat Paul in Philippi, is here intended as a very real comparison to harm they will actually experience. As an apostle, Paul will employ the "rod" of Jesus' authority to call judgment, curse them with illness, ailment or death, or condemn to Satan those who oppose him and the gospel. They will feel pain, suffer horribly, and be mutilated. Paul is able to cast curses by distance, at the reading of his letter, or even employ soul transportation and possession to at-

58. Koester, "Wisdom and Folly," 82–83.

59. 1 Cor 2:8; this is a very interesting statement in that it may indicate the opponents were Jews, as he similarly associates Jewish opponents with the rabble that killed "the Lord Jesus and the Prophets" (1 Thess 2:15), and should be cursed, separated from God (Gal 1:8).

60. 1 Cor 1:17.

61. 1 Cor 4:1.

62. 1 Cor 4:5.

63. 1 Cor 4:1–17.

The Enemies of Paul: Demons, Satan, Betrayers, and Apostles

tack his victims. The most startling example is when Paul attacks one of his enemies.[64] Paul commands the immediate pronouncement of judgment, and so casts an effectual curse on an offender, a man who is in a physical relationship with his father's wife, which was *forbidden by both Roman and Jewish law*. He does so with the reading of his letter, which includes a terrifying, ritually formulaic divine curse:[65] "I have already pronounced judgment in the name of the Lord Jesus." This statement has a direct link to a saying of the risen Jesus, "Whatever you ask in my name, I will do it."[66] Paul then adds, "When you are assembled[67] *and my spirit is present*, with the power of the Lord Jesus, you are to deliver this man to Satan for the destruction of the flesh that his spirit may be saved in the day of the Lord Jesus."[68] This is a startling, horrific pronouncement that emphasizes Paul's deadly charismatic powers. What is the historical risk context of Paul's statement?

To begin, Paul is referring to soul or spirit transportation, where his spirit is present by incantation, or mystical call, and trance—then possession of one of those present to pronounce the curse. Paul employs what would have been considered the darkest of magic in the Roman world,[69] having condemned his enemy to Satan, to physical demonic possession and attack, and agonizing curse certainly leading to death—an excruciatingly painful dark curse. Paul's curse in 1 Corinthians is therefore similar to elements of his "magical" letter, Galatians, in that Paul is referring to deadly, immediate cursing of his enemies at the reading of his letter.[70] Here, Paul risks being associated with Jesus as an "evildoer," an illegal dark magician under Roman law and subject to immediate execution. More important, Paul is aligned with practices that would place him clearly in the context of the first-century mindset of those charismatics, exorcists and *goetes* that were feared.

Consequently, Paul does not hesitate to cast the death curse, which affirms the use a deadly curse is within his authority as an *apostolos*. This raises a troubling question. Is Paul here aligned with the practices of Jesus? Did Jesus also cast curses in his confrontation with demons and Satan. In his "woes" on Scribes and Pharisees, calling them vipers, we may have evidence that he did, which would explain the violent response of his opponents. More, Jesus curses Capernaum with a deadly curse ("you will be thrown to Hades," Luke 4:31–36) and Korazin (Matt 11:21–22). Further, using his animistic powers, Jesus curses and destroys a fig tree (Mark 11:20). Consequently,

---

64. 1 Cor 5:1.
65. 1 Cor 5:3–5.
66. John 14:13.
67. Assembled as a collective *ecclesiae* (all of the independent house churches in Corinth gather as one), for the Lord's Supper, the common meal recognizing and embracing the death of Jesus and anticipating the messianic return of Jesus as risen Lord, i.e., the eschatological tension of present and future; see discussion to follow on the Lord's Supper.
68. 1 Cor 5:4b–5.
69. See Busse, *Jesus Resurrected*, 10.
70. Betz, *Galatians*.

Paul is reflecting the same practices of Jesus, but now empowering the curse with Jesus' name. As such, Paul affirms the power to exercise such authority, just as Jesus did during his ministry. Set in the *sitz im leben* of the ancient Roman world, Paul is clearly more than a charismatic Jew. Like Jesus, his enemies considered him terribly dangerous and evil. This may have been why in Galatia, Thessaloniki and now Corinth, Paul's enemies wait until he has vacated the city.

Naming His Enemies and Rejecting Gnosis—the New *Soma* of God

Paul identifies his opponents as "Hebrews and Israelites,"[71] which Deiter Georgi has convincingly shown to be contemporary terms understood in the Roman world as itinerant Jewish pneumatics, magicians and wonder workers—those who claimed access to powers and mysteries on par with the cult of Isis, and came from God with special knowledge.

> Hadrian and Juvenal are not the only pagan authors of the second century C.E. who mention Jewish magic as a contemporary phenomenon: Apuleius, Lucian, Celsus, and Numenius do so as well. In addition, there are rabbinic and Christian attestations . . . The pagan Celsus says the [Jewish] miracle men, mantics and prophets had been seen in Palestine and Phoenicia not only by him in his own time, but also they represented an age-old phenomenon. Celsus mentions cultic preachers, pagans as well as Jews . . . [He lists various expressions of the pneumatic consciousness of such prophets, "I am God or God's child or a holy spirit]."[72]

The names Paul uses for his enemies are clearly intentional. They are a dire warning of substantive consequences for those who follow such men and turn from the *euangelion* and *agape* to the deceit of the satanic itinerants who claim to come from God with powers and *gnosis*—they are evil and will be turned over to Satan. They, like Paul's cursed enemy in Corinth, will only have their spirit saved. But this is not intended to

---

71. 2 Cor 11:22. Deiter Georgi has provided a comprehensive analysis of these designations repeated by Paul, which clearly the opponents use to identify themselves to Paul's *ecclesia*. As noted, the designation "Hebrews" had a resonant meaning in the first-century Roman world for the mysteries of the Hebrew religion, whether its esoteric rites, laws and practices, or the mysterious use of the Hebrew language. It was understood in the Hellenistic Roman world to be a term that denoted a mystery religion or cult, not unlike the Egyptian cults of Isis. Thus, Paul's opponents would claim antecedent power and authority drawing on these mysteries, confirming their claim to have gnosis and powers that required only their knowledge as *pneumatikoi*. Likewise, Georgi has confirmed using contemporary sources, including Josephus, Philo, Juvenal, that wandering Israelites were pneumatic itinerants, imbued with powers, helping the explain the aggressive expansion of Judaism to every corner of the Roman world by the first century. Many of these propagandists were wandering Jewish pneumatics, poor beggars, but known to be "holy men." Their acts were considered magic and their itinerancy was associated with a "coming" for God with mysterious and powerful knowledge. Georgi, *Paul's Opponents*, 102–5.

72. Ibid., 104.

allow escape, as they will not share in the resurrection as a newly transformed being.[73] Their doomed spirits will wander in desolate places, like the untimely dead, one of Satan's demons, being used for evil—they will suffer horrendous pain and agony. They will not be given the new, spiritual *soma* at the *parousia*.

Paul expects the *parousia*, the "day of the Lord Jesus," during his lifetime, and this *imminent event* characterizes the tension between the current order of the world, the terrorizing agony to be faced by his enemies, all of which is to accompany the collapse of the evil world with the presence of the Lord and the general resurrection "at his coming [for] those who belong to Christ,"[74] meaning both those "who have fallen asleep" as well as those still alive *in Paul's euangelion*. It is Paul's expectation that the living adherents he addresses will soon be changed, indeed, many of those hearing Paul's letter will experience a glorious transformation of their body, *the soma*, and see it with their own eyes: "Lo! I tell you a mystery. We shall not all sleep, but we shall all be changed, in a moment, in the twinkling of an eye at the last trumpet . . . For this perishable nature must put on the imperishable, and this mortal nature must put on immortal."[75] What is "sown as a body [*soma*] natural and [is] raised a body [*soma*] spiritual."[76]

Paul's description of the resurrected (or transformed) body as "spiritual" has led to much controversy, i.e., that the resurrection is purely spiritual, but the evidence is overwhelmingly contrary to this assertion—there is a new form of *soma*, which has material qualities. Paul is a Jew and Pharisee, and in verses too numerous to cite, Paul speaks of the body as the *soma*, which is a term for the body that a Pharisee understands *as the physical body*. He consistently alludes to the body in this way[77] and is also consistent in his statements as to the physical, holy (i.e., temple of the Holy Spirit), and sinful nature of the body from the perspective of a Pharisee. Further, the Pharisees were also insistent as to the physical resurrection of the *soma* at the end of the age.[78] His analogy of the seed dying to produce a more glorious body, and the body as a type of seed that must die to become "imperishable," as well as his description of the many types of plant, animal and material "*soma*" God has chosen and made, all refer to observable realities, and the miracle of God's creation.[79] *Soma* is then a physical reality, sometimes defined and the object that makes the shadow and not the shadow itself.

---

73. The theological ramifications related to the punishment invoked by Paul and the apparent indestructibility of the soul is worthy of investigation.

74. 1 Cor 15:13.

75. 1 Cor 15:51–52a, 53.

76. 1 Cor 15:44b.

77. 1 Cor refers to the *soma* thirty-five times, more than any other New Testament work.

78. This continued into the rabbinical period and is still one of thirteen fundamental tenets of current rabbinic Judaism.

79. 1 Cor 15:37–42.

For Paul, the resurrected body is a "spiritual *soma*," just as the food and drink that the Jews ate in the wilderness with Moses was "spiritual food and drink," i.e., real physical food and drink, but given by God's miracle, thus making it spiritual.[80] So it is with what is raised as "imperishable," meaning it is a spiritual *soma* whose characteristics are given by the miracle of God; but it is somehow material resurrected *soma*. It is not a *phantasm*, disembodied spirit, the wandering untimely dead, a demon or angel, or any entity that is known and experienced in the Hellenistic world of his time. Christ's new *soma* was observable with Paul's eyes, but was also encountered and thought to be just as material in visions, dreams and trances. Paul says, "Christ was the first fruits";[81] that is, the resurrected *soma* Paul is now describing what all his adherents will receive at the *parousia*, a *soma* like that of Jesus. If Paul intended to describe a transformation into an ethereal spirit he would have been clear, i.e., an "out of the body [*soma*]," just as he did when he recounted his experience being "caught away" to the "third heaven" (not "caught up" as in some translations; caught away is consistent with the ancient Jewish belief of the highest heaven being somewhere other than up or above): "I know a man in Christ who fourteen years ago was caught away to the third heaven—whether in the body or out of the body, I do not know, God, knows."[82] Paul could explain the difference firsthand—on the Day of the Lord, a transformation to a new spiritual *soma* will occur for his adherents that is exactly like that of Jesus.

Paul warns the adherents of the perilous risk of turning to his enemies. He demands that they not consort with immoral men,[83] that they practice *agape*, and literally[84] "drive out the wicked [i.e., evil doers] from among you," meaning the infiltrating *apostoloi*: "I wrote to you in my letter not to associate with immoral men; not at all meaning the immoral of this world . . . since you would need to go out of this world . . . but with anyone who bears the name of brother [who is guilty of immorality, such as the man condemned]."[85] Paul's adherents are in danger—the enemies of God are fracturing divine protection, i.e., the practice of *agape*. Now they exhibit hate, and it has infected the *ecclesia*. Even minor disputes are brought to a Roman court.[86] To drive home the seriousness of the Corinthians' crisis, Paul employs a powerfully charged word familiar to Jews, i.e., *hagios* ("separated ones/saints"), and redirects its application by placing it in a startling new context.

80. 1 Cor 10:1–5.
81. 1 Cor 15:23.
82. 2 Cor 12:2–3.
83. 1 Cor 5:9.
84. 1 Cor 5:10–13.
85. 1 Cor 5:9–10a, 11a.
86. "When one of you has a grievance against a brother, does he *dare* go to law before the unrighteous instead of the *saints*. Do you not know that the saints will judge the world? And if the world is to be judged by you, are you incompetent to try trivial cases? Do you not know that we are to judge angels?" (1 Cor 6:1–11).

Hagios is a term that has great significance for Paul personally, as well as for his Jewish adherents. Once an elitist term, Paul now designates all of his adherents as the "sainted ones" (*hagioi*), specifically, the holy ones separated by God. "Holy ones" is equivalent to the meaning of *Pharisee* in Hebrew, i.e., the self-designation of the sect of Jews who sought a renewal to ritual purity and separated from the all immorality and sin to be the chosen and elite people of God. The Pharisees focused on obedience to the law, and contemporary interpretation of it with ritual acts to maintain separation and purity, employing the Oral Torah and interpretation of it, i.e., as it kept a "fence" around the torah. Paul had held the fundamental tenets of the Pharisees—that God's love for the individual led to the revelation of himself in the "twofold law";[87] i.e., the torah and oral tradition. If the individual "internalized" the law and Oral Torah, and obeyed the precepts and teachings of them, expressed daily through ritual purity and separation from sinners, then after death they would merit the salvation by God and enjoy a physical resurrection of the body. Paul was a rigorous member of the sect[88] (he says "extremely zealous"), and expected, because of his flawless practice of its precepts, to have justified himself before God as a "saint" or holy one. But Paul radically changed his Pharisaic view and came to reject merited claims on God as legitimate, or even possible. His proclamation *that only pistis in he euangelion and practice of agape until the parousia would justify forgiveness and acceptance by God was a radical acceptance that he remained in peril as a Pharisee*. Only acceptance by God, i.e., his adoption of the new children of Israel of *pistis*, is what merits designation as a *hagios*.[89] Jacob Neusner has correctly pointed out that Paul presents the ethnic Israelites, "Israel after the flesh," as distinct from the new spiritual Israel, or "Israel after the spirit."[90] Paul's adherents are the latter and inherit the true Israel through *pistis*. The Pharisees separated themselves for sanctification, while now God separates his adherents through *pistis* for salvation—*only they* are "holy." Thus, for Paul, the former Pharisee, being a "holy one" cannot come from personal practices and earned rights, it can only be given—it is a *charismata* of divine *agape* that begins with God's revelation in the crucifixion, death and resurrection of Jesus of Nazareth. Paul's use of this term for his adherents was shocking, radical, and redefined the true *hagioi* of God. Paul's adherents, *Jews and Gentiles, men and women, slave and free, are the new true Israel, the chosen and holy ones*, separated as the children of God.

87. See *Interpreter's Dictionary of the Bible*, 660.

88. Gal 1:14.

89. Paul is clear. It was impossible to keep the law or its precepts, and Paul now recognizes the futile position he was in before his encounter with the risen Jesus. Like Paul, the holy ones, the "saints" can only be no more that humble believers who have embraced the overflowing love of the Father, fully revealed in his resurrection of his son Jesus' from the cursed death on a cross, i.e., God's "wisdom" that is folly to the Gentiles and offensive to the Jews. No one can make a claim on God before the cross of Christ; one can only come by faith to it and embrace that same faith of Jesus also in humility, hoping for God's mercy, adoption and love, and soon, resurrection and life.

90. Neusner, *Judaism*, 93.

Remarkably then, Paul expands the blessedness and power of *hagioi* to an unexpected level; i.e., the mitigation of all perilous risk arising from Satan. His adherents will be the future judges of this world, even the judges of the angels on the last day.[91] By implication, they will be judges of Paul's enemies as well! He thus radically reapplies the designation and its efficacy to every adherent of his *euangelion*—everything he thought once true has been overturned! Thus, Paul masterfully exposes his enemies' lack of "knowledge" *by revealing something completely new*—the adherents true standing as the "holy ones," the children of God, who have been set apart for salvation by their *pistis* and *agape*. Their blessed place before God stands above and apart from any errant claim to hidden *gnosis* drawn from the esoteric interpretation of *logoi* by mystagogues who practice unnecessary errant rituals and engage in abhorrent libertine sexuality.

This *radical reversal*, redefining who is "holy," is immensely powerful in disarming Paul's enemies. Paul contends that safety from Satan and death does not arise from his own unique or "special" interpretation of Hebrew Scripture, or a claim to secret *logia* of Jesus. Instead, it is comes from the *sophia* and power of God openly revealed to all, through the resurrection of Jesus and a response of *pistis* to the *euangelion*. Only this grants access to divine, protective and efficacious *agape* and the sure *elpis* of salvation at the imminent *parousia*. This is true *gnosis* of the *hagioi*. The *hagioi* live in the context of the *eschaton*, i.e., the intense eschatological expectation of the *parousia*, in which they, by *pistis* and the practice of *agape*, can endure even satanic opposition, attack and harm as they await the arrival and presence of the risen Lord and the kingdom of God. Consequently, Paul's recasting of the designation *hagios* is a brilliant rejection of the opponents' claims of exclusive, esoteric salvific authority. Paul *expects* the adherents to openly practice *agape*, and like Jesus, love the cursed, outcasts and poor, demon worshippers, adulterers, thieves, the greedy, drunkards, and robbers (unless they are a brother), because

> such were some of you. But you were washed, you were sanctified, you were justified in the name of the Lord Jesus Christ and in the Spirit of our God.[92]

The designation of *hagios* is now reserved for Paul's adherents of the *euangelion*, Jesus, as they have also been separated for God:

> To the *ecclesia* of God, which is at Corinth, to those *sanctified* in Christ Jesus, called to be saints together with all those who in every place call on the same of the Lord Jesus Christ.[93]

It is one of the most profound examples of eschatological reversal of expectations in Paul's writings.

---

91. 1 Cor 6:3.
92. Gal 6:11.
93. 1 Cor 1:2.

Paul warns them of their error and the perilous risk of not recognizing a new status before God. Indeed, Paul's *ecclesia* is not comprised of Jew or Gentile, male or female, slave or free—it is comprised of the separated ones, the "saint's of God," bound for the imminent kingdom who enter as children of the community of divine *agape* and forgiveness. The *hagioi* who are forgiven must forgive, or settle their disputes as a community with *agape* as their guide.[94] Taking disputes before a Roman or civic court evidences a rejection of their blessed place of safety and security with God.

Gnosis, the Jerusalem *Apostoloi* and Battle over the *Logia*

Paul's aforementioned questions to the *ecclesia* also reveal a much deeper risk struggle over the source and authority of the *logia* claimed by his enemies, as well as the interpretation and the *sophia* and *gnosis* they profess is revealed.

> Do you not perceive that the saints [*hagios*] will judge the world? And if the world is to be judged by you, are you incompetent to try trivial cases? Do you not know that we are to judge angels?[95]

Paul here references a saying of Jesus, which in its most original form is found in Luke:[96]

> You are those who have continued with me in my trials; and I assign to you, as my Father assigned to me, a kingdom, that you may eat and drink at my table in my kingdom, *and sit on thrones judging the twelve tribes of Israel.*[97]

Paul's intent in citing this saying is clearly an indictment of his enemies' claim to salvific *gnosis*. As he has argued before, they do not understand the *logia* of Jesus, but even more, they intentionally exclude, or worse, do not know key *logia*, which would confirm Paul's assertion of the coming *parousia*. More precisely, how can legitimate *apostoloi* claim immediate, salvific *gnosis*, when according to the *logia* of the Lord, it is his adherents, the *hagioi*, who will be the judges of even the angels on the last day. The judgment is yet to come, and Paul's enemies, due to their lack of divine *gnosis* contained in the *euangelion*, will be among those judged by the very ones they reject and scorn. Paul also radically expands the application of the *logoi*. It is no longer only the Twelve who will judge, but all of Paul's adherents. Paul gives the seat of judgment to the believing slave, woman, poor outcast, and even the Gentile, at the *parousia*.

---

94. It is interesting to note that the "Lord's Prayer" was not here employed by Paul or the Corinthian *ecclesia*. If Paul knew the Lord's Prayer he certainly would have repeated a portion of it here: "forgive us our trespasses as we forgive those who trespass against us" (Luke 11:2–4).

95. 1 Cor 6:2.

96. The saying has been altered in Matthew to an apocalyptic setting, which links judgment to the arrival of the Son of Man, Matt 19:28.

97. Luke 22:28–30.

The Enemies of Paul in Corinth

Paul turns then presses his verbal attack on the opponents by first quoting them; "All things are lawful to me," or perhaps better translated, "I have the right to do anything."[98] Based on the context, Paul's enemies are publicly practicing radical, offensive and even unlawful libertine behavior. Their libertine view of sexual morality is an outcome of their new standing as "saved" and free; their claim that knowledge that this world (i.e., the material world of death and deception) no longer has any power over them—the truth has been revealed through comprehension of the secret and hidden wisdom sayings of Jesus who is the exclusive agent of God's wisdom. They need nothing more. By implication then, for followers of the opponents, it does not matter what happens to the *soma*, or how it is treated, nor does it matter how they interact and behave with those who are unenlightened, for those individuals are part of the material world of the lost. There is nothing restricting Paul's opponents any longer. Indeed, there is nothing that can prevail in this world against them—they are "free" from it, and there is nothing "unlawful" for them, whether forbidden by religion or even Roman law.[99] They are "victors and kings."[100] The *logia* of Jesus are all that are necessary to freedom and life.

With a hint of sarcasm, Paul responds that libertine morality in the material world (once *gnosis* is obtained) and judgment of him as a charlatan (true and immediate salvation is gained only through their *gnosis*), is meritless and simple (i.e., by implication, lacking knowledge): "But with me it is a very *small thing* [in Greek, *elaksiston*, completely insignificant] that I should be judged by you or by any *human day* [many translations use the term 'court' instead of 'day,' but clearly the context demands 'day,' *emeras*]."[101] To be clear, the opponents' eschatology is radically heightened, as salvation is achieved on the day of *gnosis*. But Paul characterizes the eschatology of gnosis-salvation as nothing more than a "human day" since it is not the *parousia* of God; i.e., the Lord is still to return to the world made by God (i.e., to recall, *parousia* means "presence," and just as the resurrected body is a spiritual *soma*, a body with some new form of material substance, the return is to the physical realm, to this world). Paul is emphatic: "It is the Lord that judges me. Therefore, do not pronounce judgment before the time, before the Lord comes."[102]

Once again, the tension between the eschatology of the opponents and Paul is clear. They are saved, without fear, free in the world to act even immorally, for this world is full of deceit and evil and it no longer has hold on them by "hiding" the truth from them, or obscuring it. They have gained life, and so safety from perilous risk and death. They are free of the world, they understand its true hopelessness, *and they can mock it through their actions*, including consorting with prostitutes (or as

98. 1 Cor 6:12.
99. 1 Cor 5:1–2.
100. 1 Cor 4:5, 8.
101. 1 Cor 4:3a.
102. 1 Cor 4:5.

another member had done, taken up illegal sexual relations with his father's wife). It is evident as well that they understand their body as doomed to corruption as part of the material world. Their resurrection is purely "spiritual";[103] they abhor and reject any conception of material resurrection of the *soma*. Their lack of interest in the cross, crucifixion and resurrection of Jesus is clear—in fact, *there is no interest at all*. Paul is a deceiver, a minion of a lost, satanic world.

Paul confronts the opponents' libertine views by extending the Jewish conception of the body as a partner of the soul and spirit.[104] The physical body is not only of God, but it is the very temple of God's spirit in this world: "Do you not know that your body is a temple of the Holy Spirit within you, which you have from God? You are not your own; you were bought with a price, so *glorify God in your body*."[105] Paul warns that there are dangerous consequences in the rejection God's creation and body—he warns that they will "not inherit the kingdom of God."[106]

Paul closes his attack on the opponents by asserting his role as a "steward of the mysteries of God," he says:

> I have applied all this to myself and Apollos for your benefit, brethren, that you may learn by us not *to go beyond what is written*, that none of you be puffed up in favor of one against another.

Paul's use of "steward," *oikonomous*, is important, as he also uses this term in Gal 4:2 as a more technical term, i.e., a "guardian." The term denotes the ones chosen by the owner or master to control the household, property and distribution to the needs. They are the sole and exclusive governors, and cannot be challenged. Paul's use of the term in this sense is intentional. Special use of the *logia* of Jesus, or a secret initiation and salvific practices based on *gnosis* obtained from these *logia*, cannot be used to challenge Paul's gospel or authority since he has been appointed the role of *oikonomous*. This intent is made clear in Paul's demand that the collection of *logia* used by opponents, apparently in writing, are being misused in that they claim exclusive rights to esoteric interpretation of them that is dangerously errant, i.e., "do not go beyond what is written." A review can help elucidate the context of Paul's statement here.

Verse 6 has long been recognized as very difficult to translate, as it is a jumble that affords several translation options. John Strugnell made the claim that the words "not to go beyond what is written" (words that if eliminated ease the difficultly of translation) were not Paul's but those of an early scribe who was struggling with the translation he was transcribing. This scribe did his best and then put this comment, or "conjectural emendation," in the column to indicate he did not want to go beyond

---

103. The conception of *gnosis*-salvation is even more ethereal that our concept of spirit, it is completely other worldly, as this world obscures understanding of it other than one is free.
104. Similarly to Jesus and the depth of love for God—Luke 10:25–28.
105. 1 Cor 6:19–20.
106. 1 Cor 6:9.

what Paul had written. Eventually, other scribes incorporated this comment into the letter as new copies were produced for dissemination in the early church as collections of Paul's letters were gathered.

Despite his argument, Strugnell's conclusion must be rejected, not only based on the content of Paul's letter where his opponents' clear reliance on wisdom salvation *gnosis* and an appeal to *logia* of the Lord are evident, but also by the fact that Paul quotes a saying found no where in the canonical gospels, i.e., *Gospel of Thomas* 17, in 1 Cor 2:9. The saying is clearly from a written source, and is one that was incorporated into a more complex gnostic wisdom-salvation written collection of Jesus' sayings. Koester and Robinson have confirmed that written sayings collections existed and circulated, perhaps even at the time Paul wrote 1 Corinthians.[107] Even more, there is a connection between Paul's demand to "not go beyond what is written" and the next verses.[108] These verses are a direct reflection of some of Jesus' sayings on inheriting the kingdom of heaven, known commonly as the "beatitudes."[109] Jesus says, "Blessed are you poor, for yours is the kingdom of God; Blessed are you that hunger now for you shall be filled; Blessed are you that weep now, for you shall laugh," followed by Jesus sayings on reversal (i.e., the full now shall hunger, those who laugh will mourn and weep). There is little doubt that these *logia* could be understood as wisdom sayings, revealing to those who "sought wisdom" access to God and the kingdom by understanding one's true position and the spiritual awakening they bring. Note Paul's response: "Already you are filled! Already you have become rich! Already you are kings!" Clearly Paul's response, which at first might seem abrupt and out of context, is not random, nor is it a response to verbal accusations. Instead Paul is responding the opponents' use of other *logia* where his opponents have clearly gone "beyond what is written." What's more, Paul then applies his own reversal formula, almost exactly as the sayings attributed to Jesus: "We are fools for Christ's sake, but you are wise; we are weak, but you are strong." The pattern is unmistakable: "When reviled we bless, when persecuted we endure, when slandered we try to conciliate," echoing the words of Jesus.[110] Paul counters with reference to sayings of Jesus, clearly dem-

---

107. Robinson and Koester, *Trajectories*, 85–103, 186–87.

108. 1 Cor 4:8–10.

109. See Luke 6.17, 20–23.

110. See Matt 5:38, i.e., a saying from the beatitudes in that gospel; clearly Paul does know sayings of Jesus and the core of his gospel message, and more, he embraces it fully in an authentic continuation of it. Paul expands it to include the cross and resurrection, but the eschatological crisis is as intense and immediate, as is the call to decision for or against Abba'. It is interesting that Paul here cites the beatitudes of Matthew, a gospel that has been ascribed by the majority of scholars to a Jewish-oriented community that was most interested in presenting Jesus as the new Moses, i.e., who fulfills the law, does not destroy it. Paul, a Pharisee, must have come into contact with Jewish believers orally circulating these traditions in Antioch, or Jerusalem. It is also possible that Paul has seen, or has heard the content of the opponents' written sayings source and, by repeating these sayings, places them in an alternative context, i.e., in the context of *agape*, the practice of the *hagios* until the arrival of the Lord and judgment. While at first these sayings would seem counter to the opponents' radical behavior,

onstrating that Paul was familiar with *logia* of Jesus. By citing the saying of Jesus in this context, Paul is demonstrating their interpretation, drawn form a written source, is an errant distortion, but more to his point, they have "gone beyond what is written": Paul appeals to his adherents: "I do not write this to make you ashamed, but to admonish you as my beloved children."[111] The dichotomy is striking: Paul curses his enemies and admonishes his "children."

Paul then characterizes himself, not as their "guide" (*paidagogous*, better translated in this case as "tutor," "guide" or "custodian" [see Gal 3:2]), but as their "father." In the first century, a *paidagogos* was the trusted slave responsible for the moral training of the young children of the wealthy owner. The duties were important in the upbringing of the child, particularly young boys. Paul uses this term twice in the letter to the Galatians in reference to the function of the law as a "tutor," like a "schoolmaster": "Wherefore the law has become our *tutor* to bring us to Christ, so that we may be justified by faith. But now that faith has come we are no longer under a *tutor*."[112] Paul pushes beyond the role of *paidagogos*, perhaps because the opponents use it as a title or spiritual designation. Instead, Paul calls himself their father or *pater*, not a religious title or position, but the one who from birth, loves, admonishes and protects his own flesh and blood or adopted child; a term of intimacy and familiarity that implies a bond that extends from life and death and all between. Paul is thereby explaining the chasm between he and those who oppose him, those errant "guides." The tutor is only at the service of the father, and once dismissed, the children remain with the father. Paul is the father of these "children," not just their guide—those who are truly loved by him belong only to *Abba'*, the father of all children, including Paul and Jesus.

Perilous Risk Questions from Corinth

Paul now turns to the written questions that have arrived with "Chloe's people." It is quite remarkable to have access to several specific risk questions from a mid-first-century *ecclesiae* established by Paul of Tarsus; particularly from an *ecclesia* founded only several months before it had became embroiled in a bitter and desperate dispute with infiltrating Jewish *apostoloi* from Jerusalem. Those who sent the questions were clearly aligned with Paul. As such, they faced great personal risk. The *apostoloi of the logia* were aggressive, even violent infiltrators that had tracked Paul from Antioch to

---

that is, they are publicly immoral, why would they "bless," Paul is likely responding to a specific saying of Jesus by citing another, i.e., a perfect example of why Paul says, "don't go beyond what is written." Indeed, placing this saying in the context of libertine and radically offensive behavior, then the context of their saying of Jesus would have been, "you will be reviled, persecuted, slandered, but you are already kings!" This is very similar to a saying of Jesus, "You will be hated because of me," and not dissimilar to sayings in the *Gospel of Thomas*. This demonstrates even more strongly that Paul knows sayings of Jesus and presents another to counter the claims of the opponents.

111. 1 Cor 4:14.
112. Gal 3:24–25.

Corinth. Clearly, they employed any means necessary to disrupt and disband his *ecclesiae*, even if by force. Just as Paul had done as a violent paid "hit man" of the Jerusalem elite who was ordered to annihilate the followers of Jesus and the *ecclesiae*, they too intervened, severing subsistence incomes, leveling charges of practicing black magic, punishable by death, and raising local mobs and civic opposition to expel adherents from the city. They carried licenses that authorized them to physically abuse, beat or even kill Paul's adherents, likely citing scriptural justification. Paul had rejected the salvific *logia* of the Risen One, and thus, the *apostoloi* who were its mystagogues. Consequently, by carefully evaluating Paul's answers using risk analysis, it is possible to reconstruct the (1) *sitz im leben* of the questions and the crises within the *ecclesia* (2) *logia* contained in the enemies' source document, and (3) the risk mitigations employed by Paul to neutralize and defeat his enemies.

We must understand that the risks Paul's adherents faced were horrific. Indeed, the crisis was so real and desperate that they sent emissaries who traveled hundreds of miles by boat and foot, risking danger and death, urgently seeking answers. Were they now at risk, susceptible to demonic attack, and therefore, unprotected and doomed? Were any of the risk practices of the infiltrators legitimate, and if so, why hadn't Paul taught them? What was the Lord's Supper and was it acceptable to feast and drink till drunk? Each question is a window to the practices and threats brought by these *apostoloi*.

To establish context, it is imperative to evaluate Paul's preliminary warning: "Let each man take care how he builds upon this. For no other foundation can anyone lay than which is laid, which is Jesus Christ."[113] Paul begins by employing a christological title that encapsulates the entire thrust of his *euangelion*—"Jesus Christ." The very early trajectory of titular development leading to the combination of the name Jesus (i.e., of Nazareth), with the messianic title "Christ" (*Christus*), has long puzzled critical scholars;[114] that is, as to where, when and why this correlation was made so early in the Jesus movement, almost as if "Christ" was understood as Jesus' last name by the mid-30s, but certainly before the early 40s CE. There were many contemporary historical figures that also had similar combinations, most notably the Caesars, e.g., Julius, Tiberius or Augustus Caesar. But here to combine Jesus with Christ (i.e., the Greek form of the Jewish title, Messiah) was very risky and dangerous. It was a claim to kingship—a claim other Jewish antagonists had made in Palestine that had led to bloody conflicts with Rome. Paul is effluent in his use of this title. Indeed, in 1 Corinthians 15 he later cites a very early, well-developed formulaic creed, perhaps the earliest recorded in the New Testament, that he says defines the *euangelion*: "For I delivered to you as of first importance what I also received: '*That* Christ died for our

---

113. 1 Cor 3:10b–11a; Paul's employment of "Jesus Christ" is to assert the gospel and that Jesus is the Messiah, risen from the dead, and soon to come to deliver the kingdom and justice of God.

114. In 2010, I had a conversation with my friend and advisor, Helmut Koester, who continued to express dismay as to the origin for the linkage of Jesus' name with Christ, as if a last name.

The Enemies of Paul: Demons, Satan, Betrayers, and Apostles

sins according to the scriptures, *that* he was buried, *that* he was raised on the third day *according to scriptures*, and *that* he appeared to Kayfa, then to the twelve.'"[115] More about this creed will be provided later,[116] but it is critical to note the title "Christ" is here associated with a list of resurrection appearances, and that Paul plainly states that "Christ died for our sins according to the scriptures" (meaning the Hebrew Torah and prophets),[117] and was raised "according to the scriptures."

Paul's citation of this creed is of central import, particularly to Jews and Jewish proselytes, and so must have an early Palestinian or Syrian origin. Scholars, such as Jeremias and Koester, have cited this part of the creed as confirmation that the earliest Palestinian adherents, including Paul, linked the future coming of Jesus as the Messiah with the necessity of his death as fulfilling the "suffering servant" prophecies of Isaiah 51, i.e., the innocent blood sacrifice for sin to satiate the requirements of the law. Indeed, Paul names Jesus the "Pascal lamb" in 1 Corinthians, meaning that Jesus' death was akin to the efficacious sacrifice of the unblemished lamb at the Passover, imbuing one with safety from the infection of sin (in Hebrew, the *korban Pesakh*).[118] However, that Paul is intending to refer to the Isaiah prophecies of the suffering servant is not clear. There is no doubt, however, that the creed identifies the risen Jesus with his Messianic role (Christ), the one whose resurrection is a precursor to the coming general resurrection and arrival of the kingdom of God (just as Paul had described in 1 Thessalonians 4). Messiah/Christ is thus already understood as the title of Jesus in the *kerygma* (proclamation) of Paul and a trajectory of his predecessors. As such, "Jesus Christ" represents the risen Lord and Messiah of God who will appear at the *parousia*:

> But in fact Christ has been raised from the dead, the first fruits of those fallen asleep. For as by man came death, by a man has come also the resurrection of the dead. For as in Adam all die, so also those in Christ shall all be made alive.[119]

Paul's citation of "Jesus Christ" refutes his enemies' claim to immediate salvation via *gnosis* and the concomitant saving wisdom, *sophia*, it provides through *logia*. The statement is a warning. It is only Jesus Christ who will deliver the kingdom to God:

---

115. 1 Cor 15:3–5.

116. The use of *hoti*, or "that," before each section, gives the statement an almost scriptural reverence and defines it as an early creed that was well established.

117. It differs from the canonical gospel order and who received the appearances as well—it is important also to note that the first resurrection appearance to Mary Magdalene reported in John is completely absent, and certainly, this was historical due to its problematic nature, i.e., that a woman was the first witness, as their testimony was unacceptable and inadmissible in court or legal proceedings.

118. 1 Cor 5:7.

119. 1 Cor 15:20–22.

> Then comes the end when he [Christ] delivers the kingdom to God the Father after destroying every rule and every authority and power.[120]

To not share in this hope is to be in perilous risk—one must "beware" (*blepeto*!). It is a dire warning of risk consequences. Paul says,

> For no other foundation can anyone lay than which is laid, which is Jesus Christ.[121]

Without "Jesus Christ" as the "foundation" nothing can *stand and perilous risk and danger are real and imminent*, "for the Day will disclose it, because it will be revealed with fire and fire will test what sort of work each has done."[122]

It is for this reason that Paul employs the titular and divine name, "Jesus Christ," at the very outset of his correspondence, and repeatedly thereafter—indeed, *a remarkable nine times in the first ten verses*. Consequently, to employ sayings of Jesus without placing them in the context of "Jesus Christ" is to face perilous risk, including satanic deception. As these verses unfold, it is clear that Paul employs the divine name as (1) the foundation of his call to reject the infiltrating enemies, (2) his unassailable authority as an *apostolos* of the *euangelion*, (3) the efficacious power of the *euangelion*, (4) the still coming judgment and the Day of the Lord, and (5) *pistis* in the *euangelion*, followed by the practice of *agape*, as the only efficacious powers that protect adherents until the *parousia*. Indeed, Paul carefully establishes and ties every critical facet of his coming arguments to "Jesus Christ," beginning with his authority. Paul was appointed "by the will [*thelematos*] of God"[123] to be an *apostolos* of *Jesus Christ*, i.e., the only legitimate calling for an *apostolos*. He is the empowered representative of Jesus Christ, the risen one, the Lord and now Messiah of the coming kingdom of God. To question Paul's apostleship is to question the "will of God."

Given this context of Paul as the *apostolos* of Jesus Christ, risk analysis now allows more specific recovery of the beliefs and practices of Paul's enemies. As noted, when two entities in a common historical context perceive one another as a perilous risk, the countermeasures each employs to cancel the other out almost always isolates a verifiable historical conflict. In almost every case, the core risk issues are uncovered, and often they provide a basis for assessment of the factual nature of the escalating conflict and the countermeasures employed (e.g., actions, sayings, or events). The goal of each of these two conflicting entities in Corinth is victory, not a negotiated settlement. The questions sent to Paul are a window into that deadly conflict, and allow for recovery. While complex and challenging, when this method is applied in 1 Corinthians, the results provide unqualified conclusions about the materiality and

---

120. 1 Cor 15:24.
121. 1 Cor 3:10b–11a.
122. 1 Cor 15:13.
123. Paul's use of *thelematos* is here understood to be a special title of appointment.

likelihood that risk events will or have occurred in highly specific ways. Paul begins: "Now concerning the matters about which you wrote."[124]

Logia and Paul's Empowerment of Women in His *Ecclesiae*

The first question is directly related to the devastating impact the infiltrators have had on Paul's adherents and the dissonance it has caused. It is apparent that the adherents are witnessing deliberate, shocking and very public sexual immorality. This could only have originated with the infiltrating *apostoloi*. The conflict with enemies permeates every aspect of this letter, as well as 2 Corinthians. While Paul's advice in response to the first question is at first puzzling—"It is good for a man not to touch a woman"[125]—it becomes clear that Paul is not referring to a radical form of celibacy demanded by the infiltrating *apostoloi* (Paul is not here quoting the opponents), just the opposite. Paul is instead responding to sexual practices that are dangerous and perilous because they displace *agape*, and so are satanic. Paul's response is better rendered, "[It is well] that these men not touch a woman [a prostitute]." But more (and as noted above), the infiltrators not only consort with prostitutes, they encourage and allow incest, a capital crime and violation of not only Jewish but Roman law.[126] It is this behavior that has exacerbated the crisis and heightened the conflict between Paul's adherents and the *apostoloi*.[127]

Paul crafts his response by describing the intense and dangerous eschatological *sitz im leben*; that is, all sexual relations before the *parousia* must occur in marriage. Abhorrent sexual practices, such as those of the infiltrators, lead to judgment and death.[128] The practice of *agape* must dominate (i.e., as fully described later by Paul in 1 Corinthians 13). Paul's response condemns the behavior of the enemies as not just errant, but perilous, subject to the risk of divine judgment, and so, is susceptible to the curse of death. For Paul, marriage avoids the temptation for immorality.[129] Temptation was not simply a question of moral or ethical practice. For Paul and his contemporaries, this term represented a powerful and evil force that originated from Satan, one that sought to find weakness and separate from God. Temptation was intentional and active, evil and deadly—to be feared. Thus, embedded in Jesus' Aramaic prayer is a cry of deliverance from evil temptation. Errant practices, particularly sexual immorality, were justified by Satan, and so were intended to displace protective, divine *agape*. Consequently, one must not only avoid sexual immorality (its destroys *agape*), one must resist the tempter in the last days, or be corrupted and doomed to judgment.

124. 1 Cor 7:1.
125. 1 Cor 7:1b.
126. See discussion above on 1 Cor 5:1–2.
127. 1 Cor 5:1.
128. 1 Cor 7:7.
129. 1 Cor 7:2.

Paul instructs the adherents to let their desire and sexual behavior be so totally trusting and loving in marriage that they rely only on the partner's desires, not their own; but also, to not withhold sexual relations, except for a season of prayer if both agree, then "come back together."[130] This is the full extent to which *agape* must prevail for his adherents ensure protection from Satan. To not do so allows for the powerful influences of satanic "temptation" and errant behavior, which infects the adherent and makes them susceptible to the perilous risk of judgment and death.[131] For Paul, this is the risk of immorality in the final days before the *parousia*—alignment with Satan. As such, Paul is clear that these *apostoloi* are under satanic influence and are at great risk: "lest Satan tempt you by lack of self-control."[132] Paul knows that the libertine attitude of his enemies is based on their claim to freedom garnered from an elitist interpretation of *logia*. Paul turns this assumption on its head in a masterful stroke of eschatological reversal, when he says: "I say this by way of concession, not of command. I wish that all were as I myself am, but each has his own special gift from God, of one kind or of another."[133] Paul is even more specific: "To the unmarried and the widows, I say that it is well for them to remain single as I do."[134] For Paul, the highest *charismata* in the matter of "not touching a woman" is not to have sexual relationships, *the exact opposite* to the practices of the *apostoloi*. Paul considers celibacy "a gift from God," not because it is a higher or elitist gift, but because it allows the adherent to focus solely on *agape* in the last days. Short of this, Paul encourages marital relations to avoid satanic temptation. These are both practices Paul establishes "by concession." Consequently, it is abundantly clear that the *apostoloi* were not practicing radical celibacy.[135]

Paul next turns to instances of separation and divorce. Given the foregoing context, it is virtually certain that Paul's enemies were encouraging separation from spouses, behavior that led to or encouraged separation, or simply allowed sexual relations whether or not adherents separated from spouses. Marriages were in turmoil and many were seeking divorce, disrupting *agape* in the community.[136] In one of the rare instances where he directly references a saying of the Lord in oral circulation—the prohibition of divorce as a "command of the Lord"[137]—Paul recasts the application of the saying from a general "command" to the *sitz im leben* in Corinth, and does so

---

130. 1 Cor 7:3–5.

131. Paul's stance on equality in sexual relations is also radical in the context of his historical setting. This is just but one of many indications that Paul considered women not only as equals, but also as having all the rights of men in the *ecclesia*, and far from requiring them "to be silent" in the churches, there is no distinction of superiority of gender, which he considers an elitist claim.

132. 1 Cor 7:5.

133. 1 Cor 7:6–7.

134. 1 Cor 7:8.

135. Conzelmann, *Corinthians*, 116–17.

136. The wife from husband; it is not clear if this was prohibited by Roman law, but is was restricted under Jewish law.

137. See Jesus saying, Mark 10:10.

solely on his authority as an *apostolos* of Jesus Christ. In a rather remarkable statement, Paul *allows* divorce, demonstrating that he claimed the authority to adapt any *logia* to the *sitz im leben* of his *ecclesiae*, particularly given the intense eschatological crisis.[138] Jesus' prohibition against divorce was later crystallized in the narrative gospels, thereby allowing little flexibility. In the Gospel of Matthew, Jesus does allow divorce for "sexual immorality" (which, interestingly, would have applied in Corinth). Paul is even more liberal, and allows divorce in the case where the "unbelieving partner" desires separation by leaving the marriage relationship.[139]

> To the married I give this command (not I, but the Lord): *A wife* must not separate from her husband. *But if she does*, she must remain unmarried or else be reconciled to her husband. And a *husband must not divorce his wife*.

Why does Paul introduce *logoi* of the Lord in the context of the adherents' question on sexual immorality? The reason now must be abundantly clear—he is countering the libertine sexual practices of the *apostoloi*, drawn from *logia* of the Lord, with other *logia* that contradict their teachings. There are multiple *logia* in Q and the *Gospel of Thomas* that can be understood as a rejection of the world and immunity from its "intoxication" (i.e., evil deception), once one's true divine origin is understood and reclaimed.[140] More specifically, Paul *allows the divorce of female adherents* only. The *apostoloi* were Jewish *males*. Their influence on Paul's male adherents was devastating. As noted, Paul cursed one of these men, allowing Satan to afflict and destroy him for having committed incest.[141] Clearly, there were women adherents witnessing husbands adopting similar or even worse libertine sexual behavior. Consequently, it is apparent that the infiltrators had convinced several of Paul's male adherents to abandon his *euangelion* and engage freely in libertine sexual practices they claimed were no longer prohibited given their *gnosis-logia*.

As a result, the situation in Corinth is now clear. Paul presents the command of the Lord *from the perspective of the female* who separates, and allows divorce only *for the female* from such immoral men under the influence of the infiltrators. Paul adapts a saying of the Lord to defend further erosion of his *ecclesia*. Then to threaten his enemies, Paul absolutely forbids divorce initiated by the male, placing them in dire jeopardy. It is only they who would be in violation of the Lord's command and subject to judgment at the *parousia*. Ironically, the libertines, who are freely immoral, have afforded their spouses to be freely moral and to separate, thereby remaining under the protection of the *euangelion* and *agape*. Paul defines the opponents in this case as "unbelieving," *apiston*, more literally, the "unfaithful," or those against faith—another

---

138. Another instance in support of oral formation of the sayings tradition and the value of form critical study.

139. 1 Cor 7:15.

140. Koester and Patterson, "Authentic Sayings," 35–36; e.g., *Gos. Thom.* 56, 83–84, 42, 55.

141. 1 Cor 5:1.

term in this case for *cursed*. Indeed, Paul intentionally uses *apiston* as a specific designation of his enemies. Given the context of Paul's directive, he has placed the opponents in the deadly and perilous camp of the "unbelievers," who are controlled by satanic forces of the tempter and doomed.

The Emerging Risk Profile of Paul's Opponents

Given this context, it is now possible to recap several perilous risks crises within the *eccleisa* and the mitigations Paul employs to neutralize them. This allows the formation of the first risk profile of Paul's enemies in Corinth.

To begin, Paul has called for unity in this *euangelion*, the practice of *agape*, and has afforded women the right to divorce men who have embraced his Jewish enemies' rites and libertine practices. He has established marriage as the only legitimate context for sexual relations, further cautioning that even abstinence must be limited to avoid the infiltration and infection of Satan's influence and the displacement of *agape*. Paul then recommends that each adherent, male or female, remain in the "state they are in" due to the "impending distress," i.e., the heightened eschatological crisis and imminent *parousia*:[142] This call to remain in their current state is a mitigation to the perilous risk of libertine sexuality the enemies practice and expect followers to emulate.

> I mean, brethren, the appointed time has grown very short; from now on, let those who have wives live as though they had none . . . and those who deal with the world as though they had no dealings with it. For the form of this world is passing away.[143]

While it may appear that Paul is endorsing the very libertine practices he forbids, his demand is instead a dire warning and indictment given the imminent *parousia* and call for *agape*. Paul brilliantly undercuts their understanding by placing their claims in the eschatological context of the near judgment and presence of the Lord whose *logia* they have perverted. The adherents are not yet free—they have been "bought with a price."[144] Thus, when Paul says, "let those who have wives live as though they have none," he is not proclaiming libertine behavior, just the opposite, Paul is demanding a heightened level of *agape*, so strong that any act must up-build the to avoid satanic corruption and infection. Paul contextualizes sexual immorality in the last days as the very focus of God's enemy, just as it is for Paul's enemies. Even to those engaged, despite the nearness of the *parousia*, he counsels marriage![145]

Paul's detailed answer to the adherents' first question confirms and clarifies the disturbing nature and impact of the *apostoloi*, their immoral practices, and more,

142. 1 Cor 7:25.
143. 1 Cor 7:29–31.
144. 1 Cor 7:23.
145. 1 Cor 7:25–28.

The Enemies of Paul: Demons, Satan, Betrayers, and Apostles

their infiltration intended to destroy the *ecclesia*. As in Galatia, they may have also demanded circumcision,[146] but Paul quickly devalues any practice other than *pistis* and *agape* in the last days of the age. To empower women and maintain the cohesiveness of the community, Paul radicalizes a saying of Jesus, allowing divorce. The *logia* employed by the *apostoloi* from their written source are perverted and errantly interpreted. Indeed, the Lord is with Paul and not his enemies—only he is a true *apostolos* of the Lord Jesus Christ.

From these observations, an initial portrait of the opponents emerges, and it is startling:

- The opponents are libertine, Jewish Hebrew males from Palestine who carry special letters of recommendation by an undisputed Jerusalem authority (likely James the brother of Jesus). Paul repeatedly casts curses on them and their practices, naming them *apiston*, those against *pistis*, divine faith, i.e., they are satanic.

- They track Paul from city to city under orders and with licenses. They are vicious and even violent, employ charismatic *glossolalia* as proof of their divine state, and claim Paul, his *euangelion* and the *parousia* to be a deception.

- Paul also names them "super-apostles," but unlike Paul the *apostolos* of the *euangelion* of Jesus Christ, they are the apostolic mystagogues,[147] the guardians and guides into elitist, divine *sophia* of the Risen One, obtained exclusively through the interpretation of a secret *logia* collection, which provides the only true awakening with salvific, esoteric *gnosis*.

- Only their *logia* are the legitimate and efficacious *logoi* of the Risen One, and their practices that arise from the *logia*, which include mysterious cultic rituals and an ecstatic baptism afford the initiate entry into safety and the state of reunion with the divine—safety from an evil, satanic and deceived world, which, by implication, includes the deceiver and false *apostolos* Paul.

- They encourage sexual activity outside of marriage, even incest, which was a capital crime under both Roman and Jewish law. Such behavior actually demonstrates the illegitimacy of any worldly authority, recognizing the present order as doomed and evil, under the control of Satan, and so deadly. They are "kings" over this world.

- The enemies ridicule and abhor marriage, and consider it deceiving and an entrapment of this satanic world. Several have separated from their spouses and proclaim freedom from any moral and legal (even financial) responsibility. Such behavior threatens the survival of women and children who are divorced. Women are considered as part of the satanic world and as deceivers. Paul elevates women above men, allows divorce and even amends a saying of the Lord

---

146. 1 Cor 7:18–19.
147. Koester, "Wisdom and Folly," 84.

- to protect them by forbidding male spouses to cease legal and social support of wives and families.

- The enemies reject the *parousia*—moral judgment is not only inapplicable to them, but is itself deceptive and part of the dying world. This confirms beyond any doubt that they proclaim that salvific *gnosis* has been realized—they are now "kings."

- Their radical eschatology and realized salvation rejects Jesus as the coming one, the messiah, and they refuse to use the titular Jesus Christ because it errantly implies the parousia. The enemies only accept Jesus as the Risen One, the agent of *logia* and salvation-*gnosis*.

- Jesus' death on the cross has no meaning, i.e., Paul's *euangelion* is errant and valueless, ineffective and deadly. The adherents of Paul are doomed and remain mired in this world, which is under Satan's curse of death.

- They consider their bodies corrupted, material and evil; certainly not, as Paul claims, "the temple of the Holy Spirit."[148]

- Women have no rights or access to salvation-*gnosis*, and can be treated with contempt, i.e., women foster deception by using sexuality as a weapon of deception for evil purposes, meaning they are under the influence of God's enemy. This would presuppose that if the opponents maintained a community or *ecclesia*, it was exclusively male. (There were possibly initiation rights that would purify women and make them "male").

Evidenced by the many letters and accusations that followed and the conflict that greatly intensified between he and these "superlative apostles,"[149] Paul was engaged in a perilous conflict and risk crisis. The plethora of letters[150] to this *ecclesia* (and a "painful" visit)[151] demonstrate the significance of Paul underestimation as to the depth of the crisis in Corinth and the resiliency of his enemies. Paul had previously met severe challenges from James' infiltrators in Galatia, Thessaloniki, and Philippi, and had also survived interrogation, beatings, prison and expulsion from local authorities. But in Corinth, for first time in his itinerant ministry, Paul encountered a more sophisticated threat—Jewish salvation-*gnosis* that was based upon the *logia* of Jesus, the Risen One, with claim to licenses, apostolic authority, and backing from *apostoloi* in Jerusalem. For the opponents, there was nothing that could displace the *logia* and their saving power. *Pistis* in the cross and resurrection was irrelevant to the power of the saving gnosis the *logia* and the safety and freedom provided. Focusing on the cross, *agape* and *pistis* in a Lord yet to come, was the result of Paul's desire to fill his pockets and

---

148. 1 Cor 6:19.
149. 2 Cor 10–13.
150. As many as nine, see above.
151. 2 Cor 2:1.

provide support. Just as he acted once to destroy the *ecclesia*, now he had been deceived by Satan and was still unknowingly annihilating the church of God.

Clearly, the Corinthian conflict confirms that there were alternative itinerant missionaries that were successfully promulgating their own eschatology and expressions of salvation, and did not hesitate to infiltrate existing assemblies with the intent to disrupt or disband them. The conflict demonstrates that early Christianity was anything but copacetic. This was an epic perilous conflict between competing itinerant Jewish charismatics within the Jesus movement, claiming the mantle of *apostolos*.

Paul's countermeasures, from curses to warnings, also include unique reassurance to his married adherents that are struggling with the trauma of separation and infidelity. Paul imbues his adherents, specifically female adherents, with a special charismatic power that saturates their marriage with divine protection from satanic attack:[152] "For the unbelieving husband is *consecrated* [*hegiasti*] through his wife, and the unbelieving wife is consecrated through her husband. Otherwise, your children would be unclean, but as it is *they are holy*."[153] Paul has thereby extended the divine benefits of a believer's marriage to the *apiston*, going well beyond the training he has obtained as a Pharisee concerning unbelieving spouses,[154] as well as to the children, calling them *hagia*. Consecration for Paul means the love of God revealed in the cross of Christ is so efficacious and powerful that a believer's spouse is afforded mystical *protection and safety from the curse of death*. More, their children are *hagia*, meaning set apart for God and also guaranteed safety. This is an immensely powerful assurance given by Paul to his adherents. Thus, Paul's emphasis is on the blessing of *pistis* in the *euangelion* extends beyond all expectation, even for the *apiston* and their children. Indeed, Paul's promise is startling, as it extends the blessing of *pistis* to adherents suffering at the hands of enemies, protecting those they love and have lost.[155]

In addition, Paul's reference to children also may reflect a deliberate challenge to *logia* employed by his opponents. Fore example, in Thomas, Saying 3, Jesus says:

> (1) If those who lead you say to you, "Look the kingdom is in the sky!" then the birds of the sky will precede you. (2) If they say to you, "It is in the sea," then the fishes will precede you. (3) Rather, the kingdom is inside and outside of you. (4) When you come to know yourselves, you will be known, and you will realize that you are the children of the living Father. (5) If you do not come to know yourselves, then you exist in poverty, and you are in poverty.

---

152. Thus, emphasizing it as not only a legitimate but acceptable institution of God even in the last days.

153. 1 Cor 7:14–15.

154. The teachings of the rabbis, the Talmud and Orthodox Judaism reject intermarriages or marriage to non-believing spouses. Pharisaic Judaism encouraged marriage, but required the maintenance of its sanctity.

155. Koester, "Wisdom and Folly," 81.

The Enemies of Paul in Corinth

Here the emphasis is on only the initiate of *gnosis* as the true child of the Father, i.e., the solitary and exclusive encounter of an initiate with esoteric *logia*, divine *sophia* and salvific *gnosis*; a mystical awakening of one's true divine state, i.e., "knowing oneself." Paul rejects this elitist view. Indeed, Paul's extension of protective blessing to an entire family as a result of one adherents' *pistis* in the *euangelion* is very powerful, intensely attractive, and unexpected. Paul once again recasts the *logia* within the context of the cross and *parousia*, and salvific *pistis* in the *euangelion* of God. Even if his enemies appealed to other *logia*, such as Jesus' call to become like a child, i.e., the epitome of the true believer, the *agios*,[156] Paul's extension of the protective benefits of being a child to the adherents' family, believing or not, vacates their exclusivist claims.

Paul's mitigation to his enemies' elitist claims is striking: The *logia* were never intended for an elitist individual, but instead demonstrate the *agape* of God that is extended to all his children of *pistis*. As such, all *logia* must be set in the context of *pistis* in the *euangelion* of the cross and practice of *agape* to achieve true *gnosis*, which, if legitimately employed, protect and strengthen the *ecclesiae* of God until the *parousia*! As a result, while the opponents claim an elitist knowledge that affords them salvation, Paul, in another event of eschatological reversal, emphatically shows that any use of "child" has nothing to do "secret knowledge" or *gnosis* claimed by the opponents, but to the believing "child" who has nothing, no claim. It is the child of God who is solely gifted to safety and *elpis* at the *parousia* by the *agape* of God. *Pistis* in the *euangelion*, activates all protective blessings, which extend mystically to the entire family of that child.

For Paul, the wisdom (*sophia*) of God that brought this democratized "way" into safety from Satan and death was founded on the cross, the event that elicits *pisits* and elpis in God as Abba'—a wisdom that cannot be claimed exclusively by teachers of the law, philosophers of the age, or particularly those who claim esoteric sophia and secret *gnosis* that is accompanied by a cultic initiate baptism:

> For Christ sent me not to baptize, but to proclaim the *euangelion*. Not with *sophia logou* [wisdom sayings], lest the cross of Christ be made void [empty, or meaningless].[157]

So for Paul and his *euangelion*, the enemies by implication are far from the true *sophia* and *gnosis* of God. They are in perilous risk, and so are any who follow them based on *logia* alone.

---

156. Luke 9:46–48.
157. 1 Cor 1:17.

THE ENEMIES OF PAUL: DEMONS, SATAN, BETRAYERS, AND APOSTLES

The Consumption of Demonic Food

Paul turns to the next question: "Now concerning food offered to idols [or, concerning idol sacrifices]."[158] To reconstruct the question posed to Paul, the *sitz im leben* of the *ecclesia* must be established.

Based on the content of the letter, it is apparent that Paul's followers have witnessed the opponents or their initiates publicly feasting, perhaps also purchasing, but certainty openly eating meats (beef and fish) and foods (perhaps also, grains and fruits) "offered" to idols. These would have been ritually processed and dedicated foods of sacrificial cultic ceremonies. Those of *gnosis* do so without any concern as to its having been gifted to a pagan deity and consecrated by the priest of that temple or cult, and then ritually sacrificed to that god or goddess. Because of these esoteric ritual practices, the food was thought imbued with the spirit of the god, and therefore was considered demonically possessed by Jews and members of competing pagan cults. Even more shocking to Paul's adherents, the "man of *gnosis*" is consuming these foods during these rituals and in *the pagan temple itself at its cultic feast table*.[159] This presents a dangerous, troubling and vivid portrait of the brazen risk practices of Paul's enemies, who, though having "knowledge" (Paul uses sarcasm here, i.e., the "man of knowledge"), are *void of agape*; that is, their lack of either consideration or caring for the "conscience" of other adherents (meaning, their practices are so distressing that they threaten the community and ignore divine love) is arrogant and *intentionally dissonant*. Indeed, in the first sentence it is clear that Paul speaks directly to these practices through his comparison of those of *gnosis* (his enemies) and those of *agape* (Paul's adherents): *Gnosis*, which "puffs up," making one arrogant and subject to judgment, and *agape* that "builds up," protecting one with divine *agape* by uniting them safely to the *ecclesiae* of Jesus Christ.

Paul's provides a dire and sarcastic warning:

> If anyone imagines that he knows something, he does not know yet what he ought to know. But if one loves God, one is known by him.[160]

Here is Paul's point. Those of *gnosis* "imagine" (think by themselves) that they know (*gnosis*) *something*. Paul's word usage is carefully crafted. What his enemies claim to know *is not of God*, it is only *something*, so they do not have claim to salvific understanding (*gnosis*). If one "loves God," meaning has *pistis* in the *euangelion* which engenders *agape* for God and fellow adherents, then the adherent is *known (gnosis) by God*—they receive *elpis* until the *parousia* and judgment. The "knowing," or true and efficacious *gnosis*, originates from God in response to *agape*. Only this type of *gnosis* (i.e., being known by God through *agape*) is divine. Paul is asserting that any form of

---

158. 1 Cor 8:1.
159. 1 Cor 8:10.
160. 1 Cor 8:2–3.

salvation-*gnosis* cannot be "found" by self-discovery, or the interpretation of secret meaning in sayings of Jesus, so that one can claim salvation from God apart from divine *agape*. With "true knowledge" as the foundation of his reply, Paul emphasizes the perilous risk facing his enemies that have brought "offense" to "weaker brethren." Those who turn from the *euangelion* and participate in pagan sacrificial rituals have become not only exposed to satanic powers, but have joined with them. As a result, not only are the enemies unknown to God, but so now also are those that have abandoned the *ecclesia* of *agape*. Both are deceived and separated from God, trapped in a state of *agnosis* engendered by Satan. It is a precarious and dangerous place, subject to a deadly curse of annihilation.

To be clear, the consumption of sacrificial meat, grains and plants was understood as partaking in (i.e., actually joining to or uniting with) the substance of the god or gods; that is, the consumption particularly of cultic meat was choosing to bind one's *soma*, spirit and soul to the deity and provide any efficacious powers or safety that afforded. For Paul's Jewish followers in particular, consuming such foods was considered not just defilement, where one is made impure and tainted before God by joining with a demon, but *anathema*, a literal curse, evidenced by illness, infirmity, or death that confirmed separation from the protection of God. Jews of the *Diaspora* were regularly exposed to an abundance of meat and foods available for sale to the public after major festivals and celebrations of a cult or deity, but they avoided these foods.[161] For the Gentile converts, most of whom were struggling subsistence workers like Paul, to be able to purchase meat was a luxury, but it was abundant and made available during and after cultic festivals and celebrations at much lower costs. Gentile patrons of pagan temples often donated or purchased vast quantities of food for celebrations to honor the deity, which included elaborate civic parades on feast days. Indeed, much more was purchased than could be consumed by the priest(s) and by the cult membership.[162] Certainly, this would have been true in the metropoli like Corinth where the temple of Aphrodite and all of the Mediterranean world's various temples, cults and religions were represented.[163] Consequently, witnessing these "men of *gnosis*," the Jewish *apostoloi* and their initiates, openly feasting at pagan cultic sacrifices and ceremonies would have been horrifying, the perilous risks of which being perceived as overwhelming, particularly to Paul's Jewish adherents. These Jewish adherents may have been those Paul terms the "weaker."

The eyewitness accounts of Pausanias, a Greek historian and "tourist" of the ancient world and its temples (early 2nd century CE during the rule of Hadrian, 117–138 CE,

---

161. Even Gentile adherents of other cults may not have considered eating meat from other temples, i.e., that is would be impure and in violation of purity.

162. This would occasionally drive down the price of meat and make it more available to lower socioeconomic classes.

163. Particularly mystery religions and the Egyptian cults such as Isis, Serapis and Anubis, or Greek cults for Dionysus, Hera or other gods or goddesses of the pantheon.

The Enemies of Paul: Demons, Satan, Betrayers, and Apostles

in his *Description of Greece*[164]), record impressive celebrations. Participants were united with the deity during the consumption of sacred meat. Corinth was a major sea faring town centered between two ports, Lechaion to the west and Kenchreai to the east, and so attracted traveling merchants, seaman, athletes and tourists who would often stay for the Isthmian games held every two years. Originally, the games were held in Isthmia, 9.6 miles northeast of Corinth in the stadium a few meters from the Temple of Isthmia, also known as the Temple of Poseidon. During Paul's mission in Corinth, these games were likely held in the city of Corinth itself, not in the Isthmian stadium, as the temple and apparently the stadium had been destroyed by the Romans and were not reconstructed until the mid-50s to 90 CE, at least shortly after Paul moved his activity to Ephesus. The games were extremely popular, particularly with the nearby Athenians,[165] and they attracted renowned athletes from throughout the Roman world, particularly since these games at one time rivaled the Olympics. In addition to tourists, there were foreign colonists who sought refuge from persecution or exile from other cities and became residents; the most famously documented case is in the writings of Paul, namely, Prisca and Aquila, Jews (who may have brought Christianity to Corinth years before Paul's arrival) from Rome who were expelled by Claudius in 42 CE. Sailors who often tented when they arrived at port (i.e., for safety and to limit expenditures, as it is reported that the inns were often filthy and notoriously dangerous), visited the metropolis, both to seek worship and protection at their own cult shrine or temple deity and to make sacrifice for safe travel, and often for their own pleasures. It is clear why so many religions and cults were active in Corinth. The many temples, such as the large temple of Aphrodite in the fortress above Corinth, or Acro-Corinth, were ancient and well established for centuries prior to the destruction by the Romans. Even with the demise of Corinth in the mid-second century BCE, these temples were reestablished by 30 BCE and flourished as wealth returned to the metropolis (evidenced by the number of inscriptions uncovered by archaeologists at various shrines and temple sites). New colonists and transients, as well as athletes and fans of the games introduced many "foreign" cults to the city in short order. All of these factors led to the successful growth of active pagan religions and cultic communities and the vast and abundant ritual consumption of sacrificial meats.

Even social associations and artisan guilds, such as leather workers and tent-makers, who themselves often identified with a patron deity,[166] would purchase the excess meat. The fact that Paul refers to this practice in answer to the adherents' question would indicate that the men of *gnosis* were *regularly* eating meat that was considered as cursed, tainted food. If the opponents were simply purchasing meat, then *the opponents would be from the upper classes*, i.e., they could afford meat. Re-

---

164. See 10.32–38 or 5.13, in the Loeb Classical Library; also see Pausanias description of the cult of Heracles and the eating of meat which he witnessed while touring Corinth, 2.10.2.

165. See Pausanias on Corinth and other ancient Roman historians on the Isthmian games, including Strabo.

166. See the thorough discussion previously on Thessaloniki.

gardless, the purchase of meat, or the consumption of meat as a regular practice, meant it was intentional—i.e., to deliberately and publicly do so was an audacious demonstration of their "liberty," or in Greek, "authority" (*exousia*). Consumption of profane meat was *proof* of the efficacy of their *gnosis*, freedom from the curse because of its impotence. The "*gnostic* man" was more than just immune, he had reached such a state of authority that engaging in any formerly forbidden practice became the demonstrative *validation* of power; i.e., immune and without fear of separation from God, no longer subject to the power of God's enemies, those whom Paul terms, "the gods of heaven and of earth."[167] So, in an odd, almost bizarre demonstration of their elitist state as "kings" they announced their divine status as God's elite by doing the very thing immoral in this world.

For Paul, his enemies' claim to proof of their divine status, evidenced by harmless consumption of sacrificial meat, is based on satanic deception and ignorance. In a powerful rebuke, Paul vacates any such claim by democratizing access to cultic meats for all of his adherents: "We have all knowledge,"[168] and "we know that idols have no real existence" and "there is no God but one God." There is no doubt that Paul is now quoting his enemies. Here is what can be learned from Paul's statement. The Jewish *apostoloi* adhered to the most fundamental tenet of Judaism, "one God," as expressed in central statement of Judaism twice daily, the *Shema*, "Hear O Israel, the Lord our God, the Lord is One";[169] but also, they have moved well beyond the ritual observance of the law to what they perceive as the true and divine essence of the law, the pure wisdom of the torah, fully revealed in higher knowledge and, thus, the *sophia* achieved from the *logia* of Jesus that contain this salvific wisdom. They are of God, united with him and his essence, and have "all knowledge" and are already "kings" through understanding their true and divine nature.[170] For them, the law was originally given to restrict men from being entangled in the world through obedience to laws and precepts (i.e., the law's custodianship and wisdom to separate God's chosen from sin similar to Paul's view in Galatians), but only *until full gnosis was achieved*—and once achieved, they obtained divine freedom from the corrupt world and, ironically, its deception. Indeed, having this higher knowledge frees them from any fear of this world, which includes the *gnosis* that "idols have no existence," and by implication, "eating meats offered to idols is of no consequence," as the food of idols is but of the "gods" and "lords" of this world (i.e., of heaven and earth). The temples, lords and gods of this world, their feasts and rituals, and the meant consecrated to them are ridiculously powerless—for the opponents know they are insignificant due to the "liberty" they have gained. For Paul, their presumed liberty and sexual activity is a satanic trap designed to entangle them in deadly sin, resulting in their condemnation at the *parousia*.

167. 1 Cor 8:5.
168. 1 Cor 8:1.
169. In Hebrew, *Shema Yisrael Adonai elohienu Adnonai ehad*, Deut 6:1.
170. 1 Cor 4:8.

The Enemies of Paul: Demons, Satan, Betrayers, and Apostles

As Paul continues, he indirectly discloses his enemies understanding of Jesus' divine status, namely, that Jesus is the agent of divine wisdom, i.e., the Living One, and that *gnosis* of this wisdom, made available and confirmed in his *logia*, provides them immediate union with God, salvation and freedom from this corrupted material world. Jesus is not the future Messiah (the anointed, or Christ) to soon be present. Paul rejects this claim:

> Yet, for us there is one God, the Father, *from whom* are all things and for whom we exist, and one Lord, Jesus Christ, *through whom* are all things and through whom we exist.[171]

Here, Paul makes two points. First, God is creator of all things and it is *for him* that all things exist. This is in agreement with his enemies' view and their recitation of the *Shema*—there is but one God. But, Paul continues. As creation is from God, *humankind and the body are holy* and to be treated as such since they are of God.[172] Paul's statement contradicts their disdain for the body and its inconsequential nature, evidenced by shocking immorality and union with prostitutes and perilous behavior.[173] God has intentionally created all things, and the "goodness" of his creation includes the *soma*, the body. What they consider as radical participation in pagan cultic sacrifices and feasts, instead of demonstrating their disdain for the world and freedom, only reveals their monumental ignorance and lack of knowledge of God's good creation and the power it contains, as well as their abhorrent view of the sanctity and holiness of God's world and creation. It is Satan and his demons that must be expelled, not the world! More, meat offered to pagan demons and idols is already void of any danger for Paul's adherents—God is God, and Paul's adherents now have authority over demons and satanic forces through Jesus Christ and *agape*, even if attacked and persecuted, because of *pistis* in the *euangelion* and the protection it provides at the imminent *parousia*. The *apostoloi* make what is divine, namely *agape*, a curse, when instead, it is the power of God, and the only force God acknowledges, protects and "knows." The *apostoloi* do not even understand the *Shema*. They only demonstrate their ignorance and apostasy, and so their doom.

Paul is emphatic that the opponents err as to the power of Jesus' *logia* alone to save, and that this error places them in great danger—the impending eschatological crisis will come upon them. Paul summarizes their dilemma—*they do not have "all knowledge" by relying solely on the logia for salvation*.[174] For Paul, all knowledge is based not on secret knowledge embedded in *logia*, but in *pistis* in the *euangelion*, confirmed by evidence and practice of *agape* in his *ecclesiae*. The dire, unfolding events of salvation

---

171. 1 Cor 8:6.

172. See the presentation above on Paul's discussion of immorality and the body as the *temple of the Holy Spirit*—the true living temple of God, not one made with hands.

173. 1 Cor 6:12–20.

174. 1 Cor 8:2.

soon to come with the *parousia*, are thus summarized in Jesus' appointed titles, *Lord and Christ* of the faithful. Here Paul intentionally employs the full christological title of the resurrected Jesus to reaffirm he is *Christ and Lord* over all things. It is he *whose presence is near that will bring judgment and reward to the faithful*, i.e., he is the Christ, the Messiah long anticipated. The response of God to the love and faith of Jesus was his resurrection to life, which confirmed this son of God as *the Lord Jesus Christ*, "through whom are all things and through whom we exist."[175] Realized eschatology through *pistis* in the *euangelion* and the practice of *agape* is the power of salvific "existence" and both reveals and displaces the deadly ignorance of the *apostoloi* and their errant *gnosis*. "All things" indicates that even the hope of salvation and adoption by God were made possible through Jesus' crucifixion, death and resurrection, not his words. The believer can only then "exist" to God by *pistis* and *agape* because *Jesus is now Lord and the coming Christ*, otherwise, the adherent is not known to God.

The Jerusalem *apostoloi* and their claim to salvific *gnosis* and *sophia* has contemporaneous parallels. Indeed, while there is much literature on the Jewish background and relationship to proto or full Gnosticism,[176] there has been a growing certainty among scholars that a segment of Diaspora Judaism[177] sought revelation and salvation through divine wisdom, the highest form of the law and teachings of God. Jewish literature is filled with the foundations of gnostic wisdom movements, from documents such as 3rd Enoch to the Wisdom of Solomon, Sirach, Ecclesiastes, Job, and the Psalms; or from Alexandria and Philo and the allegorical interpretation of the torah. There is little doubt that many Jewish writings were interpreted as divine, esoteric wisdom teachings by adherents who turned from the need for ritual practice or purity to the revelation of divine wisdom. However, the achievement of true and divine wisdom and insight, which went beyond the law, or Oral Torah and ritual purity (and separation), did not always result in the realization of immediate salvation for some Jewish gnostic sects (unlike Paul's opponents for example). In Ecclesiastes, there is no discussion of resurrection, but there is enlightenment, as at death the soul seems to sleep. The implication is that this knowledge allows libertine behavior, as the end of life is senseless and meaningless, but still the soul sleeps after death—not in pain, suffering or wandering as an aimless spirit, but in a state of quiet and peace. Paul counters such claims, asserting that *the son, Jesus Christ, is the completion of the creation*, as is the believer that now "exists" only in Christ Jesus, meaning, grasping the hope of life through *pistis* in God's act in Christ Jesus, the coming Messiah with the *parousia*, and a humble response of *agape* that is known by God. Paul states that the opponents lack this knowledge when he says, "However, not all possess this knowledge." They are lost, at risk, and in peril. Paul then turns to the implication of their lack of understanding.

---

175. 1 Cor 8:6.

176. See McCrae, "Jewish Background," 81–101.

177. Judaism outside of Palestine in the Hellenistic-Roman cities of the world, such as Alexandria, Egypt—home of Apollos.

The Enemies of Paul: Demons, Satan, Betrayers, and Apostles

Yes, they, like Paul, know that idols, even if possessed by demons, now have no real substance, authority or power. Jesus Christ has overwhelmed all satanic forces. And so, "Food will not commend us to God. We are no worse off if we eat, and no better off if we do."[178] But that is not the problem with his enemies' claim to salvific wisdom. Paul warns, "Only take care lest this *liberty* of yours somehow becomes a stumbling block to the weak."[179] Paul makes clear that this is their most devastating and perilous error, and it is of such consequence that, by "destroying" their brethren by their *gnosis*, they lack *agape*, the evidence of the Spirit of God, and so are not known and condemned by God—they are without the very thing they believe they have, i.e., salvific knowledge.[180] The opponents' deadly peril is in their disruption of faith, the direct result of which is the surrender of hope for salvation, so then, they are immediately guilty of deadly "sin," thumbing their nose at God, and standing with satanic forces against God *in the most profound way*. By their pretense, the opponents are intentionally acting in disregard to the conscience and faith of others with the most devastating result—the separation of the adherent from God. Consequently, *they "sin" against the very nature* of God, i.e., *agape*, as revealed in the *euangelion*.

Paul then extends his opponents' offense to *opposition to God's divine will*. By sinning against the brethren, they also do the abhorrent, namely, they sin against God's "Christ," the Messiah who soon brings God's hope, the resurrection and transformation to life, and the *basileian tou Theou* (the kingdom of God). But the significance of this sin against Christ is centered in Paul's next statement: "And by your knowledge this weak man is destroyed, *the brother for whom Christ died*."[181] They deny the efficacious death of Jesus as the pivotal event, central to salvation, turning weaker innocent adherents away from salvific *pistis* and *agape*, which is contrary to the will of God. Paul's statement as to Christ dying for a brother is also a very personal, moving, and foundational statement for him. The horror of Jesus' crucifixion was unbearable for Paul:[182] "the Son of God, who loved me and gave himself for me," meant for Paul that he could only "exist" through the overwhelming *agape* of the son who died on the cross, and whose efficacious death eradicated the curse of the law (i.e., death, Gal 3:13–14), and replaced it with *elpis* through *pistis* and *agape*. The curse of the cross having been overcome by the resurrection, thereby destroying the power of death, was the sole demonstration of the power of God—something the *logia* of Jesus could never provide. As Paul states in Galatians, the true Israel, the *hagios*, was the community of adherents of *pistis* in the *euangelion*, those who had hope and were *now known by God* through the practice of *agape*.[183] *Agape* among the brethren was evidence of the Holy Spirit's presence for

---

178. 1 Cor 8:8.
179. 1 Cor 8:9.
180. 1 Cor 8:11.
181. Ibid.; also see Rom 14:15.
182. Gal 2:20b.
183. This must have been the foundation for later statements, such as in the book of Revelation,

Paul, allowing the bestowing of the *charismata*.[184] As such, practice of *agape* in the *ecclesiae* was the fulfillment of the entire Law and the Prophets, and so, the fulfilling of God's will.[185] Because the opponents' actions are intentionally void of *agape*,[186] theirs is a condemnation by their blatant affront to God. For Paul, the actions of the *apostoloi* are an expression of the inherent sinfulness of mankind since Adam's transgression, i.e., satanic rebellion. Their *gnosis* is arrogance and defiance, standing against his will. These are the errant children of Adam, *both Jew and Gentile*, the enemies not only of Paul, but God and his Christ—a most perilous position!

Paul as a Charlatan, Deceived, and a False *Apostolos*

It is only in this context that what appears to be an abrupt and aggressive change in Paul's tone is made coherent in this next section of the letter.[187] Paul contrasts the freedom given by divine *agape*[188] with his enemies' perilous claim to "liberty" achieved solely by their esoteric *gnosis*. Their claims to salvific *gnosis* and concomitant libertine practices ridicule God's *agape*. The enemies' *gnosis* seeks its expression in public, illegal acts of sexual misconduct; in incest and immorality; it encourages dissonance and division; it freely engages in feasting at the cultic sacrifices of demonic gods and consumption of cursed meats; and most abhorrent, it eagerly destroys the *pisits* of "weaker" adherents. Paul asserts that he has the right as an *apostolos* to practice freedom, but not if it abrogates divine *agape* and the formation of the *ecclesiae* of God and his Christ: "Am I not free? Am I not an apostle? Have I not seen Jesus our Lord?[189] Are you not my workmanship in the Lord?"[190]

While the tone of these rhetorical questions is abrupt, they are coherent with Paul's preceding discussion, and are not an "interruption in the flow of the letter."[191] Nonetheless, the change in tone has led to speculation that a large section of 1 Corin-

---

where the names of the believers were "written in the book of life" (Rev 20:5).

184. Rom 5:5.

185. Rom 13:8–10.

186. They intentionally ridicule *agape* by engaging in public sexual immorality and enjoy abasing believers by offending them through participation in pagan feasts.

187. So much so that 1 Cor 9:1–2 is often considered an insertion from another letter, see Conzelmann, *Corinthians*; *Interpreter's Dictionary of the Bible*, et al.

188. That is, because of the love of God, the joy and hope of salvation and eternal life given by faith alone make one free from fear and the sentence of death at the *parousia* if one loves as God has love; this engenders to serve on another in the eschatological assembly of Abba', just as one has been loved and forgiven.

189. This means an event in the perfect sense, namely, having seen Jesus alive, physically having seen him risen from the dead, the prerequisite of making him an apostle.

190. 1 Cor 9:1.

191. Conzelmann says for example, "Chap. 9 introduces a new theme, the apostleship of Paul," *Corinthians*, 151, and for a thorough presentation on the various reconstructions proposed by scholars, see 151–52n5.

thians, extending from 9:1 to 11:34, was an insertion from another and perhaps later correspondence of Paul to the Corinthians, although it is virtually impossible to find where it fits in the various letters that now make up 2 Corinthians. Indeed, there is no acceptable placement with other fragments that is coherent with sections of 2 Corinthians. Nor could this section be the first letter Paul mentions that preceded 1 Corinthians.[192] Those who argue that this section is an insertion claim that 1 Cor 8:13 actually continues at 12:1: "Now concerning spiritual gifts"; in other words, at the next question answered by Paul. If 9:1—11:34 is a separate letter, then, when read by itself, this mysterious correspondence would have to be Paul's response to an attack on his apostleship, remarkably because he refused to take compensation for his work like other apostles,[193] including the opponents,[194] or claim his right to be accompanied by a wife (who is also to be supported) "as other apostles and brothers of the Lord and Kayfa."[195] Yet, there is absolutely no evidence in Paul's other undisputed writings that he was charged with being a false *apostolos* because he refused compensation prior to 1 Corinthians. On the contrary, Paul's opponents labeled him a charlatan in Thessaloniki for having taken compensation! Paul believes he is entitled to compensation[196] and was in fact being supported by other *ecclesiae* (as well as his subsistence labor) while active in Corinth.[197] In 2 Corinthians 8–9, Paul speaks extensively about the collection of funds for the poor in Jerusalem. If Paul were being accused of inappropriately taking money in Corinth, then certainly there would have been an objection to Paul's collection there. Instead, there is no complaint about his collecting funds as an apostle for another *ecclesia*. Indeed, there is no evidence that other apostles took up collections, which would make such a practice even more suspicious if he was considered a profiteer. Clearly then in Corinth, Paul is accused of being a charlatan because he does not adhere to one of the *logia* contained in his enemies' written collection; one they cite as a their right, namely, a command of the Lord for entitlement of compensation. This is another clear example of Paul's claim to have the authority as an *apostolos* of Christ to interpret and apply all *logia* to the *euangelion* and his practices in establishing each. Paul's enemies specifically point to his refusal to accept compensation as conclusive evidence that he is a false *apostolos*. As such, the tone of this argument is also coherent with context of Paul's defense and mitigation of accusations. His refusal to demand compensation, drawn from a saying he well knows to be a command of the Lord, is based on his application of *agape* for the benefit of the *ecclesia* in Corinth.

As such, 1 Cor 9:1—11:34 cannot be a separate letter now lost. Indeed, its multiple subjects are all related to his right to claim "freedom" equal to or greater than

---

192. 1 Cor 5:9.
193. 1 Cor 9:3.
194. Georgi, *Paul's Opponents*, 238–39.
195. 1 Cor 9:4–5.
196. 1 Cor 9:11, 14; Gal 6:6.
197. Phil 4:15–18; see also 2 Cor 11:8–9.

that of the Jerusalem *apostoloi*—but for the sake of *agape*, Paul refuses. These include: as noted, Paul's right to claim income, but his refusal to do so; his legitimacy as an apostle for proclaiming only the *euangelion*; the nature of the divine miracles given to the Hebrews during their sojourn in the wilderness; the eating foods offered to idols; his return to the statement "all things are lawful to me" (quoting his opponents); even how to properly conduct the sacred cultic meal of union with Christ, the Lord's Supper. Clearly, as a stand-alone document, the letter makes little sense and is frankly impossible to place in a life situation that is coherent apart from 1 Corinthians and Paul's call solely to *agape*.

Paul has therefore linked his right to claim support and the opponents' attack on his lack of making such a claim both as examples of choosing *agape* over his rights and "freedom" as an *apostolos*. Exercising this claim may become a "stumbling block" to his adherents, just as devastating as the his enemies' careless behavior. To make clear the full weight of this claim, Paul repeats Jesus' *logoi* as to his right of support.[198] The context of Paul's statement indicates that the right to support was well known to the Corinthians and was in full use even by other apostles who had visited the city and the *ecclesia*,[199] including Kayfa[200] and his wife.[201]

Paul's next defense is an appeal to the behavior of Kayfa, i.e., Peter, the leader of the twelve apostles in Jerusalem. While an itinerant, Kayfa made claims for support (for he and his wife!), which apparently included Corinth. According to Paul in Galatians,[202] Kayfa was assigned the mission to the circumcised (the Jews), and Paul the uncircumcised (the Gentiles). It is possible that Kayfa had come to Corinth as part of his itinerant activity. While there is no hint of this in Acts, Paul does confirm a public dispute with Kayfa in Antioch in Galatians, an account also absent in Acts. With Kayfa in Antioch, it is certain that he extended his ministry beyond the confines of Palestine. Since Paul, along with Prisca and Aquila, were the "founders" of the *ecclesia* in Corinth,[203] and were responsible for its accelerated growth, Kayfa's activity there must have come after Paul had departed. As the itinerary provided by Acts demonstrates, Paul sailed for Ephesus with Prisca and Aquila in 52 CE, and then Paul alone continued his travel to Caesarea and Jerusalem.[204] He then arrived in Antioch in 52 or 53 CE. It was in Antioch that Paul encounters Kayfa and confronts him with his insincere behavior at meals with the Gentiles. While they part ways, shortly after

---

198. See Luke 10:7, "The worker is worthy of his hire" and later cites it outright, see also Luke 9:14

199. Including the "brothers of the Lord," James, Joses, Simon and Judas (Mark 6:3); see also 9:12.

200. Kayfa, or Peter, the leader of the twelve who lived and risked all with Jesus of Nazareth.

201. Who presumably receives full support.

202. See above, Gal 2:7.

203. Acts 16:5.

204. For the Feast of Tabernacles and with a donation for the Jerusalem *ecclesia*, clearly what Paul believed was his agreement with Kayfa, James and John, but as we have seen, not what James understood, i.e., adherence to the law and all dietary restrictions.

this confrontation, Paul is forced to write the letter to the Galatians to combat Jewish opponents requiring circumcision in early 53 CE. Since we find Kayfa in Antioch about this time, it would have been possible for him to also reach other cities, including Corinth in 54 to 57 CE, about the time Paul begins his third missionary journey and arrived in Ephesus, where he hears from Chloe's people. If so, Kayfa's missionary activity was as far-reaching as that of Paul, but unfortunately the records of his journeys do not exist, except in extra-canonical accounts such as the *Acts of Peter*.[205] If Kayfa did make it to Corinth, it would indicate that he either spoke Greek,[206] or had an interpreter who could do so. It is also possible that the local Jews had Aramaic speakers in the *ecclesia*.

Paul then extends his argument, possible reflecting a saying of Jesus, although Paul would confirm this as he does in other instances.[207] He cites specifically scriptural authority: "Do I say this on human authority? Does not the Law say the same? For it is written in the Law of Moses . . ."[208] By Paul's citing Torah Scripture, and specifically the Law, he confirms that those posing the questions, certainly including the opponents, were primarily Jews and God-fearers.[209] Paul would employ this argument only if he knew Jewish scriptural reference would carry weight; that is, the reference to the law would resonate with his audience. The example he uses is revealing: "You shall not muzzle the ox when it is treading the grain."[210] Paul is associating his labor with that of an ox turning the grain millstone. He is a servant. As the ox turns raw grain into flour for consumption and use in sustaining life, so Paul serves under compulsion to change humans into a form of newness and life. The point being that even the ox has a right to eat the grain that he crushes to flour—how much more so, Paul? Paul, like the ox at work, has a right to gather enough from his labor to survive. But, instead, Paul acted with love and concern for the adherents and even the opponents: "Nevertheless, we have not made use of this right, be we endure anything rather than put an obstacle in the way of the gospel of Christ."[211] Clearly, this section is a perfect continuation of Paul's insistence for love over freedom as expressed in 1 Cor 8:1–13. Love and care for one another trumps every right and claim in the intense eschatological life setting of the last days, even if an expression of this newly found freedom is valid, such as eating meat offered to idols. This is *agape*, radical divine love, that transcends self desire,

---

205. The *Acts of Peter* is ascribed to 150–200 CE, and relates the contest between Simon Magus and Kayfa while he was in Rome, with Kayfa victorious.

206. Palestinian Aramaic was his native language.

207. Whether this was a saying of the risen Lord, or can be placed in the context of Jesus' ministry in Palestine is not of critical importance, but it certainly has a life situation in the itinerant ministry of Jesus particularly since he was accused of being a "wine bibber—a drunkard—and a glutton," Luke 7:34.

208. 1 Cor 9:8–9a.

209. Gentiles converting to Judaism.

210. Deut 25:4.

211. 1 Cor 9:12b.

elitism and standing, because this is God's desire for his children—as love has been given, so must it be shared if one is the child of Abba'. Love stands before Paul's own rights as an apostle—for it was by love he came to his calling and hope.

Therefore, 9:1–15 is not an insertion, but a continued elaboration of his main theme—*agape*, love. In fact, it is clear that virtually all topics covered in the section that follow, from 9:1 to 11:33, can be contextualized within this theme of love for one another as the divine defining factor in a true believer who has true *gnosis*, i.e., *that they are known by God the father by their love and faith—they have existence and hope as the age passes and the Lord returns*. Indeed, love must stand before any claim to act freely in this world if it endangers the faith of another. To not do so is to turn freedom into a claim of merit before God, which can lead to the devastating consequences of sin and the curse of death, brutally emptying the cross of Jesus of Nazareth, the risen Lord, who died for the brother or sister. Consequently, Paul is consistent: "Therefore, if food (offered to idols), is a cause of my brother's falling, I will never eat meat lest I cause my brother to fall."[212]

One additional comment is appropriate before moving on to the next part of Paul's plea for love. Paul states the he would rather die "than have anyone deprive me of my boast,"[213] i.e., the boast that he does not claim his rights as a "proclaimer of the gospel," unlike Kayfa and other apostles. Paul, who is both completely free as an apostle and has every right to receive support and compensation, is so overwhelmed and guided by love that he surrenders any freedom and submits voluntarily to an unsupported, compulsory ministry for sake of love if it will save others. Paul even stresses that he had an absolute right to claim support because he did not "volunteer for his ministry," but instead, he was compelled (conscripted), by God through his selection as an *apostolos*: "For when I preach the gospel, I cannot boast, since I am compelled (literally, necessity is laid upon me) to preach. Woe to me if I do not preach the gospel! If I preach voluntarily, I have a reward; if not voluntarily, I am simply discharging the trust committed to me."[214] Thus, Paul's compulsion of ministry comes with full rights of support, just as anyone who is conscripted in the Roman army, or for that matter, an ox. But Paul unequivocally rejects this based on love and his legitimate concern that doing so may result in dissonance and accusations against him, which might result in adherents turning from the Way. His is a shocking statement of reversal for both the Corinthians and the opponents to hear, i.e., far from him being a charlatan or "weak," he is strong and immersed in love for the sake of the gospel. He denies his rightful claims, confirmed by the words of Jesus, "The worker is worthy of his hire,"[215] yet he rejects them. Instead of seeking freedom and support, he does not rebel and accepts compulsion and servitude. Servants and slaves sought just the opposite in the Roman

212. 1 Cor 8:3.
213. 1 Cor 9:15.
214. 1 Cor 9:16–17.
215. Luke 10:7.

world; that is, to achieve free status—one would never volunteer for servitude. This is why the Jewish gnostic opponents may have reveled in their supposed freedom, as *perhaps they were freedmen themselves*, as their newly realized religious freedom from the world resonated so strongly that it led to libertine actions, even violation of Roman law. Paul's submission of freedom to love displays the dominance love must have over freedom, which is itself based on the *logia* of Jesus, such as his command to love another, even the enemy,[216] and so fulfill the law of Moses and also the law of Christ. Ironically then, Paul speaks of freedom to practice love as a slave to all, which is his only basis of boasting. If he were not to do so, he would die. The opponents understand their freedom as the basis of acting as they wish, without concern or love for their brother, and do so to boldly boast of their freedom publicly as if they will never die; they are kings, but in actuality they are the sons of Satan.

Apostolos as Servant of *Agape*

The theme of *agape* over freedom continues in 9:15–18, where Paul again quotes the opponents who by inference "boast" over their freedom to disdain this world and the ignorant because they are *apostoloi*. Paul argues that this "boast" is a baseless and arrogant. Indeed, Paul's appointment as an *apostolos* by God is far from a license to arrogance and freedom—it is a call to perilous risk and servitude in the spread the salvific *agape* of the *euangelion*: "For if I announce the *euangelion*, that gives me no ground for boasting. For necessity is placed upon me. Woe to me if I do not announce the *euangelion*."[217] Paul's only "boast" is in that he opens the way to anyone who embraces *pistis* in the *euangelion* to divine *agape* as the age comes to an end. As such, Paul elevates love as the principal foundation for all action and root of his actions as an *apostolos* of God and Jesus Christ: "Make *agape* your aim," he will later say.[218]

Paul further defines the freedom to which he has claim as a true *apostolos*: "For though I am free from all men, I have made myself a slave to all, that I might win the more."[219] Paul understands that this freedom is driven by the overriding responsibility to love his brethren: "I do this for the sake of the *euangelion*, that I may share in its blessings."[220] So his "freedom" is conditioned by the *agape* he has received from God the father, who has given him *elpis* and protection from the catastrophic judgment and the curse of death awaiting God's enemies. And so, Paul offers the *euangelion* of freedom and *elpis*, "that I might by all means save some."[221] To do this, he adjusts his

---

216. Matt 5:43–48.
217. 1 Cor 9:16b.
218. 1 Cor 14:1a; Paul can boast of nothing, other than the love he has "secretly" expressed by actions on behalf of the well being of his brethren.
219. 1 Cor 9:19.
220. 1 Cor 9:23.
221. Ibid.

cultural behavior, language, vocabulary and religious practice to "become" like his hearers—whether a Jew or Gentile. He adapts his message and behavior to those he seeks by adopting their practices, standing and relationship to the world and to God as needed—this is his freedom, which is part of his compulsion, but also a compulsion revealed in the *euangelion* of *agape*. Indeed, Paul is cautious when he discusses his work with those "outside the law" when he says: "To those outside the law I became as one outside the law—not being without law toward God but under the law of Christ."[222] Paul infers that he operates under the "law of Christ," which is his letter to the Galatians is clearly defined: "Bear one another's burdens and so fulfill the law of Christ."[223] *Agape* is the law of Christ, and reflects the eschatological reversal (the "law of love," means no law or rule other than loving others, and so freedom from the law of death is assured): "For the law is fulfilled in one word [i.e., *agape*], even in this: 'You shall love your neighbor as yourself.'"[224]

What are the limits of this love for Paul? Could he violate Jewish law of purification and circumcision? He did. Could he eat food offered to idols? Yes, and more. Could he freely interpret the law anew because of the *euangelion*? Yes he did often, even rejecting circumcision, the sign of the covenant for a Jew, as a condition of receiving the love and forgiveness of God.[225] Could he reinterpret and apply *logia* of Jesus Christ as an *apostolos*? Yes, and without hesitation he does so repeatedly. So the "law of Christ" is for Paul the fulfillment of the divine command to love one's neighbor. There was little risk in violating the "law of Christ" if all action and efforts were motivated by divine *agape*, the desired objective of which was establishing *pistis* and *elpis* in the efficacious *euangelion* with the community of God in the last days before the *parousia*.

Paul's *masal*, or parable, of the athlete that then follows is also focused on freedom expressed in *agape*.[226] Just as Paul, who is free, makes himself a slave to all so that he may "win the more" because of his overwhelming drive to share the blessings of love of God, so the athlete transforms freedom into disciplined action and surrenders to the passion to compete for the prize and to win victory. *The athlete's freedom is overwhelmed by a drive to win.* It obscures everything else and gives meaning and context to all effort and the way one lives each day. There is no stopping the effort to reach victory once it is engaged, as it consumes all actions so that the prize may be obtained. So fully engaged is the athlete that ensuring proper focus and mental preparedness is a constant demand, so that it even requires disciplining the body to prepare for

222. 1 Cor 9:21.
223. Gal 6:2.
224. Gal 5:14.
225. The new sign of the covenant is the "circumcision" of the heart, meaning accepting and embracing the love of God, and loving one's neighbor, the higher torah, and divine *agape*—this is the democratization of acceptance as a child of God, becoming one of the new Israel, the adopted children of God.
226. 1 Cor 9:24–27.

competition—all for the sake of "love" of the race and hope for victory.[227] Paul uses familiar and a well-known example that would resonate with the Corinthians with the Isthmian games held there.[228] The Corinthians would have been firsthand witnesses to the life and discipline of the athletes who gave everything daily to reach their objective, i.e., victory, on the coming day of their event. Given the number of shrines found throughout the Roman and Greek cities dedicated to athletes as heroes, even honored as if they were gods, the athlete was well known, charismatic, and revered. They were larger than life, the stars of their time, and respected for their commitment and discipline to compete and achieve the prize on that day. Thus, the athlete's drive, dedication and overwhelming desire for victory were the characteristics that led to their success—and so must it be with *agape*. The Corinthian adherents, who like Paul, embrace *agape*, understand freedom as the power to embrace and practice divine *agape* until the *parousia* when they are judged. As such, the practice and dissemination of divine *agape* is the only legitimate charge of true *apostoloi* of God and Jesus Christ, as well as adherents of *pisits* who announce the *euangelion*.

Paul's *masal* of the athlete is a reflection back to Jesus' frequent use of *masal* during his pre-Easter war on Satan and demonic imperialism.[229] Using common scenes and familiar events of daily life in Palestine, Jesus' *masal* confronted his hearers with esoteric insight as to their perilous status and the impending judgment coming any day. Consequently, they demanded a decision for or against the efficacious *euangelion*. Refusal left them facing exclusion from the kingdom of God, and so, remaining under a curse of death and satanic doom. Similarly, Paul's *masal* demands a decision for the *euangelion* or exclusion and death under the curse of the law. His adherents must be as dedicated to victory at the *parousia* through *pistis* and the practice of *agape* as the athletes of the Isthmian games, or face defeat. The athlete thus becomes an eschatological metaphor for Paul's adherent.

Paul's use of *masal* with their eschatological emphasis would suggest he was aware of Jesus' own. Certainly there were also examples in his early Pharisaic training. There are numerous contemporary examples of rabbinic *masal* reminiscent also of Jesus and Paul's *masal*. However, Jesus' utilized and crafted the *masal* as an oral vehicle that spread the mysterious and efficacious power of the *euangelion* to his adherents—these mysteries of the kingdom of God held transformative, salvific power if acted upon. Paul here is stressing the same salvific power of the *euangelion* in the race to achieve victory (life) or defeat (death). This stress is epitomized in Paul's own realization of the deadly risk he faces if he fails as an *apostolos*: "Woe to me if I do not preach the *euangelion*." If Paul is at risk, his enemies are doomed, fraudulent and under satanic influence. He races for the "imperishable crown," *aphtharton stephanon*.

227. Possibly a reference to the Isthmian games and the events of foot racing and boxing.

228. See comments on the Isthmian games above, which at this time were likely still held in the city of Corinth.

229. Busse, *Jesus Resurrected*, 131–65.

Allegory and the Wisdom of God: The New Seder and the *Logia* of Christ

Paul's preparation and training in the tradition of pharisaic-scribal interpretation and application of the law[230] becomes evident in the next part of his letter, which is clearly directed at his enemies. In fact, it is this section of his letter that definitively confirms they were Jews, as he employs the Jewish *haggadic* tradition in his plea for the power of *agape* over *gnosis* and libertine immorality.

The Haggadah, Hebrew for "telling," was originally an oral narrative tradition that also provided the "order" (in Hebrew, *seder*) to employ when celebrating the Passover feast, the *Pesach*, i.e., what is to be said and done in the religious ceremony celebrating the deliverance of Israel from Egyptian slavery by the finger of God. The haggadic *seder* included a recounting of the Passover events—the exodus led by Moses and miracles of God to the arrival in the Promised Land. The Passover feast was *the* central celebratory religious meal of the Jews, whether in Palestine or in the Diaspora. The telling of the Passover was required by the law and to be remembered by all generations, and so passed from father to son;[231] the bondage and bitterness of slavery in Egypt remembered in the meal of unleavened bread (the *matzoh*) and bitter herbs (*maror*) and harsh labor of making mortar for bricks (*charoses*); the event of Passover that spared the Israelites and destroyed the first born sons of Egypt and freed the Hebrews from Pharaoh's slavery, followed by the exodus to the promised land, always dominated by the presence and miracles of God;[232] all these defined the Jews as a divine nation and, most important, as the chosen people of God (represented in the *beitzah*, *karpas* and *zaroah*).

Paul's use of this oral narrative *seder* places him firmly in the Jewish Pharisaic-Scribal tradition and practice of the *haggadic* celebration of early first-century Judaism. Consequently, only Jews and God-fearers who celebrated this central and defining feast and would understand the significance Paul's plea. While the written form of the Haggadah was composed much later (i.e., in the period from 200 CE to 500 CE during the collection of rabbinic traditions, the Talmud), the oral form of it was well established in Judaism because it fulfilled the demand of Exodus to "tell your sons";[233] thus, the oral *haggadic* narrative predated the written Haggadah by centuries. Consequently, the fundamental elements of the history cited by Paul were likely from the Scribal oral tradition, believed to have originated with Moses, then handed down verbally by each subsequent generation. To be specific, there is little doubt that the reference of Paul to the wilderness, the leadership of God in

---

230. Both the oral and written law, as well as other forms of Jewish interpretive work contemporaneous with Paul and Jesus.

231. Exod 13:8.

232. The parting of the sea, the guiding cloud and pillar of fire, the spring of water issuing from the "flinty" rock in the desert.

233. Exod 13:8.

the cloud that guided the Israelites out of Egypt, the miracles of manna and drink, and water that followed Moses, were elements of an oral haggadic tradition that were well known to first-century Jews of Palestine and the Diaspora. Paul, however, employs this typology anew: The events of Moses in the wilderness, particularly the divine provision of living waters flowing from the rock, are for Paul a precursor to the event of *Christ*, i.e., Christ of the *euangelion*, not the Living One or Risen One of his enemies' salvific *gnosis* and *sophia*. Paul's titular use here of Christ is intentional. As such, it is important to consider if Paul's terminology may in fact extend beyond scribal oral tradition and reflect the diverse interpretive work of the haggadic tradition that was developing outside of Palestine in Diaspora Judaism during the early first century CE, such as the allegorical work of Philo of Alexandria (20 BCE–50 CE), a Jew and contemporary of Paul. Did Philo or the allegorical method influence Paul in 1 Corinthians? If so, how did he use it?

Philo detailed his allegory of the law in two books that may have circulated as early as 25–30 CE. Indeed, Philo's allegories used similar images to those employed by Paul (e.g., manna and the spiritual rock with living water that followed the Israelites in the wilderness on their journey). But Philo's employment was a more radical and severe allegorical formulation that focused on the elements as revealing the salvific wisdom, or *sophia*, of God.[234] Paul's approach was not simply allegorical, nor was it solely focused on gleaning salvific divine wisdom, but was a unique blend of the allegorical and historical; allegorical in that it included such elements as the rock that provided living water *was* indeed "Christ," but also historical in that Paul points to the experience in the wilderness as an example of the experience of his Corinthian adherents. In other words, Paul's application certainly did center on the spiritual truths and typology of the wilderness experience of Moses and Israel, supported by God's historical work, but also how it was also precursor for the work of God *in providing salvation through Christ*. For Paul, this of course means the historical events of the death, burial and resurrection and their outcome—the efficacious *euangelion* of *pistis* and *agape*. By implication, these are the spiritual drink, food and living water—the living water only of *Christ*.

This strongly suggests that Paul authoritatively constructs his own allegorical interpretation, blending his with the history of the *seder*, and more, that his choice of this passage and the interpretive methods he used were intentional in confronting his enemies. Indeed, Paul may be challenging the very allegorical-topological interpretation of Scripture they employed, such as a mystical journey to salvific *sophia* revealed in the *logia* of the Risen One and *gnosis*, which very closely resembles the writings of Philo on achieving a wisdom-salvation, and perhaps like other gnostic writings, e.g., the Hymn of the Pearl). If so, Paul's interpretative words, intended to confront this view of salvation, come out of the first-century milieu of Jewish scriptural interpretation, but are unique to Paul. He combines scribal (historical), *haggadic seder* in its oral form,

---

234. *Allegorical Interpretation*, 2.86.

with a typological application to confound the opponents. By employing "Christ," Paul nullifies a purely mystical interpretation of a spiritual sojourn to *sophia* and *gnosis*, returning instead to the historical haggadic *seder* of the wilderness sojourn. These historical events are a precursor to historical events recounted in the *euangelion* of the Christ's cross, death and resurrection, which, through *pistis* and the practice of *agape*, provide the *elpis* of salvation, i.e., the "living water" until the journey in the wilderness is complete. The risk of satanic attack and doom, is ended by *pistis* in the *euangelion* until the *parousia*, general resurrection and establishment of the kingdom of God—the promise land. As Paul states repeatedly, this is the *sophia* of God.[235]

As such, the Corinthian adherents who hear Paul's letter read aloud must recognize his direct attack on his enemies' errant allegorical interpretation of the *seder* and the terrible consequences they will soon experience: "I want you to know, brethren, that our fathers were all under the cloud, and all passed through the sea, and were all baptized into Moses in the cloud and the sea, an all ate the same spiritual food and all drank the same spiritual drink."[236] Paul's emphasis is once again on the danger in the presumptive infallibility and misguided freedom that comes from satanic deception, particularly for those who witness and experience the power of God. In this case, even if one, like the Israelites in the wilderness, comes under the active guidance of God, there remains perilous risk from Satan, whom Paul identifies as *olothreutou*, the "destroyer." He makes this abundantly clear: "Nevertheless, with most of them, God was not pleased, for they were overthrown [in Greek, 'scattered'] in the wilderness." For Paul, despite the guiding cloud (i.e., the historical and active presence of God physically leading the Israelites through the wilderness), the wonder of crossing the parted red sea (the very miracle of deliverance from fear and death), and the many continuous miracles that were always present with them, such as the provision manna and life giving water flowing from a rock,[237] the Israelites became arrogant with their own knowledge and presumed power, embraced apostasy in self-worship and identify with a demonic god, and freely practiced sexual immorality. Judgment came on them and it resulted in divine abandonment, and even Moses' banishment from the promise land. Because of the *agape* of God for this children, revealed in the *euangelion* of the cross and his Christ, the *apostoloi* must learn from the failure of the Israelites' apostasy, embrace *agape*, and reject their presumed *gnosis* and immoral practices they believe demonstrates their divinity. They are deceived, as *sophia* has become their god. They must turn from their self-presumed "wisdom" to the true and efficacious *euangelion* of God, and endure in *agape* until the *parousia* to reach the promise land.

235. 1 Cor 1:18–2:16.

236. 1 Cor 10:1–4.

237. Paul identifies the rock as being Christ. This is a reference to the Gospel of John's saying of Jesus, "Everyone who drinks of this water I shall give to him will never thirst [John 4:14]," or "He that believes in me, out of him will flow rivers of living water [John 7:38]"—interestingly, this is one of a few possible references by Paul to the oral tradition that ultimately was crystallized by absorption into the Johannine tradition.

The Enemies of Paul: Demons, Satan, Betrayers, and Apostles

Paul's examples highlight the doom that followed the folly of the Israelites. The story would be quite familiar to Paul's enemies, and particularly to the Jewish adherents and God-fearers.[238] His first example denounces his enemies' revelry, their libertine eating and drinking. During the Israelites wilderness sojourn, their behavior led to immorality and arrogance toward God, willingly abusing their special standing as his chosen children—just like the Jerusalem *apostoloi*. Indeed, Paul's recasting of the passage of Num 25:1–8, is much more than an application of a moral lesson. Paul warns the Jerusalem *apostoloi* in language and training they would understand as to the dire situation faced—like the Israelites they are about to be scattered, banished and face rejection.[239] Indeed, after an act of apostasy, the Israelites began eating, drinking and dancing as if free. Despite all of the divine miracles experienced since their departure from Egypt, Moses' short absence on Mt. Horeb to receive their laws, they abandoned Moses and God, forming their own deity. They embraced idolatry, which engendered immorality,[240] and failed to grasp the work of God, seeking only safety. The Israelites abandoned *pistis* in the promises of God, discarded endurance, and rejected a future "promised land." Even Moses failed. For striking the rock twice (a show of Moses' own power, not God's, to bring forth water to the parched Israelites), he is banned from entering the promise land. The Israelites' arrogance in Shittim led them to intermingle with the local Moabite women. Marriage with foreigners was forbidden,[241] but despite this and other warnings about the possible of impurity and apostasy, the Israelites do marry and quickly assimilate Moabite practices, including cultic sacrifices and the eating meat and foods offered to Baal. For this, a plague destroyed over twenty-four thousand,[242] a devastating loss to the Israelites poised for invasion. Lastly, Paul sites the "grumbling," actually, "speaking against God and Moses," by the Israelites who are facing a difficult nomadic life in the desert.[243] Again, despite the miraculous presence of God, they reject him, calling for a return to independence and comfort. Paul is emphatic that these examples are a warning to the Jewish *apostoloi* who, like the Israelites, reject God, the *euangelion* and the *Christ*, failing to reach the "promise land," i.e., the *parousia*: "but for us they were written down for our instruction [*midrashim*], upon whom the end of the age has come."[244] With this statement, Paul radicalizes Israelite history as much more than just *midrashim*—they must be understood in the

---

238. To them as children from the age of twelve by their fathers, or from the wealthy tutors; the establishment of early Jewish education is sometimes ascribed to Joshua ben Gamla, a 1st-century CE sage.

239. It demonstrates the depth of Paul's training and understanding of the torah, and his ability to apply it as a *midrash* to the *sitz im leben* of the *ecclesia*.

240. Exod 32:4–6.

241. Deut 7:1–5.

242. Num 25:9.

243. Num 16:14, 49.

244. 1 Cor 10:11.

context of the eschatological crisis they face, and so, these example are urgent, divine warnings to his enemies.

By participating in cultic feasts and sacrifices to pagan deities, Paul's opponents have become entangled in the same deception and doom as the Israelites. Paul summarizes by warning his adherents: "Therefore, my beloved, shun the worship of idols," because "I imply that what pagans sacrifice they offer to demons and not to God. I do not want you to be partners with demons."[245] His enemies' ignorance and arrogance, and their presumptive libertine practices of entitlement over the practice of love (*agnosis*) all risk separation from God. There is little time to act. Further, they risk possession by demons. The perilous risk embedded in the eschatology of Paul is laid bare: "[for upon us] the end of the age has come."[246] The end is emerging now: "Therefore, let anyone who thinks he stands take heed lest he fall."[247] To consume foods at the cult of demons is to sit at the table of demons (*trapezes daimonion*), forbidding one from sitting at the table of the Lord (trapezes kuriou). To do so is to provoke the jealous retribution of God, i.e., *parazeloumen*.[248]

Paul next turns to the abuse of the Lord's Supper by the *apostoloi*. They reject the *agape* of God by defiling the central cultic participatory event that is the foundational practice of the *ecclesia* of the *euangelion*—consumption of the body and blood of Jesus Christ, which unites the adherent with the death, burial and resurrection of Jesus Christ, the same resurrection available to all who also embrace efficacious *pistis* and follow the command of the Lord to practice of *agape*. The deception by Satan is so effective that even the Lord's Supper becomes just another of the many meaningless and moot drunken meals in which the *apostoloi* imbibe. Indeed, it errantly commemorates for them irrelevant events and an unnecessary *parousia*.

Paul's reference to the Lord's Supper[249] (i.e., to the partaking of the "cup of blessing . . . is it not a participation [*koinonia*] in the blood of Christ," and the bread which is broken, "is it not participation [*koinonia*] in the body of Christ") is the earliest record of its practice by adherents of the Way in the New Testament. By the time Paul writes this letter around 53 CE, these words of "communion" (or participation, *koinonia*) are already well established in primitive Christian tradition as directed by Jesus, now the risen Lord, at his Passover *seder*.[250] The intermingling mystically with the bread and wine as the actual body and blood is powerful—a union of the adherent into the resurrected, living Christ. The *apostoloi*, who come drunk and ridicule the cultic ceremony of union with Christ, which is to be practiced until the *parousia*, do so because they are under the influence of demons and Satan. Paul's warnings confirm

245. 1 Cor 9:14, 20.
246. 1 Cor 10:11b.
247. 1 Cor 10:12.
248. 1 Cor 10:22.
249. 1 Cor 10:16–18.
250. Indeed, a *seder* would be likely, as there was wine first, then the breaking of bread and wine.

that his opponents participate in the collective *ecclesia* to celebrate the Lord's Supper. For Paul it is clear: The *apostoloi* of *gnosis* do not have true understanding of God (they have no real knowledge), because they treat as inconsequential the *agape* of God revealed in the *euangelion* and the cultic feast of *agape*—they claim they are free from such silliness because "all things are lawful."[251] Here Paul quotes his enemies twice, "All things are lawful to me" (*panta moi exestin!*), but refutes both because they do not build the community of agape, i.e., *ou panta sumpherei* and *ou panta oikodomei*. Paul states that if they understood the *agape* of God, they would have "true knowledge." Instead, they are void of divine *agape*: "Let no one seek his own good, but the good of his neighbor."[252] Paul's statement is a clear reference to a saying of Jesus, in fact, the pivotal saying of Jesus for Paul, "Love you neighbor as yourself."[253]

It is in this context (i.e., that seeking the good of the neighbor is participating in divine *agape*) that Paul then returns to the discussion of consuming sacrificial meat offered to demons at cultic celebrations, and brings to a conclusion the discussion of claims of libertine freedom versus the efficacious practice of divine *agape*. He does so by providing a final example; one that prioritizes all right actions during the last days of the age as being for the "good of your neighbor." Paul quotes Ps 24:1, confirming once again that his enemies are familiar with Jewish Scripture: "For the earth is the Lord's, and everything in it." This quote provides the basis of support for what follows.

As Paul sternly warns his enemies, participation in the consumption of cultic meats sacrificed to pagan demons is to join with demons. It is perilous because it is subject to the jealous retribution of God, as they willingly abrogate the first commandment and *Shema*. They are not free, but instead are deceived and possessed by the very demons they claim are impotent and now face God's retributive judgment. It is quite possible that Paul cites Ps 24:1 because the opponents' employ it to justify their actions, i.e., all things are now under their power.[254] Paul rejects this view,

251. 1 Cor 10:23.

252. 1 Cor 10:24.

253. Gal 5:14, Rom 13:8, and as expanded by Paul later in 1 Cor 13:4–8, reflecting Jesus' saying from Mark 12:31.

254. It is very possible that this psalm was actually employed by the opponents, as it clearly fits the slogan characterization Paul cites in quoting them, "All things are Lawful to me" (the capital on the Law here is intentional, as they are citing Psalms as a source of scriptural support for their claim that all is lawful, including the eating of meat offered to idols). If so, Paul's citation would have a more powerful impact in that he would be challenging directly their use of Scripture, and driving the point that Scripture cannot be used as a licensed justification to act without concern for one's neighbor, but, like Jesus, Scripture must first drive by the motivation of the heart and embody love and thus exhibit faith. I should mention once again that this type of argument recalls Jesus' own approach to Scripture in his preaching, particularly the Sermon on the Mount, i.e., "You have heard it been said by men of old, 'You shall not commit adultery', but if in your heart you look at a woman in lust, you have already done so." As noted above, it appears almost certain that a written document was in the hands of Paul's opponents and was a source for their interpretive gnosis. This document included a primitive assemblage of sayings of Jesus, not unlike the *Gospel of Thomas*, and appears to have included sayings related to the Sermon on the Mount (in Luke, the Sermon on the Plain). Paul similarly critiques their

and instead uses it to demonstrate that the good of the neighbor (i.e., the practice of *agape*) is the only context within which all Scripture must be applied. For Paul, meat sold at the market butcher (*makello*), even if it may have been used in a cultic sacrificial rite, is not participation in demonic rituals, and so, is not cursed because it originates from God's good creation. Meat served at a dinner is likewise safe. Consequently, Paul allows the consumption of meat purchased at public market—but *only* if it is not dissonant to another adherent, causing them to fall over "stumbling blocks" (*aproskopoi*) and lose *pistis*, which is a violation of *agape*. Paul makes all his adherents' first responsibility to consider the mind and conscience of one's neighbor before acting: "then out of consideration for the man who informed you [i.e., the meat set before one at dinner was offered in pagan sacrifice], and for conscience's sake—I mean his conscience, not yours—do not eat it."[255] Paul then addresses the opponents: "So, whether you eat or drink, or whatever you do, do all to the glory of God. Give no offense to Jews or Greeks or to the *ecclesia* of God" (10:31).[256] Paul stresses that God demands *agape* in everything so that "they may be saved." He then presses his case, stressing that *agape* is the demand of the risen Lord above all else, and is evidenced in his itinerant mission, teaching and authority to interpret the *logia* of Jesus: "Be imitators of me, as I am *of Christ*." In this remarkable statement, Paul directly links his practice and teachings solely to Jesus Christ.

Lastly, while Paul founded the *ecclesia* in Corinth,[257] it is possible that the Lord's Supper had been in practice when Paul arrived in Corinth, perhaps brought by Prisca and Aquila. If so, they would have brought the tradition with them from Rome to Corinth as early as 49 CE with their expulsion as Jews under the edict of Claudius. This would mean that the Lord's Supper was practiced before that time in Rome. In Act 6:9–10, Stephen, likely a Hellenistic Jew, is appointed as a deacon by the apostles to assist in service and mend a serious division, but also, he preaches to the Synagogue of the Freedmen in late 33 or 34 CE. Stephen's preaching of the Way of Jesus and the *euangelion* of salvation was successful. The Freedmen were Roman slaves, who by manumission, education, or trade, became free (under Augustus, after age 30). The origin of this practice was in Rome where the Freedmen as an association of fellows originated. It is possible that some of the Freedmen in Jerusalem communicated the new *pistis* of the Way to Roman Freedmen when traveling, and thus, carried the

---

use of it earlier in the letter, and may recall that document here. But note that if this is so, Paul recasts the sayings in the form used by Jesus, i.e., all Scripture was not to be understood as license or violation, but reveal the nature and will of God, namely, love. This may indicated that Paul was aware of the oral tradition and formulation of the antithesis that was more in line with Matthew 5, and contrary to the document held by the opponents. Consequently, it is apparent that Paul's form of challenge to the opponents' justification of action, which is based on an appeal to Scripture, is perfectly in concert with the same direct challenge made by Jesus to the Pharisees who erred.

255. 1 Cor 10:29.
256. 1 Cor 10:31.
257. Acts 18:1–7.

Lord's Supper to the capital within just a few years of the Easter event. If this is so, there is some irony: Jewish opponents stoned Stephen shortly after this event. Standing with the Jews on that day—in fact, said to be holding the coats of those who threw the stones—was the young Saul of Tarsus, i.e., Paul. Thus, it is possible that Stephen's preaching led to the *pistis* and practices that were established in Rome by the Freedmen, which in turn led to the conversion of Prisca and Aquila. Prisca and Aquila brought the Way, along with the Lord's Supper, to Corinth, where Saul, now the Apostle Paul, encountered the adherents, whose faith originated with Stephen, the man he helped murder; a full circle of traditions, originating from the murder of Stephen by Paul seventeen years before.

It must be also noted that the formality of the *logia* of institution attributed to the Lord in Paul's recitation is formulaic, often used by Paul to introduce Hebrew Scripture. This is later reaffirmed in Paul's discussion on the proper order of practice of the Lord's Supper (i.e., *oti* or "that," 11:23–26). The *ecclesiae* in Corinth must have gathered at a single location (i.e., from the two to three house churches in Corinth, 11:20) weekly to participate communally in the death, burial and resurrection of Jesus of Nazareth until the *parousia*. Paul's choice of the Greek word *koinonia* was deliberate, as it had a specific meaning, communion by intimate participation; the intimacy of the word is lost in English, but it was used to describe the marital relationship, as Bauer notes, "the most intimate [relationship] between humans."[258] And so, in the commemoration of the Lord's Supper, a sacramental, mystical and cultic participation took place. Uniting with Jesus Christ in *koinonia*, thus, was efficacious, but also radical, taking all risk by publicly uniting the adherent with this Jew's crucifixion, his death and resurrection as Christ. Paul states the *logia* concerning the broken body and blood were received "from the Lord," meaning (as it did when Paul quoted other traditions) Paul received this directly from the risen Lord by ecstatic revelation, whether in a vision, direct encounter, trance or dream. This event most likely confirmed the *logia* of institution already embedded in the earliest oral tradition. This is a most critical affirmation that Paul's encounter with the risen Lord is linked with the most important cultic event practiced each week by every adherent. More, Paul's claim to have directly received the efficacious *logia* is an assertion of his authority to understand and apply *logia* of the Lord as the *apostolos* of Christ.

Finally, it is important to recognize that the *logia* Paul cites in 1 Cor 10:15–16, i.e., "The cup of blessing which we bless, is it not a participation in [*koinonia*, communion or becoming one with] the blood of Christ? The bread which we break, is it not a participation [*koinonia*] in the body of Christ," are absent an introduction like those he will later cite in 11:18.[259] It is important to note that these *logia* are different from the tradition that Paul "received from the Lord." In fact, they are so different that it is evident that Paul is moving from *logia* of institution in 10:15–16 used during

---

258. Bauer, *Lexicon of the New Testament*, 438.
259. 1 Cor 10:17; 11:18.

the sacramental practice of communion by the *ecclesia* when they gather (with the drunkards), to words given personally to Paul in 11:23–26, i.e., the *logia* Paul received directly from the risen Lord. Thus, Paul does not need to introduce the *logia* in 10:15–16, meaning that they reflect an established oral tradition. But his *logia* have a deeply personal context, standing apart from the fixed tradition and certifying his claim to an apostolic relationship with the Christ, the coming Lord of the *parousia*.

Veiling Women in the *Ecclesiae*: A Later Emendation to 1 Corinthians[260]

Given the context of Paul's demand to be an imitator of both he and Christ, the next verses are completely incongruous both with this command and his practices, as well as other matters that follow in the letter. Any comments attributed to Paul on the subordinate role of women (particularly later in 1 Corinthians 14 that women "keep silent") are problematic, as they are entirely contradictory with his consistent portrayal of the equal or the superior role of women in his undisputed letters (Romans, Galatians and particularly both 1 and 2 Corinthians when this section is omitted). Indeed, women have prominent roles, including *apostolos*, deacons, patrons and leaders. Junia, named an *apostolos*, was not only renowned, but Paul confirms she was superior and a witness to the resurrected Jesus. Accordingly, 1 Cor 11:3–16, where Paul is said to require women be veiled, cannot be Pauline, and must be considered a later insertion and emendation to the letter. Claims that this section must be Pauline because it is found in all other ancient manuscripts and trajectories/traditions are moot. Virtually all scholars now accept that 2 Corinthians (also with a largely consistent ancient manuscript attribution) is the compilation and redaction of at least five to seven separate letters by unknown editors of Paul's correspondences.

Since the section cannot be reconciled with the leading role of women that Paul consistently acknowledges and encourages in all of his letters,[261] it is clear that this section has been either inserted or radically emended. If emended, Paul's original statement likely took one of two forms to be contextually coherent with his foregoing and following arguments:

- In a first reconstruction, Paul extols the women of Corinth as being far superior to his infiltrating apostolic enemies. As risk analysis has demonstrated, the infiltrators not only disdain women as evil, deceptive and corrupt beings,[262] they encourage their sexual abuse, as well as allow adultery and even incest for any of male initiate. The *pistis* and *agape* of the Corinthian women, which by negative

260. 1 Cor 11:1–16.

261. See Paul's letter to the Galatians 3:28, Rom 16, on Phoebe the deaconess and Junias the apostle; Chloe as benefactress; Aquila as an equal member in the ministry of Paul, and Peter's wife entitled to the same benefits as that of an apostle.

262. This study has already shown that the opponents treated women as inferior, evil and deceptive, and could be abused sexually.

historical assertion[263] confirms that women such as Chloe were leaders equal with Paul, *must not be veiled*, nor be required to shave their heads and be silent. They are authorized by Christ to continue in these roles and participate in every practice equally with men, including Paul.

- In a second reconstruction, Paul quotes the intruders. Here they demand that women be either expelled from cultic gatherings and practices, or that they be veiled (or heads shaved) and be silent. This raises the intriguing possibility that the *apostoloi* had either expelled Chloe (and so her female followers) or had demanded they she veiled or head shaved and be silent, forbidden to participate in charismatic practices. By inference, Chloe was a leader of the *ecclesia*—a deacon, *prophetaea* or *apostolos* of the *ecclesiae*—either appointed by Paul, or had preceded him there (e.g., such as Prisca). Any practices she employed, led or taught were considered arrogant and offensive. Consistent with the previous section then, Paul would have stressed that women should not be veiled, heads shaved and silenced, because they practiced divine *agape* and *pistis*, emulating both he and Christ.[264]

In his response, Paul alludes to specific practices that engendered condemnation by the infiltrators. This deserves further exploration.

In 11:2–16, the original tenor of the enemies' condemnation clearly points to what they perceived to be a perilous risk. Since women were corrupt and evil, a woman's ecstatic prayer and prophecy infected hearers, particularly men, with the satanic deception and deadly ignorance, and so, separation from salvific *sophia* and *gnosis* of the Living One. Consequently, the Jerusalem *apostoloi* witness the shocking and abhorrent: In Paul's *ecclesiae*, these women who claim to pronounce divine instruction and insight are instead aspiring evil and infecting male adherents. For Paul to allow such practices, particularly prophecy, is confirmation that he is a false *apostolos* who sides with God's enemy.

Indeed, 1 Corinthians 14 confirms that in all of Paul's *ecclesiae* women *prophesied*. He asserts that they were powerful ecstatics, endowed with or possessed by the Spirit of God. Such prophesying included *espousing sayings, or logia, of the risen Lord*, as well as the authoritative interpretation of them. These *logia* were intended for application in the *sitz im leben* of the Corinthian *ecclesia*, a community whose radical context was the impending *parousia*, i.e., a community struggling with and preparing for the final days before the return of the Messiah—all of which was the satanic corruption of the salvific *sophia* and *gnosis* provided by the Living One according to the intruders.

Consequently, as the section stands today, the authenticity of the emended passage implodes from lack of coherence with Paul's practices and the context of his

---

263. That is, it was problematic and therefore was likely historical.

264. Paul's discussion on the Lord's Supper is absent any requirement of segmentation between men and women.

correspondences.²⁶⁵ Paul would never demand submissive veiling or silencing of the very *charismata* he praises and attributes to the work of the Spirit of God. He confirms that *they pray and prophesy with equal standing to men in the ecclesia during assembly and in communion.* Paul, a former Pharisee, attended synagogues where women were segregated and separated from men, and women did veil.²⁶⁶ Paul rejects any segmentation, as the salvific *euangelion* of *pistis* and *agape* has afforded *elpis* and assurances of entering the kingdom of God at the *parousia* to all.²⁶⁷

Thus, it is not Paul, but the Jewish *apostoloi* who demand that women must be subordinate and silenced, *even forcefully removed if needed*, because of the perilous risk they present. They must be compelled to wear veils, or have their heads shaved and be silenced to contain their satanic deception. Whether a woman is veiled, or even if she shaves her head to be like a male, it makes no difference to Paul. All women adherents are equal participants in the efficacious *euangelion* and the *charismata* of God. Thus, Paul's rebuke of his opponents came by quoting them. It is their statements that reflected their vehement objection to women, and particularly their praying and prophesying.

Consequently, a reconstruction of the original words of Paul would represented something like the following:

> Follow my example, as I follow the example of Christ. I praise you for remembering me in everything and for holding to the traditions just as I passed them on to you. [omit: But I want you to realize that] The head of every man is Christ [omit: and the head of the woman is man] and the head of Christ is God. *But* every man who prays or prophesies with his head covered dishonors his head. Every woman who prays or prophesies with her head uncovered *does not* dishonor her head [add] *even if you or she shaves her head*. For if a woman does not cover her head, she might as well have her hair cut off, *there is no difference*: "It is a disgrace for a woman to have her hair cut off or her head shaved, then she should cover her head, [say the opponents]." But *if this were so, then* a man ought not to cover his head *as you, the "kings" do*, since he is the "image and glory of God." "For man did not come from woman, but woman

---

265. Paul would never have made such a demand on women, i.e., to come under domination of males. We have just demonstrated that women prayed and prophesied openly, verbally, in the *ecclesia* on an equal basis with men during assembly and communion. There is not the least bit of question that Paul accepts this, even as in the passage as it stands today. So if Paul endorses this practice, leaving aside the question of veiling or not veiling, then how can Paul state that women must be silent in the church in 14:33b–35? Again, he could not, as Paul accepts that women were to speak up, pray and prophesy in the ecclesia according to the very section where he criticizes women for not veiling. Consequently, 14:33b–35, on the basis of coherence, must also conclusively be rejected as a later insertion into the letter, again with the intent of subordinating the role of women to men, and claiming that it is a violation of God's order not to do so.

266. And were to keep silent in services—only men spoke, prayed and read Scriptures for interpretive purposes, applying Scripture to the life situation of the local Jewish community.

267. Gal 3:28.

> from man; neither was man created for woman, but woman for man." *But love abounds, and* it is for this reason that a woman ought to have authority over her own head, because *they are* messengers *of the euangelion*. Nevertheless, in the Lord woman is not independent of man, nor is man independent of woman. For as woman came from man, so also man is born of woman (i.e., Paul's remarkable statement and confirmation that men and women are equal). But everything comes from God [both man and women]. Judge for yourselves: "Is it proper for a woman to pray to God with her head uncovered?" *They cover for your sake because of their love* [i.e., they imitate me and the traditions I taught you], *but* does not the very nature of things teach you that if a man has long hair, it is a disgrace to him, but that if a woman has long hair, it is her glory? For long hair is given to her as a covering. *I praise the women for their love*. If anyone wants to be contentious about this, we have no other practice—nor do the churches of God.

Clearly, a later editor fabricated the subordinate the role of women in 11:2–16. In fact, it is in this context that is easy to see why Paul used the Corinthian women as the example of Christ's love—all was new, the *euangelion* had freed all from the bounds of constraint through *agape*.

Paul's Warning to Opponents on Misuse of the *Logia*

Paul's commendation of the women adherents of Corinth is then followed by a condemnation of the intruders, as well as other men who have apparently come to follow careless, libertine behavior because of their influence. Paul states, "But in the following instructions I do not commend you."[268] Paul then provide "instructions" about errant behavior on the part of the enemies that is again egregious, contrary to the peace of the assembly and in opposition to *agape*. Indeed, as the next section unfolds, it is apparent that the opponents intentionally become drunk and disrupt the cultic meal and sacred assembly of the *ecclesiae, i.e., when they come together as one on the first day of the week*, and celebrate its most inclusive and efficacious sacrament, the Lord's Supper—the mystical consumption and uniting with the body and blood of the risen Christ. Their arrogance and ridicule of the union with the risen Christ is so offensive that Paul invokes the *logia* of Jesus; indeed the *logoi* he states were given directly to him (i.e., *logoi* that the opponents do not know). Paul then issues a stern warning that they will be infected by a divine curse, namely, that partaking in the sacrament in arrogance is to consume the body and blood in contempt, and so, without full knowledge (*gnosis*) of its salvific power they mystically participate in the satanic murder of Jesus Christ. It is they who are in perilous risk of the curse of death!

Paul's language reflects the real and powerful union of the adherent with the risen Christ with the *Lord's* Supper. It is the "supper" that recalls the historical event of

---

268. 1 Cor 11:17.

Jesus' eating his last meal with the disciples in Jerusalem on the night of his betrayal. However, this is not called Jesus' Supper. Jesus is Lord and Christ, and so Paul's use of "Lord" is titular, and so, is significant—it is union with the risen Lord himself and all the elements that made that event powerful: The blood, the broken body and the resurrection event by God's authority and intervention, portending his return as Christ, the Messiah soon to come at the *parousia*. Thus, "Lord" expands the events from a purely historical (mundane) meal to the super-historical divine event of God's intervention in the world to break the satanic curse of death by the event of Jesus Christ for those of *pistis* and *agape*.

Paul then recounts that night's events: Jesus has come to Jerusalem to exorcise Satan and demons from the temple in his itinerant war to drive Satan and demonic possession form the land and prepare the way for the kingdom and rule of God.[269] The evening meal and practices of Jesus and his exorcists were mystically powerful and routine. They included ecstatic prayers for protection, rhythmic singing, the consumption of efficacious food and drink, a call on God's arrival with the inbreaking of the kingdom of God. Now in the very camp of Satan's control in Jerusalem, saturated with demonic powers and sought out by deadly spies and enemies, Jesus accepts the perilous risk of remaining in Jerusalem to confront Satan. Facing capture, torture and death, this danger existed not only for himself, but so for his exorcists. Consequently, that night, Jesus and his exorcists were in the most dangerous setting possible, having failed to rid the temple of satanic control and the "vipers," i.e., the Jerusalem religious elite, in the shadow of the inbreaking of the kingdom of God. Jesus imbues them with practices of protection and promise (Judas was either not there,[270] sneaks away before they go to Gethsemane,[271] or leaves[272]), but warns them that he may be captured and killed. If so, he provides a binding to him in body and blood for protection from Satan. He asks that if he is killed, they continue this ritual for their protection and union with him even in death until the kingdom arrives.[273] Paul reflects this same hope, centered in the event of the crucifixion and the resurrection: "For I decided to know nothing among you except Jesus Christ and him crucified" (1 Cor 2:2) ". . . that your faith not rest in the wisdom of men, but in the power of God" (2:5). Paul plainly says, "When you meet together [note that he does not use the word 'commune' here], it is not the Lord's Supper that you eat" (11:20).

The danger of tainting the sacred cultic meal in Corinth is perilous and deadly for the intruders: "Whoever, therefore, eats the bread or *drinks the cup of the Lord*[274]

269. See, Busse, *Fire*, 8–30, 70–88.
270. Luke 22:47.
271. Matt 26:23–35.
272. John 13:26–30.
273. Jesus recognizes the danger.
274. This statement is significant, i.e., "the blood of the Lord," which for Paul was the covenant founded on faith alone, not the law or works that justifies one before God. Jesus' blood was the

in an unworthy manner will be guilty [*enochos*, or liable] of the body and blood of the Lord."[275] To consume the flesh and drink the blood without "discerning[276] the body" is to embrace doom, the curse of death and judgment, and to participate in the satanic murder of the Christ. The consumption and mystical union with the body and blood is participation in the brutal death of Jesus, not his murder, just as it is in the reconstitution and resurrection of the Christ to life: "For as often as you eat this bread and drink the cup, you announce [assert one's communion in the same faith of Jesus Christ, the crucified and now living one] the Lord's death *until he comes*."[277] To "proclaim the Lord's death" *until he comes* is to embrace the efficacious *euangelion* and *agape*—to publicly risk all, to commitment to that death's power to neutralize Satan, and embrace God as the child, awaiting the arrival of Jesus as Messiah, the *parousia* and resurrection, expected by Paul any day.

Consequently, participating in the Lord's Supper is efficacious, and can be deadly for those who tacitly ridicule it with abusive drunkenness and disdain. For the adherent of Paul's *euangelion*, founded on the *logoi* of the Lord given directly to Paul (i.e., the intruders do not know this saying, so Paul's assertion is that his *logia* of the Lord are contrary to the inadequate and errantly interpreted *logia* source employed by the opponents), they are assured protection and safety. For the arrogant, contemptuous and drunk intruders,[278] they are under a deadly curse, the evidence of which is already apparent: "That is why many of you are weak and ill, and some have fallen asleep [died]."[279] Paul is clear. While peace and hope are active now,[280] so is judgment for those who defile the cultic uniting with the death and resurrection of the risen son, rejecting mystical union with his body and blood as inconsequential—only *pistis* unites the adherent with Jesus of Nazareth, Lord and Christ: "But, if we judged ourselves truly, we should not be judged,"[281] meaning, the discerning, adherent in the cultic meal will not suffer the judgment of weakness, illness and death.

In concluding this section, Paul says, "But when we are judged by the Lord we are being chastened [i.e., we are *corrected* by punishment], so that we may not be

---

ultimate expression of his faith, not as a blood sacrifice (this is secondary), but as the ultimate expression of total faith, trusting in Abba' even in one's death for the sake of the gospel if needed; not wanted, desired or expected, but a reality for those who, like Jesus, follow the Way of Abba'.

275. 1 Cor 11:27.

276. *Diakrinon*, to perceive with both one's eyes and one's mind, meaning to internalize the faith that led to the events on the cross—how that faith led to the Way to salvation for all believers—and how the historical man, Jesus of Nazareth, was brutally murdered.

277. 1 Cor 11:26.

278. They arrogantly drink without discerning the body of Jesus.

279. 1 Cor 11:20.

280. That is, the activity of God in the end of the age is in its passing, and so, God is active in both present and future.

281. 1 Cor 11:31.

condemned along with the world."²⁸² Paul is stating rather clearly that the *agape* of God as Abba' is so great that even those adherents who may temporarily fail to discern the body and blood of Jesus of Nazareth²⁸³ are *not* necessarily yet cursed or condemned to death, eternal judgment and separation. They have hope of recovery. Paul ends the section by appealing to *agape*, i.e., that the adherents wait for one another before beginning the Lord's Supper, and to avoid the loveless gluttony of the rich and arrogant intruders: "So then, my brethren, when you come together to eat [the communion], wait for one another—if anyone is hungry let him eat at home—lest you come together and be condemned."²⁸⁴ Apparently, there are other matters for discussion about the Lord's Supper, but Paul defers these to when he arrives in person.

The Enemies of Paul Revealed in Chloe's Questions

Paul now returns to the questions brought to him in Ephesus by Chloe's messengers. It is important to recall that, thus far, we have found that each of the questions posed to Paul have been related to the difficulties and dissension brought into the *ecclesia* by the intruders, the Jewish male *apostoloi* of Jerusalem,²⁸⁵ whose libertine practices are best characterized in their declaration, "all things are lawful to me." They show no regard or concern for the impact that their behavior has on Paul's adherents, as they hold that they have already merited freedom from a corrupt and satanic world through knowledge, *gnosis*, and saving wisdom, *sophia*. *Pistis* and *agape* that express hope in a future *parousia* are errant and moot beliefs. A future return and presence of the Lord, i.e., Paul's Jesus Christ, is a satanically influenced deception. Given Paul's responses to questions thus far, and answers to questions about to be posed, it is now possible to even more clearly identify the infiltrators' theology.

Let's first recap. To confirm, prove and even strengthen their superior status, rights and claim to freedom from the laws, rule and order of this deceived world—indeed, a world lost in *agnosis* (ignorance), mired in sin and death, dominated by evil, controlled by demons and Satan, filled with the ignorant that are alienated from God and lack salvific *logoi* of the Living One—the infiltrating *apostoloi* intentionally engage in or approve shocking and repulsive public behavior that is either illegal or contrary to Mosaic law. These acts demonstrate their divine status, like gods, and detachment from a dangerous world of deceit, perilous risk and death—they are free, like *kings on earth*,²⁸⁶ above the judgment or any law. As such, the infiltrators are *anti-*

---

282. 1 Cor 11:32b.

283. Those believers who fail to reflect on his death and what was made possible through his complete faith, trust and love of Abba'.

284. 1 Cor 11:23.

285. 1 Cor 6:12.

286. Actually in their case, only they are God's elite and elect, who are predestined to be saved, confirmed in their discovery of their true divine nature through the *logoi*.

nomian gnostic Jews (and various sects that seem to have been known to Philo), who are not bound by any law or morality because their salvation was predestined, and once discovered through *gnosis,* they are free to become libertines to the world. Torah laws bring order, and God created the world, but laws are guidance to the corrupted, and more, have become fully corrupted by interpretation. The world too and its order have become corrupted; creation itself has been corrupted by turning from God.[287] The infiltrators know this, they are the elite, and have achieved union with the Living One and reclaimed their true divine status and power.

Given this, risk analysis has provided strong evidence that Paul's Jewish enemies exhibit *antinomian gnostic* traits,[288] evidenced in his verbal attacks, deadly curses and rhetorical defenses, all to neutralize the perilous risk they present to he, his adherents and *ecclesiae,* and to the *euangelion* of the cross. The examples are numerous: Their adaptation of baptism into a mystical initiation by *gnostic* mystagogues that grant exclusive access to secret, salvific *gnosis* and divine *sophia,* both of which stand separate from and above the Mosaic law; the condemnation of all *apostoloi* of the *parousia,* including Kayfa and Paul (and the itinerant preacher Apollos), who assert that only their *euangelion* of the cross affords protection from satanic forces and the curse of death in the Mosaic law; the rejection of *pistis, agape* and the *ecclesia* as the *soma of Christ* that overcomes a divine curse; the ridicule of the cultic meal and its claim to unite (through the consumption of wine and bread, i.e., blood and flesh) the adherent with the risen Christ; their abuse of women, allowance of incest, rejection of women leaders, and denial of the legitimacy of ecstatic prophecy and use of the *logia* of the Lord; their feasting and participation in pagan temples and cultic unions with demonic gods openly, calling participation in rites and consumption of tainted and possessed foods inconsequential.

This background sets the stage for the next troubling question sent to him by Chloe. If the *apostoloi* are illegitimate, why are they endowed with powerful *charismata.* Are not these not proof of the divine source of their salvific *gnosis*? Indeed, if these *apostoloi* are illegitimate, how can they exhibit any *charismata,* particularly the same gifts Paul also demonstrates and lauds? The implication is that they have them and that they use them prolifically!

Paul begins his attack on the *apostoloi* by naming them: "Now concerning the *pneumatikon,* brethren, I do not want you to be uninformed."[289] Paul's term *pneumatikon* is often translated "spiritual gifts," but the word can be instead translated as "spiritual persons." The preceding passages analyzed using risk analysis make it clear

---

287. See Friedlander, *Philo on the Melchizedekianism,* from Alexandrian Jews; Birger A. Pearson recounts this in his book *Gnosticism, Judaism and Egyptian Christianity.*

288. Paul should also be considered an *antinomian* based on his stand on justification by faith alone, conceding that circumcision and Jewish dietary laws and practices were no longer requirements for adherence to the community of God in the last days—in essence, a displacement of the priority position of the Mosaic law, which for Paul could never save but only act as a "custodian."

289. 1 Cor 12:1.

that Paul is indeed addressing his enemies as the "spiritual persons," or the "Spiritual Ones," sarcastically. In fact, Paul's is intentional in his use of the term "brethren," setting it in contrast to the *pneumatikoi* in his introductory statement, confirms that *pneumatikoi* may have been their self-designation.

Paul's argument to neutralize the infiltrators' claim to authentic *charismata* follows a tripartite formula of Spirit, Lord, and God, which takes the form of (1) the authentic spiritual attributes of the end times (2) the need for the "body" of the Lord and its diversity in preparation for that end, and (3) the assigned stations of work appointed by God. This includes those that truly have the authority and *knowledge* to discern which spiritual gifts are from the Holy Spirit and which are erroneously practiced—those that are unhelpful to the building up of the adherent and *ecclesia* because they are absent of divine *agape*, the defining characteristic of the true spiritual *charismata* that are legitimate. Paul's seems to once again confirm that the opponents are Jewish as he begins. Paul addresses the "brethren" as Gentiles, "led astray by dumb idols,"[290] that is, they are set in opposition to the *pneumatikoi*. Paul appears to link the *pneumatikoi* and their ecstatic speech with the demonic pagan rites and ecstatic practices during processions and feasts. In essence Paul begins: "You remember the ecstatic experiences you Gentiles witnessed in pagan feasts celebrating demonic idols and now realize they were empty and meaningless to us; now the *pneumatikoi* are doing the same, but they are in danger!"

Paul's next statement is striking: "Therefore, I want you to understand that no one speaking by the Spirit [*pneuma*] of God ever says 'Jesus be cursed [*anathema*]!'"[291] From this context it is readily apparent *that this is an ecstatic cry of the opponents*, that is, "Curse Jesus!" The context is clear. The Corinthian adherents and Chloe's people have sent to Paul the question about the *pneumatikoi* and their "spiritual" outcry, i.e., *glossolalia*, "speaking in tongues." While *glossolalia* is often unintelligible and must be interpreted, in the case of the *apostoloi* this outcry was either translated or was understood. But, when set in the context of the conflict over Jesus Christ (Paul), and the Living One (the enemies), the curse becomes abundantly clear. They ridicule Jesus the man, and so the cross and death, and with it, Paul's Christ. Jesus is the Living One, the divine agent of the *logoi* that provides salvific *gnosis* and *sophia*. The *pneumatikoi* and their initiates are like *kings*. They reject the salvific concept of Jesus in the flesh as anything but a deception. Jesus, like all humans, was cursed and died, as does all corrupted flesh, so reliance on a bodily-resurrected Jesus is absurd. What Jesus was or may have been in the flesh is immaterial, an illusion, and interpretations of those events as salvific are corruptions of *gnosis*, as evidenced by Paul's *euangelion*! The circumstance for the outcry is evidently what is happening at the gathering of the *ecclesia*. The *pneumatikoi* witness ecstatic speaking among the adherents praising Jesus, the crucified Lord and Christ. In response to "Jesus is Lord," which Paul asserts

---

290. 1 Cor 12:2.
291. 1 Cor 12:3a.

comes only by the "Spirit of God,"²⁹² the *apostoloi* respond by decrying the human Jesus who died on a cross and was cursed. Jesus is the Living One, the agent of divine *gnosis* and *sophia*. They shout, "Curse Jesus!" The implication is clear and is consistent with the aforementioned shocking practices of *antinomian* gnostics: The followers of Paul are deceived and have fallen victim to corrupted interpretations, and the fate of the deceived is death. Only the *logoi* of Jesus the Living One, delivered as the agent of God, are salvific, for they contain divine *gnosis* that only the elect can grasp. The *euangelion* is another corruption of divine *gnosis* and is deadly.

Clearly, the confusion and dissension of these competing groups crying out "Jesus is Lord!" and "Jesus is accursed!" is devastating the community. Gatherings for the Lord's Supper, when the *ecclesiae* assemble, have become an intentional drunken debauchery. The ecstatic utterance of each group reveals the core of their contrasting views of their claims to salvation. The opponents completely reject dependence on *pistis in Jesus as salvific*—"Curse Jesus!" *Pistis* is not just futile, but deadly; justification by *pistis*, the power of *pistis*, and the cross as the power of God are "folly."²⁹³ For the intruding *apostoloi*, divine saving *gnosis* was always present, but was lost and obscured by corrupt interpretations, such as that of Paul, but can now be found and gained through the *logia, which they have collected*.²⁹⁴ The *logia* contain this knowledge and provide wisdom and salvation already present, and they are free to proclaim it through their own libertine expression of newfound life. Paul vehemently rejects their claim to alternate divine knowledge and salvation apart from his *euangelion*, but more, he insists that no one *speaking with the Holy Spirit* could possibly say, "Curse Jesus!" Paul thereby charges that opponents' *glossolalia* is *not of God* and, therefore, *it is evil*, and they, by implication are not children of God, but children of Satan.

Paul then provides a detailed explanation of the legitimate work of God's Spirit among the adherents and within the *ecclesia*, and describes the various expressions of it;²⁹⁵ all of support "the common good," i.e., peace, order, care and *agape* that *up-builds* the community of *pistis* until the *parousia*. *Pistis* without *agape*, and *charismata* that strengthen *agape* within the *ecclesia*, are evidence of the Spirit's presence. Those who utter *legitimate logoi* of divine *sophia* do so to "build up" the community of faith,²⁹⁶ i.e., they speak *logoi* that are imbued with *agape* for one another. As such, only the adherents have received true *gnosis* that is given by God through *pistis* alone. This true *gnosis* originates from the *pneumatou agiou*, the Holy Spirit of God, which was poured out upon the adherents because of Abba's love for the crucified son of faith.

292. 1 Cor 12:3, "No one can say 'Jesus is Lord' except by the Holy Spirit."

293. Koester, "Wisdom and Folly," 81–86.

294. Indeed, the fact that there is a written collection of *logoi* (see the previous discussion that is confirmed in Paul's argument against the use of the *logoi* as containing secret or hidden knowledge and saving wisdom), would also suggest that there was a community document for the opponents, and the intent to provide the truth to others, i.e., win converts.

295. 1 Cor 12:4–7.

296. 1 Cor 8:1–13.

Consequently, true *gnosis* is the understanding that *the cross is the wisdom of God*;[297] that is, all human knowledge and wisdom (the basis of false merit and self justification like that of the opponents) fail because they find as folly (i.e., they reject the possibility) that God's will and nature were fully revealed in the resurrection of Jesus as Christ, all because Jesus' total trust and faith in Abba', even if it meant to die on the cross.[298] On that cross, faith and *agape* became the victor over any human claim that self-achieved wisdom and knowledge would merit God's salvation. Thus, Paul rejects that God would ever reveal himself and provide safety through anything hidden or secret. God acted in the most radical and public way because of divine *agape* in response to *pistis*, not the provision of secret wisdom for a just a few. His children are the radical sons and daughters of God. Consequently, *Paul is radical (and perhaps dangerously political), not only in terms of the Way centered in a crucified and resurrected Christ and Lord, but also in his interpretation of the foundation for God's action*—he overpowered *the cruel Roman cross*, the curse of death, and made it powerless! Thus, Paul's emphasis in on the most public of all actions—the Roman crucifixion and Abba's rejection of it in the resurrection of Jesus of Nazareth—is the *sophia* of God. This wisdom opened the Way for all the children of *pistis* to *elpis*; the hope and promise of resurrection and eternal life at the *parousia* in the kingdom of God. This is the *sophia* and *dunamis theou*, the wisdom and power of God,[299] and no human wisdom could anticipate it or overcome it—*ho logos gar ho tou staurou*, the *word* of the cross being God's *sophia* has become the "roadblock to the Jews" (including the Jerusalem *apostoloi* and their initiates) and the "folly to the Gentiles." It is they who have been deceived by the satanic forces. And so, only adherents of *pistis* in the cross and power of God have the true salvific *gnosis*, which has been openly revealed to all in Paul's *euangelion*. As the community of *pistis* and *agape* that builds up the *ecclesia* of God with the *sophia* of the cross, it is they who have divine protection and hope.[300]

Paul then introduces the various works of the Spirit, proving that the community is the assembly of the children of God. The gifts are democratized, that is *they are spread among all the adherents*, not isolated to an elitist group:

> There are different kinds of gifts, but the same Spirit distributes them. There are different kinds of service, but the same Lord. There are different kinds of working, but in all of them and in everyone it is the same God at work.[301]

The first gift of the Holy Spirit Paul names is the "utterance of wisdom" or the "utterance of knowledge."[302] These are not expressions of esoteric knowledge or elitist

---

297. 1 Cor 1:18.
298. 1 Cor 1:21.
299. 1 Cor 1:18.
300. 1 Cor 12:7.
301. 1 Cor 12:4–6.
302. 1 Cor 12:8.

wisdom to the individual, but orally spoken words of powerful active *gnosis* for the community intended to deepen the corporate faith of the *ecclesia* by providing divine insight and guidance, both into the meaning of unfolding events as well applying the practice of eschatological *agape*. Such words, inspired by the Holy Spirit, provide new clarity and fuller understanding as to the meaning of the cross, the foundation of all faith that is saving to all of the Corinthians adherents, whether male or female, slave or free, Jew or Gentile—there is no distinction. Both the knowledge and wisdom of God's salvation are gifted to the community by these *logia* or by other *logoi*, whether given by prophets (see below), or simply by other gifted members of the community. Paul thus elevates divine knowledge and the wisdom of God to direct gifts of the Holy Spirit *given only to his community of faith*, not to an individual's discovery of secret knowledge and wisdom in selected *logia* of Jesus. The divine words of the Holy Spirit build up the community and teach it how to employ *agape*, both for the up building of the brethren as well as to those outside the community. They strengthen and afford risk mitigation to the threat of Satan's power and the curse of death. For the community they confirm safety and the assurance of justification and salvation as the age comes to a close and justice arrives with the kingdom. Thus, only God provides divine knowledge and wisdom through the Holy Spirit; human knowledge and claims of spiritual standing or merit are empty of salvific power, and so, they are satanic deceptions. Paul emphasizes these "gifts" (*charismata*) are of the same Spirit of God. They are *available to all adherents*. The Holy Spirit democratizes access to God's own wisdom for the Corinthian *ecclesia*. The opponents' *gnosis* is, thus, of no merit. As Paul stated at the outset of 1 Corinthians:

> For it is written, I will destroy the wisdom of the wise, and will bring to nothing the understanding of the prudent.[303]

Paul continues with the manifestations of the Holy Spirit. To be legitimate, Paul insists that each must be "for the common good."[304] For Paul, *pistis* in the *euangelion* is the foundation, source and essence of divine *gnosis* and *sophia*, as well as the result of them. All legitimate expressions of divine *gnosis* and *sophia*, which include interpretation and application of *logia*, *propheteia*, *glossolalia*, *dunamaeis*, and *exorkistes*, must be contextualized by *pistis* in the *euangelion* and *agape*. Only in this way can any of these manifestations be properly interpreted and applied, ensuring that they strengthen and benefit the common good, i.e., the adherents and the *ecclesiae*, in the last days of the age. While *sophia*, *gnosis* and *pistis* would seem to be a linear order of *charismata*, i.e., one leading to the other, Paul is not providing a prioritization. Instead, he is carefully describing the complimentary manifestations of the Spirit that have been given to Paul's adherents before the *parousia*.

---

303. 1 Cor 1:19.
304. 1 Cor 12:9.

The importance of *pistis* for Paul as the central *charismata* of the Holy Spirit cannot be overemphasized. *Pistis*, like that of Jesus of Nazareth,[305] comes from a deeply personal encounter and response to the ecstatic and salvific power of the *euangelion* of God, that when accepted manifest *charismata* and *agape* that effectively confront and can disable satanic powers—it saturates one's living soul with *elpis* and reveals the *gnosis* and *sophia* of the coming kingdom and salvation, and provides assurance that Satan and death will be destroyed. Thus for Paul, *pistis* is what actualizes the awakening and transformation of one's *nous*, *soma* and *pneuma* to this knowledge and wisdom—it is a personal charismatic event. *Pistis* then fully embraces the event of Jesus as the Christ, the crucified and risen Lord, the hope and end of all the perilous risks that surround and seek to destroy the children of God (*tekna tou Theou*) in Paul's dangerous demon-infected world. *Pistis* is mystically nourished in one's regular cultic participation in the Lord's Supper, the consumption of Jesus' blood and body, and so, a numinous union of the *teknon* with Christ in his death, burial and resurrection, i.e., the *euangelion*. *Pistis* in the *euangelion* is thus efficacious and salvific in that it subjugates God's enemies. Consequently, *pistis* is not an intellectual exercise. It is a real, personal and corporal encounter with the divine, the *charismata* of willingly and actively embracing Jesus Christ as Lord with all of its accompanying risks and powerful mitigations.[306] Its outcome is *elpis* and anticipation and longing for the *parousia*, the resurrection and the kingdom of God; its manifestation is *agape*; its collective power is *koinonia* in the *ecclesia* of the *agioi*, regardless of status, wealth or station in life. Only *pistis* allows the *agioi* participation in and union with the *soma* of Christ, the risen Lord, who has overcome Satan and the neutralized the curse and infection of death.[307] *Pistis* then is the gift of understanding of the cross as the *sophia* and *he dunamis tou Theou*, the power of God, and *gnosis* of his true nature (e.g., mercy, forgiveness and adoption of those of *pistis*), and his will evidenced in Jesus Christ—embracing love, forgiveness, mercy and humility. Indeed, the gift of *pistis* is most fully realized then when the adherent exhibits *agape* and proclaims the power of the *euangelion* to others. It is this *charismata* that allows complete insight from the Holy Spirit, and as Paul describes, makes the believer erupt in spiritual joy and physically cry out, "Abba', Father!" This ecstatic outcry is the ultimate demonstration of the *charismata* of *pistis* as originating from the Holy Spirit of God. The *charisma* of *pistis* represents the most powerful countermeasure to the *pneumatikoi* and their

---

305. The *charismata* of *pistis* brings hope and assurance that are so powerful so as to risk crucifixion and annihilation under the curse of death for God's kingdom and a war on Satan to drive him and demonic imperialism from the land; *pistis* that perceives the evidence of God's coming in *charismata* that portend the coming *parousia and kingdom of God* and the destruction of Satan and end to the curse of death. See Busse, *Fire*, 128–29.

306. Phil 3:10.

307 Including participation in the faith of Jesus shared in communion with his body and blood during the Lord's Supper.

The Enemies of Paul: Demons, Satan, Betrayers, and Apostles

claims to an exclusive salvific *gnosis* and *sophia* contained in an esoteric collection of *logia*—the battle between the cross and *logia*.

Paul next lists "cures," *charismata iamaton*. This is a very specific *charisma* of the Holy Spirit, which Paul intends to differentiate from miracles. The *charismata iamaton* were particularly exhibited by Jesus in his war on Satan (i.e., as the exorcist of demonically possessed and afflicted, such as with the touch of Jesus' hand in healing a leper;[308] his negotiation and commands to demons, the untimely dead and dark angels to come out or leave;[309] the use of special substances to effectuate expulsion of evil, such as in the mixture of clay and spittle), and in Paul's activity,[310] such as in Ephesus (where Paul was writing 1 Corinthians).

The *dunameis te out as tuchousas*, special powers, Paul practiced are described in Acts 19:11–12. This is a reliable tradition, evidenced by its unusual historical assertion[311] (i.e., it is difficult to explain why anyone would create such an odd tradition) and its accurate reference to *hikanoi de ton ta perierga praxanton*, those practicing magic. In Ephesus, Paul set up his missionary endeavor by finding work in his trade as a leatherworker or tentmaker (see above for Paul's itinerant missionary strategy). As noted, a *skenopoios*, or leatherworker, lived an extremely arduous, physically difficult existence of working long days (sunrise to sunset), often in very poor conditions. Most were poor and contracted for three to five years, or were indentured or simply slaves. Leatherworking and tent making were particularly damaging to the fingers and hands. Wages for a full day's labor were barely able to provide subsistence food and shelter. Paul, along with Prisca and Aquila, likely pooled their wages meet their needs. Located in small downstairs shops with little ventilation and light, Paul would have tied shredded cloths around his wrists and head to prevent sweat from reaching his hands. Perspiration made leather slippery and dangerous when using utilizing knives, awls, hooks and needles. The tradition states that "unusual" *charismata iamaton* were performed through indirect contact with Paul—in Greek, *ou tas tuchousas*, "not ordinary," perhaps better translated, "unusual." It seems that "handkerchiefs" and "aprons" that had touched Paul's skin, *chrotos*, could be taken to those possessed with demons of affliction and illness and laid on the infection or the body. These cloths apparently carried efficacious powers, and were successful in expelling demons. The cloths were not considered to contain magical spells or concoctions, but carried the sweat of a known charismatic (i.e., like Jesus' spittle), a divine substance thought in the ancient world to have repulsive powers, dangerous to demons and other evil spirits. A similar

---

308. Mark 1:40–45, forbidden in his time, and terribly dangerous.

309. Luke 8:26–39; John 5:1–18; Mark 2:1–12.

310. John 9:6, certainly historical; and even the passing of a shadow (Acts 5:15, the shadow of the Apostle Peter).

311. Since it appears that the handkerchiefs were most likely the sweat handkerchiefs Paul wore around his wrists and head during long hours of leatherwork, no one would have thought to create such an unusual practice; consequently, it is a reliable tradition.

The Enemies of Paul in Corinth

tradition, i.e., healing by touching a garment or sacred item, is associated with Jesus found in Mark,[312] and continues to be a practice today. In Mark, a woman touches the garment of Jesus and is freed of a demonic malady. Jesus felt the power "leave him," so the encounter was incidental. In Acts, these expulsions were described as at "the hands of Paul," meaning that they were no accident. Indeed, Paul encouraged their use. This, of course, had a tremendous impact on the success of Paul's effort in Ephesus, and the fame of these healings as powerful events (*dunameis*) led to copycat attempts by local charismatic Jews in the city (which was met with disaster). Interestingly, the report states that those able to conjure spirits and perform magic (such as sorcerers and exorcists) burned their magical scrolls, which were filled with incantations used for this very purpose, i.e., to control evil spirits, cure and heal for a price. Such practices have been confirmed in magical papyri.[313] The effect of Paul's *charisma* exceeded those who were considered in his world to be able to mitigate, negotiate and control the capricious and deadly attacks of dark forces and evil, particularly on the poor, like subsistence workers and the disenfranchised. Paul may be citing this *charisma* because it was widely known that he especially held such powers, which others could confirm, perhaps including the infiltrators.

Paul then moves to the next *charisma* of the Holy Spirit, the miracle, or *energemata dynameon*, literally the "operation of powers."[314] With regard to Paul, there is no clarity here as to specific events in his activity that is more demonstrative of *energemata dynameon* than the exorcism of the possessed woman in Philippi.[315] There is no question that his was an "operation of power," as Paul was "grieved" at what he witnessed, and how her possession was used for monetary gain by her keepers, even though she was tormented. Other examples may have included Paul's resuscitation of a young man who had apparently died (i.e., the young man, Eutychus, who fell asleep because Paul spoke "on and on" and out of a third floor loft[316] and seemed as dead;[317] Paul embraced him and felt life within him and he recovered), the blinding of Bar-Jesus the sorcerer on Cyprus (for turning Sergius Paulus from the Way),[318] various miracles at Iconium;[319] and his surviving a stoning.[320]

---

312. Mark 5:21–34.

313. See Ogden, *Magic*, 13–40, 277–90.

314. 1 Cor 12:10.

315. Acts 16:18.

316. This was in Alexandrian Troas, a very large Hellenistic-Roman seaport on the Adriatic. The site covered almost a thousand acres, including the typical public buildings, only a handful of which remain. If like other Roman cities, there were certainly three story buildings, likely apartments like those near the forum in Rome.

317. Due to Paul's long sermon, still referenced today in many sermons as an anecdote for a preacher's long and laborious sermon; Acts 20:9.

318. Acts 13:6–11.

319. Acts 14:3.

320. Acts 14:9–20.

Paul next addresses the *charisma* of prophecy, or *propheteia*. *Prophetiae* are charismatic revelations drawn from Hebrew Scripture, events, or *logoi* of the Lord that are given to selected individuals for the defense, edification, comfort, or propaganda of the *ecclesiae*. For Paul, *prophetiae* included new insights into the interpretive relevance of torah or prophetic writings to the Jesus event, including events surrounding his life, death and crucifixion (i.e., the *euangelion*), but also, the proper interpretation of his *logia*, as well as the provision of new *logoi* of the Lord to counter threats, thereby protecting and up-building the *ecclesia* while mitigating perilous risks encountered by and in the *ecclesiae*. Interpretive understanding of the *logia* was given by revelation of the Holy Spirit, but certainly also by the risen Lord. This *charisma* is claimed by Paul, who acknowledges that he had "received from the Lord" several instructions for the edification and up-building of the *ecclesia*, which included (as noted) *logoi* that included dire warnings for those errantly participating in the Lord's Supper.[321] This prophetic revelation was the active relationship of *logia* of the risen Jesus with the efficacious power of uniting in the blood and body, death and life of Christ. Hortative preaching and teaching in the context of the prophetic *charisma* strengthened *pistis* by mitigating perilous risks, confirming the *euangelion* and the coming *parousia*, otherwise, there was no point in prophecy itself.

First Corinthians demonstrates beyond doubt that it was within the prophetic activity of the early church where many of the *logoi* of the Lord originated and were dynamically combined with oral stories and traditions to address the *sitz im leben* of the *ecclesiae*. Clearly in Paul's *ecclesiae*, a post-Easter reinterpretive reflection as to the meaning of events and *logia* of Jesus during his itinerant war on Satan was taken. This creative activity continued until the Jesus tradition was crystallized in written gospels, particularly the synoptic and the Johannine traditions. The prophetic tradition itself must have first centered on the *passion narrative*, i.e., the story of Jesus' death, crucifixion and resurrection, for in it we find the earliest use of Isaiah 53,[322] as well as *logia* repeated by Paul,[323] as well as new *logoi* of the Lord, and later, the formation of the *euangelion* itself.[324]

As noted, Paul insists that all legitimate *propheteia* be conducted solely in the context of the *euangelion*, and must strengthen *pistis* and *agape* or be errant and dangerous. As such, Paul's prophetic speaker provided intensely relevant insight and meaning into what was unfolding in the *sitz im leben* of the *ecclesia* of *agape*, negating any esoteric and elitist interpretation, such as that claimed by the infiltrators. Paul's

---

321. 1 Cor 11:23–26; see the detailed analysis above on this tradition that Paul says he personally "received from the Lord."

322. The interpretive words of the prophet Isaiah applied to the events at the cross is certainly an example of the prophetic tradition development.

323. See 1 Cor 2:9, and many other allusions including direct reference to the beatitudes as noted before.

324. 1 Cor 15:1 forward; it is clear what Paul means by *gospel* in ch. 15 is the entire passion tradition, as well as related sayings.

description of each *charismata*, particularly *propheteia*, continues then to carefully mitigate the risk of disruption and dissonance among his adherents related to the infiltrators' claims of superiority—particularly, that they alone have exclusive and legitimate access to divine *charismata* confirming them, not Paul, to be the *pneumatikoi* and valid *apostoloi* of the Living One. It is his contextualization of legitimate *charismata* within the framework of the *euangelion*, *pistis* and *agape* that renders the *charisma* of the *pneumatikoi* as not simply errant, but a cursed deception of Satan. As later Paul asserts, "He who prophesies speaks to men for their up-building and encouragement and consolation . . . he edifies the church."[325] Thus, the bestowal of the prophetic voice was a critically important *charisma* to Paul, maintaining the dynamic and adaptive power of the efficacious *euangelion* to the context of the successful growth and expansion of the *euangelion* into new cities, social and religious strata. Consequently, prophets were highly regarded by Paul. His prophets are linked to and demonstrate cohesiveness with *pistis* in the *euangelion*, which can be tested by witnesses, and thus, is in stark contrast to unintelligible *glossolalia* of the infiltrators.

It is no accident then why Paul next states that there are those who can "discern (*diakriseis*) between the spirits,"[326] meaning distinguish between demonic influence and the Spirit of God. This gift allows for critical examination the prophetic utterance and is required by Paul. *Without this gift present, prophetic speaking is to be silenced.* With the gift of discerning present, Paul is very specific about how prophetic speech should be conducted in public among the members of the *ecclesia*: "Let two or three prophets speak, and let the others [i.e., the other prophets that can discern the speaking] weigh what is said. If a revelation is made to another sitting by, let the first be silent. For you can all prophecy one by one, so that all may learn and all be encouraged; and the *charimsata* of the prophets are subject to the prophets."[327] And so, at the most nascent stages of the formation the *ecclesiae*, there were those who discussed and "weighed" (*kai oi alloi diakrinetosan*) the prophetic speech and vibrant and emerging oral tradition and, thus, defined "orthodoxy"—it was the prophet (and those that discern, i.e., the other prophets) who Paul ranks second only to the *apostolos* in the "body" of Christ.[328] In Corinth, it is likely that these prophetic speakers were those chosen by Paul to lead the *ecclesia* after his departure, perhaps in including Chloe.[329]

---

325. 1 Cor 14:3–4.

326. 1 Cor 12:10.

327. 1 Cor 14:29–32.

328. It is likely that from the prophetic speakers (and discerning groups), formed the first "elders," or later, those designated as an "elder," such as John, the author of the letters now ascribed to the apostle—as he simply refers to himself as "the elder."

329. Paul's establishment of a group of prophetic speakers and discerners who are responsible for the "orthodoxy" of the oral tradition under the efficacious *euangelion* is important and merits even further research and comparative and contemporary analysis in the development of the oral, and later, synoptic tradition.

While all *charismata* are of the same Spirit and the Spirit has been disseminated to all (not just to the Jerusalem *apostoloi*), Paul will use this democratization of the *charismata* to contextualize and criticize the opponents' actions that are contrary to the "common good," *agape*, and edification of the *ecclesia*. Paul has intentionally left *glossolalia*, speaking in tongues, for last, as this is the *charisma* claimed by the opponents to be proof of their divine status. While the prophetic speakers must have other prophets that can test and discern the accuracy of their insights and sayings, for Paul those that utter unintelligible words (*glossolalia*, literally "tongue speaking"), or *spiritual language*, must also have interpreters, and the words must edify the *euangelion* and strengthen *agape*, or they must be silent. Paul will return to this with some intensity and rigor, but for now, he has established the context for the next stage of his discussion of Spirit, Lord, and God.

The *Ecclesia* and the Spirit of God

Paul next links the *charismata* to the active possession by and ecstatic activity of the Spirit among only the adherents of his *ecclesiae*; indeed, exclusively to those who embrace *pistis* in Jesus Christ and the *euangelion*. Paul asserts that it is the Spirit of God that discerns how the *charismata* will be apportioned: "All these are inspired [i.e., charismatic power, operations or manifestations, or *energei*] by one and the same Spirit, *who apportions to each one individually as he wills*."[330] For Paul, the work of the Spirit is intelligent; it is intentional in fostering *agape*; it apportions the *charismata* for the benefit of the adherent, but the *charisma* is conjointly intended to strengthen the *ecclesia*, and so, the *charismata* are, as Paul declares, like the various members that make up one cohesive body: "For just as the body is one and has many members, and all the members of the body, though many, are one body, so it is with Christ."[331] Paul then expressly states that each member is mystically part of the body of Christ. As such, the *charismata* of the Spirit are not for elitist, they are *given to all adherents* for the benefit of the corporate body of adherents, the *ecclesia*, who are mystically united with Christ. Indeed, Paul obliterates any claim to special position based on possession of *charismata*. By implication, the intruders make exactly this claim: "For by [or 'in'] one Spirit we were all baptized into one body[332]—Jews and Greeks, slaves or free—and

330. 1 Cor 12:11.

331. 1 Cor 12:12.

332. The implication of Paul's statement, "For by [in] one Spirit [*kai gar en heni pneumati*] we were all baptized," is important, as it could be interpreted in two ways. First, the translation of *en* as "by" would tend to turn the translation to an active role of the Spirit, i.e., that the Spirit was active in helping to lead the adherent to *pistis* by being baptized in the name of the Lord Jesus Christ, which is followed by the Spirit awarding "gifts" to each individual for the up-building and common good. This understanding would eliminate baptism as the work of an individual to obtain spiritual gifts and standing in the *ecclesia*, i.e., an elitist act of merit. Second, the translation of *en* as "in one Spirit" implies that the *pistis* of the adherent upon hearing the *euangelion* that leads to baptism joins the adherent with the Spirit in baptism. It was this *pistis* in the salvific *euangelion* that was efficacious and

all were made to drink of one Spirit."³³³ The *charismata* are equal manifestations of one dynamic, intentional and active Spirit of God, and are only valid if used to build up the "body," i.e., the *ecclesia* of the *euangelion*.

Paul is severely criticizing the *apostoloi* who disdain the body and world as corrupted and evil. For Paul, just as the body is designed by God, so the *ecclesia* is designed by his living, active Spirit³³⁴—the *ecclesia* is the eschatological assembly of *melos* (organs, members or parts) that make up a living, healthy and active body, so *no part is inferior to the next*, and all have their purpose. It is God's purposeful activity and intentional design to gather his children together into on body, the *ecclesia*, before the *parousia* through the salvific *euangelion* and efficacious *pistis*, *agape* and *elpis*,³³⁵ and to endow them with *charismata* of the Spirit that provide mitigation of risks arising from attacks, both human and otherwise. To deny this, or to claim superiority and reject any member, is to reject God's design, which by implication is to reject the *ecclesia* as the work of God's Spirit. The infiltrators do just this, and so are at great risk. The *pneumatikoi* would object to Paul's analogy of the body,³³⁶ particularly rejecting the sexual or "unpresentable parts,"³³⁷ i.e., as anything worthy of consideration or as members of God's higher creation!³³⁸ But Paul anticipates this. He makes it clear that these parts are indeed modest, and as such they are to be treated with even more modesty. Far from being rejected, they are to be accepted and given more care - the *agape* of the community is to be heightened for the weaker and inferior members, which is the will of God, and reflects the essence of the *euangelion*, which embraces the disenfranchised, the poor and outcasts. All are to be honored as members of the body of Christ; *they cannot be rejected* because they too are part of the whole creation and make the body what it is.

Paul's description of the body focuses primarily on the eye, ear, hand, nose, and feet³³⁹ (all of the most critical elements related to *sensory and serving*), and appears to be unique when compared to other contemporary writings.³⁴⁰ Paul attacks the

---

then validated as authentic by the Spirit's bestowal of *charismata* for that adherent, thereby supporting the up-building of the *ecclesia* and strengthening of *agape* until the *parousia*. Those *charismata* bestowed can be transformative or supportive, but regardless, each is an equal *charisma* of the Spirit for the *ecclesia*. Either translation supports Paul's contention that the baptism of the *pneumatikoi* is an act of magic, a mystical initiation rite that makes a demand on *charismata*, calling on their bestowal at baptism—exactly the practice the mystagogues of *gnosis* and baptism; the *pneumatikoi*; the Jerusalem *apostoloi*.

333. 1 Cor 12:13.

334. 1 Cor 12:24.

335. It is not going too far to say that Paul, the Pharisee, has in mind the tradition of creation from Gen 1:26, in the image of God man is made.

336. E.g., see *Gos. Thom.*, Saying 112.

337. 1 Cor 12:23.

338. The opponents despise sexuality by holding it meaningless and also powerless over them.

339. Paul infers this by his use of smell, *osphresis*.

340. It is apparent that Paul is not referring to the famous fable of Livy, Menenius Agrippa, where

deadly error of the *pneumatikoi*: "The eye cannot say to the hand, I have no need of you."[341] Paul is intentional in his choice of allegorical members of the body and their comparisons. For example, Paul addresses the *pneumatikoi*, the *apostoloi* of *gnosis*, when he employs a comparison of "the eye." The "eye" would be a complimentary designation, the window to knowledge and wisdom. But, he associates the *ecclesia* and the individual members with the work of "the hand," and recasts the accusation making this comparison. The infiltrators dismiss the mundane manual work of the hand, i.e., the *ecclesia* and its practice of *agape*, as pointless and meaningless. For Paul, *agape* is the essence of the Spirit and the efficacious *euangelion* until the *parousia*: "On the contrary, the parts of the body which seem to weaker are indispensable."[342] He mitigates their rejection of the *ecclesia* and all adherents as the recipients of divine protection and favor: "But God has so composed the body, giving greater honor to the inferior part, that there may be no discord in the body, but that *the members may have the same care for one another*."[343] The *euangelion* is a divine creation, active and of *agape*. As the *ecclesia* is strengthened by the intentional diversity of gifts provided, it becomes efficacious in the proclamation of the *euangelion*, *agape* and *elpis* through the presence of Christ evidenced in the *charismata*, and so, the *ecclesia* is the living presence of Christ.

Just because Paul's adherents' "ears" cannot understand the *glossolalia* of the *pneumatikoi*, they are not inferior or ignorant and doomed. Paul is clear about the the failure of the infiltrators to understand the true Spirit of God, and the presence of Christ in it, evidenced by the diversity of *charismata*: "If the whole body were an eye, where would be the hearing," meaning that the work of the prophets, apostles and others who speak and teach would not be able to edify the *ecclesia* if esoteric knowledge alone prevailed among elitists, and if secret *gnosis* were legitimate *charismata*. Such would be contrary to the very nature of the *charismata* awarded by the Spirit of God: "But as it is, God arranged the organs of the body, each one of them, as he chose."[344]

The opponents are thus not part of the body of Christ; they are not members of the God's *ecclesia*, nor do they share in its legitimate *charismata* given by the Spirit. Lacking *agape* and membership in the *ecclesia* of God and Christ, they face the doom so near. With the impending *parousia*, those creating dissonance are both dangerous

---

Agrippa tells the story of the conspiracy of the body parts against the stomach, i.e., we cannot find our analogy here. One can look to Paul's use of the Greek word *melos*—it is sometimes used as a technical term for the physical extremities, members or organs of the body. The use of the body, *melos*, as a metaphor is familiar to the literature of Stoicism, and is found in Judaism as well (Philo's allegorical work, for example), but again, we cannot find a strong parallel that compels a direct correlation with Paul's effort here and the type of emphasis he gives to the whole and parts. While such examples (i.e., of allegorical use of the body) do point out that in literature contemporaneous with Paul the analogy to the body was in wide use, *Paul's is unique.*

341. 1 Cor 12:21.
342. 1 Cor 12:23.
343. 1 Cor 12:24b–25.
344. 1 Cor 12:18.

and at great risk.³⁴⁵ It is clear that they have rejected the *charismata* of the *ecclesiae* because it fails to elevate, emphasize and publicly acknowledge *glossolalia* as the pinnacle of all spiritual gifts. For he *pneumatikoi*, *glossolalia* is paramount, and confirms for them their status and union with the divine.³⁴⁶ Their perilous risk is in their failure to acknowledge the *euangelion* and *soma* of God, the Spirit and all of the *charismata* as equally divine, and practice the greatest of all *charisma*, *agape*.

The Legitimate *Charismata*

Paul now moves to an organization of eschatological appointments *given by God*, all of which have one sole purpose—the protection and up building of the assembly, the *agioi* and *tekna tou Theou*, who corporately comprise the *ecclesia*, the living "body of Christ" until his presence at the *parousia*.³⁴⁷ The appointments are *not powers or authorities* over others, but *servant-leader* roles, that is, those who are entrusted with gathering and sustaining the assembly of the sacred *tekna tou Theou* as their servants and caretakers, as well as *growing* the *ecclesia* as the last days of the age come to a close. All must ensure that the *charismata* of the Spirit are employed with and for *agape*, meeting the dynamic needs of the *ecclesia* that faces daily opposition and attack by opponents and demonic powers. Paul's listing of appointments reflects those who are provided important unifying *charismata* of the Spirit: "And God has appointed in the *ecclesia* first apostles, second prophets, third teachers, then workers of miracles, then healers, helpers, administrators, speakers in various kinds of tongues."³⁴⁸ It is no accident that Paul places the *charisma* claimed by the *pneumatikoi*, i.e., *glossolalia*, at the bottom of his list.³⁴⁹

345. Far from simply a political organization of a new society or social organization, the *ecclesia* was a community of faithful, trusting believers of the Way in the last days; those who waited with hope the justice and mercy of the Lord Jesus Christ.

346. Paul discredits *glossolalia* as demonstration of divine status by using his analogy of the body. To do so, he brilliantly argues and demonstrates that one gift, particularly the one claimed by the infiltrators, could not possible be sufficient, as it denies the miraculous work of the Spirit among all adherents, and therefore denies that the presence of Christ (working with and through the Spirit) is with them: "If the foot should say, 'Because I am not a hand, I do not belong to the body.' That would not make it any less a part of the body. . . . If the whole body were an eye, where would be the hearing?" Paul thus ensures that the adherents come to the knowledge that it is only the democratized *charismata* of the Spirit, not one elite dominating *charisma* that evidences the presence of God.

347. 1 Cor 12:27–34.

348. 1 Cor 12:28.

349. The order is fascinating, and much of the intent is now lost on current readers, as most organized denominations today reject the role of prophets (it is certainly still active), assigning this only to the "age of the apostles," meaning that prophetic and charismatic influenced ended with the apostolic age, i.e., with the death of the last apostles at the close of the first century CE. Certainly, this study is only focused on the historical context of Paul's letter in about 54 CE. Nonetheless, as noted above, the role of the prophet was in the interpretation and application of *logia* of the Lord to the current situation within the historical *ecclesia*, that is, until the sayings (whether of Jesus of Nazareth or the risen Lord) were crystallized in the gospels—the gospels which formed around the passion narrative and

Apostolos and Paul's Appointment by God as *Apostolos* of the Risen Christ

The list of *charismata* that Paul presents identifies God's "appointments" that he alone designates as valid for the protection and strengthening of his *ecclesiae*. This list rightfully begins with the witnesses to the life, death and resurrection of Jesus of Nazareth, or through a special encounter with him, namely, *the apostolos*. This differentiates those who claim access to salvation via *gnosis* from those who were selected by Jesus and were witnesses to his resurrection, or those chosen by God for this itinerant ministry before birth (*ho aphorisas me ek koilias metros mou kai kalesas dia tes chariots autou*),[350] and given an encounter or revelation, such as Paul. Indeed, there were different events and techniques that led to receiving the appointment as an *apostolos*.

First, selection by Jesus ultimately led those chosen (men and women, originally all exorcists) to join with him in his itinerant war on Satan, his "inner circle."[351] They exorcised demons and attempted to drive Satan from the land in preparation for the arrival of the kingdom of God having been given charismatic powers by the Spirit (bestowed by Jesus through various techniques, including breathing on the disciple). Those that subsequently encounter Jesus in very specific and definitive post-resurrection events became witnesses to and *apostoloi* of the salvific *euangelion* of the risen Christ (see Busse, *Jesus, Resurrected*).[352] Second, Paul asserts that God selected others through special intercession (i.e., his encounter with the risen Jesus on his way to persecute the adherents in Damascus). Third, the action of the Spirit (e.g., the selection of Matthias[353] using ecstatic prayer and dice) identified others to be *apostoloi*. Paul's list of James and others who later were named witnesses, that is, those named in Paul's listing of resurrection witnesses in Corinthians, were not necessarily named *apostoloi*.[354] Indeed, James is not identified as an *apostolos* in the noncanonical Gospel of James, or in the pseudepigraphical canonical letter attributed to James, where his is identified as "servant" (doulos) of Jesus Christ and God.[355] Others that Paul names *apostolos*, such as Junia, we know little about.

---

attracted sayings and other anecdotes over time.

350. Gal 1:15.

351. There is Kayfa, Andrew, James and John who were Jesus' closest followers, given access to him in some of his most pivotal moments; then there the other eight men that made up the residual of the twelve apostles, as well as a group of at least six to eight women, several of who were *apostoloi*, that are named, Mary of Magdala being the first to receive a resurrection encounter; finally, there is Jesus family, his brothers, and most prominently, James; Paul's list certainly includes all of these men and women, as he mentions "other apostles" and "over five hundred brethren."

352. In one of the most moving scenes in the New Testament, Jesus builds a coal fire and cooks fish and has bread waiting for the disciples on shore of Galilee in a dawn breakfast for them.

353. Having been both a witness to the resurrected Jesus and with him since his baptism by John (i.e., the beginning of his war on Satan) was the required criterion for Matthias to be counted as a candidate to replace Judas Iscariot.

354. 1 Cor 15, the earliest listing of resurrection witnesses in the New Testament.

355. Josephus identifies James as "the brother of Jesus" (*Antiquities*, 20.200), Paul similarly names

Paul links his appointment to *apostolos* and the legitimacy of his *euangelion* to *his receiving a unique resurrection experience and revelation* by God. God provided direct revelation to Paul: "He was pleased to reveal his son to [or 'in'] me."[356] Paul was subsequently given another special revelation, where he was elevated to the "third heaven," that is, the sacred place of where God and the risen Lord reside. There he heard sacred *logoi* that could not be repeated. As Paul notes, an *apostolos* has no claim on God, just the opposite. His apostleship made him the least of all the *tekna tou Theou*. As such, he is charged with the successful dissemination of the *euangelion* before the *parousia*,[357] evidenced by the establishment of *ecclesiae*, or face doom. The countervailing perilous risks of accepting or denying this appointment were monumental. As such, Paul stresses that he, like other *apostoloi*, were compelled to bear the weight and burden of gathering the children of God through the difficult and dangerous itinerant life of proclaiming the *euangelion*, eliciting *pistis*, and thereby establishing God's *ecclesia*, the *soma* of Christ, in *agape*. To resist or delay would be tantamount to abandoning the *agioi* to Satan in the crisis of the impending judgment. It is noteworthy that Paul never acknowledges the Jerusalem *pneumatikoi* as *apostoloi* in Corinthians; he only sarcastically names them "super-apostles," thereby ridiculing their claims to salvific gnosis and libertine freedom. For Paul, legitimate *apostoloi* are only those men and women who adhere to, announce and practice advancing the *euangelion* of *pistis* and *agape*.

Propheteia

Paul's rejection of *glossolalia* as the penultimate *charisma* is further emphasized by the "second" of God's appointments listed—that of *prophet*. As noted, Paul associates this *charisma* with divine insight and interpretation of Scripture, prophecy, *logia*, revelations, dreams and other ecstatic experiences to the *sitz im leben* of the *ecclesia* and to the *euangelion*. The Spirit's provision of scriptural relevance, expressed in citation or paraphrase of torah or prophetic Scripture and its fulfillment in the event of Jesus Christ and the cross, is clearly evident. This included relevance of Scripture to specific events surrounding Jesus' birth, itinerant activity, death and crucifixion, as well as to *his logoi*. The *charisma* of prophetic speech also allowed the introduction of new *logia* of the risen Lord, or could draw from oral tradition of *logia*, which were then applied as needed. Hortative preaching and teaching in the context of the prophetic *charisma* of the Spirit was efficacious. It brought mitigation of evil spells and curses, encouragement during times of attack and persecution, explanation of events and their meaning in the context of the *parousia*, and protection from demons and Satan in the form of practices and rites to be performed, such as the Lord's Supper. Prophetic *logoi* were to be tested by two to three other prophets using a ritual practices established by Paul, thereby ensuring

---

him such in Gal 1:19.

356. Gal 1:16.

357. 1 Cor 4:9–13.

that the outcome of the prophetic speech and its guidance resulted in edification and strengthening of the *ecclesia*, the *euangelion*, practice of *agape* and elicitation of *elpis*. If is noteworthy that Paul by inference also claims this *charisma*.[358]

Formation of the Jesus Tradition:
The Prophetic Movement in Paul's Ecclesiae

The prophetic tradition first formed in the gatherings and practices introduced by Paul. Other oral traditions also formed around the passion narrative, i.e., the story of Jesus' death, crucifixion and resurrection, for in it we find the earliest use of Isaiah,[359] as well as sayings repeated by Paul,[360] such as the well developed words of the Lord's Supper, and later, the "gospel" tradition of the resurrection appearances.[361] The prophetic speaker then provided intensely authoritative and relevant insight and meaning into what was unfolding in and around the *ecclesia* by providing Scripture, *logia* or oral traditions to contextualize an event or attack as eschatological, i.e., explaining and confirming the events in the context of the in-breaking of the kingdom of God, thereby validating and strengthening the *pistis* of the adherents experiencing the *charismata* and *elpis* for and expectation of the soon arrival of Christ and the *parousia*. This process of prophetic validation is confirmed not only in Corinthians, but also in Paul's letter to the Galatians. Paul confirms that he presented his prophetic revelations, his encounter with the risen Lord and his *euangelion* to those of "repute." Paul asserts that he was given the charismatic "right hand" of *koinonia*, their confirmation that his experiences and prophetic interpretations were legitimate *among the Gentiles* (*not* among the Jews). Other oral forms, such as parables, miracle stories, dialogues, all guided by the prophetic utterance, were drawn into circulation to address the *sitz im leben* of the early *ecclesiae* until crystallized into narrative collections, i.e., the "gospels," and independent written sayings sources, such as the *Gospel of Thomas*, or in extended passion narratives, e.g., the Gospel of Mark. And so, methodologies such as form criticism, have fundamentally uncovered the history, development and use of traditions and *logia* preserved, adapted and created by the prophets of the early church, thereby capturing the work of the *charisma* of the Spirit within the prophetic movement of Paul's *ecclesiae*. The prophetic speakers are largely to be credited with the development of the oral forms and stories that moved through various stages as they were applied to the life situation and experiential needs of the adherents as primitive Christianity expanded into a syncretic Hellenistic-Roman

---

358. 1 Cor 14:1–5.

359. The interpretive words of the prophet applied to the life and death of Jesus.

360. See 1 Cor 2:9, and many other allusions including direct reference to the beatitudes as noted above.

361. 1 Cor 15:1–2; it is clear what Paul means by gospel in ch. 15 is the entire passion tradition, as well as related sayings.

world dominated by satanic and evil forces and tyrants that were soon to be displaced by the kingdom of God and his Christ.

Didaskolos

Paul moves to the third appointed *charisma* in the *ecclesia*, that of the "teacher," i.e., the *didaskalos*. The Greek word *disaskalos* is used only three times by Paul and only in his undisputed letters, with two of the three instances found in 1 Corinthians. The use of *didaskalos* was not uncommon however in the Synoptic Gospel tradition,[362] usually set in the context of controversy dialogues[363] (that is, where Jesus is challenged by enemies—usually minions, spies or informants of the Jerusalem elite—or sometimes by sympathetic scribes or Pharisees),[364] or where Jesus is asked to exorcise demons by parents or guardians.[365] The controversy dialogues and exorcisms usually result in a saying of the Lord that is the apex of the narrative event, certainly one that the *ecclesia* recognized as authoritative and useful for their own life situation; for example, whether or not taxes should be paid to Caesar:[366] The capstone of this particular dialogue narrative is a pronouncement saying, certainly one of Jesus' most important sayings in the context of the first-century Roman world for the *ecclesiae*: "Render to Caesar the things that are Caesar's and to God, the things that are God's." Adherents are instructed by the Lord as *didaskolos* to honor all taxes and duties due to the empire.[367] Of course, the decision to resist taxation or duty would result in persecution and social separation from the political order of the day, and perhaps also arrest and execution for sedition. Certainly, Paul knew this saying and commands its practice to the *ecclesiae*.[368] In the early stage of oral transmission and Paul's itinerant activity (i.e., 33–50 CE), indeed dating to Jesus' war on Satan, the issue for both adherents and their violent opponents centered on this question and charges of sedition and blasphemy. Clearly, Paul's *ecclesiae* faced exactly this accusation, and so a dangerous perilous risk crisis. This specific saying, known to Paul, attempted to mitigate that risk by presenting the opponents' accusation (i.e., confirming adherents were not cult members of a seditious movement).[369] Consequently, the *didaskolos* played a critical role in the ap-

---

362. Twelve times in Matthew and Mark, sixteen times in Luke, surprisingly with fewer parallels that at first one might imagine.

363. Since the saying is set in the context of a historical event (the narrative) during the life of Jesus, the recollection either comes from a witness, or is recalled by inspiration of the Spirit to a prophet of the risen Lord Jesus (this *does not* mean the event did not happen), which may then be applied by a *didaskalos*.

364. Luke 10:25, as to his action or understanding of torah or oral tradition.

365. Luke 8:49.

366. Matt 22:15–22.

367. Since the empire and the world were rapidly coming to an end with the return of the Messiah.

368. Rom 13:5–7.

369. For example, Jesus' response mutes legal witnesses—at least three—that attempt to convict

plication of *logia*, traditions and even prophecy to the *sitz im leben* of Paul's *ecclesiae*, allowing for defense and mitigation of perilous risks and threats.

Indeed, as *ecclesiae* were established in various cities, towns and villages of the Roman empire by itinerant *apostoloi* such as Paul or Kayfa (40–65 CE), their *sitz im leben* was unique to their challenges and risks, but were all characterized by a heightened eschatology of an impending *parousia*. Most adherents already struggled with subsistence survival in an imperial and hostile social and religious world—a struggle that was also susceptible to attack by demons, the rule of oppressive laws and onerous taxes, slavery and indentured servitude, hunger and starvation; a social world that required participation in pagan cultic and civic festivals and required public submission and oblation to the emperor as divine. Only guidance from the risen Lord as teacher, echoed in the use of *logia* by the *apostolos, propheteia, and didaskalos* as to how to mitigate various crises, helped to refine practices and responses to conflicts and how each were to be incorporated into the community facing the last days of the age.

Eventually, when the first generation of *apostoloi* and leaders had been murdered, executed or died (i.e., 36–90 CE), reliance on these *logia* and oral traditions became of paramount importance to the communities that had allegiance to them, and needed to fill their authoritative void—certainly, a perilous risk crisis.[370] In the canonical gospels, *logia* and traditions were placed around the passion narrative and therefore became crystallized, especially those *logia* and traditions that mitigated danger,[371] opposition, or explained the emerging problem concerning the delay of the *parousia*. The controversy dialogues were exceptionally useful, particularly those where Jesus is called "teacher" (e.g., Matt 22:15–22), as they effectively functioned as the authoritative instruction of the Lord to the wider *ecclesiae* as the written gospels emerged and displaced the oral trajectory. These traditions could be used to confirm to both secular authorities and opponents (Roman and local administrators and magistrates) that early Christians and their *ecclesiae* were no threat;[372] indeed, *that the object of its worship had commanded adherence to political authority, and also piety and God's justice*—certainly a noble answer that was acceptable in Roman society and impossible to

---

him of treason. The response becomes a source for the community's contemporary experience facing opponents who make similar accusations, in this case Diaspora Jewish opponents, who are generically labeled "Pharisees."

370. The Gospel of John is a clear example, but so too, the Gospel of Mark facing the destruction of Jerusalem.

371. For example, the formation of the Gospel of Mark coincided with the destruction of Jerusalem (68–70 CE), and the community's expectation of God's messianic, retributive Son of Man.

372. Thus, the controversies that arose in Jesus' life situation were not dissimilar to those faced by the expanding Way, and so these sayings of Jesus were pliable and useful for those, inspired by the Spirit, who were appointed by God as *didaskalos*, those who could readily apply them to the life situation of the *ecclesiae*.

condemn.[373] In the context of the Roman world a *didaskalos*[374] was respected, and the fact that the Christian Lord had instructed adherence to Roman and provincial taxation, represented the central command as to one's duties to the empire. This type of instruction as to one's place and responsibility in a terminal and hostile world, indeed one's role and responsibility as an adherent of the risen Lord anticipating the *parousia*, surely set the standard for *didaskaloi* in Paul's *ecclesiae*. As such, other *logia* embedded in controversy dialogues ascribed to the Lord as *didaskalos* functioned similarly and carried authority useful to the *didaskaloi* of Paul's *eccelsiae* (see other examples such as Mark 2:1–36, 11:27–12:44). These detailed social responsibilities that were cap stoned by the Lord's command to love one's neighbor.[375]

Consequently, the Lord as "teacher" provided a cadre of *logia* and traditions that provided not just guidance, but eschatological rules and commands that adherents must embrace in relation to social and political matters, many of which mitigated accusations and charges, thereby neutralizing perilous risks to the *ecclesiae*. Clearly the *ecclesiae* were susceptible to accusations of sedition, that is, for worshiping a crucified Jew whom they titled Lord and Savior—the same epithets attributed to the divine Caesar. Jewish opponents often charged them with blasphemy, as evidenced in Paul's letters. Consequently, the "teacher," such as those appointed by God in Paul's *ecclesiae*, would draw from *logia* of Jesus as Lord and *didaskalos*, providing authoritative guidance for such crises and conflicts, or their own teachings and interpretations arising from new *logia* given to *propheteia* and *apostoloi* by the risen Lord under the guidance

---

373. This particular saying on taxation is a good example of the timeless power of such sayings for the early church in a dynamic and challenging historical context. In this case, Jesus' saying is remembered because he is able to confound his opponents with a pronouncement that is apolitical, it escapes the charge of fostering sedition; where action (paying taxes) and service (rendering God his due love and respect) are both sublimated to God's justice alone without disenfranchising the listener from the responsibilities to ruling authorities, in other words, the saying was dynamic and applicable to multiple life situations of the *ecclesia* pointing to service to God and yet responsible citizenry. Later, both the church and individual adherent needed to answer the question, "Is allegiance to your coming Messiah, the Lord Jesus Christ [i.e., 'messiah' understood commonly as a political king, meaning a rejection of the current order—were they dangerous and subversives], or to Caesar?" Jesus' saying separates political from religious duty, but with the emphasis on service to God, allows for action for God to legitimize life decisions in the context of good citizenry. If Jesus were to instruct followers to not pay taxes, he would be calling for rebellion and raise expectations that he was a messianic pretender, like Judas the Galilean, CE 6, who rebelled against the census of Quirinius (Roman governor in the province of Syria, which included Palestine), imposed to raise taxes. This was the popular expectation, a political-military messiah, and was adopted by Pharisees and Sadducees, Zealots and the Essenes (an expectation that Jesus severely criticizes). That the saying had broad application to other life situations of the *ecclesia* is abundantly clear. Later the saying was used to prove that believers were to be good citizens of Rome—i.e., Jesus instructed his followers to pay taxes (Paul echoes the essence saying his introductory letter to the *ecclesia* in Rome, Rom 13:1–3, about 54/55 CE)—as early Christianity sought a futile legitimacy from Rome from the time of Paul to the fourth century when the emperor Constantine legalized Christianity and made it the state religion (i.e., the Edict of Milan, 313 CE).

374. *Didaskalos* was a familiar and respected designation in Hellenistic-Roman society, so calling Jesus "teacher" was relevant and meaningful.

375. Busse, *Fire*, 41–42.

of the Spirit. This would suggest that the *didaskalos* had access to a malleable oral tradition, including a collection of sayings at the time of 1 Corinthian's composition, to cite or expound upon if needed, or to use as a catalyst for new teachings on current issues, and to strengthen and sustain the *pistis* and *agape* of the *ecclesia*. But was this the only role of a *didaskalos* in Corinth?

While the Synoptic Gospels confirm the use of controversy sayings of Jesus for just this purpose, we do not initially find direct evidence that such sayings were presented by a *didaskalos* in Corinth; we only have *logia* cited by Paul. But, as noted, these were indeed used to contest and challenge the legitimacy of the claims and practices employed by the infiltrators, as well as provide the basis for a death curse being placed upon them.[376] Paul confirms that he taught "traditions" to the Corinthian adherents, which must have included *logia* of Jesus, whether from his war on Satan or from post-crucifixion encounters, Paul makes no distinction.[377] Certainly, the *didaskaloi* of Paul's *ecclesiae* emulated him and how he used *logia*. Consequently, while it is clear within the oral tradition that Jesus was addressed as "teacher," and that the *logia* embedded within the controversy dialogues and traditions were used combat and neutralize opponents based on evidence in both the synoptic tradition and 1 Corinthians, it is important to ascertain whether Paul intended a *didaskalos* to function only in this way in Corinth. Is the *charisma* of "teaching" the gift of defending the *ecclesia* from opponents by *confounding them* with *logia* of Jesus thereby neutralizing them and mitigating perilous risk? Or was the gift of "teaching" instead a didactic exemplary *charisma* that could be disassociated from *logia* of Jesus? In other words, does evidence suggest that it was also the *charisma* of exemplifying and extolling actions or practices that strengthened *agape*; that is, observable practices and actions of a *didaskalos* that evidenced the Spirit, strengthening the "body of Christ"? Since Paul rarely appeals to *logia* of Jesus, or to his ministry, or controversy dialogues from the oral tradition that were absorbed in the synoptic and Johannine traditions, it is most likely that the gift of teaching was indeed didactic, i.e., also an exemplary *charisma*.

Jesus demonstrated his teaching through what Norman Perrin and Joachim Jeremias describe as "parabolic actions,"[378] or actions that reveal, display and "teach" the nature and the will of God in the context of the inbreaking of the kingdom. Paul certainly displayed this same understanding of parabolic actions, as evidenced in his own life and itinerant mission founded on the *charisma* of *agape*. This understanding of "teaching" seems then to extend the role of a Spirit-gifted *didaskolos* beyond the employment of *logia* to *an active, exemplary role of demonstrating how to apply agape and live in it through actions that edify and build the ecclesia in the last days.*

---

376. The drunken participation in the consumption of the Lord's blood and body, making them susceptible to a death curse via association as a participant in his murder—they are guilty.

377. See 1 Cor 11:1–2; 2:9; and references to the beatitudes noted earlier in our study.

378. Perrin, *Rediscovering*, 107; Jeremias, *Parables*, 227.

So then, how would the *didaskalos* activate protective *agape* and thereby strengthen and edify the *ecclesia in Corinth*, and does this explain Paul's ranking of "teacher" as third in appointments by God and the Spirit? The Gospel of John provides the most provocative example of how the role of a *didaskalos* served for the edification and *agape* within the *ecclesia*, i.e., to strengthen and sustain it in the practice of *agape*, and so ward off Satan a demonic attack. In John, we find Jesus transforming the role of a teacher from didactic instructor to a demonstrator of *agape*, the selfless service of love to others.[379] *Jesus reverses the roles of servant and master and asserts that the action of agape by example is the true role of the teacher*: "If then, the Lord and Teacher, washed your feet, you also ought to wash one another's feet." The Gospel of John records a completely different set of traditions in the context of Jesus' last night with his close followers, including the assassin, Judas.[380] No longer are the Lord's Supper, bread and the wine the central shared event recorded that evening, underscoring the significance of the practice of love for one another as the ultimate act of the Lord-Teacher. Given this, the *charisma* of teaching was the ability to transform Torah Scripture and prophetic sayings and apostolic guidance into active examples of *agape* within the *ecclesiae* to up-build it and strengthen it, thereby protecting it. "Teaching" then meant displaying *agape* in tangible, sometimes shocking examples of service and care to the brethren to strengthen the adherents and assembly. Consequently, the traditional the role of a teacher, which was applied to Jesus by his exorcists, was literally turned on its head when Jesus took on the role of servant by humbly washing feet as if a slave, the lowest servant-performed task (that is why Kayfa is said to have refused Jesus). Jesus teaches the central place of *agape* is in actions, that is, he is "teaching" the disciples to render humble trusting service and *agape* to each other—*didaskaloi* then are the protectors of the *ecclesiae* by not only defending it with *logia*, but by the efficacious practice of *agape*. *Apostoloi* "plant," *propheteia* "water" and *didaskaloi* "grow" and protect the *ecclesiae* from all enemies, human and otherwise, by acting to ensure that *agape* permeates all things.[381]

This same emphasis on the master as servant is recorded in the passion narratives in the synoptic tradition at the Lord's Supper. But here the tradition of washing feet was jettisoned (or was not known) and replaced with a summary statement—a saying of Jesus about the true role of a master (i.e., teacher) and love: "But you are not like that, the greatest among you should be like the youngest, and the one who rules like the one who serves. For who is greater, the one who serves or the one who sits at the table? But I am one among you who serves."[382] Jesus' table service transformed

---

379. John 13:14.
380. John 13:10–11.
381. Busse, *Fire*, 76–77, 115, 122–23; Busse, *Jesus Resurrected*, 154.
382 Luke 21:26, 27.

the role of teacher/master to one who through the *charismata* of *didaskalos* tangibly demonstrated the Spirit's presence through *agape*.³⁸³

In Paul's *ecclesiae*, the *charisma of the didaskalos* was then the unique and powerful role of displaying and demonstrating the essence of torah and prophetic Scripture, sayings and traditions from Jesus, and guidance of the apostles through efficacious acts of *agape*, thus evidencing the presence of the Spirit of God, thereby validating its power to protect from evil, demonic influence and the curse of death in the shadow of judgment to come in the near *parousia*. Just as Jesus extends his role of *didaskalos* to a new level of action and service by washing the feet of his disciples at dinner (i.e., a parabolic action), so Paul understands the *charismata* of teaching as the gift of evoking powerful and protective *agape*, which brings about not just assurance but practices that evidence the Spirit of God is present, strengthening the *ecclesia* and warding off evil and death.

Confirmation of Charismata and the Practices of Paul's Ecclesiae

The infiltrating *apostoloi* who claim they possess the penultimate *charisma*, namely *glossolalia*, which is witnessed by Paul's adherents as unintelligible heavenly, or angelic language, cite it as the absolute proof they have achieved "kingly" status exclusively through their efficacious *gnosis* extracted from the *logia* of Jesus.³⁸⁴ By implication, they reject Paul's order of appointments, especially his claim to be an *apostolos*.³⁸⁵ True *apostolos* are, like they, *pneumatikoi*, guides and mystagogues, whose rites and practices lead initiates into revelatory *gnosis* and *sophia* that is salvific. Consequently, Paul's claim to be an *apostolos* of the *euangelion* is not inconsequential—it is the claim of a deceived fool or a satanic charlatan. As a deceiver, he is guilty *agnosis*, a most serious charge, i.e., leading his adherents into ignorance, thereby mystically leaving them mired in a satanically corrupted world that is infected with the curse of death.

In response, Paul asserts that only he and his adherents have the legitimate *charisma* of *glossolalia*, and that his is even more effusive. More, he has stressed that the *charisma* of *glossolalia* is only one of the many *charismata* of the *pneumatos hagiou*, and as such, the "same Spirit" that awards legitimate *glossolalia* also awards various *charismata* to every adherent as it wills. None provide proof of having achieved divinity, as legitimate *charismata* are provided by God only to strengthen the *ecclesia*, and its *pistis* and *agape* until the *parousia*, thereby protecting the *ecclesia* from the attack and infiltration of Satan and his demons. While all *charismata* are of equal in value, as

---

383. And the omitted tradition of washing the feet of the disciples—it is not a tradition that may have been known to the synoptic editors and writers, or was did not fit within the life situation at that time; I have to acknowledge that Paul does not mention the practice itself, but certainly understands his life as a kind of "parabolic action," see 2 Cor 11:16–33.

384. As the agent of saving wisdom of God, not as coming Messiah.

385. Notice that Paul lists *glossolalia* last, behind even "helpers" and "administrators"—it is placed last because it provides the least benefit is building *agape* and strengthening the *ecclesia*.

all help sustain and protect the living "the body of Christ" from the dark forces, *glossolalia*, unless interpreted and found to edify and strengthen the *ecclesia*, is to be silenced. By inference, Paul calls on the *apostoloi* (repeated later) to be silent! Legitimate *charisma* must foster *agape* for the benefit of the *ecclesia* in the last days. More, only this full array of *charismata* evidences the actual presence of the true Spirit of God. And they must be proven and tested: Even a prophet that is gifted with application of torah and Scripture and the *logia* of Jesus (including those of the risen Lord) to events and crises faced by the *ecclesiae* are subject to the further interpretation and evaluation of other prophets within that *ecclesia*. Their prophetic words must be "checked," or better confirmed and validated, by fellow prophets. And more, *they must then be translated into actions*[386] and practices of *agape* by the *didaskalos* to actualize the application of the prophet's utterances given by the Spirit to the adherents and *ecclesia*. Only the true *apostolos*, who is the catalyst for spread of the *euangelion*, the efficacious gospel of divine protection and *agape* given by God in the last days of the age, has access to all of these *charismata*, not just *glossolalia, and employs them as provided by the Spirit to build God's community for the kingdom of God*. *Pistis* in the *euangelion* of Jesus as Lord and Christ is made salvific, if maintained to the *parousia*, or if one dies and "sleeps," awaiting the metamorphosis of resurrection into a new and divine *soma*. Consequently, *glossolalia* is solely a confirmation of unity with the legitimate Spirit of God, the *ecclesia* of *pistis* and *agape*, and *elpis* of salvation.

Paul rejects then all elitism, arrogance or claim to special standing apart from his *euangelion* and *ecclesiae* because they are contrary to *agape*. Paul, employing the *logoi* of Jesus, warns there is perilous risk—that they will become like demons that devour the innocent and unprotected if they continue errant practices that ignore *agape*:

> You, my brothers and sisters, were called to be free. But do not use your freedom to indulge the flesh; rather, serve one another humbly in love. For the entire law is fulfilled in keeping this one command: "Love your neighbor as yourself." If you *bite and devour each other*, watch out or *you will be consumed by each other*.[387]

Paul's list of the "acts of the flesh" is remarkably similar to the traits identified thus far in an analysis of the characteristics of the opponents in Corinth. Paul warns that such practices lead to the curse of death:

> The acts of the flesh are obvious: sexual immorality, impurity and debauchery; idolatry and witchcraft; hatred, discord, jealousy, fits of rage, selfish ambition, dissensions, factions and envy; drunkenness, orgies, and the like.

---

386. A prime example is Paul's workshop ministry and his refusal to take compensation to prevent any suspicion of personal motive and remove any burden.

387. Gal 5:13–15.

I warn you, as I did before, that those who live like this will not inherit the kingdom of God.[388]

The risk of the dissolution of the *ecclesia* from the influence of such demonic opponents was not only real, but also fraught with danger for Paul, for if the *ecclesia* disbands, his commission as an apostle of risen Christ had failed, and the son whom he loves will find him wanting when he is present.[389] Consequently, this is a complex matter of interactions never before experienced, but Paul's complete confidence and faith are based on his knowledge that the *Spirit's selection of gifts and appointments are intentional.*[390] For Paul, *charismata are numerous, unlimited, but all of equal importance because they are given by the Spirit* and must be practiced with *agape*, while the appointments of the Spirit ensure the interaction of *charismata* strengthen the bonds of love in the *ecclesia*. Thus, Paul is not intending to establish hierarchical or ecclesiastical order with these instructions; only ensure that "love abounds,"[391] for the *ecclesia* is composed of the children of God that are under attack. This is important to understand given that Paul then provides a general list of the other *charismata*: ". . . then workers of miracles, then healers, helpers and administrators [not in the sense of hierarchical power], *and speakers in various types of tongues.*"[392] Paul's complete list of appointments demonstrates the emphasis on up building of the *ecclesia* in *agape*. He turns to the least of the gifts, *glossolalia*.

Glossolalia

It is obvious that Paul intentionally lists *glossolalia last*, and that he describes the legitimate gift of the Spirit differently than how it is manifested among the opponents in Corinth,[393] i.e., for Paul *glossolalia* is speaking in "various types of tongues." Paul's choice of words is important. The opponents practice *glossolalia* as unintelligible language—there is no interpreter—which is understood by them to signifying full reception of divine knowledge and their reclaimed divinity, and so, escape from deadly ignorance. *Glossolalia* demonstrates the achievement of salvation brought by the divine messenger, the *Soter*, the Living One, Jesus. It is an individual *charisma* having been achieved through their struggle to break through ignorance (with the help of a

---

388. Gal 5:19–21.
389. See 1 Cor 2:20.
390. 1 Cor 12:4, 7.
391. See Phil 1:9.
392. 1 Cor 12:28b.

393. If Paul would have recognized the appointment and the gift of *glossolalia* first, and not broadened the definition of it beyond the practice of the opponent, the primitive church would have become nothing more than gnostic cult or another mystery cult, where transformation and miracle define the initiate's success and position with the cult deity, not the democratization of gifts for the purposes of establishing the *community of love* that anticipates the soon arrival of God in history.

guide, the "super-apostles," and special rites, including esoteric baptism), to not only comprehend but embrace the transformative *dunamis* of divine *gnosis* and *sophia*, and so, it is an elitist gift. But as noted, Paul places *glossolalia* as the last appointment for this reason, as it is of God and the Spirit only if it edifies *agape* and protects the *ecclesia* of God—it acts as a democratized, not elitist, *charisma*. The infiltrators *glossolalia*, as noted, is disruptive, arrogantly employed—it edifies only the speaker,[394] is unilateral,[395] and fails to serve *agape*. For Paul, *glossolalia* is not a *charisma* of the Spirit unless there is *charisma* of interpretation, which then engages the prophets and teachers.

Paul is aware that those outside the *ecclesia* recognize *glossolalia* as miraculous, a proof of power,[396] as it has attracted potential adherents.[397] Paul and his adherents have evidently invited outsiders into the assembly who witness the translation of heavenly language, or languages, into words, practices or knowledge of divine *agape*. Paul not only confirms he has this *charisma*, but more abundantly than any of the opponents.[398] Indeed, like them, when he speaks in heavenly tongues he does not "use his mind,"[399] meaning, it is an ecstatic experience that comes from the Spirit as channeling the divine words through the chosen speaker. Such words are most typically as an utterance of praise, a song, or perhaps a poem, but all for the edification of the "body" of Christ *by praising God*.[400] Paul also understands *glossolalia* more expansively than the opponents, i.e., also as the gift of understanding and speaking in foreign languages unknown to the adherent (but this gift he does not specifically indicate he has), such as described in Acts.[401] In fact, Paul does not distinguish between the gifts of speaking in heavenly ecstatic or unknown foreign languages because both require the *charisma of interpretation*. What the opponents are experiencing is dangerous. It should be silenced and forbidden. Paul effectively neutralizes the legitimacy of the infiltrators' practice of *glossolalia*, and the subsequent claims made. Then in a dramatic and beautiful didactic poem, Paul describes the efficacious and salvific *euangelion* of "the more excellent Way,"[402] the way of *agape*.

394. 1 Cor 14:4.

395. 1 Cor 14:23, 27.

396 See 14:22; unfortunately an understanding that is distorted and in perfect harmony with the arrogance of the opponents who engage in public libertine behaviors and sexual promiscuity to demonstrate their divine position and merit before God—*glossolalia* would be publicly employed to "awe" others and neglect its purpose to build up the *ecclesia*. *Glossolalia* was known to have been practiced in the cult of Apollo and other mystery cults.

397. See Acts 2 and the thousands added to the church in one day—the key difference in Acts versus the opponents' experience is that the speakers in Acts were understood in "various languages."

398. 1 Cor 14:8.

399. 1 Cor 14:9.

400. 1 Cor 14:14, 16–17.

401. See the description of "tongues of fire" in Jerusalem during Pentecost, Acts 2:1–4, which was the outpouring of the Spirit allowing uneducated Palestinian and Galilean Jews to speak intelligibly to Diaspora Jews on pilgrimage to the city during the religious holiday in their own foreign language.

402. 1 Cor 12:31b.

The More Excellent Way: Efficacious *Agape* as Mitigation to Satan and the Curse of Death

It is important before beginning an excurses on Paul's designation of adherents to the *euangelion* as participants in "the more excellent Way" to recognize Paul's use this designation as both intentional[403] and transformational.[404] Paul embraces this designation as the sole and proper label of the charismatic *pistis* of his adherents in the salvific *euangelion* of Jesus Christ, whose mitigation of perilous risks, including demonic attack and death, is repeatedly confirmed by the *charismata* and practice of protective divine *agape*, "the Way," instead of choosing others that concurrently circulated. The risk question is why this designation versus others that concurrently circulated and does its use neutralize risks introduced by the infiltrating Jerusalem *apostoloi*?

To begin, it is clear that Paul selects *hodos*, "the Way," intentionally. We know this because there were other contemporary designations of the Jesus movement, albeit those of enemies, which will be explored below. *Hodos* was likely the earliest self-designations adopted by the exorcists of Jesus post resurrection.[405] It appears in all layers of the Jesus tradition (the Synoptics, Q), as well as in Acts, Paul's undisputed letters and the Johannine tradition. As such, this was the designation adopted by Jesus' exorcists and their earliest adherents before Paul's encounter with the risen Lord on the road to Damascus, and was still in use when Paul met Apollos in Ephesus. Paul specifically says that he is "a follower of the Way" when under examination of the Roman Governor of Samaria, Marcus Antonius Felix in 56–58 CE, on accusations brought by Ananias (i.e., the Roman appointed High Priest that turned Jesus over to the Romans).[406] Claiming to be a follower *of the way* versus a follower of Jesus Christ as Lord, i.e., a dangerous Galilean messianic movement or a movement associated with the practices of dark magic and evil that led Jesus to be crucified as an "evil-doer" (see below), echoes a risk choice by the remaining exorcists to mitigate peril of capture, torture and execution. It reflects a risk term used in secrecy among a fringe affiliation of those hunted, considered outcasts and criminals by authorities, clearly an apolitical affiliation that would help avoid detection or retribution. Another risk mitigation would be the use of *hodos* also as a claim to a moral or philosophical path of life, practices that were deemed virtuous or even holy, versus charges of participation in the cult of Jesus that not only expects but also engages in cult practices, the consumption of flesh and blood, and calls on and urges by these magical practices the termination of demonic imperialism and the overthrow of all authorities, including Rome, at the *parousia*—exactly the charges later brought by Roman accusers. Conse-

---

403. Paul adopts the most primitive designation of the adherents for their *pistis* in the *euangelion* as "the Way" known from New Testament traditions.

404. Paul expands the primitive meaning of the Way to the level of new theological and interpretive work by Jewish scholars such as Philo of Alexandria—this will be made more clear below.

405. See Acts 9:1–4.

406. John 14:6; see also Acts 18:25; 19:9, 23; 22:4; 24:14, 22.

quently, *hodos* is consistent with a practice of perilous risk mitigation, and stand in contrast to others employed.

Paul's adherents in 1 Corinthians clearly know *hodos* to be their self-designation. Indeed, by stating at the outset that he will show them the *huperbolen hodos*, Paul confirms this and concurrently rejects exclusivist claims to *hodos* made by the intruders. Indeed, a half-century later, the Didache verifies that the early church had resisted competing practices and theologies linked to *hodos* by the developing an authorized description of the authentic *hodos*, and then describing the two "ways," the errant and the true way of God. In 1 Corinthians, Paul then must intentionally have employed *hodos* because the Jerusalem infiltrators claimed *hodos* and their esoteric practices and salvific *gnosis* drawn from their collection of *logia* to be its only legitimate expression. Paul seeks to mitigate this claim by showing the *huperbolen hodos*, which will stand in contrast to the deadly *hodos* of his enemies.

Another designation, one that very early and paralleled "the Way," was the label given to the followers of Jesus by fierce and violent opponents (e.g., such as those aligned with Saul of Tarsus, bent on the annihilation of the followers of Jesus), i.e., aristocratic sympathizers with Rome, as well as the Roman authorities who executed Jesus and who dispatched other messianic rebellious movements;[407] namely, "the Nazarenes."[408] This label had dangerous connotations. It intentionally tied those who followed Jesus with his condemnation as the crucified "evil doer" of Galilee. Similar to the derogatory use of "Galilean" as rebels, hicks and the ignorant, this more specific identification of the Nazarenes was intended to point to the village in Galilee famous for producing the possessed sorcerer of Nazareth. Consequently, while both were slanderous and implied a rebellious citizenry based on history and reputation,[409] Nazarenes were considered dangerous—the dark magician's disciples, exorcists and sorcerers, consorts with evil and Beelzebul. Tertullus, the advocate speaking against Paul who represented Ananias,[410] used this term before Felix by calling Paul a "ringleader of the sect of the Nazarene."[411]

By contrast the followers of Jesus used term "the Way" to neutralize various risks. It was an "open term," meaning it had an invitational tone and actionable character adherents must exhibit publicly that Paul does not hesitate to claim is from God. The "Way" implied practices that were demonstrable and observable, beneficial to those in need and hungry—personal and charismatic actions contrary

---

407. It preceded the destruction of the temple certainly.

408. Most likely a Semitism for "sons of the Nazarene."

409. Corinthian also implied drunkenness, debauchery, and sexual promiscuity.

410. Ananias, son of Nebelos, was high priest from approximately 46–60 CE, described as complicit with the Romans, which ultimately led to his death by the hand of his own people.

411. See Acts 24:5b, Paul causes riots and is accused of desecrating the temple by bringing a Gentile into its sacred precincts.

to those who followed Beelzebul or consorted with demons.[412] Practicing "the Way" however did not necessarily imply it was always apolitical, as the Essenes who were contemporaries of Jesus and Paul also designated their community as "the way."[413] The Essenes labeled themselves "sons of light," "the poor," and community of "the perfect of the way." It is clear that the Essenes community and teachings, at least as represented in the Qumran Dead Sea Scrolls,[414] differentiated their practices of the Way by contextualizing them in a dualistic contention between God and his enemies, where there were polarizing peoples of the "light" or "darkness" and that a war between the sons of both was about to be waged.[415] Of course, the *ecclesia* of *agape* had little to do with this view of "the Way"[416]—that is, until the *parousia*, which brought divine intervention (i.e., not attack of the Sons of Light), death and judgment to the wicked, and the destruction of the enemies of God.

In 1 Corinthians, Paul provides the earliest and most elaborate description of the *huperbolen odon*, "*the more excellent*" *way* for followers of Jesus *pre-parousia* that is found in the New Testament. It is important to point out that Paul is intentionally expanding the original designation of "the Way," to the "*more excellent* Way." Samuel Sandmel notes that "Judaism and the Church [had] moved along the road to separation."[417] Paul was not saying, like later generations of Christians and subsequent formal doctrines made claim, that the Jews are to be rejected. On the contrary, for Paul there was no distinction between Jew and Greek (i.e., Gentile); all had equal access to "the Way," the higher torah, and so, it was the "more excellent Way," which by implication, rejected any form of elitist *gnosis*. As such, Paul understood his *ecclesia* as different from both paganism and Palestinian Judaism, or any form "human wisdom" and *gnosis*—it was the new *agioi*, the *tekna tou Theou*, the fulfilled expression and presence of the eschatological salvation of God that was encountered and activated

---

412. That is, publicly in acts of charity, kindness, fairness, and love, whether in the village or metropolis—Acts 2:42–47, "They devoted themselves to the apostles' teaching and to fellowship, to the breaking of bread and to prayer. Everyone was filled with awe at the many wonders and signs performed by the apostles. All the believers were together and had everything in common. They sold property and possessions to give to anyone who had need. Every day they continued to meet together in the temple courts. They broke bread in their homes and ate together with glad and sincere hearts, praising God and enjoying the favor of all the people. And the Lord added to their number daily those who were being saved."

413. Dead Sea Scrolls, *Rule of the Community*, "the perfect of the way."

414. See Allegro, *Dead Sea Scrolls*, "War of the Sons of Light and Sons of Darkness."

415. Literally a physical war in the eschatological context of the annihilation of the enemies of God in the final battle of good versus evil; this battle did occur after the destruction of Jerusalem in 70 CE, as Josephus reports the Essenes were instigators in the war against Rome and that they were likely exterminated by the Romans near Qumran.

416. Paul does allude to dualistic language in 1 Thessalonians, perhaps indicating that some of the Jews there had some affiliation with the Essenes: "You are all children of the light and children of the day. We do not belong to the night or to the darkness. So then, let us not be like others, who are asleep, but let us be awake and sober," 1 Thess 5:5–6.

417. Sandmel, *Jewish Understanding*, 65–71, in particular, and also 63.

by *pistis* in the efficacious and salvific *euangelion* of Jesus as the crucified Lord, now Christ; that *pistis* and the *ecclesia* endowed Paul's adherents with various *charismata* of the Spirit, confirming *elpis* in the immanent general resurrection and *parousia*, strengthening and assuring the *ecclesia* of its safety from peril; that its practice of divine *agape* repulsed satanic forces and deadly deception of enemies (including the infiltrators) until that day. Consequently, Paul can "turn on the Jews, and even speak vulgarly of them (Phil 3:2; also Gal 5:12), but he cannot forget he is a Jew."[418]

As such, Paul, a Hellenistic Jew who eventually operated outside the influence of the literalist view of the law in Palestine,[419] is able to absorb the influence of Greek thought on the written, or "lower" law, and contrast it with the "natural" law, which is the *"higher" law that reveals the very will and nature of God.* Writers contemporary with Paul, such as the Philo of Alexandria,[420] the Hellenistic Jewish philosopher[421] and theologian,[422] claimed through their examples how the law of Moses only reflected this *higher*, natural law of God. Adhering to the rituals and literalist interpretation of the written law could not lead one to attain salvation, nor could the law even be maintained perfectly by any individual. Indeed, Greek philosophy condemned written law as the tool of both the good but also tyrants who twisted it to their own desires,[423] and so, identified any written codification with the *lower* law. Sandmel asserts that Paul himself recognized this dichotomy and sought the higher law,[424] but only in the context of his *euangelion*, the tangible expressions of it being the *ecclesia* of the cross, *pistis* and *agape* until the parousia. He was the *apostolos* of this higher law, the more excellent way, that trumped the written law, secret *logia* or elitist *gnosis*.

Thus, to Philo and to Paul, the written law could only point out transgressions, and so, both sought out the higher law to embrace the very nature and will of God. The inadequacy in the law was for Sandmel clearly reflected in Paul's outcry, "Wretched man that I am, who will deliver me from this body of death,"[425] a statement that preceded Paul's conversion and encapsulated the struggle imbedded in Paul's personal encounter with the higher, natural law of God.[426] It was only when Paul embraced *pistis*

---

418. Ibid., 63–64.

419. Such as the separatists such as the Pharisees and Sadducees.

420. 20 BCE–50 CE, a contemporary of Paul.

421. Under the significant influence of Stoicism, i.e., God's essence flows into the material world and infuses it with divinity revealed in divine reason, the *logos*.

422. Using philosophy, he demonstrates that the law of Moses reveals the divine reason and universal truths of God.

423. Sandmel, *Jewish Understanding*, 65.

424. Paul's statement that he was "zealous" for the traditions of his father may have meant that he moved beyond the literal to the "higher" law, so he could justify brutal persecution and "lay waste" to the church because the followers of Jesus the evildoer was a minion of Beelzebul and perverted Scripture and God's will and nature.

425. Rom 7:24.

426. Sandmel does not attribute this to Paul's resurrection encounter with Jesus, but more of an intellectual inspiration that preceded the event.

in the *euangelion* of Jesus Christ that he was able, by revelation of God and encounters with the risen Lord, to understand the essence of the higher law and escape the curse of death. Paul found *pistis* in the *euangelion* of Christ crucified to be the essence of the "higher law," i.e., through *faith alone* in the efficacious and salvific *euangelion* one received God's forgiveness, acceptance and *agape*. God's will and nature become active—that is, he is *Abba'*, the father of the *tekna tou Theou*, who protects each adherent of *pistis* by his *agape*. And so, Paul's adherent in the *euangelion* embraces *agape*, which is the essence of making active and present in this world the higher law of God, i.e., the "more excellent way."

Paul uses numerous examples to demonstrate that the "lower law," the written law, pointed to the "higher" natural law of God, which for Paul is that *pistis* in the *euangelion* activates divine *agape* and justification, just as it had for Abraham, the father of the faith. Paul, and Jesus of Nazareth, summarized the entire law by blending adherence to it[427] with submitting to its "natural" expectation found in loving one's neighbor, i.e., complete faith in the *euangelion* of *agape*.[428] Abraham, Isaac and Jacob *were justified by their faith alone*, just as *pistis* in the *euangelion* results in *agape*. The conclusion then is powerful and important, and its implications are helpful in understanding Paul's plea for the opponents to adopt "the more excellent Way," namely, to embrace the nature and will of God, which is not only beyond *logia* and law, it is only active and fully efficacious in the *euangelion* and its outcome, *pistis* and active divine *agape*. Thus, 1 Cor 13:1–13 is clearly consistent with the context of the preceding content, if not its culmination. The *huperbolen odon* he describes is completely foreign to separatism, elitism, dualistic conflict, or the arrogant and dismissive behavior of Paul's opponents. *Agape* stands apart from and above all of these, yet defines and fulfills the law. Paul therefore expounds on the Way of God, the "higher law" or "more excellent way," to the Corinthians. Indeed, 1 Cor 13:1–13 is the earliest and most pure form of the outcome of *pistis* in the *euangelion* proclaimed and instituted by Paul of Tarsus, *apostolos* of Jesus Christ.

In 1 Corinthians 13, we find Paul's presentation of the "higher law," the divine love of God,[429] *agape*, which both envelopes and defines the life and practices of the baptized, faithful and justified adherents in the last days of the age. This section on *agape* is clearly from Paul's own hand—it is not only coherent with the context Paul's life situation in Corinth but also reflects the core message he proclaims in all of his undisputed letters to his *ecclesiae*, or to individuals.[430] Even more, Paul has been anticipating this section of the letter almost from the beginning. Each of the foregoing situational issues he addresses builds toward *agape*, the *more excellent way* for the *tekna*

---

427. Matt 22:37, by loving God with one's entire heart, soul, strength and mind.

428. See Matt 22:36–40; Jesus makes equal this second statement of love for one's neighbor, i.e., and the "second is like it . . ."

429. God, who comes to his new children as Abba', the intimate relationship of child and father.

430. 1 Thess 3:11–12; Gal 5:13–15; Phil 1:9; Rom 12:9–13; Phlm 1:9.

tou Theou—the adopted child of God. While his initial words are directed certainly at the infiltrators,[431] they are also addressed to the *ecclesia* as well as each adherent. Paul's comparison of divine *agape* with the human arrogance of the infiltrators condemns, indeed curses, their destructive influence on the *ecclesia*. Thus, the majority of the negative comparisons Paul makes[432] in 1 Cor 13:1–13 are already embedded in the earlier sections of the letter, i.e., Paul summarizes his foregoing criticism and his pleas and appeals, by describing by contrast *the excellent Way* with the errant and doomed way of the infiltrators.

On the whole, Paul's didactic poem in 1 Corinthians 13 may be properly described as the "Pauline beatitudes." According to Matthew's gospel, Jesus "sharpened the law" and provided the higher torah by elevating the essence of the law above legal or ritual stipulations to the adoption of divine attributes (i.e., the higher law),[433] culminating in Jesus' call to love *even one's enemies*. Paul similarly elevates *agape* to the divine attribute of the true and adopted *tekna tou Theou*, leaving by comparison the errant practices subject to judgment, error and rejection. Even more, now in the days of blessing with the outpouring of the Spirit awarded to each of the new children of Abba', it is especially the *charismata* that must exemplify divine *agape*—indeed, they are selected by the Spirit to edify and strengthen both the brethren and become inspiration for those outside the community to seek admission to the Way and to *elpis*. Consequently, *there are two concurrent paths or ways of practice operative in Corinth*. For Paul, one mitigates the perilous risk of death and satanic destruction through *agape*, while the other is errant, cursed and deadly because it rejects *agape*. Those who encounter the *euangelion* and embrace it with *pistis* and *agape* are endowed with the protection. The infiltrating *pneumatikoi*, the Jerusalem *apostoloi* who make claim to salvific *gnosis*, encourage chaos and dissension, are arrogant and divisive, and engage in libertine practices that not only ignore *agape*, but ravage it intentionally. It is they who face the curse of death. For Paul, the contrast of paths between the adherents and the opponents could not be more stark or dangerous.

Consequently, Paul identifies two paths in 1 Corinthians 13, namely, *the Way of excellence, huperbolen odon*, and the *Way of emptiness*, what Paul calls "nothingness." Of course, by implication, Paul stresses that the end of the infiltrators' elitist practices will be annihilation, as they are doomed. And so Paul begins by clearly addressing the perilous risk facing the *pneumatikoi*: "If I speak in the *tongues of men and of angels, but have not love*, I am a noisy gong or clanging symbol."[434]

There is no doubt that here Paul is describing the opponents' *glossolalia*.[435] Without interpretation and therefore understanding (comprehension), the sounds they ut-

---

431. 1 Cor 13:1–3 in particular, but also in the contrasts of love and emptiness in 4–13.
432. Literally, Paul is comparing "two ways."
433. Reflected in Matt 5:17–48.
434. 1 Cor 13:1.
435. The cult of Dionysus included ecstatic speech during intoxicated celebrations, where they

ter, primarily what they claim as divine or heavenly language[436] is not just empty and worthless, but satanic and deceptive. The indecipherable sounds are compared to "a noisy gong [*chalkos echon*] or clanging cymbal [*kumbalon alalazon*]," both instruments used in pagan cultic rituals and processions, i.e., the music of demons. It is possible that instruments were used in the *ecclesia* during gatherings to accompany early hymns, songs or chants to represent to presence of the Lord or the Spirit.[437] A special and very ancient pair of cymbals (or possibly a plate that was struck) was in the care of a special priest used in the second temple. The sound was unique but harmonious, remembered, and was used to give the signal for the Levites to chant the psalms.[438] Paul's reference is to pagan instruments used in cultic worship, processions, rituals and feasts. For Paul to associate the *glossolalia* of the *pneumatikoi* with pagan cultic instruments was to identify the origin of their *logoi* as demonic, and that the risk of annihilation (i.e., the way to "nothingness") will be the outcome of their practices.

The term "tongues of angels" (*glossais angelon*) is deliberately chosen by Paul, and designates speaking in an angelic dialect(s), or a form of "heavenly speaking." Since there are no New Testament examples of angelic dialect other than a possible allusion to such language heard by Paul in 2 Cor 12:4 during his own heavenly experience,[439] or Heb 1:4, the mention of the name of Jesus as superior to that of the angels,[440] we must look at contemporaneous Jewish or Hellenistic literature.

There is one striking passage in the *Testament of Job*,[441] which is a Jewish pseudepigraphical document that addresses "endurance in troubled times."[442] Several angelic dialects are accessible once one achieves *gnosis*. Job transfers his worldly and spiritual possessions to his sons and daughters.[443] His daughters receive his "better inheritance," that is, his spiritual knowledge or *gnosis*. When they do, they are released from concerns and desires of the world and are free to pursue the new spiritual prowess and access to heavenly realm and angelic beings, including even the *archai*, cherubim and other heavenly beings. Job provides them with magical "bands" or "sashes" that

---

cried out "*Eue Saboe*," untranslatable words.

436. Namely, the "tongues of angels."

437. Or that some offered this talent when the *ecclesiae* came together; if they were inappropriate, do recall that Paul criticizes these gatherings for the Lord's Supper as having deteriorated into an offensive drunken, festive event instead of an event of *koinonia* and love; if positively used, I must add that they could have accompanied early Christian hymns as hymns were presented in Corinth during the gathering of the whole ecclesia as Paul states in 14:26.

438. Hirsh, *Jewish Encyclopedia*, "Cymbals."

439. "And I know that this man was caught up into Paradise [*paradeison*]—whether in the body or out of the body, I do not know, God knows—and he heard ineffable words [*arreta remata*, or *unspeakable declarations*] that cannot be told, which man may not utter."

440. See Hebrews, about 85 CE, twenty years after the execution of Paul: ". . . having become as much superior to angels as the name he has obtained is more excellent than theirs."

441 Composed between 100 BCE to 100 CE.

442. See Nickelsburg, *Jewish Literature*, 247.

443. Testament of Job, 48–50.

provide this access, and they obtain the ability to speak to various ranks of angels in their language. This is intelligible only to those angels, and is accessed through secret *gnosis*, that is, special *logia* provided by Job through the bands and sashes. Notably, it is the *women* who are given access to the angelic dialects.[444] Originating in Egypt[445] the Testament of Job is roughly contemporaneous with Pauline writings. As such, the role of the women as the true holders of *gnosis* and angelic language begs the question: Did the infiltrating *pneumatikoi* include women who accompanied the Jewish male *apostoloi* to Corinth, evidenced both by his admonitions and in his answer to the questions sent to him?[446]

To begin, there is no evidence that women exclusively spoke *glossais angelon*, or exhibited the *charisma* of *glossolalia*, or that there were Jewish women *pneumatikoi* in Corinth,[447] as Paul never confronts Jewish women, and more, he flatly says he has this *charisma* himself. It is also unlikely that Apollos of Alexandria would have brought such ecstatic practices to Corinth. Apollos, a male Jew and follower of John the Baptist, did not exhibit *glossolalia*, but was a gifted *didaskalos*.[448] Indeed, risk analysis has confirmed that the infiltrators were Jewish males from Jerusalem who disdained and demeaned women, considering them corrupted and evil, and so, shunned them (that is, other than for gratuitous sexual relations to demonstrate that as *pneumatikoi* they were free from a corrupted, satanic world). As a result, there is no correlation between the women portrayed in *Testament of Job* and the infiltrators in Corinth. Paul only infers that the *charisma* of *glossias angelon* was claimed his enemies, those of *gnosis*.

Paul next moves to the "higher" *charismata*, that is, he moves from speaking in tongues (*glossolalia*), to prophecy (*propheteia*), the *charisma* that Paul previously listed as second only to that of *apostolos*. In a devastating warning as to their perilous risk, Paul states:

> And if I have *prophetic powers*, and *understand all mysteries* [*sophia*] and *knowledge* [*gnosis*], and if I have faith [*pistis*] so as to remove mountains, *but have not love, I am nothing* [*outhen eimi*].[449]

---

444. Women did participate in the cult of Demeter.

445. Again, one might postulate a connection with Apollos from Alexandria, Egypt, although Acts is clear that Apollos was "eloquent," but that he was a follower of John the Baptist, not a Jewish gnostic movement or background in wisdom literature—exposure is possible, if not likely, however.

446. In other cults, such as that of Demeter, there were religious festivals for women exclusively, such as the Thesmophria. Other cults included ecstatic language.

447. While this might appear helpful as an explanation for the awkward passage in 1 Cor 14:34 concerning women who should keep silent in the *ecclesia*, i.e., Paul would be supposedly silencing the unruly women opponents by forbidding them to speak in indecipherable heavenly dialects. However, as has been demonstrated, the passage about the silence of women *is unquestionably not from Paul's hand*. It is contrary to his many statements on the equality and importance of women in the *ecclesia* and the Way—Chloe, Phoebe, and Junias are all examples previously discussed.

448. 1 Cor 3:6.

449. 1 Cor 13:2.

In this remarkably complex and important indictment of his enemies' grave error, one that captures the essence of the conflict with the *pneumatikoi*, Paul cites the specific *charismata* claimed by the infiltrators to be exclusively theirs and as proof of their divine state (i.e., *propheteia*, *sophia* and *gnosis*). He links these *charismata* with a saying of the Lord on the efficacious power of *pistis*, but then subjugates both the *charismata* and even the *logoi* of the Lord to the *charisma* and practice of *agape*. *Propheteia*, *sophia* and *gnosis* are only valid (i.e., of the Spirit of God) if they strengthen *agape* within the *ecclesiae*, the "body of Christ," until the *parousia*. Those who practice them without *agape* have "nothing," and are deceived and susceptible to peril. Consequently, Paul is sternly warning the *pneumatikoi* that they face annihilation. Paul also contextualizes use of the *logia*: Even the most authoritative *logoi* of the Lord are subservient to the test of *agape* or they become errantly interpreted and employed leading to "nothingness." As such, Paul forcefully rejects any esoteric interpretation of *logia* of the Lord, particularly those that have been collected by the *pneumatikoi*, if they conflict with the *euangelion* and fail to fortify *agape* and protect *ecclesia* from satanic force. Based on Paul's association of *propheteia* with *gnosis* and *sophia*, it is clear that the *pneumatikoi* claim that prophecy informed which *logia* to collect, the salvific *gnosis* and *sophia* they revealed, which in turn awoke them to their divine condition, making them "kings" over the corrupted world.[450]

Paul is the first witness to the formation of esoteric written sayings documents in the New Testament. The oral malleability evidenced in Paul's use of *logoi* and *logia* of the Lord, where legitimate prophetic or didactic interpretation of them is *agape* dependent and set in the context of the *euangelion* and the *sitz im leben* of the *ecclesia*, is lost. Such alternate trajectories have been documented by Koester, Robinson and others,[451] and continued into the second century, with altering versions of sayings being employed for vying theological purposes.[452] Once interpreted and vested with exclusivist "certainty," written collections of *logia* by their nature became schismatic to competing claims. This, of course, included Paul's subjugation of *logia* and *logoi* of the Lord to the *euangelion*, *pistis* and *agape*, and intense expectation of immanent *parousia*, as contained in his letters. As such, it is clear that Paul first encounters this competing trajectory in the infiltrators' *logia* document.

---

450. Circulating orally for fifty years before being compiled in 80–85 CE. Koester and Patterson, *Authentic Sayings*, 36; sayings that reflect the beatitudes are found in Q and Thomas, conclusively demonstrating the existence of written sayings documents very early, and certainly before the composition of the gospels. Koester and Patterson both agree that they did exist and may have been the earliest trajectory among Jesus' followers, i.e., the efficacious nature of *logia* from the risen Lord, and an adherents response to them, provided salvation.

451. See Robinson and Koester, *Trajectories*.

452. Marcion, 85–159 CE (his *Gospel of the Lord*, that is, Marcion's extensive revision of sayings of the Lord in Luke, eliminating references to the Law and Prophets which he considers part of the deceitful evil god who opposes the God of Jesus): the collection of Valentinus, the early gnostic Christian theologian, 100–160 CE.

As noted, Paul's "and if I have faith, so as to remove mountains"[453] is an oral saying of the Lord that was later incorporated into the synoptic tradition, i.e., Mark and Matthew. Mark may represent the earliest form of the two: "Have faith in God. Truly, I say to you, whoever says to this mountain, 'Be taken up and cast into the sea,' and does not doubt in his heart, but believes that what he says will come to pass, it will be done for him."[454] The version in Matthew is as follows: "For truly I say to you, if you have faith as a grain of mustard seed, you will say to this mountain, 'Move from here to there,' and it will move, and nothing will be impossible to you."[455] In both sayings, Jesus calls on complete and utter faith and trust in God, releasing all presumptions and worldly reliance, placing incredible and astounding trust and hope in God's unbounded power, *not one's own power*, and certainly not in one's ability to move mountains at will. If one is aligned with God's will, nothing is impossible.

Paul's version seems to be similar to that found in the Synoptics. However, in the context of 1 Corinthians, the emphasis and tone have shifted to a criticism of the saying. Paul is not criticizing the saying itself, but *how the opponents have employed it*. Recall that Paul has quoted other sayings and does not hesitate to critique them, or placed them in new context or life situation,[456] particularly when they are used to confront him or his *euangelion*. Now the saying appears to be a metaphor for the *pneumatikoi* as "kings." Indeed, there are two alternate sayings that deserve mention—both have an emphasis on individual power gained through proper prophetic interpretation (i.e., gaining divine *gnosis* and *sophia*) of special *logia*. They are found in a collection of *logia* that make up the *Gospel of Thomas*; namely, Sayings 48 and 106. Saying 48 reads as follows: "If two make peace with each other in this one house, they will say to the mountain, 'move away,' and it will move away." The other is Saying 106, "When you make the two one, you will become the sons of man, and when you say, 'Mountain, move away,' and it will move away." Both sayings are esoteric, but reveal an individualistic self-awareness and reconciliation of two into one; that is, a reconciliation of opposites, the divine and human being are reunited into what has been described as the "solitary one." When this reconciliation is achieved one achieves "peace" or becomes the "sons of men." But more, when revelatory reconciliation occurs, individual power is overwhelming and transformative—nothing is impossible, and the material world, i.e., the "mountain," and its rules and laws thought to have control over the individual are not just meaningless—they can be cast away. The new "one," through *gnosis*, is united—the two opposites are reconciled into a divine, solitary being—and the world is void of power. This mirrors the stance of the infiltrators in Corinth, evidenced by their libertine behavior and their sarcastic arrogance and rejection of Paul and the *euangelion*. It is Paul and his adherents who are lost, mired in a world where mutual

---

453. 1 Cor 13:2b.
454. Mark 11:23.
455. Matt 17:20.
456. See above, 1 Cor 2:9 and *Gos. Thom.* 17.

and selfless love is blinding and binds them to a misguided slavery of dependence on others and in service to a community of the lost. For the infiltrators, *agape* is ignorance and loss. *Pistis* in the *logia* and the salvific *gnosis* they provide bringing union via an awakening to *sophia* is the essence of power and freedom.

The Mark of the Enemies: Branding and Tattoos

Paul continues his critique of the *pneumatikoi* in 13:3. There are two very distinct translations of this passage and both have a claim to authenticity because either can be traced to ancient manuscript traditions that diverge simply by one Greek verb. The more difficult reading is this: "And if I give away all and give up my body in order *that I may boast*" (the Greek word is *kauchesomai*, "that I may boast"). The alternate reading (and the one found in most translations of the New Testament) is this: "And if I give away all and give my body *that it may be burned*" (the Greek word here is *kauthesomai*, that [my body] may be burned). The more difficult reading is usually the one preferred by textual critics because, as noted earlier in our study, the more difficult reading generally is the original, i.e., a more difficult reading is later adjusted or clarified. However, in this case, either translation presents difficulties to commentators. As a result, the majority of translations employed by commentators are expanded to emphasize a much more altruistic interpretation of Paul, one that has really no correlation to the life situation in Corinth. In other words, *they assume that Paul is addressing the adherents, not the opponents* (contrary to the context of vv. 1 and 2), and that he is inferring that selfless martyrdom is a common practice among the adherents. For example, "And if I give away all my possessions [to the poor, or to feed the poor], and give my body to be burned [i.e., in martyrdom, a sacrifice for the faith], and yet do not have love it profits me nothing." This saying later was widely quoted as a reference to Christian martyrdom, and that one's life, if sacrificed, is to be given in love.

Yet, this much expanded and, frankly, inferred translation is fraught with a myriad of problems. First, it does not fit the context of Paul's confrontation with the infiltrators in vv. 1–2, i.e., where he attacked and warned the infiltrators about their dangerously errant use of *logia*. It is clear that the *pneumatikoi* had no interest in voluntary martyrdom, but instead freely and intentionally enjoyed every forbidden and outlawed pleasure—this is the *sitz im leben* of Corinth. Second, Paul provides no evidence of any kind in 1 or 2 Corinthians that the his adherents were faced with a state sanctioned persecution resulting in the risk of imprisonment, execution or murder (martyrdom), nor for that matter was the risk of violent death expected before the arrival the Lord based on the eschatology and tone of Paul's letters from 49 to 58 CE.[457] Indeed, to this point there had been no sanctioned executions or

---

457. Certainly, Paul would have mentioned a persecution as a sure sign of the ending days of the age, as he states that when "the Lord Jesus" returns, "he will subjugate all powers under his authority"

violent persecution by Roman authorities recorded by any historian, only the expulsion of the adherents from Jerusalem by the Chief Priests and Herod Agrippa 1,[458] and the expulsion of Jews from Rome, i.e., the edict of Claudius (ca. 49 CE).[459] The first severe persecution came under Nero, 64–68 CE, which according to Christian tradition led to the sanctioned execution of Kayfa and Paul[460] and hundreds of adherents in and around Rome. There is no doubt that Paul met violent opposition in Philippi and threat of imprisonment (and perhaps death).[461] Since he was not a Roman citizen as Acts claims, he could not appeal to protection under Roman citizenship.[462] Paul encountered violent Jewish opponents in Galatian cities, including Iconium and Lystra (as well as Gentile opponents),[463] and in other cities, such as in Ephesus, where he "fought with beasts." Acts records that when the ruler of the Corinthian synagogue, Sosthenes, failed to have Paul condemned by the proconsul Gallio,[464] he was beaten by fellow Jews.[465] Yet, there is simply no evidence of a general, sanctioned persecution or even violent, organized opposition in Corinth or other Hellenistic cities at this time. Consequently, interpretations that assume Paul is addressing adherents in relation to the possibility of accepting (or even contemplating) martyrdom, and more, that this it would be meaningless without *agape*, are completely unfounded and simply do not fit the *sitz im leben* evidenced in the Corinthian correspondence. Since it is clear that Paul is addressing the infiltrators in vv. 1–3, it is important to study the two variant interpretations in the light of their behavior and in the context of Paul's earlier comments about them.

Taking first the most frequently adopted translation, "and if I deliver my body to be burned," one must ask what this statement meant in its historical context, and more, what relation it may have to the infiltrators and their behavior. Martyrdom, as we have seen, has no place in this context. It is possible that "to be burned" might imply an act of submitting the body to punishment, but this was typically conducted in relation to bringing the body into submission—far from the expected practice of a libertine in Corinth. Consequently, the alternate answer may be to abuse the body, to exploit it to prove its material and temporary nature, as well as to use it as means of pleasure or, as noted before, a public and arrogant display of superiority over all

---

(1 Thess 4)—that time had not come, nor had any Roman persecution.

458. About the time of the death of James son of Zebedee, 44 CE.

459. Likely resulting from violent opposition of Jews to followers of Jesus making inroads in the capital.

460. By tradition, both apostles died under Nero's persecution, which was a local persecution it appears. There is no reason to doubt that Paul was present in Rome. The tradition of Kayfa in Rome is very ancient.

461. Acts 16:22.

462. Roetzel, *Paul*, 19–22.

463. Where he was stoned and presumed dead, Acts 14:19–20.

464. Ca. 51–52 CE, Acts 18:12–17.

465. Although this was more likely by Gentiles, not Jews (see above).

worldly things, including taboos and common and religious morality. "To be burned" can imply something rather radical in the ancient world, namely to be *voluntarily branded*, which included stitch/ink, scars and burning. Indeed, branding the body was used to publicly signify slavery, which, of course, was a mark of the lowest social status and servitude (unless it was the mark of the emperor). The most severe observable branding was brutal and used to indicate a master's punishment for lawbreaking, running away ("FUV," Latin for "*Fugitivus hic est*"), or falsehood (branded with a "K" for "*Kalumnia*," a liar). The branding (i.e., tattooing) could be made on the arms, legs, face or forehead. For those being punished for a crime, particularly for running away, the actual infringement was branding so it could be identified immediately, thus, the most problematic slaves were branded on the forehead. While there is evidence that some venerated ancient Greeks, including a Cretan named Epimenides, a leader of Orphism, were tattooed, and even Ptolemy Philopater was branded with Dionysiac brand marks (possibly tattoos), the predominance of brands were reserved for slaves, criminals or outcasts, including those expelled from cities.[466]

Since branding was usually a form of public acknowledgment of servitude and lowest class, being intentionally or voluntarily branded would be surprising, if not shocking. If the *pneumatikoi* were consistent in their public display of disdain for worldly rules and conventions relating to position, status and superiority, they could employ branding as a startling display of contradiction; namely, being branded to imply they were slaves, but then publicly engaging in every libertine act possible to demonstrate their status as free and superior ("kings"), a form of perversion of social norms and shocking public display of contradictory superiority. Consequently, they would have scoffed at and ridiculed the most demonstrable and accepted social practice of ancient world, particularly in the Greco-Roman world (certainly in Corinth), *being branded as slaves, but acting as kings*. Thus, for the infiltrating *pneumatikoi* to voluntarily have their bodies branded, most likely in intentionally conspicuous places and with the most radical marks that would be known, and then behave as libertines (beyond all laws and contrary to the marks on their bodies) would be a public display proclaiming their status.[467]

Paul does not condemn being branded, as certainly some of his adherents had been marked based on their social origin.[468] What Paul criticizes is that branding used to offend and shock others and mock social norms is completely contrary to "*the more excellent Way*," where selfless *agape* would result in a radical act, e.g., giving up

466. Paul was expelled from Philippi, and could have been branded for example.

467. In relation to Paul's comment on branding, two other additional insights are appropriate to explore. With regard to the infiltrators, there is a wisdom saying in the *Gospel of Thomas* worth noting: "Whoever is near me is near the fire!" (Saying 82). It is possible that a similar saying may have been part of the collection of the wisdom *logia* of the opponents in Corinth. If so, the opponents may have understood that branding was public affirmation of being "near the living fire," that is, having attained salvific *gnosis* through *logia*.

468. The slave Onesimus, Phlm 10; 1 Cor 1:26.

one's social standing for another—voluntarily taking their place as slave or servant. Paul's emphasis captures perfectly the character and intent of a saying of Jesus, where Jesus shockingly demands that if one is compelled to bear the equipment of a soldier one mile, one should go two miles.[469] This act would imply voluntarily entering into temporary slavery, thereby showing such remarkable *agape* that the witness to the event might seek the *euangelion*. It is interesting that this saying is imbedded in the collection of *logia* from Matthew 5 (the Beatitudes), where, as we have noted, several of the *logia* employed by the Jerusalem *apostoloi* may have originated.

Given this, Paul's tacit acceptance of the practice of branding is question-begging. It suggests that Paul's adherents might have known such saying of Jesus, i.e., introduced by Paul or other *apostoloi* who visited Corinth (e.g., Kayfa). If so, following from Jesus' own admonition for radical acts of *agape*, some of Paul's adherents might have voluntarily taken a brand or mark to identify themselves as "servants" and "slaves of the Lord Jesus Christ," just as servants would bear the marks of their owners, lords and masters. The slaves and servants of the "house of Caesar" wore these marks with distinction and were treated with great respect. Consequently, this practice, signifying oneself as the slave or servant of Caesar, may have been embraced by some of the early adherents in Corinth to designate themselves as "slaves and servants of Christ." Paul clearly does state that he is "compelled" to preach the *euangelion*, and that he (and the other apostles) are like the lowest caste, slaves and servants, and that he "bears the marks of the Lord Jesus on his body."[470] Was this an early practice or rite? The Corinthian followers of Paul, as an act of *agape* and service drawn from a saying of Jesus and Paul who bore a brand, may have also adopted a similar brand to signify their commitment to Jesus Christ and *agape* (service) for others. Consequently, Paul accepts the practice, but rejects the radical turn the *pneumatikoi apostoloi* have given it. This is coherent with the *sitz im leben* in Corinth and Paul's letter. Their brand was likely not an offensive symbol (see below).

With regard to the Corinthian *ecclesia*, as noted earlier, "Freedmen," former slaves, among the circle of Pauline adherents.[471] The Roman recolonization of Corinth was primarily made up of Freedmen,[472] and as noted earlier, "Chloe's people" who were sent to Paul were certainly slaves and likely Freedmen. These well-known "Freedmen" (those particularly of Caesar's house who became adherents in Corinth and whose mark was widely and immediately recognized throughout the Roman Empire) may have voluntarily accepted a new brand or mark—that of their new master, "the Lord

---

469. Matt 5:41.

470. Yet, in this case, he probably means the wounds and scars of the beatings and physical abuse he has suffered for the good news; but it is also possible he has accepted a branding mark as well; a mark would of course support the assumption that Paul could not be a citizen of Rome and so is beaten.

471. See the very impressive and influential work by Wayne Meeks, *Urban*, 21–23.

472. Meeks, *Urban*, 55.

The Enemies of Paul: Demons, Satan, Betrayers, and Apostles

Jesus Christ." But to do so could be fraught with perilous risk. Freedman of Caesar's "household" (*familia caesaris*), such as Gaius Julius Polybius,[473] despite having risen to substantial power and standing, were not immune to penalty for inappropriate behavior and suffered execution for outward acts of defiance, and more important, *disloyalty*. To accept an alternate mark as a former Freedman of the house of Caesar would have been a startling public act of submission to a new master and Lord, i.e., a crucified Roman criminal, Jesus of Nazareth. Such an act could have resulted in significant risk; i.e., accepting the "mark" of the Christ, the new Lord, even if it was obscure (e.g., and *ichthys* or *ankyra*, see below). It would be this kind of overt act that could foster persecution of Roman authorities; i.e., adopting a new master, an executed criminal, particularly over the *familia caesaris*, would be considered seditious.

Consequently, placing the infiltrators (i.e., those who were engaged in offensive libertine practices and branded themselves with an offensive mark considered rebellious to authorities) among Paul's adherents (i.e., those who were branded as servants of Jesus Christ and practicing *agape*) clearly resulted in tension and risk that would be visual and visceral. Whether or not all of the Corinthian adherents submitted to branding as a commitment to service to the Lord, it is certain that it was a practice known to Paul and his followers via his reference to it without criticism. Thus, branding was present and likely practiced in Corinth by Paul's adherents as a public mark of servitude to their Lord and Master, Jesus Christ,[474] and by the *pneumatikoi* to assert their freedom from all authorities, allowing them to engage in brazen sexual and social acts. Consequently, they must have been branded with a prominent mark that would be shocking—namely, a *stauros*, or cross.[475]

In 54–58 CE, the most offensive symbol was an "open cross," for it was the symbol of horrendous, brutal death of a violent or seditious criminal, an enemy of the state and society—the perfect symbol for the arrogant and offensive *pneumatikoi* who claimed individual salvation and status as "kings," i.e., as more powerful than the Roman authority and executioner's cross. The *stauros* was most likely branded on the face or forehead. It would have been shocking anywhere in the Roman world (i.e., to Gentile and Jew alike) to see this image branded or tattooed on the forehead, and then witness immoral, libertine and offensive behavior shouted defiance—that even crucifixion has no power, as it had no power: "I, the *knowing one*,[476] am free, a king, able to ridicule even the symbol of authority—it is nothing." If they held Docetic views, the branding of the *stauros* also asserted that the crucifixion of Jesus, the Living One,

---

473. Around 40 CE; he was a Freedman of the Emperor Claudius.

474. Like the slave of the "house of Caesar," e.g., Augustus or Claudius Caesar, the ecclesia and "family" of Jesus who is Christ, i.e., Jesus Christ.

475. Not because the cross is offensive any longer today, but because it would be perceived today as sacrilegious in where it would be placed so prominently. However, I have recently witnessed a cross having been tattooed on the forehead of a youth—it was shocking and was offensive to some for the reasons noted.

476. What Koester in *Trajectories* correctly terms "the Solitary One."

was a farce, just as was later depicted in the gospel of Judas and the "laughing Jesus"[477] on the cross. Ironically, Paul presses *pistis* in the *euangelion* of the cross as salvific if accompanied by *agape*, while the infiltrators use the cross as an empty symbol to ridicule the world's ignorance, corruption and impotence and practice sexual immorality, disdain for cults and the gods, and even Roman authority. Both are similarly radical in the Roman world and could be conflated by authorities as the same seditious and perverted "superstition."

If they employed the cross as a face brand or tattoo, this must have been its earliest employment as a symbol associated with Christ,[478] and because of its offensive nature, would explain why it did not reappear until the second century, hidden away in catacombs (usually as an anchor, see below), and then only publicly as a cross on a sarcophagus in the fifth century. Interestingly, the cross was condemned as a pagan symbol in the third century CE by church fathers. As noted, the earliest image was most likely the *ichthys*, the fish, or the anchor, *ankyra*, reflecting the locale and profession of the first *apostoloi*, the fishermen from Galilee—Kayfa, Andrew, James and John. The anchor was predominant, however, and is found in many catacombs and on first-century monuments.[479] It was widely used because its top cross bar hid the appearance of the cross, and so it was obscure. The *ichthys* was also popular because it was the symbol referenced by Jesus of Nazareth's in various sayings.[480] It was likely one of these symbols that was adopted by Paul's adherents, perhaps as noted the Freedmen, in Corinth, and may have become the brand mark that was used. The contrast of the loving act of branding the hand, wrist or arm by the adherents in Corinth ("I am a slave/servant of Christ"), thereby recognizing Jesus as Lord and Master, with the horrifying tattoo or branding of a brutal cross on the face or forehead by the infiltrators is remarkable and striking.

Paul then states: ". . . and give up my body in order that I may boast." The alternate translation, which has an equal claim to ancient manuscript tradition, must now be explored. Of the two translations, the more difficult reading is the second: "And if I give away all and give up my body in order *that I may boast* . . . [Greek, *kauchesomai*, 'that I may boast']." The challenge is to understand the meaning of this statement in the context of the *sitz im leben* of 1 Corinthians.

---

477. Gospel of Judas, 120–160 CE.

478. Again, not that the opponents were associating themselves with the cross, unless they were Docetics, who believed that Jesus was the agent of wisdom, and whose physical appearance was an illusion, meaning that his death on a cross was purely illusory. This was later portrayed as the "laughing Jesus," where Jesus watches as those who believe they are crucifying him but do not understand it is but an illusion.

479. Primarily Roman catacombs, or underground burial grounds that wound underneath specific sections of Rome.

480. E.g., "I will make you fishers of men," Mark 1:17; see also Matt 12:40; 14:17; Luke 5:6; 24:42; John 2:16; and 1 Cor 15:39.

As an analysis has shown, the infiltrators intentionally practiced offensive and immoral behavior, consorting with prostitutes openly and dining willfully in pagan temples at celebratory feasts, consuming sacrificial meats of pagan idols, i.e., demons, without fear. They are sexually abusive to women and treat them with disdain and disrespect as corrupted beings. More, they reject and dismiss Paul as anything other than ignorant and a charlatan, ridiculing his authority and the *euangelion* he proclaims. Indeed, the world itself is corrupted and is mired in satanic ignorance. They are free of this corruption, having achieved union with their divine self through the *logia* of the Living One, awakened by esoteric *gnosis* to salvific *sophia*; free not only from religious laws, but also secular Roman law. As proof of their divine union, they claim special *charismata*, particularly an array of angelic *glossolalias*, which are unintelligible to those lost in ignorance. They brand themselves with shocking images, perhaps the stauros on their forehead or face, an offensive symbol of death.

It is possible that Paul's statement is directed at these practices of bodily abuse and boasting, i.e., "giving up their bodies," as proof of their superior status (above all laws, rules and conventions), because they are free, divine and protected—the "Solitary Ones." If this is Paul's emphasis, he is criticizing the core of their radical practices; that is, that they are errantly "giving up their bodies." Instead their claims and practices are meaningless and empty, "nothingness," because they are without *agape*. To "give up my body that I may boast" is characterized by Paul as an impossibly irreconcilable, stark contrast between selfless *agape* and selfish, elitist enlightenment.

Either translation, i.e., "give my body to be burned," or "give my body that I may boast," focuses on the practices of the infiltrators that stand in stark contrast to the *euangelion* and its outcome, *agape*. Either fits the context of the *sitz im leben* in Corinth when properly analyzed. While the later is a more difficult translation, the more difficult reading, once the concept of reference to martyrdom is rejected, is actually to "give my body to be burned." It is in this translation that the abhorrent practice of offensive branding is discovered. Paul is *de facto* drawing a line between his enemies and the adherents, the "kings" and the followers of the "more excellent Way"; between "nothingness" and the *agape* of God.

The Power of *Agape* over All Enemies

After Paul addresses the errant views and practices of the opponents, he turns to the characteristics of *agape* for the followers of the Way.[481] Paul describes *agape* in terms of it opposites; that is, the specific characteristics of *agape* that are completely lacking in the infiltrators' practices, and by contrast then, those expected of Paul's adherents. There is no question that Paul is making these contrasts to be didactic and so reveal the "more excellent Way" of *agape*. Some commentators assert that Paul does not provide

---

481. 1 Cor 14:4–7.

a definition of *agape*. When looking at the carefully selected words Paul employs to present the "ways" of *agape*, there are clearly two operative results. The first is that Paul utilizes words that imply active and unavoidable involvement beyond oneself with others. For example, *makrothumeo, chresteuomai* (see below) clearly indicate active *agape*. Consequently, Paul is doing more than making a contrast of expected behaviors (i.e., of feelings or emotions that are good or bad), he is engaging in powerful teaching, that is, by engaging in *agape* through the ways he describes, one is protected by the power of God and the Lord Jesus Christ from satanic deception and death. The adherent that embraces *pistis* in the *euangelion* of Christ and becomes active in *agape* mystically enters into an efficacious, salvific relationship with God as Abba' *by loving others selflessly,* and so becomes justified before the *parousia* and is adopted as a *tekna tou Theou*. This child literally enters into a living relationship with the Lord who has overcome Satan and death, thereby embracing the "more excellent Way." This is the *sophia* of the cross, and Paul's efficacious gospel in its most pristine form. *So the contrast of behaviors is much more significant than having or not having a trait of love; it is a contrast of wisdom teachings—the wisdom of God, agape, versus esoteric wisdom errantly extracted from the logia and false gnosis, what Paul terms "nothingness."*

Paul's use of the words "arrogance or boasting" is a contrast of wisdoms, not emotive behavior. Failure of engagement in loving one's neighbor, i.e., what is demanded by *agape*, separates one from others, and so, distances one form the true wisdom and Way of God. This means that the infiltrators' errant arrogance and public boasting, their intentional shocking behavior, immorality and ridicule of religious and secular laws, represent the empty claims of the deceived, the children of evil. Unfortunately the specific contrasting words Paul selects when translated into English equivalents have lost all of this powerful meaning—they are benign. For example, in v. 4, Paul says, "*hey agape markrothumei*," which is translated, "Love is patient." But the word *markrothoumei* means much more that an attitude of being patient with someone. It means to be actively patient by bearing and caring for the needs and burdens of others. The word *chresteuomai* is translated as "kind," but again, this is not an emotion or attitude, the word is the active employment of kindness to others, or better said, "to show oneself kind."[482] The common translation of *zeloun*, "jealous" could as easily be translated as "zealous," which better fits the behavior of the infiltrators, for the statement would then read in v. 4b: "love is not zealous for oneself or conceited." In v. 5, Paul selects a word in direct contrast to *agape*, translated in most translations as "rude," but the word actually in better translated with its full meaning, "acting indecently" (*askemonei*); again, the word implies much more than an attitude, it is an intentional action that affects others. This is also true with the common translation of *parokunein*, irritable. The English translation is "love is not irritable," but the correct translation should be focused on the action of the individual, not an emotion,

---

482. Conzelmann notes that this word and usage only occur in Christian literature, *1 Corinthians*, 224.

thus "love does not incite others to anger or disgust," i.e., the very experience of the adherents who are "incited" intentionally by the infiltrators. Paul stresses, "This is not love." It is clear that Paul is starkly contrasting the *sophia* of God revealed in *agape* with the errant and perilously dangerous *sophia* claimed by and evidenced in the practices of the infiltrators.

The second operative result is that Paul may be contrasting sayings of Jesus used by the infiltrators (i.e., in their written document) with *logia* Paul employs. Recall that Paul freely employs *logia* of Jesus to fit the context of the Corinthian *sitz im leben*, even criticizing their use, particularly when they are cited to condemn or reject Paul's *euangelion* or his appointment as an *apostolos*. For example, given what can be gleaned from Paul's criticism of the opponents in 1 Corinthians, it is highly likely that their *logia* source employed the well-known (and controversial) wisdom saying of Jesus, "Wisdom [*sophia*] is known [justified] by her own children [or deeds]," or "Wisdom is justified by all of her offspring" a saying from Q (Matt 11:19, par. Luke 7:35). Such a saying could easily be understood as an esoteric reference to achieving *gnosis* and, thereby, becoming a "child of wisdom." As such, the *pneumatikos* is self-understood to be a "Solitary One," i.e., an elitist and personified child of divine wisdom (i.e., salvific wisdom of God). And if so, this would justify a claim to be libertines, free from the social, political and religious norms of society and of religious morality—a libertine by right having achieved salvific gnosis-wisdom. Thus, having achieved this status, i.e., being united with divine *sophia* and being "her" child, elitist's actions that are shocking and abhorrent become intentional public displays of power and propaganda that confirm divine status as a "Solitary One." Indeed, the contrasts he provides between the children of *agape* and the children of *sophia-gnosis* demonstrate the errant behavior of the *pneumatikoi*. Consequently, Paul defines true wisdom as active, communal, purposeful and powerful *agape*—God's very will and nature. *Agape* "always protects, always trusts, always hopes, and always preserves others";[483] it is active and continuous, not incidental and sporadic, and is intimately linked with the protection and edification of the *ecclesia* until the *parousia*.

Paul continues, *he agape oudepote ekpipte*, "love never fails." Some translations attempt to capture the permanence of *agape* with "love never *ends*." However, "never fails" is more accurate because it conveys *agape's* mystical permanence and power, i.e., it is from God and trumps all *charismata* because *agape is the full expression of all charismata*. Individual *charisma* are only partial and temporary expressions of it that will end, but *agape* (patience that bears the needs of others, kindness that also carries the concerns and fills those needs) will never fail to mystically protect the adherent and the *ecclesia* until the *parousia* from satanic deceit, deviance and practices that continue to render one subject to the curse of death. Indeed, *ekpipte* means more than "fail," as it should be better translated "never becomes powerless." This difference between the temporary character of the *charismata* and the permanence of active

---

483. 1 Cor 4:7.

agape is carried forward in Paul's continuing critique of the infiltrators' reliance on the *charismata* of *glossolalia* as evidence of their superior and protected state. Paul states: "Where there are prophecies, they will be discarded [i.e., end, or pass away], where there are tongues, they will cease; where there is knowledge, it will pass away." Paul states plainly that all *charismata* are temporary—they fill the need of establishing, strengthening and edifying the *ecclesia* until the *parousia*. Only *agape* is permanent, "mature" and "perfect" because it is the outcome of the efficacious *euangelion* and *pistis*, and the expression of the essence, will and power of God, evidenced in the cross and resurrection of Jesus Christ.

Paul confirms the temporary, utilitarian nature of the *charismata* when he addresses the prophetic interpretations and application of Scripture and *logia* of the Lord to the *sitz im leben* of the *ecclesia*: "For what we know [*ginoskomen*], we prophecy [*prophetegomen*] *in part*; but when the perfect comes *the partial will pass away*."[484] The *charismata* up-build and edify *agape* within the *ecclesia* until the *parousia* and presence of the Lord; they are a signal of the end times, the eschatological presence of the Spirit of God before the return and the arrival of the kingdom of God. The Greek translation of "in part," *ek merous*, carries a more definitive meaning than that found in most translations, "in part." A more appropriate translation in context is "immaturely" or "innocently" (i.e., without full experience).

Paul's contrast of immature knowledge and prophecy with a full "maturity" still to come sets the stage for his next use of the metaphor of the child and adult (an accurate translation of the original Greek renders the child/adult metaphor more intelligible): "When I was a child, I was *speaking* like a child, I was *thinking* as a child, I was *reasoning* as a child. When I became an adult [literally in Greek, *a man*], I made useless the things of the child." He links the *charismata* of speaking in tongues (*glossolalia*), knowledge (*gnosis*), and reasoning[485] as practiced by the intruders as "immature," *like the effort of a child*. Once the way of an adult is understood (by context, the limitless practice of *agape*), the childlike thinking is abandoned for *agape*, the more excellent way, the way of God. The contrast is striking; the *pneumatikoi* misunderstand the purpose and temporary nature of the *charismata*—they are the children of error and at risk. Indeed, Paul asserts that the adherent knows that *charismata* are nothing more than a utilitarian gift, the focus of which is to fully establish *agape* and neutralize Satan until the parousia. Only *agape* is the full expression and mystical power of God's *sophia*, and so, is his will and nature. Thus, Paul counters any claim to have obtained divinity in esoteric *gnosis*, or that a salvific state is confirmed by *glossolalia*. Paul's analogy stresses that both the adherent and *pneumatikoi* must still strive for "maturity," also called by Paul "perfection" (v. 10, *to teleion*). As noted, *teleion* comes only from

---

484. 1 Cor 13:9.

485. Interesting here that Paul uses "reasoning," in place of prophesying, which confirms that prophecy was associated with interpretation.

embracing the wisdom of God, his will and nature, which for Paul is only expressed fully in *agape* arising from *pistis* in the *euangelion*.

As noted, Paul consistently chooses his words and analogies (as well as his *masal*) carefully. As such, Paul certainly selects the analogy of a child because the *apostoloi pneumatikoi* cite *glossolalia* as proof of their divine status as a pure, united and divine "child." *Logia* in other sayings collections confirm this. Indeed there are several wisdom sayings attributed in the *logia* collection of the *Gospel of Thomas* related to the child or children in addition to one notable saying already cited, i.e., "Wisdom is justified by her children."[486] Paul's enemies likely share similarities with these *logia*.

The *Gospel of Thomas* describes the child as asexual, pure and untainted, and as a new being—the "two becoming one" as the divine self, and what has been termed the "Solitary One." The individual has been awakened to their divine origin and can be united again through *gnosis* and *sophia*. The *Gospel of Thomas* is such a sayings document that provides an awakening via *gnosis* and *sophia* through the *logia* of the "Living One" to the enlightened children of the true kingdom. As noted, the similarities between the Corinthian libertine infiltrators and the community of Thomas (evidenced in just the first five *logia* in Thomas, as well as the other *logia* and relationship to the beatitudes that have been discussed) are striking. A similar written *logia*-source undoubtedly made up the core of the their document, if not sections of the *Gospel of Thomas*. Indeed, Thomas underscores the exclusive and salvific nature of the *logia* collection: "Whoever discovers the interpretation of these sayings will not taste death."[487] This perfectly reflects the claims of the infiltrators.

Once one obtains knowledge, the result is radical and unsettling, for all that was considered important no longer has meaning or power. In fact, the seeker now "reigns" like a "king":

> Let one who seeks not stop seeking until one finds. When one finds, one will be disturbed one will marvel, and will reign over all.[488]

This mirrors Paul's comment about the Corinthian opponents already noted: "Already you are kings!"[489] Salvation and power over all former moral and legal conventions are available to the opponent, just as is seen in the behavior of the opponents in Corinth. False "leaders," such as Paul, who say the kingdom of God is yet to come (it is found elsewhere), are deceived, errant and mistaken:

> If your leaders say to you, "Behold the kingdom is in heaven," then the birds of heaven will precede you. If they say to you, "It is in the sea," then the fish will precede you. Rather the kingdom is within you and is outside of you. When

---

486. Matt 7:35.
487. *Gos. Thom.*, Saying 1.
488. *Gos. Thom.*, Saying 2.
489. 1 Cor 4:8.

you know yourselves, then you will be known, and you will understand that you are the children of the Living Father.⁴⁹⁰

The result of "knowing oneself" (i.e., discovering through the *logia* the truth as to one's true divine origin and nature) leads to "being known" and unification with the divine. Unification means a return to one's original nature, thus, the metaphor of the childlike state, summarized in the concept of the "Solitary One," *the child who speaks in babbling language, but by doing so, proves they speak divine language.* This is also confirmed in Thomas, Saying 4:

> Jesus said, "The person old in days will not hesitate to ask a little child of seven days about the place of life, and that person will live. For many of the first will be last, and will become a single one" [i.e., a Solitary One].

This unification of the opposites⁴⁹¹ is also expressed in Saying 22 and 27. Indeed, these four sayings, when combined with Thomas' wisdom beatitudes, confirm the libertine practices and assertions made by the opponents of Corinth as proto-gnositic, i.e., an early form of nascent Christian Gnosis, where the *logia*, not the cross, provide salvation to the adherent.

There can be little doubt now that the infiltrators had a collection of *logia* not unlike that in Thomas. It is coherent with the *sitz im leben* of the Corinthian *ecclesia* and the risk mitigations Paul and his enemies employ to neutralize the other. It is the battle over soteriology: *pistis* in the *euangelion* of the cross and the coming *parousia* versus *sophia-gnosis* obtained through powerful *logia*. Thus, it is quite possible that Paul in v. 11 is alluding to a saying, e.g., Saying 4, they employ. Thus, Paul's emphasis is on the opponents' lack of understanding, that is, they lacking maturity. His call is that they give up "childish ways," i.e., as Solitary Ones. Paul sharply contrasts the childish "way" of the opponents with "the more excellent way" of maturity in *agape*.

The Dim Mirror

Paul next employs the metaphor of the "dim" mirror. Corinth was one of the major Roman-Hellenistic cities that produced high quality mirrors, evidenced by important archaeological finds there.⁴⁹² In fact, scholars often cite Corinth as one of the most renowned production centers for mirrors, primarily because of the city's reputation for bronze production and its ability to fabricate reflective, silver bronze used in mirrors⁴⁹³—This made Corinthian mirrors highly desired. Excavations of tombs

---

490. *Gos. Thom.*, Saying 3.
491. Neither male nor female, only the spiritual being, and as such "perfect," or childlike.
492. Along with Argos, Sikyon, Sidon and Kleonai; for Sidon, see Pliny, *Natural History*, 36: 66.93.
493. See Pausanias, 2.3.3; there are other features of gods and goddesses that can be associated with Corinth since bronze statues are reflected also in archeological finds, include a bronze box mirror from the 3rd century CE.

and gravesites have produced a wide array of mirrors, but when combined, seem to suggest a similar "style" associated with the city. Mirrors in the first century were made using highly polished brass, bronze or glass coated with tin, or, as in Corinth, silver. Usually they were small and round (i.e., disk-mirrors) with a diameter of about 2.7–8 inches. On the reverse were various scenes, from seated or standing goddesses (Aphrodite), to nymphs (or other divine figures, including Pan and Eros); not uncommon were ornate geometric designs or simple "birds feet" lines. There were many styles, including handheld or pedestal, but the most ornate and rare were designed for a table or stand (e.g., a folding or box type that when opened revealed the mirror in the lid). Pausanias states that *mirrors were used in divination*,[494] where the mirror was lowered into a well and touched, or was dipped into the water, so that when extracted, the water-streak formation revealed to the diviner a message, e.g., if sick would recover, worsen, or even die.

Paul discusses both of these analogies, the child and mirror, back to back. In the first analogy, "speaking, understanding and reasoning as a child," Paul has referenced and responded to a specific claim made by the infiltrators. They point to *glossolalia* as the divine angelic language of a Solitary One—*the full child of wisdom*. But for Paul, their claim to have obtained divine knowledge (*gnosis*) and reasoning (*propheteia*), evidenced in their form of *glossolalia*, instead reveals they are like immature children, lacking true understanding and reasoning because it fails to engender divine *agape*. Indeed, all legitimate Spirit-awarded *charismata* facilitate the strengthening of *agape* in the *ecclesia*, only to fade away as *agape* permeates and protects the assembly in the final days. *Charismata* are only "dim images" of what is to come with the *parousia* and Jesus Christ. It is this analogy that brings the mirror to mind. The mirror only reflects, but cannot capture anything more than just that. As a result, it seems possible that the connection for Paul between analogies is centered in the dangerous incompleteness of their knowledge. Especially in Corinth, the reference to a mirror could be understood this way—even the most carefully made mirror could do nothing more that reflect a "dim image" and nothing more of the true self. As incomplete was that image, so too was their immature, childlike understanding and claims to divinity based on *glossolalia* alone. They are in peril.

But Hans Conzelmann has provided another striking insight. He notes that children sometimes served in religious practices related to mirrors.[495] Indeed, mirrors were used in divination ceremonies among various Hellenistic mystery cults, and *there are many allusions to mirrors in later gnostic writings* (2nd to 3rd century CE). One of the more prominent gnostic documents includes all the key elements noted by Paul, and so it merits further evaluation. The *Hymn of the Pearl* includes a boy (child), wisdom as salvation and a transformative experience with a mirror, where the true

---

494. That is, catoptromancy; see VII, 17–27, "they lowered the mirror on a fine cord, judging the distance so it does not sink deep into the spring."

495. Conzelmann, *Corinthians*, 227n95.

nature of the self is rediscovered. Remarkably, the hymn is embedded in the *Acts of Thomas*,[496] purportedly the same Thomas as the author or catalyst for the formation of the *Gospel of Thomas*;[497] the sayings source that in some form (perhaps an earlier collection still in a formative state) may have been employed by the opponents.[498] The connection between each of these literary sources, and the fact that the *Gospel of Thomas* was the final form of an earlier collection of sayings that were known very early in Corinth by 54 CE, lends support to the view that there was a "school" of Thomas' traditions; better said, there was a trajectory of the Thomas tradition not unlike that of the synoptic or Johannine traditions that had a claim to nascent orthodoxy, i.e., the *logia* of Jesus of Nazareth, but in this case, saving power was gained in properly understanding Jesus' *logia*.

In the hymn, the mirror is distinctly referenced as both the reflection of the true and divine self, and concurrently the image of the fallen and lost human that is the poor reflection of divinity. When a boy was sent by the King of kings to Egypt to exchange gold and silver for a single invaluable pearl,[499] he becomes distracted and lost in the material world, and having lost his way is doomed. When a message from the King awakens him to his task (i.e., to return the pearl), he makes his way successfully to the point where he must he recall his former glorious state, represented by his beautiful robe, but he cannot—*until he sees his reflection in a mirror*:

> I could not recall my former splendor. But when I saw my garment reflected as in a *mirror*, I perceived my whole self as well. And through it I recognized and saw myself. For, though we derived form one and the same we were partially divided, and then again we were one, with a single form.[500]

The mirror plays a pivotal role in the hymn, and becomes the defining event for an awakening by revealing the true state when the lost child looks into it.

Paul's statement seems to take for granted a practice where a mirror was employed, and instead of it revealing the truth, he claims that one looked into it "dimly," or "darkly," or perhaps better translated, to look in and *speak an enigma or riddles*.[501] If Paul truly meant to convey the meaning of "enigma," a riddle or mystery, he may be citing a practice of the opponents, where they participate in a mysterious cultic ceremony, looking into a mirror to see their "true selves," just as the child did when he recognized both his glorious self and his human body. While the *Hymn of the Pearl* certainly is dated decades after Paul's activity in Corinth, the poem may actually

---

496. 200–225 CE; Didymos Judas Thomas.

497. 100–160 CE.

498. As we have demonstrated, the opponents unquestionably knew a similar document and logia that were challenged by Paul; see 1 Cor 2:9.

499. See Jesus' saying in the synoptic tradition on the parable "of the hidden treasure," Matt 13:45–46.

500. *Hymn*, 75–78.

501. Greek is *ainigmata*, also enigma in English; mysterious or *to speak in riddles*.

capture a practice that was very ancient and employed in early wisdom or esoteric cults, mystery religions and later gnostic trajectories, *the ceremony of recognition*. This seems more plausible because the hymn itself includes a subtle emphasis on conversion and as it conveys the journey of the archetypal gnostic.[502] With the additional reference in Pausanias to the use of a mirror in determining the health or fatal illness by looking into it (and so, with other practices of divination), Paul may be referencing a similar practice among the intruders.

The ceremony of recognition may have contained a reenactment of the journey of the child (speaking in *glossolalia* during the journey and in preparation for viewing the true self in a mirror,[503] followed by an acknowledgment that *gnosis* and saving wisdom have been attained)—a practice perhaps employed by Paul's opponents. Once freedom from the corrupted world of vanity and deceit (elements evident in the *Hymn of the Pearl*) and misguided human convention had been achieved, one was able to exercise that freedom through any means, from libertine disdain for human rules, religion and laws to abstinence.[504] Since Paul is very selective in his choice of words throughout 1 Corinthians, it is no accident that he references both the child and the mirror, but critiques their use by altering the understanding of their relationship to the *euangelion* of Jesus Christ and the impending *parousia*. Consequently, it is likely that Paul is referring to a cultic rite, practice or recitation using a mirror. The intruders' reenactment of a "journey" from ignorance to *gnosis* and wisdom-salvation (i.e., such as that found in the much later *Hymn of the Pearl*), leads Paul's to employ the two documented gnostic images—the Solitary One and *gnosis*, child/mirror, back to back.

If the *journey of recognition* was indeed the practice to which Paul refers, then it is important to understand how he also criticizes its legitimacy by shifting its claim to the immediate recognition and achievement of divinity to a future hope. With regard to the change in timing, we may actually find confirmation that the practice of a gnostic-like journey leading to immediate salvation for the initiate was in place. Indeed, Paul uses these same images from practice that has been relayed to him, and then clearly critiques both. The child's journey (v. 11) is now a childish effort in speaking, knowing and reasoning that should be "put away" (*katergeka*, literally "discarded"), because "I have become a man" (*gegona aner*). Paul uses the image of the *aner*, the human, in the fullest sense; as a *mature man*—certainly not saved but yet residing in safety and protection from evil and Satan in the last days before the *parousia* and presence of the Lord. He is mature in his own *gnosis* of the *euangelion* and *pistis*, empowered and protected by divine *agape*. The enigmatic experience of witnessing the gnostic divine self in a mirror and receiving enlightenment of one's true nature

---

502. That is, the journey of the boy child sent by the King of kings to discover the one pearl, wisdom, temporarily loses but then finds himself, his true nature and his divine saved state.

503. The divine language of the child—possible under the influence of hallucinogens or intoxicants.

504. Perhaps as indicated by the encounter witnessed in the mirror, i.e., the form of the robe obtained.

is altered into a different enigma, "mystery," that is nothing more than an image of the self that will not achieve its complete saved state until the Day of the Lord, i.e., in the immediate future, when all will be fully revealed. Paul continues, "Now I know in part [*merous*, again the incomplete state], but *then* [i.e., when the presence of the Lord arrives], I shall know just as I am known."[505] For Paul, any claim that *gnosis* or an esoteric journey can reveal all, or achieve divinity, is impossible, as all has yet to be revealed; certainly the image obtained in the mirror is incomplete, and perfection in speaking, thinking and knowing as a child cannot represent divine perfection, for such knowledge is immature.

Paul then summarizes *the Way* as a journey that stands apart from the *journey of recognition*. The Way is the journey *to* adoption as a child of God, granting grace and safety to the adherent at the *parousia*—it is not a journey of the lost divine child to salvific recognition and return to the divine. Indeed, the Way is characterized by the adherents' *pistis* and *elpis* in the transformative event of God's action in the cross (death, burial and resurrection of Jesus Christ)—that *pistis* engenders *elpis* and *agape*. Paul shows that both *pistis* and *elpis* are the result of this journey, i.e., the perilous risk of embracing the wisdom of God revealed in the cross of Jesus. The Spirit of God then assesses the adherent and provides *charismata*. These *charismata* are given to the adherent to confirm one to be a prospective child of God's *ecclesia*, the living body of the Christ. But the *charismata* do not confirm salvation as claimed by the opponents; only that the adherent has been joined to the body of Christ, which awaits the *parousia*. *Agape* is the object of the journey until that day, as even the *charismata* will fade away. Indeed, the Way is a journey still in process until the *parousia*. That Paul recognizes *pistis*, *elpis* and *agape* as defining *the Way* is confirmed by his usage of this triad in other letters. In addressing the Thessalonians, Paul states: "Whenever we pray, we remember before God your faith, hope and love";[506] also, "Since we heard of your faith in Christ Jesus and of your love for all the holy ones; because of the hope which is laid up for you in heaven."[507] Paul's entire thesis on salvation by faith alone, leading to hope and the overwhelming outpouring of love "into our hearts," is central to his presentation in Romans: "Now hope does not disappoint, because the love of God has been poured out in our hearts by the *hagiou pneumatos*, the Holy Spirit, who was give to us."[508] Even the short letter of Paul to Philemon contains the three key elements of the Way.[509] So, Paul concludes the section on *agape* with the central tenets of the *more excellent Way*, that is, the journey of adherent in God's Way, until the *parousia* and presence of the Lord.

505. 1 Cor 13:12.
506. 1 Thess 1:3.
507. Col 1:4–5.
508. Rom 5:5.
509. Phlm 5–7.

The Pursuit of *Agape* and Valid *Charismata*

Paul now returns to the central message in his emphatic and passionate summary to the adherents: "Make *agape* your aim!"[510] The Greek word used by Paul for "aim" is *diokete*, which is a present *active verb* meaning "Be pursuing!" The pursuit is more than an objective. Paul is insisting that it is a present and active journey, the Way of *agape*, which must dominate and stand at the foundation of the crisis of the present time. As such, the perilous risk of satanic attack, deception and the curse of death, as well as mitigation of that risk through *pistis* and *elpis* in Jesus Christ, demands present, bold, fearless and active *agape*, which is strengthened and fully evidenced by the presence of legitimate *charismata* that serve but one purpose—the edification and strengthening of the *ecclesia*, which is enveloped in this protective *agape*.

Paul continues: "Pursue love (!), and earnestly desire the *charismata*, especially that you may prophesy."[511] The link between *agape* and the *charismata* is reaffirmed by Paul, consistent with the foregoing analysis on Paul's insistence that legitimate *charismata* build up the power of protective *agape*, thus the outpouring of democratized forms of *charismata* to every adherent. Paul's emphasis on the *charisma* of prophecy asks all adherents to "desire" it, which is much more accurately rendered by the Greek word *zeloute*, "be zealous!" It is *propheteia*, the voice and instruction of the divine that for Paul absorbs Scripture, prophetic writings, *logia* and *logoi* of the risen Lord. Using these divine sources, *propheteia* powerfully mitigates risks faced by the *ecclesia* and affirms right standing and *agape* in the crisis of the last days. It engenders *agape* by resisting desperate satanic attacks, including the infiltration by enemies out to destroy the *ecclesiae* by introducing alien claims and practices, i.e., those contrary to the *euangelion* of Jesus Christ. Prophecy was the penultimate gift in the ancient world. The recovered practices of various pagan mystery religions, as well as through oracles,[512] the cult deity spoke through a priest, priestess or designated sacred individual, such as the Sybil or Pythia. In the tradition of Judaism, God spoke through chosen prophets, and so too, the prophetic tradition was carried forward through Priests and High Priest, and in the Pharisaic tradition, the interpretation and application of oral law, familiar to the Jewish adherents and to Paul.[513] These special conduits had highly valued the *charisma of propheteia*. Now that divine gift is evidenced in the *ecclesia*, confirming for Paul the presence of the Spirit of God, validating his *euangelion*, and marking the legitimate continuation of the ancient prophetic tradition through Jesus Christ—prophecy upbuilds *pitis*, *elpis* and *agape* and is the undisputed seal of divine presence. In the final days of the age, and contained within the prophetic tradition,

---

510. 1 Cor 14:1.

511. 1 Cor 14:1.

512. Such as in Delphi, familiar, even famous, to many of the Gentile believers.

513. It is important to note that Paul never refers to Jesus of Nazareth as a prophet, but as the son, the Lord and Christ.

was God's promise that there would be an outpouring of his Spirit in the "last days" *on all of his children*.⁵¹⁴ Paul is therefore referencing that promise—the Way is the journey and pursuit of *agape* until the *parousia*, and while the adherent should desire *charismata* to up-build, strengthen and protect the *ecclesia* in the last days, *propheteia* is of immense importance in maintaining and protecting the body of Christ because it draws in the total validation evidenced by the divine voice among God's chosen people, i.e., *not glossolalia*.

Paul is clear: "He who prophesies speaks to men for their up building and encouragement and *consolation* [*paramuthian*, i.e., comfort, meeting the life situation needs of the *ecclesia*]."⁵¹⁵ Interpretation and application of sayings of the Lord was only legitimate if appointed and Spirit-possessed prophets (who were checked by other prophets) employed them for the strengthening of the *ecclesiae* in *agape* (except if the application of *logia* or *logoi* were by an *apostoloi* such as Paul, i.e., one who proclaimed the efficacious *euangelion* of the cross and *parousia*, to strengthen *agape* and *ecclesiae*). As such, many *logia* known today in Paul's writings, the synoptic and Johannine traditions originally circulated among these early Christian prophets of Paul's *ecclesiae*. These prophets perceived how these divine *logoi* and *logia*, as well as Scripture and prophetic wrings, were to be used by the *ecclesiae* in the context of Paul's *euangelion*. The "check" that was conducted by other prophets within the community led to assurance of proper application and interpretation of the Scripture or saying to the *sitz im leben* of the *ecclesia*. This very early institution and practice of the prophetic tradition by Paul in his *ecclesiae* led to the approval and authentication of various *logia*, a form of nascent "orthodoxy."⁵¹⁶ Indeed, the prophetic movement was largely responsible for the development of the oral tradition, particularly *logia*. Thus, the *logia* (by the nature of their interpretation, under the influence of the prophets) were for the edification of the *ecclesia* and the adherers; in other words, those who were participants in the community of *agape* and the Way in the last days.⁵¹⁷ Any saying that failed to do so, or was claimed to have "secret" *gnosis* apart from the context of the *euangelion* and *agape*, could not be held as valid.

Paul asserts, once again, that *glossolalia* is subservient to *propheteia*, as well as the other *charismata*: "He who speaks in a tongue edifies himself, but he who prophesies

---

514. Joel 2:28–32.

515. 1 Cor 14:3.

516. This would included the *logia* collection of the opponents that Paul critiques, "do not go beyond what is written," 1 Cor 4:6.

517. Sayings now embedded in the synoptic, Johannine or other traditions (e.g., Thomas) originally came from the appointed prophets of the first century—the first generation of Christians. Understanding this trajectory of the oral tradition, which not only included sayings of the Lord but also the application of Scripture in an interpretation of his life and ministry post-Easter, is not questioning the "authenticity" or "historicity" of the tradition, but the place of origin so as to fully understand the rich context and use of the saying in its original setting.

edifies the *ecclesia*."⁵¹⁸ This statement confirms again that the *pneumatikoi* did not provide interpretation, but spoke in ecstatic language solely to demonstrate personal status (e.g., angelic language that revealed the level of their divine status), both to adherents and to outsiders. Paul confirms as legitimate only *charismata* that are for the "edification" (*oikodomei*) of the *ecclesia*, including *glossolalia*: "He who prophesies is greater than he who speaks, unless one interprets, so that the *ecclesia* may be edified."⁵¹⁹ When interpretation is made (and interpretation is also a *charisma*), Paul elevates *glossolalia*. He does so because *glossolalia* that "edifies" effuses the *ecclesia* with protective *agape*; that is, it provides a "revelation," a "prophecy," "gnosis," or "teaching"⁵²⁰ that build or strengthen the *ecclesia* against all enemies, and so, *agape*. As a result, valid *glossolalia* yields *serves the other charismata*—this is its sole purpose.

By employing "revelation," *apokalupse*, Paul refers to specific, overwhelming and transformative, charismatic encounters with the divine that provide a revealing, an awakening and understanding as to the salvific *euangelion*, which in turn evoke a compelling response that fosters dissemination of the *euangelion*, strengthens the *ecclesia* and activates *agape*. A revelation can thus shatter the perception of perilous risks by contradicting their validity, dramatically compelling new risk mitigation responses, sometimes entirely counter to previous actions. As such, a revelation is more than an insight, and is a manifestation of the divine for Paul. Indeed, Paul's transformative post-crucifixion encounter with Jesus is characterized as a manifestation,⁵²¹ and he uses this term for the manifestation and actual presence of Jesus Christ at the *parousia*.⁵²² Paul typifies his transportation to the "third heaven," i.e., the divine place of God and Jesus Christ, as a revelation in 37–38 CE, citing the year and point in time that cataclysmically altered his life. In this case, he was manifested in heaven by the power of God where he encountered secret *logoi* and *gnosis* that confirmed the *euangelion*. Such revelations displaced his understanding of deadly satanic risks, leading him to abandon his attack on the surviving exorcists and followers of Jesus, whom he had once believed were sorcerers and "evildoers" like Jesus, possessed by Beelzebul.⁵²³ His life as a paid informant and assassin, of violence and murder, ended that day. This manifestation included clarity of divine will, compelling a risk response or doom. In his defense to the infiltrators in Galatia, Paul writes, "For I would have you know, brethren, that the *euangelion* which was preached by me is not man's gospel. For I did not receive it from man, nor was I taught it, but it came through a revelation of Jesus Christ."⁵²⁴ Paul asserts that he received the efficacious and salvific *euangelion* directly

518. 1 Cor 14:4.
519. 1 Cor 14:5.
520. 1 Cor 14:6.
521. Gal 1:12.
522. 1 Cor 1:7.
523. Busse, *Jesus Resurrected*, 216–22; *Fire*, 169.
524. Gal 1:11–12.

from the risen Christ, that is, a *full revelation*—a complete understanding of the divine activity, its purpose and meaning, how to embrace and practice the outcome of the revelation, and what was to come. For Paul, divine revelation is fully revealed solely in the *euangelion*, and any other revelation is satanic. In Corinth then, a revelation would have been a significant event, certainly critically important for the *ecclesia*, building *agape* and clarifying its role in its battle with Satan.

Paul's reference to revelation in relation to *glossolalia* then is critically important. Unlike the claims of the infiltrators, the *charisma* of *glossolalia* is not simply a confirmation of *gnosis* and divine status espoused in unintelligible babble, which signifies the angelic level of *gnosis* achieved. The divine *charisma* of *glossolalia* brings forth revelation concerning the *euangelion* and Jesus Christ that is intelligible, overwhelming and must be actionable for the *ecclesia* and *agape*. Paul claims to have the *charisma* of *glossolalia* more than all, but he restricts its use to provision of all *charismata* for the benefit of the *ecclesia*. Indeed, his own manifestation by the power of God to the "third heaven" included hearing divine *logoi*, yet Paul asserts that divine *logoi* are not to be uttered, for to do so is unlawful. By implication, whatever the infiltrators espouse is false, not a *charisma* of the Spirit, and so is demon possession. Paul even refuses to repeat these *logoi* to promote his status; instead he is humbled by his weakness to serve the *euangelion*.[525] Consequently, legitimate *glossolalia* serves as a conduit of divine revelation that is intelligible, powerful and for the edification and benefit of *agape* and the *ecclesia* as it counters satanic forces in the last days. Like Paul who was transformed, so too have been Corinthian adherents been radically changed, and any new *apokolupeis* are provided to measurable aid in that transformation, engendering *pistis*, *elpis* and *agape* until the *parousia*.

Finally, Paul makes reference to musical instruments, ones very familiar to the Gentile Corinthians—the flute, the harp and the horn, all of which were sacred instruments used in pagan worship. Paul's inference is striking: Without understanding how to play these instruments in pagan ceremonies, the sounds that come out are like "*speaking into the air.*" Recalling again that Paul is deliberate in his choice of words, what can this mean? Some commentators suggest a contemporary, intellectual understanding on Paul's statement; that is, that the infiltrators are simply "blowing hot air" or wasting one's breath. But in first-century Corinth, this statement meant something much more ominous. It is a dire warning from Paul that the intruders' *glossolalia* is far from angelic language. It is worse than flutes, harps and horns, that, when played incorrectly in pagan service, not only fail to please the pagan deity, i.e., a demon, *but call retribution upon the errant player(s)*. They are inviting attack by "speaking into the air," i.e., inviting evil retribution upon themselves.

---

525. 2 Cor 12:2–5.

Perilous Risk for the Adherents

Having warned the infiltrators of the danger they face, Paul now turns to the adherents that have been swayed, those who now embrace and rely on *gnosis*, not *agape*, and claim the *charisma* of *glossolalia* as evidence of their full and complete divine status. Paul appeals to them by citing a common example. By noting the multiplicity of languages in the world (*gene phonon* or "kinds of languages"),[526] Paul implies that each has a meaning and interpretation; if a foreigner cannot understand the language spoken then it is not only useless, it is pointless. The intruders' *glossolalia* is useless since there is no interpretation to the *ecclesia* or the *euangelion*. Paul acknowledges the desire for *charismata*, but again appeals to a return to *agape*: "Even so, since you are zealous for the spiritual gifts [i.e., the swayed adherents], let it be for the edification of the *ecclesia* that you may excel."[527] Thus, if *glossolalia* is unintelligible, it cannot benefit of the community, it is not of the Spirit and can lead to deception. Paul's reference and call for the adherents to "excel" links directly back to his original appeal to embrace the more "excellent Way," i.e., that all *charismata* must build up the *ecclesia*, and so, the valid desire for *glossolalia* is based on *agape* for the strengthening of the community.

For Paul, such edification can only begin with rites of *interpretation* (*diermeneue*),[528] which is also a *charisma* given by the Spirit: "For this reason anyone who speaks in a tongue should pray that he may interpret what he says. I will pray with my spirit, but I will pray with my mind also; I will sing with my spirit, but I will sing with my mind also." Here, Paul demands interpretation be accompanied by ecstatic prayer that is intelligible (*prosuche*), allowing that prayer is the Spirit may be in word or in song, just as the interpretation may also be in word or song. Paul identifies characteristics of prayer practiced in charismatic and ecstatic rites of his *ecclesia*. Paul admonishes those who pray ecstatically in *glossolalia*, whether in word and song, must do so not just in the Spirit, but also *with the mind*, the *nous*, in order to excel in *agape*. Paul's use of the word *nous* is, as always, a deliberate one.

It appears that Paul is referencing the term *nous* in sense of the gnostic terminology found in later literature, that is, *nous* as the highest living cognitive soul,[529] the divine element that is made alive by *gnosis* and brings full consciousness as to one's divine origin—the awakening, or what is term in the Gospel of Mary, "the Moment of Awakening." If so, Paul accepts his enemies' acknowledgment of the *nous*. But then, he radically transforms their use and understanding of its function from the source of a solitary "awakening" into a more transparent and communal meaning, namely, that of

---

526. 1 Cor 14:10.

527. 1 Cor 14:12.

528. 1 Cor 14:13–15.

529. For Plato, the immortal part of the soul, the higher mind; the *Gospel of Mary*, a gnostic document of the 3rd century CE, cites Jesus as describing the nous as the part of the being that recognizes him in the "Moment of Vision" and is the individual's divine essence, greater than and "between" the soul and spirit; there are multiple examples in gnostic literature.

the divine intellect and reasoning whose only legitimate function is to discern and then employ the *charismata* if they build *agape* and edify the community—this is the divine, higher function of the *nous*. Paul asserts that the legitimate *charisma* of *glossolalia* is also governed by the *nous*, meaning that ecstatic speaking in song or prayer "in the Spirit" that is unintelligible excludes the highest gift, namely, the application of the *nous* with interpretation to strengthen the community and its protection with *agape*.

Given the context of the passage and Paul's practice of referencing his enemies' slogans, words and practices, it is quite apparent that Paul is indeed intending to transform the word *nous* as understood by them (i.e., the individual "soul" awakened by *gnosis* to salvation), into the divine evaluative "gift" that searches and validates other *charismata* through the highest expression of God and divinity, *agape*. It is not simply evaluative in the sense of testing, but more in the sense of screening and filtering by evaluating if the prayer spoken or sung in *glossolalia*, once understood, edifies and strengthens *agape*. Thus, the gift of the *nous* evaluates if the prayer or song is valid for the edification of the *ecclesia* through understanding. If not, the adherent either rejects the ecstatic experience or ensures it will not be debilitating or destructive. In doing so, Paul boldly seizes their term and contextualizes as a divine *charisma* guided by *agape*.

From Paul's description of the activity of the intruders during the gathering of all the *ecclesiae* in Corinth for the Lord's Supper, it is apparent that they intentionally publicly practiced a full range of *glossolalia*, from speaking in indecipherable, heavenly or angelic language to ecstatic prayer and ecstatic singing.[530] This is the first and only indication in the undisputed writings of Paul where *singing in tongues* is mentioned. Paul warns that blessing the prayers and songs of the intruders' *glossolalia* with "amen"[531] is forbidden if adherents cannot understand what is being said, revealing another practice in his *ecclesiae*.

> Otherwise when you are praising God in the Spirit, how can someone else, who is now put in the position of an inquirer, say "Amen" to your thanksgiving, since they do not know what you are saying? You are giving thanks well enough, but no one else is edified.[532]

It is apparent that the general assembly of *ecclesiae* adopted some of the elements of the Jewish Hellenistic synagogue.[533] The law and prophets were read with comment or interpretation (the role of Paul's *propheteia*), and prayer and singing of hymns were conducted.[534] Paul mentions the affirmation of giving thanks to God with the word

---

530. 1 Cor 14:14–15.

531. See below on "amen," a term familiar to the Diaspora synagogue.

532. 1 Cor 14:16–17.

533. The information is very sparse on the first-century synagogue practices, however, some basic elements are known to have been present.

534. Conzelmann, *Corinthians*, 238.

The Enemies of Paul: Demons, Satan, Betrayers, and Apostles

"amen," specifically a term used by Jews from the earliest times,[535] and undoubtedly in the synagogue setting. Thus, the infiltrators' and adherents' practices as established by Paul reflect a Hellenistic Jewish synagogue background.[536]

Paul's Authority over the Opponents' *Glossolalia*

Paul then expresses thanks to God (*eucharisto*) for his *charisma* of *glossolalia* of tongues. The common interpretation is as follows:

> I thank God that I speak in tongues more than all of you. But in the church I would rather speak five intelligible words to instruct others than ten thousand words in a tongue.[537]

But this interpretation does not fit the intensity of Paul's warnings, i.e., that he simply claims he can outdo them in the volume of speaking. To understand the magnitude of the difference between Paul and the intruders, it is important to carefully evaluate Paul's claim that he can speak in multiple heavenly languages.

First, his thanks to God are linked with the diversity of charismatic powers, particularly *glossolalia*; *panton umon mallon glossais lalo*, "I speak in *more tongues* than *all* of you."[538] When the intruders ultimately challenge the legitimacy of Paul's spiritual prowess and standing as an *apostolos*, Paul must defend himself and identifying where he heard and learned these spiritual languages,[539] i.e., in the "third heaven," the very spiritual objective of his enemies. Paul denies he is boasting, but stating fact; that is, he can speak and interpret several heavenly languages. Yet, he counts this as nothing if the words cannot edify and build *agape* in the *ecclesia*.

Paul summarizes this theme again: "I would rather speak five words with my mind (*nous*) in order *to instruct* others, than ten thousand words in a tongue." Paul's sets aside his charismatic gifts so that his mind, the *nous* (see above), the inspired intellect driven by *agape*, can "instruct" others and build up the *ecclesia*. Paul's ability to speak in multiple languages must facilitate service and teaching (one of the appointments), so as to edify. But, the word Paul uses, *katecheso*, or "I should be instructing," is an unusual Greek word for him. By selecting it, Paul sharpens the expectation for any interpretations that comes from *glossolalia*, i.e., it cannot simply be a repetition of words, but instead the interpretation must be a *catechism*—better said, an application of divine *logoi*

---

535. Num 5:22; Deut 27:15–26; Isa 25:1; Jer 3:19; 11:5, et al.

536. Conzelmann, *Corinthians*, 236–37; he rightly isolates the elements Paul describes to the Hellenistic synagogue, as the shorter "amen" replaced the longer affirmation used in temple services, "Blessed be the name of the glory of his kingdom for ever and ever."

537. 1 Cor 14:19–20.

538. Publicly stating that he was greater in his ability to speak in tongues than "all" of them would indicate that this could not have been disputed—this is historical proof that Paul did speak in heavenly, as well as foreign language.

539. 2 Cor 12:1–6.

of heavenly language to fortify the *agape* of the *ecclesia* in the last days. Paul's comparison would then render the practice of *glossolalia* in the Corinthian *ecclesia* as relegated to the fringe of practices that are to be admitted in its gatherings and services—it is to be allowed only if it edifies instruction and *agape* in the last days.[540]

Paul addresses those who have been swayed by the intruders: "Brethren [*adelphoi*], do not be children in your thinking, babes in evil, but in thinking be mature."[541] Paul characterizes the intruders' claim to divine standing as *agnosis*, ignorance—"do not be children in your thinking." Paul's phrase, "babes in evil," extends their ignorance to having become deadly and deceptive, the work of Satan. They are the children of evil. "Be mature in your thinking," meaning, reject the evil ones!

Paul then sternly warns and makes clear to the *adelphoi* the evil children's impending doom by employing a free quotation from prophetic Scripture:[542]

> By men of strange tongues and by the lips of foreigners will I speak to this people, and even then they will not listen to me, says the Lord.[543]

Paul's point is poignant: The *pneumatikoi* utterly fail to understand God's activity present in *glossolalia*, are deceived by evil and are at terrible risk. He calls on the *adelphoi* to recognize what the *charismata* of *glossolalia* signifies—the near and still pending intervention of God in *agape* that is evidenced in the work of the Spirit among both Jews *and* Gentiles.[544] The Jewish *apostoloi* must awake to the realization that *glossolalia* is a democratized divine *sign*. Isaiah's prophecy demonstrates this, as it never signified the achievement of salvation, but the call to respond to God's activity in history. Just as the Israelites failed to heed the significance of the cataclysmic changes about to occur with the arrival of foreign tongues among them, so the intruders ignore what the tongues reveal about the impending intervention of God. Isaiah confirms the reign of

---

540. Paul does not forbid it, for it is a recognized gift that he has obviously endorsed, and in which he practices. But even more, it was witnessed and experienced by the earliest followers dating to the event at Pentecost, shortly after the resurrection encounters with Jesus of Nazareth. Indeed, it was likely well known as *the* historical event that signaled the outpouring of the Spirit and the fulfillment of the prophecy of Joel (2:28–32).

541. 1 Cor 14:20.

542. Paul's quotations are sometimes free renderings of the "Scripture," which in first-century Judaism included both the Law and the Prophets, but in this case Paul seems to be referencing a Greek translation of the Hebrew Scriptures other than the Septuagint, one which Conzelmann identifies as known also to one Aquila, a Jew who ultimately translated the Hebrew Scriptures into Greek in 128 CE (Conzelmann, *Corinthians*, 242n17); regardless, the point is the remarkable knowledge of Paul and that his statement in Gal 1:13–14 is certainly accurate: "... and I was advancing in Judaism beyond many of my contemporaries among my countryman, being more extremely zealous for my ancestral traditions." Paul was a well-trained Jew who thoroughly knew the law and could accurately cite passages from memory and apply them, as well as engage in effective Midrash. This also indicates, once again, that the opponents he addressed were Jews.

543. Isa 28:11–12.

544. That is, as a tangible witness to the glorious presence of God among them, thereby strengthening the *agape* of the assembly as it awaits the Lord.

God is coming and *glossolalia* is *one of many charismata* and appointments given by God and his Spirit, which are all intended to edify and strengthen his people; but even more, they are intended to influence a response from those *outside the assembly* bringing more to the *euangelion*. For Paul, this is particularly the function of the *charismata* of *glossolalia*: "Thus, tongues are a *sign* not for adherents, but for unbelievers."[545] The intruders' claim to divine status, evidenced by their practice of *glossolalia*, is not just an error—it is the demonstration of ignorance by the children of who are evil, the children of Satan. Instead of gaining adherents, the chaotic experience, void of meaning and *agape*, presents itself just as Paul describes, like "madmen" speaking into the air:

> If, therefore, the whole church assembles,[546] and all speak in tongues, and outsiders and unbelievers enter, will they not say that you are mad![547]

The intruders then prevent the Spirit from the operative purpose of *glossolalia* in the *ecclesia*; that is, as an eschatological sign of God, a *charisma* whose divine speaking must be conducted with the *nous* to provide *agape* and edification through its prayers, songs, prophecies and catechism to the community; and as a call to the wayward and lost to seek the Way. They appear as *madmen* (*hoti manesthe*), i.e., the possessed, driving away potential adherents, and so, are evil. Like the Israelites, they fail to heed the weighty meaning of the sign of *glossolalia*; they face the same errant destruction that came upon those people.

The Practice of Prophecy in Paul's *Ecclesiae* and the *Logia* of Jesus Christ

With the function and proper use of *glossolalia* now established (and dire warnings as to is misuse by Paul's enemies made clear), Paul points both the intruders and adherents to the preeminent *charisma*, *propheteia*—the gift of insight, interpretation and application of Scripture and *logia* of the Lord to the *sitz im leben* of the *ecclesia in the final days*. Paul also focuses on the power and importance of this *charisma* for the *apistos* (literally, the "unbelievers"), or *idiotes* (the inquirer, layman or the ignorant),[548] that come into the assembly while "all" are prophesying (just as "all" were speaking in tongues):

> But if all are prophesying and the unbeliever or layman enters, he is *exposed* by all and is *convinced* by all. And thus, the secrets [*krupta*, "hidden things"] of the heart [*kardias*] are revealed; and so falling down on his face, he will

---

545. 1 Cor 14:22.

546. All of the house churches come together in one house or hall, again indicating the size of the assembly was forty to one hundred believers.

547. 1 Cor 14:23.

548. Paul be could be referring to those outside of the tradesmen, the leatherworkers, whose "guild" embraced the Way as was evident in other ecclesia such as Thessaloniki—indeed it is possible.

worship God and *report* that God is truly among you [i.e., he will proselytize, proclaiming to Way to others].⁵⁴⁹

Paul's statement has received many interpretations, from a prophetic ability to see into the heart (a kind of clairvoyance), to the prophet's employing Scripture and *logia* of the Lord to convince the *apistoi* of their affront to God (their sin), and the hope of rescue from doom by embracing the Way. While this later interpretation seems to fit with Paul's theology as to the nature of universal sin found in his letter to the Romans,⁵⁵⁰ it does not fit the historical context of the perilous risks and challenges Paul faces in Corinth. Indeed, Paul is describing actual events he had witnessed, i.e., the actual activity and impact of the prophet practicing the rites or rituals the *charisma* of the Spirit, and how the outcome has transformed those witnessing the *charisma* from ignorance to *pistis* in the *euangelion* and practice of *agape* (understanding of the doom of the impending crisis and the perilous risk of their *sitz im leben*), leading to the mitigation of perilous risk by embracing the Way and *agape*. How so?

Paul's description of the prophet's activity in Corinth must be considered both historical and accurate, not only because there were other witnesses who could corroborate it (including the intruders), but also because Paul's account is troubling, and so free of interpretive embellishment. There was drunkenness, hunger, dispute, avarice, arrogance and contention—not *agape*. Indeed, the gatherings of the local *ecclesiae* at one assembly "on the first day of the week" (i.e., for the cultic meal, the ingestion of blood and body of the crucified and resurrected Lord) are described as far from idyllic—just the opposite. They were chaotic, unorganized, and made even more complex and confusing by the entry of Paul's vociferous enemies who espoused superiority over adherents and shouted out in ecstatic prayer and song unintelligible *glossolalia*; words they claimed came directly into them from angels and the divine—*a kind of ecstatic angelic possession*. Paul's description confirms then that *apistoi* experienced uncontrolled *charismata*, from *glossolalia* to *propheteia*. Yet, remarkably, the *apistoi* are personally overcome by *propheteia* and share with the prophet an ecstatic experience. Paul's description of this impact, which is transformative, is striking.

Paul describes the powerful *charisma* of prophecy as it unfolds in an encounter with *apistoi*. The *kardia* (the inner secrets, even shame)⁵⁵¹ and *sitz im leben* of the individual are not only revealed by the prophetic *logoi*, but the doom faced. These secrets are revealed so completely in *logoi* given by the Spirit (perhaps publicly, but certainly privately) that it is physically and mentally overwhelming to the individual, driving them to the ground. *Logia*, Scripture and insights render the unbeliever vulnerable to the dire risks at hand. This is not an intellectual revelation—they are infected with death and face annihilation that will come upon them any day. An awakening of the

---

549. 1 Cor 14:24–25.
550. Rom 6:1–23.
551. See 2 Cor 2:4, *aishunes*.

The Enemies of Paul: Demons, Satan, Betrayers, and Apostles

individual's *nous by revelation and understanding that only the Spirit of God could know* is experienced. Unlike the intruders' awakening that creates the Solitary One, the new adherent of the *ecclesia* is confronted by the crisis of their infection and doom, but also the mitigation of risk of death available to them through *pistis* in the *euangelion*, which in turn engenders signs of acceptance by God, the *charismata* of the Spirit, which builds the community of *agape* of the last days.[552] Paul is speaking from his own intense personal experience of a similar encounter.[553] The "secrets of the heart" were laid bare.[554] The prophetic encounter with the Spirit by the individual awakening to the infection and crisis at hand is reflected in the synoptic tradition, particularly Mark 13:11, where the *logoi* of Jesus (almost certainly *logoi* or the risen Lord) address the "piercing the heart" of even his enemies.[555] The overwhelming encounter of the *apistoi* results in what Paul calls *conviction* (*elegchetai*), and cries out, "God is really among you!"[556] The *apistos* is "exposed," i.e., completely laid bare, and so, devastated and in terror. Consequently, Paul provides the earliest and most intimate and descriptive account of the ecstatic encounter of an *apistos* with the *charisma* of the Spirit of God, *propheteia*.

Prophetic *logoi* are reflected in the speech[557] attributed to Kayfa at *Shavu'ot* (Pentecost) to a gathering of *apistoi* immediately after they witness *glossolalia*; remarkably, the same type of prophetic activity demonstrated in Corinth that also follows *glossolalia*[558]—certainly this is no coincidence. As recorded in Acts of the Apostles, Kayfa's prophetic utterance of what had recently transpired (i.e., an interpretation of Scripture with insight and application to the *sitz im leben* of the *apistos*), what it meant (*logia* of the risen Lord recast with prophetic interpretation of Scripture), and what will soon be experienced, which reveals their doom and the cataclysmic risk and danger they face[559] (the personal prophetic utterance to transform the heart

---

552. John 1:47–49.

553. Gal 1:16.

554. "It is hard for you to kick against the pricks," the reference to the first-century farmer who used a goad to prick the oxen while tilling the field, and when the oxen kicked back, the prick went in deeper—certainly another way of referring to being pierced to the heart.

555. This saying is immensely powerful and moving, as it comes from the first generation of missionaries, the world of Paul and the apostles, and those who were facing the first intense and organized persecution of Christians by Nero in 64–65 CE following the fire in Rome as recorded to Tacitus, *Annals* 15:44, 2–8; this was most certainly *a prophetic saying* of the risen Lord to his *ecclesiae*.

556. 1 Cor 14:25.

557. The speech reflects a more sophisticated and refined theology and Christology, and so, reflects the editorial and redactive work of a later Christian editor in 80–90 CE.

558. See Acts 2:37.

559. Acts 2:40, where Kayfa, "with many other *logoi* he warned them; and he pleaded with them, 'Save yourselves from this corrupt generation.'" This one statement underplays the central place such prophetic *logoi* actually took. The eschatological crisis here is muted, i.e., "save yourselves from this corrupt generation," as the pending *parousia* for Paul in 1 Corinthians is urgent, imminent and perilous. They are not saving themselves from a corrupt generation, but from annihilation, satanic powers and death.

of the individual listener through *agape*, reaching to the "secrets of the heart"). The speech ends with the statement, "Now when they heard this they were 'pierced' [literally, pricked or punctured; *stung*; *katenugesan*] to the heart." In the first century, this statement, "pierced to the heart," was a colloquialism for "shattered," that is, a radical change to the mind (*nous*) and perception of reality that is transformative. In the general sense, this public event has very individual impact, and in the Corinthian *ecclesia*, the *apistoi* experienced personal revelations and an awakening of the *nous*—but the characteristics and sequence of events (*glossolalia* to *propheteia*) fits the experience in Corinth. Notably, *propheteia* fails to accompany the unintelligible *glossolalia* of the intruders. Certainly, Kayfa's speech must somewhat reflect the Corinthian prophetic experience,[560] i.e., "that they may learn and all be *exhorted* and *convicted*."[561]

Paul describes the prophetic impact on the *apistos*: "And so, falling on his face,[562] he will worship God and declare that, 'God is really among you.'"[563] Prophecy and the work of the Spirit powerfully combined to transform the *nous* of the individual, "penetrating the heart," *convicting* to humility and creating awe that acknowledges the actual presence of God's Spirit. Corinthian prophets then, like the prophetic speech of Kayfa, did not reject the *apistoi*, which stood in stark contrast to the intruders.

Conflict over the *Charismata*

After explaining the critical role and purpose of prophets and prophetic activity in the Corinthian *ecclesia*, Paul provides the earliest description of *koinonia*, the fellowship of adherents, i.e., the gathering of the house churches on the "first day of the week."[564] In the case of the Corinthian *ecclesia*, the assembly numbered between fifty to one hundred twenty adherents. It was a unique and socially diverse gathering, all bound together by *pistis* in the *euangelion*, *charismata* and *agape*, set in a framework of intense eschatological expectation: Jews and Gentiles, male and female, rich and poor, elite and low social status, all equal as the *hagios*, the holy ones, the *tekna tou* and protective *agape*[565]—the democratized new "Israel of God" awaiting the *parousia*.[566]

560. There were at least three prophets in Corinth according to Paul's letter.

561. 1 Cor 14:31.

562. The most humbled and reverent position in Judaism and the ancient middle east (also to this day); all of the prophets did so, see Ezek 9:8; also see Gen 48:12 (Joseph) and Ruth 2:10; this was the position Jesus took in his prayer in the Garden of Gethsemane, Matt 26:39—this confirms that only an eyewitness could have reported this.

563. 1 Cor 14:25.

564. There is no question that the Gentile *ecclesia* adopted the first day because it was the day of the resurrection; it is unknown if the Jerusalem *ecclesia* under James and the remaining apostles met on that day—since the Jerusalem believers formed a communal association, they may have met daily in common meals until its size made that practice prohibitive, evidenced by the adoption of the deacons who delivered meals [to Gentile widows] in the place of the apostles.

565. See Gal 3:28.

566. Gal 6:16.

Paul addresses his adherents: "What does this suggest, brethren? When you come together [i.e., in one assembly for the cultic meal, the Lord's Supper], each one has,"

- a *hymn* (i.e., literally a psalm, *psalmon*, such as those sung or perhaps recited at the beginning of synagogue services);

- a *lesson*, i.e., a teaching, *dedoxen*, likely drawn from the core of the primitive oral tradition predating the gospel narratives; namely, the oral recount of the last week of life, betrayal, death, and resurrection of Jesus of Nazareth, and other oral traditions and sayings that had already become attached to that narrative—the content of the primitive gospel is confirmed by Paul himself in 1 Cor 15:1–5, as Paul refers to the *euangelion* as this core, already quoted as if Scripture indicated by the use of *oti*, i.e., "that," followed by a formal statement; the teaching could also come from the law;

- a *revelation*, i.e., *apocalupsin*. Like Paul who was transformed, so too have been Corinthian adherents be radically changed, and any new *apokolupeis* are provided to measurable aid in that transformation, engendering *pistis*, *elpis* and *agape* until the *parousia*. The "revealing [or manifesting] of things formerly hidden" set in the context of the intense eschatological fervor in Corinth served the plethora of *charismata*, and so could be related to *propheteia* or *glossolalia*; the "revelation" to which Paul refers was surely focused on revealing the nature of the coming cataclysmic events of the last days, the return of the Lord and arrival of the kingdom of heaven; as revelation was a *charisma*, what was revealed certainly helped to form the earliest traditions as to the *parousia*, i.e., similar to Paul's own revelation of the sequence of events in 1 Thess 4:15 that he received by revelation "from the Lord";

- a *tongue*, i.e., *glossolalia*, the center of Paul's dispute with the opponents described previously, which Paul discounts as even useful without interpretation;

- or an *interpretation*, i.e., *hermeneian*; it is not clear if Paul intends *interpretation* for speaking tongues or for prophecy, but it seems clear in this case Paul is referring to the interpretation of tongues, as he is about to stress order in the *ecclesia* of Corinth, something completely lacking in the confusion created by the rampant *glossolalia*, and other *charismata*, in Corinth.

It is interesting that Paul begins his description of the gatherings in Corinth with the *hymn*, more accurately translated, *a psalm*. A hymn or psalm was sung or recited at the beginning of services in the Jewish synagogue, and also at its conclusion. Jesus is reported to have sung a psalm with his disciples after finishing the meal in Jerusalem, a *Seder*, just before they took the evening journey to the Garden of Gethsemane for protection, rest and prayer.[567] Paul's placement of the psalm at the beginning of his list of

---

567. Matt 26:30.

activities in the *ecclesia* may reveal Paul's own imposed *assumption as to how the order of the fellowship is to be conducted arising from his background in the style of the Hellenistic Jewish synagogue*.[568] This could have come from Jews or God fearers who had left the synagogue and joined the *ecclesia*. Of course, this would also imply that the early adherents understood themselves as members of sect of Judaism, i.e., the legitimate extension of God's promised people at the end of the age, the "new Israel."[569]

Paul's second element as well, "a teaching," *dedoxen*, was also familiar in the Hellenistic synagogue, usually coming after a reading of the law.[570] Again, Jesus was asked to read and provide a teaching in the synagogue of Nazareth, although his response was instead a *prophetic interpretation*.[571] Consequently, Scripture and interpretation, in this case prophetic interpretation, must have been intended to follow. These features confirm that worship and fellowship in Paul's *ecclesia* were modeled on the practices of the Hellenistic synagogue. Based on Paul's remaining description, much of what was chaotic.

Paul confirms that while he employed some traditional elements of synagogue worship in the Corinthian *ecclesia*, his dominant concern was for the orderly expression of the *charismata*, particularly prophecy, to ensure the strengthening of *agape* for protection of *ecclesia* from satanic attack. As such, it is here that Paul establishes a protocol for distilling and approving *logoi* that emerge via the *charisma* of prophetic speech. A collective group of prophets, chosen by the Spirit, perform this role. More, they are to follow a process of confirmed interpretation, "the *charisma* of the prophets is subject to the control of the prophets."[572] By this statement he acknowledges that the prophets were guardians of the oral tradition and *logia*, as well as conduits for new traditions and *logoi* and *logia* of the risen Lord, as well as the application of Hebrew Scripture to the events unfolding in the *sitz im leben* of the *ecclesia*. Most important, they were to ensure that satanic deception did not infiltrate the *ecclesia* or its *adherents*.

Paul confirms he established the appointment of prophets, and that they were operative while he had been present. As such, the disruption of order in the *ecclesia* is completely associated with entry of the intruders. Just as with the troubling, drunken behavior of the intruders at the Lord's Supper (which rendered the central sacrament of *koinonia* with the risen Lord chaotic, offensive and subject to divine retribution), the infiltrators also *intentionally* disrupt the order of practices established by Paul by overwhelming them with loud, unintelligible *glossolalia*. Paul limits *glossolalia*, requiring order and the *charisma* of interpretation, and then acceptance of the translation only if it strengthens the *ecclesia* in *agape*.

568. See Chijioke Iwe, *Jesus in the Synagogue of Capernaum*.
569. Rom 9:27.
570. As we have seen, Paul's use of "the law" includes the meaning of both Torah and Prophets.
571. Luke 4:16–21.
572. 1 Cor 14:29–31.

The Enemies of Paul: Demons, Satan, Betrayers, and Apostles

He states: "If any man speaks [*lalei*] in a tongue [*glosse*], then it should be two, or at most [*pleiston*],[573] three on each occasion,[574] and one after the other; and someone is to be interpreting."[575] Contrast this with Paul's statement on prophesying: "In the case of prophets, however, two or three *should speak* [or 'let them speak,' *laleitosan*], and the others should *test* [*diakrinetosan*, not simply to 'judge' right or wrong as some translations adopt, but to evaluate, sift, weigh, sort through carefully and thoughtfully] what is said."[576] The difference between these statements is striking. It is clear that Paul only reluctantly allows *glossolalia* into the fellowship gatherings, *and only if there is active interpretation*: "But if there is no interpreter, *let the man keep silent* in the *ecclesia*, and let him speak to himself and God."[577] But with regard to prophecy, Paul strongly encourages active discussion, and even more, requires that other prophets evaluate and test each statement: "You can surely all prophesy, one after the other, so that all may learn and will be exhorted [the word 'exhorted,' *parakalontai* may also be translated, 'encouraged']."[578] In effect, Paul silences the intruders during the assembly by censuring *glossolalia*; if there is no *charisma* of interpretation, then they are to "keep silent." Conversely, he ensures that prophecy, guided by *agape*, is to dominate the *charismata* because all essential testing and judgment as to what is acceptable for "learning" and "exhortation"[579] are to be weighed by the prophets.

It is an effective mitigation to the disruption and claims of the intruders. Paul establishes order by asserting that *prophetic agape* must be the preeminent characteristic of the assembly and the boundary of the employment of *charismata*. To further solidify the preeminent position of the *agape prophets* as unassailable, Paul states, "The gifts of the prophets are under the prophet's control";[580] i.e., no one can usurp their authority in the order of God's appointments, not even an *apostolos*, such as Paul, and particularly the Jerusalem *apostoloi*. This rejects anyone who would claim that prophetic *charismata* are subject to *glossolalia*. Consequently, the infiltrators' claim to have superior standing via *gnosis* and point to the *charisma* of *glossolalia* as confirmation of their standing as "kings" is to not only be rejected, *Paul implies is should be silenced because it is evil, and not of the Spirit of God*. Thus, Paul successfully dismisses the intruders' insistence that other *charismata* as subservient to *glossolalia*. "God is not the God of disorder [*akatastasia*, i.e., that brought into the *ecclesia* by the

---

573. Paul uses this limiting term to devalue tongues in comparison to the employment of other gifts, particularly prophesy.

574. The "occasion" of the gathering of the joint *ecclesiae* into one assembly on the first day of the week.

575. 1 Cor 14:27.

576. 1 Cor 14:29.

577. 1 Cor 14:28.

578. 1 Cor 14:31.

579. Perhaps better translated as "encouragement."

580. 1 Cor 14:32.

apostoloi[581]], but of peace." Paul thereby condemns the intentional disruption of the fellowship meetings as proof they are not of God. This rejection is true for all of the *ecclesiae*, "as in all the *ecclesiae* of the *hagios*."

Paul thereby firmly establishes the critical and pivotal role of the prophets in Corinth—all subject to *agape* and the *euangelion*. The distinction is critically important in that next to the *apostoloi*, the prophets become the most influential men and women in the formation of the oral tradition and formative practices in early Christianity. The prophets became the purveyors of orthodoxy and heresy, beginning in their small groups organized and encouraged by Paul.[582] Through the *charisma* of the Spirit, *agape* prophets began to interpret and apply Scripture to the life and teachings of Jesus of Nazareth in light of the Easter event to the *sitz im leben* of the *ecclesia*; they also incorporated *logia* from the rich oral tradition, which included new sayings of the risen Lord (e.g., those provided by Paul, evidenced in the Corinthian correspondence), all for the purpose of edification and to strengthen *agape* in the *ecclesia*.

Paul's elevation of the prophets to a dominant role within his *ecclesiae* renders the intruders' undecipherable *glossolalia* useless. Consequently, if the intruders make claims as to their standing based on *glossolalia*, or assert elitist standing based on *glossolalia*, that contradict the judgment of the prophets, then *they are to be ignored*: "If anyone thinks he is a prophet or a *pneumatic* [*e pneumatikos*], then he must recognize that what I have written to you is a *command of the Lord*," i.e., the risen Jesus, Lord and Christ.[583] Paul is abundantly clear—his *paraenesis* on the order and priority of *charismata* during the gatherings have been validated by a new "command [*entole*] of the Lord." As such, it is not Paul that is being rejected—they are rejecting Jesus Christ. To recognize that Paul cites a new *command* of the Lord is to understand that Paul makes claim to an active relationship with Jesus Christ not shared by the intruders. Paul's description of his apostleship is thus made abundantly clear—he is the "bondservant" of Christ,[584] a *doulos*. Paul therefore effectively mitigates the disruption and claims of the opponents in the *ecclesia* of *agape* by imposing an *entole* of the risen Lord as his *apostolos*. Given that the Corinthians are commanded by the Lord to submit, Paul concludes: "Therefore, my brethren, strive after [i.e., 'long for,' or 'be eager for'] prophecy and do not forbid speaking in tongues, but let everything be done decently [*euschemonos*, respectfully, i.e., *for edification*], and according to the order [i.e., *taxin*, as it has been ordained by command of the Lord Jesus Christ]."[585]

---

581. See Conzelmann, *Corinthians*, 245.

582. 1 Cor 14:29–33.

583. 1 Cor 14:37.

584. Phil 1:1; Rom 1:1, a "bond servant." Paul became a voluntary "slave," a *doulos* ("bondservant"), who was "purchased with a price," see 1 Cor 6:20 into freedom from slavery to death. As a result, he voluntarily belongs completely to Jesus as his Lord and master, a service he cannot deny because of the wondrous things he has seen and the separation from God as Abba' that would result.

585. 1 Cor 14:39–40.

Paul drives the point home by employing additional *logoi* of the Lord: "If anyone does not know [*agnoei*], then *he will not be known*."[586] In the context of Paul's statement on the *entole* of the Lord, which immediately precedes these words,[587] it is clear he addresses the intruders (the *pneumatics*). He cites a saying of the Lord that they employ. But he alters its meaning, linking the saying anew to the requirement (by command of the Lord) that they recognize (i.e., *know*) the subservient place of *glossolalia* to that of both prophecy and *agape* in the *ecclesia*. By implication, they stand alone and apart from God and the salvific *euangelion* of *agape*. Indeed, Paul reverses the intruders' claim to be "kings"—they are not even known by God, and so, are facing doom.

That Paul is quoting from the opponents' collection of *logia*[588] is confirmed by a positive version of the saying in the *Gospel of Thomas*. It reads: "When you know yourself then you will be known."[589] There are primarily two possibilities with regard to Paul's version of the saying. Either Paul has turned the saying from a positive statement to a negative intentionally (which has other ramifications requiring additional discussion, see below), or it is an earlier, more primitive form of the saying. The *pneumatic* will "not be known" by God, *agnoeitai*. They face annihilation in their own ignorance.

A comparison of the intruders' and Paul's version of the saying demonstrates that Paul worked from a written document, as Paul confronts the opponents with a shift in eschatology that is consistent with the emendation of a literary source:

> When you know [*gnoei*] yourself then you will be known. (*Gospel of Thomas*, Saying 3b)

> If anyone does not know [*agnoei*, is ignornant], they will not be known. (1 Cor 14:38)

That Paul must know this saying in written form is evident from the subtle, but precise word change he makes in crafting his negative version of it and the dramatic change that results in the saying's new and urgent eschatological outlook. Thus, Paul's interpretation and change in the saying is best understood only if he is citing the saying and emending it. Certainly, this provides strong support for the earlier interpretation of Paul's statement, "Do not go beyond what is written,"[590] i.e., as having nothing to so with a scribal emendation,[591] but instead with Paul having the document and the collection *logia* employed by the opponents. That Paul consistently corrects erroneous

---

586. 1 Cor 14:38.

587. That is, the primacy of prophecy and edification over the spiritual ecstasy of the pneumatics expressed in unintelligible *glossolalia*.

588. See 1 Cor 2:9 et al.

589. *Gos. Thom.*, Saying 3b.

590. 1 Cor 4:6.

591. Strugnell, "Plea," 555–58.

use of *logia* employed by the intruders would also tend to explain why Paul rarely quotes sayings of Jesus, and instead, only critiques them in 1 Corinthians; that is, they are already a source of grave contention, resulting in trajectories of interpretation that are contrary to his *euangelion*.

Paul, Resurrection and the Risen Lord

Paul moves to the most disturbing and devastating claim of the opponents; *namely that the resurrection has already occurred*. For the intruding *pneumatikoi*, Jesus is the divine *logos*, the redeemer that descended as the Spirit, the Living One, free from materiality or human form. As the divine *logos*, he is the envoy and agent of powerful *gnosis* that provides salvific *logia*, which when understood, awaken the soul and unites the divine into the Solitary One, the child of *sophia*. The journey of awakening and reunion with the divine is confirmed by the *charisma* of *glossolalia*, which awards a divine-like status, free of the world of ignorance and death, where this material world, its corruption and deceit, can be rejected and ridiculed. A physical resurrection then would be absurd. Resurrection back into corruption is unthinkable.

For Paul, the world is the creation of a good and loving God. The fall into death and corruption was the result of rebellion against God. Paul understands man's position as hopeless and separated from by this sin and error. Jesus came as the redeemer, becoming the sacrifice to destroy sin and death. It is only *pistis* in the efficacious *euangelion* (i.e., the death, burial and resurrection) and the practice of *agape* that can neutralize the curse of death and repair the rift created by mankind, and so, provide *elpis* in the resurrection and entry into the kingdom of God at the *parousia* for the *tekna tou Theou*. For Paul, it was Adam who introduced sin and death into the world and set in motion the law and the long awaited Messiah who would displace this order.[592]

And so, it is satanic deceit that the intruders deny Jesus' physical death on a cross under the curse of the law and his resurrection appearances that broke that curse. Paul now addresses this last pivotal issue and deadly error of the opponents—denial of the death, burial and resurrection of Jesus of Nazareth.

Mitigating the Perilous Risk of Salvific *Gnosis*: The Resurrection of Jesus

To refute the intruders rejection of Jesus' resurrection as paramount to salvation, Paul cites a very early, well-developed unit of tradition in 1 Cor 15:3–5. It antedates 1 Corinthians. Its formulaic structure has mnemonic quality, suggesting it was circulated orally as an independent unit. Indeed, Paul introduces the tradition using two important terms; that he "received" (*paralabon*), and then orally "delivered" (*paradoka*) it to the Corinthians. These terms unequivocally confirm an oral

---

592. As reflected in Rom 5:12–21.

background for the unit, as they are technical terms employed by rabbis to describe the passing of reliable and sacred oral tradition, such as the Oral Torah, the *Mishna*. Paul's use of these terms may reflect his Pharisaic training, which was significantly reliant on the accurate transmission of a substantial body of sacred oral tradition. Paul is thereby introducing powerful and salvific tradition, what he considers to be equivalent with Hebrew Scripture; namely, the efficacious *euangelion*, the core of which is the call to *pistis* in the death, burial *and resurrection* of Jesus of Nazareth. The *euangelion* in turn engenders *pistis*, *elpis* and *agape*—only this is salvific result mitigates all risk and neutralizes the power of Satan.

Further analysis of the unit is revealing. First, each line begins with *hoti* (i.e., "that"). Paul and other contemporary writers typically use *hoti* to introduce or quote sacred oral traditions, laws or sayings, or written Hebrew Scripture. Consequently, *hoti* is confirmation that Paul considers this oral unit on par with Scripture—it was unassailable. Second, a comparison of each line and the tradition as a whole with Paul's language and style in his undisputed letters (particularly 1 and 2 Corinthians, 1 Thessalonians, Romans and Galatians) clearly demonstrates that it is not Pauline. As such, its origin (to which is appended the earliest listing of resurrection appearances in the New Testament) must have originated very early and among the first post-crucifixion witnesses of the resurrection, most of whom were said by Paul to be alive and active. Paul defends its accuracy because there are witnesses who could corroborate or reject it.[593] The existence and circulation of independent oral tradition of the *euangelion*, one that predates Paul's post-crucifixion encounter with Jesus, would seem to contradict Paul's claim in Galatians that he received the *euangelion* by revelation, *apokalupseos iesou christou*,[594] not from any man. However, the circulation of an independent oral form and a revelation or manifestation to Paul of Jesus Christ is not mutually exclusive. Paul's emphasis is on the resurrection as the pivotal event in history includes an equally emphatic insistence on the death and burial of Jesus. As such, his emphasis on *burial* and *death* empties any claim by the intruders that Jesus was a "spiritual" agent of *gnosis* and wisdom.

Paul then provides dire warning for those who would abandon the *euangelion* for the *gnosis* of the infiltrators. He begins: "But I make known to you [*gnorizein*], brothers" just as he had begun his warning in his defense of the *euangelion* to the Galatian *ecclesiae*.[595] Paul then confirms that this is the same "*euangelion*, I preached to you," that was "accepted [by you]." The word "accepted," *paralambanein*, means that it is a living acceptance, active, and operative—it has mystical and infusive salvific powers for the adherent. Indeed, the acceptance of the *euangelion* by *pistis* mitigates deadly risks, allowing them standing in the *elpis* of salvation,[596] but only "if you stand fast";

---

593. 2 Cor 12:2-4; Gal 1:16 are possibilities to this event of revelation.
594. Gal 1:12.
595. Gal 1:11.
596. 1 Cor 15:2.

i.e., they must actively continue in their *pistis* in the *euangelion*, which is evidenced by the practice of *agape*. Consequently, the condition of safety (that is, "standing" in the *elpis* of salvation that neutralizes the curse of death at the *parousia*) is dependent on continuing in *pistis* in the *euangelion*, which for Paul means active *pistis* in death, burial and resurrection of the historical man, Jesus of Nazareth. If they hold fast, i.e., to *pitsis*, they are adopted, protected and accepted as a *tekna tou Theou*, brethren of Jesus Christ, Lord and Savior.

Following his warning, Paul presents the oral tradition that he "received":

> *That* Christ died for our sins according to the scriptures; and *that* he was buried; and *that* he was raised on the third day according to the scriptures.[597]

As noted, the *charismata* of *propheteia* and even *glossolalia* would cite *logia*, logoi, and, as noted here, Hebrew Scripture to confirm the *euangelion*. The oral unit here seems to reference the Suffering Servant tradition of Isaiah 53, i.e., "that Christ died for our sins." If this is allowed, this may be the earliest association of Jesus with the Suffering Servant tradition, i.e., he was *the* Suffering Servant Paul and other Christian writers assert was prophesied by Isaiah, i.e., a christological claim for Jesus. As such, this would reflect rather sophisticated and developed "Christology" very early in the formation of the oral tradition. However, this may be reading too much into the unit. As Conzelmann correctly notes,[598] the idea of atonement is not fully developed here and that statement may instead be emphasizing "substitution," i.e., that Jesus died so that "you" by faith may live, i.e., Jesus' example of complete faith, even to death, made accessible the Way for all to be saved by faith alone. In fact this interpretation more accurately reflects the context of Paul's arguments in 1 Corinthians, as well other scriptural references employed by Paul. However, we are witness to the earliest stage of Christian prophetic practices and the formation of tradition that united Scripture and interpretation to the *euangelion* of Christ's death, burial and resurrection—what later became the passion narrative in the synoptic and Johannine traditions, as well as other noncanonical gospels. Paul in his letter to the Romans more fully expands on this theological concept.[599] Nonetheless, while the oral tradition here links Christ's dying for "our sins" to Isa 53:5–12, it does not identify Jesus as the sole atoning figure, *the* Suffering Servant, but as a man who, like all of Israel, was a suffering servant of God, who was appointed Christ post-crucifixion according to Paul and others.

For Paul, the resurrection was the proof of the impending *parousia*, the eschatological event that portended judgment, the destruction of Satan and death, the general resurrection and arrival of the Christ with the kingdom of God. So, the unit stresses that this miracle of resurrection on "the third day," signifying certain death had been overcome by the miracle of God, has neutralized Satan and the curse of death for

---

597. 1 Cor 15:3b–5.
598. Conzelmann, *1 Corinthians*, 255n59.
599. E.g., Rom 3:24.

Paul's adherents who embrace the gospel. The tradition of the "third day" being the day of the resurrection is *universally attested* in all strata of canonical and several non-canonical writings.[600] By dying on a Friday, before the Sabbath, restrictions forbade work and purity laws prohibited disturbing the body until the "first day" of the week (*shenee* in Hebrew, *Kahd B Shabaa* in Aramaic). Thus, the tradition of the "third day" in the unit confirms the day of the death and resurrection of Jesus as witnessed events, and events and timing that are governed by Jewish law.

Paul associates the raising of Jesus on the third day with fulfillment of "scripture," i.e., "according to the scriptures." What does Paul mean? Paul could be referring to the Psalms: "because you will not abandon me to the grave, nor let your holy one see corruption."[601] Indeed, Acts 13:35 places this very scriptural reference on Paul's lips. In fact, Jesus also referred to the third day in relation to his proclamation of the *euangelion* and the "sign of Jonah,"[602] that is, the near fullness of the inbreaking of the kingdom of God evidenced in his proclamation, exorcisms and war on Satan. Prophetic interpretation of this saying of Jesus, linking it to a prediction of the resurrection, may have occurred in a post-Easter setting, i.e., the prophetic activity of the *ecclesiae*. But clearly, Paul is not referencing Jonah. Additionally, in Kayfa's speech at Pentecost,[603] Acts does not actually have him reference the "third day," he only infers it. As noted, Kayfa's prophetic speech is an example of how early oral tradition developed among Christian prophets and applied Scripture to the resurrection tradition. However, the Kayfa speech does not seem shed any additional light on Paul's own reference to Scripture.

There is a prophecy from Hosea (one of the Minor Prophets, 750 BCE), particularly 6:1–2, which is striking:

> Come, let us return to the Lord; for he has torn us, that he may heal us; he has struck us down that he may bind us up. After two days he will revive us; on the third day he will raise us up that we may live before him.

Hosea would have been one of the prophets familiar to Paul.[604] When combined with Ps 16:10, the prophecy from Hosea would have provided sufficient support for early Christian prophetic association of Scripture with the third day and resurrection. It is worth noting, however, that Paul may have added the statement, "according to the scriptures," as scholars have identified other elements that may have been appended to the original

---

600. E.g., the *Gospel of Peter*, where the religious leaders beseech Pilate for a three day "guard" at the tomb; also see the *Gospel of the Hebrews*.
601. Ps 16:10.
602. Matt 12:39–40.
603. Acts 2:27.
604. Gal 1:14.

oral form by Paul.[605] If so, we have the melding of an established oral tradition with Paul's addition, referencing his own revelations from the Lord.[606]

Paul continues with the oral tradition by listing the first recorded appearances of the risen Lord found in the New Testament: "and that [*hoti*] he appeared to Kayfa, then to the twelve."[607] The word "appeared" (*ophthe*), literally means that "he was seen," not as a ghost, apparition, or one of the untimely dead (see the appearances of ghosts, demons and the untimely dead in *Jesus, Resurrected*), but was seen with the eyes and recognized as present. Interestingly, the appearance to Kayfa is not found in the canonical gospels with the exception of a brief reference in Luke, "It is true, the Lord has risen and he has appeared to Simon [the Semitic name of Kayfa]."[608] The nature of the tradition in Luke with only a glancing reference to the appearance to Kayfa indicates that the tradition was so well known and established that only a brief reference was required.

Paul then adds the last element to what scholars believe was part of the original oral unit: "then [he was seen], by the Twelve." At the time of Paul's writing, the assassin and informant, Judas Iscariot, one of the original Twelve, was dead.[609] If so, who then make up the Twelve?

Acts relates the selection of Matthias as the replacement for Judas, i.e., the new Twelve, who were all "witnesses" to the resurrection.[610] But Paul's use of the designation "the Twelve" is so specific that it implies there was an established cohort of Twelve apostles, that is, as if they were still well known and alive. But even this is problematic. We know that Herod Agrippa I, the grandson of Herod the Great who ruled form 41–44 CE arrested one of the apostles, James the brother of John. James was likely arrested because he was mistaken for James the brother of Jesus, the leader of the Jerusalem *ecclesia*. James was killed on orders of Agrippa "by the sword" (i.e., to prevent his ghost from returning for retribution as one of the untimely dead). So in 54–56 CE, when Paul wrote 1 Corinthians, "the Twelve" must have included James' replacement. But more puzzling, in the sequence of appearances, Kayfa is separated from "the Twelve." This would suggest that a replacement may have been appointed for Kayfa as well who became the leader of "the Twelve." If so, and what is suggested

---

605. Even Conzelmann for example confirms that just one line of the formula, "that he was raised," likely circulated itself independently and may have been the core around which the rest formed, *Corinthians*, 255.

606. In this case, I think this conclusion is correct, as Paul freely expands the formula rather dramatically so that it extends even to himself. As noted, Paul does not hesitate to adapt sayings of Jesus or other traditions and apply them as needed for the purpose of edification and building up the ecclesia, or to defend his gospel. If Paul can adapt, correct and even reject sayings of the Lord under his appointment as an apostle of Jesus Christ, he can certainly amend oral traditions relating to the gospel.

607. 1 Cor 15:5.

608. Luke 24:34.

609. Paul's exclusion of Judas from those having "fallen asleep" implies that Judas was not considered one who would be resurrected.

610. Acts 1:12–26.

The Enemies of Paul: Demons, Satan, Betrayers, and Apostles

by Paul's reference, is that "the Twelve" represented a permanent order of *apostoloi* that was maintained under the leadership of Kayfa, i.e., the exorcists of Jesus. Indeed, Acts records that there was a defined group, and a careful process of selection was to be used. Kayfa elicits the support of his fellow *apostoloi* to select by inspiration of the Spirit, through the "casting of lots,"[611] a replacement for vacancies. The criteria for candidacy as to the process of inclusion into "the Twelve" was as follows:

> Therefore it is necessary to chose one the men who have been with the whole time the Lord Jesus went in and out among us, beginning from John's baptism to the time he was taken up from us. For one of these *men* must become with us a witness to the resurrection.[612]

As with his later speech concerning the *charismata* of *glossolalia* during Pentecost, Kayfa cites scriptural support for replacing Iscariot.[613] Thus, we must assume it is Kayfa once again who ensures the continuation of the Twelve through another election for the replacement of James. It is certain that Kayfa did not form the Twelve,[614] but that he continued maintaining a core group, the selection of which must have included exorcists and charismatics like those trained and chosen by Jesus in his war on Satan.[615] It is likely that twelve were chosen by Jesus because it represented the eschatological reconstitution of the twelve tribes of Israel in preparation for the arrival of the kingdom of God—what Joachim Jeremias identifies with the term "Parabolic Actions," the new Israel that would arise in the last days.[616] Koester noted that the historical personage of Jesus is most likely reflected in the practices of his followers.[617] The identification of "the Twelve" confirms that there was a select group of witnesses who joined with Jesus in his war on Satan, but for Paul most importantly who were known to have encountered Jesus post-crucifixion. Thus, it is obvious that Paul need not define "the Twelve."[618]

---

611. As previously noted, the method by which spiritual decisions were rendered even by the high priest, i.e., trusting God and the Spirit to influence the decision.

612. Acts 1:21–22.

613. Pss 69:25; 109:8, which for an untrained Galilean fisherman is rather surprising and must be attributed to prophetic *charismata* similar to that experienced in Corinth.

614. As some scholars claim, or that it was a post-Easter creation of James the brother of Jesus.

615. See Busse, *Fire*, 67–69; *Jesus Resurrected*, 8, 22–29.

616. Jeremias, *Parables*, 248.

617. Koester, *Jesus*, 250.

618. While they have been well known by number, the exact list of names was not secure, as there are differences in the list of names between the Synoptic Gospels. Is it possible that some of the differences could have been attributed to later additions to the Twelve that were inserted into the list, or is it likely as most scholars assume that these men had different names applied (e.g., Kayfa, Cephas, Peter, Simeon, all used for the leader of the Twelve).

The Twelve, Oral Tradition, and the Formation of the Gospel Narratives

In 54–55 CE, when Paul writes his letter, Kayfa was the recognized leader of the followers of Jesus in his war on Satan, and as the earliest post-crucifixion witnesses to the risen Jesus. Of course, this leads to an important observation regarding the ultimate displacement of the oral tradition and the formation of the written gospels. With the first persecution under Herod Agrippa 1 in 41–44, and the organized persecution under Nero in 64–66 CE, and then finally the siege and destruction of Jerusalem by the Romans under Titus and Vespasian by 70 CE, the first generation of witnesses of Jesus of Nazareth, particularly from the baptism by John to the resurrection, had been either been widely disbursed, imprisoned, had died, or were martyred. Kayfa and the Twelve, Paul and many of the other "apostles" mentioned by Paul, were no longer available as authoritative sources of the oral tradition.

After the destruction of Jerusalem there is no mention of the Twelve again as an operative group,[619] although the document called the *Didache* (i.e., the teaching of the twelve apostles) may date to late in the first century CE or early second, and was clearly an attempt to consolidate an early rendering of "orthodoxy" by assigning these core teachings to the men who lived and worked with Jesus of Nazareth. Assigning written documents to the Twelve, such as the Didache, confirms the continued influence and importance of the Twelve, long after they had long passed. The authority of the *apostoloi* after their deaths led to the posthumous creation of pseudepigraphical letters, that is, those who wrote in the name of an apostle as their student or representing their "school of thought." The letters of 2 Thessalonians, Ephesians, and Colossians may be such examples, or may have been expanded or consolidated from actual letters from Paul. First Timothy and Titus are also examples of pseudepigraphical works, as they clearly do not reflect the language or theology of Paul, and attempts to describe them as different on the basis of scribal style in recording Paul's dictation or his circumstances (awaiting a serious trial in Rome that may result in execution) cannot fully explain the difficulties, particularly in eschatology, theology and language adequately.[620] Aside from these letters, there are multiple others, such as 2 Peter, James and perhaps Jude, and outside the canon of the New Testament there are literally dozens of others that were rejected by the various leaders of churches in the second through fourth centuries.

---

619. Kayfa had been murdered under Nero, by tradition crucified head downwards; as the leader of the Twelve was gone, the group must have disbanded to itinerant missions or died.

620. In the summer of 1978, I had the opportunity to speak to Howard Kee at Boston University (where I had been accepted into the PhD program in New Testament after graduation from Reed College in Portland, Oregon), about 2 Timothy and the very personal and emotional appeal of Paul to Timothy to come before winter, and his having "fought the good fight"—Paul is ready to lay his life down as a "libation." Dr. Kee agreed that 2 Timothy likely did contain at least fragments of an authentic letter of Paul that were expanded by one of his students or later followers who continued his "school" of influence. There was no purpose or possibility in a later writer providing such intimate personal reflection.

The point is that the authority and influence of the writings of Apostles or the Twelve continued long after their end. Of course, this absence dramatically increased the perilous risk to the community of failing to collect and record in written source documents the sayings, biographical events, parables and miracles of Jesus of Nazareth, all of which ultimately were set as a framework around the core *gospel*, i.e., seen in light of Jesus' death, burial and resurrection, i.e., exactly what Paul has described in 1 Cor 15:1–5.

First Corinthians 15:3–5 is an example of how oral traditions, particularly ones as significant as this summary of "the gospel," were "living" traditions under the authority of *propheteia* or *apostoloi*, and were freely and dynamically adapted to the meet the challenges in the *sitz im leben* of an *ecclesia*. Here an oral unit was taken from the *kerygma* and practices of the early church, most likely from statements of confession by adherents at baptism, and then set in a new context (as well as expanded) to confront enemies and mitigate the risks they presented. Adaptation of these oral units was therefore employed regularly as a powerful risk mitigant.

Oral traditions and *logia* were therefore pliable, particularly during this period of growth and expansion. While Paul's addition of "according to the scriptures" was a subtle but significant emendation of the central creedal formula of efficacious faith,[621] and it displays Paul's emphasis on scriptural authority to strengthen his presentation of the *euangelion* and to confront the opponents with authoritative citations they would have to acknowledge, the original confessional structure was retained as his framework. In borrowing the creed from confessional liturgy, Paul's emendation and application to the situation in Corinth was effective, as the infiltrators could no longer appeal to Scripture as the basis of their rejection of the salvific nature of the resurrection of Jesus of Nazareth; whether citing Scripture as dismissive proof or by claiming that sufficient evidence was simply absent in Scripture. Paul is not interested in listing the scriptural texts from the Law or Prophets,[622] but simply expressing that they exist. This, of course, may imply that Paul's "according to scripture" inferred specific passages that were well known to the Corinthians, i.e., that Paul employed Scripture in the course of his proclamation to them. If so, Paul demonstrably ties the historical event of the resurrection and the efficacious *euangelion* to the Jewish prophetic expectations that he selects. Since there was no other significant expansion or emendation to this oral unit other than this change, Paul's adaptation was focused on strengthening the oral tradition's impact *in Corinth* to the *euangelion*. Consequently, 15:3b–5 demonstrates that many oral traditions and *logia* were adapted to the life situation of

---

621. It is highly significant that Paul adds the words "according to scripture," as this influenced believers (and even scholars today) to engage a quest to discern which "scriptures" are those to which Paul alludes.

622. Paul does not quote the specific Scriptures to which he refers—we can only infer what these passages may have been and so in essence we are also emending the formula by presuming which Scriptures Paul references and applying our own understanding to them.

the church at the time of Corinthian correspondence, but carefully chosen exclusively to support Paul's *euangelion*.

It is noteworthy that this particular unit of oral tradition (along with others soon to be discussed) may have served their final purpose in Corinth, as this unit is not found in later canonical or noncanonical writings, including the *Didache* (references to a more developed theological association of Jesus' death as an expiation for sin are found in Deutero-Pauline writings, such as Eph 3:12; Col 1:22; Heb 9:14, 26, 28; and 10:10; as well as 1 Pet 2:21). By 69 to 85 CE when the Synoptics were compiled, the unit was no longer in use, and so was not absorbed from the oral tradition into the written gospels. Instead, the passion narrative of the death, burial and resurrection in its comprehensive form, particularly as represented in Mark, had displaced it and dominated the canonical gospels. Evidence of the early formation of traditions that became the gospel passion narrative is found in 1 Corinthians—Paul's introduction of words of the Lord concerning the Last Supper, and certainly elements inferred by this oral creed in 1 Cor 15:3b–5. This indicates there was a rich history of oral development of the passion narratives until their assimilation into the Synoptic Gospels.

Proof of the Resurrection: Paul's Additional Witnesses

Paul adds an extended list of witnesses to the post-crucifixion appearances, i.e., the events and names of those who encountered and interacted post-crucifixion with the risen Jesus of Nazareth. This is the earliest and most comprehensive list of encounters found in the New Testament, but surprisingly *excludes all appearances to women* that ultimately were incorporated and given priority in the synoptic tradition,[623] and were further expanded and given even higher priority in the Gospel of John.[624] Paul includes none of these.[625] It is these very traditions that would appear to have the greatest claim to authenticity due to their problematic nature, i.e., the witness of women was not accepted in Jewish legal proceedings and such reports were treated (just as the gospels report) as "idle tales."[626] Was Paul's omission intentional, and was it based on this reason? If so, the omission might be another example where oral traditions were selected and then adapted to meet the specific perilous risks in the *sitz im leben* of an *ecclesia*. But then how would omission of appearances to women edify and strengthen the *sitz im leben* of a particular *ecclesia*? And in the case of 1 Corinthians, specifically how would such an omission mitigate the perilous risks emerging from Paul's opponents?

We begin with Paul's view on women. Understanding that there is overwhelming evidence of Paul's equal acceptance of women in his undisputed writings (including

---

623. Mark, Matthew and Luke-Acts, 69–85 CE.

624. 95–100 CE.

625. Most strongly confirmed by the appearance to Mary the Magdalene, which is very old: John 20:11–18.

626. Luke 24:11–12.

working closely with them as colleagues, *apostoloi*, teachers and leaders, and as recipients of *charismata*, including *propheteia*)[627] and that analysis has demonstrated 14:34 to be non-Pauline and a later insertion,[628] Paul's omission of appearances to women could be considered intentional, as he clearly accepts and endorses their authoritative role, and so, fully accepts them as valid witnesses.[629] But did he know these traditions? Clearly, his association with women *apostoloi*, including Junia, who was renown and preceded him, as well a Maria (a Semitic name), and others, would certainly confirm that he knew of the post-crucifixion encounters with women (and one cannot discount that Kayfa and John, whom Paul met in Jerusalem according to Galatians, also recounted these events). Consequently, Paul must have known of appearances to women *apostoloi*. His omission of them here suggests that he was facing both a cultural prejudice and radical religious bias[630]—certainly not of the Corinthian *ecclesiae*, but of the opponents.[631] Indeed, comprehensive analysis has convincingly demonstrated that Paul is addressing the *pneumatikoi*, proto-*gnostic* Jewish *male apostoloi* as his enemies in Corinth; those who not only disdained women but also deliberately practiced abuse and shocking illegal sexual activity (incest) to publicly demonstrate their superiority over and liberation from the evil material world. These men considered women corrupted and in this world of satanic infiltration and influence, deceptive and worthless. As such, there is sufficient evidence to suggest that Paul has carefully selected only males to populate his expansion of the oral resurrection tradition. He has intentionally cited living male witnesses to confront his enemies' rejection of the resurrection of Jesus. Indeed, Paul's compilation lists encounters solely with *Jewish males*, many of whom are residing in Jerusalem. Several are not specifically mentioned in either the synoptic or Johannine traditions. Therefore, Paul's omission of women and inclusion of those he selects serves both to confirm the identity of the infiltrators and mitigate the threat present. The list clearly demonstrates the significant threat they present. Paul provides a powerful list to neutralize their claims to apostolic authority and legitimacy, derived from special licenses and letters of recommendation they carry. Consequently, as demonstrated by the tenets of risk analysis, Paul's impressive list of significant names confirms the perilous threat his enemies present, which must

---

627. Including Junias the apostle and Phoebe the deaconess; Chloe who is a benefactress and leader of a house church—the list is long and undeniable.

628. See earlier analysis. We do not have Paul's original letter in front of us.

629. Also of note, in the Roman/Hellenistic society of Paul's day, women were afforded certain rights in the testimony of court actions and in divorce, where they could also claim property rights. Women were priestesses and religious officials and were patrons and benefactors (like Chloe) to temples and a wide variety of religious cults. They were civic leaders, merchants and advisors. Paul is not addressing Hellenistic Roman men. His careful choice of resurrection encounters confirms that he is speaking to elitist *libertine Jewish males*.

630. And also, in Mary's case, a tendency in tradition to shift the emphasis from Jesus' humanity to his divinity.

631. Again, Chloe is very influential and a Patron, as are other women who embrace Paul's ministry.

include their claim to authority as having come from Jerusalem. The only name that would carry such weight of course is James, the brother of Jesus.

Paul's supplemental list of resurrection appearances follows those to Kayfa and the Twelve. While the structure is not as formulaic as 3b–5, it is connected to it by "thereafter" (*epeita*), which places an intentional stress on a sequential series of events passing in time, which is confirmed by Paul's final comment, "Last of all . . . he appeared to me."[632] Consequently, it is neither a random collection of later witnesses nor an order of witnesses by their importance. By introducing a sequential order, Paul appears to suggest that his encounter (34–37 CE) was the temporal terminus for resurrections events, i.e., there had been no others since his up to the Corinthian correspondence in 52–56 CE. As such, Paul may be claiming that his encounter with Jesus[633] was the last of the encounters of the legitimate *apostoloi*.[634] Indeed, he understands witness encounters with the risen Jesus as completely unique, God given, and the criterion of appointment as a Jesus *apostoloi*: "the seal of my apostleship."[635] While Paul calls Apollos an *apostolos*, his exclusion from the list suggests he was instead understood to be a "messenger," but not a post-crucifixion witness.

Since Paul's list implies a timeline and orderly account of the resurrection events with Jesus, there are some surprises. For example, James' encounter with the resurrected Jesus would have come *after* the appearance of more than "five hundred" brethren "at once." What was the timeframe between these encounters? This event is not specifically mentioned in the canonical gospel accounts, nor can it be found with certainty in noncanonical materials. It could be an indirect reference to either (1) the outpouring of the Spirit that occurred at Pentecost[636] or (2) perhaps the ascension.[637] Whatever this event may have been, it is still *known to over five hundred* witnesses, most of who were still able to confirm it. James' absence is noteworthy, i.e., he may have still rejected Jesus post-crucifixion at first as he had done during his itinerant war on Satan.[638] But within a very short time, the author/editor of Acts reports that James and his brothers were present with the eleven apostles in the "upper room,"[639]

632. 1 Cor 15:8.

633. 1 Cor 9:2.

634. Georgi, *Paul's Opponents*, 36: Paul's terminus with his encounter with Jesus as being the end of apostolic appointments is intended to invalidate other claims. But more, Georgi notes that this terminus means that faith, pistis, is not "enveloped in a timeless, mystical experience of identity [like his opponents' claim], but that faith also has a past and thereby the dimension of time." This links the event of an encounter with the risen Jesus with time, and so, a future, i.e., the *parousia*, which for Paul is an essential element of true salvific faith.

635. 1 Cor 9:2.

636. This is problematic as the resurrected Jesus is never mentioned as having been at this event—this tradition is about the ascendency of Kayfa as leader and spokesman of the Way.

637. Acts 1:5–11, the event where Jesus is taken up out of their sight on Mt. Olivet, yet, according to Acts 1:15 the total number of believes was only about one hundred twenty.

638. Mark 6:4; John 7:3–5.

639. The "brothers of the Lord," Acts 1:14.

The Enemies of Paul: Demons, Satan, Betrayers, and Apostles

as well as Mary his mother and other women/*apostoloi* from Galilee, i.e., within eight weeks after the resurrection and returning from the ascension. Whether this tradition was added later and intended to show that the rift between Jesus and his family had been resolved is uncertain, but it is impossible to rely on it as confirmation as to when James encountered Jesus post crucifixion. The resurrection event with James is therefore undocumented.

Why list an appearance to five hundred? Certainly, it is overwhelming evidence of mass witness to Jesus' death, burial and resurrection. But more, Paul counters his enemies' claim to have attained salvation and safety by establishing tension between the event of the physical resurrection of Jesus (an event that can be confirmed by hundreds of witnesses) and the present activity of the Spirit and the *parousia* still to come: "Then he was seen by over five hundred brethren *at one time*, of whom *the majority are still alive, although some have fallen asleep.*"[640] Here Paul's emphasis is not only on the massive number of witnesses to the event but the death of some of those who encountered Jesus (those who have "fallen asleep"), as it emphasizes that the *parousia* with the general resurrection is still future. Indeed, those men who shared a post-crucifixion encounter with Jesus had yet to attain salvation, as well as those "who have fallen asleep." Consequently, Paul has appended to the original oral formula his own list of encounters to supplement it with a specific and intentional purpose; i.e., not only to establish the certainty the resurrection of Jesus of Nazareth but more importantly to establish that the salvation claimed by the intruding *apostoloi* cannot have been achieved for it has not yet come.[641]

It is important to note that Paul's citation of the resurrection encounter with the five hundred brethren and his admission that some of them had died is not without *some real risk*. In Thessaloniki, the death of an adherent was a serious and destabilizing problem within the *ecclesia* (i.e., Paul's adherents were distraught over the death of some adherents). Had they lost access to the general resurrection? Paul mitigates their concern in Thessaloniki by elevating the role of those who "died in Christ"—it is they who would be first to be raised. Why was this then not a problem in Corinth, as Paul mentions the death of some of the five hundred almost intentionally?

It appears that Paul learned from his experience, establishing practices and rituals to reinforce the interim period between the resurrection and *parousia*. Indeed, there is evidence of this in Corinth, centered in his emphasis on the *charismata*, the practice of *agape*, the "more excellent Way," as temporary—*charismata* will fade away while *agape* will become fully active at Christ's return. For Paul, the outpouring of *charismata*

---

640. Paul uses the Greek word, *ekoimethesan*, which is term describes an interim state between death, judgment and resurrection.

641. This eschatological view is consistent with that expressed by Paul throughout his undisputed writings: 1 Thessalonians, Galatians, and 1 Corinthians (and with Jesus' eschatology as well). If Paul is interested in only in an overwhelming list of "proofs" he would have stopped with Kayfa and the Twelve, adding perhaps James, i.e., particularly since James is named in the gnostic *logia* collections similar to those in the *Gospel of Thomas*; see above.

within the *ecclesiae* and presence of the Spirit, and resulting *agape* among those "in Christ," are mitigants to satanic attack until evil is defeated. Deception and falling victim to the curse of death before *the parousia* are overcome by those of *pistis* in Paul's *euangelion* (i.e., the death, burial and resurrection of Jesus), union with the risen Christ in the cultic meal, and the practice of protective *agape* (including the employment of *charismata* provided by the Spirit to strengthen the *ecclesia* in *agape*), all of which engender sure *elpis*. As a result, those who die "in Christ" only "sleep" until the *parousia*. Paul's established rituals serve to reaffirm the mitigation of the curse of death until the *parousia*, i.e., the efficacious Lord's Supper, the order and use of *charismata*, particularly *propheteia*, and even charismatic hymns celebrating release from the fear of death: "Oh death, where is your victory, oh death where is your sting."[642] Remarkably, this early hymn indicates that a liturgy had begun to emerge, arising from Paul's teaching on death as powerless over the adherent (i.e., it is "sleep").

James, the Brother of Jesus, as Paul's Opponent

Paul continues with his list of witnesses: "Then he appeared to James [i.e., the brother of Jesus], then to all the apostles."[643] What is striking is Paul's construction, i.e., that the appearance to James was then followed by appearances to "all of the apostles," an undefined group. Unlike the five hundred, there is no indication that this was a mass encounter. Paul does not use the words "at once." As a result, these were some form of post-crucifixion encounters with a different circle of *apostoloi*. Speculation as to the identification of these *apostoloi* is typically focused on the "seventy" who were sent out to proclaim the gospel by Jesus.[644] While they were witnesses to Jesus during his war on Satan in Palestine, there is no indication that some or all of them had a post-crucifixion encounter (presuming this tradition is reliable). Whatever theses encounters may have been, Paul segments these *apostoloi* into a different group. Why does Paul separate James and the *apostoloi* from the others?

Risk analysis of Galatians, Thessalonians and 1 Corinthians consistently demonstrated that Paul carefully selects both words and structure. As such, it is clear that the paring of James with "all the apostles" is intentional. In other words, like Kayfa and the Twelve, Paul is paring James with "all" (*pantes*) the *apostoloi*—the placement of "all" at the end of the sentence underscores this emphasis. Why does Paul do this? The first inference is that Paul is relegating James to the "remainder" of all the other apostles— the second-tier group. James is the notable standout in this group of "all" the other apostles. If this is Paul's intent, he diminishes James' standing as a primary witness (unlike other noncanonical traditions that claimed James as first witness).[645] So, while

642. 1 Cor 15:55.
643. 1 Cor 15:7.
644. Luke 10:1–12.
645. See M. R. James's translation, *Gospel of the Hebrews*; James is also given preeminence in the

notable as Jesus' brother, Paul positions James as another of the many *apostoloi* to have had an encounter, and most important, that this encounter was different than that experienced by Kayfa and the Twelve. By implication then (i.e., in diminishing the status of James), Paul gives preeminence to Kayfa over James, both as witness and as leader of the Twelve, the inner circle of exorcists chosen by Jesus of Nazareth.[646] However, Paul may be intentionally segmenting and diminishing James' importance for a more urgent risk purpose relating to the infiltrators in Corinth.[647] James may have been the *leader of a separate group of apostoloi*, i.e., "*all the other apostles.*" In fact, James may have appointed these *apostoloi*,[648] having provided them with a post-crucifixion encounter different than that claimed and experienced by Kayfa and the Twelve. Just as Kayfa maintained the circle of the Twelve with well-defined and rigorous criteria of qualification,[649] so too James qualified his own circle of *apostoloi* based on his own criteria and experiences. Was James then "ordaining" *apostoloi* to form his own community, as well as exerting his authority over an expansion into the Hellenistic/Roman world with a *euangelion* different than Paul's? Almost certainly, he was, and there is substantial risk evidence to support it.

We know from Galatians that James exercised significant authority to independently appoint and send a chosen emissaries as his personal representatives and messengers (i.e., *apostoloi*) to carry out his orders at Antioch, and subsequently in Paul's Galatian *ecclesiae*. They were to infiltrate, spy and then dismantle Paul's *ecclesia* by rejecting the adherents to his *euangelion* and practices[650]—those whom Paul calls the "ones of the circumcision" (*tous ek peritomes*), or "circumcision party." This label should not be mistaken for the only difference between Paul's *euangelion* and that of James, i.e., that Paul's non-Jewish adherents must be circumcised. It is an intentional, offensive and demeaning label used by Paul, which he uses again to identify them as evil.[651] Indeed, while Paul does not specifically identify these men in Galatia as *apostoloi*, it is clear that they were authorized and endorsed by James to act, and that they "proclaimed another *euangelion*" that "perverted the *euangelion of Christ*."[652] To pervert the *euangelion* of "Christ" (i.e., as noted, the title Paul employs to designate the efficacious *euangelion* of Jesus' crucifixion, death and resurrection) would be to reject *pistis*

Gos. Thom., Saying 12.

646. This may be another reason why Paul links Jesus' name with Christ, i.e., to ensure that the human person Jesus, the son of God who was crucified and buried, was the Jesus he witnessed risen as Christ, just like Kayfa and the Twelve. He is not the Risen One, the Living One—he is Jesus Christ.

647. See below; the reason for this may be that the opponents' acknowledge James as their leader or hold James "the just" as their sponsor—recall the *Gos. Thom.* 12 records the preeminence of James the Just for whom "the world was made."

648. James and "all" the apostles *that he appointed* or were associated with him.

649. Similar to Acts 1:21–26.

650. Gal 2:12.

651. See Phil 3:2, they are like "dogs," "evil workers."

652. Gal 1:7.

in the *euangelion* as the key salvific element of justification before God at *the still to come parousia*. James' *euangelion* must have held a future *parousia* to be moot, displacing it with the salvific power of the *logia* of the Living One, i.e., similar to the *Gospel of Thomas*, which cited James as the ultimate authority over wisdom-*logia*, and as the one for whom "the world was made."[653] Indeed, the *Gospel of Thomas*, with its emphasis on salvific *logia* and James as its leader, only alludes to the death of Jesus (Saying 65), *but does not* mention his crucifixion, resurrection or the *parousia*, and so, is void of a future messianic role for Jesus or a return and judgment. Indeed, the title "Christ" does not appear in any of the *logia*. Instead, the *Gospel of Thomas* starts: "Whoever finds the interpretation of these *logia* will not experience death." Since it is apparent that the *Gospel of Thomas* (which may, as noted, date as early as 50 CE) reflects many of the *logia* and practices of the infiltrating male Jewish *pneumatikoi apostoloi* from Jerusalem found in 1 Corinthians, as well as cites James as its authority, this document is a reliable reflection of the written *logia* document carried by the Jerusalem *pneumatikoi apostoloi*, and so, James' *euangelion*. Consequently, it is virtually certain that James was appointing his own *apostoloi*, those who embraced his own *euangelion* of the salvific *sophia-logia*. Does risk analysis support this conclusion?

To begin, risk analysis demonstrates that when two entities are in conflict, the mitigations employed by each evidences the scope and peril of the risk encountered. Placing a deadly curse on the Galatian intruders and the source of their *euangelion* strongly suggests that Paul is attempting to neutralize a very well-known figure with great authority, and by implication, the authoritative figure standing behind their *euangelion*, such as a group of *apostoloi* sent by a one claiming undisputed authority to rebuke Paul, and Kayfa, and so the Twelve and John. The only figure mentioned by Paul in all of these cases was James. Paul's casting of a curse therefore demonstrates that he was using the most powerful mitigation available—a death curse—to neutralizing a most powerful foe—James. Consequently, it is virtually certain that James represented a distinct segment of *apostoloi* within primitive Christianity that was in a perilous risk conflict with Paul and his *euangelion*. Only James, the brother of Jesus, could have empowered a separate trajectory and *euangelion* apart from Paul's salvation by *pistis* in the *euangelion* of Christ. Kayfa must have fallen victim to James' control and oversight in Jerusalem, thus, Kayfa's withdrawal from Paul, his *euangelion* and his adherents in Antioch.

Paul also identifies the leader of the infiltrators as having received a different *euangelion* from "an angel from heaven,"[654] one that he taught to his *apostoloi*. Paul says,

---

653. *Gos. Thom.*, Saying 12.
654. Gal 1:8.

> I will have you know brethren that the *euangelion*, which was preached by me is not man's *euangelion*. For I did not receive it from men, nor was taught it to me; but it came by a revelation [*apokalupseos*] of Jesus Christ.[655]

Paul is clear about the source of his *euangelion*, it is an ecstatic encounter directly with the risen Lord, i.e., a revelation of Jesus Christ, not from an angel in heaven. In Paul's world, dark angels and demons that were under control of the Angel of Darkness espoused deceit and turned humans from God with lies, including various gradations of dark angels and demons. Their presence, activity and war with God (and the Prince of Lights) are documented in contemporary literature of Paul's time, particularly in the Dead Sea Scrolls.[656] Only at the judgment would their powers be curtailed. Consequently, Paul considers the source of the alternate *euangelion* of the *tous ek peritomes* as evil,[657] from an angel (i.e., a dark angel), because he contrasts it with the direct revelation he has received from the risen one, Jesus *Christ*, and the salvific *euangelion* of *pistis* and *agape* that sustains adherents until the judgment. *Paul clearly sates that these apostoloi are demons; that Satan disguises himself as an Angel of Light, which is exactly what the apostoloi represent!*[658] It is this false angel of light that has deceived the Galatians; they have been bewitched, just as it had the Corinthians.[659] The alternate *euangelion*, its source, its promulgator and followers, are therefore are of Satan and are cursed. In fact, associating this alternate *euangelion* with an angel is consistent with the infiltrators' claim to undecipherable angelic *glossolalia* being proof of their divine status (albeit they believe it is from a heavenly origin). As noted, the *Gospel of Thomas* ascribes to James exactly this role, that is, overseer and custodian of the *logia* of Jesus the Living One.[660]

Further risk evidence confirming James to be the leader of the Corinthian infiltrators is corroborated in the form of Paul's defense of his former life as a persecutor of the Jerusalem church, which is only found in Galatians and 1 Corinthians. Certainly, James and others turned to Paul's violent background, i.e., the deceit he used

---

655. Gal 1:11–12.

656. Beginning with the Watchers in Jubilees and in Qumran, CD II:17–21, 4Q180; the spirit of truth and falsehood, 1 QS III:15–19; the Angel of Darkness and Prince of Lights, 1 QS 3:13–14:26; leader of the fallen angels and demons is called by many names, Belial, Mastema, Satan, Beelzebub, Angel of Darkness, e.g., 1 QH–a XII: 12–13, leads in the war against God until he is defeated; Belial deceives and can even take possession of members of God's community, CD XII, 2; the angels and demons under the control of the Angel of Darkness are known as "spirits," "demons," "messengers," and "angels of destruction," 1 QM 13:10–12, 4Q510 1:4–8; they can infect humans with deceit and doom, cause illness and can be expelled by exorcism, 4Q266 6i:5–7; Until Belial is defeated, those chosen by God must be protected, 4Q444, 4Q 510–11. See Philip Alexander, "Demonology of the Dead Sea Scrolls," 331–53; John J. Collins, "Powers in Heaven: God, Gods, and Angels in the Dead Sea Scrolls," 9–28.

657. Gal 1:1–11; Phil 3:2.

658. 2 Cor 11:12–15.

659. Gal 1:8 and 3:1.

660. Opt. Cit., Saying 12.

The Enemies of Paul in Corinth

to infiltrate the *ecclesiae* and murder followers, proving that Paul was an agent of Satan, a charlatan, and *apostolos* of an errant *euangelion*. He was not to be trusted, and was feared. Paul has to recognize this background then cite the authority for events that led him to abandon the life of violence in Galatian and Corinth to neutralize their accusations. He does this because it is the same infiltrators from Jerusalem the have come to destroy his work, citing his bloody history. His defense includes his visit to Jerusalem, a meeting with James and Kayfa, and the extension of the "right hand" of fellowship.

Finally, it is clear that James was publicly known as Paul's opponent.[661] In fact, there are traces of this opposition throughout the traditions associated with James, from the *Gospel of the Hebrews*[662] to the letter ascribed to the "school" of James that firmly contradicts salvation by *pistis*—a document that is primarily composed of wisdom *logia*. Consequently, James was known as a both the leader of wisdom *logia* as well as the authoritative custodian and arbiter of Jesus' powerful *logia*, a *trajectory that is unquestionably acknowledged* by scholars.[663] As such, we have James as he was known to Paul from his Galatians and Corinthian correspondences: Paul's opponent, leader of the male Jews of Jerusalem known as the "circumcision party" and "pneumatikoi"; James who ordered his *apostoloi*,[664] bearing licenses with a collection of salvific *logia* to discredit Paul and his errant *euangelion*, and dismantle his *ecclesiae*.[665] Paul faces off against a James who declared the world evil and in conflict with God:[666]

> Unfaithful creatures! Do you not know that friendship with the world is enmity with God? Therefore whoever wishes to be a friend of the world makes himself an enemy of God.[667]

Paul rejected such "human wisdom" and any secret salvific *gnosis* as available only to an elite group who had access to a collection of special *logia*. Instead, while he accepts them as valid, he freely adapts and conforms these same *logia* to confirm his *euangelion* of the cross and *agape*. Paul rejected their abuse of women (accepting them as equals), libertine practices, and circumcision as a prerequisite to Gentile admission to the kingdom of God. His *euangelion* was accessible to all: Jew or Gentile, slave or free, male or female, all those who embraced the *euangelion* of *pistis* and *agape* as the *agioi*, the adopted *tekna tou Theou*. It is they who were validated by *charismata* to be in the "body of Christ" through the practice of *agape in the world* until the *parousia*. It

---

661. Gal 2:12.
662. Which claims that James was the first to receive a resurrection experience.
663. Robinson and Koester, *Trajectories*.
664. See Georgi, *Paul's Opponents*, 32–38.
665. This is why Paul rebuts rejection of James by recounting that later James "gave him the right hand of fellowship" in his letter to the Galatians.
666. Jas 2:14.
667. Jas 4:4.

is no wonder that James and his *apostoloi* considered Paul an enemy, but not just any enemy—he was an enemy of God, just as Paul considered his opponents, including the infiltrators in Corinth, of Satan.

In sum, there is clear and substantial risk evidence that James was behind the infiltration and perilous conflict created in Corinth, just as he was in Galatia and Antioch, and that the infiltrators cited him as their source of authority, the angel of light, providing licenses and letters of recommendation authorizing their actions against Paul. Consequently, Paul's inclusion James with "all the apostles" in his list of witnesses must be intentional. How do we reconcile Paul's inclusion of James and his *apostoloi* in the list of post-crucifixion encounters and yet the striking conflict between them and James' rejection of Paul's *euangelion*? The answer requires careful and complex evaluation.

In his letter to Galatians, Paul states that Kayfa, James and John, the so-called "pillars" not only validated his *euangelion*, but agreed to place virtually no restrictions on him.[668] Clearly, Paul has to make such a defense, i.e., that James once had supported his *euangelion*. But there is a significant difference between Paul's meeting with James reported in Acts (80–90 CE) and Paul's recount of meeting in his letter to the Galatians (49–52 CE). In Galatians, Paul reports only a single practice he is to follow after he received the "right hand of fellowship"; namely, remembering the poor, "which I was glad to do."[669] But in Acts, it is James who speaks to the assembly after Kayfa and is said to have made an appeal in support of Paul's ministry[670]—a fiction. Indeed, the outcome of the requirements placed on Paul after James' speech are requirements that fall under Jewish law, namely, not eating meat from strangled animals, digesting blood, sexual immorality[671] and eating meat offered to idols.[672] What is striking is that this list is exactly the practices found in Corinth among the libertines of the *sophia-logia*, James' *apostoloi*! Clearly, Acts is attempting to obscure and recast James' deadly conflict with Paul in the early Christian movement via an attestation by James of Paul's *euangelion*. By doing so, the author/editor of Acts separates Paul's enemies from James, now his supposed supporter. Acts also mitigates the James-Paul conflict over circumcision, again glossing over the enmity evidenced in Galatia between them. James' requiring circumcision was a *de facto* attempt to invalidate Paul's inclusiveness of uncircumcised Gentiles and others by "*pistis* alone," forcing instead a radical, exclusivist adoption of "another" *euangelion* from an angel in heaven.

668. Gal 2:10.

669. Ibid.

670. This is fascinating—Kayfa is more sympathetic to Paul in Acts, and even though Paul confronts him in front of the *ecclesia* at Antioch after James sent spies into the assembly and disrupt their table fellowship. Kayfa was in fact sitting at table with Paul and other Gentiles, which by implication meant that Kayfa was sympathetic to Paul as is apparently confirmed by Paul in Galatians and 1 Corinthians.

671. Likely associated with ecstatic Gentile celebrations and pagan religious feasts; see above.

672. Acts 15:19–21.

Additional attempts to gloss over the conflict between James and Paul in early Christianity are evident. Jerome's recounting of the tradition from Hegesippus, a Christian writer, asserts that James was more rigorous than any in his purity and practice of the law;[673] that James was so revered for his adherence to the law that he was allowed in the "holy place," and that his knees were calloused like a camel's for praying so frequently in the temple. Clearly, such traditions are an attempt to harmonize James' activity with other martyrs of the faith such as Paul. James' murder was that of a martyr under the corrupt Jerusalem elite, but more, his practices were not in conflict with Pauline Christianity. Indeed, Pauline Christianity dominated at the time of Jerome's writing.

We come closest to the actual perilous risk conflict in non-Christian reports, as well as the James trajectory evidence in noncanonical sources. For example, James' abridgement of the law, perhaps for his *euangelion* of the Risen One that was a "higher law," is suggested by Flavius Josephus' independent report of his murder (early 60s CE). Josephus, a Jewish-Roman historian, states that James and his followers (*his apostoloi*?) held to non-traditional practices and views on the law. Josephus reports that the murder of James was based on his "breaking the law," that he was stoned under the law for his abrogation of it.[674] This certainly contradicts Hegesippus. In addition, later traditions in the *Secret Book of James* (i.e., the *Apocryphon of James*, 100–150 CE, a text which evidences earlier oral traditions and a sayings source dating perhaps to 1 Corinthians)[675] and *1 and 2 Apocalypse of James* (125–200 CE) state that the risen Jesus appointed James his successor (by revelation); that only James assigned *apostoloi* their itinerant missions (and so could revoke these assignments); that he was exclusively given secret "passwords" (i.e., the *sophia-logia*) to access the highest heaven (and so hear angelic speech and *glossolalia*); and that he was the "Guardian of Heaven's Gate" (i.e., only this *euangelion* was salvific since James was the only true interpreter of Jesus' *logia*, and so, salvific *gnosis*). In *2 Apocalypse of James*, Jesus kisses James and states that he has revealed to only him (i.e., passed to him by an infectious kiss) what only heaven and the angels have known (salvific *gnosis*). These traditions, also propaganda for gnostic Christianity, clearly and more accurately reflect the risk conflict in Corinth.

As such, Paul's inclusion of James in the list of witnesses recognizes James' claim to have received a revelation or encounter with the risen Lord, now the Living One, but that an "angel of light" has overtaken and influenced James, one that Paul considers to be the angel of Satan who has perverted the *euangelion* of Christ. Consequently, is it evident that James and his original trajectory never rejected a form of resurrection of Jesus, that is why Paul mentions the appearance to James in his list of witnesses[676]

673. Hegesippus, 5th book, *Commentaries*.
674. Josephus, *Antiquities*, 20.9.
675. Koester, *Gospels*, 187–200; Cameron, *Other Gospels*.
676. If these men link themselves to James, Paul's citation of his witness would set the stage to

(the infiltrators are thereby confronted by this admission) and identifies a group of "other apostles" that are associated with him who were appointed by James. Whether by the *euangelion* of *pistis* (i.e., Paul) or by salvific *gnosis* gleaned from the *logia* of wisdom-torah given by the new Moses, Jesus is for both the Living One and Lord. But this is the crux of their struggle and conflict, and where both attempt to mitigate the perilous risk of the other.

The False *Apostoloi Christou* in Corinth

Paul labels the infiltrators "super-apostles" (*huper apostoloi*), a sarcastic title or epithet,[677] as they are evildoers, *apistoi*, deceivers, having "transformed" themselves into false *apostoloi* of Satan. They had ridiculed and dismissed any efficacious authority in Paul's letters (empty of any power to curse or condemn), his *euangelion* (*agnosis* and deadly errant), and even his use of *logoi* (void of *gnosis*):[678] "For his letters, they say, are weighty and strong [*ischurai*], but his physical presence is weak and his *logoi* are inconsequential."[679] The description of Paul's physical characteristics came *before* Paul's "painful" visit to Corinth.[680] This confirms that some of the infiltrators (recall that they had arrived *after* Paul had left for Ephesus)[681] had previously seen and heard Paul; perhaps at Antioch or Jerusalem, or in another *ecclesia*; or that they were the "circumcision party" and spies in Galatia—they knew him by sight and had used these attacks before. More important, they reject the legitimacy of his apostolic status.[682] Their attacks only strengthened after his first letter arrived, evidenced by Paul's desperate defense and response.[683] That his mitigations utterly failed is most assuredly demonstrated by the almost complete absence of Paul's demand that they embrace *pistis* and *agape* in 2 Corinthians.[684] In fact, *agape* is remarkably absent in all of the seven letters that make up 2 Corinthians. Paul is so much on the defensive, and must guard his authority and legitimacy, that his attacks, threats and curses lead to remorse and "pain." Paul even

---

refute their claim that this is no resurrection.

677. Georgi, *Paul's Opponents*, 18–60, particularly 32–39. Super-apostles has gained prestige, they could perform signs, and had mystical rites that preceded *gnosis* and salvific *sophia*.

678. See 2 Cor 11:5; 12:11.

679. 2 Cor 10:10.

680. 2 Cor 2:1.

681. 1 Cor 16:19.

682. See Paul's defense, including his revelation in paradise, the "third heaven," 2 Cor 12:1–5.

683. See 2 Cor 10:1–12:11.

684. Paul does ask the believers to forgive the errant opponents if they become humbled; he also certainly cites the love of God, 2 Cor 5:21, that responded to the faithful service of Jesus of Nazareth; and, Paul describes the believer is in the "acceptable time of the Lord," the time of salvation, and as servants of God living rightly because they recognize and embraced the hope of salvation, living in "genuine love" until that day, 2 Cor 6:6.

apologizes for making his defense by calling it "folly" (*aphrosune*) that he is speaking "out of his mind" (*paraphronon*, as a madman).[685]

The *apostoloi* make authoritative claims based on pure Jewish heritage as Hebrews. Paul provides his own claims to Hebrew lineage and privileges. The implication of Paul's defense is that the infiltrators challenge even Paul's legitimacy as a Jew. It is clear that Paul was being marginalized even as a legitimate heir of his race, tribe and tradition. Simply speaking, they charged that Paul was evil, possessed by Satan or one of his demons, a complete charlatan, and a profiteer. They bring up old charges used in Galatia, Thessaloniki and Philippi, i.e., that Paul stole their money, leaving town and them forgotten. Paul reminds the Corinthians that he paid his own way.[686] Paul says that these *apostoloi* claim their authority is from "*another Jesus*," i.e., not Paul's. So effective are they that many of Paul's Corinthian adherents have abandoned the *euangelion*.[687] In response, he gives a stern warning: Those who have abandoned the *euangelion* have received "a different *spirit* from the one you [Paul's followers] received."[688] Paul's *euangelion* is of God, evidenced by the *charismata* of the Spirit, all of which strengthen *agape*—the infiltrators' spirit, evidenced by *glossolalia*, possesses them with deception by the false angel of light, i.e., Satan. They are cursed and doomed.

As noted, these *apostoloi* understand Jesus' *logia* as the *new torah, the higher wisdom torah of salvation*, and the fulfillment of the promise of salvation echoed in the Torah, Prophets and oral law (*Mishna*). Not that they rejected the temple or law itself, but that its true message and intent for God's elite had been fully revealed by this *sophia* and *gnosis* in the *logia*, that is, as to God's true desire and nature, and as a result, the true nature of the one's divine state for those who attain true *sophia* and *gnosis* and treat with disdain this corrupted world under Satan's control. Consequently, they made exclusivist claims and practice public arrogance toward an evil world. Even in the Matthean tradition is there similar evidence of this trajectory (i.e., of Jesus as the agent of wisdom torah). Indeed, the parallels between the special material peculiar to Matthew and the opponents' similar *logia* have been previously highlighted and are striking (i.e., the *logia* of beatitudes). More, in Matthew, Jesus is portrayed as the new Moses, the deliverer of the new torah,[689] but who rejects those who deny or wish to omit even "one iota."

And so, all *logia* of Jesus that confirmed the "new law" of salvation by *sophia* and *gnosis*, not a future resurrection, were collected orally and then transferred in written esoteric sayings documents, such as Thomas:

---

685. 2 Cor 11:23.
686. 1 Cor 2:2; 9:19.
687. 2 Cor 11:4.
688. 2 Cor 11:4.
689. See Suggs, *Wisdom*; Robinson and Koester, *Trajectories*.

> These are the secret sayings that the *living Jesus* spoke and Didymos Judas Thomas *recorded*.[690]

Evidence has shown that the *logia*-document of the Corinthian infiltrators must have similarly reflected immediate access to salvation and freedom from the evil world:

> And he [Jesus] said, "Whoever discovers the interpretations of these sayings will not taste death."[691]

But more, once the *sophia* and *gnosis* were achieved, libertine freedom was available:

> Jesus said, "Those who seek should not stop seeking until they find. When they find, they will be disturbed. When they are disturbed, they will marvel, and *will reign over all*. [And after they have reigned they will rest]."[692]

There was no need to look outside of oneself or to a future *parousia*, or to an *apostolos* who proclaimed only a crucified messiah and promise of future resurrection:

> . . . for the kingdom was inside and outside of you.[693]

The evil world is to be rejected and abhorred, even abused if desired:

> Look, I have cast fire upon the earth and I am guarding it until it blazes.[694]

If there are doubts, the successor of Jesus and heir to the *logia* is the "Just." The Thomas *logia* trajectory is explicit about the authority of James as successor of Jesus:

> No matter where you are you are to go to James the Just for whose sake heaven and earth came into being.[695]

They are no longer obligated to follow the ritual practices of the law for even these can lead to worldly deception. They are free of the world, saved, and are encouraged to resist or be lost:

> If you fast, you will bring sin upon yourselves, and if you pray, you will be condemned, and if you give to charity, you will harm your spirits.[696]

It is the time to reject the world and human deception, certainly *agape*, as they are in the throws of a confrontation; that is why the infiltrators must display public rejection on all things considered sacred, for it is the wisdom of God:

---

690. See *Gos. Thom.*, introduction to the Sayings source.
691. *Gos. Thom.*, Saying 1.
692. *Gos. Thom.*, Saying 2.
693. *Gos. Thom.*, Saying 3.
694. *Gos. Thom.*, Saying 10.
695. *Gos. Thom.*, Saying 12b.
696. *Gos. Thom.*, Saying 14a.

Jesus said, "Perhaps people think that I have come to cast peace upon the world. They do not know that I have come to cast conflicts upon the earth: fire, sword, war. For there will be five in a house: there'll be three against two and two against three, father against son and son against father, and they will stand alone."[697]

The religious purists, like Paul, are rejected as deceivers and errant:

Damn the Pharisees! They are like a dog sleeping in the cattle manger: the dog neither eats nor [lets] the cattle eat.[698]

The search is over, for the beginning of the search for salvation is its end if the seeker finds that salvation has always been present in the *sophia* and *gnosis* of the *logia*—one's divinity is revealed and union is attained:

Have you found the beginning, then, that you are looking for the end? You see, the end will be where the beginning is. Congratulations to the one who stands at the beginning: that one will know the end and will not taste death.[699]

Self-realization of one's true divine state brings immediate recognition that one is already saved, free and powerful. The intruders are like children (of wisdom) throwing off their clothes, i.e., their traditional understanding and convention, freely to embrace their true nature as children of the divine, the Solitary Ones, the saved ones.[700] It is a complete transformation—a substantive change that is overwhelming, a true experience of enlightenment and transference, free from the corrupted world of Satan.[701] It is only Jesus, "The Living One," whose *logia* have both the authority and power to save immediately through *sophia-gnosis*, and bring about union now with the divine:

Jesus said, "Whoever drinks from my mouth *will become like me*; I myself shall become that person, and the hidden things will be revealed to him."

As guardian of the sacred *logia*, James the Just became the "clearing house" for what became the trajectory of wisdom-salvation.

The Relationship between Kayfa, Paul, and James

It is often assumed that Kayfa and Paul were enemies based on the events in Antioch as related by Paul in his letter to the Galatians,[702] and his reminding the Corinthians

---

697. *Gos. Thom.*, Saying 16.
698. *Gos. Thom.*, Saying 102.
699. *Gos. Thom.*, Saying 18.
700. *Gos. Thom.*, Saying 21.
701. *Gos. Thom.*, Saying 22.
702. Gal 2: 11–15.

about Kayfa's claim to lodging and monetary support.[703] However, risk analysis speaks against this conclusion.

Paul does report that he opposed Kayfa "to his face" before them all.[704] Some scholars assume that Paul lost this confrontation with Kayfa over dietary restrictions and was forced to depart Antioch.[705] This is inaccurate based on our analysis of 1 Corinthians and Galatians. Paul uses this encounter as a powerful mitigation to his enemies' charges, i.e., that Kayfa rejected Paul, his practices and *euangelion*, just as James had done. Paul instead uses this event to confirm that Kayfa, leader of the twelve *apostoloi*, was in agreement with Paul's dietary and admission practices—until James' spies infiltrated. More, after the confrontation, Paul's silence on Kayfa reaction would imply that Kayfa acknowledged Paul's appeal as valid—thus, Paul's silence. In Galatians, *Paul is not focused on Kayfa, but on James.* Indeed, it appears that Kayfa is the one who withdrew from the confrontation. Consequently, the antagonist in Paul's recounting of this event is not Kayfa, it is James, who is labeled the leader of "spies," who "takes away freedom" and "preaches another gospel . . . another Jesus"—it is he and the *apostoloi* attached to him who are "accursed!" Paul's point is clear—even Kayfa was persuaded by James! Paul thereby implies that Kayfa was a victim of James' oppression, just as he is the target of perilous and intense opposition. *Paul never mentions Kayfa in a negative context*, nor does he mention Kayfa as in conflict with his missionary work—not once. Paul does reference Kayfa's itinerant missionary work, and he accepts it.[706] Did this event in Antioch become a catalyst for the missionary work of Kayfa, just as it did for Paul? Most likely it did and would explain why Kayfa is mentioned as having baptized some of the followers in Corinth after Paul departs, i.e., that he briefly conducted his missionary work there in Corinth, baptizing some of the adherents, likely Jews.[707] Kayfa did not instruct those baptized to separate from Paul's followers, but to join the *ecclesia*. Thus, in 1 Cor 15:6–7, Paul seems to be separating the leadership of Kayfa and the Twelve from James and "all the apostles." These then are the well-known "parties" emerging in Christian origins. Therefore, based on 1 Corinthians we confirm the existence of two parties, i.e., that of Kayfa and Paul and another of James.

703. 1 Cor 9:5.

704. That is, all of those in the gathered *ecclesia* of Antioch.

705. Notably, Koester, *Introduction*, 113–14.

706. 1 Cor 9:5.

707. How do we know that Kayfa was in Corinth and did baptize? Paul confirms he personally baptized very few of the Corinthian adherents, such as the house of Crispus (1 Cor 1:14; Crispus was the chief ruler of the synagogue, Acts 18:8). Paul also notes that there were adherents who received baptism by Apollos. Certainly Apollos was in Corinth. Others were simply baptized into "Christ," i.e., they said, "I belong to Christ," by those appointed by Paul, likely the administrators or prophets. Since Paul, Apollos and the local prophets baptized and were unquestionably in Corinth, Kayfa must have been present as well. Consequently, there is little doubt that Kayfa visited Corinth, likely after Paul's departure. Paul has no issues with Kayfa's baptism, or his adherents among these others in the *ecclesia*.

But Paul also mentions a third person in his letters—John. If the Johannine tradition can be shown to also emphasize the physical resurrection of Jesus and reject James and the trajectory of *gnosis* then we can confirm that Paul's order of resurrection appearances reveals a nascent schism and perilous conflict that became fierce for generations.

Paul and John

A third trajectory is made evident in Paul's letters, one that justifies further risk analysis. Once again, it is a trajectory originating in Jerusalem. That it was a separate, authoritative tradition is made certain by Paul's stress to his readers as to what happened; namely, that he received "the right hand of fellowship" from James, Kayfa and *John*, "who were reputed [understood] to be *pillars* [*stuloi*, or 'the ones seeming to be the pillars']."[708] Some commentators incorrectly assume that only these three were present at Jerusalem when Paul attended the first "council," and this is why he only mentions the three. Such an assumption is largely is based on a bias that John's presence was of little consequence, i.e., just another one of the eleven (or twelve?) exorcists/*apostoloi* that happened to be in Jerusalem at the time of the council. But we learn from Acts 15 that Paul and Barnabas were sent to Jerusalem "to the *apostoloi* and elders,"[709] and that they were "greeted by the *ecclesia and the apostoloi* and the elders." As previously noted, the report in Acts of the council meeting and agreements reached was developed to gloss over the actual rift between Paul and James. Nonetheless, there is no reason to object to its report that most if not all of Jesus' remaining exorcists/*apostoloi* were in Jerusalem. Indeed, these may have been some of the *apostoloi* listed in the synoptic tradition with the addition of Matthias (replacing Judas) and the women exorcists who had been deleted from the tradition.[710]

Since several *apostoloi* were present in Jerusalem, it is certain that Paul is, once again, intentional in his choice of words *and* names. He selects only these three specific leaders among those present and cites their endorsement of his *euangelion* via the "right hand of fellowship." Therefore, Paul's citation of John's endorsement is also unique and significant. John is placed on equal standing with the brother of Jesus and Kayfa the leader of the Twelve. Consequently, the implication is clear: Paul is employing John's name and endorsement as a powerful risk mitigation, just as he had done by citing Kayfa's. Since Paul does not need to explain who John is, it confirms that this John was widely known and respected in Galatia by 50 CE. Who was this John, and specifically, why does Paul employ John's name as a risk mitigation?

The Johannine tradition became one of the most dominant trajectories in early Christianity by the late first and early second century. Indeed, the oldest extant

---

708. Gal 2:9b.
709. Acts 15:2b.
710. Luke 6:14–16.

The Enemies of Paul: Demons, Satan, Betrayers, and Apostles

fragment of the New Testament known today is the Rylands Library papyrus P52 that dates to 100–117 CE.[711] Since this fragment was found in Egypt it is obvious that this *euangelion* trajectory had been spread a relatively impressive distance since its place of origin is almost unanimously identified as Asia Minor by scholars,[712] and by later tradition per Eusebius, more specifically to Ephesus, Roman capital of Asia. John, the son of Zebedee and Salome, was the younger brother of James. The family resided in Bethsaida (Beth-saida, literally "fishing village" or "village of the fish god"). Both James and John were trained exorcists, subsistence fishermen before joining Jesus. Jesus gave them their exorcist names as *Boanerges* (Aramaic for the "sons of thunder," Mark 3:16–17). They also stayed in Capernaum when Jesus adopted Kayfa's home as his own before entering into his war on Satan.

Yet, the Gospel of John cannot with certainty be attributed to this John. However, there are traditions within it that claim a direct witness stood behind them and was its authoritative source. The use of "the beloved disciple," the intimate dialogues between Jesus and this disciple, and his close association with Kayfa and Jesus' favorite exorcists, makes a strong case that many of the gospel's traditions originated with John, just as later tradition attests. It is clear that the community intended minimally to give strong credence to John's oral influence, if not his hand in its composition before his unexpected death, which rocked its community: "This is the disciple who is bearing witness to these things, and who has written these things; and *we know* that his testimony is true."[713] Indeed, the gospel confirms that a definitive witness, one who lived in Palestinian and knew conditions among the Jews there,[714] provided many of the oral traditions. Thus, a Palestinian Jew, likely John, and the community that recognized his authority is most certainly the primary source of its core traditions.

The Jesus portrayed in these traditions is significantly different than the one presented in the Synoptics. More, the sources of tradition used in the gospel do not seem to know the Synoptics (other than elements of the passion narrative), and so, it represents an independent trajectory. Jesus speaks in mysterious, esoteric dialogues about God the Father. Jesus states he is "one" with the Father, while the disciples must "eat [Jesus'] flesh and drink [his] blood" to be one with him. The prologue of the gospel is an elegant poem about the "word [*logos*] becoming flesh" and that the word "tented [or dwelled] among us," suggesting that Jesus was transformed into the personified *Logos* of God, the one who speaks with the authority of salvation and was preexistent, i.e., "face to face with God," taking human form. As such, this introduction seems to suggest that salvation comes through the power of the *logia* of Jesus, the *Logos*, and that confession upon hearing his *logia* is immediately efficacious, affording salvation. Yet, the gospel also presents very stark, graphic and even disturbing material encounters

---

711. John 18:31–33.
712. Such as Koester, *History*, 203.
713. John 21:24.
714. A more thorough discussion is provided below.

with Jesus post-crucifixion, which makes impossible any claim to access to salvation through the *logia* and *gnosis-wisdom* alone. Indeed, the gospel demands that the adherent accept *pisits* in the efficacious death and physical resurrection of Jesus, as well as a return and judgment.[715] Interestingly, *it is the Apostle Thomas* who demands that he will not believe until he actually examines and puts his fingers inside the crucifixion wounds on the body. It is only when Thomas confirms a materially resurrected Jesus that he confesses and cries out, "My Lord and my God!"[716] Thus, the entire trajectory of Thomas, or those like it—a trajectory as we have demonstrated is present and opposing Paul in Corinth—is rejected in this one *pericope*. Indeed, it is decisively displaced by a demand to accept the material resurrection of Jesus, not a metaphorical or spiritual resurrection.[717] Consequently, the Johannine trajectory is founded on the resurrection of Jesus of Nazareth as undisputed, and event that is most assuredly, and ironically, confirmed by Didymus Thomas.

This leads us to the repudiation of James. It is striking that James is not even mentioned by name in the Gospel of John. Instead, the brothers of Jesus (which included James) are dismissed as *apistoi*, and are criticized and ridiculed: "For even his own brothers did not believe in him."[718] This is a significant and intentional debasement of the James' trajectory and authority by the community of the beloved disciple. Indeed, even though Jerusalem lay in ruins at the time of the composition of the gospel, the failure to call to memory and status of James is almost shocking. James' reputation has been so radically diminished that he almost vanishes, being *marginalized as an unbeliever*, an enemy. This would suggest that a dramatic schism had developed that was never repaired between James and the Johannine community (i.e., John). There is not even and attempt to sanitize James' reputation, something done for Thomas. The silence is deafening. Therefore, from a risk perspective we must conclude that James was ultimately at enmity with three early Christian movement leaders who all held to efficacious *pistis* in the *euangelion* of the risen Jesus and the coming *parousia*—Paul, Kayfa and John. By the end of the first century, the trajectory of James became even more radicalized than in Corinth. What is evidenced in Paul's order of resurrection appearances then is an early recognition of separate parties and nascent schisms.

While the community of John marginalizes James, it elevates others, particularly women. This elevation of women is striking. It is a dominant trajectory and its importance to the structure of John is irrefutable. The Gospel of John's oral sources, and so its original legacy, are intertwined with numerous of these key traditions passed on by women *apostoloi*. More, they are inseparable from the traditions associated with the "beloved apostle." In virtually every case, either the beloved disciple or specifically named women (who notably travel with Jesus' exorcists) are cited as direct

---

715. John 3:16; 21:22.
716. John 20:24–29.
717. E.g., Docetism, i.e., that Jesus only seemed to be in a body but actually it was an illusion.
718. John 7:35.

The Enemies of Paul: Demons, Satan, Betrayers, and Apostles

witnesses and the sources to the events recorded, and were considered as having equal standing with the beloved disciple. Consequently, it is certain that the beloved disciple endorsed their inclusion, as the community attributed the authority for the formation and authority of the gospel tradition to him alone.[719] As such, the inclusion of women *apostoloi* in this trajectory warrants further investigation. Indeed, the frequent use of *pericope* concerning women that are both unique to this gospel and powerful in their placement and content, or are pivotal to transformative events, is striking.[720] The gospel bases much of trajectory on these traditions—it is reliant upon them as a major source and framework in the formation of the tradition and presents it with careful, and deliberate respect. Indeed, the respect given them is equivalent to that afforded Kayfa and other *apostoloi*, i.e., all witnesses to the resurrected Jesus. We begin with the post-crucifixion encounters.

At the gospel's conclusion, the details of the first encounter are provided. This first post-crucifixion encounter was not with Kayfa, contrary to the claim in the synoptic tradition.[721] Here, the first encounter was with Mary the Magdalene, one of Jesus' leading exorcists and *apostoloi*.[722] Only Mary could have shared this event, making it of immense importance to John who understood it as indisputable validation of the resurrection of Jesus to the first "*apostolos*." This encounter finds credence on multiple levels: It was (1) culturally very problematic (i.e., it records the first appearance to a woman; inadmissible as evidence in Jewish court);[723] (2) it was rejected by the apostles when they heard it (i.e., negative attestation, as it does not put the apostles in a very positive light); and (3) it displaced the first appearance to Kayfa, the leader of the Twelve. It also provides extraordinary details that reflect knowledge of (4) Jerusalem; (5) the service of gardeners in local Palestinian tombs; (5) the location of the tombs outside the city walls later confirmed by archaeology; (6) the tomb's structure that is distinct to the area and similar to other first-century Jewish tombs found in the vicinity; and (7) that the event was post-Sabbath.

Indeed, just as Magdalene's post-crucifixion encounter with Jesus is given pre-eminence over all others, virtually all traditions originating with *apostolic women* are the most prominent and pivotal in the gospel. From Jesus' first charismatic "sign" (i.e., the water to wine at the wedding at Cana,[724] reluctantly performed at the request of Jesus' mother), to necromancy in the raising of Lazarus from the dead and Jesus'

---

719. John 21:23.

720. John 2:1–11; 4:1–42; 11:1–45; 12:1–8; 19:25–27; 20:1–2, 11–18.

721. Recall that Paul is not claiming Kayfa was the first, but he is listing intentionally the order of appearances to fit the context of his confrontation with Jewish male opponents in Corinth reflected in an early creedal formula.

722. For an extensive discussion of Mary the Magdalene as an exorcist who participated in Jesus' war on Satan, and first to encounter Jesus, see Busse, *Resurrected*, 106–17.

723. Neusner, *Modern Study of the Mishnah*, 194–95, and *Tractate Sanhedrin*, chs. 1–3.

724. John 2:1–11.

dialogue with Martha,[725] all are pivotal moments pre- and post-crucifixion. In fact, Jesus' acknowledgment that his war on Satan was not simply prophetic was revealed, not to Kayfa or the Twelve, but to a Samaritan and woman at Jacob's well.[726] She not only believes him (i.e., has *pistis*), she becomes his "*witness [marturouses] of the word [logos]*" to her people; that is, she was commissioned to witness and garner *pistis*—an apostolic commission.[727]

In another striking pericope, Jesus provides the most explicit description of the transformative power of *pistis*, indeed its salvific nature, to neutralize annihilation under the curse of death. This dialogue is with Martha, who is desperate and grieving over the death of her brother.[728] Jesus is so moved by her and her sister's *pistis* that in tears he performs necromancy, risking all because it is immediately punishable by death under Roman law.[729] This event is absent in the synoptic tradition, but is described in intimate and accurate detail. The Lazarus event becomes the watershed event arming Jesus' enemies to have him put to death as a dark magician, an evildoer and minion of Beelzebul. Consequently, it is this tradition that records the catalyst for the Jesus' death, burial and subsequent resurrection. And it is to these women that power of *pistis* in overcoming the curse of death is revealed, i.e., by *pistis* in Jesus as Christ. The prominence of women in the Gospel of John is therefore indisputable.

Consequently, looking solely at these traditions it is clear that the Gospel of John places women as the pivotal apostolic witnesses in Jesus' ministry. As such, the association of the Johannine tradition with the elevation of these apostolic women may help to explain the importance of John as one of the three "pillars" and Paul's use of John as a risk mitigation to the Corinthian infiltrators.

The "Beloved Disciple" and Paul's "John" as the "Pillar"

Like the trajectory of the *apostolic women*, the tradition of the "beloved" disciple is intimately linked with major pivotal events in Jesus' activity. It betrays a definite and unique knowledge of these events and of Palestine that can only be attributed to a Palestinian Jew and witness, particularly a subsistence worker turned exorcist. Indeed, much of the gospel is written in very simple Koine Greek,[730] the language that could

---

725. John 11:1–45.

726. John 4:4–42; the culturally shocking scene of the disciples returning to see Jesus speaking with a Samaritan could only be remembered by an eyewitness.

727. Not only was a personal discussion with this Samaritan woman forbidden (Jewish men were not allowed to talk alone with women as recorded here), it was considered heretical. This is why Jesus' tone (particularly in Koine Greek) is harsh, but still he breaks social norms and not only speaks to her, but commissions her. Most important, it is the elevation of women to the most prominent roles in the Johannine gospel tradition.

728. John 11:21–27.

729. See Busse, *Resurrected*, 1, 60–63.

730. The Greek in John is not unlike that of the recitation, or dictation of an educated Galilean

be associated with a peasant. Of course, only a witness could have reported the many non-public dialogues of Jesus related in the gospel. These facts strongly support the conclusion that a witness stands behind the traditions in John, one who also knew and conversed with the women *apostoloi*. Indeed, this is the assertion of the "beloved disciple" and the community that recognized his authority.

Most important is the placement of the "beloved disciple" at the crucifixion of Jesus, where he witnesses "blood and water" flowing from his side, indicating the physical proximity of the disciple to Jesus, but more, that he witnesses a transformation in Jesus' body had begun. The water flowing from the wound in Jesus' body (i.e., from the Roman lance to ensure he was dead) was recognized by the beloved disciple as the beginning of the transformation from death to life, "the spirit *and water* [life]."[731] Such "signs" were drawn from a miracles tradition that identified Jesus as blessed and from God. Rudolf Bultmann was the first to capture an outline of the more primitive gospel of the "beloved disciple" that preceded the "midrash," or longer theological narratives explaining the theological themes in the gospel.[732] While he associates the miracles, such as the one in Cana, with a written source behind the gospel, it is more likely that these "signs" were also linked to the reminiscences of apostolic women who were present at these events, and were intertwined with the witness of the beloved disciple who knew these women and honored their traditions.[733] The conclusion of the gospel clearly makes this claim, and the evidence supports it.[734]

In this regard, there is an intensely personal event recorded in the gospel, one of immense import to the beloved disciple that the community preserved, and was remembered in all subsequent generations of adherents, i.e., *Jesus' dying request that the beloved disciple care for his mother*:

> When Jesus saw his mother and the disciple whom he loved standing near, he said to this mother, "Women behold your son!" Then he said to the disciple, "Behold, you mother."[735]

Here Jesus asks the beloved disciple to care for his mother after his death, *not his own brother, James, or any of his family!*[736] This is a startling tradition. The authority and memory of James is thereby obliterated. The status of the beloved disciple is elevated to be "one of the pillars." He becomes the conduit of a different trajectory of traditions that included the other apostolic women—her sister, Mary the wife of

---

worker, with the ability to speak Greek and Aramaic (there are many "Aramaisms" in John).

731. However, understanding the gospel's emphasis on assuring the physical death of Jesus, it could have also been seen as the sign he was surely dead.

732. Bultmann, *John*, 1941.

733. Perrin, *Introduction*, 225.

734. See John 20:30–31.

735. John 19:26–27.

736. This also provides sure evidence that Joseph, Jesus' father, was also unavailable.

Clopas, and Mary the Magdalene—the only exorcist to have not fled to Galilee after Jesus' murder.[737]

Mary's care was the last and most urgent request given by Jesus from the cross before his death.[738] It stands as a reliable tradition to its negative connotations with regard to Jesus' own family, having rejected him and thought him to be possessed by Satan. That this disciple did just as requested is highly likely given the recitation of the tradition by the community document: "And from that hour that disciple took her to his own *home*."[739] Consequently, it is virtually certain that Mary resided with John, the "beloved disciple," in Jerusalem, as Paul confirms John's presence there in his Galatian correspondence. John's designation as a "pillar" is then certainly tied to his role in preserving the traditions of the apostolic women, particularly Mary the mother of Jesus.

In sum, Paul's citation of these three men to his adherents in Corinth was intended to unequivocally demonstrate that his *euangelion* and apostleship had been validated by those *apostoloi* who represented the leading traditions of his time. It is a strong mitigation to the risk of James' *apostoloi* claiming that Paul's *euangelion* is of Satan. Paul warns that James had once endorsed his *euangelion*, but is now cursed; but he was not alone in this endorsement—John and Kayfa, whom Paul supports, had done so, making James therefore the outcast of the "pillars."

The Resurrection Creed or the *Logia*

It is at this point that Paul places himself in his expanded list of the post-crucifixion encounters with the risen Jesus: "Then, *last of all*, he was *seen* by me."[740] Paul uses the verb "to be seen" (*ophthe*; see the discussion on Paul's use of this verb and its significance above), meaning that Paul encountered a manifestation of Jesus that he could see with his eyes, and so, was unmistakably material and present with him; i.e., it was not an apparition, phantasm or spirit that "appeared," which is the word commonly and incorrectly found in many translations.

Paul continues, ". . . as to one who was *untimely born*."[741] Conzelmann translates this same statement as follows: "[he appeared to me] . . . as if to an abortive creature."[742] Paul is implying that at the time of his "birth," i.e., his physical encounter with the risen Jesus, he was unformed, not yet ready for birth, actually portraying himself as something as shocking as a monster. In ancient Roman law, the Law of the Twelve Tables (*Leges Duodecem Tabularum*), which was the foundational law of the Roman Republic and later Roman law itself, Table 4 (only remaining in fragments) reads, "An

737. See Busse, *Jesus Resurrected*, 106–20; John 19:25.
738. John 19:27.
739. John 19:27b.
740. 1 Cor 15:8.
741. Ibid.
742. Conzelmann, *Corinthians*, 259.

The Enemies of Paul: Demons, Satan, Betrayers, and Apostles

obviously deformed child must be put to death." Paul is not comparing himself to an aborted child. Instead, he is comparing himself to a birthed child who was deformed and who only deserved death by law. But the question remains as to why did Paul chooses the analogy of a deformed child worthy of death?

Paul provides this context: "For I am the least of the apostles, and I am not worthy to be called an *apostolos*, because I *persecuted the ecclesia of God*."[743] As in Galatians, Paul again admits his most heinous past as a paid spy, a "hit man," and assassin of the Jerusalem religious elite. He did more than identify and persecute followers of the evildoer Jesus and his exorcists. To use his own words, he "laid waste" to the *ecclesiae* and their adherents, tracking them as far as the Roman Decapolis city of Damascus (about 136 miles from Jerusalem). The Jerusalem elite licensed his violence, including murder, against these men and women, authorizing the pursuit and neutralization of any adherents of the cult of Jesus. They were not only criminals and blasphemers, they were evil and under Satan's control like their master, and because they controlled demons in his name, were dangerous. They embraced this condemned dark magician and crucified Roman criminal as Lord, and continued not only to control demons of Beelzebul at will, but practiced dark magic in his name (including necromancy and curses). Some followers were able to contact and conjure his spirit, clearly for evil purposes, i.e., infect and destroy enemies. Even their practices were abhorrent—they gathered to consume his flesh and blood to absorb his evil power each week. Paul was therefore authorized to annihilate this cult and it followers. He could seize property, bring adherents by force before Roman authorities for punishment or execution, immediately form mobs and stone them; he could forbid victims from practicing subsistence trades and revoke production licenses (e.g., fishing). These powers forced victims into starvation, and destitution. Without subsistence wages, debtors prison and the dissolution of families resulted. And this is exactly what Paul means he did. The Romans agreed that the cult of Jesus was comprised of seditious criminals. Paul was the leader of the first organized deadly persecution of the Jesus movement.[744] While it may be shocking to consider, risk analysis would suggest that Paul may have employed the same protocol in his mission to disrupt and destroy the *ecclesiae* as he did later to spread the *euangelion*; that is, he went directly to the synagogue assemblies on the Sabbath, or feast with local trade guilds including leather workers, but in this case to target and identify adherents for destruction.

743. 1 Cor 15:9.

744. Acts 8:3, "But Saul laid waste to the *ecclesia* of God, entering house after house, dragging off both men and women to prison"; Acts 9:1, "Now Saul, still breathing threats and murder against the disciples of the Lord, went to the high priest and asked him for letters to the synagogues at Damascus, so that if he found any belonging to the Way, men or women, he might bring them bound to Jerusalem"; Acts 22:4, "I persecuted this Way to the death, putting into prison both men and women"; "And I said, 'Lord, they themselves understand that in one synagogue after another I used to imprison and beat those who believed in you"; and most important, Acts 26:10, "And this is just what I did in Jerusalem; not only did I lock up many of the saints in prisons, having received authority from the chief priests, but also when they were being put to death I cast my vote against them."

Remarkably then, Paul is putting his standing with the Corinthians at significant risk with a most amazing self-condemnation, admitting he was a violent spy and assassin. Why would Paul do this? The answer must begin by seeking the origin of Paul's analogy of the child.

In the *logia* of Jesus there are numerous *logia* that describe the adherents' proper response to the call of God as proclaimed by Jesus. In these sayings, Jesus rejects anyone's claim of merit before God, and calls for the true adherent to revert to the childlike state; that is, humbling oneself completely like a child to a parent in trust and *pistis*. Koester acknowledges that the sayings and metaphors of the child have a strong claim to authenticity, i.e., that they can be traced to Jesus of Nazareth and his ministry (without the filtering of the nascent oral history of transmission of such sayings that were adapted to meet the life situation of the growing movement).[745] As Koester notes: "The metaphor of the child—again derived from a genuine saying of Jesus (Mark 10.15 par.), becomes an important symbol for the true adherent in whose religious experience the opposites are reconciled," meaning the recognition of "present blessedness." Koester also notes that the image of the child became the image of the radical eschatological agony Jesus introduces in his proclamation, which later became the catalyst for development and retention of the early proto-gnostic and gnostic sayings, such as in the *Gospel of Thomas*:

> Other prophetic sayings of Jesus in the form of beatitudes, some of them quoted [in the *Gospel of Thomas*] without significant alterations (Sayings 54, 68, 69 = Matt 5:3, 11, 6), are used to describe this same state of present blessedness; thus, all these designations by which Jesus identified the heirs of the kingdom—the children, the poor, the hungry, those who suffer persecution—ultimately mean in the *Gospel of Thomas* the "Solitary One."[746]

The *Solitary One*, or the one that stands as united with the wisdom of God, is in the androgynous blessed childlike state—where immediate salvation or "blessedness is achieved"—by understanding one's origin and divine place. Koester summarizes this as follows:

> In the agonizing eschatological divisions which have been ushered in by Jesus (Luke 12:51–53 // Matt 10:34–36, quoted in Saying 16), the adherent stands as the Solitares . . . Jesus radicalized the traditional apocalyptic expectation of the kingdom; his message demands that the mysterious presence of the kingdom in his words be recognized.

Thus, the *Gospel of Thomas*, and *logia* collections like those in Corinth that found saving power, "blessedness," in the words of Jesus (i.e., as opposed to Paul's *euangelion* of *agape* and *pistis* and the coming *parousia*), were the only authentic and efficacious

---

745. Robinson and Koester, *Trajectories*, 174–75.
746. Ibid.

trajectory to unity with the divine and salvation. Any other *euangelion* was empty, of deceit and evil. The emphasis on the power of the risen one's *logia*, now under the control of James and his higher wisdom torah (see above) was the sole way to achieve wisdom and salvation of salvation's presence, one's true blessed state.

> But the disclosure of the mysterious presence of the kingdom is no longer an eschatological event [of the future]; it has become a matter of the interpretation of Jesus' words . . . thus, "whoever finds the explanation of the se words will not taste death." (Saying 51)

As noted in the Thomas tradition, James is cited as the authority for the powerful, saving *sophia-logia*, and we have established, James did indeed oversee the *logia* of wisdom salvation, i.e., Jesus as the new Moses of the perfect law of wisdom-torah. The saying then of reconciliation of the self into the state of the child must have been part of the collection of *logia* used by the intruders against Paul's unacceptable malformed state:

> These children who are being suckled are like those who enter the kingdom. . . . When you make the two one, and when you make the inner as the outer . . . and as the above the below, the male and female into a single one . . . then you shall enter the kingdom of God. (Saying 22)

For the intruders, Paul's *euangelion* was not simply errant, it was another satanic and evil deception—i.e., it was of "another spirit." Consequently, Paul was malformed—*he was twisted and evil, far from being one of the children of the kingdom*. Clearly then, Paul uses the metaphor of the malformed child because this is how he is labeled, using one of the *logia* like Saying 22.[747] Paul's *euangelion* demonstrated that he had not made "the inside like the out"—he had not made the salvific transformation through *gnosis* into a Solitary One.

Not only was Paul mired in deadly ignorance but also was the *apostolos* of it. His ignorance was perilous and deadly, as he continued to espouse a *euangelion* that laid havoc to the true kingdom of God (*basileia tou Theou*), *just as he had done as a paid hit man and assassin in Jerusalem* (which some of the *apostoloi* from Jerusalem knew and witnessed). For them, Paul was continuing his evil attack on the kingdom, but instead of violence, he deceived and obscured salvation with a *euangelion* of the *parousia*. Paul was under satanic control, still persecuting the *ecclesiae of God* through his rejection of them, and by implication, *his rejection of James*. Consequently, the infiltrators link Paul's violent past with rejection of the *logia* of the Living One. Paul is like the evil, malformed child.

Paul understands their accusations and use of *logia* to emphasize his malformed evil state.[748] He cannot dispute their charges or that he was a violent persecutor of

---

747. *Gos. Thom.*, Saying 22, detailed above.
748. See 2 Cor 11:1–33.

the Way.⁷⁴⁹ Paul acknowledges their accusations, taking the offensive: "For I am the least of the *apostoloi* and do not even deserve to be called an *apostolos*, because I persecuted the *ecclesia* of God."⁷⁵⁰ He admits his life of violent opposition to God's "pillars," then makes a bold claim; namely, that his appointment as an *apostolos* resulted from an act of *charis*, or grace of God: "But by the grace of God, I am what I am, and his grace toward me has not been in vain, but I have labored more than all of them [i.e., the 'pillars'], *yet not I*, but the grace of God that was within me."⁷⁵¹ Paul's only claim in response to the accusations of the enemies is that while he was worthless and doomed he was given favor and grace that only divine *agape* could bring, just as that given to the Corinthians, which is the proof of the real presence of God and the vindication of his position. Paul claims this grace was "within him," i.e., he too contained divinity, but that it was not he but God who revealed it and brought it forth. Paul shifts from defense to offense, now addressing the infiltrators' claim that there is no resurrection of the dead.⁷⁵²

Paul begins his attack with an affirmation, something often overlooked, but of critical importance: "*Whether it was either I or they, so we preach and so you believed.*"⁷⁵³ The "they" implies that Kayfa, the Twelve *and James* acknowledged Jesus' resurrection for salvation, i.e., they witnessed and would acknowledge that Jesus was not dead but alive, validating his divinity. Clearly, this is where divergence occurred, and in a world alien to our own (where demons, satanic powers and dark angels, illness and death were feared), improper practices and errant understanding literally meant perilous risk, woe and doom. As such, 1 Corinthians allows a reconstruction of the infiltrators' view of Jesus as the Living One.

As noted, the James' trajectory emphasized the saving power of Jesus' *logia* as salvific through wisdom-torah. It evident that neither James nor his original trajectory ever rejected a form of resurrection of Jesus, that is why Paul mentions the appearance to James in his list of witnesses⁷⁵⁴ (the infiltrators are thereby confronted by this admission) and identifies a group of "other apostles" that are associated with James and who were appointed by him. Indeed, these *apostoloi* must have experienced a form of encounter with the Living One, likely via the *logia* and salvific revelation it provided, i.e., as a having come to them from the Living One. Since the infiltrators claim James as their divinely appointed champion, Paul's inclusion of him in the list of witnesses to the resurrection sets the stage to challenge their claims of sole legitimacy and authority apart from a future resurrection. Whether by the *euangelion* of

---

749. That is why it is reported that "he who once persecuted the Way is now a believer," Gal 1:23.
750. 1 Cor 15:9.
751. 1 Cor 15:10.
752. 1 Cor 15:12.
753. 1 Cor 15:11.
754. If these men link themselves to James, Paul's citation of his witness would set the stage to refute their claim that this is no resurrection.

pistis (i.e., Paul), or by salvific *gnosis* gleaned from the *logia* of wisdom-torah given by the new Moses, Jesus is for both the Living One and Lord. But for Paul, Jesus' resurrection is the "first fruits" of the *parousia*, with the general resurrection still to come for those of *pistis* and *agape*.

The wisdom-torah trajectory found in Jesus' *logia* develops a pattern of esoteric salvific *gnosis*, that when selected sayings were assembled correctly, the *logia* provided a new divinely inspired view of one's true nature and status given by the Risen One.[755] It is a divine wisdom so dramatic that it leads to reliance solely on the saving power of those words, the "higher-torah" of truth.

> A woman in the crowd said to him: Blessed is the womb that bore thee, and the breasts that nourished thee. He said to her: *Blessed are they who have heard the word of the Father and have kept it in truth.* For there shall be days when you will say: Blessed is that womb which has not conceived, and those breasts which have not given suck.[756]

The *logia* provided *gnosis* as to one's divine state.

> Jesus said: When you see your likeness, you rejoice; but when you see your images which came into being before you—they neither die nor are made manifest—how much will you bear?[757]

Once understood, complete freedom from the world of human misery and error was gained.

> Jesus said: Perhaps men think that I am come to cast peace upon the world, and know not that I am come to cast divisions upon the earth, fire, sword, war. For there shall be five in a house; there shall be three against two, and two against three, the father against the son and the son against the father, and they shall stand as Solitaries.[758]

This blessed state, the uniting of the inner and outer into a new child, granted libertine rights, which when publicly displayed "awake" others possible to saving and liberating power of wisdom-torah from this corrupt world.

> Jesus saw some infants at the breast. He said to his disciples: These little ones at the breast are like those who enter into the kingdom. They said to him: If we then be children, shall we enter the kingdom? Jesus said to them: When you make the two one, and when you make the inside as the outside, and the outside as the inside, and the upper side as the lower; and when you make the male and the female into a single one, that the male be not male and the female

---

755 *Gos. Thom.*, Saying 70: "When you bring forth that in yourselves, that which you have will save you. If you do not have that in yourselves, that which you do not have in you will kill you."

756. *Gos. Thom.*, Saying 79.

757. *Gos. Thom.*, Saying 84.

758. *Gos. Thom.*, Saying 16.

> not female; when you make eyes in the place of an eye, and a hand in place of a hand, and a foot in place of a foot, an image in place of an image, then shall you enter [the kingdom].[759]

As the followers gained momentum, they became itinerant preachers, spoke in angelic tongues, and claimed the right (by a saying of Jesus) for support. The basis of their authority was solely linked to the *logia* of Jesus that provided divine, transformative and salvific wisdom,[760] and the authoritative guardian of the *logia* trajectory, James, "for whom heaven and earth were made."[761]

Thus, James, who sent the "super-apostles" to follow Paul and Kayfa with licenses to disrupt and then discredit Paul,[762] would not have authorized them to reject a risen Lord. As noted, Paul knows this because he lists James as a witness to the physical resurrection. Yet still, there is no future resurrection of the dead, particularly in a physical form; salvation is present now in its original and incorruptible form.[763] They follow the "son of the Living One,"[764] the divine one who brings higher law, the pure Sabbath, that the current religious leaders who are "drunk" with this world could never understand. They refer to dead prophets![765] The divine ones are the Solitary Ones.[766]

Could a Pharisaic Jew who became a follower of James ever have rejected the general resurrection, replacing it with wisdom-*gnosis*, discovering the "higher torah" and blessed state? Absolutely, as the collected *logia* stressed the miraculous in-breaking of the kingdom of God in the *logia* alone, which meant that "some standing here will not taste death before they see the kingdom of God coming with power,"[767] or "the kingdom of God is within [among] you."[768] To remain a Pharisee and not recognize that one's union with the divine is accessible now is to be deceived and face doom.

> Jesus said: The Pharisees and the scribes have received the keys of knowledge; they have hidden them. They did not go in, and those who wanted to go in they did not allow. But you be wise as serpents and innocent as doves.[769]

---

759. *Gos. Thom.*, Saying 22.
760. *Gos. Thom.*, Saying 1.
761. *Gos. Thom.*, Saying 12.
762. That is, as he did in Galatia after discovering that the agreement he, Paul and Kayfa reached on dietary and other ritual adherence to the law was abridged by Paul and Kayfa in the *ecclesia* of Antioch.
763. *Gos. Thom.*, Saying 18.
764. *Gos. Thom.*, Saying 37.
765. *Gos. Thom.*, Saying 28, 43, 52.
766. *Gos. Thom.*, Saying 49, 50.
767. Luke 9:27.
768. Luke 17:21; *Gos. Thom.*, Saying 3.
769. *Gos. Thom.*, Saying 39.

The Enemies of Paul: Demons, Satan, Betrayers, and Apostles

The promise of the arrival of the kingdom meant that all who resist would be destroyed.[770] *Logia* warn of violent separation and struggle, a demonstrated rejection of the evil ones and the world, even brother, mother, sister and children. What was to come was only violent death to enemies, as the *logia* led to life when comprehended, i.e., the moment of awakening and unity, and one's rule over the world.

> Jesus said: He who seeks, let him not cease seeking until: finds; and when he finds he will be troubled, and if he is troubled, he will be amazed, and he will reign over the All.[771]

The *logia* defined the world and the enlightened ones as in a violent struggle. Radical rejection of the human world and its errant and deceitful interpretation and application of the law was in order, but more, there is freedom from it.

> Jesus said: I have cast fire upon the world, and behold I guard it until it is ablaze.[772]

> Jesus said: I stood in the midst of the world, and I appeared to them in flesh. I found them all drunk, I found none among them thirsting; and my soul was afflicted for the sons of men, for they are blind in their heart and they do not see. For empty came they into the world, seeking also to depart empty from the world. But now they are drunk. When they have thrown off their wine, then will they repent.[773]

True law was higher wisdom of one's situation, status and divine nature, so that insight, *gnosis* and reuniting with the divine through wisdom were gained. Indeed, the radical nature of this understanding through sayings in the collection provided not only authorization but also required the demonstration of one's freedom as evidence of the blessed state.[774] Much like the *charismata* within the *ecclesiae* of Paul, the opponents' recognized their gift of *glossolalia* as this preeminent demonstration of reaching directly to the words of the third heaven, to God and to the angels, and more, to the realized resurrection already obtained; *in other words, for them the general resurrection had already begun through their gnosis and the saving wisdom it provided.* Indeed, there was no waiting necessary for a general resurrection, as the blessed state was present and had been realized through knowledge of the wisdom of God—the most radical eschatology. They must separate from the world to achieve *gnosis*,[775] but once *gnosis* is achieved they may do what they will in order to demonstrate freedom from

---

770. Recall Ezra and the discussion above on the judgment and violent death of sinners by God's chosen one.
771. *Gos. Thom.*, Saying 2.
772. *Gos. Thom.*, Saying 10.
773. *Gos. Thom.*, Saying 28.
774. *Gos. Thom.*, Saying 81.
775. Saying 27: "If you do not abstain from the world, you will not find the kingdom..."

the corrupted and evil world and their disdain for it.⁷⁷⁶ But even more, the *logia* also *called for* and *authorized* rejection of the errant and cursed people who were already rejected by God—they were lost—and accordingly, the *logia* included a proclamation for public demonstration of freedom through the shocking actions affirming this rejection.⁷⁷⁷ Whether these were Hellenistic Jews, Alexandrian Jews, Sadducees, or Pharisees, it is certain that they embraced the salvific *sophia-logia* trajectory, rejecting a general resurrection. The Gospel of John recounts this claim quite clearly:

> Then Jesus said to them: Truly, truly I say to you, Moses gave you not the bread from heaven, but my father gives you true bread from heaven. For the bread of God is he that comes down from heaven and gives life unto the world . . . I am the bread of life. He that believes in me shall never hunger . . . or thirst; Truly, truly I say to you, he who hears my word and believes on him that sent me has eternal life and shall not come to judgment, but is passed from death to life.⁷⁷⁸

While this is likely not from the collection of *logia*, it summarizes the radical eschatological view embraced in 1 Corinthians by Paul's enemies as a result of their interpretation of them—the wisdom (and blessedness) coming from *sophia-gnosis*.

The Imminent Expectation of the *Parousia*: The Opponents' Deadly Danger

The infiltrators rejected a future general resurrection as well as the reconstitution of a body.⁷⁷⁹ This is the basis of Paul's next comment: "Now if Christ is proclaimed as raised from the dead, how can a group of you say that there is no resurrection of the dead."⁷⁸⁰ Paul's use of *kerrusetai*, the "proclamation," refers to that which he has just established, namely the uniformity of witnesses, including James from whom they seek their authority—James, who would confirm to have encountered in some form a post-crucifixion living Lord. For Paul, Jesus is indeed a raised being, transformed into *something completely new*. Paul describes this form as a *pnuematikon soma*, a

---

776. Saying 14: "If you fast, you will bring forth sin for yourselves. If you pray, you will be condemned. And is you give alms you will do harm to your spirits. And if you go into any land and wander from place to place (and) if they take you in (then) eat what they will set before you. Heal the sick among them! For what goes in you mouth will not defile you, rather what comes out of your mouth will defile you."

777. Saying 55, on hating father and mother; Saying 56, the corpse is the world, disdain it as it is unworthy; Saying 81, they are kings and have the power over the world; Saying 104, they sin if they fast and pray; Saying 42, be passers by in the world (use it as one sees fit, but do not be caught in its deception); and possibly Saying 35, where the strong man of the house (the world) is bound, allowing it to be looted. Regardless, they are "kings over all," Saying 2.

778. John 6:32–35; John 5:24.

779. Whether the spiritual soma, *pnuematikon soma*, 1 Cor 15:44, or the more traditional Jewish expectation of a physically reconstituted body, Ezekiel—see above.

780. 1 Cor 15:12.

spiritual body that has substance and materiality.[781] This concept is exactly the same as described in the Gospel of John, where Jesus' presence is suddenly with the eleven disciples who are hiding behind locked doors, yet unlike a spirit, the disbelieving Thomas is able to touch Jesus' physical body in its mutilated, but raised form.[782] However, this is not the experience of James' followers, nor does it reflect necessarily the experience of James himself or the *other apostoloi*. Paul's own experience seems to be very different than John's gospel account.

Paul then takes a bold risk. He offers fodder to his enemies' position about his *euangelion* of Jesus *Christ* and the coming *parousia* and resurrection:

> But if there is no resurrection of the dead, then Christ has not been raised; if Christ is not raised, then our proclamation [*kerygma*] is in vain [*kenon*, better rendered as 'empty'] and your *pistis* is in [empty].[783]

Paul's comment is in response to a saying of Jesus found in Thomas, which must be very similar to that found in the *logia* collection of the infiltrators: "That resurrection which you seek has already come, but you do not recognize it."[784]

Paul begins with a warning to his adherents. All is at risk and salvation is voided if there has been no resurrection of Jesus, one that portends a future *parousia* and general resurrection for those of *pistis* and *agape*. If not, Jesus is then no longer Lord and Christ.[785] Paul then lays out the risks to not only himself, but to Kayfa *and James*: "We [meaning all of the witnesses in the list] are even found misrepresenting God [a stronger and more accurate rendering of *pseudomartures* is 'false witnesses' or 'charlatans'], because we testified of God the he raised Christ, whom he did not raise if it is true that the dead are not raised."[786] Paul extends the result: "Those who sleep [have died] have perished [Paul uses the emphatic verb to demonstrate the horrible realization of the finality of death for those adherents, *apolonto*] . . . and we are of all men most to be pitied."[787] In dramatic voice, Paul admits that the opponents' charges against him if true indeed make him a charlatan. But if Paul is a charlatan, so are the rest of the *apostoloi, even James*! Jesus is living post the crucifixion. Paul's attempt to recast the infiltrators' and James' acceptance of Jesus' resurrection as a commitment to a future *parousia* is an attempt to deny the legitimacy of individualist resurrection and the *logia* trajectory.

---

781. A complete discussion of this topic is provided above.
782. John 20:24–29.
783. 1 Cor 15:13.
784. Saying 51, and Saying 1, "Whoever finds the meaning of these words will not taste death."
785. The appellation given to Jesus like "Caesar," the long promised king sent by God, Jesus Christ, just like Julius Caesar.
786. 1 Cor 15:16.
787. 1 Cor 15:16–19.

Paul now asserts the validity of the resurrection of the dead, and with it the proper eschatological perspective given the reality of his own experience: "But in fact [literally, 'but now,' meaning right at this moment he is alive and is risen], Christ has been raised from the dead, the first-fruits of those who have fallen asleep."[788] Paul employs a description of the transformation they can observe from death to new life, and a changed *soma*, referring to wheat and grain that is planted and transforms; but more, how all things, even celestial bodies, have different bodies; that like a seed that must be planted and die to be transformed into its true glorious self: "What is sown is perishable, what is raised is imperishable."[789]

With the validity of a resurrection argued via a list of witnesses (a list that includes the infiltrators' champion), and with a description of the resurrected transformed body explicitly provided, the foundation and context of Paul's urgent eschatological appeal has been established. To further his argument, Paul rejects the radical and immediate transformation claimed by them by adding another saying of Jesus in their collection to his argument:

> Adam came from great power and a great wealth. But he did not become worthy of you. For if he had been worthy, then he would not have tasted of death.[790]

Paul states:

> For as by a man came death, by a man has also come the resurrection of the dead ... But each in his own order: Christ, the first-fruits, then at his coming, those who belong to Christ.[791]

Paul describes the sequence of events of the *parousia*, leading to the annihilation of death:

> Then comes the end, when he delivers the kingdom to God, even the Father, after destroying [better, "abolishing" *katargese*] all [or every] rule, all authority and all power.[792]

Paul presents a time on earth when Christ will rule, subduing all of these "enemies" are subdued and destroyed and the Scripture that foretold these events are fulfilled: "For God has put all things in subjection under his feet."[793]

---

788. 1 Cor 15:20.

789. 1 Cor 15:42.

790. Saying 85.

791. This is similar to those "sleeping" as delineated in his earlier letter, 1 Thess 4, then those alive who will greet him like Romans and Greeks who greeted the returning and victorious Lord or Caesar outside the city walls.

792. 1 Cor 15:24.

793. 1 Cor 15:27, parallel Ps 8:6.

The Enemies of Paul: Demons, Satan, Betrayers, and Apostles

What does Paul mean by Christ's subjugating "all authority . . . power . . . rule?" Paul is not referring to political and social categories here, that is, where Christ becomes a political king, but to powerful opponents considered most threatening in the Hellenistic-Roman world—the world of demons, Satan, evil principalities and celestial powers that were believed to control or destroy humans, torture or torment and kill, or infect them with the curse of death. The dangerous nature of Christ's enemies and their power is most clearly evidenced by Paul's statement: "The last [*eskatos*] enemy destroyed is death."[794] In the ancient Hellenistic-Roman world, *death was considered as the ultimate disease or scourge*; an enemy that ultimately enveloped every human being and ended life, brought about by the forces of demonic and evil powers—but regardless *it was the strongest and most feared enemy*. This was true for Paul's enemies as well. Would not death be overcome for all who believed by *pistis* in Christ? For Paul, death was the infection brought into humankind by the rebellion of Adam, just as it was for his enemies. Consequently, the end of death meant its overthrowing. It is not the logia of *sophia-gnosis* that accomplishes this. It is only *pistis* in Jesus *Christ*, the resurrected one and Lord who is still to come with the *parousia* to rescue the children of God and reconstitute the kingdom of God, that is salvific.

For Paul, the resurrection of Jesus was the beginning of *elpis* in the coming transformation to new life for those of *pistis* in the cross and resurrection at the *parousia*. The spiritual *soma* of Jesus portended what the adherents would also receive if they continued in *pistis* and embraced *agape*. As such, final days, which awaited the coming Day of the Lord, indeed, the eschatological age of transformation, had begun. For Paul, Jesus was not just the first, he was the *only one* thus far raised, i.e., the first of the eschatological harvest, or "first fruits" (for Paul, an eschatological term applied to this monumental and still unique event) of the kingdom. Judgment is yet to come upon all, and in the interim adherents who die "sleep." Paul is stressing that all things known, particularly the most powerful enemy, death, had already begun to be defeated in Jesus Christ, but the end had not yet come. Thus, the infiltrators were deceived, lost, and subject to judgment at the *parousia*. As they promulgated the false *euangelion* of salvific *gnosis*, perhaps even unknowingly, they operated as agents of Satan. They were possessed, even tragically so, infected still by the curse of death and under Satan's power.

The place of death in the eschatological schema of Paul's *euangelion* is centered in the tension between the world that is doomed and dying under the influence of Satan, and *pistis* in the salvific *euangelion* of Christ crucified that provides the sure *elpis* of adoption as a *tekna tou Theou* into the *basileia tou Theou* at the *parousia*. Consequently, death is one of the weightiest of all matters discussed by Paul in his conflict with the infiltrators. His adherents are being told that they are dead in *agnois*—followers of a charlatan, a false *apostolos* and an enemy of God. They are void of the salvific *gnosis* of the Living One. But Paul counters that it is the infiltrators who face sure death and are

---

794. 1 Cor 15:26.

cursed by rejecting the true *sophia* of God, the *euangelion*.[795] The resurrection of Jesus Christ is the power of God. It is the *pneumatikoi* who are to be counted among the final opponents of God, the last enemies who will be neutralized by Jesus Christ[796] (the *eskatos* or last thing). The new creation at the *parousia* will not be "flesh and blood,"[797] but the spiritual *soma* because the "perishable does not inherit the imperishable."[798] As such, Paul stresses that the infiltrators could not possibly have attained life and transformation for they are still flesh and blood. They remain perishable and have not attained the status of imperishable. Thus, their claim that there is no resurrection of the dead (i.e., that they by implication have already passed from death to life) is the claim of a cursed enemy of God and seals their fate.

As such in 1 Corinthians 15, Paul provides the earliest description of events relating to the order of death's elimination. Those "in Christ" will be transformed into a spiritual *soma*; then the enemies of God will be destroyed, *the last of which is death*; the kingdom will then be handed over to God the Father. Paul's description of the *eskatos* concludes with the most unusual act of all, certainly startling to the adherents living in a Roman world and contrary to their personal witness in history with regard to earthly rulers and kings: Christ, the Messiah of God, the appointed ruler who conquers all of the most feared enemies, including death, *will then surrender all of his authority and subject himself to God*—the ultimate act of *agape* and submission. For Paul, the tension between the present in-breaking of the kingdom[799] and the future destruction and subjugation of all enemies with the final delivery of the kingdom to God did not leave the present state void; it was filled with Paul's, Apollos' and Kayfa's itinerant mission of salvation through *pistis* in the *euangelion* of Jesus Christ.

Baptism for the Dead

One of the most mysterious practices recorded in early Christian literature is baptism on behalf of, or over (*huper ton nekron*), the dead. At first read, Paul seems to accept the practice since he does not condemn it. But to assume Paul accepts the practice is to ignore the eschatological risk context of Paul's arguments against the infiltrators' claims and the perilous crisis and context he has been mitigating.

It seems ironic to Paul that those who claim there is no resurrection of the dead are being baptized on behalf of the dead to free them from death! Such a practice would be powerfully appealing to any of Paul's adherents who had lost loved ones

795. See Gal 1:9 and 1 Cor 15:1–4.
796. That is, not by an individual through a self merited achievement of secret gnosis that saves.
797. 1 Cor 15:50a.
798. 1 Cor 15:50b.
799. Evidenced by (1) the historical and physical resurrection of Jesus, (2) the arrival of the Spirit and the *charismata*, and (3) the formation of the *ecclesia*, the community of the "more excellent Way" founded on *agape* until the *parousia*.

prior to reception of the *euangelion*. Paul's adherents know that the *agioi* who have died prior to the *parousia* will be the first raised, but others who had died would be left to the judgment of God. The implication of Paul's statement is that baptism on behalf of the dead is immediately salvific and efficacious, and so, is a practice of the *pneumatikoi*. As such, there is no evidence that Paul's adherents would have employed a baptism for the dead. This is further supported by Paul's statement: "Else what will they do, the ones being baptized on behalf of the dead."[800] Paul is speaking to and about the infiltrators who practice baptism for the "dead"—i.e., an esoteric rite they bring to Corinth. Since they are already "kings" they claim to have attained salvation, or "blessedness," through *gnosis* (i.e., since they have passed or been transformed from death to life through *gnosis* and its *sophia* to a new being and state). It can hold only power for those who have "died" to the world and attained the reunion with divinity through *gnosis*. In other words, they hold that *only they have the power to raise the dead to the third heaven* by being baptized on their behalf—they have the power of granting access into life as *apostoloi* of the *logia*, the *pneumatikoi*, mystagogues and guides of the Living One appointed by James. It would appear that these *apostoloi* are baptized on behalf of the "dead" as a means of propaganda for their own *euangelion* to turn to *gnosis*, i.e., to "gain life." Consequently, baptism is not the submission to *pistis* in the cross and resurrection, providing then access to *agape* and *elpis*, which are validated by the *charismata*, thereby assuring safety from the curse of death at the *parousia*. Baptism has become an elitist rite for which they claim sole possession and control—it has nothing to do with *pistis*, but instead salvific *gnosis*.

The infiltrators' concept of baptism may reflect aspects of the gnostic "redeemer" myth,[801] i.e., just as Jesus was transformed through wisdom and became all knowing, so too are they who embrace the wisdom revealed in his *logia* and receive life. As such, the *pneumatikoi* assert that they have sway over eternal life. Only those empowered by *gnosis* and *sophia* can practice authorizing "blessedness," who will live and rise to the third heaven. Truly, these would be then the "super-apostles," just as Paul sarcastically labels them.

Now it becomes abundantly clear why there is great consternation and crisis in Corinth, and why Paul immediately tackles the question of baptism and *sophia* at the outset of his correspondence, and makes subservient all *sophia* and *gnosis* to the *euangelion* of the cross (i.e., *pistis* in the cross and resurrection).[802] The response of the adherents is to cite the legitimacy of their baptism by giving the authoritative individual who performed the rite, whether Kayfa, Apollos or Paul. This also explains why Paul is emphatic and counts the individual who performed the baptism as nothing when compared to the *faith of the individual* who submitted humbly in trust be-

---

800. 1 Cor 15:29.

801. An example, the *Stromta* of Valentinus (185 CE), as quoted by Clement of Alexandria; see also Iraneus.

802. 1 Cor 1:21–23.

fore God, making one's trusting plea for forgiveness and acceptance without claim of merit, status, heredity or ritual works. Paul eliminates any claim to status in baptism, whether it is from Kayfa or the infiltrators: "Is Christ divided?"[803]

As such, the *pneumatikoi* have made the claim that only they can baptize legitimately. The esoteric rites of their baptism provide immediate salvation, confirmed by the *charismata* of *glossolalia*, the sign of achieved divinity and presence in the third heaven (i.e., they have already achieved "blessedness"). It is uncertain if there was any use of water, but since these were Jewish males it is likely a ritual sprinkling, dipping or washing. Water was thought to absorb evil in the ancient world.[804] According to later gnostic practices, simple words were used with water and oil. Indeed, baptism for the dead (or by the "dead to the world," by the *pneumatikoi*) was a common practice employed by gnostics, confirmed in later literature as part of the trajectory of that began as wisdom-salvation associated with the *logia* of Jesus. Baptism on behalf of the dead was recorded in the second-century *Pistis Sophia* (291–292), and was performed by the Marcionites (ca. 150 CE).[805] A gnostic leader or designee performed baptism for the dead individual, including answering for the corpse. This means that in Corinth, the *pneumatikoi* claimed that any other baptism was invalid. Their efficacious baptism brought he unification of opposites.[806]

---

803. 1 Cor 1:13.

804. Busse, *Jesus Resurrected*, 34–41; Van der Toorn et al., *Dictionary of Demons and Deities*, 236: "They held power during dangerous situations and times: Chiefly at night, during sleep, during a wind storm or an eclipse, or heat of mid-day, and especially in child birth." These were poor peasants whose worlds were inundated with other worldly forces out of their control. Multigenerational families huddled in small rooms with a central small courtyard, cooking with a simple stone oven, living subsistence existence. In Galilee they were totally reliance on local resources, primarily bread, olives and fish diet, where the whims of evil forces haunting Galilee could quickly force them into starvation. Dwellings made them susceptible to illness and diseases, as they were made of rough basalt stones, filled with mud and pebbles, covered with twig and mud roofs. Every day was a struggle for existence. That Beelzebul haunted the waters is confirmed by Hull: "Beelzebul has a demonic child who haunts the Red Sea (*T. Sol.* 5.11) and has been trapped there against his will (*T. Sol.* 25.7)." See Hull, *Hellenistic Magic*, 104. That Jesus is accused of being possessed by Beelzebul and is able to control the fish for the benefit of subsistence fishermen (to deceive them according to his enemies) presents an interesting correlation between possession of the waters of Galilee, under the control of Jesus (and thus Beelzebul), and the Red Sea, by Beelzebul's son. Jesus' enemies must have understood this connection. Also see Bar-Ilan, *Exorcism by Rabbis*: "Some springs have a complete family of spirits living in each; it is understood that hot springs, as in Tiberias (Galilee), are heated by spirits (acting on the basis of the commands of King Solomon). It can be generalized that there is hardly a source of water in the land of Israel without a spirit (one or more)." Bar-Ilan cites as additional support the *Pesachim* 112 p. 1, two baraitot: "The Rabbis learned: One should not drink water from rivers or lakes at night. And if he drinks, he risks his life because of the hazard. What hazard? The hazard of demons." Also cited by Bar-Ilan, "Haunted Springs," 153–70.

805. The gnostic Christian movement founded in Rome by Marcion, a rich tradesman turned theologian, who amended the gospels and letters of Paul so as to provide a gnostic bias. Marcion was excommunicated in 144 CE by the bishop of Rome.

806. See above, and Sayings 84, 114; Saying 51 records the radical eschatological perspective of reconciliation: "His disciples said to him, 'When will the rest for the dead take place, and when will the new world come?' He said to them, 'What you are looking forward to has come, but you don't know it.'"

The Enemies of Paul: Demons, Satan, Betrayers, and Apostles

In sum, since the practice of baptism for the dead continued for generations, primarily in gnostic writings, and Paul intentionally uses "they" to describe those who participate in or perform the rite, it seems abundantly clear that the opponents did practice baptism for either (1) literally the dead because they claimed the power to transform the deceased from death to life, or (2) baptized only their converts as the only legitimate authority to do so since they were "dead" to the world. Consequently, Paul does not reject the practice because it was not a practice of his adherents.

The Perilous Risks Faced by Paul and the Shame of His Enemies

Paul's next comments are difficult to translate from the Koine Greek, and are coherently challenging in the context of his previous statements. Many translations do not adequately consider the context of the immediate preceding section, which documents the intense conflict between Paul and the infiltrators over the nature of death and resurrection ("blessedness"). As a result, the correct translation of Paul's next comments *must be based on Paul's eschatology*, which is the context for his criticism and rejection of baptism for or by the dead.

Paul, speaking to his adherents, has just critiqued and rejected the infiltrators' baptism on behalf of, for, or as the only legitimate *apostoloi*, the dead of the world.[807] He then follows with several provocative statements: "As for us, why do we endanger ourselves every hour?" Paul continues, "I face death every day," or "I die every day!" He makes the claim that he can boast in "Christ Jesus our Lord" about "them" (the adherents or the opponents?) and that he "fought with beasts in Ephesus."[808] Knowing that Paul is, as always, intentional in his choice of words, how do these statements relate to the context of his critique of the opponents' form of baptism?

We begin with a well-established translation of Paul's letter and then turn to the Greek text. The Revised Standard Version reads as follows:

> Why am I in peril every hour? I protest brethren by my pride in you, which I have in Jesus Christ our Lord, I die every day! What do I gain if, humanly speaking, I fought with the beasts at Ephesus? If the dead are not raised, "*Let us eat and drink for tomorrow we die.*" Do not be deceived, "Bad company ruins good morals."[809]

It is obvious that the RSV translation results in a rather awkward convoluted string of thoughts, particularly given the preceding context of Paul's critique of the infiltrators'

---

807. Or, as we have seen, the "dead to the world," i.e., the enlightened gnostic opponents, being baptized for the converts to bring them to blessedness, or life.

808. Paul was writing from Ephesus, but there is no evidence that the literally fought in the theatre of Ephesus or anywhere else in Ephesus with beasts, i.e., as in a gladiatorial contest, nor metaphorically with "beasts," other than the single riot over the falling trade in statuettes of Artemis, the local deity, led by one Demetrius the silversmith (interestingly, another craftsman like Paul), Acts 19:33.

809. 1 Cor 15:30–32.

The Enemies of Paul in Corinth

baptism. Frankly, they are quite puzzling. But, this is the point—this translation falls short of connecting Paul's comments with his risk mitigations against the infiltrators' claims. Certainly, Paul's statement must somehow relate to the threat they represent as "kings." What can the risk context tell us?

First, Paul sternly warns the *pneumatikoi* about their impending peril, indeed, the doom they face. Theirs is deadly rebellion against God. Paul *quotes one of the most well known indictments in all of Jewish Law and the Prophets*, namely Isa 22:13: "Let us eat and drink for tomorrow we die." As Paul has detailed, the *pneumatikoi* eat (i.e., the careless ingestion of demonic foods), drink (i.e., drunkenness), and even go further—they encourage illicit and illegal sexual activity (i.e., incest, consorting with prostitutes, and all means of sexual and social behavior that violates Jewish and Roman law). Certainly, as Hebrews and pure Israelites, they know of Isaiah's dire warning, as it went unheeded and led to the utter destruction of Israel. God's judgment was devastating. Paul employs this divine warning because it echoes the very eschatological situation and context in which the enemies reside. God's impending intervention in the *parousia* and the "destruction all dominion, power and authority" of all enemies is their fate. Like the Israelites who ignored the divine warning thinking they had *sophia* and *gnosis* and lived arrogantly, so too, the *pneumatikoi* face the most dire of consequences. They rebel against God and fail to recognize the impending judgment. What is clear is that Paul's quotation is intended to punctuate his dire warning.

Second, and then mysteriously, Paul quotes from a comedy by Menander,[810] indeed a play about a prostitute named Thais, citing the central theme of the now lost work:[811] "Bad associations corrupt good ethics," the only time in the New Testament the word *ethe*, or "ethics," is used. Of course, at first this seems quite odd. Why would Paul cite the pivotal line from an ancient Greek comic playwright in the context of his eschatological threat and warning, placing it beside the revered prophet Isaiah? There can only be one explanation; namely, that Paul is again warning the *pneumatikoi*, but this time sarcastically by drawing from pagan wisdom found in a comic play. It is the prostitute Thais that makes Paul's point. Thais warns of dire consequences for arrogant behavior. *Ironically, the "wisdom" of Thais the prostitute is greater than that of the pneumatikoi!* Paul's sarcasm is clear; he ridicules them. When this letter was read aloud audible laughter must have resulted. So, Paul not only condemns but ridicules the *pneumatikoi*.

What can Paul mean when he says that he "dies every day"? The traditional translation fails to take into account the very perilous risk imbedded in Paul's eschatological confrontation with the infiltrators. Indeed, the Greek translation can as easily be rendered as follows: "Daily I die as a result of your boasting [arrogance], which I have [the right to boast], in Christ Jesus." Paul's point here is about *agape*,

---

810. 342–291 BCE, a Greek playwright, the quotation is from *Thais*, 218.

811. We have only fragments, but it is mentioned elsewhere and other works by later playwrights may have expanded Menander's play.

that is, his personal, daily agony over their arrogance and their failure to embrace the salvific *euangelion*. Their rejection places both Paul and the *pneumatikoi* equally in danger of the impending eschatological crisis. If the *parousia* were to occur that day, Paul too might perish for his failure to turn them to the *euangelion*. When he stands before the Lord Jesus Christ, he must account for them as opponents and enemies of his *ecclesia*, "the seal of his apostleship" that failed.[812] If his *ecclesia* fails, he fails and faces the judgment. Consequently, the *pneumatikoi* by their rejection of the *euangelion* leave both he and they in terrible peril.

Paul's last reference is about his fighting the "beasts" in Ephesus: "If according to man I fought with the beasts in Ephesus, what does it profit me?" Other translations also render the statement: "If humanly speaking I fought with the beast of Ephesus, what good does it do?" Most exegetes understand this statement as figurative, as Conzelmann believes that as a Roman citizen,[813] Paul could not have been condemned to the beasts, unless his citizenship had been stripped. But Paul was not a Roman citizen as noted, and this passage is further confirmation that citizenship was later fabrication of the early church.[814] Paul could have faced imprisonment and like later Christians been condemned to such contests with gladiators—not uncommon for criminals. Indeed, there is strong archeological evidence of gladiatorial contests in Ephesus. Several tombs and inscriptions associated with gladiators have been identified, including some that show the more popular were held as heroes.

Organized gladiatorial contests were first brought to Ephesus in 69 CE by Lucillus, the commander of the Roman garrison in Ephesus (long after Paul's time there). But gladiatorial competition, perhaps even seasonal contests that preceded those organized by Lucillus, were in fact commonplace in the larger cities. Ephesus certainly would have been one of these. The city was the preeminent Asian seaport with as many as two hundred thousand residents at its height. It was honored as the "first city" of Asia, and received special imperial favor from Antony and Cleopatra, and even later after their defeat by Augustus Caesar at Actium. Augustus approved construction of the most prized temple of the imperial cult, the Temple of Dea Roma and Divus Julius, which honored the god Roma and Augustus' adoptive father, Julius Caesar. This temple likely stood in the center of the state agora in the upper administrative section of the city.[815] Consequently, the population, honors given to the city, and the immense size of the theatre and its stadium would certainly provide opportunity for seasonal or special contests during Paul's lifetime that are now lost.

812. 1 Cor 9:2.
813. See Conzelmann, introduction to *1 Corinthians*, 277n130.
814. *1 Corinthians*, 277; of course by tradition Paul was condemned to death under Nero (Eusebius, *Chronicles*), and was beheaded, a death reserved for citizens (*Duodecim Tabulae*), on or near the Ostian road just outside of Rome—Roman citizens could not be crucified or condemned to beasts. For a list of scholars and the rationale that speaks against Paul's citizenship, see Roetzel, *Paul*, 19–22.
815. Which I would identify at the centre of the State Agora, not at the traditional site located on tourists maps.

Gladiatorial battles with wild animals also find supporting archaeological evidence. Skeletal wounds found on remains attributed to gladiators indicate death by animal attack.[816] They cannot be attributed to battle or to the Charon. The Charon dispatched wounded gladiators. Dressed as the gatekeeper to Hades, he determined if the gladiator was dead using a hot poker. If not mortally wounded, the Charon struck the gladiator on the side of the head with a pointed mallet. This left a square hole in the skull just before the ear that is easily discernible, not gashes from claws or teeth. The theatre of Ephesus had iron rails that would contain gladiatorial combat with animals. If not at the theatre, they could have also been held at the stadium, which held up to twenty-five thousand spectators.

Since the archaeological evidence is indisputable, one of the "main" attractions in Ephesus' gladiatorial events would have been a battle with a "beast," i.e., a lion or bear. This makes Paul's reference to fighting the wild beasts not just intriguing or metaphorical, but evidentiary and possible in Ephesus. In fact, the pseudepigraphical 2 Timothy records Paul as saying that he escaped the "mouth of the lion,"[817] which would suggest a tradition of Paul's former encounter in an arena. But notably, Paul's list of sufferings in 2 Corinthians 10 *does not mention any such event*. Consequently, Paul, who is in Ephesus at the time he composes 1 Corinthians, may have been employing a popular saying widely known from Ephesus to describe a deadly encounter, not recounting a literal fight in the arena.

If Paul meant this figuratively, we must grapple with how this statement advanced his eschatological argument that the end was yet to come and the last enemy to conquer would be death. Could this be a straightforward admission that his struggle with enemies (i.e., "beasts) in Ephesus would be pointless if there is no resurrection to come? In this case, this interpretation is logical and contextually coherent. The first difficulty would be explaining how the opponents would know that he had experienced significant risk and stress in Ephesus, which is presumed by his comment. One possible answer is that the Chloe's people brought back word of Paul's struggles and, perhaps, the fierce opposition from the Jewish community or the local trade guild(s), such as that led by Demetrius the silversmith reported in Acts.[818] While there are no Artemis silver shrines in existence today (almost all ancient silver has been melted down, other than coins), there are inscriptions in Ephesus that describe the donation or gift of shrines and idols, certainly some of which were silver. Even more, archaeological evidence is plentiful that small statuettes of Artemis, Aphrodite, Meter and Hekate were produced in mass, and this evidence includes the discovery of a sculptured hand holding a small

---

816. The wounds fit the teeth marks from either a lion or bear.

817. 2 Tim 4:7.

818. It is interesting that Alexander the coppersmith, a Jew, tried to defend Paul before the crowd, as obviously he would not have been producing such statuettes, but more importantly, he was a tradesman and a Jew. This lends support to the structure of Paul's missionary strategy, that is, to approach those of the synagogue and those in trade guilds who were related to his, or were Jews.

statuette of Artemis in Ephesus.[819] Coins of Ephesus also show figures holding similar statuettes. The Temple of Artemis drew cult followers and those who wished to honor the goddess from all over the Roman world. This indicates a thriving trade for the local artisans or guilds. If Paul's activity reduced production, retribution was inevitable. Consequently, the impact on the local trade, sale and dedication of statuettes of the goddesses Artemis[820] would need to have been noticeable, so as to raise serious risk to Paul. Paul provides no indication that he had been quite so successful, such as noted in Acts, and so this explanation is speculative.

What is evident is that if this were simply a popular saying, Paul's citation would be the third he uses in confronting the opponents, all of which would be known to them—Isaiah, Meander, and then a famous aphorism relating to Ephesus, i.e., the "fighting the beasts of Ephesus," the greatest of heroic struggles. In this case, Paul would be ridiculing the opponents' claim to being "rich" and "kings," a social status equivalent to that given "heroes," some of who were considered divine. Paul is saying that if he were a hero, like those that defeated the beasts of Ephesus, the greatest achievement of popular and heroic culture of his day, it would mean nothing in the context of the eschatological crisis.

Paul ends with a detrimental assessment of their wisdom-*gnosis* and the perilous standing with God: "Awake! to being right with God and do not sin [thumb your nose at him]; those [to whom I speak] have no *gnosis* of God—to your shame I speak."[821] Here Paul uses gnostic terminology, and clearly the language of the opponents. *Eknepsiate*, from the verb *nephein*, is translated by many commentators, "Awake," but it is more appropriately translated as "become sober," that is, as a command, "be sober!" The contrast between sobriety and intoxication are *gnostic* terms, particularly in later gnostic literature, and so, may have had a place in the language of Paul's opponents.[822] Here, use of the word "sober" meant to achieve an awakening through *gnosis* gleaned from a collection of *logia*, which provided wisdom and insight into one's true state, i.e., already divine and saved. One was no longer "intoxicated," i.e., deceived by the world, but was free and "sober." Paul use of the word could have a dual meaning, i.e., *Eknepsiate* could also be used in an *eschatological sense*, that is, to become sober to the eschatological crisis faced and the end times approaching as opposed to being unprepared and "drunk."[823] This demand for eschatological sobriety is found in the

---

819. I must mention too that these statuettes where purchased by local residents for placement in home sanctuaries, and were purchased by tourists who came to Ephesus to honor Artemis.

820. She dominated the city of Ephesus over all male gods.

821. 1 Cor 15:34.

822. See *Odes of Solomon*, 11.6–8, as a good example; there are countless examples.

823. See 1 Tim 3:2 as an example; 1 Thess 5:8, is set in the eschatological context of the last days: "But since we belong to the day, let us be sober, putting on faith and love as a breastplate, and the hope of salvation as a helmet."

literary tradition associated with Kayfa, particularly in the pseudepigraphical first letter ascribed to him.[824]

His last statement, directed at the opponents, presents a dire warning: "I say this to your shame." Paul employed this same word, *entropen*, "shame," earlier in the letter and in an eschatological context.[825] There, Paul condemns the opponents for failing to correctly judge even internal disputes, an egregious failure of "gnosis" since they were to be "judges of the world" at the *parousia*. They are pitiless, going to public court to settle petty issues, failing to recognize their blessed role in the last days and God's *agape* as the new and divine criteria for all judgment and *gnosis*. To be "shamed" then is to say they are in a hopeless state that they must recognize, accept and repent, for they stand in opposition to God. Thus, Paul ends this appeal by "shaming" the opponents. With his point made, Paul then turns to another condescending and arrogant question posed by the opponents to the adherents, and also, the most intriguing to generations of adherents—the nature of the resurrected body.

The Nature of the Resurrected Body

Paul introduces the question: "But someone asks, 'How are the dead raised? With what kind of body do they come?'" These are clearly questions posed by the *pneumatikoi* who, as noted, reject as absurd and unnecessary bodily resurrection. This is evidenced by Paul's response: "You foolish one!" Paul has *never* addressed the adherents as "foolish" (i.e., *aphron*). More, he employs a play on words; *a* = "without," and *phren* = "understanding," or "foolish," clearly a reference to the opponents. Paul is not simply calling them "fools," he is accusing them again of being "without understanding" about the *eschatos*, meaning they are in perilous danger.

Paul then provides various examples of physical transformation from death to life that are observable, all of which provide irrefutable proof that resurrection and transformation are the ultimate miracles in God's good and creative design. He begins with the simplest analogy, the seed: "What you sow does not come to life unless it dies."[826] Paul states what is an observable fact to both the adherents and opponents. How can the opponents be so ignorant as to not to notice what happens when a seed is buried and "dies," but is then transformed into a new "body," becoming more glorious and full than its last form? Paul provides a more specific examples, but first clarifies that what is sown at death is not the final body. Just as the seed that dies, one's true and full being is only realized following the death of the body and resurrection to full and new life given solely the miracle of God.

Again using observable events, Paul cites "bare grain" perhaps of "wheat" or "some other kind . . . God gives to it a body as he wished and to each of the seeds

---

824. See 1 Pet 4:1–7.
825. 1 Cor 6:5.
826. 1 Cor 15:36.

their own body." Paul's analogy is witnessed and commonplace, but still is a miracle. This same analogy is found in the Talmudic literature, where Rabbi Meier also uses the transformation of a seed as evidence for the physical resurrection of the body—a miracle: "If a kernel of wheat is buried naked and will sprout forth in many robes, how much more so the righteous."[827] This type of analogy of seed to plant and transformation would also explain Paul's use of Jesus of Nazareth's resurrection as the "first fruits," that is the first transformation to the substance of new resurrected body, particularly that of the seed.

Paul's analogy of the seed may reflect a saying in the collection of *logia* employed by the *pneumatikoi*, a saying that is found in *Thomas*, Saying 9. Here the seed that is spread out in the ground is scattered. Most of it is killed or choked off, and only the seed that falls to the *good ground* "bears fruit." The rendering of this saying in the context in Thomas focuses on revelation, i.e., that the hearer is awakened that they are receiving the divine *logos* and are among those of the "good ground." This awakening brings immediate transformation, "bearing fruit of *gnosis*," reuniting them with their divine self and with the divine. The form of the saying is virtually the same as that found in Matt 13:1–23, but Matthew provides a very detailed and different explanation. Here, Jesus is the teacher of divine wisdom. In Matthew's version, one must understand the distribution of the "word," or *logos*, i.e., the spreading of the *euangelion* of salvation that he brings as God's Christ and the enemies that it will face before the *eschatos*. As such, Matthew casts the *mashal* as a wisdom teaching, namely, the recognition of how Satan attacks and destroys the *euangelion*, and even the children of God that may have received it but by deceit and corruption have abandoned it. Indeed, it is the "evil one" that can snatch the *logos*, whether by persecution or enticement and entanglement in sin and rebellion against God. Thus, in Matthew the *logos* is the salvific *euangelion* of Jesus Christ, the crucified one who is raised and is to come again—a very Pauline Jesus. It is clear that this is the way Paul understood this *mashal* and why he may be referencing it here as a mitigation against its use by the infiltrators. The seed is the perfect example of God's miracle in Jesus Christ, as well as the resurrection, not the salvific hidden *sophia* of *gnosis* contained in *logia*.

To Paul, the new *soma* is a "spiritual body," but it has a unique substance and form. It has physical characteristics, which for Paul was first observed in his encounter with the resurrected Jesus witnessed with his eyes. Even more, the fact that those who have "fallen asleep" have yet to have made the transformation, evidenced in the eschatological order of Paul's apocalypse in 1 Thessalonians and 1 Corinthians, presses his point: Only at the returned presence of the Lord does the resurrection occur and *only then* will both those who have not fallen asleep and those who are still alive will also be transformed:

---

827. See, *b. Sanhedrin* 90b.

> We shall not all fall asleep, all we shall be changed, in a moment, in a glance of an eye at the last trumpet [*salpiggi*]; for a trumpet will sound and the dead will be raised incorruptible, and we shall be changed.[828]

The miracle of the resurrection is not given solely to the dead, but to all of the *tekna tou Theou* at the *parousia*, an event Paul expects to see in his lifetime.

As such, Paul provides a new and radical eschatological expansion of the nature of death for the adherent who is "in Christ," which redefines the intermittent state of death as a part of the unfolding of God's plan and transformative care for the adherent of the *euangelion* and *agape* prior to the *parousia*. For Paul, the *euangelion* of Jesus Christ is so efficacious and salvific that those adherents who die now "sleep" safely, whether "in the spirit or body, I do not know, only God knows."[829] Thus, during the interim between bodily death and the *parousia*, the adherent is immediately taken to the "third heaven" to be with the risen Christ, remaining with him until the *general resurrection*, where all adherents will rise with a new, eternal *soma*:

> Therefore, being always of good courage, and knowing that while we are at home in the body we are absent from the Lord—for we walk by *pistis*, not by sight—we are of good courage, I say, and prefer rather to be absent from the body and to be at home with the Lord.[830]

In another undisputed letter, Paul writes to the Philippians:

> For to me, to live is Christ and to die is gain. But if I am to live on in the flesh, this will mean fruitful labor for me; and I do not know which to choose. But I am hard-pressed from both directions, having the desire to depart and be with Christ, for that is very much better; yet to remain on in the flesh is more necessary for your sake.[831]

This statement characterizes Paul's eschatology. Death, or "Sleep" for the adherent, means the opportunity to be with Christ *until the general resurrection* and the delivery of the kingdom to God, something that cannot be obtained by the Solitary One through *gnosis*. Paul's risk response to the infiltrators' question is unequivocal: Only upon the arrival of the Lord Jesus Christ does God gives his *tekna tou Theou* a spiritual *soma*, one that has glorious substance. Until that day, *pistis* in the *euangelion* and *agape* provide protection and afford the adherent who dies a place with the risen Lord. Paul's carefully constructed examples are intended to unquestionably demonstrate that resurrection is already present in the observable world, but the *pneumatikoi* are blinded as *apistoi*. They remain in *agnosis*, failing understand that resurrection into a new *soma* is not only possible but is God's design. The implication of not accepting this evidence is Paul's perilous

---

828. 1 Cor 15:51–52.
829. 2 Cor 12:2.
830. 2 Cor 5:6–8.
831. Phil 1:21–24.

warning, i.e., that they will not participate in the glory of the resurrection unless they turn and accept *agape*, the "more excellent Way." Like the miracle of the seed, so will be the miracle of the resurrected body for Paul's adherents, both of must be transformed by the power of God into a new form and substance.

It is when "this corruptible must put on incorruption, and this mortal shall have put on immortality" that the prophet's saying would be fulfilled: "Death is swallowed up in victory. Oh death, where is your victory? Oh death, where is your sting?"[832] This appears to be a unique conflation of two prophetic sayings found in Isaiah[833] and Hosea.[834] This quotation of Hosea comes from the Septuagint, the Koine Greek translation of the torah.[835] The translation reads as follows: "Where is thy victory [literally, victory such as in a lawsuit], O death? Where is thy sting, O Hades?" So, Paul's freely renders from the Septuagint. The saying from Isaiah reads: "He swallowed up death forever." Paul is familiar with the saying due to its clear association with the power of God over death. He links the two using the word "victory," *nikos*. Paul's use of these sayings and final victory prophetically confirms a future general resurrection at the *parousia*, and only after the kingdom is delivered to God and death has been abolished (the "last enemy" to be destroyed). Paul employs prophetic Scripture because his enemies are Jews who have been trained in the Law and Prophets. It is on the basis of the coming resurrection for those of his *euangelion* that Paul makes the emotional and joyous outcry: "But thanks be to God, who gives us the victory through our Lord Jesus Christ!"[836]

Paul's citation of Scripture linking death and the law is important. Paul defines the "sting" (*kentron*) as the deadly curse brought about by "sin" contained in and revealed by the law.[837] This is an interesting and important reference to the law as the "power of sin," meaning it cannot reverse or cure the curse of death, but instead confirms its infection. Further transgression must stop until redemption comes. Why would Paul bring up this topic with the infiltrators?

As noted, the infiltrators claimed to have achieved an immediate state of blessedness solely by *gnosis* and *sophia* gained via the *logia* of the Living One. Their libertine demonstration of authority over all forbidden actions, i.e., that their "higher" new wisdom-torah had not only freed them, but also demanded that they publicly demonstrate superiority over the corrupted world. Their practices of intentionally breaching the law to show its impotence confirmed that the law was empty of power.

---

832. 1 Cor 15:55–56.

833. Isa 25:8.

834. Hos 13:14.

835. This translation was completed by tradition in Egypt by seventy Jewish scholars (thus the Greek word use, Septuagint or "seventy"), between the 250 BCE to about 100 CE, and became the fundamental translation that would have been known to Paul and his contemporaries.

836. 1 Cor 15:57.

837. 1 Cor 15:56.

Paul challenges this view by employing his own interpretation of the function of the law. The law is both powerful and deadly, and to further violate it is to become mired in its curse in *agnosis*. For Paul, the law confirms transgressions and rebellion, all related to the inherited death brought into the world by one man, Adam. Paul's view of the entry of death into history is based on the torah's record of the entry of sin into the world through the act of Adam, a man.[838] *Like an infection or plague*, death became dominant and inherent in humankind through one man, and humankind is left without hope other than the promise of God to act on their behalf in the last days and with the promise of a resurrection of the righteous:[839] "And so it is written: The first man Adam was made a living soul;[840] the last Adam a life giving spirit."[841] Paul's assessment of Adam is virtually the same as Ezra in the apocrypha: "Oh Adam, what have you done, for though it was you who sinned, the fall was not yours alone, but is ours also who are your descendants."[842] Ezra says: "[Adam] transgressed and was overcome, burdened with an evil heart, as are all who descended from him."[843] The law's function is to teach, to instruct and prevent further descent into the control of Satan and death. For Paul, only the new man, Jesus Christ, has brought the *elpis* of life for those of *pistis* in the *euangelion*, and who immerse themselves in protective *agape*, thereby fulfilling law until the *parousia* and their adoption into the *basileia tou Theou*.[844] And herein lies the difference between Adam and Jesus Christ for Paul. The death brought by Adam was universal, but the Way to life is only available to the new children of God: "And the free gift is not like the effect of that one man's sin." Grace, mercy, the "free gift" are given to all those *who respond in pistis and practice agape*, there is no *gnosis* aside from that contained in the *euangelion* that can displace the curse of death, and so end the power of the law.

The reference to Adam raises the possibility that the infiltrators had access to *logia* of Jesus that spoke of Adam and sin, and Paul is critiquing their interpretation. There are three sayings in Thomas that reference Adam, which may reflect an earlier tradition. The first is Saying 46:

> Jesus said, "From Adam to John the Baptist, among those born of women, no one is so much greater than John the Baptist that his eyes should not be averted. But I have said that whoever among you becomes a child will recognize the [Father's] kingdom and will become greater than John."

---

838. See Rom 5:12–21.
839. Ezek 37:1–28.
840. Gen 2:7.
841. 1 Cor 15:45.
842. 4 Ezra 7:118.
843. 4 Ezra 3.1.
844. Rom 5:12–14.

The Enemies of Paul: Demons, Satan, Betrayers, and Apostles

This saying has parallels with the synoptic tradition in the materials ascribed to Q: "I tell you, among those born of women none is greater than John; yet he who is least in the kingdom of God is greater than he."[845] The difference between the two traditions is striking. Both relate to John and his prophetic work and imply his role as a precursor. In the gnostic saying, Jesus claims that no person that has been born is greater than John the Baptist *unless* that person becomes a child, which in this case means "the Solitary One," one who unifies the "inside with the outside" through *gnosis*. In the moment of awakening, recognition as to one's divine status is achieved, and this *gnosis* leads to *sophia* and salvation, i.e., the reunification of the self with the divine becoming the Solitary One. The image of the child symbolizes this reunification. Alternatively, the Q version contextualizes John as great, but that the least in the kingdom of God is greater than he. Some scholars see this Q saying as a diminishing of John, that is, an attempt to reduce the standing of John among the adherents, as there continued to be followers of John who were not familiar with Jesus in Ephesus when Paul arrived some twenty-five years after John's death,[846] and later, followers that rejected Jesus as Messiah.[847] However, this saying places John above Adam and all of his descendants. Adam then is seen as inferior and marginalized. In both cases, the child and the adherent are greater than John.

The second is Saying 85: "Jesus said, 'Adam came from great power and great wealth, but he was not worthy of you. For had he been worthy, [he would] not [have tasted] death.'" In this saying, Adam obviously became detached from his origin, which was divine, as he lost his "power" and "wealth," meaning his forgot his place of origin and become corrupted, or sinful. Consequently, this saying is a wisdom saying. According to Jesus, the hearer must recognize that humankind since Adam has become lost and worthy of death like Adam, and knowledge ("wealth and power") has been displaced by ignorance (i.e., "poverty"). Thus, understanding of one's true nature is to return to richness and power, thereby reuniting with one's divine origin. This "awakening" makes one greater than Adam. Adam then is *the prototype of the ignorant man* who came from the divine but turned away and become lost in the world of material deception—he was deserving of death. As one comes to recognize Adam's failure, *gnosis* is obtained and *sophia* is revealed.

What Saying 85 tells us about Adam in the early collection of gnostic-wisdom *logia* is that Adam was the progenitor of all humans who have become lost, and, as a result, have died based on unworthy and deadly behavior in the corrupted world. And in so doing, Adam became ignorant giving up the great power and wealth he

---

845. Namely, Matt 11:11 and Luke 7:28.

846. Acts 18:24–46.

847. Many scholars hold that the synoptic tradition's rendering of John, particularly his statement that he is unworthy to "untie the thongs of his sandals" (Luke 3:15–18), is designed to subjugate John to Jesus, and establish him as the precursor, but that John's prophetic role was never tied to Jesus, other than the indisputable historical fact that John did baptize Jesus.

once "owned," i.e., life. For Paul, Adam's failure was his disobedience to God and thus his affront, which infected the world with death, entering the heart of every human descended from Adam. The similarity between Paul's portrayal of Adam and that of the Thomas collection is surprising. In both, Adam is representative of the failure of all humans except the enlightened ones (the Solitary Ones) or in Paul's case, those of *pistis* in the *euangelion*, i.e., the humbled adherent that envelope themselves in *agape*. The difference between the two, however, is unmistakable. The Thomas saying presupposes that this elitist knowledge brings wisdom-salvation instantly in that one is no longer like Adam who died in ignorance—one is instantly free of death, i.e., at physical death there is no need for future resurrection, as the spirit is already united through wisdom-gnosis with the divine, its place of origin, so radical eschatology is evidenced. This leads to either an aesthetic/monastic life to avoid entrapment in the material world, or like the infiltrators in Corinth, libertine behavior and public demonstration of the power since the world and entrapments no longer have any hold on them.[848] We have already identified Paul's assertion that sin has been overcome by the inauguration of the "last days" or *eschatos* through the historical resurrection of one man, Jesus of Nazareth, the new Adam. It is only *pistis* that brings the hope of salvation at the final judgment and life with God the arrival of the kingdom. Thus, Paul could be responding to the opponents' use of a saying like Saying 85. Paul recontextualizes their saying, rendering the sin of Adam as responsible for the death of all humankind, thereby emphasizing the resurrection of Jesus as the beginning of a new salvific era for those in *pistis* and practicing *agape* at the *parousia*.

Lastly, there is a corollary reference to Adam in Thomas that may shed additional light on Paul's reference. Saying 106 is as follows: Jesus said, "When you make the two into one, you will become children of Adam, and when you say, 'Mountain, move from here!' it will move." As noted earlier, a portion of this saying, i.e., about faith and moving mountains, was critiqued by Paul.[849] Paul is not criticizing the saying, but how the opponents used it to advance their gnosis-salvation claims. For Paul, *logia* of the Lord must advance the activity of the expansion of the *ecclesia* and *agape* by *pistis* in the event of the cross. In Saying 106, there is a conflation of the three topics; the saying about faith to move mountains, a call to return and become a "child of Adam" and the requirement to unite the outside and inside, or become a Solitary One. What then does this saying mean to the gnostic, and also perhaps to the opponents in Corinth?

Adam at one time had "power and wealth," but lost his way, and became either deceived or distracted by this world, and forgot (or became ignorant of) his divine

---

848. Saying 110 also captures the interpretation that can lead to either type of interaction with the world: Jesus said, "Let one who has found the world, and has become wealthy, renounce the world," and similarly with Saying 112, Jesus said, "Damn the flesh that depends on the soul. Damn the soul that depends on the flesh."

849 See 1 Cor 13:2.

origin. Only *gnosis* and the *sophia* gained from understanding one's true nature and origin can reunite one with the divine source, i.e., and so become a "king!" that is, regain immediately one's "power" and "wealth." To "return" to Adam and become a child of Adam is to return to the primal state of power and wealth, that is, become the Solitary One uniting the self with its divine origin ("making the two one"). This "power" allows the gnostic complete freedom from humankind (again, see sayings 110 and 112) and all of the entrapments created. Faith to move mountains is *not intended* as the ability to literally move a mountain, but for the infiltrators, the regained power and authority to be united with the divine source. Their return to Adam pre-rebellion, the divine state, is their goal, not future resurrection, and certainly not *agape*. But for Paul, a return to Adam is a return to the curse of death. Consequently, Paul is warning the opponents that whether their goal is to embrace Adam or any figure other than Jesus and the coming *parousia* is to embrace death.

Paul's Plea to His Adherents

Paul ends this section with a plea to his adherents. Paul says, "Therefore my *agapetoi* [beloved] *adelphoi* [brothers], be firm, unmovable, abounding in the work of the Lord always, knowing that your labor in not in vain."[850] This term of endearment, *agapetioi*, is Paul's direct expression of unmovable, deep and personal love for those he has brought to the *euangelion*. He appeals to them to stand fast in their *pistis*, "knowing," or better, "being fully aware [*endontes*]," that it is secure. Paul's use of *endontes* is intentional, acting as a countermeasure to the intruders' claim to special *gnosis*, but more, reminding those of *pistis* that they now have been made aware that it is errant deception and deadly.

The "Collection" for the *Agioi* in Jerusalem

Paul begins this section by answering the last question sent by Chloe's people: "Now concerning [*peri de*] the collection for the saints [*agious*]." This is the same formulaic structure he has used throughout his letter when answering the questions sent to him.[851] Paul has chosen to answer this question last. The previous questions dealt with serious matters related to the infiltration of the *pneumatikoi* (plus the corollary questions that arise from the formal questions), including: sexual relations in the last days;[852] divorce;[853] circumcision;[854] virginity and marriage;[855] purity restrictions

---

850. 1 Cor 15:58.
851. See 1 Cor 12:1.
852. 1 Cor 7:1–2.
853. 1 Cor 7:12.
854. 1 Cor 7:18.
855. 1 Cor 7:25.

The Enemies of Paul in Corinth

including consuming meat offered to demons and attending demonic festivals;[856] the legitimacy of Paul's apostleship (freely adapting the *logia* of Jesus);[857] the proper behavior of men toward women;[858] risks of ingesting the sacraments of the Lord's Supper; use of the *logia* of the Lord (given directly to Paul);[859] the nature and order of *charismata* of the Spirit and their purpose for edification of *agape* and the body (the *ecclesiae*) of Christ;[860] the order of divine appointments in the *ecclesia*, diminishing the role of *glossolalia*;[861] rejecting *gnosis* for the "excellent Way" of *agape*;[862] the proper order practices at the full assembly of the *ecclesiae*;[863] the validity of the resurrection of the dead;[864] the general resurrection and parousia;[865] how the dead are raised and the nature of the resurrected body;[866] and the *euangelion* and the end of death.[867] The question is: Why did Paul place the question of collection of monies for the Jerusalem *ecclesia* and the means by which it should be gathered last?

The collection for the Jerusalem *ecclesia* continued to be an issue in Corinth for some time, as one of Paul's later letters (now represented in 2 Corinthians chs. 8 and 9), provides extraordinary detail, not as at to the process of collection, but about recognizing the need to give "out of abundance" because of *agape*. Paul agreed to a collection with the pillars, James, Kayfa and John. Economic distress in Jerusalem led Paul (then Saul) and Barnabas to collect support for the Jerusalem *ecclesia* well before this agreement was made. At their later council,[868] Paul committed to certain conditions to gain support for his *euangelion* and his itinerant, and limited, mission to the Gentiles. But the nature of his commitment, as noted, differs significantly between his own account in Galatians and the report provided almost generation later in Acts.

Just as Jesus and his exorcist shared a common purse, his exorcists continued this practice in post-crucifixion period. Any income or possessions were surrendered or sold. Kayfa and the Twelve held the funds and controlled distribution.[869] The immanent

---

856. 1 Cor 8:1.

857. That is, Paul not taking support as commanded by Jesus which brings to question the legitimacy of him as an apostle, 1 Cor 9:1.

858. 1 Cor 11:1.

859. 1 Cor 11:17.

860. Diminishing the value of *glossolalia* as a gift from first to last, 1 Cor 12:1.

861. 1 Cor 12:27.

862. 1 Cor 13:1.

863. 1 Cor 14:23.

864. Via the first list of witnesses recorded and the "first fruits" (resurrected Jesus) of the end of the age, the raising of Jesus of Nazareth, 1 Cor 15:1.

865. Given only to Paul, 1 Cor 15:23.

866. 1 Cor 15:35.

867. 1 Cor 15:51.

868. Acts 15, see above, which included the "pillars," other apostles and elders; see also Gal 2; this counsel occurred in 49–50 CE.

869. Acts 2:45–47.

parousia supported such temporary measures and a collective commune. Distribution was based on need, but particularly emphasized the disenfranchised and outcasts, widows and orphans. But the delay of the *parousia*, coupled with the outpouring of need and the disastrous famine in Syria/Palestine in 45–48 CE,[870] coupled with the persecutions that arose,[871] depleted all funds of the Jerusalem *ecclesia*[872]—they were starving. Later, the distribution of monies created logistical and social issues, as the Hellenized Jews and "God-fearers" complained about the lack of support provided to their widows. The distribution of the wealth and service was expanded with the appointment of deacons, most of whom were Gentile or God-fearing Romans or Greeks.

Paul presents the question, "Now concerning the contribution for the *agioi* [saints]."[873] Paul's identification with the Jerusalem *ecclesia* was still critical, as he still maintained the support of Kayfa and likely John, and was committed to honoring his agreement made in the presence of the other *apostoloi*.[874] Throughout all of Paul's undisputed letters, the collection is a prominent feature of his instructions.[875] He is very careful, however in Corinth. Paul is *not* requiring that he take the collection to Jerusalem, but with their permission will do so, or will be accompanied by whomever they wish:

> And when I arrive [back at Corinth], I will send those whom you accredit by letter to carry your gift to Jerusalem. If it seems advisable that I should go, they will accompany me.[876]

The implication is that Paul does not want to be accused again of being a profiteer, a charlatan.[877] The *apostoloi* from James who track Paul charged him with just this: when Paul gathers up enough funds, he departs, leaving adherents in disarray, robbed and foolish.[878] In Thessaloniki, Philippi, Galatian and Corinth, Paul has had to defend against these charges, stating that he has refused compensation. Paul's refusal to accept support from the adherents at Corinth is ironically used by the infiltrators as evidence he violates a *command* of the Lord, i.e., one of the *logia* they cite to prove he is a false

---

870. Non-Christian reports of the famine during in Palestine, and during the rule of Claudius, include Dion Cassius (LX. 11), Tacitus (Annals XII. 13), and Josephus (Antiquities XX. 2. 5 and 5. 2). The events recounted place the famine between 45–48 CE.

871. After the death of Stephen, Acts 11:19.

872. Acts 11:27–30.

873. 1 Cor 16:1.

874. See above, Paul never criticizes Kayfa, but recounts in Galatians their dispute that led to Kayfa's admission that Paul had the justification to proceed in his ministry, which is further supported by Paul's citing Kayfa as authorized to travel with his wife.

875. Gal 2:10; Rom 15:29, and as noted a separate letter now contained in 2 Cor 8, 9.

876. 1 Cor 16:4.

877. See 2 Cor 11:7–9.

878. By implication, abandoning the believers, leaving them to face intense criticism and persecution by Jewish opponents sent from James and other splinter groups that formed, such as the proto-gnostic opponents in Corinth, so that their lives are completely disrupted.

apostolos. Paul must acknowledges this as a saying of Jesus, but he rejects its application appealing to *agape*, that is, to his choice of not being a burden—"working with his hands night and day," Paul relieves them from any financial obligation.

The collection became an established practice in all of Paul's *ecclesiae* on "the first day of the week."[879] Paul's use of the "first day" evidences his Semitic background, as in Hebrew the days of the week other than the Sabbath had no name, but were simply numbered (i.e., the Sabbath was also known as the "seventh day"). This simple statement is of immense importance as it is the *earliest reference* in the New Testament to the day Paul's *ecclesiae gathered*[880] to celebrate the Lord's Supper, reflecting the same day Jesus of Nazareth rose from the dead. To assume Paul identified the "first day" for other social or religious reasons is possible as well, but is more speculative.[881]

Paul asks that they "give out of their abundance," *ho ti ean euodotai*, i.e., "whatever he is prospered," meaning whatever God provided the adherent that can be set aside above basic subsistence needs. These sums were likely meager for most. However, the word *euodatai* is applied to all adherents—rich and poor, and all social classes and means. Thus, Paul is not calling for the surrender of all goods (as in the communal practices of Jerusalem as portrayed in Acts), but a gift of *agape*. As such, the collection for the "poor" of Jerusalem was unique in primitive Christianity. We learn of no other similar gift for other "saints."

Ultimately, the collection is, as Paul knows, his one unifying act of the Gentile churches with Jerusalem, fulfilling his commitments. Paul's letter to the Romans captures the character of this giving most clearly, and interestingly, Paul reports that he delivered the contribution to Jerusalem himself.[882] It is his most powerful mitigation to James and accusations that he is a dangerous charlatan and under the control of satanic forces. Paul is confident that the confrontation over the validity of his *euangelion* has been resolved. The contribution for the *agioi* of Jerusalem punctuates his legitimacy. This is the reason Paul addresses this question last.

Paul's Travel Plans and Return to Corinth

Paul's indicates that if he passes through Macedonia (the Roman province into which Paul would have entered from Asia and Ephesus), he may spend the winter with the adherents in Corinth. If so, Paul would have left the Ephesus and sailed west to Thessaloniki or Philippi before winter when weather created tremendous risk due to high

---

879. See, Gal 2:10; 1 Cor 16:1; as he also instructed his "churches in Galatia—thus we know that this letter came after that to the Galatians.

880. 1 Cor 16:2.

881. The day after market and pagan services occurred, or perhaps the day of guild and trade association gatherings.

882. Rom 15:25–29.

winds and unpredictable storms that had overwhelmed ship crews for centuries.[883] Paul acknowledges in 2 Corinthians the dangers of sea travel, which are particularly accentuated during the inopportune season.[884] The treacherous weather was primarily most dangerous in mid-November through March. In fact, Roman law prohibited sea travel from November 10 to March 10 with the safest sailing from May to September. The grain ship that was almost lost in Acts[885] was over two hundred feet long. The strong wind that captured the ship forced the crew to run cables to protect it from breaking apart. Aside from the danger of the sea, there was danger on land. The ship would have ported almost every day and travelers had to disembark to find lodging. Port lodging was notoriously dangerous, and most sailors stayed aboard or tented near port for safety. Passengers were at even greater risk if they were rumored to have carried valuables. Indeed, a plot developed to kill Paul and take the collection, probably by simply throwing him overboard.[886] But there was little choice. Land travel was much too long and arduous a journey, as Ephesus was on the west coast of Asia Minor, and even with the excellent roads and security of the Roman provincial patrols, there were still significant risk of robbery from bands of thieves and robbers. The travel time Ephesus to Corinth it was at least a month's journey. So, sea travel up from Ephesus to Troas and across to Philippi or Thessaloniki was the most accommodating, as well as direct route.

At this point, Paul is not presuming he will accompany the collection for he says, "so that when [I arrive in Corinth] you may speed me on my journey, wherever I go."[887] It is noteworthy that Paul does imply that they will provide some monetary assistance for his journey to "speed" him on his way. So, while Paul refuses support for his ministry to avoid accusation of thievery, he is willing to accept funds for his trip, as this appears to be a voluntary and discretionary expense on their part (it is not an obligation).

Paul also acknowledges that his ability to stay with the Corinthians is completely dependant on the will of the Lord, i.e., "if the Lord permits," or better, if the "master [*kurios*] is permitting it." This active relationship with the risen Lord includes vision and revelatory instructions, the destinations approved and the time allotted to remain at each location: "I hope to tarry with you a little time, if the Lord permits."[888] Paul refers to this active relationship when describing his presence in Ephesus (i.e., the location from where he writes to the Corinthians): "But I will remain in Ephesus until

---

883. See the description and even the name given to the type of ferocious wind encountered in Acts 27:17–20, the *Euroclydon*.

884. 2 Cor 11:25; Paul says he had been shipwrecked three times, including on his way to Rome after his appeal to Caesar; again see Acts 27.

885. Acts 27:9.

886. Acts 20:3.

887. 1 Cor 16:6.

888. 1 Cor 16:7.

Pentecost; for a great door has opened to me for effectual work, but there are many opposing."[889] The "great door opened to him" has been opened *to him* by God. What is the origin of Paul's reference?

The "great door" may be a reference to a physical location in the ancient world, which when opened portended miraculous events were about to occur, or that momentous proceedings were about to be witnessed. While Paul is likely recalling such a place or event, it must be noted that there is no Greek article preceding "door," which if present would more surely have indicated that he had a specific place in mind. There was a famous door that would have been known to Paul—a *thura megale* in the Jerusalem temple precincts, but the location is now uncertain (perhaps leading down fifteen steps the court of women). Indeed, the Nicanor gate[890] on the Temple Mount was made of Corinthian copper (or brass), which looked like gold, and was famous for its beauty and size. More, in the Talmud there is a tradition that the doors of the temple opened miraculously, certainly a miracle, as it required over twenty men to open the Nicanor doors. Other miracles were associated with the Nicanor gate.[891] It was due to the miracles (never named) that the door was not covered with gold or silver like others. It was these doors that some archaeologists believe led to the inner temple, which housed the holy of holies. Paul's point may be referencing this event or the miracles associated with the doors—certainly something that would be known to the Jerusalem infiltrators, and perhaps to the Corinthian adherents. Just like the miraculous events portended by the Nicanor doors opening in Jerusalem and the miracles associated with them, a miraculous opportunity has been given to Paul in Ephesus. Consequently, Paul is not dissuaded by the opposition he is facing, as the "great door" has been opened to him is something completely unexpected. Paul characterization of the opposition he faces in Ephesus is significant, *antikeimenoi polloi*, which should be literally interpreted "many opposing."

This short statement, "the opening of a great door," in Paul's letter is often overlooked. It is easy to take for granted the singular, pivotal events Paul's understood as charismatic and miraculous, that is, as the work of the risen Lord and of God. The "great door" opening was to Paul a result that could only come through the active presence of God—a validation that must put the opponents and Corinthians on notice. Paul is sharing his joy and surprise, and his hope and excitement about these events with the Corinthians adherents to validate his apostleship and active relationship with the risen Lord. Paul knows also that having success in Ephesus would confirm for the Corinthian adherents that the *euangelion* of Jesus Christ is the only legitimate and

---

889. 1 Cor 6:9.

890. Named after the Alexandrian Jew who donated the gate doors.

891. According to the Mishnah, the east gate, with two rooms attached (Mid. 1:4, also see Yoma 3:10).

salvific message of God. In doing so, Paul is witness to the eschatological incursion of God, as well as the emergence of God's future promise still to arrive.[892]

The Miracle in Ephesus: One of Three Events

Paul has been in Ephesus up to a year when he writes to the Corinthians. Since Paul later acknowledges that Prisca and Aquila are with him,[893] and we know that they are leatherworkers like Paul, it is certain that he has followed his traditional itinerant strategy entering a major metropolis. Arriving with his mobile toolbox, or more likely his folding leather bag of tools and hooks, Paul contacts with others in the local trade to find work. He looks for a shop with sleeping quarters above and begins his long days of labor (literally night and day) to earn a mere subsistence living to pay for his room and board. He then attends the trade/guild events and assemblies, learning more about those in the guild, both Jews and Gentiles, but particularly Jewish tradesmen. Concurrently, he attends and then is invited to speak as a guest in the local synagogue on the Sabbath, proclaiming Jesus of Nazareth the Lord and Christ. Paul begins teaching daily in the workshop setting, as local slaves and freemen working for owners or masters, as well as wealthy patrons and customers, deliver and pick up orders. Soon, those who want to learn more of the Way meet with him. Then by invitation Paul speaks in homes. Aquila and Prisca follow Paul and conduct a similar activity, coordinating their contacts.

Ultimately, with enough funds in hand, Paul, Prisca and Aquila rent a "house," likely either an apartment in a larger Roman villa, or perhaps one in a municipal apartment house. It is also possible that they rented the upper floor above a shop, where, as noted, artisans slept at night, allowing them to work late hours. Theirs becomes the first *ecclesia*, or "house church." The strategy was to establish the *ecclesia* as soon as possible. That this was accomplished early in the entry into Ephesus, or any metropolis, is certain. Confirmation is found in the timing of the Corinthian correspondence. In less than a year since he left Corinth, Paul states, "The *ecclesia* in the house of Aquila and Prisca greets you." It would appear that at this early stage, the house church had not grown beyond the home of his two colleagues, otherwise would have added the other *ecclesiae*, or simply used the plural.

---

892. Paul's comment confirms (1) the continued *active* involvement of the risen Lord in his ministry and success in expanding the good news in major Hellenistic-Roman cities (and this also validates his appointment, the "seal of his apostleship"); (2) that what he wills, such as visiting with the Corinthians and remaining with them, is not up to him but up to the risen Lord, i.e., he has active communication with the risen Lord who directs his actions; and (3) that the tangible results he is experiencing, *such as those that occurred in Corinth and are still evident in the charismata*, are most certainly events brought about by God and the Spirit, confirming the end of the age is near. These events validate that the *euangelion*, the good news of the Way (the more "excellent" Way), is from God. For Paul, his ministry is confirmed by the actions of the Spirit and intervention of the Lord Jesus Christ, as only this can explain his success and opening "great doors."

893. 1 Cor 16:19.

The Enemies of Paul in Corinth

It is uncertain what the new event may have been, that is, the opening of a "great door." It may have been related to one of three events recorded in Acts. First, after he failed in the synagogue and met significant opposition there, Paul moved his activity to the *schole*, the school or "hall," of Tyrannus[894] so that he might speak freely,[895] disputing with the Jews "daily." This was obviously a well know location in Ephesus and so came to have value as a place frequented daily by Paul.[896] It is possible that a Gentile God-fearer provided this hall for Paul's use and this opened a "great door" for spread of the *euangelion*. Indeed, this would have occurred early in the incursion there, as Paul left the synagogue after three months of disputing, and we know from Corinthians (see above) that the house church was still meeting in the home of Prisca and Aquila. Consequently, Paul's allusion to the "great door" may have been referencing access to a prestigious location to speak.

If Paul was disputing daily in the hall of Tyrannus it undoubtedly was at a time that would have allowed for minimal interruption to his leatherworking and subsistence income. In fact, in the Western Textual tradition[897] this version of Acts adds the words, "he argued in the hall of Tyrannus from the fifth to the tenth hour,"[898] or from 10 a.m. to about 4 p.m., about the time when work was suspended for the midday meal and then for the afternoon rest (the Mediterranean afternoon "nap," similar to a Spanish *siesta*), that is, usually during the heat of the day. The hall would have been available during this time, and so, would likely have been offered freely to Paul. Since the word *schole* can be translated literally as "school," Paul may have been offered an academic/Stoic setting for his teaching as a debating scholar or philosopher, but at a lower tier evidenced by the time of the day provided. The fact that the *shole* is named does suggest it was a well-known location for such events, i.e., where foreign philosophers or speakers were welcomed. Paul would have publicly "argued" just as other popular philosophers and rhetoricians of the day. It is also possible that the "hall" was a *guild or trade hall*, that is, Paul was invited to speak freely in the trade hall of his leatherworking guild (see above on the discussion in Thessaloniki). Since this was the *modus operandi* of Paul (i.e., to set up his workshop ministry and then develop support from his guild

---

894. Either Tyrannus was himself famous (i.e., this is why the editor of Acts mentions him), or he became a follower of the Way and offered Paul the hall, and thus, became well known to believers throughout Asia. Since the Greek *tyrannus*, is translated as "tyrant," but in Greek, this could mean a ruler of the city, i.e., an honorary name. Indeed, there have been inscriptions found which include the name Tyrannus. Several inscriptions in Asia Minor and in Ephesus date to the first century CE, one in particular on a column with the inscription of "Tyrannus." And so the move from the synagogue to the hall of his trade guild, the Hall of Tyrannus, was a significant event, just as stated by Paul.

895. Acts 19:9.

896. This is why it is remembered in Acts, i.e., one of the few physical locations ever mentioned in the New Testament where Paul, or any apostle was active, but the location is now lost to history.

897. Examples from the Western Textual tradition usually include expanded sections that seem to provide a better explanation of various traditions and statements, e.g., Codex Bezae, 5th CE, written in uncials, or capital letters in Latin or Greek from the 3rd to the 9th century CE.

898. Acts 19:9.

while preaching in the synagogue on the Sabbath), Paul may have been using a guild meeting house to present the *euangelion* of Jesus Christ.

However, the amount of time that Paul is said to have spoken daily at the hall of Tyrannus (according to the Western Textual tradition) would indicate a significant commitment of a well-known location, and may have created financial difficulty for Paul without some form of additional assistance. As noted, the leatherworker's day was long and difficult, stretching from dawn to dusk, resulting only in a short breaks to earn small subsistence wage, even assuming one lived in the loft above the shop.[899] Consequently, it is clear that others must have financially supported Paul to make up for the missed hours, even if they were during the afternoon *siesta*. Support may have come from a local benefactor, or perhaps another *ecclesiae*, thus allowing Paul to speak and debate. Acts reports the following: "This continued for two years, so that all the residents of Asia heard the word of the Lord, both *Jew and Greeks*."[900]

For "all of the residents" to have heard of the *euangelion* and the Way, Paul must have attracted substantial attention, which leads to a second possibility. Acts continues: "And God did extraordinary miracles by the hands of Paul, so that aprons [these were Paul's workman's aprons and handkerchiefs tied around his wrists and head to absorb sweat] were carried away from his body to the sick and diseases left them and the evil spirits came out of them."[901] Paul's association with the risen Jesus—a man who could call on the efficacious name of his master for the expulsion of demons, spells and evil spirits—combined with his democratized proclamation of life for all social classes by *pistis* in salvific *euangelion*, was a powerful combination. The sweat of a charismatic such as Paul was thought to carry the divine or supernatural power and authority of the individual, which was repulsive and dangerous to demons and evil spirits. It could nullify curses, spells or poisons. Anyone who thought they could find relief for suffering or possessed family or relatives through the clothing, spittle, rites, command or touch of a shaman like figure, would be sought out. Frankly, payment for the aprons could have been a source of financing for Paul. Certainly, the expulsion of illness and possession would have brought regional fame and positive social attention, i.e., that Paul's attending audience was comprised of *both* "Jews and Greeks." The overwhelming of dark forces can mitigate, even eliminate, ethnic, social religious barriers and perilous risk.

Paul's charismatic reputation and fame were also facilitated by the broad support he received from fellow artisans and trade guild members in the city. In fact, it is just as likely that those subsistence artisans who became adherents may have carried Paul's *euangelion* far beyond Ephesus as his emissaries. How would this have happened? Ephesus was home to the temple of the goddess Artemis, one of the seven wonders of the ancient world. Ephesus was also the center of many festival celebrations, including

---

899. 1 Thess 2:9.
900. Acts 19:10.
901. Acts 19:11–12.

Magna Mater and *Attis*, as well as the ecstatic celebration of the goddess Cybele, the *Ephesia*. The portability of leatherworkers and tent makers allowed them to travel from city to city as they followed a festival calendar (just as in Corinth for the games), moving to the next celebratory event. Ephesus undoubtedly attracted other craftsmen to the city during these celebrations and festivals, both Jews and Gentiles. Indeed, there is no dispute among scholars as to whether Hellenistic Jews and Greeks were members of the same trade associations—they were, which was particularly true for subsistence wage leatherworkers. Consequently, during Ephesian festivals and celebrations, not only did both Jews and Gentiles come to the Roman capital of Asia and hear of the charismatic Paul, but so did other craftsmen who would then return to their home city and new workshop settings. Paul's charismatic powers validated his proclamation of the Way. Paul calls fellow craftsmen and women to become his "fellow workers" for Christ. Indeed, Paul does not differentiate the term *synergoi* "fellow workers" between those who work with him for the Lord and those fellow workers in the trade, most notably, Prisca and Aquila. Here he uses the same terminology, which is clearly drawn from the language of his trade association and guild. Consequently, the report that both Jews and Greeks "heard the word of the Lord" is better explained by the mobility of the leatherworkers that came to the Ephesian festivals and then moved to the next festival or returned home, all having visited the hall of Tyrannus and, hearing Paul's proclamation, became adherents. These *synergoi*, both Jews and Greeks, would have carried the *euangelion* to other *metropoli*. Thus, Paul was influencing a new group of itinerant missionaries who not only practiced his trade, but also embraced his missionary strategy, including the workshop ministry.

A third possible incident that opened a "great door" is recounted in the events surrounding the sons of Sceva, a Jew and "Chief of the Priests." When his seven sons failed to exorcise a demon,[902] the results were disastrous. The "wounding" of the sons who fled naked after trying to perform their exorcism by invoking the name of Jesus became known to "all the Jews and Greeks," and "fear fell on them all [dwelling in Ephesus], and the name of the Lord Jesus was magnified." This event may fit Paul's designation of the "great door" being opened, and while providing new adherents, it also recounts how Paul became feared. As a result, "many brought their books" and burned them.[903] These were scrolls that carried magical incantations in secret symbols (indecipherable words, except to priests and initiates) associated with the cult of Artemis called the *Ephesian Grammata*. These included books of spells for protection and healing, some of which apparently were made of stitched leather, including sayings on belts and other items as well.[904] Can Paul have equated something as momentous

---

902. Acts 19:14–17.

903. Acts 19:18.

904. Anaxilas, *Harp-Maker*, from Athenaeus, Deipnosophistae XII. 548C, "Oiling his skin with yellow unguents, flaunting soft cloaks, shuffling fine slippers, munching bulbs, bolting pieces of cheese, pecking at eggs, eating periwinkes, drinking Chian wine, and what is more, carrying about, on little

and frightening as the failed exorcism with a "great door?" The final statement in this tradition in Acts is important: "Thus by the might of the Lord [other translations have instead, 'the name of the Lord'], the word increased and was strong."[905] Certainly, these events would qualify as notoriety and it is clear that the editor of Acts states explicitly that the "word," i.e., the good news, increased and was "strong." However, the issue is the timing of these events. The statement by Paul in Corinthians (as noted above) seems to indicate an event early in his ministry in Ephesus. For this reason, the timing would suggest that the opportunity to speak in the Hall of Tyrannus and the miracles that occurred during this phase were the "great door" opened to Paul.

Paul's citation of these events would be added proof of his status as a legitimate *apostoloi* to both his opponents and to the Corinthians, both of who may have been made aware. Paul's employment of the "great door" and the name of Tyrannus are therefore intentional and dramatic.

Paul's Supporters in the Last Days

Paul has decided then to stay in Ephesus until Pentecost. Pentecost, literally fifty days after Passover, is known in Judaism as *Shavou't*, the festival of weeks, which celebrated the *giving* of the torah to Moses (and the continual giving of it to Israel), but also had agricultural significance in that it celebrated the giving of the "first fruits" being harvested. The harvests were brought to the temple in thanks as free will offerings. The offering consisted of two first fruit loaves of new meal and *ephah*, leavened and baked. *Shavou't* actually does not have a fixed date on the calendar, but used a method of counting from the second day of Passover and seven weeks.[906] Typically, this would have left Paul in Ephesus until late May to mid-June, or still in the best season for travel by sea, then through Macedonia to Ephesus. Since Paul is traveling through Macedonia, he may have taken a ship to Thessaloniki, or Philippi, not directly to Corinth as noted. This route would have saved several weeks of land travel. It is difficult to ascertain if Paul is remaining in Ephesus to celebrate Pentecost, but it seems he uses this festival as the demarcation point.

What this does demonstrate is that Paul is first and foremost adhering to the Jewish traditions and calendar celebrations of his ancestors. Second, it clearly indicates

---

bits of stitched leather, lovely Ephesian letters." Also, Plutarch, Moralia 706E, "For just as sorcerers advise those possessed by demons to recite and name over to themselves the Ephesian letters, so we, in the midst of such warblings and caperings, 'Stirred by frenzies and whoops to the tumult of tossing heads,' if we bethink ourselves of those hallowed and venerable writings and set up for comparison songs and poems and tales of true nobility, shall not be altogether dazed by these performances." The most famous *grammata* were associated with six or four words that can be found in many inscriptions. Attempts by early writers to interpret them failed.

905. Acts 19:20.

906. The first night is generally reserved for reading and studying of the torah, and sometimes celebrants stayed up all night. It is current tradition, but also may have been so in Paul's time, the book of Ruth was also read.

that Paul is writing to those who understood what this date meant as to the time of year, i.e., both his Jewish adherents and the opponents. As noted, Paul links the stay to the "great door" that had been opened. Whether Paul associated his departure after Pentecost with events at the Hall of Tyrannus, including demonic exorcisms that occurred, is uncertain. Paul is still unaware of the significance of these events and how they might change his travel plans. Paul may have extended his stay extending given the many letters to the Corinthians that followed 1 Corinthians. It is certain, however, that Paul did make a short "painful" visit to Corinth to face the opponents, which was followed by the "letter of tears."[907] This letter is now lost. Such a visit could have come after Pentecost as Paul intended. This would particularly be the case if events did indeed spiral out of control, which is indicated by the troubling letters that now make up Second Corinthians. As Paul ends his correspondence, he lists those who are share in the perilous risks of his itinerancy for the *euangelion* of Jesus Christ.

Timothy

Paul notifies the Corinthians aware that he has sent his "fellow worker"[908] Timothy to them.[909] Timothy, Paul's loyal and devoted assistant and "beloved child," *agapeton teknon*,[910] has been dispatched: "For this cause I have sent to you Timothy, who is my beloved and faithful child in the Lord to remind you of my *ways* in Christ, as I teach in them everywhere in every *ecclesia*." The "ways" of which Paul is speaking is *agape*, the more excellent Way, the highest expression of the torah that he describes in 1 Corinthians 13, and is the central theme of his entire letter—the efficacious *euangelion* of the cross, *pistis*, *elpis* and the practice of *agape* and *charismata*, while awaiting the *parousia*. This is evident by the context given by Paul's preceding statement. While they claim to be "kings," Paul and his fellow workers exhibited *humility and love* on their behalf. They have given up any claims of merit, rejecting even subsistence support. Their safety is to be found only in *pistis* and *elpis*, and their service through *agape*—this despite their brutal life and treatment in the world and attacks by Satan. And so, Paul sends his most beloved "child" to them, Timothy, and asks that he not be despised, nor put in fear. Indeed, this is not the first time that Timothy has assisted Paul in delivering his messages or strengthening Paul's *ecclesiae* as his personal emissary after his departure: "We sent Timothy, our brother and God's servant in the gospel of Christ, to establish you in the faith and to exhort you, that no one be

---

907. 2 Cor 2:1.
908. Rom 16:1.
909. 1 Cor 16:10–11.
910. 1 Cor 4:17.

moved by these afflictions."[911] Timothy remained a devoted disciple of Paul, even to his imprisonment in Rome.[912]

The son of a Hellenistic pagan father (a Gentile who is unnamed by Paul) and a Jewish mother, Eunice,[913] Timothy came to the *euangelion* by her mother during Paul's activity in Galatia. Timothy was a young man at the time of Paul's arrival in Lystra, perhaps twenty (48 or 49 CE). Paul had just been escaped from Iconium,[914] where there was an attempt to kill him. When Paul arrived, he exorcised the demon of a lame man[915] and was immediately proclaim Zeus, and his companion Barnabas was identified as Hermes (the herald of Zeus). Paul and Barnabas resisted and forbade sacrifice in their honor, an honor bestowed only to gods. Disaster soon came when Paul's Jewish opponents arrived from Antioch,[916] Iconium and Derbe. They incited a riot, stoned Paul, and literally dragged him out of the city believing he was dead to the city dump.[917] Paul's wounds were severe, with several blows to the head. Nonetheless, Paul regained consciousness and under his own power left for Derbe, a journey of almost sixty miles. Paul intentionally returned not only to Lystra but also to Iconium and Antioch (most likely Pisidian Antioch in Asia Minor, a center of Jewish opposition to his *euangelion*), risking his life. Paul's enemies must have understood his survival from death as either an act of God or protection by dark or satanic forces, thereby making any further attacks on him dangerous and subject to risk and retribution. Paul returned to Lystra (perhaps beginning in 49 or 50 CE) as he began his second itinerant tour. After receiving a good report from the *ecclesiae* there,[918] Paul asked Timothy to join with him. From that time, Timothy became Paul's closest associate with the exception of Luke.[919]

Timothy joined Paul, fully knowing the perilous risks, persecution and difficulties he would face, which included threats and attempts on own life: "You, however, know all about my teaching, my way of life, my purpose, faith, patience, love, endurance, persecutions, sufferings—what kinds of things happened to me in Antioch, Iconium and Lystra, the persecutions I endured. Yet the Lord rescued me from all of them."[920] Paul's emphasis on the intervention of God is of critical importance: Paul's rescue punctuated and validated the legitimacy of his apostolic mission and his *euangelion*

911. 1 Thess 3:2.
912. Phlm 1:1.
913. 2 Tim 1:5.
914. Acts 14:5.
915. Acts 14:8.
916. Likely, followers of James even though this was before the Apostolic Council.
917. Acts 14:19; see also 2 Cor 11:25 where Paul historically confirms his stoning.
918. "The brothers from Lystra and Iconium spoke well of him," Acts 16:2.
919. 2 Tim 4:11.
920. 2 Tim 3:10, 11—this in one of many passages that clearly demonstrates that 2 Timothy is either an authentic letter of Paul, or a fragment of an authentic letter, contrary to the opinion of most critical scholars.

because it was God who intervened against Satan and his demons—repeatedly. But this intervention carried with it great risk for Paul and Timothy. They must not fail to successfully promulgate the *euangelion* and establish and maintain *ecclesiae* to the *parousia* or face doom. The perilous risk of failure outweighed the perilous risk of denying the revelatory encounter with Jesus Christ, making and facing torture, or even death. The mitigation was the *euangelion* and the immanent *parousia*. Anyone who joined with Paul faced these risks.

Timothy accepted this peril and several high-risk assignments for Paul; whether to Athens, Thessaloniki, Philippi, Iconium or Corinth, as the named emissary of a controversial and accused Jewish charlatan, and as one who proclaimed a crucified Jew resurrected, Savior and Lord. In at least two of the cities that Timothy entered, Paul had been attacked and almost murdered. Not unlike the *apostoloi* appointed by James, Timothy was Paul's emissary, his *agapeton teknon*, beloved child and "fellow servant," imbued with authority. And not unlike the James' *apostoloi*, Timothy was also permeated with charismatic powers, but like Paul, his *charismata* were not limited to *gnosis* and *glossolalia*; they included the practice of soul projection, casting divine curses, exorcism, visions and trances—all the *charismata* Paul encouraged in the *ecclesiae*. Timothy carried Paul's efficacious letters (which contained powerful orders, as well as efficacious curses and blessings), and so, was licensed to act for Paul, Jesus Christ and the Holy Spirit. In prison facing uncertainty and perhaps death, Paul includes Timothy's own personal greeting to the Roman *ecclesiae*: "Timothy, my fellow worker, sends greetings."[921]

When Paul reminds the Corinthians that Timothy is on his way,[922] it is obvious that Timothy had left long before the letter was written, most likely immediately after the arrival of Chloe's people.[923] In fact, it is clear that Paul expects Timothy to arrive after the letter has been received. This would mean that Paul had instructed Timothy to stop and visit other *ecclesiae* in Macedonia (after crossing from the port at Troas in Asia Minor), such as Thessaloniki and Philippi. But here, Paul not only reminds the Corinthians that Timothy was on the way (i.e., repeating his earlier comment),[924] he warns them about mistreating Timothy, which is puzzling.

Paul demands that Timothy not be rejected or despised when he arrives in Corinth. Indeed, it is curious why Paul feels it is necessary to explain how the Corinthians are to behave toward Timothy. Why would Paul have to defend Timothy, particularly if Paul was addressing adherents and not the infiltrators? Why would Paul say to adherents: "See that you put him to ease among you [literally, make him not be in fear among you], for he is doing the work of the Lord, as I am. So let no one despise him. Speed him on his way in peace that he may return to me." That the adherents,

---

921. Rom 16:21.
922. 1 Cor 16:10, following his early comment in 4:17.
923. 1 Cor 1:11.
924. 1 Cor 4:17.

those who have just been asked to practice the "more excellent Way" of *agape*, would be literally commanded to not threaten Timothy is question begging. It is clear that Timothy travelled at Paul's bequest without hesitation and, as noted, at great risk. Consequently, Timothy does not appear to have been a fearful emissary. Indeed, why would the Corinthian adherents even consider hate or attack him? The question then is if there is any evidence in other Pauline correspondence that can give us a clue as to why Timothy would engender such a radical response from adherents, i.e., that he was despised and would be threatened?

To determine what if any issues there might have been with Timothy (i.e., issues that required Paul to provide for his defense), Paul's undisputed letters can be consulted. However, Romans, 1 and 2 Corinthians, Galatians, 1 Thessalonians, and Philippians provide no insight. For example, in Philippians Paul says: "I have no one like him, and he is genuinely anxious for you [i.e., Timothy, despite being with Paul in prison, is concerned for Philippian *ecclesia* and not himself] . . . Timothy's character [or 'worth'] you know, how as a *son with a father* he has served with me in the *euangelion*."[925] Consequently, Paul's undisputed letters provide nothing about Timothy that would suggest he is despised, or why anyone would threaten him. Commentators have offered a wide variety of explanations, most of which go beyond the written evidence available, or are not coherent with what is known. For example, it simply cannot be as some purport that Timothy is despised and hated because he is the loyal follower of Paul, that is, he is seen as an adversary, spy and untrustworthy (i.e., like James' spies in Galatia). The evidence against this is quite clear. Paul is openly sending Timothy to the *ecclesia* in Corinth, so why would he be considered a "spy" and untrustworthy or a danger, and why would Paul take the time to warn them or make the request for their support if this was the case? What then might be the reason for Paul's appeal?

To begin an analysis, the most insightful comments come from a what universally held to be a pseudepigraphical letter, 2 Timothy, which is a personal letter purportedly written from Paul to Timothy from prison in Rome. Paul is condemned and awaiting execution. This letter is commonly identified with Paul's "second imprisonment in Rome," during the officially sanctioned mass persecution and legal murder of Christians under Nero Caesar in about 64 CE. Yet, 2 Timothy is clearly a letter whose Pauline authorship and origin is widely disputed for sound reasons, particularly among critical scholars.[926] The "Pastoral Epistles," or 1 and 2 Timothy and Titus (so called because Paul is addressing pastoral practices he expects from all of the church leadership being established, including that of Timothy and Titus), do *collectively* appear be addressing issues that would have arisen long after the apostolic period, that is, when church hierarchy needed to be firmly established to maintain order with the passing of the last generation of witnesses and their immediate followers (i.e., by 110–140 CE), as

---

925. Phil 2:20a, 22.

926. Perrin, *Introduction*, provides their most coherent argument, as does Kummel in his *Introduction*.

well as the rise of Gnosticism within the early Church. However, it is fascinating that none of these letters were disputed by virtually any of the early church "fathers."[927] The Ante-Nicene fathers (from Ignatius to Polycarp) rejected several other letters attributed to Paul as pseudepigraphical, e.g., 3 Corinthians, the letter of the Corinthians to Paul, the letter to the Laodiceans, the Epistle to the Alexandrians, the Acts of Paul and Thecla, the Apocalypse of Paul, the Prayer of the Apostle Paul, a letter to Seneca, and others. This raises a question as to why the "Pastoral" letters would have been accepted as authentic so early, while many others were not. Consequently, before rejecting the Pastorals, it is important to consider whether any of the letters, or contents within the letters to Timothy, do have a claim to authenticity, even if it is a fragment of an original letter that was later embellished by a pseudepigraphical writer to meet a current life situation. If any of these letters or fragments thereof is Pauline, do they give any clue as to why Timothy needed to be rigorously defended by Paul?

Examining the content of the Pastorals, one is immediately struck by significant issues that speak against Pauline authorship—language, style, eschatology, and terminology, particularly in 1 Timothy and Titus. What is most startling is the attitude toward women in 1 Timothy and Titus. In 1 Timothy, Paul says: "Let a women learn in silence with all submissiveness [*hupotagge*, 'subjection']. I do not permit [the emphatic, *ouk epitrepo*] women to teach or to exercise authority over a man, but to be in silence."[928] As has been firmly established, Paul could not have written this, as he considered women as equals or his superior, having leading roles, including that of an *apostolos*. Paul clearly states, "There is neither Jew nor Greek, male nor female."[929] What is ironic about 1 Timothy and Titus and Paul's demand for women to be silent is his comment in 2 Timothy, that is, Timothy came to the faith *by his mother*, Eunice. Clearly, the writer(s) of 1 Timothy and Titus do not know this tradition. Other problematic examples can be found. First Timothy 3:15 continues: "Yet woman will be saved through bearing children, if she continues in faith and love and holiness with modesty." This is followed by Paul's supposed appeal to appoint male leadership, "The saying is sure: If any one aspires to the office of bishop [*episkopos*], *he* desires a noble task ... [must] be above reproach, the husband of one wife."[930] The writer of 1 Timothy is intentionally subverting the equal role of women accepted by Paul. This combined with the terminology and eschatology that is not consistent with the undisputed letters of Paul confirms that 1 Timothy is pseudepigraphical.

---

927. E.g., Irenaeus, 180 CE; it is found in the Muratorian fragment, 170 CE; omitted, as expected by Marcion and others gnostics who would have rejected their eschatology; there many be references to some of the letters in the writings of Polycarp, 132 CE, Ignatius 110 CE, and perhaps Clement of Rome in 95–98 CE.

928. 1 Tim 3:11–12.

929. Gal 3:28; Paul may have either introduced or repeated a baptismal formula as noted by Patterson, *Lost Way*, 227–28.

930. 1 Tim 3:1–2a

Unfortunately, another pastoral and personal letter addressed to Paul's fellow worker, Titus,[931] has similar devastating flaws. With regard to women, the writer of Titus says:

> Bid the older women likewise to be reverent in their behavior, not to be slanderers or slaves to drink; they are to teach what is good, and to train the young women to love their husbands and children, to be sensible, chase, domestic, kind and submissive to their husbands, that the word of God may not be discredited.[932]

Of course, this subservient role defined for women in Titus is problematic, but more, it reflects much different eschatological viewpoint than that described by Paul in his undisputed letters. This could not have come from a Paul facing death who expected the *parousia*. It is a complete reversal of Paul's eschatological perspective.[933] For Paul, the urgency of the impending *parousia* negated the need for longer-term, well defined social roles, certainly those defined by gender. The Lord's return was near and time to proclaim the *euangelion* and save as many as possible was short—*maran 'atha*, "Lord Come!" Paul shouts.[934] The tension between the current period, which was soon to pass away, and the inbreaking of the kingdom of God had not only removed social barriers, but negated them, including gender. This is why Paul reluctantly accepts marriage, but appeals to the adherents to be free from worldly responsibilities.[935] Consequently it is apparent that the eschatology of 1 Timothy and Titus is distinctly non-Pauline.[936] Thus, Titus is pseudepigraphical and reflects a different time in the history of the church, when the *parousia* was seen as distant, and no longer imminent; where church hierarchy and social roles predominated the eschatological view of times. The letter was written in the name of Paul because his letters continued to exert tremendous influence. It was a time when the church was locked in a confrontation with alternative views of the meaning of Jesus and the word, primarily defined by the conflict with Gnosticism, the rejection of the evil god of the Old Testament (Marcion), and a recasting and careful editing of early writings, from the gospels to letters of Paul. Consequently, one cannot ascribe this change in perspective to Paul's situation in prison. The conclusion is unavoidable: 1 Timothy and Titus are both pseudepigraphical writings. Consequently, virtually nothing can be garnered from 1 Timothy or Titus about the historical issues relating Paul's defense of Timothy. Better

---

931. Titus, an uncircumcised Greek or Roman; see Gal 2:1–3 and 2 Cor 8:6.

932. Titus 2:3–8.

933. For Paul, the end of the age and the good news of love and forgiveness extended to all and demanded the elimination of all barriers, as well as the introduction of the democratized *ecclesia*, the new assembly of Israel, where there is neither "male nor female, Jew or Gentile, rich or poor." The believer, no longer male or female, was a new creation *in* Christ Jesus, who was the new Adam.

934. 1 Cor 16:21; Paul is speaking Aramaic, the language of Jesus in Palestine.

935. 1 Cor 7:25–31, 36–40.

936. 1 Tim 3:1–7.

said, no historical value is available from 1 Timothy that might provide insight into Paul comments in 1 Cor 16:10.

But we are still left with a troubling dilemma. The early church fathers unanimously adopted these letters as authentic. Of course, the simple solution is the obvious one, namely, that the letters reflected the times and needs of the church, so were authorized. But would the early church fathers fall silent in opposition to their authenticity for convenience? Absolutely not, for there were several other writings, as noted above, that they could have adopted which could have similarly served the church well in those times. The only answer that is logical is that one of the letters, or portions of it, must have been unquestionably considered authentic. Since it is certain that 1 Timothy and Titus were pseudepigraphical, we are left with 2 Timothy. With regard to 2 Timothy, is there Pauline material embedded in the letter coherent with the context of Paul's eschatology and activity, and would this material reveal something about Timothy that provides additional insight into Paul's comments in 1 Cor 16:10?

The first thing that is striking is that 2 Timothy is intensely personal. Paul is in resigned to his death and execution.[937] There is no hope of appeal—death is certain, and the impending time until his execution is a great burden, not because Paul is concerned for himself, but because he is worried about his closest friend and coworker who is "in tears," Timothy. Paul says, "As I remember your tears, I long night and day to see you that I may be filled with joy."[938] Devastated by their separation and the reality that he may never see his "beloved son" again, Paul's depression is heightened because all of his fellow-workers had abandoned him—they all fled, except one. That Timothy knows the men mentioned is certain, as Paul only has to provide their first names; Demas, Crescens and *Titus*.[939] The one adherent who remained with Paul at his own great risk was Luke.[940] Indeed, the very people who have lived and worked with Paul and faced so many dangers were gone. Demas had been with Paul during his first imprisonment (his escorted "house arrest"),[941] but now, at the second and fatal imprisonment, he had forsaken him: "For Demas, in love with this present world has deserted me and gone to Thessaloniki."[942] The desertion of Demas represents the earliest evidence for the crisis that developed in the early 60s CE, that is, the death of the original witnesses combined with the obvious delay of the *parousia* had created unparalleled dissonance.

With the reality of Paul's arrest and death sentencing fully understood, Demas, Crescens *and Titus* have lost all hope.[943] What is remarkable is that *Titus* is men-

937. 2 Tim 4:6.
938. 2 Tim 1:4.
939. 2 Tim 4:9–10.
940. Col 4:14.
941. Phlm 24.
942. 2 Tim 4:10.
943. 2 Tim 4:10a.

tioned as a deserter. This provides additional evidence that speaks against the Pauline authorship of Titus, and underscores its pseudepigraphical origins. More important, this lends significant credence to the Pauline authorship of portions of 2 Timothy, as this negative historical fact would have certainly been covered up or edited, i.e., that Titus was a deserter. *What this demonstrates then is the probability that at least portion of 2 Timothy were widely known as an authentic and undisputed letter of Paul.* This also means that the addition of two letters, 1 Timothy and Titus, were "bookends" to 2 Timothy, redefining some of its comments by implying Paul was released instead of killed as expected in 2 Timothy, allowing him to write Titus. The need to silence leading women portrayed in Titus was then interpolated back into the pseudepigraphical 1 Timothy, along with the same eschatological bias. Male leadership, using Paul's name in order to clarify issues for the later church likely in the early to mid-second century, developed 1 Timothy and Titus. Paul's condemning statement was then reinterpreted to mean that only Demas was a deserter, and that Paul had sent Titus away to Dalmatia. Yet, the linguistic similarities between these two letters is striking, further supporting the conclusion that they were developed together and reliant on the other. Perhaps the letters contained fragments of more original communication from prison, but it is virtually impossible to recreate their original form.

Pauline authorship, at least of certain portions of the letter,[944] can be further confirmed. First, the intense personal nature of many comments suggests authenticity, and these comments are coherent with Paul's eschatological outlook as reflected in his authentic writings. For example, Paul looks for the simple things that are left in this world for him, particularly to see his fellow-worker and "son in the faith" Timothy. He is pained at the possibility that he will never be with him: "Do your best to come to me

---

944. It is appropriate to exercise some caution about the uniformity of 2 Timothy, that is, to acknowledge that some of Paul's statements and quotes may be later additions. In a survey of the letter, there are some statements that can be identified. They include: "If we have died with him, *we will live with him*; if we endure we shall also reign with him; if we deny him he will also deny us." This is an early Christian hymn. It betrays a theology of martyrdom and assurance that a martyr's death brings life, which can be construed as a much later development within Christianity; "Jesus Christ, risen from the dead, *descended from David*, as preached in my gospel" (to my knowledge, Paul does not appeal to Jesus' lineage from David). There are several Greek words unique to 2 Timothy that are not found in other genuine letters. Yet, the preponderance of evidence, aside from these examples, confirms the letter to be the final and personal correspondence of Paul to Timothy, coherent with Paul's eschatology. Many of the possible issues noted must be taken in the context of Paul's dire circumstances, and the Christian hymn of assurance could most certainly come at the time of the great persecution, or even long before Nero's state sanctioned persecution, i.e., during the persecution of the believers in Palestine and in Jerusalem, particularly after the murder of James, the brother of John, and the arrest of other key leaders. Why would a pseudepigraphical writer compose a personal letter that has no political, theological or hierarchical agenda other than to prevent Timothy from denying his faith and coming to him before he is executed? The very nature of the negative assertion that the letter implies, i.e., that Paul's closest companions, including Timothy, had abandoned him, makes any claim that the letter is spurious doubtful. Thus, it is justifiable to conclude that historically valid information about Paul's closest and most dear companion is contained in this letter.

soon,"⁹⁴⁵ and with even more urgency asks for Timothy to come to him before winter when travel is impossible by sea and too long and dangerous a journey by land.⁹⁴⁶ Some scholars believe that Timothy was in Ephesus, and Paul mentions he has sent Tychicus there.⁹⁴⁷ At the conclusion of the letter, Paul requests that Timothy greet Aquila and Prisca who were in Ephesus,⁹⁴⁸ his long time companions and fellow leather workers who have been instrumental in his workshop ministry, protecting Paul at their own risk and in hosting the nascent house churches.⁹⁴⁹ Consequently, Timothy is in the port city of Ephesus in late summer, probably the year 64 or 65 CE. Paul's touching and simple request to Timothy is that bring his cloak, the *philones*, which was a woolen or thick upper mantle or cloak, usually worn to protect from weather, similar to the Roman *paenula*. But the word for cloak can also mean *travel bag*, and so Paul could be requesting his tool bag or a carrying case as well. Most likely, however, it is a simple cloak, like that worn by slaves or the poor, but warm. Winter is approaching. Paul also requests the books and parchments that he left at the port of Troas. This statement has historical veracity, as by ship, the route for Timothy would have stopped at Troas before crossing to Philippi or Thessaloniki. Timothy would likely have camped overnight in Troas, or stayed with other adherents who were holding these items for Paul, before sailing on the next day. Paul's instructions clearly speak to a historical situation and are geographically accurate. This is course lends additional credence to the authenticity of portions of the letter.

Additional confirmation of the Pauline authorship is evident. Paul reminds Timothy of the risk and opposition he faced in Iconium, Lystra and Antioch when they first met. Clearly, this is a personal reminiscence that is intended for the reader alone. But more, Paul describes his experience in these cities much differently than Acts.⁹⁵⁰ Paul says: "You have observed my teaching, my conduct, my aim in life, my faith, my patience, my love, my steadfastness, my persecutions, my sufferings, what befell me at Antioch, at Iconium, and at Lystra, what persecutions I endured."⁹⁵¹ According to Acts, Paul met opposition in each of these cities, but it was only in Lystra that Jews from Antioch of Pisidia and Iconium arrived, created a mob that called for Paul's death (based on blasphemy), and then stoned him, dragging his body out of the city for the birds and dogs to devour. Paul's comments in 2 Timothy indicate that his treatment in the cities of Antioch and Iconium was actually much more severe than portrayed in Acts, and that Timothy witnessed this. But more to the point, such personal information would be extraneous detail in a pseudepigraphical work. The conclusion is obvious—there are

---

945. 2 Tim 4:9.
946. 2 Tim 4:21.
947. 2 Tim 4:12.
948. Acts 18:2–3, 19; 1 Cor 16:9.
949. Rom 16:3–4.
950. Acts 13:14–52.
951. 2 Tim 3:10–11.

portions of this correspondence that only two men who witnessed these events would understand obscure references to their first encounter.

Even more important, unlike 1 Timothy and Titus, 2 Timothy is absent any reference to the subservient role of women,[952] or call for the male domination of the church and a well-defined and developed male hierarchy. In 2 Timothy, Paul is severely critical of his male colleagues. He cites their cowardice, personal failure and desertion in the last days—the most devastating of all accusations. He even describes their destinations, another detail that would be extraneous to a pseudepigraphical letter. The criticism of Demas also evokes the genuine Pauline eschatological outlook as to passing of the present age. Paul says, "For Demas, in love with *this present world* [*nun aiona*, the 'present age'], has deserted me and gone to Thessaloniki."[953] Thus, Demas' desertion is not just the forsaking of his relationship with Paul, but it is the abandonment of the salvific *euangelion* and eschatological promise that the Lord's return is imminent, i.e., the core of Paul's eschatological proclamation.[954]

Second Timothy also reflects the same nascent emergence of Gnosticism that Paul resists in 1 Corinthians, i.e., where Paul repeats the theme that those who claim access to salvation through elitist gnosis using sayings of Jesus are in fact *not known by God*; that is, Paul uses a play on words by employing the term *gnosis*—what they claim they know is the very evidence that they have no understanding and thus are *not known by God*:

> Avoid disputing about words [*logosmaksen*, i.e., such disputing the meaning of sayings, or *logoi*, of Jesus], for they won't affect the ones you argue with [i.e., they are using the *logoi* for their own purposes and since they claim they gain special insight through the collection, they will not abandon what their collection of sayings imply] . . . their talk will eat away like gangrene. Among them are Hymenaeus and Philetus, who have swerved [literally, "misaimed"] from the truth by holding that the resurrection has already passed [exactly parallel to 1 Cor 15:2–3; 1 Cor 4:7–9]. They are upsetting the faith of some.[955]

The impact of these men on the *ecclesiae* through their selective use of the sayings of Jesus had not become a widespread eschatological division of the Way (they are obviously still in Ephesus), or created a split within the *ecclesia* in Rome and elsewhere, certainly something that did occur in the mid-second century with the rise of Marcion.

Consequently, in 2 Timothy there is little to indicate that those who deny the resurrection of Jesus are any more than a limited nuisance, or that Timothy himself

---

952. That they must be silent, only questions their husbands, only teach other young women how to submit to their husbands, and not hold ecclesiastical position.

953. 1 Tim 4:10.

954. See above, 1 Cor 15 and 1 Thess 4.

955. 2 Tim 2:16–18.

The Enemies of Paul in Corinth

is capable of confronting them successfully (i.e., as they did in Corinth). In contrast, the conflict between these infiltrators and adherent is fully engaged in 1 Timothy: "In later times some will depart from the faith by giving heed to deceitful spirits and doctrines of demons . . . who forbid marriage and enjoin abstinence from foods."[956] Clearly, this was a feature of late, well developed ascetic Gnosticism, as Eusebius states: "The so-called Encratites proceeding from Saturninus and Marcion [i.e., around 144 CE], preached against marriage, annulling the original creation of God, and tacitly condemning him who made male and female. They also introduce abstention from what they called 'animate' things in ingratitude to the God who has made all things, and they deny the salvation of the first created man."[957] Clearly, this is not the nascent opposition faced by Paul in Corinth, nor the libertine practices the opponents embraced to demonstrate the they were "already kings." James was dead and new leadership had developed.[958] Tertullian similarly describes the gnostic system that had developed under Saturninus.[959] What is even more striking is that the highly developed Gnosticism to which pseudepigraphical 1 Timothy refers came at a time when women were taking the prominent role in various sects, such as Valentinian Gnosticism.[960] As we have seen, 1 Timothy attempts to quiet women and diminish their role. Now it is obvious why, i.e., because women dominated contemporaneous gnostic sects in the mid-second century. Literature from this period confirmed that women were playing a more and more prominent role in many gnostic trajectories and its theology.[961] But, this is not the case in 2 Timothy. Paul references *two men* who are "upsetting the faith of some," there is no mention of women leading this effort. Indeed, Hymenaeus and Philetus use *logoi* of Jesus as the basis of the dispute, i.e., an elitist claim that the secret and hidden knowledge they obtain from the *logia* of Jesus merits immediate salvation, versus Paul's gospel of the cross, resurrection and *parousia*. Clearly, 2 Timothy has a claim to be a source for information on Timothy, and why Paul may be offering a defense on his behalf.

What then does 2 Timothy tell us? To begin, it is important to set the context of Paul comments and his appeal. Paul is in Rome about 63 CE, and certainly was in the city by early summer of 64 CE. On July 18 or 19 of that year, a cataclysmic fire started in the local vending shops near the Circus Maximum, "where it joins the Palatine and Caelian hills." The evening was a warm summer night and the flames moved rapidly, fanned by winds and the firestorm that was created, eventually burning three of the eleven sections of Rome. According to Tacitus (*Annals*), a Roman historian who was

---

956. 1 Tim 4:1–3.
957. Eusebius, *Ecclesiastical History*, 4:29.
958. Josephus, *Antiquities*, 20:9, likely 62 CE.
959. *Against Heresies*, book 1.
960. See, *Letter to Flora*, 4:11–13.
961. See the *Gospel of Phillip*, the *Gospel of Mary*, the *Dialogue of the Savior*, and, as noted above, the *Gospel of Thomas*.

nine years old when the fire broke out,[962] the conflagration lasted for five days, but other accounts say the fire was much worse, damaging as many as eight sections of the city and continued for six days and seven nights. Rumors quickly spread that Nero had intentionally set the fire to level sections of the city,[963] particularly around Palatine hill where the imperial palace lay. A destructive fire would allow for significant rebuilding, including an enormous new palace villa, which Nero did ultimately construct. The new palace, the Domus Aurea, included a huge bronze statue called the Colossus Neronis (over 30 meters high), and a man-made lake. Discontent arose quickly,[964] as thousands were displaced and the loss of life was enormous and from all social classes. But even Tacitus, who detested Nero, confirmed that the emperor was not in Rome when it burned. Nero was in Antium at his coastal resort where it was cool and safe, i.e., from similar fires that must have occurred.

Nero rushed to the city, opening up his own property and gardens to the displaced and financed provisions and food from his own wealth. Nonetheless, the disaster enraged the citizens as rumors spread that Nero sang as he watched Rome burn and that men with torches claimed they had been acting on orders. The emotions and protests grew, as did demands for justice. Nero recognized that quick action was necessary to prevent rioting. He learned of a Jewish sect that was so vile that even the local populace hated them.[965] By August or early September, Nero claimed that he had received confessions from "chrestians," and other members of this sect. Tacitus' report is as follows:

> Therefore, to quell the rumors, Nero falsely accused and executed with the most exquisite punishments on the most hated class called chrestians, who were infamous for their abominations.

It seems Tacitus hated only Nero more than Christians. Tacitus bluntly reports that the sect got its name from Christus, who was a Jew executed as a criminal in the "most extreme way" (i.e., he was crucified) under Pontius Pilatus, procurator of Judea. While he calls the sect of the chrestians "an evil superstition," and states that "chrestians" are vile and "deserved to made an example by the consequences of their crimes," eventually the horror of Nero's acts (e.g., lighting his gardens at night with the burning, oil covered crucified corpses of Christians) led the "people [to begin] to pity them."

With regard to Paul and the historicity of 2 Timothy, Tacitus makes a very interesting statement: "Arrest was made by all those who confessed." Generally, historians assume that these Christians were tortured in order to gain a confession, or

---

962. 55–117 CE.

963. *Annals*, XV.38.

964. *Annals* XV.44.

965. Although Josephus reports there were more that eight thousand Jews in Rome, *Antiquities* 2.80, there was obvious prejudice against them; also Juvinal's satire, Satire 14.96f., as there is ample evidence Jews were already held in low regard due to their rebellious nature, although they continued to tolerated by imperial Rome.

that the "confession" related to an admission of starting the fire. Instead, it is just as likely that well-known leaders of the "chrestians" in Rome were identified and arrested. Consequently, it is certain that Paul, one of the most controversial leaders of the "chrestians," would have been well known, particularly having been brought to Rome under escorted arrest. The original charges brought against him were seditious enough, i.e., having caused a riot in Jerusalem, not dissimilar to the events in Rome. Indeed, according to Acts,[966] Paul had been escorted to Rome after his appeal to Caesar on the orders of Porcius Festus, the Roman Procurator of Palestine.[967] Paul's appeal certainly would have marked him as a leader of that "rabble," and thus a troublemaker of the superstition of evildoers, sorcerers and magicians. Given the widely known tradition of Paul's execution in Rome, scholars have been puzzled by the ending in Acts, i.e., with Paul freely receiving visitors.[968] But the explanation is simple: Paul was transferred from house arrest to prison, and then condemned. Everyone in the Christian community knew what happened to Paul after the fire in Rome. Does Paul's known itinerary support this conclusion?

Acts reports that Paul remained in Rome for "two years, at his own expense, and welcomed all who came to him, preaching the kingdom of God and teaching about the Lord Jesus Christ quite openly and unhindered" after he arrived. Paul was under "house arrest" according to Acts,[969] allowed to live separately with the soldier to whom he was assigned by the Prefect of the Praetorian Guard. Acts is correct in reporting there was only one Prefect at this time, as usually there were two, but in 62 CE only one was named, Afrianis Burrus. This occurred during the late spring of 62 CE to the early summer of 64 CE. This type of prisoner arrangement was the most relaxed, as Paul enjoyed a tolerant guard (for visitors and guests just as reported). But by late July or early August 64 CE (*Augustus mensis*, or *sextilis mensis*), Paul is literally in "bonds" (*desmon*), meaning he his chained by feet or hands, or perhaps to a wall or to the guard's hand by a *halusi*. This means that Paul was held in the Praetorian prison or camp (depending on the extent of damage from the fire). It is also probable that Paul was still assigned to the same guard.

Would Paul have been in Rome, still under house arrest, when the devastating fire occurred? Paul arrived in Jerusalem for Pentecost in the late spring of 58 CE. He was arrested and kept for two years in Caesarea while he defended himself three times before Procurators Felix and then Festus. After his "appeal to Caesar," Paul leaves for Rome under the escort of a centurion named Julius in the late winter of 61 CE. While Paul warns Julius about travel in winter (this would have been October to early December), Julius ignores him and orders departure for Crete. They end up shipwrecked on Malta. Paul finally arrives in Rome in the late winter of 61 CE or early spring of

---

966. Acts 28:23–28.
967. Appointed under Nero, 58 to 62 CE.
968. Acts 28:23–31.
969. Acts 27:1.

62 CE. With the "two years" of house arrest reported in Acts, this would put Paul in Rome about the time of the fire. Thus, it is unlikely that Paul ever left Rome, but instead died under orders of Caesar.

Consequently, it is virtually certain that Paul was in Rome during the fire and died after being accused of and condemned for being a leader of the sect that instigated it. Just as Tacitus reports, Paul would freely admit he was a Christian. Yet, he was already an affirmed adherent and well known to the Romans, there was no need of confession. Since Paul was roughly contemporaneous with Jesus of Nazareth, he would have been in his early sixties at the time of the fire, by standards then an old man, a *presbytes* (a designation that Paul ascribes to himself in Philemon 9). Despite being an "old man," Paul was now a feared "evildoer" like Jesus the Nazarene and his "chrestians." Paul would die by the sword to protect his killers (the executioners and those who condemned Paul) from retribution as one of the untimely dead.[970] Paul confirms that he has been classified "an evil doer," *kakourgos*, which is a technical term, given to those charged with evil practices of dark magic, which in this case also included firing Rome. The word is commonly translated "criminal," but as we have seen repeatedly, we must resist benign interpretations, as Paul is deliberate, and richly, often vividly, chooses his words. It is clear that Paul had been condemned to die in this startling change of circumstances and is waiting for his execution date to be set, thus the urgency sending the letter. Since Paul appeals for Timothy's visit before winter, it is likely early September of 64 CE. It is difficult to be certain when Paul was beheaded, but what is certain is that it was swift, and clearly before summer of 65 CE.

All of these factors are coherent with the *sitz im leben* of 2 Timothy. Paul's situation is dire, matching these deadly circumstances and contradicting the reports in the pseudepigraphical Titus that he was released.[971] Indeed, Paul has accepted that

---

970. See Busse, *Jesus Resurrected*, 45, 57, a ritual sword.

971. Some scholars hold that Paul had made an appeal and escaped death in Rome by citing the following from the letter: "At my first defense no one took my part, all deserted me" (2 Tim 4:16). Yet, in context, Paul is talking about his experience in Ephesus, i.e., Timothy's location when Paul writes the letter. Consequently, Paul is warning Timothy to avoid Alexander the Coppersmith (see above), "who did me great harm . . . beware of him yourself, for he strongly opposed our message" (4:14a, 15). There is no precise identification of who this Alexander may be. He is obviously a tradesman, but it is unlikely he was a craftsman like Demetrius, who made small silver shrines or statuettes of Artemis, the patron goddess of Ephesus. Alexander was a Jew, and he would not have been involved in idol production for Artemis. However, some have pointed to Acts 19:32–34 and the riot following Paul's miracle in Ephesus: The assembly was in confusion: Some were shouting one thing, some another. Most of the people did not even know why they were there. The Jews pushed Alexander to the front, and some of the crowd shouted instructions to him. He motioned for silence in order to make a defense before the people. But when they realized he was a Jew, they all shouted in unison for about two hours: "Great is Artemis of the Ephesians." Obviously, as a Jewish leader, Alexander was associated with the Jewish troublemaker, Paul, and thus, was shouted down by the crowd. There is absolutely no reason why Alexander would make a defense on behalf of Paul, but he might make an appeal as a Jew to defend the local Jewish populace from rioting and retaliation. Paul's actions could have placed the Ephesian Jews at great risk. If so, this Alexander, a well-known and skilled craftsman, would have immediately become an aggressive opponent of Paul and the Way there, making every effort possible to

any final appeal to the judicial authorities would be futile: "I have fought the good fight, I have finished the course, I have kept the faith. Now there is laid out for me the righteousness crown, which the Lord will render to me, the righteous judge, at that day."[972] Paul is certain about his approaching execution, he says, "For I already being poured out, and the time of my departure has arrived."[973] He has not been tortured, for if he had he certainly would have mentioned it in his discussion of suffering as a "good soldier" of the Way. Only something as dramatic as the fire in Rome and the condemnation of "chrestians" accounts for Paul's uncompromising condemnation. It is clear that Paul could not even make an appeal, as he mentions nothing, but implies he was summarily condemned.[974]

The situation related to the desertion of Demas, Crescens and Titus, described by Paul bitterly in 2 Timothy, also reflects the events early in the officially sanctioned,[975] imperial persecution, that is, within sixty days of the great fire and Paul's arrest.[976] Paul is writing to Timothy reflecting on these events. It seems most probable that the timing of Paul's letter is well into the persecution with hundreds if not thousands already martyred, and with the day of his execution soon to be set. If so, the date of the letter could perhaps extend into late summer of 65 CE (still before the restrictions on winter travel). Either Nero or city officials may have been keeping Paul for a later execution as a spectacle with a planned and announced public execution date. The later timing of his death would help explain how Onesiphorus (a Latinized Greek name meaning "bringing advantage or benefit"), arriving from Ephesus, could have still "eagerly sought him out" and provided assistance without himself being captured and sentenced,[977] i.e., he would have arrived after most of the Christians had been captured.

A much later *Acts of Paul and Thecla* recounts how Paul preached in the house of Onesiphorus, but gives us no other helpful details. Historically valid is the conclusion that if visitors were not in Rome or associated with the fire, in all likelihood they could visit Paul without fear. In fact, the Roman historian Suetonius says nothing of a persecution after the fire,[978] but does talk about Christians being sporadically harassed by the local populace. Consequently, there is no evidence that the persecution extended beyond Rome, and the successful desertion of Demas, Crescens and Titus, indicates that suspected Christians were not tracked down. This conclusion would also make

---

put distance between the Jews and Paul's *ecclesia*. Consequently, it is clear that Paul cannot be referring to a first appeal in Rome or to a subsequent release.

972. 2 Tim 4:8.
973. 2 Tim 4:6.
974. See 2 Tim 1:8.
975. 2 Tim 4:9–10.
976. Only Luke remained, 2 Tim 4:11.
977. 2 Tim 1:16–17.
978. See 69–120 CE, *De Vita Caesarum*, Nero.

historical sense of Paul's request that Timothy come quickly and "bring Mark," i.e., that they could travel to be with Paul without fear. Again, as visitors, they could not be associated with the fire or be condemned.

As a result of the foregoing analysis, the *sitz im leben* of 2 Timothy provides a reliable context to explore Paul's view of Timothy, and perhaps shed light on why Paul must make a defense on his behalf to the Corinthians a decade earlier. In analyzing this situation, we look to Paul's comments to detect the issues facing Timothy. Closer examination of 2 Timothy demonstrates that Paul's appeal is not to convince Timothy to come at risk of his life, for he asks that Timothy also bring "Mark, for he is useful to me." Paul could never have put both Timothy and Mark at risk, nor would he ask for them to "bring the books and above all the parchments" if he believed they would be captured, tortured, imprisoned or killed. We know that this first imperially sanctioned persecution of *chrestians*, the *local* superstition that started the fire, demanded torture or coercion to obtain the names of any others who were in or near Rome. Thus, it is clear that the capture of *chrestians* was restricted to Rome and vicinity as noted. Without fearing a visit to Paul, it is Paul's imprisonment and death sentence that must have shaken Timothy to his core and left him in such severe doubt—Paul believes the dissonance related to his death will lead to Timothy's abandonment of the *euangelion* due to the delay of the *parousia*.

To confirm that the delay of the *parousia* had eroded Timothy's faith in the *euangelion*, we must look to Paul's appeal, particularly his introductory comments. And as has been demonstrated in each of the foregoing analyses of Thessalonians, Galatians and Corinthians, Paul's salutation always evidences the main issue and current situational crisis. In 2 Timothy Paul says: "Paul, an apostle of Christ Jesus, *according to the promise of life which is in Christ Jesus*, to Timothy, my *beloved* [*agapeto*] child."[979] The central issue of Paul's letter to Timothy is affirmation of the impending *parousia*, Paul's eschatological proclamation of the *euangelion* remains valid. Paul understands that his situation is an eschatological confirmation that the end of the age is near and the resurrection is not only assured but also that it is imminent. Timothy must not understand the times in any other way but reassurance that the Lord is near.[980] Paul extends his confidence in the impending events by adding his endearing term for Timothy, i.e., *agapeto*, "beloved." Paul stresses that nothing that is about to occur could possibly sever the relationship between them; in fact, for Paul, the coming events confirm their relationship and solidarity in the *euangelion* and resurrection that they have proclaimed in countless cities and towns over hundreds of miles in danger, peril, starving and also joy. Paul sees his death as the very reason to be assure in his Lord[981] and knows that soon, on "that day," he will receive his "crown of righteousness!"[982]

979. 2 Tim 1:1–2a.
980. 1 Thess 5:2.
981. 2 Tim 1:12.
982. 2 Tim 4:8.

Paul thereby identifies his death as an eschatological event of confirmation of the impeding *parousia*. As Paul expects the *parousia* in his lifetime, his untimely death is only further confirmation it is near, otherwise he would be alive to witness it. Thus, Paul's use of *pisits*[983] is not to be understood in any broad sense of doctrine or a "religion," or a comprehensive and developed high theology of Christianity (or as some scholars claim, evidence that 2 Timothy is pseudepigraphical). The "faith" to which Paul refers is the salvific *pistis* of his *euangelion*; the charismatic, powerful transformational *pistis* that unites Paul's adherent with the living Christ as an adopted child of God; God, whose divine action in destroying the curse of death via the cross, death, and resurrection of Jesus, engenders *elpis* and *agape*, as well as confirmatory *charismata* until the *parousia* and kingdom arrive.

Paul understands this salvific "faith" as the same that Timothy adopted and embraced, the same given to him by his mother, Eunice, and grandmother, Lois.[984] But now Timothy may abandon *pistis* and *elpis*, and the efficacious *agape* of God. Timothy is in perilous danger of remaining under the curse of death. This suggests that Timothy has reverted to a life of rebellion, abandoned morality and had become a libertine like Paul's opponents. Timothy, Paul's closest associate and own "child" has abandoned Paul's *euangelion* of *pistis*. Paul says, "For God did not give us a *spirit of timidity*, but a *power of love* and self control."[985] The word Paul uses for "timidity," *deilias*, can also be translated "fear," but more severely as "cowardice." Paul may be saying, "God did not provide us a *pneuma* of cowardice." He then offsets the "spirit of cowardice" (i.e., that *deilias* is a condition of weakness, or spirit, *pnuema*, not from God but inspired by God's enemy), with the power, *dynameos*, of "love," *agape*, i.e., the "more excellent Way," and then adds, "and power of self-control." The power of *agape* engenders the *dynameos* of "self control," or better "sound mind," because the *more excellent Way* "does not seek its own way,"[986] i.e., like that of Paul's opponents, the *pneumatikoi* libertines. Timothy also has abandoned *elpis* in the *parousia*, and with it *agape* and has become, or is in the process of becoming a libertine. Paul demands: "So shun from youthful passions and aim at righteousness, faith, love and peace, along with those who call on the name of the Lord from a pure heart."[987] What Demas, and Crescens and Titus have done, i.e., literally fled Rome in terror after the great fire and Paul's arrest, abandoning him in a crisis a fear and disillusionment, Timothy also has done "in tears."[988] That Timothy was with Paul in Rome is certain but he has left and abandoned Paul's *euangelion*.[989]

983. 2 Tim 1:5.
984. 2 Tim 1:5.
985. 2 Tim 1:7.
986. 1 Cor 13:5.
987. 2 Tim 2:22.
988. 2 Tim 1:4a.
989. See Phlm 1.

Did Paul send Timothy away to protect him from arrest and possible execution? Certainly, this would be one explanation why Timothy *shed tears*, but the evidence in the letter speaks emphatically against this. Other commentators assumed that the "tears" were shed over the news that Paul had been condemned to die when it reached Timothy in Ephesus. The evidence in the letter also speaks against this. It appears that Timothy left Paul in Rome personally shattered, disconsolate and in confusion; doubting all that he had witnessed and believed about the last days: "Think over what I have said, for the Lord will grant you understanding in everything."[990] Paul confirms this when he says: "Do not be ashamed then of testifying to our Lord, nor of me his prisoner, but share in the suffering of the gospel in the power of God."[991] Paul's disappointment and hope is that he can appeal to Timothy, and that he is still in communication with the *ecclesia* in Ephesus, for in his conclusion he asks Timothy to greet Prisca and Aquila,[992] the companion of both Paul and Timothy while in Corinth. Paul betrays a naïveté, or perhaps a simple hope, that Timothy has not been lost to the libertines. His pleas to Timothy express this hope in multiple references to his confidence in the pending promise of life and "day" of the Lord:[993] Indeed, what is being witnessed is precisely what is to be expected in the last days and struggle between God and Satan: "I have fought the good fight. I have finished the race. I have kept the faith. Henceforth there is laid up for the crown of righteousness, which the Lord, the righteous judge, will award me on the day, but also to all who have loved his appearing."[994]

Timothy's abandonment of Paul in Rome, his denial of the impending *parousia* and return of the Lord, and radical shift to libertine behavior tell us much about Paul's defense in 1 Cor 16:10–11. First, Timothy was a radical itinerant activist and charismatic zealot of the Way who, like Paul, left all and proclaimed the *euangelion* of the cross and the *parousia*. "There is no one like him," Paul stated.[995] He suffered persecution, hunger, beatings and imprisonment like Paul. But more, he defended Paul repeatedly, and was the coauthor of at least some of the letters that make up 2 Corinthians, as well as Philippians and 1 Thessalonians—all letters of conflict and crisis. Timothy was inexorably linked with Paul and his conflicts, as well as with his *charismata*, revelations, exorcisms, and possessions. He witnessed demonic attacks, and satanic opposition. But more, Timothy must have also carried out these practices under Paul's authority.

With the events in Rome and Paul's pending execution, Timothy was radically disenfranchised. The dissonance was clearly shattering. He, of all Paul's "fellow-workers" had abandoned the *euangelion*. This would suggest the Timothy was not timid

---

990. 2 Tim 2:7.
991. 2 Tim 1:8.
992. 2 Tim 4:19.
993. 2 Tim 1:1, 10; 2:8, 10, 11–13; 4:1, 8, 18.
994. 2 Tim 4:7.
995. Phil 2:19–23.

and quiet as often suggested, but was aggressive and volatile. Paul says, "Put him at ease among you."[996] Paul is warning both his adherents and the infiltrators to be cautions, not to raise Timothy's anger, leading him to respond with charismatic acts he has in his power, including death curses and judgments, all as Paul's personal apostolic representative. Paul knows that his letter with reach Corinth before Timothy, and Paul is anything but hesitant about cursing and judging enemies that are disrupting and abandoning the *euangelion*. Indeed, the name Timothy could have been feared. Paul mentions Timothy's soon arrival as a dire warning. We know that Timothy went to Corinth immediately, aware of the significant opposition and turmoil that was waiting for him.[997] It is impossible to assume that Paul sent Timothy before he received the full report from Chloe's people, so Timothy must have been fully informed and armed with all charismatic authority and instructed by Paul about what he is to do first: "He will remind you of my Way of life in Christ Jesus, which agrees with what I teach everywhere in every church."[998] Thus, Paul has provided clear direction to Timothy about the infiltrators and their reliance on *gnosis*, and that they have turned from "the more excellent Way" when he says: "[Timothy] will remind you of my way of life in Christ Jesus," i.e., the life of power and *agape* in the expectation of the arrival of the risen Lord soon to come with the *parousia* and deliver the kingdom of God.[999]

Apollos

Risk analysis of Apollos, the Alexandrian Jew who became a follower of the Way, is first set in the context of perilous risk. In other words, is there evidence that Paul was forced to neutralize competing risks from Apollos, or vice versa? With regard to context, according to Acts,[1000] Apollos had a broad knowledge of "scripture" (i.e., the Torah, oral and written, and Prophets), but knew only about the baptism of John.[1001] He "accurately preached" the Way of Jesus in Ephesus, but had not received the baptism into Jesus as the Messiah. It was Aquila and Prisca who invited Apollos to their house when they heard his eloquent speaking and "more correctly explained the Way of God." There has been speculation that Apollos is the source of the reliance on the *logia* of Jesus among Paul's opponents since the allegorical interpretation of Scripture (e.g., Philo), as well as "higher torah" and wisdom, has roots in Alexandria. Yet, there is no indication that Paul objects to his teaching or tries to restrict Apollos' interaction with the Corinthians. In fact, Paul says, "As for our brother Apollos, I strongly

---

996. 1 Cor 16:10a.

997. 2 Tim 4:17.

998. 1 Cor 4:17b.

999. Paul knew he was not making Timothy's arrival any easier, that is, by challenging the opponents' claim to already be kings and having achieved salvation.

1000. Acts 18:26.

1001. Patterson, "Apollos," in *Lost Way*, 227–29.

urged him to visit you with our brethren, but is was not his will to come now."[1002] Acts portrays Apollos as an important part of the success in Corinth:

> And when he wished to cross to Achaia, the brethren encouraged him, and wrote to the disciples to receive him. When he arrived he greatly helped those who by grace believed, for he powerfully confuted the Jews in public, showing by the scriptures that *the Christ* was Jesus.[1003]

Consequently, the context speaks against a risk conflict between Apollos and Paul. Apollos was committed to the *euangelion* of Paul, i.e., the *euangelion* of Jesus Christ.

More specific information comes directly from Paul. He describes Apollos as an important teacher who supplemented his efforts in Corinth. Paul "planted" the "seed" of the *euangelion*,[1004] clearly an allusion to a saying of Jesus.[1005] As noted, a similar saying is found in the *Gospel of Thomas*,[1006] which may have been part of the infiltrators' *logia* collection. But Paul does not follow the context of the saying in Thomas, and instead says, "He [Apollos] watered." So, it is unlikely that Paul is associating the saying with Apollos. Instead, he alters it intentionally to separate both he *and* Apollos from *sophia-gnosis*. As such, Paul confirms that the *euangelion* of both he and Apollos were one and the same. Paul credits the success of both men to the power of God: "but God gave the increase."[1007]

Eschatological Relationships and *Agape*

As Paul closes his letter, the change in tone is almost startling. It is as if he has decided abruptly to end the letter and send it on its way, which has been dictated to Sosthenes.[1008] Paul had finished answering all of the questions sent to him by Chloe's people and communicated a warning that Timothy is coming. As a result, Paul concludes the main body of his letter by providing a *paraenesis*, an exhortation, in this case to admonish and encourage the adherents to maintain their *pistis* in the face of conflict and opposition. Paul says to them: "Be watchful, stand firm in your faith, be courageous, be strong. Let all that you are doing be done in *agape*."[1009] Paul's directive, "be courageous," *andrizesthe*, actually translates as "play the man."

1002. 1 Cor 16:12.
1003. Acts 18:27–28.
1004. 1 Cor 3:6.
1005. Luke 8:1–15.
1006. *Gos. Thom.*, Saying 9.
1007. 1 Cor 3:6.
1008. Sosthenes is cited as the coauthor of the letter in 1 Cor 1:1; that Paul did not write the main body of the letter himself is indicated by his statement, "I, Paul, write this salutation with my own hand," 1 Cor 16:21.
1009 1 Cor 16:13.

Paul's use of *andrizesthe* is interesting. This word appears in the Apostolic Fathers (recorded by Eusebius), in the *Martrydom of Polycarp*, ch. 9. Polycarp, bishop of Smyrna in the second century, is captured and condemned to death under a local Roman persecution during the rule of the Stoic emperor Marcus Aurelius (166–167 CE). A description is given as Polycarp[1010] enters the arena to be examined before being executed under the Roman persecution: "Now when Polycarp entered into the arena there came a voice from heaven: 'Be strong, Polycarp, and play the man [the same word used by Paul].' No one of our people saw the speaker, but those present heard the voice" (9:1–3). This clearly demonstrates that the word *andrizesthe* was used in martyrdom literature and language as much as one hundred years after Paul's letter to the Corinthians.

While it is speculative to assign the report in *Marytrdom* to the influence of Paul's letter, what is certain is that the pattern of the admonition was well known and popular, i.e., it was used to engender a state of courage and personal strength in the face of crisis, even a crisis facing death. Paul has employed it here in a new combination, i.e., *agape* and *andrizesthe*, that risking death for the *euangelion* and *agape* is the commitment of his adherents, not simply to be diligently watchful in a crisis. Consequently, Paul's *paraenesis* must have been a colloquialism in the first century, as it is the only instance of its use in the entire New Testament. Given this, Paul is doing something quite interesting. He is blending a popular admonition with the command to love: "Let all that you do be done in love [*agape*]." For Paul, both the fundamental and driving factor that can engender confidence in the face of any perilous risk crisis is efficacious divine *agape*. Paul argued in both his letters to the Corinthians and Romans that the "more excellent Way" of *agape* is stronger than even death. It is the power of God, and so is imperishable. As such, God acknowledges the adherent who embraces *agape* with *pistis* and *elpis*. *Agape* is for Paul the ultimate *paraenesis*, as it embraces the full scope of who the *tekna tou Theou* are as the age comes to an end. Indeed, all of the *paraenesis* underscores the eschatological stress of the impending changes that are soon to arrive. For Paul to admonish the adherents to "Be watchful, stand firm in your faith, be the man, be strong" is to remind them of the perilously close end of the age, surely something Paul expects them to witness during their lifetime. And so, we find in this short *paraenesis* the essence of Paul's expectation of the imminent events about to unfold, and the powerful assurance that they have been given and must share, divine love, *agape*, no matter the risk.

It is the practice of *agape* that is the unequivocal evidence that the adherent has embraced the *eschatos*, and in *pistis* embraces the salvific *euangelion*, which is the *sophia* of God. Paul encapsulates the power of *agape* and its unshakable power most notably in 1 Corinthians and Romans. In describing the "more excellent Way," Paul summarizes the characteristics of *agape* that evidences a bond with Abba' that is unbreakable: "Love

---

1010. 69–153 CE, and a disciple of the Apostle John.

bears all things, believes all things, hopes all things, and endures all things. Love never ends."[1011] Paul also echoes this more fully in his letter to the Romans:

> Who shall separate us from the love of Christ? Shall tribulation, or distress or persecution, or famine, or nakedness, or peril, or sword? As it is written, "For thy sake we are being killed all the day long; we are regarded as sheep to be slaughtered." For I am sure that neither death, nor life . . . nor anything else in all creation, will be able to separate us from the love of God in Christ Jesus our Lord.[1012]

Paul's *paraenesis* that "let all that you do be done in *agape*," can also be translated, "All things of you let be in *agape*." It is more than the doing of things, it is the absorption of *agape* as the new source of thinking, being and action, and thus, being united with Jesus Christ and God the Father. It is only this radical divine *agape* that binds one directly into an adoptive, eternal relationship with God. While seemingly more awkward, this second translation more accurately captures the permeation of love that fills the entire being, and reflects Paul's intent.

Stephanas, Titius Justus

In his concluding remarks, Paul provides guidance on the treatment of the "house of Stephanas," and the "coming of Fortunatus and Achaicus."[1013] There are several rather remarkable issues in this short passage that require detailed analysis. First, Paul's motivation for his comments concerning for the house of Stephanas must be carefully explored, for he calls for the Corinthian adherents to be subject (*upotassesthe*) to him and his house: "I urge you to be subject to such men and to every fellow worker and laborer," because "they have devoted themselves to the service of the holy ones [the saints]." Second, Stephanas is mentioned as the one to whom the Corinthians adherents are to be subject. Why? Third, what happened to Stephanas? In Romans[1014] it is Gaius in whose home Paul is residing. More, why in Romans or in Acts is Stephanas never mentioned, but both do refer to Titius Justus, the God-fearer whose house was adjacent the synagogue of Corinth where Paul meets and lives?

In 1 Cor 1:16, Paul mentions Stephanas in passing, and that he, Paul, baptized him. In this early portion of his letter, it is clear that Paul is dictating to Sosthenes when he states, "I am thankful that I baptized none of you except Crispus and Gaius, lest anyone should say that they were baptized in my name," because he suddenly recalls that he forgot to mention Stephanas. Paul immediately corrects himself, as if in an afterthought, "I did baptize also the household of Stephanas." This correction clearly shows that at this

---

1011. 1 Cor 13:7–8a.
1012. Rom 8:35–36, 39.
1013. See 1 Cor 1:15–18.
1014. See Rom 16:23.

point in his letter Paul was dictating, whereas in other portions of his letter, Paul has carefully prepared his dictation[1015] particularly in response to the questions brought to him by Chloe's people. So who was this Stephanas?

Paul confirms that Stephanas was baptized as one of the first adherents in Corinth, i.e., as Paul calls Stephanas, the *aparke*, the "firstfruits" of Achaia, i.e., the Roman province whose capital was Corinth. Paul obviously practiced baptism early in his itinerant missionary work in each city, as he was the only one available to do so. Later, as we know from 1 Corinthians, others did baptize—Kayfa and Apollos. Stephanas in never mentioned in Acts,[1016] only Crispus, the ruler of the synagogue, and the God-fearer who became Paul's benefactor, Titius Justus (Acts 18:7, the owner of the home adjacent to the synagogue in Corinth from which Paul was expelled). Chloe is also not mentioned. Despite the absence of references to Stephanas in Acts and Romans, Paul's comments in 1 Corinthians confirm he is known to the adherents, and more, that they are to "submit" to him.

Why would Paul call on the Corinthians to "submit" to the house of Stephanas? What "service" could Stephanas have provided that would have led Paul to call for submission? The most plausible explanation is drawn from the first-century examples of Roman benefactors. As noted, when a benefactor provided substantial financial support and "backing" to a local temple, then he or she was afforded certain rights and respect from the adherents, including respect and "submission" as a responsibility. Roman benefactors had statues erected in their honor in the temples, or could have their names inscribed on the temple itself—of course that right and honor was not afforded to early benefactors of the Way since the world as it was known was soon to change dramatically and so no statues or inscriptions were needed. So what type of "submission" would be expected?

In Roman society, patronage was a well-established and honored ritual with specific expectations and traditions. There was private and public patronage. Public patronage (most likely what Paul is referring to in his letter) was usually associated with a very wealthy individual, either a man or women, particularly in the case of widows who could manage their own wealth. The patron provided financial support *and security* to a group, such as an *ecclesia* or trade association, or could finance the construction of a building (such as a temple) or sponsor a religious association. There could also be some form of manumission for certain lower-class slaves and members of an association purchased by the patron, which created a *patronus* and *libertus* relationship. This certainly could have been the case in Corinthian *ecclesia*. Paul's instructions to Philemon indicate that a request for manumission should be without cost, but not without obligation to work for or serve the patron. The patron could protect the individual from lawsuits, judicial actions, even prosecution, or provide food and financial sustenance to maintain the well being of an individual or a social

---

1015. See 1 Cor 13–14.
1016. Acts 18:1–18.

or religious community. Patronage could also entail a financial commitment to the succeeding generations of a family. In most cases, the patron was respected through service and support, including social and political support. The grateful response of those benefited often led to expressions of gratitude and respect in public places, such as in the market or state *agora*.

Paul's description of Stephanas would seem to identify him as a patron of the Corinthian *ecclesia*. However, the description Paul provides about his "service to the saints" coupled with his demand that adherents "submit," suggests that Stephanas purchased the freedom of slaves, i.e., the *liberti*, who have since abandoned their obligations to Stephanas given the immanent *parousia*, or have been influence to do so by the infiltrators. Paul's admonition to the Thessalonians to continue their work and self-support despite the immediacy of the impending end of the age is reminiscent of this crisis.[1017] In both cases, the norms of support were being relaxed creating risk and dissonance within the *ecclesia* that could threaten its survival. Paul demands that those receiving the benefits of patronage must reciprocate with *agape*, just as Stephanas' patronage, likely centered in manumission, was exorcised in *agape*. Paul's *ecclesiae* were a complex experiment in radical *agape*, where all was new, transformative, challenging, urgent, and yet demandingly introspective about what must change with *agape*, underscoring how social norms collided with the *parousia* and coming the kingdom of God. Of note, Paul's call to recognize the *agape*-patronage relationship demonstrates that when Paul writes 1 Corinthian in the early 50s CE, there were no ecclesiastical offices or hierarchy, e.g., as deacon (*diakonos*) or elder (*presbuteros*), the ecclesiastical offices that are described in the pseudepigraphical 1 Timothy.

What happened to Stephanas? He is not mentioned in Acts or Paul in his letter to the Romans. Romans, if written from Corinth where Stephanas is portrayed as a patron, makes his absence even more puzzling. However, this dilemma may be related to Paul's greeting in the letter. He mentions Gaius, "who is host to me and the whole church."[1018] Paul's association with Gaius raises another explanation. Recall that when Paul (according to Acts) first arrived in Corinth, he was expelled from the synagogue and lived with Titius Justus whose house was adjacent to it. It is likely that in this house Paul first gathered the adherents, forming the first *ecclesia*. If Paul lived with Titius Justus, his host, why less than two to three years later does Paul identify Gaius as "his host?" More, if Stephanas was a patron to whom the Corinthian adherents were to be subject,[1019] why does Paul say that Gaius is "host of me and the whole church"[1020] as if Gaius is now their patron? If Gaius is Paul's "host" and Gaius is also patron of the Corinthian adherents, is it possible that Gaius, Titius Justus and Stephanas are one in the same person?

1017. 1 Thess 4:11.
1018. Rom 16:23.
1019. 1 Cor 16:15.
1020. 1 Cor 16:23.

In 1 Cor 1:16, Paul explicitly mentions that he baptized Gaius and separately recalls (as an afterthought) that he *also* baptized "the *household* of Stephanas." It would appear that these are two different individuals, *except* that Paul makes an interesting distinction—while he immediately cites the baptism of Gaius, he then remembers also baptizing the "household" (*oikon*) of Stephanas. In a careful reading of this section of the letter, Paul recalls this event as if he uses an intimate name for a beloved friend and brother—a given nickname if you will. Indeed, the name Stephanas means "crowned," possibly a special name given to Gaius by Paul for his services and his reward to come at the *parousia*. Paul remembers the man Gaius, but then the household of beloved friend and patron whom he lovingly renames, Stephanas. Paul often describes the crown, the athlete's victory symbol, as the goal for which to strive and the award he has obtained for his faith as he faces his impending death.[1021] As such, Paul gives Gaius the name as an honor, signifying achieving his prize to come for the *agape* and support of the Way, i.e., that the name Stephanas was an agnomen (a Roman nickname) of Gaius. There are examples of this in early writings: James *the Just*,[1022] Kayfa for Simeon (used by Paul), *Boanerges* (i.e., the "Sons of Thunder"), for James and John (given by Jesus). These are just a few examples and represent a practice that began with Jesus and his exorcists.[1023]

Consequently, it is likely that Gaius and Stephanas are the same person. There is also a more practical reason for the giving of an agnomen in early Roman society. It was given when there were many in a family or an assembly or trade association with the same name. Gaius was a common name. Indeed, there were four individuals named Gaius associated with Paul or the Apostle John. Gaius of Macedonia was a traveling companion of Paul,[1024] and Gaius of Derbe accompanied him on his third missionary journey[1025] along with Sopater of Borea (who is mentioned with Paul in his letter to the Romans). There was also a Gaius who John calls "Gaius the beloved." Lastly, there is Gaius whom Paul baptized in Corinth and also joins Paul in sending his greetings to the Roman *ecclesia* who is Paul's host.[1026] This Gaius was neither Gaius of Derbe nor Gaius of Macedonia who accompanied Paul to Ephesus. Because both men may have with Paul in Corinth, Paul must have employed an *agnomen* for his host and patron, Gaius by renaming him Stephanas. Thus, there is little doubt that Stephanas and Gaius are the same individual, and that Stephanas was the "nickname," or better the "*ecclesia* name" given to him by Paul. Since Gaius is also Paul's host, we must also assume that Titius Justus, Paul's host, are also one and the same person. Taking this a step further, it is possible that Gaius and Titius Justus is the same individual, i.e., Gaius

---

1021. 2 Tim 4:7.
1022. Assigned to James by libertine or gnostic Christians, see the *Gos. Thom.*, Saying 12.
1023. See Busse, *Jesus Resurrected*, 112–13.
1024. Acts 19:29.
1025. Acts 20:4.
1026. Rom 16:23.

The Enemies of Paul: Demons, Satan, Betrayers, and Apostles

Titius Justus, his Roman *praenomen*, *nomen*, and *cognomen*. This would explain why Stephanas, the loving patron, is not mentioned in Acts or Romans, and why Paul is staying with Gaius, i.e., Titius Justus, his original host in Corinth.

Fortunatus and Achaichus

Paul also mentions two other men in a risk context, i.e., that they have "refreshed" the *pnuema* of both Paul and the *ecclesia*.[1027] Fortunatus and Achaichus have done more than provide a report; they have exorcised charismatic powers. What were these powers?

To begin, Paul underscores their importance. Fortunatus and Achaicus are also to receive "recognition" from the Corinthian adherents. Little is known of these two, but what is certain is that they are from Corinth, are companions of Stephanas, and are returning with Paul's letter to the *ecclesia* at Corinth. Fortunatus is a Roman proper name turned to Greek form. A man named Fortunatus is mentioned at the end of the letter ascribed to Clement, an early leader of the Roman *ecclesia*. Clement is writing to the *ecclesia* in Corinth about their expulsion of church leaders, a familiar theme for this dynamic assembly. Paul's woes and the difficulties with the Corinthian *ecclesia* seemed to have continued for decades after his death. Clement is a pseudepigraphical writing attributed to Clement of Rome, who is believed to be the former fellow-worker with Paul[1028] and later the leader of the Roman *ecclesia* at the beginning of the persecution by Domitian in 95 or 96 CE. Internal evidence would seem to support a pre-second-century date, as the persecution of Nero is over and there is nothing in the letter that would indicate it should be dated to the *sitz im leben* facing the church in the mid- to late second century. Consequently, Clement is commonly dated to about 96 CE. We learn nothing else about Fortunatus other than he is elderly and residing in Corinth. Hippolytus of Rome[1029] records the church tradition about the seventy apostles sent out by Jesus (*The Seventy Apostles of Christ*, all related to the tradition recorded in Luke),[1030] and actually provides their names, including that of Fortunatus. There is also the legend associated with Justus, a follower of Paul,[1031] who was shipwrecked on the way to Rome. While in southern Italy in Salento near Lecce, Justus baptized Orontius and his nephew, Fortunatus (found in twelfth-century church document). They became leaders in the church there and were eventually martyred under Nero for not giving oblation to the divinity of Caesar. Unfortunately, this is a late tradition and little more is learned. Finally, there was the tradition regarding Hermagoras and Fortunatus who were reported to

---

1027. Acts 16:17.

1028. See Phil 4:3.

1029. 179–226 CE, a follower of Irenaeus, who was a disciple of Polycarp, who was a disciple of the Apostle John.

1030. Luke 10:1–20.

1031. Acts 18:7

have died also during or immediately after the persecution of Nero. Tradition has Hermagoras chosen by Mark to become the evangelist and leader of a church in northern Italy, Aquileia. Hermagoras selected Fortunatus as his deacon. However, this tradition can only be traced to the eighth century and has no foundation or substance for and understanding of the Corinthian Fortunatus.

What is known is that Fortunatus was from Corinth and travelled with Stephanas to see Paul, and that Paul stated that he deserved the respect of the adherents for services provided. Stephanas and Achaicus "supplied what was lacking from you." This could imply that the three men brought financial support to Paul during his stay, or that they brought a donation for Paul to carry to the *ecclesia* in Jerusalem. This may be the better of the two possibilities since Paul was asking the Corinthian adherents to begin their collection for his trip to Jerusalem, and never asked them for any kind of support.[1032] Unfortunately, this solution is made unlikely since Paul also adds, "For they have refreshed [*anepausan*, 'set at ease'] my spirit and yours."[1033] It is clear that Paul is referencing an important charismatic power they employ for the *ecclesia* and Paul. To "refresh the *pnuema*" suggests that Fortunatus and Achaicus were *propheteia*. Paul admonishes the *ecclesia* that they are to be recognized, or acknowledged (*epiginoskete*), for their *charisma*. Since there is no direct reference to monetary support (nor has Paul expected or asked for such), and Paul had already addressed the donation to the offering for Jerusalem,[1034] these men must be considered guardians of the *euangelion* for the benefit of the *ecclesia* and *agape*, applying Scripture, *logia* and new sayings of the Lord to build up the *pnuema*. Since they "refreshed" both Paul and his adherents' *pnuema*, they provided insight and understanding about Paul's *sitz im leben* and that of Corinth given the present crisis, assisting Paul during the conflict with the infiltrators.

The Holy Kiss

Paul now provides his final thoughts to the *ecclesia* at Corinth. He dictates a touching ending to this remarkable and complex letter by sending greetings on behalf of others he loves, but then poignantly adds his instructions as to how the adherents are greet each other with *agape*, the *philemati agio*, the "holy kiss."[1035] Paul is not content to simply share warm greetings from those with him (greetings are extended at a distance and by words to the Corinthians from Ephesus), but includes a *paraenesis* that is striking in its historical setting.

Paul knows that the most personal of greetings, a kiss, demands direct contact with others in the *pistis* of Jesus Christ regardless of status, position or gender. The kiss transforms social standards and becomes a democratizing event in the assembly

---

1032. 2 Cor 11:7.
1033. 1 Cor 16:18.
1034. 1 Cor 16:1–4.
1035. 1 Cor 16:20; Rom 16:16.

of the last days. In the contemporary historical context, the kiss was often shared among friends of the same social class and standing, but rarely as a common act of acknowledgment and *agape* across social or gender barriers. For example, in Palestinian Judaism the Pharisee males greeted each other and their dinner guests with a kiss.[1036] There are contemporary examples as well, the most notorious of which is the kiss that the betrayer Judas gave to Jesus in the Garden of Gethsemane to infect Jesus with a disabling curse, allowing the temple soldiers and mob to take Jesus safely by force.[1037] For Paul, the *philemati agio*, "holy kiss," provides efficacious protection, the opposite of a curse, much more than a blessing. In Palestine, the kiss was given by placing the right hand on the left should and then a kiss was given to the left cheek. But regardless of how the kiss was given, it carried charismatic powers of divine *agape*, and so protection from evil, demonic and satanic powers.

Those in Asia

Paul sends greetings on behalf of the "churches of Asia" and his dearest friends and coworkers, Aquila and Prisca. With regard to the *ecclesia* of Asia, Paul is referencing the western Roman province of Asia, which included some of the *ecclesiae* he had visited or established. Paul is referring to unaffiliated, decentralized *house churches*, such as that in the home of Prisca and Aquila. The establishment of these simple house churches facilitated the rapid expansion of early Christianity via the effort of itinerant *apostoloi*, such as Paul, as well as adherents of the Way, whether merchants, artisans, sailors, or even soldiers, i.e., those who took with them the *euangelion* to the far reaches of the empire, including the *poleis*, villages and towns of Asia Minor. Paul's "churches of Asia" is likely a collection of a dozen or less house churches.

Prisca and Aquila

Much has already been said about the close relationship Paul had developed with his good friends and fellow leatherworkers, Prisca and Aquila. Paul had met them in Corinth (Acts 18:3) after they had been expelled from Rome after the edict of Claudius (49 CE). They may have been some of the first converts in Rome. It does not appear that Paul brought them to the faith. They had come to Corinth had set up shop as leather workers and tentmakers, their portable trade. As noted, leatherworking and tent making were in high demand in Corinth. This demand came from many healthy economic sectors of the local and merchant economy in Corinth, as well as the shipment of leather and Cilician goat hair tents for export from the dual ports surrounding Corinth. Demand was also bolstered by the reemergence of Corinthian

---

1036. See Luke 7:45; while Jesus was invited to dinner and entered the home of a Pharisee, he was not given the customary kiss: "For you did not give me a kiss."

1037. Matt 28:9, see Busse, *Jesus*, 45.

games (the Isthmian game, 50–60 CE), where temporary housing (tents and shelters), as well as normal trade needs (awnings, military tents and supplies), were required. Paul, as was his customary practice, sought out fellow tradesmen, and since Aquila and Prisca were Jews, Paul joined with them and worked "night and day" to support himself. They became his closest fellow workers and followed Paul to Ephesus, where they opened their home as an *ecclesia* and helped in the success there of which Paul speaks. After Paul left Ephesus, Prisca and Aquila eventually returned to Rome,[1038] as Paul sends his greeting to them there.

Paul credits them with saving his life.[1039] His endearment for them is revealed in his letters. Prisca is also known as Priscilla. This is the diminutive form of her name, i.e., an endearing and more intimate form, and is used by Paul in his final letter and greeting to her. Prisca and Aquila are never mentioned apart, and remain the most identifiable early Christian couple and coworkers. It is important that Paul mentions Prisca first, as it is Paul's intent to show the equality of all adherents "neither male nor female" in the Way, and also shows his respect and love for her. It is with these two dear friends, who witnessed the powerful *charismata*, exorcisms and Paul's interaction with the risen Lord.[1040] Paul includes them in his greeting to the Corinthian adherents, indicating they were well known and respected.

Sosthenes and Paul's Signature

Paul then provides his personal signature to the letter: "I, Paul, write this greeting with my own hand."[1041] The signature and greeting confirm the letter to be authentic and authoritative. This, of course, also shows that the letter was dictated, likely to Sosthenes, the former ruler of the Corinthian synagogue. It appears that Sosthenes was Paul's *amanuensis*, a term originally applied a Roman freedman who served a master as a personal secretary, but here applied to Sosthenes as a voluntary servant and scribe for Paul. Sosthenes is not treated as coauthor, such as Timothy and Silas in 1 Thessalonians, i.e., where Paul continually uses the first person plural, "we give thanks." Paul adds his own personal signature. In Gal 6:11, Paul's acknowledges that his handwriting is very large, perhaps indicating that the long years of his trade and accompanying arthritis have made it difficult to use his hands, forcing him to write in large letters.

Paul's Curse on Enemies

Then abruptly, Paul adds a deadly curse to the letter; indeed, the strongest curse and pronouncement that could be brought against any enemy in the ancient world: "If

---

1038. Rom 16:3.
1039. When he escapes Ephesus after the riot of Demetrius the silversmith, Acts 19:24–29.
1040. Apollos, Acts 18:26.
1041. 1 Cor 16:24.

anyone has no love for the Lord Jesus Christ, let him be cursed! Lord Come!"[1042] Paul's curse is directed at the infiltrators. In Galatians, Paul adds a similar curse to the beginning of his letter: "As we have said before and now I say again, if anyone is preaching to you a *euangelion* contrary to that which you received, let him be cursed." The curse is deadly. Paul in essence casts the darkest of curses on his enemies, i.e., let any enemy be cursed [infected] with death, and so, be completely and totally annihilated and separated from God.[1043] In Judaism, the individual so cursed was severed, excluded from the Jewish nation and the promise of salvation, and separated from God and the Torah. From 1 Corinthians, we know that the infiltrators had literally cursed the name of Jesus. Paul's concluding words therefore are a curse of death.[1044]

Paul uses *phelei* for "love" in his curse, "those who do not *love* the Lord," which is the only instance of its use in all of Paul's undisputed writings. Phileo is love that is warm, personal, having great affection for Jesus Christ, something the infiltrators reject. Indeed, the Johannine tradition includes the juxtaposition of *agape* and *pheleo* in the discussion between Jesus and Kayfa in an appearance by the lake of Galilee.[1045] In fact, the Gospel of John uses *pheleo* ten times, more than any other New Testament tradition or letter. The most striking example is John 5:20: "For the Father loves [*phelie*] the Son, and shows him all things that he himself is doing; and the Father will show him greater works than these, so that you will marvel." This saying, like Paul's, stresses the kind of love and affection that only the adherents demonstrate toward Paul and Christ.

Paul then adds, *Maran atha*, the Aramaic cry, "O Lord Come!" Paul is using the efficacious and early Christian Aramaic plea to call upon the Lord (who hears this cry!) to return now and bring judgment on all enemies, making effective his curse. It is a dire warning, affirming the Lord to come. Paul's use of *Maran atha* is an eschatological cry to the risen Lord; it is powerful, sobering, even frightening, and for the infiltrators, creates terrible perilous risk that cannot be mitigated. Paul brings forth and makes present the *eschatological crisis facing the opponents with his own cry of awakening*—"Lord, come!"

Paul's Blessing on Adherents of the Way

Paul then addresses adherents and bestows an efficacious blessing on them: "The grace of our Lord Jesus Christ be with you."[1046] This is the blessing that Paul provides

---

1042. 1 Cor 16:22.
1043. Gal 1:8.
1044. Even in 1 Cor 13:5–10.
1045. John 21:15–17.
1046. 1 Cor 16:23.

in Romans,[1047] 2 Corinthians,[1048] 1 Thessalonians,[1049] and Galatians;[1050] i.e., the blessing he provides in all of his undisputed letters. Paul's blessing is not a statement of hope, or a wish for wellbeing, or the expression of a general belief that God may interact with the adherent if asked by another. Paul's apostolic blessing is as powerful and efficacious as his curse. It is his call on the living Lord Jesus Christ—the son of Abba', raised from the dead, the Lord who listens to and hears Paul and guides his mission as an appointed *apostolos*—for his intervention now with his adherents; to shower each with divine protection, the *charismata* of the Spirit, and efficacious *agape*. *Charis* was a word that carried the reality of the active presence of and interaction with God as Abba' and the *overwhelming protection of the agape, divine love, here and now*. Consequently, it is an eschatological blessing.

Finally, Paul's concluding remark is both personal and touching, and it summarizes the theme of his entire letter—*agape*, "the more excellent Way." Paul simply says, "My love [*agape*] be with you everyone in Christ Jesus."[1051] It is a remarkable statement of humility and solidarity with the Corinthian adherents, as it reflects the essence of Paul's personal devotion to those whom he brings to the Lord Jesus Christ, uniting them with the *euangelion* and Christ for salvation at the *parousia*. They are his seal of apostleship, his presentation to the risen Lord; that he has fulfilled his appointment to the Lord to bring the efficacious and salvific *euangelion*, *pistis* and *agape* to the adherents, the new *tekna tou Theou*. "My love be with you all" is the personal expression of his unity with his adherents in the coming of the Lord.

Consequently, Paul's is an eschatological expression that confirms the position both he and the adherents share in the last days of the age; namely, living in the *agape* for each other until the Lord is present. Death no longer has any hold on the new child of God. *Pistis* and *agape* grab and pull the children of Abba' away from the perilous risk of death that comes to the world with the passing of this age. It is Paul's call on *agape* that makes all equal and worthy as they assemble in the new order, the *ecclesia*, awaiting the Lord. For Paul, the divine event in history is *agape*, revealed in the death, burial and resurrection of Abba's son, Jesus Christ, and in the coming resurrection, judgment and inbreaking kingdom of God.

1047. Rom 16:20.
1048. 2 Cor 13:14.
1049. 1 Thess 5:28.
1050. Gal 6:18.
1051. 1 Cor 16:24.

Bibliography

Adna, Jostein. "The Encounter of Jesus with the Gerasene Demoniac." In *Authenticating the Actions of Jesus*, edited by Bruce Chilton et al., 279–301. Boston: Brill, 1999.
Allegro, John. *The Dead Sea Scrolls*. New York: Penguin, 1956.
Anderson, Charles C. *The Historical Jesus: A Continuing Quest*. Grand Rapids: Eerdmans, 1972.
Aune, David. *Prophecy in Ancient Christianity and in the Mediterranean World*. Grand Rapids: Eerdmans, 1991.
Avioz, M. *Josephus' Interpretation of the Books of Samuel*. London: T. & T. Clark, 2015.
Avshalom-Govi, Dina, and Arafan Najar. "Migdal." *Hadashot Arkheologiyot: Excavations and Surveys in Israel* 125 (2013) 121–73.
Barclay, John M. G. *Pauline Churches and Diaspora Jews*. Grand Rapids: Eerdmans, 2011.
Bar-Ilan, Meir. *Exorcism by Rabbis: Talmud Sages and Their Magic*. Translated by Rachelle and Saul Isserow. https://faculty.biu.ac.il/barlim/exorcism.html#(38).
Bar-Ilan, T. Canaan. "Haunted Springs and Water Demons in Palestine." *Journal of the Palestine Oriental Society* 1 (1920–21) 153–70.
Barr, James. "Abba Isn't Daddy." *Journal of Theological Studies* 39 (1988) 28–47.
Bauer, Walter. *The Greek English Lexicon of the New Testament and Early Christian Literature*. Chicago: University of Chicago Press, 1979.
Bennema, Cornelius. "The Giving of the Spirit in John 19, 20." In *The Spirit and Christ in New Testament and Christian Theology*, edited by I. Howard Marshall et al., 93–99. Grand Rapids: Eerdmans, 2012.
Ben-Zvi, Yad Yitzhak. *Studies on the Texts of the Desert of Judah 10*. Jerusalem: Magness, 1992.
Berstein, Peter L. *Against the Gods: The Remarkable Story of Risk*. New York: Wiley, 1996.
Betz, Hans Dieter. *Galatians: A Commentary on Paul's Letter to the Churches in Galatia*. Philadelphia: Fortress, 1979.
———. "The Letter to the Galatians." In *The Interpreter's Dictionary to the Bible*, edited by Keith Crim, et al., supplementary volume, 352–53. Nashville: Abingdon, 1976.
Blake, William. *The History of Slavery and the Slave Trade, Ancient and Modern*. Columbus, OH: Miller, 1857.
Bohak, Gideon. "Amulets." In *Eerdmans Dictionary of Early Judaism*, edited by John Collins et al., 328. Grand Rapids: Eerdmans, 2010.
Bolt, Peter. "Life, Death and Afterlife in the Greco-Roman World." In *Life in the Face of Death: The Resurrection Message of the New Testament*. Grand Rapids: Eerdmans, 1998.

BIBLIOGRAPHY

Boobyer, G. H. *St. Mark and the Transfiguration Story*. Edinburgh: T. & T. Clark, 1942.

Borg, Marcus. *The Lost Gospel of Q: The Original Sayings of Jesus*. Berkeley: Ulysses, 1996.

Bornkamm, Gunther. *Jesus of Nazareth*. Translated by James M. Robinson. London: Hodder and Stoughton, 1960.

Bousset, Wilhelm. *Kyrios Christos: A History of Belief in Christ from the Beginnings of Christianity to Irenaeus*. Nashville: Abingdon, 1970.

Bowker, John. *Jesus and the Pharisees*. London: Cambridge University Press, 1973.

Boxer, B. M. "Wonder-Working and the Rabbinic Tradition: The Case of Hanina ben Dosa." *Journal for the Study of Judaism* 16 (1985) 42–92.

Brooten, Bernadette. *Women Leaders in the Ancient Synagogue*. Brown Judaic Studies 36. Atlanta: Scholars, 1982.

Brown, Raymond. *The Community of the Beloved Disciple*. Mahwah, NJ: Paulist, 1979.

———. "Roles of Women in the Fourth Gospel." *Theological Studies* 36 (1975) 688–99.

Bultmann, Rudolf. *Form Criticism*. Translated by Frederick Grant. New York: Harper, 1962.

———. *The Gospel of John: A Commentary*. Translated by G. R. Beasley-Murray et al. Philadelphia: Westminster, 1971.

———. *History of the Synoptic Tradition*. Translated by John Marsh. Oxford: Blackwell, 1972.

———. *Jesus and the Word*. Translated by Louise Pettibone Smith and Erminie Huntress Laterno. New York: Scribner, 1958.

———. *Primitive Christianity in Its Contemporary Setting*. Translated by R. H. Fuller. New York: Meridian, 1956.

———. *Theology of the New Testament*. Edited by Kendrik Grobel. New York: Scribner, 1955.

Burton, Dan, et al. *Magic, Mystery and Science: The Occult in Western Civilization*. Bloomington: Indian University Press, 2004.

Burton, Ian. *The Perception of Risk*. New York: Taylor and Francis, 2000.

Busse, Roger S. *The Essentials of Commercial Lending*. Portland: WKB, 1995.

———. *Jesus, Resurrected*. Eugene, OR: Wipf & Stock, 2016.

———. "The Son of Man in the Synoptic Tradition." BA thesis, Reed College, 1978.

———. *To Be Near the Fire*. Eugene, OR: Wipf & Stock, 2014.

Cameron, Ron. *The Other Gospels: Non-Canonical Gospel Text*. Philadelphia: Westminster, 1982.

Canaan, T. "Haunted Springs and Water Demons in Palestine." *Journal of the Palestine Oriental Society* 1 (1920–21) 153–70.

Carter, Warren. *The Roman Empire and the New Testament*. Nashville: Abingdon, 2006.

Castelli, Elizabeth. "Virginity and Its Meaning for Women's Sexuality in Early Christianity." *Journal of Feminist Studies in Religions* 2 (1986) 61–88.

Charlesworth, James H. *James, Jesus and Archaeology*. Grand Rapids: Eerdmans, 2006.

———, ed. *Jews and Christians: Exploring the Past, Present and Future*. New York: Crossroad, 1990.

———. *The Old Testament Pseudepigrapha: Apocalyptic Literature and Testaments*. Garden City: Doubleday, 1983.

Chestnutt, Randall D. "The Dead Sea Scrolls and the Meal Formula." In *The Dead Sea Scrolls and the Bible: Scripture and the Scrolls*, edited by James Charlesworth, 1:397–401. Waco, TX: Baylor University Press, 2006.

Chijioke Iwe, John. *Jesus in the Synagogue of Capernaum: The Pericope and Its Programmatic*. Rome: Gregorian University Press, 1999.

Cohen, Shaye. *From the Maccabees to the Mishna*. Louisville: John Knox, 2006.

Collins, J. J., and R. A. Kugler, eds. *Religion in the Dead Sea Scrolls*. Grand Rapids: Eerdmans, 2000.
Conzelmann, Hans. *1 Corinthians*. Translated by James W. Leitch. Edited by George MacRae. Philadelphia: Fortress, 1975.
———. *An Outline of the Theology of the New Testament*. Translated by John Bowden. New York: Harper, 1968.
———. *The Theology of St. Luke*. Translated by Geoffrey Buswell. New York: Harper, 1961.
Costa, Tony. "Exorcisms and Healings of Jesus within Classical Culture." In *Christian Origins and Greco-Roman Culture*, edited by Andrew Pitts and Stanley Porter, 125–45. Leiden: Brill, 2013.
Craffert, Peiter. *The Life of a Galilean Shaman: Jesus of Nazareth in Anthropological-Historical Perspective*. Eugene, OR: Cascade, 2008.
Crossan, John Dominick. *The Cross That Spoke: The Origins of the Passion Narrative*. San Francisco: Harper, 1988.
———. *The Historical Jesus*. San Francisco: HarperCollins, 1992.
———. *In Fragments: The Aphorisms of Jesus*. New York: Harper, 1983.
———. *In Parables: The Challenge of the Historical Jesus*. New York: Harper and Row, 1973.
———. *Sayings Parallels: A Workbook for the Jesus Tradition*. Philadelphia: Fortress, 1986.
Cullmann, Oscar. *The Christology of the New Testament*. Translated by Shirley C. Guthrie and Charles A. M. Hall. Philadelphia: Westminster, 1963.
Culpepper, R. Alan. "John 21:24–25: The Johannine Sphragis." In *John, Jesus and History*, edited by Paul N. Anderson et al., 2:349–64. Williston, VT: SBL, 2009.
D'Angelo, Mary. "Reconstructing 'Real' Women in Gospel Literature: The Case of Mary Magdalene." In *Women and Christian Origins*, edited by Ross Kraemer and Mary D'Angelo, 105–28. New York: Oxford University Press, 1999.
Daube, David. "Jesus and the Samaritan Women." *Journal of Biblical Literature* 69 (1950) 137–47.
Davies, Stevan. *The Gospel of Thomas and Christian Wisdom*. Oregon House, CA: Bardic, 2005.
Davies, W. D. *The Setting of the Sermon on the Mount*. London: Cambridge University Press, 1964.
Denaux, Adelbert. *Studies in the Gospel of Luke: Structure, Language, Theology*. Berlin: Tilburg Theological Studies, 2010.
Dickie, Matthew. *Magic and Magicians in the Greco-Roman World*. London: Routledge, 2001.
Dodd, C. H. *Apostolic Preaching and Its Development*. New York: Harper, 1964.
———. *Parables of the Kingdom*. New York: Scribner, 1961.
Donfried, Karl Paul. *Paul, Thessalonica and Early Christianity*. Grand Rapids: Eerdmans, 2002.
Drabek, Tomas E. *Human Systems and Response to Disaster: An Inventory of Sociological Findings*. New York: Springer-Verlag, 1986.
Plessis, Paul du. *Borkowski's Textbook on Roman Law*. Oxford: Oxford University Press, 2010.
Ehrman, Bart D. *The New Testament*. Oxford: Oxford University Press, 2004.
———. *Peter, Paul and Mary Magdalene*. Oxford: Oxford University Press, 2006.
Eisenman, Robert. *The Dead Sea Scrolls and the First Christians*. Edison, NJ: Cascade, 1996.
———. *James the Brother of Jesus*. New York: Viking, 1997.
Eshel, Esther. "Jesus the Exorcist in Light of Epigraphic Sources." In *Jesus and Archaeology*, edited by James Charlesworth, 183–85. Grand Rapids: Eerdmans, 2006.

Bibliography

Evans, Craig A. "Jesus and Psalm 91 in Light of the Exorcism Scrolls." In *Celebrating the Dead Sea Scrolls: A Canadian Contribution*, edited by Peter W. Flint et al., 541–55. Atlanta: SBL, 2011.

———. "Jesus and the Jewish Miracle Stories." In *Jesus and His Contemporaries*, 214–43. New York: Brill, 1995.

Felton, D. *Haunted Greece and Rome: Ghost Stories from Classic Antiquities*. Austin: University of Texas Press, 1999.

Ferguson, Everett. *Baptism in Early Church History: History, Theology and Liturgy in the First Five Centuries*. Grand Rapids: Eerdmans, 2009.

Finkelstein, Louis. *The Pharisees: The Sociological Background of Their Faith*. Vols. 1 and 2. Philadelphia: Jewish Publication Society of America, 1946.

Fishoff, Baruch, et al. *Acceptable Risk*. London: Cambridge University Press, 1984.

Fitzmeyer, Joseph A. *The Dead Sea Scrolls and Christian Origins*. Grand Rapids: Eerdmans, 2000.

Flint, P. W., and J. C. VanderKam, eds. *Dead Sea Scrolls after Fifty Years: A Comprehensive Assessment*. Vol. 2. Leiden: Brill, 1999.

Foerster, Werner. *From the Exile to Christ: A Historical Introduction to Palestinian Judaism*. Translated by Gordon E. Harris. Philadelphia: Fortress, 1964.

Frayer-Griggs, Daniel. "Spittle, Clay and Creation in John 9:6 and Some of the Dead Sea Scrolls." *Journal of Biblical Literature* 132 (2013) 659–70.

Freyne, Sean. "The Charismatic." In *Ideal Figures in Ancient Judaism: Profiles and Paradigms*, edited by G. W. E. Nickelsburg and J. J. Collins, 223–58. Chico, CA: SBL, 1980.

———. *Galilee, Jesus and the Gospels*. Philadelphia: Fortress, 1988.

———. "Herodian Economics in Galilee." In *Modeling Early Christianity*, edited by Phillip Esler, 23–46. New York: Routledge, 1995.

———. *Jesus, a Jewish Galilean: A New Reading of the Jesus Story*. New York: T. & T. Clark, 2004.

———. "Jewish Immersion and Christian Baptism: Continuity on the Margins?" In *Ablution, Initiation and Baptism: Late Antiquity*, edited by David Hellholm, 1:221–53. Grand Rapids: Eerdmans, 2009.

Funk, Robert W. "The Apostolic *Parousia*: Form and Significance." In *Christian History and Interpretation*, edited by William Farmer et al., 249–68. Cambridge: Cambridge University Press, 1967.

Funk, Robert W., and the Jesus Seminar. *The Acts of Jesus: The Search for the Authentic Deeds of Jesus*. San Francisco: Harper, 1998.

Furnish, Victor Paul. *The Love Command in the New Testament*. New York: Abingdon, 1972.

———. *2 Corinthians*. Garden City: Doubleday, 1984.

Gager, John. *Curse Tablets and Binding Spells from the Ancient World*. New York: Oxford University Press, 1992.

———. "The Social Practice of Magic in the Ancient Greco-Roman World." In *Philadelphia Seminar on Christian Origins*, vol. 14, set 1 minutes, October 5, 1976.

Georgi, Dieter. "Forms of Religious Propaganda." In *Jesus in His Time*, edited by Hans Schultz, translated by Brian Watchorn, 123–31. Philadelphia: Fortress, 1971.

———. *The Opponents of Paul in Second Corinthians*. Philadelphia: Fortress, 1986.

Gerhardsson, Birger. "Memory and Manuscript: Oral Tradition and Written Transmission in Rabbinic Judaism and Early Christianity." PhD diss., Uppsala University, Sweden, 1961.

———. *The Origins of the Gospel Traditions*. Philadelphia: Fortress, 1979.

Goldberg, Gary. "The Coincidences of the Emmaus Narrative of Luke and the *Testimonium* of Josephus." *Journal for the Study of the Pseudepigrapha* 13 (1995) 59–77.
Grant, R. M. "One Hundred Fifty Three Fishes (John 21,11)." *Harvard Theological Review* 49 (1949) 273–75.
Graves-Brown, Carolyn. *Dancing for Hathor: Women in Ancient Egypt*. Auklund, New Zealand: MPG, 2010.
Hachlili, Rachel. *Jewish Funerary Customs, Practices and Rites in the Second Temple Period*. Boston: Brill, 2005.
Hanson, K. C., and David C. Oakman. "The Galilean Fishing Economy and the Jesus Tradition." *Biblical Theology Bulletin* 27 (1997) 99–111. Also available at http://www.kchanson.com/ARTICLES/fishing.html.
———. "The Social Impact and Implications of Herod's Temple, Temple and Elite." In *Palestine in the Time of Jesus*, 146–51. Minneapolis: Fortress, 1998.
Hartvigsen, Kirsten Marie. "Matthew 28:16–20 and Mark 16:9–20: Different Ways of Relating Baptism to the Joint Mission of God, John the Baptism, Jesus, and their Adherents." In *Ablution, Initiation and Baptism: Late Antiquity, Early Judaism*, 657–709. Berlin: de Gruyter, 2011.
Hawkins, Cameron. "Contracts, Coercion, and the Boundaries of the Roman Artisanal Firms." In *Work, Labour, and Professions in the Roman World*, edited by Koenraad Verboven and Christian Laes, 36–39. Boston: Brill, 2017.
Hayman, Aaron. *Toledot Tannaim we-Amoraim* [The history of the Tannaim and Amoraim]. 3 vols. Jerusalem, 1964.
Hengel, Martin. *Crucifixion*. Philadelphia: Fortress, 1977.
———. *The Four Gospels and the One Gospel of Jesus Christ: An Investigation of the Collection and Origin of the Canonical Gospels*. Harrisburg, PA: Trinity, 2000.
———. *The Son of God: The Origin of Christology and the History of Jewish Hellenistic Religion*. Philadelphia: Fortress, 1976.
Hock, Ronald F. "Paul's Tentmaking and the Problem of His Social Class." *Journal of Biblical Literature* 97 (1998) 555–64.
———. *The Social Context of Paul's Ministry: Tentmaking and Apostleship*. Philadelphia: Fortress, 1980.
Horsley, Richard. *Archaeology, History and Society in Galilee*. Valley Forge, PA: Trinity, 1996.
———. "High Priests and the Politics of Roman Palestine." *Journal for the Study of Judaism* 17 (1986) 23–55.
———. *Jesus and the Spiral of Violence*. San Francisco: Harper, 1987.
———. *The Message and the Kingdom*. Minneapolis: Fortress, 1997.
Horsley, Richard, and K. C. Hanson. *Bandits, Prophets and Messiahs*. San Francisco: Harper, 1985.
Hull, John M. *Hellenistic Magic and the Synoptic Tradition*. Studies in Biblical Theology, 2nd series. London: SCM, 1974.
Isaac, E. "(Ethiopic Apocalypse of) Enoch (Second Century B.C.–First Century A.D.)." In *The Old Testament Pseudepigrapha: Apocalyptic Literature and Testaments*, edited by James H. Charlesworth, 5–89. Garden City: Doubleday, 1983.
Jackson, H. M. "Ancient Self-Referential Conventions." *JTS* 50 (1999) 1–34.
Janowitz, Naomi. *Magic in the Roman World*. London: Routledge, 2001.
Jeffries, James. *The Graeco-Roman World of the New Testament Era: Exploring the Background of Christianity*. Downers Grove: InterVarsity, 1999.

Jenott, Lance. *The Gospel of Judas*. Studien un Texte zu Antike und Christentum. Tubingen: Siebek, 2011.

Jeremias, Joachim. *Abba*. Gottingen: Vandenhoeck & Ruprecht, 1966.

———. *The Central Message of the New Testament*. Philadelphia: Fortress, 1965.

———. *The Eucharistic Words of Jesus*. London: SCM, 1966.

———. *Jerusalem in the Time of Jesus*. Philadelphia: Fortress, 1967.

———. *Jesus' Promise to the Nations*. London: SCM, 1956.

———. *New Testament Theology: The Proclamation of Jesus*. New York: Scribner, 1971.

———. *The Parables of Jesus*. New York: Scribner, 1972.

———. *The Prayers of Jesus*. London: SCM, 1967.

———. *The Problem of the Historical Jesus*. Philadelphia: Fortress, 1964.

———. *Rediscovering the Parables of Jesus*. New York: Scribner, 1966.

Jewettt, Robert. *The Thessalonian Correspondence: Pauline Rhetoric and Millenarian Piety*. Philadelphia: Fortress, 1986.

Johnson, Maxwell. *The Rites of Christian Initiation: Their Evolution and Interpretation*. Minneapolis: Order of St. Benedict College, 2007.

Kahneman, Daniel, et al. *Judgment under Uncertainty: Heuristics and Biases*. Cambridge: Cambridge University Press, 1982.

Kasemann, Ernst. *Testament of Jesus: Study of the Gospel of John in the Light of Chapter 17*. Translated by G. Krodel. Philadelphia: Fortress, 1978.

Kee, H. C. *The Origins of Christianity: Sources and Documents*. Englewood Cliffs, NJ: Prentice Hall, 1973.

———. "Testament of the Twelve Patriarchs." In Charlesworth, *Old Testament Pseudepigrapha*, 775–828.

———. "The Transfiguration in Mark." In *Understanding the Sacred Text*, edited by John Ruemann, 85–94. Valley Forge, PA: Judson, 1972.

Kelber, Werner H. *The Oral and the Written Gospel: The Hermeneutics of Speaking and Writing in the Synoptic Tradition, Mark, Paul and Q*. Philadelphia: Fortress, 1983.

Kimball, Charles. *Jesus' Exposition of the Old Testament in the Gospel of Luke*. Sheffield: Sheffield Academic, 1994.

King, Karen. *The Gospel of Mary: The First Woman Apostle*. Santa Rosa, CA: Polebridge, 2003.

Kloppenborg, John. "Collegia and Thiasoi: Issues in Function, Taxonomy and Membership." In *Voluntary Associations in the Ancient Graeco-Roman World*, edited by John Kloppenborg and Stephen G. Wilson, 16–30. London: Routledge, 1996.

———. *Excavating Q: The History and Setting of the Sayings Gospel*. Minneapolis: Augsburg, 2000.

———. *The Formation of Q*. Philadelphia: Fortress, 1989.

Kloppenborg, John, et al. *Q-Thomas Reader*. Sonoma, CA: Polebridge, 1990.

Klutz, Todd. *The Exorcism Stories in Luke-Acts: A Sociostylistic Reading*. Society for New Testament Studies Monograph Series 120. Cambridge: Cambridge University Press, 2004.

Koch, Klaus. *The Growth of the Biblical Tradition: The Form-Critical Method*. Translated by S. M. Cupitt. New York: Scribner, 1969.

Koester, Helmut. *Ancient Christian Gospels: Their History and Development*. Philadelphia: Trinity, 1992.

———. "Apostle and Church in the Letter to the Thessalonians." In Koester, *Paul and His World*, 24–32.

———. "Archaeology and Paul in Thessalonike." In Koester, *Paul and His World*, 38–54.

———. *Cities of Paul: Images and Interpretations from the Harvard New Testament Archaeology Project*. CD-ROM. Minneapolis: Fortress, 2005.

———. "Egyptian Religion in Thessalonike: Regulation for the Cult." In *From Roman to Early Christian Thessalonike*, edited by Laura Nasrallah et al., 133–50. Cambridge: Harvard University Press, 2010.

———. "Ephesos in Early Christian Literature." In Koester, *Ephesos*, 119–40.

———. *Ephesos: Metropolis of Asia*. Valley Forge, PA: Trinity, 1995.

———. "First Thessalonians: An Experiment in Christian Writing." In Koester, *Paul and His World*, 15–23.

———. *From Jesus to the Gospels*. Philadelphia: Fortress, 2007.

———. "GNOMAI DIAPHOROI: The Origin and Nature of Diversification in the History of Early Christianity." In Robinson and Koester, *Trajectories through Early Christianity*, 114–57.

———. "The Gospel of Thomas: Does it Contain Authentic Sayings of Jesus." *Bible Review* 6 (1990) 28–39.

———. "The Historical Jesus: Some Comments and Thoughts on Norman Perrin's Rediscovering the Teachings of Jesus." In Perrin, *Christology and a Modern Pilgrimage*, 123–36.

———. *Introduction to the New Testament: History and Literature of Early Christianity*. Vol. 2. Philadelphia: Fortress, 1984.

———. "The Memory of Jesus' Death and the Worship of the Risen Lord." *Harvard Theological Review* 91 (1998) 335–50.

———. "One Jesus and Four Primitive Gospels." In Robinson and Koester, *Trajectories through Early Christianity*, 158–204.

———. *Paul and His World: Interpreting the New Testament in Its Context*. Minneapolis: Fortress, 2007.

———. "The Structure and Criteria of Early Christian Beliefs." In Robinson and Koester, *Trajectories through Early Christianity*, 205–31.

———. "Wisdom and Folly in Corinth." In Koester, *Paul and His World*, 80–85.

Kraemer, Ross. *Her Share of the Blessings: Women's Religions among Pagans, Jews, and Christians in the Greco-Roman World*. Oxford: Oxford University Press, 1992.

———. *Maenads, Martyrs, Matrons, Monastics: A Sourcebook on Women's Religions in the Graeco-Roman World*. Philadelphia: Fortress, 1988.

Kummel, Werner Georg. *Introduction to the New Testament*. Translated by H. C. Keen. Nashville: Abingdon, 1975.

Lauterbach, Jacob. *Rabbinic Essays*. New York: Ktav, 1973.

Layton, Bentley. *The Gnostic Scriptures: A New Translation with Annotations and Introductions by Bentley Layton*. Garden City: Doubleday, 1987.

Lewis, I. M. *Ecstatic Religion: An Anthropological Study of Spirit Possession and Shamanism*. Middlesex, UK: Penguin, 1971.

Litwa, M. David. *Iesus Deus: The Early Christian Depiction of Jesus as a Mediterranean God*. Philadelphia: Fortress, 2014.

Lohse, Eduard. *Colossians and Philemon*. Edited by Helmut Koester. Translated by William R. Poehlmann and Robert J. Karris. Philadelphia: Fortress, 1971.

Longenecker, Richard N. *Biblical Exegesis in the Apostolic Period*. Grand Rapids: Eerdmans, 1975.

Luedemann, Gerd. *The Resurrection of Jesus*. Philadelphia: Fortress, 1994.

Luijendijk, Annemarie. *Forbidden Oracles? The Gospel of the Lots of Mary*. Studien und Texte zu Antike und Christentum 89. Tubingen: Siebeck, 2014.

Lunn, Nicholas P. *The Original Ending of Mark: A New Case for the Authenticity of Mark 16:9–20*. Eugene, OR: Pickwick, 2014.

Maccini, Robert. *Her Testimony Is True: Women as Witnesses in the Gospel of John*. Sheffield: Sheffield Academic, 1996.

Madden, Patrick J. "Jesus Walking on the Sea: An Investigation of the Origin of the Narrative Account." *Beihefte zur Zeitschrift fuer die neutestamentliche Wissenschaft* 81 (1997) 30–156.

Malina, Bruce, and Richard Robaugh. *Social Science Commentary on the Gospel of John*. Philadelphia: Fortress, 1998.

Marxsen, Willi. *The Resurrection of Jesus of Nazareth*. Philadelphia: Fortress, 1971.

McCrae, George. "The Jewish Background of the Gnostic Sophia Myth." *Novum Testamentum* 12 (1970) 81–101.

McDowell, Markus. *Prayers of Jewish Women: Studies of Patterns of Prayer in the Second Temple*. Tubingen: Siebeck, 2006.

Meeks, Wayne A. *The First Urban Christians: The Social World of the Apostle Paul*. New Haven: Yale University Press, 1983.

Meier, John. *A Marginal Jew: Rethinking the Historical Jesus*. Vol. 1. New York: Doubleday, 1991.

Meyer, Marvin. "Making Mary Male: The Categories 'Male' and 'Female' in the Gospel of Thomas." *New Testament Studies* 31 (1985) 554–70.

Moffatt, James. "The First and Second Epistles to the Thessalonians." In *The Expositor's Greek New Testament, Thessalonians*, edited by W. Robertson Nicoll, 189–93. Grand Rapids: Eerdmans, 1961.

Morrison, Gregg. *The Turning Point in Mark*. Eugene, OR: Pickwick, 2014.

Nasrallah, Laura, et al., eds. *From Roman to Early Christian Thessaloniki*. Cambridge: Harvard University Press, 2010.

Neusner, Jacob. *From Politics to Piety: The Emergence of Pharisaic Judaism*. Englewood Cliffs, NJ: Prentice-Hall, 1973.

———. *Judaism When Christianity Began*. Louisville: Westminster Knox, 2002.

———. *The Modern Study of the Mishnah*. Studia Post-Biblica 23. Leiden: Brill, 1973.

Neyrey, Jerome. "The Loss of Wealth, the Loss of Family, the Loss of Honor: A Cultural Interpretation of the Original Four Makarisms in Q." In *Modelling Early Christianity: Social-Scientific Studies of the New Testament in Its Context*, edited by Phillip Esler, 139–49. New York: Routledge, 1995.

Nickelsburg, George. *Jewish Literature between the Bible and the Mishnah: A Historical and Literary Introduction*. Philadelphia: Fortress, 1981.

Nickelsburg, George, and J. J. Collins, eds. *Ideal Figures in Ancient Judaism: Profiles and Paradigms*. Chico, CA: Scholars, 1980.

Nigdelis, Pantelis. "Voluntary Associations in Roman Thessalonike: In Search of Identity and Support in Cosmopolitan Society." In *From Roman to Early Christian Thessalonike*, edited by Laura Nisrallah et al., 13–48. Cambridge: Harvard University Press, 2010.

Ogden, Daniel. "The Ancient Greek Oracles of the Dead." *Acta Classica* 44 (2001) 167–95.

———. *Magic, Witchcraft and Ghosts in the Greek and Roman World*. Oxford: Oxford University Press, 2009.

Pagels, Elaine. *The Gnostic Gospels*. New York: Random House, 1979.

———. "Visions, Appearances and Apostolic Authority: Gnostic and Orthodox Traditions." In *Gnosis*, edited by U. Bianchi et al., 415–16. Gottengen: Vandenhoeck and Ruprecht, 1978.

Parsons, Mikeal. "Narrative Closure and Openness in the Plot of the Third Gospel: The Sense of Ending in Luke 24:50–53." *Society of Biblical Literature 1986 Seminar Papers* 25 (1986) 203–22.

Patterson, Stephen J. *Beyond the Passion: Rethinking the Death and Life of Jesus*. Minneapolis: Fortress, 2004.

———. *The God of Jesus*. Harrisburg, PA: Trinity, 1998.

———. *The Gospel of Thomas and Christian Origins: Essays on the Fifth Gospel*. Boston: Brill, 2013.

———. *The Gospel of Thomas and Jesus*. Sonoma, CA: Polebridge, 1993.

———. *The Lost Way*. New York: Harper, 2014.

———. "Paul and the Jesus Tradition: It's Time for Another Look." *HTR* 84 (1991) 23–41.

Pearson, Birger A. *Gnosticism, Judaism and Egyptian Christianity*. Philadelphia: Fortress, 1990.

———. *The Pneumatikos-Psychikos Terminology in 1 Corinthians: A Study in the Theology of the Corinthian Opponents of Paul and Its Relation to Gnosticism*. Missoula, MT: Scholars, 1973.

Perrin, Norman. *Christology and a Modern Pilgrimage: A Discussion with Norman Perrin*. Edited by Hans Deiter Betz. Missoula, MT: SBL and Scholars, 1974.

———. *Introduction to the New Testament*. New York: Harcourt Brace Jovanovich, 1974.

———. *Jesus and the Language of the Kingdom*. Fortress: Philadelphia, 1976.

———. *Rediscovering the Teachings of Jesus*. New York: Harper, 1976.

———. *The Resurrection according to Matthew, Mark, and Luke*. Philadelphia: Fortress, 1977.

———. "Towards an Interpretation of the Gospel of Mark." In *Christology and a Modern Pilgrimage*, 1–78.

Pidgeon, Nick, et al. *The Social Amplification of Risk*. Cambridge: Cambridge University Press, 2003.

Plevnik, Joseph. *Paul and the Parousia*. Eugene, OR: Wipf & Stock, 2014.

Plummer, Alfred. *The Gospel according to S. Luke*. Edinburgh: T. & T. Clark, 1975.

Reynolds, Benjamin. *The Apocalyptic Son of Man in the Gospel of John*. Tubingen: Siebeck, 2008.

Rivkin, Ellis. *A Hidden Revolution: The Pharisees Search for the Kingdom Within*. Nashville: Abingdon, 1978.

Robinson, James M. "Jesus: From Easter to Valentinus (or to the Apostles' Creed)." *Journal of Biblical Literature* 101 (1982) 3–5.

———. *The Nag Hammadi Library in English*. Leiden: Brill, 1988.

———. *A New Quest for the Historical Jesus*. New York: Macmillan, 1968.

———. "On the Gattung of Mark (and John)." In *Jesus and Man's Hope*, edited by David Buttrick, 1:116–18. Pittsburgh: Pittsburgh Theological Seminary, 1970.

Robinson, James M., and Helmut Koester. *Trajectories through Early Christianity*. Philadelphia: Fortress, 1971.

Ross, M. "One Hundred and Fifty Three Fishes." *Expository Times* 100 (1988) 345–57.

Rothschild, Clare C. *Baptist Traditions and Q*. Wissenshaftliche Untersuchungen zum Neuen Testament 190. Tubingen: Mohr Siebeck, 2005.

Rousseau, John. "Exorcism." In *Jesus and His World: An Archaeological and Cultural Dictionary*, edited by John Rousseau et al., 178–79. Minneapolis: Augsburg, 1995.

Sanders, E. P. *The Historical Figure of Jesus*. London: Penguin, 1993.

———. *Paul and Palestinian Judaism: A Comparison of Patterns of Religion*. London: SCM, 1977.

Sanders, Jack T. *The New Testament Christological Hymns: Their Historical Religious Background*. Edited by Matthew Black. Cambridge: Cambridge University Press, 1971.

Sandmel, Samuel. *A Jewish Understanding of the New Testament*. New York: University Publishers, 1956.

Scharlemann, M. S. "Transfiguration." In *The International Bible Encyclopedia*, edited by Geoffrey Bromiley, 4:886–88. Grand Rapids: Eerdmans, 1988.

Scherrer, Peter. "The City of Ephesos from the Roman Period to Late Antiquity." In Koester, *Ephesos*, 1–26.

Schmithals, Walter. *Gnosticism in Corinth: An Investigation of the Letters to the Corinthians*. Translated by John E. Steely. New York: Abingdon, 1971.

Schutz, John. *Paul and the Anatomy of Apostolic Authority*. Louisville: Westminster, 2007.

Schweitzer, Albert. *The Mysticism of Paul the Apostle*. New York: Seabury, 1968.

———. *The Quest of the Historical Jesus*. Preface by F. C. Burkitt. Translated by W. Montgomery. Baltimore: Johns Hopkins University Press, 1998.

Shillington, George. *Jesus and Paul before Christianity: Their World and Work in Retrospect*. Eugene, OR: Cascade, 2011.

Sim, David C. *Apocalyptic Eschatology in the Gospel of Matthew*. Cambridge: Cambridge University Press, 1996.

Slovic, Paul, and Elke Weber. "Perception of Risk Posed by Extreme Events." Paper presented at the Risk Management Strategies in an Uncertain World conference, Palisades, New York, April 12–13, 2002. https://www.ldeo.columbia.edu/chrr/documents/meetings/roundtable/white_papers/slovic_wp.pdf.

Slovic, Paul, et al. "Risk as Analysis and Risk as Feeling: Some Thoughts about Affect, Reason, Risk, and Rationality." *Risk Analysis* 24 (2004) 311–22.

———. "Trust, Emotion, Sex, Politics, and Science: Surveying the Risk Assessment Battlefield." *Risk Analysis* 19 (1999) 689–700.

Smith, David. *"Hand This Man Over to Satan": Curse Exclusion and Salvation in 1 Corinthians 5*. London: T. & T. Clark, 2008.

Smith, Morton. *Jesus the Magician*. San Francisco: Harper, 1978.

Strauss, David Friedrich. *The Life of Jesus Critically Examined*. Edited by Peter C. Hodgson. Translated by George Eliot. Philadelphia: Fortress, 1972.

Streeter, B. H. *The Four Gospels*. London: Macmillan, 1951.

Strugnell, John. "A Plea for a Conjectural Emendation in the New Testament with a Coda on 1 Corinthians 4:6." *Catholic Bible Quarterly* 36 (1974) 555–58.

Suggs, M. Jack. *Wisdom, Christology, and Law in Matthew's Gospel*. Cambridge: Harvard University Press, 1970.

Talbert, Wendell Lee. *Idol Meat in Corinth: The Pauline Argument in 1 Corinthians 8 and 10*. SBL Dissertation Series 68. 1985. Reprint, Eugene, OR: Wipf & Stock, 2004.

Taylor, Joan. "The Name Iskarioth." *Journal of Biblical Literature* 129 (2010) 369–85.

Thatcher, Tom. "I Have Conquered the World." In *Empire in the New Testament*, edited by Stanley Porter et al., 140–63. Eugene, OR: Pickwick, 2011.

Theissen, Gerd. *The Social Setting of Pauline Christianity: Essays on Corinth*. Edited and translated by John H. Schutz. Philadelphia: Fortress, 1982.

Thomas, Christine. "At Home in the City of Artemis: Religion in Ephesos in the Literary Imagination of the Roman Period." In Koester, *Ephesos*, 81–117.

Throckmorton, Bruce, Jr., ed. *Gospel Parallels: A Synopsis of the First Three Gospels*. New York: Nelson, 1957.

Tomson, Peter. "The Johannine 'Jews.'" In *Anti-Judaism in the Fourth Gospel*, edited by Reimund Bieringer, 197–99. Louisville: John Knox, 1963.

Toorn, Karel van der, et al., eds. *Dictionary of Demons and Deities in the Bible*. Cologne: Brill, 1999.

Van Wahlde, Urban. *Gnosticism, Docetism and Judaisms in the First Century*. London: T. & T Clark, 2015.

Vermes, Geza. *Post-Biblical Jewish Studies*. Leiden: Brill, 1975.

Walters, James. "Egyptian Religions in Ephesos." In Koester, *Ephesos*, 281–310.

Wassertein, Abraham, ed. *Flavius Josephus: Selections from His Works*. New York: Viking, 1974.

Wendt, Heidi. *At the Temple Gates: The Religion of Freelance Experts in the Roman Empire*. Oxford: Oxford University Press, 2016.

White, L. Michael. "Urban Development and Social Change in Imperial Ephesos." In Koester, *Ephesos*, 27–79.

Wright, David F. *The Historical Jesus*. Edited by Craig Evans. London: Routledge, 2004.